IMPERIAL IDEALS IN THE ROMAN WEST

CW01082562

This book examines the figure of the Roman emperor as a unifying symbol for the western empire. It documents an extensive correspondence between the ideals cited in honorific inscriptions for the emperor erected across the western empire and those advertised on imperial coins minted at Rome. This reveals that the dissemination of specific imperial ideals was more pervasive than previously thought, and indicates a high degree of ideological unification amongst the aristocracies of the western provinces. The widespread circulation of a particular set of imperial ideals, and the particular form of ideological unification that this brought about, not only reinforced the power of the Roman imperial state, but also increased the authority of local aristocrats, thereby facilitating a general convergence of social power that defined the high Roman empire.

CARLOS F. NOREÑA is Assistant Professor of History at the University of California, Berkeley. He is the co-editor, with Björn C. Ewald, of *The Emperor and Rome: Space, Representation, and Ritual* (Cambridge, 2010).

IMPERIAL IDEALS IN THE ROMAN WEST

Representation, Circulation, Power

CARLOS F. NOREÑA

CAMBRIDGE
UNIVERSITY PRESS

University Printing House, Cambridge CB2 8BS, United Kingdom

Cambridge University Press is part of the University of Cambridge.

It furthers the University's mission by disseminating knowledge in the pursuit of education, learning and research at the highest international levels of excellence.

www.cambridge.org
Information on this title: www.cambridge.org/9781316628966

First published 2011
First paperback edition 2016

A catalogue record for this publication is available from the British Library

Library of Congress Cataloguing in Publication data
Noreña, Carlos F.
Imperial ideals in the Roman West : representation, circulation, power /
Carlos F. Noreña.
p. cm.
Includes bibliographical references and index.
ISBN 978-1-107-00508-2 (hardback)
1. Rome – History – Empire, 30 B.C.–284 A.D.   2. Emperors – Rome – History.   3. Political culture – Rome – History.   4. Imperialism – Social aspects – Rome – History.   5. Ideals (Philosophy) – Political aspects – Rome – History.   6. Signs and symbols – Political aspects – Rome – History.   7. Power (Social sciences) – Rome – History.   8. Inscriptions, Latin – History.   9. Coins, Roman – History.   10. Rome – Politics and government – 30 B.C.–284 A.D.   I. Title.
DG271.N67   2011
937'.06 – dc22   2011008366

ISBN 978-1-107-00508-2 Hardback
ISBN 978-1-316-62896-6 Paperback

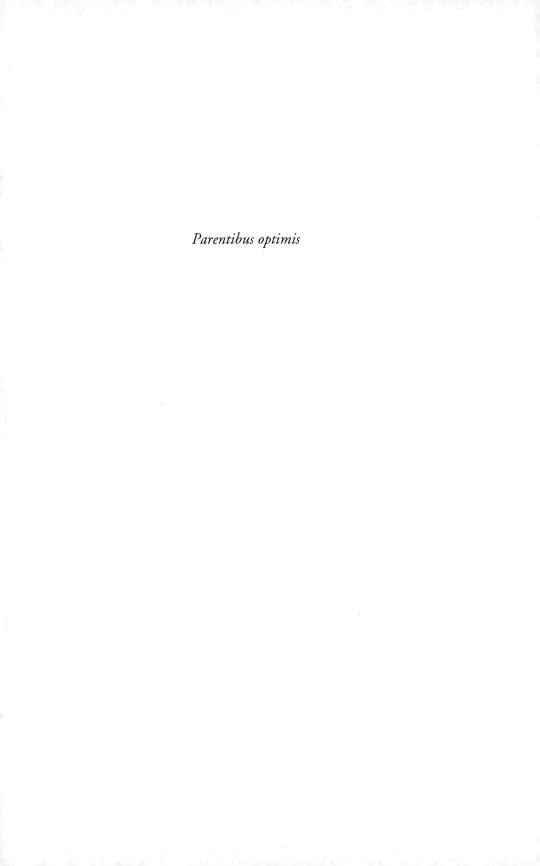

Parentibus optimis

Contents

List of illustrations

List of figures and tables

FIGURES

xiv

TABLES

List of maps

Acknowledgments

I have long dreamed of this moment, thinking, wrongly, that to write up these acknowledgments would be an easy task compared to the labors of writing the book itself. But as I stare at my computer screen, and contemplate the full extent of my debts, I now realize how difficult it will be to express the depth of my gratitude to the many teachers, colleagues, friends, and family members (overlapping categories, in a number of cases) who have made this book possible. *Fortuna* has been very kind to me indeed.

Imperial Ideals in the Roman West began as a doctoral dissertation at the University of Pennsylvania written under the supervision of Brent Shaw. Brent not only provided expert guidance on a topic that lay somewhat outside his own considerable area of research expertise, but also, more important, taught me how to think like an historian. His influence on my whole approach to the Roman empire, and to the discipline of history more generally, has been profound. To the other members of my dissertation committee, Ann Kuttner and Bill Metcalf, my debts are hardly less significant. From Ann I learned both how to "read" visual language and how to integrate the analysis of image and text, while Bill taught me more or less everything I know about Roman numismatics. He also provided me with the raw hoard data upon which my sample of silver coins was built. Without this extraordinary act of generosity on Bill's part, this book could not have been written.

I have incurred further debts in the process of transforming this study from a dissertation into a book. Ramsay MacMullen read the entire dissertation and responded to it with fifteen pages of single-spaced comments and questions that were uniformly incisive, challenging, critical, and illuminating. I seriously doubt that he will agree with all of my conclusions here, but I do hope that he will recognize his influence on the final product. My former colleagues in the Department of Classics at Yale, especially Susanna Braund, Christina Kraus, and John Matthews, offered further guidance and counsel at this crucial stage. Elizabeth Meyer and Greg Woolf read a detailed and lengthy book prospectus and helped me to sharpen my questions and strengthen my arguments. Some of these arguments were first tested out on audiences at Brown University, the Whitney Humanities Center (Yale University), the New England Ancient Historians Colloquium (University of Connecticut, April 2005), and the American Philological Association Annual Meeting (Montreal, January 2006), while a number of the ideas were first floated in the bracing atmosphere of graduate seminars at Yale ("Roman Imperial Ideology: Text and Image," Spring 2005) and Berkeley ("Culture and Empire in the Roman West," Fall 2006). I am most grateful for all the useful feedback I received in these talks and seminars from colleagues and students alike.

When it came time to assemble these arguments into book chapters, I turned for critical feedback to Kathleen Coleman, Erich Gruen, Ted Lendon, Carlos G. Noreña, and Josephine Quinn, all of whom provided most helpful comments on different parts of the manuscript. I have also received much useful advice from my colleagues in the Department of History at Berkeley, especially Beth Berry, Susanna Elm, Robin Einhorn, David Johnson, Emily Mackil, Michael Nylan, Peter Sahlins, and James Vernon. To each of them, as well as to the anonymous readers for the Press, I offer my warmest thanks.

I benefited from different types of assistance in the final stages of preparing the manuscript for publication. Philip Stark and his team in the Department of Statistics at Berkeley checked (and improved) my statistical formulas and calculations, while Darin Jensen and Mike Jones in the Department of Geography prepared the maps. Elena Stolyarik at the American Numismatic Society and Lynda Clark and Adrian Popescu at the Fitzwilliam Museum, University of Cambridge, helped me to acquire images. My gratitude goes to each of them. I would also like to thank the *Journal of Roman Studies* for permission to reprint parts of my article that appeared in volume 91 (2001). Finally, I would like to thank the editorial team at Cambridge University Press for bringing this book to publication, especially Michael Sharp, Joanna Garbutt, Elizabeth Hanlon, Mary Morton, and Christina Sarigiannidou.

These brief acknowledgments will be particularly incapable, I fear, of expressing all that I owe to my family: to my wife, Elizabeth, for her unwavering support through the inevitable ups and downs that come with the writing of a book like this; to my son, Carlos, for companionship and good cheer (and for typing a few sentences from chapter 5 into the computer); and to my daughter, Laura, for being such a lovely reminder that some things are more important than Roman history. But by far the deepest debt of all is owed to my parents, Carlos G. and Maria I. Noreña, whose love, support, and encouragement for so many years has made all the difference. I dedicate this book to them as a very small token of gratitude for all that they have given and continue to give to me.

Berkeley, CA
July 2010

Abbreviations

Abbreviations of personal names and texts follow those of the *Oxford Classical Dictionary*, and of modern periodicals, those of *L'Année Philologique*. Other abbreviations are as follows.

AE	*L'Année epigraphique*
AJN	*American Journal of Numismatics*
BMCRE	*Coins of the Roman Empire in the British Museum*
CIL	*Corpus Inscriptionum Latinarum*
CRAI	*Comptes rendus de l'Académie des Inscriptions et Belles-lettres*
EJ	V. Ehrenberg and A. H. M. Jones (eds.) *Documents Illustrating the Reigns of Augustus & Tiberius* (Oxford, 1955).
FdA	*Die Fundmünzen der Antike*
IGRR	*Inscriptiones Graecae ad Res Romanas Pertinentes*
ILLRP	*Inscriptiones Latinae Liberae Rei Publicae*
ILM	*Inscriptions latines du Maroc*
ILS	*Inscriptiones Latinae Selectae*
Inscr.Ital.	*Inscriptiones Italiae*
IRT	*Inscriptions of Roman Tripolitania*
JRS	*Journal of Roman Studies*
LIMC	*Lexicon Iconographicum Mythologiae Classicae*
LTUR	*Lexicon Topographicum Urbis Romae*
OGIS	*Orientis Graecae Inscriptiones Selectae*
OLD	*Oxford Latin Dictionary*
ORF	*Oratorum Romanorum Fragmenta* (2nd edn.)
P.Oxy	*Oxyrhynchus papyri*
RE	*Realencyclopädie der classischen Altertumswissenschaft*
RG	*Res Gestae*
RIB	*Roman Inscriptions of Britain*
RIC	*Roman Imperial Coinage*
RPC	*Roman Provincial Coinage*

RRC	*Roman Republican Coinage*
RS	*Roman Statutes*
SB	D. R. Shackleton Bailey (ed.) *Cicero: Letters to Atticus*, 7 vols.; *Epistulae ad Familiares*, 2 vols.; *Epistulae ad Quintum Fratrem et M. Brutum* (Cambridge, 2004).
SCPP	*senatusconsultum de Gnaeo Pisone Patre*
Syll	*Sylloge Inscriptionum Graecarum* (3rd edn.)
Tab.Siar.	*Tabula Siarensis*
TLL	*Thesaurus Linguae Latinae*

CHAPTER I

Introduction

MONARCHY, CULTURE, AND EMPIRE IN THE ROMAN WEST

The Roman empire, like all empires, may be seen as a particular config-uration of power. Controlled by an interlinked set of central institutions and layered aristocracies, this configuration of power reached its widest extent, deepest penetration, and greatest stability between the late first century BC and early third century AD. One feature of this 250-year period that distinguishes it from the previous two and a half centuries, when the Roman state was creating its overseas empire, was the existence of a sin-gle, empire-wide ruler, the emperor, who functioned in part as a unifying symbol for the far-flung territories and widely scattered inhabitants of the Roman world. There were no symbols of comparable resonance under the Republic. Two features of the period that distinguish it from the two and a half centuries that followed were, first, a broadly shared conception of the ideal emperor as an ethical and beneficent ruler, and second, the absence of competing symbols of equivalent distinction and empire-wide reach. For in the later empire, the emperor was often constructed as a distant and frightening autocrat, while the rise of Christianity brought with it a new and increasingly autonomous symbolic system that transcended the imperial order. As we will see, the significance of these distinctive features of the period between the late first century BC and the early third century AD went beyond the realm of symbols and ideas. Indeed, the existence of a single ruler, systematically represented as a moral exemplar who provided a range of benefits to his subjects, and standing alone as the only symbol of empire-wide scope, not only reinforced the power of the Roman imperial state, as I will argue, but also increased the collective authority of the local aristocracies upon which the empire's social and political order was based.

   In order to sustain this argument, discussion will focus on the specific imperial ideals that defined the emperor as an ethical and beneficent ruler; on the mechanisms by which these ideals came to be diffused throughout the empire; and on the reasons why the circulation of these particular ideals helped to underpin the empire's steep social and political hierarchy. Though some of the conclusions will pertain to the empire as a whole over the long term (*c.* 200 BC to AD 400), this study will concentrate, for reasons discussed below, on the western empire between AD 69 and 235. Before turning to the specific parameters of this study, however, and as a way of underlining the importance of unifying structures in the Roman world, we first need to consider the sheer size and diversity of the Roman empire at the peak of its power in the mid-second century AD.

Coming to grips with the size of the Roman empire is a constant challenge. Conventional metrics of the empire's magnitude, such as surface area (*c.* 2.5 million square miles in the mid-second century AD) or population (*c.* 60–70 million), are impressive enough, and standard cartographic depictions of the empire "at its height" – fixed, monochromatic, and stretching from the Atlantic to the Euphrates and from the Danube to the Sahara – are suitably imposing.[1] The effects of such distances on the experience of time and space in the empire can be difficult for the modern observer to appreciate. For even though the communications infrastructure of the empire was relatively advanced by the standards of the ancient world, it was limited by pre-modern technology.[2] It will be important to bear in mind just how slowly most persons, objects, and ideas circulated throughout this world.

More striking is the sheer diversity of the Roman empire. In geographical and ecological terms, the empire was deeply fragmented.[3] Stretching across four modern time zones, the empire embraced three continents and included multiple geological and climatic zones ranging from coastal plains, rugged mountain ranges, and high plateaus to fertile river valleys, deserts, and thick forests, all differentiated by temperature, rainfall, flora, and fauna. Nested within these broad zones were the countless microregions of the Roman imperial world, sometimes no larger than a single hillside or coastal inlet, within which the majority of the empire's inhabitants, more or less insulated from one another, spent most of their lives.

The human geography of the Roman empire was nearly as heterogeneous. The very different pre-conquest histories of the many areas brought under Roman imperial control gave rise to considerable internal diversity.

---

[1] Population: Scheidel 2007: 45–9.
[2] For the speed of communications, see e.g. Casson 1971: 281–99; Millar 2002–6 [1982]: 2.173–5; Duncan-Jones 1990: 7–29; Ando 2000: 121–2.
[3] Horden and Purcell 2000, with Shaw 2001; Potter 2004: 10–23.

Here the big divide was between east and west. At the dawn of Roman overseas expansion *c.* 240 BC, the Italian peninsula sat at the far western edge of a world-system centered on the eastern Mediterranean and running as far east as the Hindu Kush.[4] This was a world of large, centralized states, ruled, for the most part, by kings, and characterized by elaborate social stratification, economic complexity, technological innovation, widespread urbanization, and a highly developed historical consciousness based on authoritative literary texts. Most of the western Mediterranean and continental Europe, by contrast, stood as a tribal periphery of this world-system, with simple political structures, rudimentary social and economic organization, low levels of urbanization, and no literary tradition.[5] At the intersection of these regions lay a central zone, the "Hellenistic West," comprising southern Italy, Sicily, Punic North Africa, and the southern Iberian peninsula, which served as a sort of "gateway" for the spread of political structures and cultural forms from east to west.[6] These different regions of the Mediterranean basin, then, were at very different stages of political development in the last centuries of the first millennium BC, when all were simultaneously incorporated by the Roman state into a single imperial system.[7] And it goes without saying that within these broad zones, there was considerable diversity of historical experience prior to the Roman conquest. The Roman empire contained within its administrative boundaries a myriad of distinctive regional and local histories.

Historical variation meant cultural diversity. This could be illustrated in many ways. In the religious sphere, for example, countless deities, sacred objects and spaces, ritual practices, and beliefs co-existed in a profoundly pluralist imperial order.[8] Artistic diversity was perhaps less pronounced but significant nonetheless, with different traditions and styles, as well as different modes of artistic production and ways of seeing, prevailing in

---

[4] I use the term "world-system" to denote a large-scale, multipolar, and loosely bounded civilization characterized by broadly similar political, economic, and social structures. There are now many useful introductions to the historical evolution of the eastern Mediterranean – the "Hellenistic world" – prior to the Roman conquest; see, e.g., Erskine 2003, with full bibliography.

[5] For a broad overview of the pre-Roman, Iron Age western Mediterranean and temperate Europe, see Dietler 2007.

[6] On the "Hellenistic West," a rapidly developing field, see the papers collected in Prag and Quinn forthcoming.

[7] This is not meant to imply a crude, evolutionary model of development, but rather to point to varying levels of social and political complexity at different stages in the (variable) processes of state-formation in the ancient world; see briefly Goldstone and Haldon 2009: 24–7.

[8] Religious diversity: e.g. Turcan 1996; Rüpke 1997; Beard, North and Price 1998. For a recent attempt to delineate some of the unifying features of religion in the Roman empire, Rives 2007.

different parts of the empire.[9] Dietary patterns, too, were quite variegated across the empire, determined not only by the availability of specific crops, but also by regional and local preferences for different types of meat.[10] Perhaps the most obvious marker of cultural diversity in the Roman empire was language. We tend to think immediately, and too often exclusively, of the major Latin west/Greek east divide, but it must be emphasized that this bifurcation in the language of high culture in the Roman empire was only the most conspicuous crack in the linguistic façade of a truly polyglot realm that comprised scores of local languages and dialects.[11] It is probably safe to assume that most subjects of the Roman empire could not communicate with one another.

There were, of course, several unifying forces in the Roman empire, but all must be qualified in one way or another. The Mediterranean sea provided a measure of cohesion, especially as a catalyst for the communications that promoted local, regional, and interregional interaction between the geologically discrete, but functionally interdependent, microregions of the Roman world. But the sea itself was very large, extending some 2,300 miles from west to east, and very differentiated, effectively broken up into numerous separate waters by islands, peninsulas, a sprawling maze of disjointed currents, and a highly variable coastline. The economy of the empire as a whole was based on agriculture, and long-distance trade was substantial enough to ensure the regular movement of goods between regions, but there never emerged a single, fully integrated, market economy in the Roman empire.[12] Though the basic dynamics of the urban/rural dichotomy were roughly the same everywhere, the geographical distribution of cities and urban systems throughout the empire was rather lopsided, with much higher densities in the east and along the Mediterranean coast.[13] And while the Roman imperial state did impose a degree of administrative uniformity on its sweeping territories, this never approached the sort of homogeneity that we take for granted in a modern nation-state.[14] Indeed,

---

[9] Artistic diversity: e.g. Scott and Webster 2003; Brilliant 2007; for varieties of visual literacy, viewing, and subjectivity, see also Elsner 2007.

[10] King 1999.

[11] Linguistic diversity: Neumann and Untermann 1980; Harris 1989: 175–90. For bilingualism with Latin, see also Adams 2003, and for regional variation of Latin itself, Adams 2007.

[12] Agrarian economy: e.g. Horden and Purcell 2000: 175–297; Kehoe 2007: 550–9. On markets and degrees of economic integration in the Roman empire, see, e.g., Duncan-Jones 1990: 48–76; Howgego 1994; Hopkins 2002 (1995/96); Temin 2001; Morley 2007.

[13] It is also worth noting that the multitude of cities, towns, and villages throughout the empire was organized in an intricate mosaic of varying formal status.

[14] Taxation, for example, was far from uniform, and even though the tenets of Roman law applied, in principle, to all Roman citizens throughout the empire, in practice it seems that local laws prevailed

the central state during the first two centuries AD never attempted direct rule over its widely dispersed subjects, channeling the bulk of its material and human resources into the armies stationed along the frontiers and devolving most of what passed for day-to-day administration onto semi-autonomous communities.[15] This, too, resulted in local and regional diversity. Finally, the diffusion of Roman citizenship from one end of the Mediterranean world to the other was a remarkable and characteristic feature of the Roman empire, but its spread was very uneven, both socially and geographically.[16]

Overall, then, the picture is one of diversity and fragmentation. One conspicuous exception to this empire-wide diversity was the Roman emperor. If nothing else, every inhabitant of the Roman empire shared a single ruler.[17] And the Roman emperor was no mere ornament in the Roman imperial superstructure. Partly as an important actor in his own right, and partly as a deeply resonant symbol, the Roman emperor had a deep impact on both the political system and the cultural fabric of the Roman empire.

It is surprisingly difficult to fit the Roman emperor neatly into standard typologies of rulership. On the one hand, the emperor served as something like a civilian magistrate, formally endowed by the institutions of the *res publica*, "commonwealth," with a collection of precisely defined constitutional powers. There was no public investiture or coronation ceremony for new emperors. In fact, most emperors made an elaborate show of initially refusing imperial power, subsequently rejecting all sorts of prerogatives and honors for the duration of their reigns.[18] At the root of this anomalous posture of monarchic *recusatio* was the venerable republican framework out of which Augustus and his successors had fashioned the political system known to later commentators and modern scholars as "the principate" (*principatus*). As is well known, Augustus in particular was careful to ensure

---

more often than not. On taxation in the empire, see, e.g., Neesen 1980; Brunt 1990 (1981): 324–46, 531–40; Corbier 1991; Lo Cascio 2000: 36–43, 177–203. On Roman law and local law, Galsterer 1986; Crawford 1988; Lintott 1993: 154–60.

[15] Accounts of different aspects of this arrangement in Jacques 1984; Garnsey and Saller 1987: 26–40; Reynolds 1988; Burton 2001.

[16] On Roman citizenship, see Sherwin-White 1973; Shaw 2000: 361–72; Inglebert 2002b; Garnsey 2004; for Roman citizenship as a benefit of empire, see below, 104.

[17] In some parts of the empire, especially in the east during the first century AD, many inhabitants actually lived under what Millar has called a "two-level monarchy," subject both to a local king and to the Roman emperor (2002–6 [1996]: 2.229–45). But the Roman emperor was clearly superior.

[18] On imperial *recusatio* at accession, see Huttner 2004; cf. Béranger 1953: 137–69 (note the long list of emperors, from Augustus through Theodosius, for whom this ritual is attested, 139–40); Wickert 1954: 2,258–64. See also Wallace-Hadrill 1982: 36–7 and Talbert 1984: 359–61 for imperial refusal of honors in general.

that each of the powers and honors voted to him could be represented as consistent with Republican precedent, and throughout the imperial period the emperor articulated his formal power largely through Republican symbols and titles.[19] In these respects, then, the Roman emperor does not look very much like a conventional "absolute monarch."[20]

On the other hand, the formal powers with which the emperor was invested were in fact absolute, and he was acknowledged by the Roman jurists as being, uniquely, "above the law."[21] Indeed, ultimate decision-making authority in the Roman state came to rest with the person of the emperor, as the multiple, discrete points of decision-making characteristic of the Republic were eventually subordinated to the will of a single ruler. The reigning emperor also normally controlled the transmission of imperial power. Though the Roman imperial monarchy is historically distinctive for its high degree of dynastic discontinuity, individual emperors nevertheless regularly designated their own successors – often, in the absence of direct male descendants, from outside the nuclear family – and for most of the period down to AD 235 these publicly named heirs acceded to the imperial throne without incident.[22] And finally, the emperor very nearly monopolized all the key symbols of political power, especially in the city of Rome.[23] Later observers were quite right to refer to the political system established under Augustus as a monarchy.[24]

[19] Different perspectives on the "emperor as magistrate," with references to earlier studies, in Veyne 2002a; Rowe 2007. For Republican elements in the emperor's titulature, prominent at least through the reign of Constantine (cf. *CIL* 5.8011 = *ILS* 697), see Hammond 1959: 58–91.

[20] As exemplified, for example, by the absolutist kings of early modern Europe; for a recent overview of the scholarship on early modern absolutism, with a focus on the reign of Louis XIV, see Beik 2005, with abundant references.

[21] The emperor's absolute power is stated quite explicitly in the sixth clause of the *lex de imperio Vespasiani* (*CIL* 6.930 = *ILS* 244 = *RS* 1.39, ll. 18–20): *utique quaecunque ex usu reipublicae maiestate divinarum hum[an]arum publicarum privatarumque rerum esse censebit, ei agere facere ius potestasque sit . . .* For the argument that this clause means exactly what it says, and was intended to grant absolute power to the emperor, see Brunt 1977: 109–16; *contra*, Crook 1996: 120 ("residual emergency powers" only). The emperor's *imperium* was also formally superior to that of all other magistrates: cf. Dio 53.32.5; *CIL* 2²/5.900, ll. 34–6, with Eck *et al.* 1996: 158–61. Emperor "above the law:" *Dig.* 1.3.31 (Ulpian): *princeps legibus solutus est*; for the general perception that the emperor was above the law, see also Sen. *Ep.* 7.2, *Clem.* 1.1; Plin. *Pan.* 65.1; Suet. *Cal.* 14.1; Dio 53.18.1.

[22] In general on the transmission of imperial power, Hammond 1956. For Roman dynastic discontinuity in world-historical perspective, see Scheidel forthcoming; cf. Hekster 2001 on adoption and fictive kinship in the second century.

[23] See, e.g., Veyne 1976: 675–730; Zanker 1988a; Benoist 2005; Ewald and Noreña 2010.

[24] For explicit references to the Augustan regime as a monarchy, see, e.g., App. *Hist. pr.* 14 (τὰ Ῥωμαίων ἐς μοναρχίαν περιῆλθεν); Dio 52.1.1 (ἐκ δὲ τούτου μοναρχεῖσθαι αὖθις ἀκριβῶς ἤρξαντο). Implicit references abound, e.g. Sen. *Ben.* 2.20, 6.32; Suet. *Aug.* 28; Tac. *Hist.* 1.1, *Ann.* 1.1.1, 1.2.2, 1.3.1, 1.4.1, 1.9.4, 3.28, etc. No contemporary author referred to Augustus as a monarch, but many passages reflect a clear recognition of his monarchic power, e.g. Vitr. *pr.* 1–2; Hor. *Carm.* 1.12.49–52, 3.14.14–16,

It would be misleading, however, to conceptualize the emperor as an omnipotent monarch capable of dominating his far-flung empire. The structural limitations to the practical power of Roman emperors were simply too great. Aristocratic competitors could be very dangerous, especially those in command of legions stationed in the periphery. From such potential pretenders to the throne the threat of usurpation could never be extinguished entirely.[25] Less acute but more constant pressure came from those groups within Roman imperial society that were capable of meaningful collective action in the public sphere. Especially significant were the senate, the *plebs urbana* of Rome, and the legionary armies. With these influential collectivities the emperor was in constant dialogue, both real and symbolic, interacting with each in a highly prescribed manner calculated to elicit the public displays of consensus, or "acceptance," upon which imperial legitimacy ultimately rested.[26] And even when the emperor did decide to act, he faced the stubborn problems of time and space noted above – a constant challenge to the effective communications, mobilization of resources, and concentration of power necessary to achieve desired ends.

There were, then, multiple constraints on the independent power of the emperor. There was also real institutional continuity before and after Augustus.[27] This does not mean, however, that the transition from republic to monarchy made little difference to the political system of the Roman empire. No one will claim that the advent of monarchy at Rome triggered a fundamental redistribution of wealth and power throughout Roman society. But it did create a major new actor within the larger configuration of power that comprised the Roman empire. Part of this complex process was documented by Syme in *The Roman Revolution*, in which "the revolution" had less to do with the transition from republic to monarchy than with the extensive changes in the composition of the senatorial order brought about

---

4.5.1–2, *Ep.* 2.1.1–4; Ov. *Fast.* 1.531–2, 2.138–42, *Trist.* 4.4.13–16. On these passages, see Millar 2002–6 (1973): 1.267–70, arguing that Augustus' reign was openly monarchic and universally seen as such; *contra*, Gruen 2005. Further discussion of the distinctive nature of Roman imperial monarchy below, 315–17.

[25] The political history of the first two centuries AD is punctuated by usurpers making violent bids for imperial power, some unsuccessful (e.g. Vindex in 68, Saturninus in 89, Avidius Cassius in 175), others successful (Vespasian in 69, Septimius Severus in 193); for analysis and discussion, see Flaig 1992.

[26] Flaig 1992, esp. 94–131 (senate), 38–93 (urban plebs), and 132–73 (army). For the workings under a single emperor, Trajan, of what Flaig calls an *Akzeptanzsystem*, see Seelentag 2004. On the connection between consensus and legitimacy, Weber 1968 (1921): 1,121–48, esp. 1,125–6, with Flaig 2010 ("acceptance").

[27] Legislative assemblies, for example, are attested as late as Nerva (*Dig.* 47.21.3.1), and electoral assemblies were still meeting in the early third century (Dio 37.28, 68.20.4).

by the violent triumph of Augustus' "party." Where Syme went astray was in his implicit disregard for the symbolic forms of political life, an interpretive stance signaled most clearly by a famous programmatic statement: "In all ages, whatever the form and name of government, be it monarchy, republic, or democracy, an oligarchy lurks behind the façade; and Roman history, Republican or Imperial, is the history of the governing class."[28] For despite the underlying continuity of political institutions, Republican ideology, and oligarchic power, the change in the "form of government" was in fact critical – if not for the reasons normally given.

One impediment to understanding has been a tendency to conflate the reigning emperor with the institution of monarchy. No emperor was as powerful as his public image would suggest, but the advent of monarchy was nevertheless a decisive moment in the political and cultural history of the Roman empire, above all because it brought with it the emergence of a new symbol, the emperor, a simple but potent idea with tremendous resonance. The very existence of this symbol, and the different uses to which it could be put by different actors, reconfigured several power networks within the Roman world, as I will argue, intensifying mechanisms of social control and solidifying the hegemony of the Roman imperial state. In the transition from republic to monarchy, that is to say, it was not so much the political dimension of the change that mattered, but the symbolic one. This has not been sufficiently emphasized in recent accounts of the impact of the Augustan revolution on the political system of the Roman empire.[29]

One clue suggesting that the advent of monarchy at Rome had far-reaching effects on the politics and culture of the Roman world is chronological. A number of broadly interrelated changes and processes converged in the decades straddling the turn of the first millennium, coinciding with the advent of monarchy under Augustus. Changes in the organization of state and empire were especially momentous. The explosive and ceaseless imperial expansion of the last two centuries BC decelerated rapidly. Henceforth conquest was sporadic and comparatively brief. The administration of the provinces was rationalized. New conceptualizations of imperial territory and administrative space came to the fore, road systems were systematically

---

[28] Syme 1939: 7.

[29] See, for example, Eder 2005 and Rowe 2007, both putting too much emphasis on institutional continuities between the Republic and Augustan/Julio-Claudian periods. And those studies that do focus on the cultural and symbolic aspects of the Augustan age (and of the early empire in general) do not draw enough attention to the effects of these changes on political structures and configurations of power; see below, n. 35 and 13–14.

developed, the provincial census was initiated, and the collection of tax regularized. In brief, an aggressive conquest state was replaced by a more stable tributary regime.[30] At Rome, several new discourses arose, on time, religion, law, science, and language, and as a result knowledge became increasingly differentiated and professionalized. Literature, art, architecture, domestic space, and forms of public display (especially oratory) were all developing rapidly and in dynamic ways. Together these changes amounted to what has rightly been called a "cultural revolution."[31] In the provinces, the processes of urbanization accelerated, especially in the west.[32] Indeed, the western empire experienced its own cultural revolution during this period, a process often described under the rubric of "Romanization," as many of the objects, practices, and beliefs characteristic of Roman Italy, from monumental architecture, public space, and religious ritual to clothing, tablewares, and nomenclature, began to be widely adopted – and adapted – throughout the western provinces. Rome had had an overseas empire stretching back to the mid-third century BC, but the formative period of provincial cultures in the west did not really take off until the late first century BC.[33]

All of these changes were chronologically coincident with the transition from republic to monarchy at Rome. It is naturally difficult to disentangle how, precisely, such political and cultural changes were related to one another, and to determine where ultimate causation lies. Too much was happening at the same time for this convergence to have been merely coincidental. It is equally unrealistic to posit Augustus himself as the architect of these empire-wide transformations. We must look for deeper causes. Some scholars favor political explanations, arguing (or implying) that the emergence of monarchy drove the cultural changes characteristic of the

---

[30] Deceleration of conquest: Gruen 1996; Rich 2003. Provincial administration: Eck 2000; Eich 2005. Conceptualization of administrative space: Nicolet 1991. Road systems: Rathmann 2003. Provincial census: Lo Cascio 2000: 205–19. Collection of tax: see above, n. 14. Imperial state as tributary regime: Bang 2008.

[31] Knowledge and discourse: Wallace-Hadrill 1997, 2005, 2008: 213–58; Moatti 1997; on time and calendrical reform, see also Feeney 2006. Literature: Galinsky 1996: 225–87, 2005: 281–358 (essays by Barchiesi, Griffin, White, and Galinsky). Art and architecture: Zanker 1988a; Hofter 1988; Galinsky 1996: 141–224. "Cultural revolution" at Rome: Wallace-Hadrill 1989, 1997, 2008; Habinek and Schiesaro 1997; cf. Gruen 1990, 1992.

[32] Cf. MacMullen 2000: 7–10, 30–5, 51–5, 93–9, with references to earlier studies.

[33] Studies on the meaning and usefulness of the term "Romanization" continue to proliferate at a dizzying pace; Woolf 1998: 1–23 offers a sensible introduction. Adoption of Italic "way of life": MacMullen 2000; cf. Ward-Perkins 1970 for architectural change in the western provinces, and Wallace-Hadrill 2000 and 2008 for changes in material culture more broadly. "Formative period" of provincial cultures: Woolf 1995.

period.[34] Some have suggested that cultural change was primary, and that the transition from republic to monarchy should be seen as a product of that change.[35] Others have sought to dissolve the dichotomy between political and cultural change altogether, arguing that each was part of the same "process."[36] Consensus remains elusive.

One approach is to see these broadly simultaneous changes – the shift from a republic to a monarchy and from conquest state to tributary empire, the cultural revolution at Rome, and the cultural transformation of the western empire – as the product of a more general convergence of "social power" in the Roman world.[37] As a measure of the capacity to control territory, resources, and persons, social power arises from a number of different sources, especially control over meaning and values, material resources, physical force, and administrative infrastructure.[38] These various sources of power are organized and actualized in different ways, and are usually controlled by any number of different social actors. In the Roman empire, the key actors were the institutions and associated personnel of the central state; the most influential collectivities within the empire, especially the senate and the army; and the layered aristocracies of the Roman world, both imperial and local.[39] In attempting to situate the changes summarized

---

[34] Syme 1939 is still the best-known politics-driven account of this transformative period. Zanker 1988a is a celebrated overview of the visual sphere in the Augustan age, but art and architecture are seen throughout as the products of – and therefore secondary to – underlying political and social conditions.

[35] This has been the dominant approach of the 1990s and 2000s, very much a product of "the cultural turn" of these decades (cf. Steinmetz 1999b: 1–3). Representative works include Galinsky 1996 and Habinek and Schiesaro 1997, who write of "the centrality of culture, both as an explanatory phenomenon and as an analytical category" (xvi); the primacy of culture also characterizes much of Woolf's work (1995, 1996, 1998, 2001, 2005), e.g. 2005: 110: "The shift to autocracy at Rome, in other words, was *just another component* of the cultural transformation of the Mediterranean world" (author's emphasis).

[36] E.g. Wallace-Hadrill 2005: 81: "The present argument neither explains political change by cultural change, nor the opposite. It attempts to show that the two processes of change were deeply enmeshed with each other, indeed *were one and the same process*" (my emphasis).

[37] For what follows, see Mann 1986 (esp. 1–33 for the general model of "social power") and 1993; further discussion below, 322–3.

[38] These represent what Mann calls, respectively, "ideological," "economic," "military," and "political" power (1986: 22–8).

[39] There was, of course, substantial overlap between these three categories (a senator from Baetica serving as a provincial governor in Asia Minor, for example, or an equestrian from North Africa serving as a legionary officer on the Rhine frontier, simultaneously belonged to all three). I follow Bendix in characterizing the aristocracy as that segment of society that controlled landownership and monopolized a position of honor and prestige through claims to superior birth and morality (1978: 106), and Kautsky in stressing aristocratic participation in imperial administration and warfare (1982: 79–98, 144–66); cf. Trigger 2003: 147–54. The aristocracies (or "elites") of the Roman empire were "layered" in the sense that there always existed important subdivisions within this larger ruling class; the most important for our purposes was the division between an upper tier of "imperial"

above within the context of social power in the Roman world, we must remain sensitive not only to different types of power, but also to the different networks within which these types of power were organized, and to the different actors controlling these networks. Explaining this convergence, in other words, is rather more complicated than simply analyzing the relationship between "politics" and "culture," as the question is normally framed.

The vital link that enabled the convergence of social power in the Roman world was forged between the central state, on the one hand, and the local aristocracies of the empire, on the other. This bond was based on a simple trade. Local aristocrats throughout the empire helped to maintain order and to collect taxes in the interests of the central state, which in return provided these local "big men" with markers of status, especially Roman citizenship and, where necessary, with armed force.[40] Closely related to local administration was civic benefaction, the customary practice by which these same local aristocrats voluntarily expended their own wealth on the physical development and adornment of their cities. In the western empire in particular, this voluntary civic benefaction was the engine that drove urbanization and the making of the cities in which the cultural transformation that began in the late first century BC was most visible.[41] Both the upper-tier aristocrats who controlled the central state and the lower-tier aristocrats who controlled the municipalities of the empire had a strong incentive to maintain this arrangement, since both benefited from it. And the results are everywhere manifest in the early imperial period, above all in the political stability of the state, dominated by an imperial aristocracy headed by an emperor; in the territorial stability of the empire, maintained by a large and expensive army that was financed by the taxes

aristocrats, i.e. members of the senatorial and equestrian orders in the imperial administration, and a lower tier of "local" aristocrats, i.e. the members of the municipal ruling classes of the empire. For the senatorial and equestrian orders as a composite *Reichsaristokratie*, see (e.g.) Hopkins 1983: 44–5, 110–11. It should also be stressed, finally, that the emperor himself, and the imperial family in general, did not stand apart, but belonged to the imperial aristocracy; cf. Kautsky 1982: 235–7, and below, 315.

[40] For the administrative arrangements, see works cited in n. 15 above; for the central state's contributions to the bargain (esp. citizenship and armed force), see also Brunt 1990 (1976): 267–81, 515–17; MacMullen 1988: 104–18; Lendon 1997 (*passim*); Woolf 1998, esp. 24–47; Shaw 2000: 362–73. For similar arrangements in other pre-industrial empires, see discussion in Eisenstadt 1963, esp. 115–221; Bendix 1978: 218–43; Kautsky 1982, esp. 132–43; Sinopoli 1994: 164–5, 2001: 197–9; Trigger 2003: 207–9.

[41] On civic benefaction in the Greek and Roman world, Veyne 1976 remains fundamental. For regional studies of benefaction and urbanization in the early Roman west, see, e.g., Wesch-Klein 1990 (North Africa); Woolf 1998: 106–41 (Gaul); Melchor Gil 2001 (Spain); Lomas 2003 (Italy); for the eastern empire, see most recently Zuiderhoek 2009. For more detail, see below, chapter 5.

collected by local aristocrats; and in the replication of Roman/Italic cultural forms throughout the western empire, requiring a sustained expenditure of material resources by these same local aristocrats, whose own wealth, social status, and political power were all enhanced by their active participation in the Roman imperial system.

None of this is meant to imply that the convergence of power networks, harmonization of interests, and resulting intensification of Roman imperial power was complete or unproblematic. The political stability of the central state and the territorial stability of the empire were occasionally threatened by large-scale violence from within and from beyond the empire's borders, especially in the second half of the second century AD. The sectional interests of the different key actors could always come into conflict, too, especially over the limited agricultural surplus of the empire, shared by the central state and the empire's landowners and extracted through taxes and rents, respectively.[42] And the intensive, infrastructural power of the central state was never sufficient to intervene regularly in the daily lives of the empire's subjects. The point is simply that the degree of convergence, harmonization, and intensification in the Roman empire was significantly higher between the late first century BC and early third century AD than it was in the two and a half centuries that came before and after.

Attention to overlapping power networks may elucidate the specific processes that drove the general convergence of the late first century BC, but it does not by itself solve the problems of causation and chronology. Why did this convergence of power networks and the resulting intensification of Roman imperial power occur at all, and why did it occur when it did? Part of the answer, I argue, lies in the simple fact that the Roman world was now ruled, for the first time, by a single ruler, a monarch. The emperor played several critical roles in this convergence, both as a social actor and as a symbol – and this distinction, which deserves more emphasis than it is normally given, is critically important.

As a uniquely powerful actor in his own right, on the one hand, the emperor functioned as the ultimate arbiter between still fiercely ambitious senators, suppressing the violent aristocratic competition that had destroyed the Republic and effectively re-directing this energy towards the larger goals of the central state, especially in the maintenance of a large territorial empire – less expansion and plundering, more administration and

---

[42] For this structural competition over a limited agricultural surplus, see, e.g., Hopkins 2002 (1995/96).

development.[43] In this way, political, military, and economic power, and the networks within which each was organized, were harmonized to a degree that had never been reached under the Republic. And this arrangement was ultimately beneficial to the aristocrats themselves since it facilitated their collective dominance.[44] In addition, the emperor could dispense marks of honor, status, and authority to equestrian officials and local aristocrats in the provinces, unilaterally distributing privilege and power throughout the empire in a manner that the Rome-based, Republican oligarchy never would have tolerated, but that was clearly advantageous to the imperial system as a whole.[45] Again, this resulted in an unprecedented extension and harmonization of political, military, and economic power networks throughout the empire.

As a potent symbol, on the other hand, the figure of the Roman emperor was useful to all the beneficiaries of the imperial system, above all because this symbol was uniquely capable of generating a degree of ideological unification throughout an otherwise highly diverse and fragmented empire, helping to universalize the particular claims of the Roman imperial state and to legitimate the social and political order upon which the state was based. In this way, ideological power was effectively harnessed for all the key actors within this larger configuration of power – local aristocracies, the Roman senate, and the Roman army (collectivities); lower-tier and upper-tier aristocrats (individuals); and, critically, the ruling emperor himself – in a manner that would have been nearly impossible without a resonant, unifying symbol of this sort.[46]

The general convergence of social power in the Mediterranean world of the late first century BC, then, triggered in part by the advent of monarchy at Rome, generated an unprecedented extension and intensification of institutional, collective, and aristocratic power – an amalgamation that we

---

[43] Senatorial competition in the downfall of the Republic: e.g. Brunt 1988: 32–45. Suppression of aristocratic competition (and public display) under the monarchy: Eck 1984, 2005, 2010; Campbell 1984: 348–62; Talbert 1984: 362–4, 425–30; Roller 2001: 97–108.

[44] The benefits of a strong, centralized, and universalistic state for the individual power of particularist aristocrats is a key theme of Eisenstadt 1963; cf. Mann 1986: 170–1.

[45] It was precisely the unwillingness of the ruling elites of other ancient, republican, city-state empires (e.g., Athens and Carthage) to distribute power and privilege in this way that hindered state-formation and prevented large-scale extensions and intensifications of imperial power; cf. Scheidel 2006. Such policies could cause tension between monarchs and aristocrats, another example of sectional interests coming into conflict; the *locus classicus* from the early empire is the debate under Claudius on the admission of Gallic aristocrats to the Roman senate; see Tac. *Ann.* 11.23–5 and *ILS* 212, with Griffin 1982. In general on the continuous struggle between monarchs and aristocrats, and their mutual interdependence, see Weber 1968 (1921): 1,006–69; cf. Motyl 2001: 12–38.

[46] This point will be argued in detail in subsequent chapters.

may call, as a convenient shorthand, "the Roman empire" – that endured down to the early third century AD. While the empirical focus of this book is on the definition, representation, communication, and circulation of imperial ideals and values, the very constituents of ideological power, these symbolic dimensions of the Roman monarchical system were never divorced from the cruder and more coercive operations of military and political power. The convergence and intensification of imperial power in the early Roman empire is the larger context in which the circulation of imperial ideals must be seen.

THE COLLECTIVE PRODUCTION OF A SYMBOLIC SYSTEM

I have argued that one key to the general convergence of social power in the late first century BC was the existence of an emperor, in part because of the deep symbolic resonance of a single, empire-wide ruler. But in order for the idea of the emperor to have had any real impact on political structures and cultural forms, it had to be widely diffused. That it was widely diffused is not in doubt. Another defining feature of the early Roman empire, in fact, was the rapid and extensive proliferation of imperial symbols, in many different forms, a multifaceted process through which the idea of the emperor was spread from one end of the empire to the other, contributing to the emergence of a new, empire-wide symbolic system.[47]

This symbolic system centered on the figure of the Roman emperor was made up of many different objects, ideas, and practices.[48] Visual representations in a wide range of media helped to maintain the emperor's existence in the collective consciousness of his subjects. Scattered literary references suggest that the emperor's image was nearly ubiquitous, especially in public contexts, a picture amply confirmed by the material record, which indicates that imperial statues were erected in large numbers in the public spaces of cities big and small. Public monuments, too, helped to diffuse the idea of

---

[47] For the purposes of this study, I will define "symbolic system" as a complex of interlocking symbols that is relatively coherent, insofar as these symbols share the same logic and reinforce one another; relatively extensive, insofar as these symbols are diffused through space; and relatively stable, insofar as the production of these symbols endures over time. Of the various symbolic systems that together constituted the semiotic component of Roman imperial culture, the particular system that we are investigating here was the one comprised of those symbols, whether objects, ideas, or practices, that in one way or another expressed the idea of the Roman emperor. This formulation owes much to Geertz's definition of the symbol (e.g. 1973: 91, 208: n. 19), but departs from Geertz in its explicit acknowledgment that multiple symbolic systems can operate simultaneously within a given culture (in the semiotic sense); "symbolic system" and "culture," in other words, are not being used interchangeably, as they seem to be in Geertz's work.

[48] For details, discussion, and references for what follows, see below, 200–18.

the emperor, especially the temples and other complexes associated with what we call "the imperial cult." Less dramatic than statues and public buildings, but far more numerous, were the imperial coins produced at Rome and disseminated throughout the empire, bringing imperial images and ideals to every corner of the Roman world, and in constant circulation between the public and private spheres. Other small-scale objects, such as medallions, gems, seals, lamps, and mirrors, also conveyed images of the emperor, especially in domestic contexts. In the western empire in particular, the early imperial period also witnessed a dramatic proliferation in the number of epigraphic texts, many of which presented the emperor's names and titles in monumental letters, usually associating the emperor with some positive quality or action. Literary texts also worked to diffuse the idea of the emperor far and wide. Finally, imperial travels in the provinces not only invested local places with the temporary aura of centrality, but also gave the emperor's subjects a rare opportunity to see their ruler in person.

All of these symbols, from the largest monumental complex for emperor worship to the smallest cameo, from the ceremonials associated with an imperial visit to the ideals expressed in honorific dedications to the emperor, together constituted a complex, "modular" symbolic system that revolved around the figure of the Roman emperor. The key question for the thesis of this book is whether this system had any impact on the convergence of social power summarized above. In brief, to anticipate my conclusions, I will attempt to show that this symbolic system helped to legitimate the political supremacy of a single ruler; naturalize and universalize the experience of Roman imperial power; facilitate the cohesion of the dispersed local aristocracies of the empire; and reinforce their differentiation from, and dominance over, the masses. I also hope to show that all of these things went together, and that this nexus of ideas, symbols, and political authority – in both its empire-wide and local aspects – helps us to understand how the Roman empire actually worked as a configuration of power.

Before proceeding to the empirical core of the argument, however, we must first confront, at least in a preliminary manner, the problems of agency, intent, and motive in the production of this symbolic system. In terms of agency, the most important point to note here is that many different actors, both collective and individual, participated in the process.[49] For this reason alone, simple, top-down models of communications and arguments framed in terms of "propaganda" are ill-suited to the interpretation

---

[49] For more detail on what follows, see below: 214–17, 218–19, 240, 245–6, 314–16.

of this process as a whole.[50] Some of the actors who produced imperial symbols were associated with the central state or the imperial regime itself, others were not. They range from the emperor and his inner circle to anonymous provincial subjects. For the sake of convenience, we may call those actors connected with the central state "official," and those acting independently of it "unofficial." In practice, as we will see, there existed a wide spectrum between official and unofficial, rather than a binary opposition, but this is a useful way to organize the material for the moment.

The problem of intent in the production of imperial symbols is both more difficult and more straightforward than the problem of agency. To recover the specific, self-conscious intention behind the production of any one imperial symbol is usually impossible. The surviving evidence simply does not bring us to that level of subjectivity. At a more general level, however, it is clear that imperial symbols produced in the public sphere were broadly intended to honor, celebrate, commemorate, or idealize the figure of the emperor. It is also clear, despite the multiplicity of groups and individuals involved in the production of these symbols, that most, and certainly the most important for the idealization of the emperor, were produced by the central state, on the one hand, and by local aristocrats, whether acting individually or collectively, on the other.

Of the multiple symbols that made up this particular symbolic system, the most significant for our purposes were the specific ideals and values associated with the figure of the emperor, especially virtues and benefits. As we will see, the specific virtues and benefits communicated by the central state on various media were frequently replicated by local aristocrats, especially in the language of honorific dedications made to the emperor. The broad lexical and ideological correspondence that arose from such communication and replication makes it difficult to disentangle the various motives of the key actors involved, but understanding why these different actors actively produced these mutually reinforcing symbols of imperial authority is crucial for my larger argument. For even though both the central state and local aristocrats sought to idealize the emperor, and even though the ways in which that idealization was expressed were often similar, and sometimes identical, the motives of these two sets of actors, though compatible, were quite distinct.

The communication of imperial ideals by the central state was itself complex and multifaceted, and various motives were usually at play – a

---

[50] This is not to say that propagandistic elements were absent from all parts of this collective process; see below, 18, 318–19.

senatorial decree, for example, was not often driven by the same concerns as an imperial edict, even though both were "official" according to the definition offered above. Furthermore, it is usually impossible to specify who, precisely, was responsible for the production of any one image or text. We will return to these issues in chapter 4. Here the question is what motivated the central state in general, and the imperial regime in particular, to communicate imperial ideals and values in the first place. Some scholars have argued that such communications were intended to shape public opinion in the interests of the imperial regime, and should therefore be seen as a form of political propaganda. Asserting the regime's autocratic control over the official media of communications, its deliberate falsification of the truth, and the drive to obtain consensus for imperial rule and the authority of the reigning emperor, a number of scholars have also drawn explicit parallels between the Roman state and the totalitarian regimes of the mid-twentieth century.[51] Other scholars, disputing the Roman imperial regime's capacity to control the various media of communications and highlighting the limitations of pre-modern technologies, have rejected the proposition that imperial coins, statues, and monuments could function as instruments of political propaganda.[52] Veyne has gone even further, denying that imperial representation had any persuasive content whatsoever, and arguing that such representation should be seen instead as nothing more than *faste monarchique* ("monarchic display") – the "irrational" public expression of imperial power for its own sake.[53]

The pendulum of scholarly opinion has now swung away from the interpretation of the various official media of communications as vehicles of propaganda.[54] But the idea of imperial propaganda should not be abandoned altogether. One obstacle to consensus, especially in Anglo-American scholarship, has been a somewhat crude understanding of just

---

[51] Syme 1939 is a classic interpretation along these lines. "The purpose of propaganda," he wrote, "was threefold: to win an appearance of legality for measures of violence, to seduce the supporters of a rival party and to stampede the neutral or non-political elements" (154). This conception of propaganda informs the whole book, culminating in the chapter entitled "The Organization of Opinion" (459–75). For other interpretations of imperial propaganda, see, e.g., Sordi 1974 and 1976 (emphasizing its subtle, hidden nature, and its regular distortion of the truth); cf. Hannestad 1986, esp. 9–14 for explicit defense of the term "propaganda" in the study of official imperial imagery.

[52] The most rigorous and theoretically informed critique of the notion of Roman imperial propaganda is Eich 2003. For other arguments against the idea of propaganda in the early Roman empire, see also Levick 1982; Wallace-Hadrill 1986: 67; Zanker 1988a: 3 and *passim*; Galinsky 1996: 20–41.

[53] Veyne's thesis, developed over a series of trenchant essays (esp. 1990, 2002b, and 2005: 379–418), is of course more complex than this paraphrase suggests.

[54] Representative studies in Weber and Zimmermann 2003; Enenkel and Pfeiffer 2005.

what propaganda is.[55] It is especially important to distinguish between different types of propaganda. Ellul, for example, has offered a well-known typology, distinguishing in particular between "agitation" and "integration" propaganda. While agitation propaganda seeks to change attitudes, according to Ellul's definition, integration propaganda seeks to bolster them. The former is more visible and widespread, is often subversive, and bears "the stamp of opposition," while the latter aims instead at "stabilizing the social body," making it "the preferred instrument of government."[56] This distinction is useful, and helps to explain why the imperial regime ever bothered to communicate a set of ideals and values associated with the reigning emperor. In general, there was not much in the way of agitation propaganda in the Roman imperial period. During the high empire in particular, there was little need to change attitudes and – even more important – the actual mechanics of imperial communications would have made it almost impossible to do so. That the regular, long-term dissemination of imperial ideals was instead intended, at least in part, to reinforce belief in the legitimacy of Roman imperial rule seems more plausible. This does not mean that such efforts were always successful, nor does it preclude an element of the irrational ostentation that Veyne sees as characteristic of monarchic display. But the official communication of imperial ideals by the central state necessarily entailed a positive valuation of imperial rule, which in turn entailed a degree of persuasion, even if only implicit. Moreover, one of the media available to the imperial regime, the coinage, was particularly well suited to the slow, long-term diffusion of ideas upon which such integration propaganda depends.[57] As a preliminary conclusion, then, we may say that the central state, in idealizing the figure of the emperor through a set of ideals and values associated with him, was motivated at least in part by the goal of reinforcing the legitimacy of Roman imperial rule.[58]

---

[55] See, for example, Ramage 1997, 1998, and 2000, on Augustus' "propaganda" in Gaul, Spain, and North Africa, respectively, a useful compilation of evidence with almost no discussion of intent or impact in the dissemination of Augustan symbols in these regions.

[56] Ellul 1973, esp. 61–87, on the different types of propaganda, and 70–9 on "agitation" and "integration" propaganda in particular. Though the value of Ellul's typology has been acknowledged by Roman scholars (see, for example, Kennedy 1984; Evans 1992; Galinsky 1996: 39–41), his central insight into the very different means and functions of different forms of propaganda, and the different sorts of media through which these forms could be disseminated, has not had much impact on studies of Roman imperial ideology.

[57] For the mechanics of coin production and circulation, and both the limitations and potential of the imperial coinage as a medium of communications, see below, 191–200.

[58] *Contra* Lendon 2006, who argues that the imperial regime never required such "strategies of legitimation." We will revisit this issue in the conclusion (chapter 6).

Many of the specific imperial ideals and values communicated by the central state were replicated in the language of local honors for the Roman emperor, especially on the inscribed bases for honorific statues dedicated to the emperor. Most of the statue bases on which this honorific language appeared were set up by local aristocrats.[59] Why they should have expended their own resources on such honorific displays is not obvious. As I will argue in chapter 5, these local honors for the emperor are best seen as symbolic gestures aimed not at the emperor himself, who saw only the tiniest fraction of them, nor at the central state, which did not require such displays of loyalty, but rather at an internal audience. It was, in brief, local representation for local purposes. This formulation is consistent with much recent work on Roman imperial culture, but what will be emphasized is that these local honors for the emperor did not just serve the interests of the community as a whole, by representing imperial power in what had become a familiar symbolic language.[60] Such honors also, and more deliberately, served the narrower, sectional interests of the local aristocrats themselves. By idealizing the emperor, symbolically associating themselves with him, and universalizing an imperial order in which they were clear beneficiaries, these aristocrats were effectively reinforcing their own, local authority. The idealization of the figure of the Roman emperor at the local level, then, was not motivated by a sense of loyalty to Rome, nor by a desire to articulate local identity in a provincial setting, but rather by a strategic calculus on the part of local aristocrats that such an idealization served their own interests.[61]

So while the central state communicated a set of ideals and values mainly in order to strengthen belief in the legitimacy of Roman imperial rule, the local aristocrats in the provinces replicated these same ideals and values mainly in order to secure their own privileged place within the empire's social and political hierarchy. Though the central state and these local aristocrats had different goals, then, their motives in idealizing the emperor were ultimately compatible, since this collective idealization manifestly served the distinct interests of both sets of actors.

---

[59] Details on collective and individual authorship in Introduction to Part II, 181–2, and 219, 267–70.

[60] The now conventional view, for which Price 1984 was seminal.

[61] This interpretation may be contrasted with that of Ando 2000, who emphasizes provincial loyalty and the culture of loyalism in the Roman empire, and that of (e.g.) Revell 2009, who interprets the incorporation of Roman imperial symbols into local contexts primarily as a means of expressing local identity. Though these perspectives are not wholly incompatible with mine, the emphases are very different. Further discussion, including the aristocrats' understanding of their own interests, in chapters 5–6.

The logistics of communications in the Roman empire, and the various mechanisms and processes by which specific ideas could be disseminated from Rome and almost simultaneously replicated throughout the provinces, are complex topics. So too is the ideological unification that arose from such long-distance communications between "center" and "periphery," which partly transcended the internal diversity of the empire by providing a common symbolic framework within which the dispersed communities of the empire, and especially their local ruling classes, could imagine their particular place within a much larger political order, and which helped, as a result, to stabilize this larger configuration of power. These and related problems will be examined in detail in subsequent chapters.

With respect to the collective production of this symbolic system centered on the figure of the emperor, one final, major point needs to be stressed, and that is the critical importance of the specific ideals and values that were attached to the emperor. It is, in fact, in the changing nature of the particular ideals and values associated with the emperor, and in their variable effects on the political system and cultural fabric of the empire, that the heart of my argument lies. In tracing the impact of these ideas on the convergence of social power in the early Roman empire, we will be able to draw on some of the recent scholarship on processes of state-formation in general.[62] As we will see, this comparative context can shed useful light on the roles played by ideas and culture in the development of large states such as the Roman empire. Where we will get less guidance from theorists of state-formation, though, is in understanding the particular resonance of the emperor as an especially capacious symbol. For what is often missing from studies that explore the circulation of ideas in large-scale political systems is sufficient attention to the ideas themselves. Once it has been shown how a set of ideas functions – sometimes as an expression of political power, sometimes as constitutive of it, often both – or by what media and infrastructural means these ideas are disseminated, the analysis usually proceeds directly to the structure of the political system itself. In some of the most influential work on state-formation, in other words, and indeed in much of the scholarship on the impact of imperial ideology on the cultural and political framework of the Roman empire, the function of ideas is carefully examined, but the ideas themselves are treated as incidental.

For the thesis argued in this book, however, the underlying ideas really do matter. The very idea of the Roman emperor – a monarch ruling over

[62] See below, 310–13.

some sixty million subjects – was already quite powerful, and was by itself enough to support some measure of ideological unification within the Roman empire. But the symbol of the Roman emperor could be articulated and expressed in many different ways, and even subtle changes in these different modes of representation could alter the discursive and ideological nature of this symbolic system – with important implications, as we will see, for the nature of the relationship between the central state and local aristocrats. It is not just the diffusion of the idea of the emperor, then, but rather the diffusion of multiple ideas of the emperor, conceptualized and articulated in very specific ways, that we must examine. For it is only through careful attention to the particular ideas, ideals, and values associated with the emperor, and to their changing historical contexts, chronological and geographical patterning, and, above all, degree of prominence in relation to one another, that we can fully grasp the impact of this symbolic system on the political structures, social hierarchy, and cultural fabric of the Roman empire.

TOWARDS A QUANTIFICATION OF IMPERIAL IDEALS

The importance of examining specific imperial ideals and values has long been recognized, of course, and indeed many detailed studies have been devoted to the systematic analysis of the various ideals associated with the Roman emperor. Most studies of this sort have concentrated on a single concept – generosity, justice, valor, victory, peace, abundance, etc. – and many have sought to explain individual expressions of the ideal in question (on an imperial coin, for example, or in a literary text) by reference to short-term, topical concerns or to personal circumstances in the life of the reigning emperor. This general approach to imperial ideals, positivist in orientation, has produced significant results and remains useful.[63] In order to understand the complex symbolic system centered on the figure of the emperor, however, it is also necessary to consider larger sets of interrelated imperial ideals, over the long term, and in particular to assess the changing structural relationships between these ideals, whether such changes were the result of short-term, conscious decisions or not. Sensitivity to the different temporalities within which these ideals were diffused throughout the empire is also vital. Such analysis cannot proceed by anecdotal reference to particular coin designs, single inscriptions, or individual literary texts alone – the standard approach. It is only possible through quantification.

---

[63] Extensive references to traditional studies of individual imperial ideals in chapters 2–3 below.

The use of quantitative methods in pre-modern history is usually hampered by the paucity of the sorts of quantifiable data upon which such methods rely. As a result, most quantitative approaches in ancient Greek and Roman history have depended on comparative evidence from other, better-documented societies, or have employed a combination of estimates and formal models as a way of generating some numbers to work with. In addition, the application of quantitative methods in ancient Greek and Roman history has been limited almost exclusively to subjects in economic or demographic history.[64] But as I hope to show in this book, quantification can also shed important light on matters of cultural and political history – ideas, symbols, communications, and power – and does not, in this case, depend on recourse to comparative evidence or elaborate models.

The "quantification" of imperial ideals refers to the numerical measurement of the frequency, in different media, of specific ideals or sets of ideals, in relation to other ideals or sets of ideals, over the short, medium, or long term. It is designed to provide an empirical basis for assessments of the changing commonness or rarity of different ideals and values over time. And it is precisely by charting these variable frequencies that we can gain a new and empirically grounded perspective on the changing contours of the symbolic system discussed above.

By far the most useful source for the quantitative analysis of imperial ideals and values is the Roman imperial coinage. The messages conveyed by the designs on imperial coins were unambiguously official, according to my definition (above, 16), and the coins themselves were mass produced and in constant circulation from one end of the empire to the other and over the long term. What the imperial coinage provides, in brief, is direct access to official representations of the emperor on the most widely disseminated medium of communications available to the central state. In addition, and equally important for our purposes, imperial coins have survived in tremendous bulk and are therefore susceptible of meaningful quantification. The raw, numerical data provided by coins is unparalleled in its volume, objective dating, and unbroken chronological span over several centuries.[65] These data have long been mined for information related to

---

[64] See, for a representative example, Bowman and Wilson 2009, a series of quantitative studies of the Roman imperial economy; the papers in de Callataÿ forthcoming, based on a conference on the theme of "Long-Term Quantification in Ancient Mediterranean History," share this traditional focus.

[65] Especially significant, as we will see, is the very fine chronological resolution of (most) Roman imperial coins, which enables a much higher degree of precision in the analysis of both short- and long-term trends than is normally possible in other, material-based approaches to the study of ancient empires (cf. Sinopoli 1994: 190).

economic history in general and monetary history in particular, but have only begun to be exploited by students of imperial imagery, ideology, and communications.[66]

The numismatic evidence employed in this book draws on a sample of over 185,000 coins minted at Rome between 69 and 235.[67] On the basis of this sample it is possible to measure the changing relative frequencies of different coin types, and the ideals they expressed, by year, by imperial reign, or for the whole period 69–235. As a result, it is possible, for the first time, to place arguments about the "importance" of different imperial ideals and values on a solid empirical footing, and to measure with some precision the varying degrees to which these concepts related to one another as parts of a larger ideological and semiotic system.

More limited quantification of imperial ideals is also possible on the basis of public inscriptions. The small proportion of inscriptions that have survived makes precise calculations impossible, but it is nevertheless possible to delineate some broad patterns in the frequency and use of both official ideals, in imperial edicts, senatorial decrees, and milestones, which helps to contextualize the evidence from the imperial coinage, and unofficial ideals, especially in honorific decrees, which provides a very useful counterpoint to "the official line." The epigraphic evidence is based on a corpus of 575 inscriptions erected in Rome, Italy, and the provinces, especially in the western empire, between 69 and 235.[68]

Three general points about the use of quantitative evidence in this book should be stressed at the outset. First, the basic calculations employed are very simple. Some of the discussion in subsequent chapters will make use of statistical formulas and terminology, and the collection of data would not have been possible without the use of a computer, but the various numbers and figures cited in the text, mainly percentages, are essentially the product of "pencil-and-paper" methods. Second, I have not engaged in quantification for its own sake. The quantitative data have been collected and cited in order to support a broader argument about ideals and values, symbolic systems, and political power. It goes without saying that most of the questions raised by a study of this sort cannot be answered by

---

[66] For two preliminary studies, see Noreña 2001 and 2003. For some economic and monetary analyses based on the quantification of coins, see Carcassonne and Hackens 1981; Carradice 1983; Duncan-Jones 1994, with Metcalf 1995; Hobley 1998; Harris 2006a: 20–2; Howgego 2009; see also Howgego 1992: 2–4 for sensible comments on the limits to numismatic quantification in general.

[67] The composition and nature of the numismatic sample is discussed in detail in the Introduction to Part I. The sources and data are presented in full in appendices 1–8.

[68] For the composition and nature of this epigraphic corpus, see discussion in the Introduction to Part II, as well as appendices 13–15.

numbers alone. And finally, despite the fact that some of the numerical data cited below will be expressed in precise figures, which will inevitably be quoted by other scholars for their own purposes, the evidentiary base for these numbers, though large by the standards of ancient history, is usually capable of supporting only rough estimates and broad orders of magnitude – and for the most part that is all that is necessary for the arguments I make in the chapters that follow.[69]

OVERVIEW

This book is a study of the nexus between representation, communications, and power in a large, pre-industrial empire. It begins from the proposition that the Roman emperor was central both to the political system and to the cultural matrix of the Roman empire. That is hardly a novel claim, of course, but where the book seeks to offer something different from conventional studies of the emperor in the Roman world and of Roman imperial ideology, and something more compelling, is both in its conceptualization and interpretation of the emperor's centrality, and in the new method it develops for analyzing it. The main goals of the book, that is to say, are both substantive and methodological. The keys to understanding the emperor's centrality, as I have suggested and as I will argue in more detail in subsequent chapters, lie in the separability of the emperor as actor and the emperor as symbol; in the variety of compatible yet discrete interests that the latter could be made to serve; and, above all, in the many different ways in which the idea of the emperor could be expressed, some of which, as we will see, had important implications for how the figure of the emperor, as a symbol, could affect the distribution of social power in the Roman empire. And it is precisely because of the relationship that I propose between the different symbolic constructions of the emperor, on the one hand, and the distribution of social power, on the other, that it is so important to assess the relative importance of these different symbolic constructions in empirical and indeed numerical terms, and why the quantitative analysis of the ideals and values attached to the emperor can not only provide new insights into imperial representation, but can also (ultimately) provide the foundation for a new account of what made the period of the high Roman empire different from what came before and after.

---

[69] For a good discussion of the proper use of quantitative evidence by historians, see Stone 1987: 17–19, 32–40; this may be contrasted with the overly optimistic account in Fogel 1975.

This is the "big picture" that the book as a whole hopes to elucidate. Most of the evidence in the empirical core of the book, however, will focus on the western empire between AD 69 and 235. The dates correspond to the period when the typology of the imperial coinage was especially diverse, and when inscriptions that employed specific honorific terms for the emperor were most numerous.[70] Because one goal of the book is to document precise lexical correspondences between various official and unofficial media, as a way of illuminating the collective production of a single, coherent symbolic system centered on the figure of the emperor, the geographical focus is necessarily on the western empire, where the majority of unofficial inscriptions were written in Latin, the language of official communications. In addition, the bronze coinage, an important body of evidence for this book, circulated almost exclusively in the western empire. By "western empire" and "Roman West," then, I refer, in a loose way, to that large segment of the Roman empire in which the majority of bronze coins minted at Rome happened to circulate, and in which most public inscriptions happened to be written in Latin.[71]

So there are several pragmatic reasons for the focus on the Roman West. But there are historical reasons, too. For this focus is also justified by the very different political and social systems of the eastern and western Mediterranean worlds prior to the Roman conquest. Unlike the eastern empire, which had had long experience with centralized monarchic regimes and ruler worship, the west, for the most part, had no pre-existing symbolic frameworks in which to incorporate the figure of the Roman emperor.[72] So when the local aristocracies of the western empire sought the appropriate terms in which to praise their ruler in inscriptions erected on his behalf, they really had nowhere to turn for inspiration but to the "official line." The municipal epigraphy of the western provinces, therefore, to a much greater degree than that of the eastern provinces, is a very sensitive indicator of the extent to which specifically *Roman* imperial ideals were circulating beyond Rome and by unofficial channels.

These chronological and geographical parameters are not, however, exclusive. Comparative evidence from the Roman East will be employed in a key case study in chapter 5, and evidence from before 69 and after 235 will be cited where relevant. While the quantitative evidence from the

---

[70] The reasons for this patterning in the evidence are discussed below, 236–43.

[71] In practice this means the western half of the empire, stretching as far east as Dacia and Lower Moesia in the north, and Tripolitania in the south; for a map of the inscriptions employed in this study, which effectively illustrates the Roman West in (epigraphic) practice, see map 1 (186–7).

[72] See above, 2–3.

western empire between 69 and 235 represents the empirical foundation of the book, the larger argument that it is meant to support will bear on the empire as a whole over the long term.

But we will have to build up to that larger argument in a cumulative manner, starting with the quantifiable evidence. The investigation in Part I, "Representation," will begin with a detailed analysis of the specific ideals and values through which the figure of the emperor was officially repre-sented by the central state, both as a moral exemplar and paradigm of personal virtues (chapter 2), and as the author of a wide range of both concrete and affective benefits for the inhabitants of the Roman world (chapter 3). In these two chapters we will touch only in passing on the frameworks and logistics of communications in the Roman world, and our attention will remain focused on the ideals and values themselves and on the manner in which they were represented, both discursively and iconographically.

In Part II, "Circulation," the discussion turns from the representation of imperial ideals and values to their chronological and spatial diffusion throughout the Roman West. The first chapter in Part II begins with an examination of the mechanics of coin production and circulation, and then investigates the official communications networks of the Roman empire, drawing in particular on the combined evidence of imperial coins and official inscriptions (chapter 4). The next chapter assesses the symbolic "response" of local communities to the ideals disseminated by the central state, documenting a high degree of lexical correspondence between the honorific terms employed in dedications to the emperor and those dissem-inated on official media of communications (chapter 5). In both chapter 4 and 5, special attention is paid to questions of agency and intent in the production of these imperial symbols.

The concluding chapter (chapter 6) returns to the role played by Roman imperial ideals and values in reinforcing both the power of the central state and the authority of local aristocracies, pulling together the various strands of the central thesis on the emperor's symbolic function in contributing both to the ideological unification of the empire and to the general con-vergence of social power between the late first century BC and early third century AD.

PART I

Representation

Introduction to Part 1: Representation

The two chapters of Part 1 examine the official representation of imperial ideals, with a focus on imperial virtues (chapter 2) and the benefits of empire (chapter 3). Though these two chapters draw on a range of evidence, the principal source for Part 1 is the imperial coinage. The purpose of this introduction is to explain the composition of the numismatic sample upon which the arguments of chapters 2 and 3 are based, and to describe the overall typology of the imperial coinage, as reconstructed through quantitative analysis, during our period.[1]

For this study I have assembled a sample of 185,561 coins minted at Rome between AD 69 and 235. Of these coins, 148,421 are silver, and 37,140 bronze. Because some of the coins in the overall sample were hybrids, forgeries, or unidentified coins, the actual number of coins employed in the calculations below is 179,285, of which 142,798 are silver, and 36,487 bronze.[2] The chronological parameters of this sample have been set by the nature of the numismatic evidence itself. Though it is not clear when the central mint was transferred from Lugdunum to Rome, the move had certainly taken place by the accession of Vespasian in 69. All the coins in the sample, in other words, may safely be regarded as both central and official.[3] And in iconographic terms, it is only with Vespasian that the imperial coinage begins to show the consistent diversity in type content

---

[1] The methodological comments that follow draw upon Noreña 2001, esp. 148–52, which should be consulted by those interested in fuller discussion and references.

[2] Of the 148,421 coins that make up the silver sample, 5,623 (c. 4 percent) were hybrids, forgeries, or unidentified coins; of the 37,140 coins that make up the bronze sample, 653 (c. 2 percent) fell into one of these categories. I will use the term "bronze" as a shorthand for the various base-metal denominations of the imperial coinage, which were in fact composed of orichalcum (sestertii and dupondii) and copper (asses and quadrantes).

[3] For the dating of the mint's transfer, Metcalf 1989. Note that several mints outside of Rome were producing coins during this period, and that it is not always clear where a given coin was minted (cf. Wolters 1999: 45–61). Since many of the coins produced outside of Rome are indistinguishable from those of the central mint, they should not affect the analysis undertaken here since they still represented, in effect, an "official" version of imperial ideals.

that makes a study of this sort most illuminating.[4] The choice of 235 as the terminal date for the numismatic sample is a bit more arbitrary, but in the rapid sequence of relatively short-lived imperial reigns that followed the death of Severus Alexander, the typology of the imperial coinage was ultimately transformed, and should probably be seen as part of the long-term transition to the very different world of the later empire.

From my sample of just under 180,000 coins it is possible to measure the relative frequencies of different coin types – and the ideals they expressed – by year (or by any other chronological division), by imperial reign, or for the whole period 69–235, on both silver and bronze denominations. In the absence of surviving mint records, the best method for determining the relative frequency of imperial coin types is the tabulation of coins known to us from published hoards, and indeed the vast majority of the coins which make up the sample come from hoards. Other methods are flawed or inferior. The number of specimens in the major coin collections, for example, is not an accurate indicator of frequency, as most curators seek to purchase rare coins rather than common coins already well represented in the collection. As a result, the most common coins tend to be grossly underrepresented in the major collections.[5] Extrapolation from the number of known dies is also problematic, since the number of coins struck per die is unknown (and, in principle, unknowable).[6] Finally, while the number of different types illustrated in *RIC* can provide a rough-and-ready guide to frequency, this method is necessarily less accurate than one based on the larger numbers of coins derived from the hoards themselves.[7]

In antiquity, coins were withdrawn from circulation and hoarded (i.e., concealed) for a number of reasons.[8] There is no good reason to believe that the specific designs they bore was one of them. That is an important point, because the hoard evidence is being used here as an index of the various coin types that were being produced by the central mint and that were in circulation at any one moment. Most coins were withdrawn from circulation and hidden in order to protect them from theft or loss, or

---

[4] Cf. Buttrey 1972a.

[5] So Volk 1987: 141; cf. Carradice 1998: 97 on the inaccuracy of scarcity ratings in the first edition of *RIC*, based on 29 major collections (xxi–xxii), which "depart wildly from what the hoards imply." Note that the second edition of *RIC* 2 (*RIC* 2.1, from Vespasian to Domitian, edited by Carradice and Buttrey), published in 2007, now employs the hoard evidence in assessing scarcity.

[6] See below, 193, n. 11. Many more die studies will have to be undertaken and published before the evidence from dies can be properly compared with the hoard evidence.

[7] For some calculations based on the frequency of types in *RIC*, see Manders 2008.

[8] In general on hoarding and coin finds, see Grierson 1975: 124–39; for the ancient world, see also Crawford 1983b: 187–207; Buttrey 1999; von Kaenel and Kemmers 2009.

because they were deemed to be undervalued and of potentially greater value at some later date (under Gresham's Law). These are fundamentally economic concerns, and it is most unlikely that coin types had anything to do with such calculations.[9] It is true that individual coins could be withdrawn from circulation on the basis of their designs for dedication at sanctuaries (though there is not much concrete evidence for this) or even for the purpose of forming a private collection – the emperor Augustus, for example, was said to own a collection of old and foreign coins – but such isolated dedications and collections will have had very little effect on the overall profile of coin hoards and coin populations in the Roman empire as a whole.[10] And because there is no reason to expect a correlation between specific designs and the individual coins chosen for hoarding, the fact that we only have access to those hoards that were not recovered in antiquity has no bearing on the sample. There is no *a priori* reason why a sample based on a number of separate hoards cannot be an accurate indicator of the variable relative frequencies with which specific designs were minted.

Though the sample of 179,285 coins is more than sufficient as a database of coin types, it represents only a tiny fraction of the total number of silver and bronze coins produced by the central mint between 69 and 235.[11] How representative of mint output is this sample? Here it will be necessary to treat the silver and bronze samples separately, since they were collected from slightly different sources.

The silver sample is based on a collection of 105 hoards buried between AD 80 and 267.[12] In assessing the representativeness of this sample, the major question concerns the very lopsided geographical distribution of the hoards that have been used to generate it, with nearly three quarters of the coins coming from hoards in the Balkans and along the Danube (table Int. I.1). The effect of this pronounced geographical imbalance on the validity of the sample depends entirely on the circulation patterns of silver coins. If silver coins tended to circulate only in regional or local pools, then this sample will not be representative of empire-wide circulation

[9] Those designs that happened to be on coins hoarded for their economic value will be somewhat overrepresented in the hoards, but the very large number of designs in circulation at any one time, together with the size and chronological spread of the sample, largely mitigates this unavoidable problem.

[10] For a case study of reverse types found in sanctuaries (on antoniniani minted in the mid-third century AD), concluding that "it is not possible to clearly demonstrate a positive selection of coin types in sanctuaries," see Kaczynski and Nüsse 2009 (quoted, 107). Augustus' coin collection: Suet. *Aug.* 75.

[11] For some estimates of the total numbers of coins minted during our period, see below, 193.

[12] Appendix 1.

Table Int. 1.1 *Regional sources for tabulations of silver coins, AD 69–235*

Region	Number of hoards	Number of coins	Percentage of total
Danube/Balkans	37	105,776	71%
Britain	34	16,276	11%
West Continent	17	16,016	11%
The East	14	8,817	6%
Italy/North Africa	3	1,536	1%
Total	105	148,421	100%

Sources: see appendix 1.
Note: "West Continent" includes Germany, Gaul, and Spain, and "The East" includes all Greek-speaking provinces; this classification follows Bolin 1958 and Duncan-Jones 1994. "Percentage of total" refers to the number of coins, not the number of hoards.

patterns, and will not, as a result, be a very useful guide to the relative frequency of the various designs produced by the central mint. If, however, silver coins freely circulated throughout the whole of the empire, then this sample will indeed be representative of circulation and mint output, despite the fact that the hoards are so unevenly distributed in space. The only way to establish the circulation patterns of coins is to compare the frequencies of specific types in different hoards from different parts of the empire.[13] In a series of studies addressed to this question, Duncan-Jones has consistently argued that local populations of silver coins display marked dissimilarities from one another, proving that silver coins tended to circulate only in regional clusters.[14] Against Duncan-Jones' data we can set the substantial evidence for the long-distance movement of silver coins throughout the empire.[15] More important, Duncan-Jones' own figures can be interpreted in different ways. Most of his claims of dissimilarities in regional coin populations, in fact, are based on minor discrepancies that, for our purposes, are almost negligible; indeed, what is quite remarkable is just how homogeneous coin populations throughout the empire actually

[13] It should be noted that the statistical validity of the sample depends only on the range and velocity of coin circulation, not on the modes by which the coins circulated – the ongoing debate between state intervention and the market as the main engine of distribution (on which see, e.g., Lo Cascio 2007), in other words, has no bearing on this issue.
[14] Duncan-Jones 1989; 1994: 172–9; 1996; 1999; 2003; 2005, esp. 471–87.
[15] So Howgego 1994: 12–16; Wolters 2006: 26–7.

Table Int. 1.2 *Regional sources for tabulations of bronze coins, AD 69–235*

Region	Number of coins	Percentage of total
West Continent	22,356	60%
Italy	8268	22%
North Africa	2711	7%
Britain	2439	7%
Danube/Balkans	1366	4%
Total	37,140	100%

Sources: see appendix 2.

were.[16] By the second half of the third century the hoard evidence does point to the regional circulation of precious-metal coins, and it is unlikely that the empire as a whole ever formed a single, homogeneous circulation area.[17] The regional dissimilarities that did exist in our period, however, were not very significant. Despite the very uneven geographical spread of the hoards used to generate the sample of silver coins, then, regional bias should not affect its representativeness with respect to circulation and mint output.

The coins that make up the bronze sample come primarily from the West Continent and Italy (table Int. 1.2). Unlike the silver coins, which all come from published hoards, the bronze coins in the sample come from a combination of hoards, excavations, stray finds, and local museum collections. The sources vary according to region. For Germany (West Continent), the Netherlands (West Continent), Luxembourg (West Continent) and Slovenia (Danube/Balkans), I have relied on the volumes of the *Fundmünzen der Antike* (*FdA*) series, which list all ancient coins discovered from hoards, sites, and stray finds.[18] The coins from Britain come from a combination of published reports and local museum collections, while those from Italy come entirely from local museum collections.[19] Finally, I have added to the sample the evidence from two of the largest bronze coin hoards, Garonne (West Continent) and Guelma (North Africa).

---

[16] Negligible discrepancies in Duncan-Jones' figures: Noreña 2001: 151, n. 26. Homogeneity of coin populations throughout empire: Howgego 1994: 14.

[17] Regional circulation in later empire: Callu 1983.   [18] See appendix 2.

[19] For Britain, Gaul, and Italy, I have incorporated into the sample the tabulations published by Hobley 1998 (cf. 1–2 on his methods of data collection, and 141–4 for further details on the sites and collections examined).

This combination of different sources should not affect the general validity of the bronze coin sample since, as I have argued, the designs on coins were incidental to their hoarding, loss, and recovery in antiquity.[20] The use of local museum collections to determine the relative frequency of coin types must also be distinguished from reliance on the holdings of the major collections. Unlike the major collections, which extend and diversify their holdings through the purchase of coins from every corner of the empire, local museums depend, for the most part, on material from local excavations alone, and should therefore provide a reasonable index of the type content of local coin populations.[21]

One factor that may affect the validity of the bronze coin sample as a whole is regional bias, since there are some indications from our period that base-metal coins, unlike precious-metal coins, tended to circulate in local or regional pools. In his study of the coin finds at Bath, for example, Walker demonstrated that the base-metal coins that arrived in Britain rarely left the province, and that certain bronze types from the mint of Rome circulated only in Britain. But this seems to have been an extreme case.[22] While other studies have documented the mainly local circulation of base-metal coins in other areas, nowhere in the western empire was the range of circulation as restricted as it was in Britain.[23] It should also be noted that base-metal coins produced by the central mint at Rome were intended for circulation in the western empire only, as the base-metal denominations

---

[20] See discussion in Hopkins 1980: 113–16, with figure 4, on the "striking similarity" in patterns of coin populations whether drawn from stray finds, hoards, or local museum collections.

[21] Hobley 1998: 2 cites evidence for the similarities between local museum collections and locally excavated material. It should also be noted that all the evidence from Britain and Italy and much of the evidence from Gaul comes from the tabulations published by Hobley, whose study of the circulation of imperial bronze coins in the western provinces is restricted to the period AD 81–192. The discrepancy in dates between our two samples means only that the bronze evidence for the period 81–192 will be somewhat more accurate than the evidence for either 69–81 or 193–235, on the principle that larger coin finds will be more representative of circulation (on this point, cf. Reece 1981; Volk 1987), and that the totals by type for the period 69–235 as a whole will slightly favor those types minted more heavily during the period 81–192.

[22] Walker 1988. Among the types that circulated only in Britain were the Britannia types of Hadrian and Antoninus Pius; see discussion in Howgego 1994: 13–14, and below, chapter 4. It should be noted that the concentration of Britannia types in Britain seems to have been an anomaly. Indeed, Hobley's evidence did not reveal any other examples of province types circulating specifically in the province they commemorated (1998: 53); cf. Reece 1973.

[23] Kraay 1956 showed that coins countermarked in the Rhine military camps tended to circulate locally, a conclusion supported by Kemmers' detailed study of the coin finds at the legionary fortress and *canabae* at Nijmegen (2006), and by her case study of Severan coinage in several western provinces (2009). Hobley 1998 has also revealed several dissimilarities in the type content of regional coin populations. Not all of Hobley's conclusions, however, are supported by the evidence he adduces; see my review in *AJN* 11 (1999), 160–4. For local circulation of bronze coins in the eastern empire, see Jones 1963; Howgego 1994: 13.

Table Int. 1.3 *Relative frequency of iconographic categories
on the imperial coinage, expressed as a percentage of all
reverse types, AD 69–235*

Iconographic category	Silver (N = 142,798)	Bronze (N = 36,487)
personifications	55%	57%
gods and goddesses	29%	23%
objects	9%	7%
emperor/imperial family	7%	9%
geographical representations	<1%	4%

Note: Percentages are rounded off to the nearest whole number.

of the eastern empire were supplied by local and regional mints there.[24] In general, then, it is likely that the bronze coin sample is slightly skewed in favor of those coins that happened to circulate in the West Continent region, from which 60 percent of the coins in the sample were taken, with the result that conclusions drawn from this sample will have to be more tentative than those drawn from the more representative silver sample.[25]

On the basis of the silver and bronze coin samples we may make some preliminary remarks about the overall typology of the imperial coinage for the period 69–235. The obverse was dominated throughout this period by the portrait of the reigning emperor.[26] The reverse types that accompanied the obverse portrait may be divided into five broad iconographic categories: personifications of ideals and values; gods and goddesses; emperors and members of the imperial family; inanimate objects; and geographical representations.[27] Measuring the relative frequency of these five iconographic categories for the period 69–235 as a whole indicates that personifications were overwhelmingly the most common types, on both silver and bronze coinages (table Int. 1.3). Gods and goddesses were

[24] For local and regional mints in the Roman empire, the precise locations and operations of which are sometimes obscure, see the introductions to *RPC* 1 and 2.

[25] Dependence on coins from Gaul and the Rhineland also means that the sample contains comparatively few Severan coins, since Severan bronze does not seem to have circulated in large numbers in these areas in the third century, for reasons that remain unclear; on this problem, see Buttrey 1972b; cf. Kemmers 2009: 142–6, showing that the survival rates of Severan bronze are higher in civilian and especially ritual contexts than in military ones.

[26] For the numismatic portraiture of the emperor, see Bastien 1992–94, with Crawford 1983a on the prominence of the imperial portrait in the overall typological scheme of the imperial coinage; cf. King 1999 for the imperial portrait on coins as an expression of power.

[27] Cf. Noreña 2001: 154, n. 41, for discussion of the criteria used for assigning different types to these categories.

also fairly common on both silver and base-metal denominations, while types from each of the other categories were minted in relatively small numbers.

The fact that the relative frequencies of the different iconographic categories are so similar across metals illuminates an important aspect of mint organization, showing clearly that the typological programs of both the silver and the bronze coinages were being dictated from a single, central source. The size and chronological breadth of the sample – just under 180,000 coins covering a span of 167 years – militates strongly against the possibility of mere coincidence in these data. The main implication of this finding is that there could not have existed during our period a separate and autonomous senatorial mint responsible for the production of the bronze coinage, as is still sometimes argued.[28] Further evidence discussed in chapters 2 and 3 will support this conclusion.

Individual designs in any of the iconographic categories represented in table Int. I.3 could express ideals or values attached to the Roman emperor. Representations of gods could denote particular spheres of divine action that the imperial regime wished to highlight as part of some larger message – Mars and warfare to commemorate the emperor's defeat of a foreign enemy, for example, or Ceres and fertility, to advertise the agricultural prosperity brought about by imperial beneficence. Objects such as altars, religious implements, or temples could allude to the emperor's sacred authority. The emperor himself could be shown in any number of guises, each emphasizing a different aspect of his ideal function within the state. And geographical representations could establish a symbolic linkage between the emperor and the peoples and places of empire. Of all the iconographic categories, however, personifications were the most effective for the representation and communication of imperial ideals, and it is no accident that these were the most common iconographic types. Personifications, human figures that give visual shape and concrete embodiment to abstract ideas, enabled the expression of a very wide range of complicated concepts through a simple but flexible pictorial vocabulary, articulated mainly by means of these personifications' defining attributes and adjuncts. Accompanied by the short legends that were regularly employed on the imperial coinage, these personifications of imperial ideals represented a potent combination

---

[28] For the view that there existed under the empire an autonomous senatorial mint responsible for the bronze coinage (which goes back to Mommsen and the theory of a "dyarchy" between emperor and senate), see Burnett 1977: 45–57, 59–63; Lo Cascio 2000 (1991): 43–50, with references. On type selection in general, see below, 191–2.

of image and text.[29] In light of their expressive range and power, then, as well as their overwhelming predominance on coins, personifications will be at the center of the iconographic and discursive analysis of the imperial coinage in chapters 2 and 3.

[29] On the use of personification in Roman visual language, see, e.g., Hamberg 1945: 15–45; Toynbee 1956; Hölscher 1980: 273–9; Kuttner 1995: 69–93; Clark 2007: 11–13 (and *passim*); cf. Shapiro 1993 for the Greek roots of this visual and semantic system, and Kantorowicz 1957: 114, n. 80, for the continuity of this mode of expression into the medieval period.

CHAPTER 2

Values and virtues
The ethical profile of the emperor

MONARCHS AND VIRTUES

In his *Panegyricus*, a speech of thanks (*gratiarum actio*) to Trajan for a suffect consulship (AD 100), Pliny bombards his listeners with no fewer than thirty individual virtues ascribed to the emperor. The sheer variety of these personal qualities is worth noting. The Roman people admire Trajan, as Pliny assures his audience in one concentrated burst, for his sense of duty (*pietas*), restraint (*abstinentia*), clemency (*mansuetudo*), humane character (*humanitas*), moderation (*temperantia*) and good nature (*facilitas*) (*Pan.* 2.6–7). Trajan rules with mildness (*indulgentia*, 21.4), truthfulness (*veritas*, 54.5), probity (*sanctitas*, 63.8), integrity and attentiveness (*integritas* and *diligentia*, 92.2), shows both generosity (*liberalitas*) and justice (*iustitia*) in his giving of public games (33.2), administers justice with fairness (*aequitas*, 77.3), and provides security to his subjects through his overall excellence (*bonitas*, 30.5). And despite this superabundance of virtues, the emperor's personal behavior is not haughty or overbearing, but is instead characterized by a sense of decency (*pudor*, 2.8), respect for propriety and temperateness (*modestia* and *moderatio*, 3.2), thriftiness, kindness, and self-control (*frugalitas*, *benignitas*, and *continentia*, 3.4), candor (*simplicitas*, 4.6), good faith (*fides*, 67.1), cheerfulness (*hilaritas*, 4.6), friendliness (*comitas*, 71.6) and, perhaps most important from Pliny's perspective, respect for the senate (*senatus reverentia*, 69.4). He does not, of course, overlook Trajan's capacity to rule an empire, making sure to note that the emperor possesses the necessary industry and bravery (*labor* and *fortitudo*, 3.4), alertness (*vigilantia*, 10.3), endurance (*patientia*, 59.3), strictness and authority (*severitas* and *gravitas*, 4.6). It is an impressive list of virtues indeed.

As we will see, the choice of specific qualities with which to praise or honor the Roman emperor was often significant. It also provides us with a means to map the changing currents of imperial ideology and to assess the variable resonance of the virtues advertised on behalf of the emperor.

More important for the time being, though, is the fact that the main criterion employed by Pliny to distinguish between the "good" emperor, Trajan, and his "bad" predecessors, especially Domitian, is neither action nor achievement, but rather personal character. In fact, the speech as a whole is a very good example of how the formal celebration of an idealized Roman emperor could be grounded in the emperor's personal virtues.[1]

In praising Trajan's exemplary character Pliny was able to draw on a venerable tradition, reaching back to the fourth century BC, in which sets of virtues were ascribed to or proclaimed by monarchs as a moral basis and justification for their rule. This ideal association between rulers and virtues was in fact fundamental to conceptions of monarchy in the ancient world. It also represents one of classical antiquity's main contributions to western political thought, as the traditions of lauding monarchs for their personal virtues, and of rationalizing monarchical rule through the celebration of the ruler's perfect character, retained their vitality for many centuries after Pliny's panegyric of Trajan. One way to understand the nature and expression of Roman imperial ideals, then, is to examine the officially advertised virtues of the emperor. It will not be enough, however, to catalog the many different virtues assigned to Roman emperors. Only by determining which of these virtues were singled out and emphasized beyond all others, and to what degree, and by examining their official representation, in both text and image, will it be possible to discern the ethical profile of the Roman emperor. That is the principal aim of this chapter. But in order to contextualize the virtues of the Roman emperor, to appreciate their deep genealogies, it will be useful to consider first the long-term evolution of the idea in Greek and Roman political thought that monarchs could be defined largely through their personal character, and that they should in fact possess certain virtues.[2]

Formal attribution of virtues to rulers did not become an urgent concern until the early Hellenistic period, when monarchic regimes came to dominate the Greek world, but many Hellenistic ideas about the character of the ideal king, as well as the conceptual frameworks in which these ideas were developed, had their origins in earlier Greek thought. The notion

---

[1] On the *Panegyricus* in general, see Durry 1938; Radice 1968; Fedeli 1989a; Bartsch 1994: 148–87; Seelentag 2004: 214–96; Roche 2011.

[2] The following discussion is intended to provide a brief, diachronic overview of the ascription of virtues (both individually and in sets) to rulers (both real and imagined) in the Greek, Hellenistic, Roman, and late Roman periods. For more detailed consideration of the rather different social and political contexts in which Hellenistic and Roman monarchic ideals in particular were developed and deployed, see below, 314–16.

that a ruler must possess specific virtues was first examined systematically in rhetorical and philosophical texts of the fourth century BC, in the generation preceding Alexander's conquests.[3] The maturation of speculative and abstract thinking during this period, as well as the emergence of a whole range of new literary genres, provided writers sympathetic to monarchy with a much broader canvas than had previously existed for the exposition of a monarch's virtues and for the celebration of the ideal human qualities that underpinned royal action and achievement. One effect of these developments was the rise of a monarchic ideology in which the personal virtues of the ruler occupied a central position.

Of particular importance in the formative stage of this new conception of monarchy were the writings of Isocrates (436–338 BC) and Xenophon (c. 428–c. 354 BC). Their most significant and influential innovation for this nascent ideology, especially for the practice of associating monarchs with virtues, was the development of encomiastic prose biography.[4] In the *Evagoras*, the earliest surviving prose encomium (c. 365 BC), Isocrates declares (22–3) that his subject possessed exceptional moderation (*sōphrosynē*), courage (*andreia*), wisdom (*sophia*) and justice (*dikaiosynē*). Several years later Xenophon composed a prose encomium of his own, on the Spartan king Agesilaus (*Agesilaus*, c. 360 BC), praising Agesilaus not only for the four virtues attributed to Evagoras by Isocrates (4, 5, 6.1–8), but also for his reverence for the gods (*eusebeia*, 3), "patriotism," charm (*to euchari*, 8.1), "geniality" (8.2) and foresight (*pronoia*, 8.5).[5] And in his encomiastic masterpiece, the *Cyropaedia* (late 360s BC), the Persian king Cyrus is presented as an ideal monarch. Xenophon introduces Cyrus (1.2.1) with a comment on his reputation for having been most humane (*philanthrōpotatos*), most

---

[3] The personal virtues of rulers did not command much attention in pre-classical Greek thought. The *basileis* of the Homeric epics and Hesiod's poems, for example, were defined less by their virtues than by their service to the community, whether in war (e.g. *Il.* 12.310–21) or through the dispensation of justice (*Theog.* 83–6; *Op.* 219 ff.), and by a sort of generalized and absolute superiority, as expressed in Peleus' advice to Achilles "always to be the best (*aristeuein*) and to remain preeminent (*hupeirochos*) above the others" (*Il.* 11.784; cf. 6.208). In this early Greek ideology of political rule, individual human qualities were subordinated to achievement, status, and power. For a useful overview of political thought during the archaic period, see Raaflaub 2000, esp. 29–37 on Homeric and Hesiodic *basileis*, drawing attention to various constraints on their power; cf. Hadot 1972: 568–73 for "monarchic" ideals from Homer to Pindar.

[4] On the emergence of biography in general in the fourth century, Momigliano 1993 (1971): ch. 3. Russell and Wilson 1981: xv–xix trace the history of encomium and its influence on later rhetorical theory and practice.

[5] "Patriotism": Xenophon calls Agesilaus a lover of his city (*philopolis*, 7.1), a lover of Hellas (*philellēn*, 7.4), and a hater of Persia (*misopersēs*, 7.7); "geniality" (8.2): he is optimistic (*euelpis*), cheerful (*euthumos*), joyous (*hilaros*).

studious (*philomathestatos*), and most ambitious (*philotimotatos*), and near the end of the work explores the many ways in which Cyrus had been a model of *aretē* (8.1.21), with particular attention to his devotion to the gods (8.1.23), commitment to justice (8.1.26), moderation and self-control (*sōphrosynē* and *enkrateia*, 8.1.30–31), humanity (*philanthrōpia*, 8.2.1), and concern and care for his friends (*therapeia* and *epimeleia*, 8.2.13). It is true that the bulk of the work explores Cyrus' character not through individual virtues, but through concrete actions, but the underlying emphasis nevertheless remains on character as the key prerequisite for ideal rulership.

In general, the *Evagoras*, *Agesilaus*, and *Cyropaedia* reflect an emerging perception that personal character was vital to rulership, and that monarchy, as opposed to tyranny, was best construed as arising from the paradigmatic virtues of the monarch himself.[6] A related set of ideas can be traced in the major philosophical treatises from the first half of the fourth century BC that addressed the relationship between virtue, citizenship, and the state, especially Plato's *Republic*, *Statesman*, and *Laws*, and Aristotle's *Politics*. An important goal of these works was to establish formal typologies of different constitutions (*politeiai*), including monarchy.[7] In defining monarchy, and in particular in distinguishing it from its corrupt form, tyranny, Plato and Aristotle do not, like Isocrates and Xenophon, offer up a catalog of royal virtues, but there is in these texts a similar emphasis on the personal character of the monarch rather than on the institutional features of monarchy as such.[8] Both philosophers were certainly capable of advancing structural

---

[6] Other works by Isocrates and Xenophon reveal a similar, if less intense, interest in royal character. In *To Nicocles* (*Or.* 2, *c.* 372 BC), for example, a work in the "mirror of princes" genre, Isocrates advises the Cypriot king to be more thoughtful than others (*phronimōteros*, 10), to be best and most just (*beltistos, dikaiotatos*, 20), and to practice moderation (31, 33), while in *Nicocles* (*Or.* 3, *c.* 368 BC), a celebration of monarchy written as if delivered by Nicocles himself, Isocrates devotes a major portion of the speech to an exposition of the king's virtues (29–46), above all justice (29, 31–5, 44–5) and moderation (29, 36–41, 44–5).

[7] E.g. *Rep.* 338d, 445d, 544c; *Statesman* 291d–e, 302c–e; *Laws* 393d ff.; *Pol.* 3.6–13, 1278b–1284b; cf. Isoc. *Pan.* 130–3 for a similar typology of rule by one, rule by some, and rule by all. The roots of this constitutional taxonomy appear to go back to the second half of the fifth century BC, as illustrated by the Persian "constitutional debate" in Book 3 of Herodotus (3.80–2).

[8] In the *Republic*, Plato identifies the "most kingly" man (*basilikōtatos*) as the one who is best (*aristos*), most just (*dikaiotatos*), happiest (*eudaimonestatos*), and who is truly a king over himself (580c), a string of qualities akin to those cited in the laudatory biographies, while in the *Statesman* he defines the ideal statesman (*politikos*) as the one who has mastered the extremely difficult "art of ruling" (*politikē technē*) (292e ff.) and who would guide the state with virtue (*aretē*) and knowledge (*epistēmē*), distributing justice (*ta dikaia*) to all (301d). Aristotle, too, accentuates the virtue of the ideal monarch. Kings should be chosen, he argues, not because of their lineage, but on the basis of their personal life and conduct (*Pol.* 2.9, 1271a). And though Aristotle views absolute monarchy as a primitive and generally undesirable form of government (*Pol.* 3.15, 1286b1–9; 3.17, 1288a1–5), he insists that if a man of outstanding virtue should ever be found, he should indeed have monarchic power over everyone else (3.17, 1288a15–29).

or practical arguments in favor of the institution of monarchy – in the *Statesman*, for example, Plato claims that any body of laws, no matter how wise, is always general in nature, and therefore inferior to the ideal ruler, who can adapt laws to particular circumstances (295a) – but in general they share with Isocrates and Xenophon a fundamentally ethical conception of rulership.

The growing interest in monarchy in the first half of the fourth century BC should be seen against the backdrop of political and ideological change in the Greek world. The defeat of democratic Athens in the Peloponnesian War, the violent oligarchic revolution that toppled the democracy, and the restoration and reformation of democracy there encouraged reflection, especially among the Athenians themselves, on different constitutional forms and their associated strengths and weaknesses. And on the periphery of the Greek world, powerful rulers such as Mausolus of Caria, Jason of Pherae in Thessaly, and above all Philip II of Macedon began to encroach upon the autonomy of Greek city-states, which awakened the Greek imagination to the possibilities of strong, one-man rule – in providing leadership for a panhellenic crusade against the Persian empire, for example, as Isocrates advocated. In such conditions, theoretical engagement with monarchy, as an idea, flourished.[9] Then, following the formation of several large, independent kingdoms in the wake of Alexander the Great's far-flung conquests, monarchy became the prevailing form of government in the enlarged Greco-Macedonian world of the Hellenistic period (323–30 BC). For the first time, Greek ideas about monarchy were conditioned by the ubiquitous and dominant presence of real monarchs.

Theories of monarchy proliferated in the Hellenistic age.[10] The number of treatises "On Kingship" (*peri basileias*), usually addressed to an individual king in the manner of Isocrates' *To Nicocles*, demonstrates the intensity of contemporary interest in and philosophical speculation on monarchy. Produced by representatives from all the major philosophical schools, these works evidently explored, among other topics, the moral basis of monarchic rule, but none of them survives and it is impossible to determine how much emphasis was placed on royal virtues in general or to identify the particular

---

[9] See, once again, Momigliano 1993 (1971): ch. 3 on the relationship between Greek political thought and changing power structures in the fourth century; cf. Balot 2006: ch. 6, esp. 184–7 on the "monarchic solution" to contemporary problems.

[10] Useful introductions to Hellenistic kingship theory and royal ideology in Goodenough 1928 (suggestive, but drawing mainly on pseudo-Pythagorean texts usually dated to the second and third centuries AD; see below, 53); Schubart 1937 (inscriptions and papyri); Dvornik 1966: ch. 5, esp. 241–69; Hadot 1972: 580–92; Préaux 1978: 181–388; Walbank 1984; Smith 1988: ch. 5 (portraits); Bilde *et al.* 1996; Hahm 2000: 458–64; Ma 2003; Balot 2006: 269–76; Eckstein 2009.

qualities that were stressed.[11] That Hellenistic kingship could be defined without reference to any virtues whatsoever is clear from the most famous definition of all, preserved in the Byzantine Suda but deriving (it seems) from an early Hellenistic source: "Monarchy: it is neither nature (*phusis*) nor justice (*to dikaion*) that gives monarchy to men, but the ability to command an army and to govern competently" (Suda, s.v. *basileia*, 2). And there can be no doubt that success in warfare was crucial to the stability and legitimacy of Hellenistic monarchies.[12] Nevertheless, ethical conceptions of kingship did not disappear during the Hellenistic period, as a scatter of contemporary theoretical texts reveals, and a profusion of honorific decrees and titles shows that royal virtues were prominent in the official discourse of the main Hellenistic monarchies. From such sources we can reconstruct the broad outlines of Hellenistic kingship theory and royal ideology, so important to the later development of Roman imperial ideology.

The relevant contemporary texts are the pseudonymous *Rhetoric to Alexander*, preserved among the works of Aristotle (but clearly post-Aristotelian), which begins with a fictional letter from Aristotle to Alexander (1420a–1421b); the pseudonymous *Letter of Aristeas to Philocrates*, probably written in the mid-second century BC, which narrates the visit of Jewish sages to the court of Ptolemy II Philadelphus in Alexandria, including a series of questions and answers on the nature of kingship (187–292); and Philodemus' *On the Good King according to Homer*, from the very late Hellenistic period (mid-first century BC), which explores the proper functions of the king. In addition, the first book of Diodorus Siculus' *History* seems to preserve a portion of Hecataeus of Abdera's *On the Egyptians*, dating (probably) to the late fourth century BC, which includes an idealized portrait of the early Egyptian kings written from the perspective of the Ptolemaic court in Alexandria (1.70–1).[13] Royal virtues play a role in all these works, but they are mobilized for different purposes. In the *Rhetoric to Alexander*, the author includes moral worth as one of the particular concerns of the king and implies that justice is essential to kingship, but these ideals are subordinated to reason (*logos*), the defining human quality

[11] The authors and titles of these works are known mainly from citations in Diogenes Laertius (third century AD). Authors of works *peri basileias* include Theophrastus, Demetrius of Phalerum, and Strato among the Peripatetics (following the lead of Aristotle himself); Zeno, Cleanthes, Sphaerus, and Persaeus among the Stoics; and Epicurus.

[12] Emphasized by Austin 1986; Eckstein 2009.

[13] For the *Rhetoric to Alexander*, see briefly Hahm 2000: 458–61, with references; cf. Balot 2006: 269–73; Aristeas: Murray 1967; Philodemus: Murray 1965; Hecateus (via Diodorus Siculus): Murray 1970.

according to which the king should organize his own life to the advantage of the state as a whole (cf. 1420a11–27). Traditional royal virtues are more to the fore in the *Letter of Aristeas*. Ptolemy II is instructed in the importance of humanity (*philanthrōpia*, 188), justice (*dikaion*, 189), and foresight (*pronoia*, 190), and told that he must be reasonable (*epieikēs*, 188) and show clemency (*makrothumia*, 188) to his subjects, all with a view to providing peace and justice for his kingdom (291–2). The main novelties in the *Letter of Aristeas* are the prominence accorded to self-control (*enkrateia*), labeled the essence (*horos*) of kingship and the most powerful type of rulership (*archē kratistē*) and repeatedly evoked as necessary for the good king, and the notion that God is the ultimate source of royal virtue, a principle that imbues conventional Greek ethics with an eclectic blend of Jewish theology and Egyptian regal tradition.[14] It is the king's role in promoting peace and concord that is highlighted by Philodemus, who employs the examples of Odysseus and Nestor to illustrate the point that the good king must display reasonableness (*epieikeia*) and gentleness (*praotēs* and *hēmerotēs*) in order to prevent discord and violence.[15] And Hecataeus presents the early Egyptian kings not so much as paradigms of virtue, but rather as rulers who exercised self-control and who remained, as a result, subject to the laws.[16]

Ideas about monarchy in the Hellenistic age, then, included some notable innovations, in particular the elevation of self-control as a major virtue, the attention to human reason as an organizing principle for monarchic behavior, and the ascription of royal virtue to God. In general, though, the ethical conception of kingship that pervades these texts continued the tradition established in the fourth century by Isocrates, Xenophon, Plato, and Aristotle. But the discourse of royal virtues was not limited to philosophical or theoretical texts. The personal qualities of the king were nearly omnipresent in the documentary record, too, especially in royal letters and in municipal honorific decrees for kings.[17] Hellenistic monarchs were regularly lauded for courage (*andragathia*), a crucial quality in a violent world in

---

[14] Self-control as essence of kingship: 211; most powerful type of rulership: 221–2; necessary for the good king: e.g. 211, 248, 255–6, 276, 279. God as source of royal virtue: e.g. 187–8, 205, 230, 265, 273.

[15] These virtues are cited in column VI of the papyrus on which the text is preserved; see Murray 1965: 168, and 176–7 on the resonance of these qualities in late-Republican Rome.

[16] Diod. Sic. 1.70.1–71.1.

[17] Convenient collection of evidence in Schubart 1937; cf. Bertrand 1990 and Ma 1999: ch. 4 for the relationship between inscriptions, public language, royal discourse, and monarchic power (and see below, ch. 5, for a similar approach to municipal inscriptions in the Roman empire). Citations below given *exempli gratia*.

which success in warfare could be construed as the very basis of monarchy.[18] When the fighting was done, successful governance of a kingdom depended on the king's non-martial virtues, including cerebral qualities such as understanding (*phronēsis*) and foresight (*pronoia*).[19] An all-powerful monarch was also expected to display the proper attitude of benevolent concern for his subjects, which could be labeled as magnanimity (*megalopsychia*), goodwill (*eunoia*), consideration (*epimeleia*), kindness (*eugnōmosynē*), or affection (*philostorgia*).[20] In more concrete terms, such concern could be demonstrated through material benefactions, which reflected the king's generosity (*philanthrōpia*) or munificence (*megalomereia*), or through the provision of justice (*dikaiosynē; to dikaion; eunomia*).[21] Nothing was possible without the support of the gods, of course, and indeed Hellenistic kings were routinely honored for their piety (*eusebeia*).[22] And underpinning all these qualities was the king's overall excellence (*aretē*).[23] Saturated with such ethical terminology, the diplomatic and honorific language of the Hellenistic kingdoms contributed to a thriving discourse, also reflected in the literary texts discussed above, in which ideal monarchy was imagined primarily in moral terms.

The proliferation of royal virtues in official letters and honorific decrees for kings suggests the prevalence of an ethical conception of kingship in the Hellenistic age, but the various epithets chosen by Hellenistic monarchs, perhaps a better guide to official ideals, convey a rather different impression.[24] Several royal epithets celebrated military victory

---

[18] *Andragathia*: OGIS 219, l. 34 (Antiochus I); OGIS 332, l. 23 (Attalus III). The ambition (*philotimia*) of the Hellenistic king also found expression in the military sphere: cf. OGIS 219, l. 13 (Attalus I), with Schubart 1937: 8.

[19] *Phronēsis*: OGIS 332, l. 25 (Attalus III). *Pronoia*: OGIS 270, l. 3 (Attalus I); OGIS 56, l. 19 (Ptolemy III); OGIS 763, l. 10 (Eumenes II). Further references in Schubart 1937: 8.

[20] *Megalopsychia*: OGIS 229, ll. 6–7 (Seleucus II); cf. Schubart 1937: 5. *Eunoia*: OGIS 248, l. 34 (Antiochus IV); OGIS 332, l. 2 (Attalus III); Syll.³ 390, l. 19 (Ptolemy II); OGIS 55, l. 23 (Ptolemy III); further references in Schubart 1937: 8–10. *Epimeleia*: Syll.³ 390, l. 19 (Ptolemy II); OGIS 56, l. 10 (Ptolemy III). *Eugnōmosynē*: Schubart 1937: 11–12. *Philostorgia*: OGIS 247, l. 6 (Seleucus IV); OGIS 331, l. 42 (Attalus III).

[21] *Philanthrōpia*: OGIS 270, l. 5 (Attalus I); cf. Schubart 1937: 10–11 (often nominal: *to philanthrōpon*). *Megalomereia*: OGIS 332, l. 26 (Attalus III). For the benefactions of Hellenistic kings, Bringmann 1993. *Dikaiosynē*: OGIS 140, l. 10 (Ptolemy VIII); *Dikaios* (of an action): OGIS 219, l. 7 (Attalus I), OGIS 223, l. 32 (Antiochus II), OGIS 224, l. 8 (Antiochus III). *Eunomia*: OGIS 56, l. 13 (Ptolemy III). Further references to royal justice in Schubart 1937: 6–8.

[22] *Eusebeia*: Welles 1934, no. 26, ll. 14–15 (Seleucus II [?]); OGIS 244, l. 28 (Antiochus III); Welles 1934, no. 62, l. 5 (Attalus II [?]); OGIS 383, l. 14 (Antiochus I of Commagene); cf. Schubart 1937: 6 (often adverbial: *eusebōs*).

[23] *Aretē*: OGIS 56, l. 18 (Ptolemy III); OGIS 219, ll. 15, 34 (Antiochus I); OGIS 248, l. 33 (Antiochus IV); OGIS 332, l. 22 (Attalus III). Further references in Schubart 1937: 5.

[24] For what follows, see briefly Smith 1988: 49–50; more specialized studies of Hellenistic royal titulature cited in Goodenough 1928: 98, n. 137.

(e.g. *Nikatōr, Kallinikos, Nikēphoros*), especially among the Seleucids; others advertised dynastic harmony (e.g. *Philadelphus, Philopatōr, Philomētōr*), especially among the Ptolemies; some implied the divinity of the king (e.g. *Epiphanēs, Sōtēr*).[25] Among epithets alluding to ethical qualities, only "Benefactor" (*Euergetēs*) was employed by any of the major dynasties (the Ptolemies), while other virtue epithets, such as "The Pious" (*Eusebēs*) or "The Just" (*Dikaios*), were confined to kingdoms on the periphery of the Greco-Macedonian world, such as Cappadocia, Parthia, and Bactria.[26] The titles the kings chose for themselves are salutary reminders that Hellenistic royal ideology was hardly limited to the ethical qualities of the good monarch.

Over the course of the Hellenistic age, then, the institution of monarchy was equipped with a formidable ideological apparatus, with roots reaching back to a series of seminal works produced in fourth-century Athens. Philosophy, rhetoric, honorific language, and official terminology all contributed to the portrait of the "good" Hellenistic king. Nothing was more important to that portrait than royal character. And though conceptions of ideal rulership were not solely ethical, as the Suda and royal epithets are enough to show, emphasis on the king's virtues was a consistent and often prominent feature of contemporary discourses on monarchy and on individual kings. This bundle of classical Greek and Hellenistic ideas about kingship would eventually have a major impact on Roman imperial ideology. The ideal of the good king with his canonical royal virtues was not blindly adopted at Rome, however, nor did Augustus and his successors simply model themselves on Hellenistic monarchs. Instead, Roman writers and aristocrats responded creatively and critically to Greek ideas about monarchy, and appropriated them for their own purposes. In this respect the development of Roman conceptions of monarchy should be seen as one aspect of the much bigger and multilayered process of "Hellenization" at Rome.[27]

---

[25] *Nikatōr*: Seleucus I, Demetrius II, Seleucus VI; *Kallinikos*: Seleucus II, Demetrius III, Antiochus XII; *Nikēphoros*: Antiochus IV; *Philadelphus*: Ptolemy II, Attalus II, Antiochus XI, Philip I; *Philopatōr*: Ptolemy IV, Ptolemy VII; *Philomētōr*: Ptolemy VI, Attalus III, Ariarathes VII; *Epiphanēs*: Antiochus IV, Antiochus VI, Antiochus VII, Antiochus XI, Antiochus XII, Seleucus VI, Philip I; *Sōtēr*: Ptolemy I, Antiochus I, Seleucus III, Demetrius I, Attalus I, Eumenes II, Ptolemy IX.

[26] *Euergetēs*: Ptolemy III, Ptolemy VIII, Mithradates V of Pontus, Nicomedes III of Bithynia.

[27] The problem of Hellenization at Rome is an unwieldy and complex topic. Good introductions to the main issues in Rawson 1989; Gruen 1990 and 1992; Wallace-Hadrill 2008. For the Hellenization of Roman political thought in particular, see also Dvornik 1966: 453–83. See also below, 314–16, for further discussion of distinctively Hellenistic and Roman "modes" in the elaboration of monarchic ideals and values.

There were several conduits between Rome and the Greek East for the absorption and assimilation at Rome of the ideas and practices that encouraged an association between monarchs and virtues. First, in the religious sphere, numerous Greek concepts, such as Victory (Nikē), Peace (Eirēnē), and Concord (Homonoia), encountered primarily in Magna Graecia, were given cult at Rome (but with Latin names: Victoria, Pax, Concordia, etc.), almost all as the result of *vota* made in wars fought between the late fourth and early second centuries BC.[28] Some of these concepts, especially Virtus and Pietas, were not only human qualities, but virtues of Hellenistic kings as well (*andreia/aretē* and *eusebeia*). The spread of such cults was therefore one way in which the political ideals of the Greek world in general, and of Hellenistic monarchy in particular, began to filter into Roman society.

The third and second centuries BC also witnessed increasing interactions, in the military, diplomatic, and private spheres, between high-ranking Roman senators and Hellenistic kings.[29] The record was mixed. We tend to think of Roman aristocratic disdain for kings, epitomized by Popillius Laenas' browbeating of Antiochus IV, but we should not forget the examples of Scipio Africanus corresponding on friendly terms with Philip V, or the favorable reception given to Eumenes in Rome in 190/89.[30] More important than the treatment of any one king, though, was the fact that Roman aristocrats were becoming accustomed to the realities of monarchy.

Contemporary with these developments was the increasing familiarity with Greek constitutional theory and Hellenistic political thought among educated Romans. Again, the resulting attitudes towards monarchy were ambiguous. On the one hand, there was open hostility. Cato, for example, could fulminate against Eumenes on the grounds that a king was by nature a "flesh-eating creature"; on the other hand, the true king was seen as a virtuous ruler, to be distinguished from a tyrant, an idealization of monarchy reflected, for example, in the tradition that Scipio Aemilianus studied the

---

[28] Other cults introduced during this period include Fortuna, Salus, Spes, Fides, Libertas, Pietas, Honos, Mens, Ops, and Juventas. On the introduction of these cults at Rome, see Clark 2007: 29–72, with emphasis on the dynamic Roman tradition about the origins of these "divine qualities," and the way in which interaction with them helped to establish a sense of community at Rome; see also Fears 1981b: 833–69, for emphasis on their religious trappings in particular (temples, altars, sacrifices, etc.).

[29] For what follows, see discussion and references in Rawson 1975; cf. Hölscher 1990. See also Gruen 1984 for a comprehensive account of the political, diplomatic, and military contexts in which these interactions took place.

[30] Popillius Laenas and Antiochus IV: Polyb. 29.27; Cic. *Phil.* 8.23; Vell. Pat. 1.10.1; Val. Max. 6.4.3. Scipio and Philip V: Polyb. 10.9.3; Livy 37.7.15. Eumenes: Polyb. 21.18; Livy 38.52.

Cyropaedia for his own edification.[31] Even Cato, when the occasion suited, could describe a king, Ptolemy VI, as "best and most generous."[32] That monarchy could be viewed by aristocratic Romans as a beneficial form of rule is especially clear from the mid-Republican tradition on Rome's own regal period, in which all the kings except Tarquinius Superbus received (mostly) favorable reviews from both poets and historians.[33] By the end of the second century BC, in other words, aristocratic Romans had become familiar with theoretical arguments in favor of monarchy and with many of the virtues expected of the "good" king.

Finally, the emergence of Greek-style honorific practice at Rome in the first century BC, in which collective honors, especially statues voted by the senate, were exchanged for the benefactions of individuals, created the necessary framework for the routine, official celebration of powerful aristocrats. Alien to the traditions of the Republic, in which aristocrats competed with one another through self-promotion, this honorific system eventually became one of the primary means by which specific ideals, including virtues, were attached to individual emperors.[34]

So the language of virtues, Greek political theory, and a Greek-style honorific system were absorbed at Rome along a number of different but overlapping trajectories, and all during a period when aristocratic Romans were interacting more and more with Hellenistic kings. These diverse ideas, practices, and experiences eventually coalesced at Rome in the regular association of rulership with specific virtues, an ideological nexus with unmistakably Greek origins, but very well suited to the discourse of Roman political power. In considering this nexus, it is important to remember that these virtues, human qualities that were much discussed in non-religious texts, were also personified and worshiped as objects of public cult. Indeed, it is precisely the simultaneous location of these concepts in both the divine and discursive fields that makes their association with groups, individuals, and (especially) rulers so resonant.[35]

---

[31] Cato: Plut. *Cai. Mai.* 8.8. King distinguished from tyrant: Polyb. 6.3–4, 7. Scipio Aemilianus and *Cyropaedia*: Cic. *Tusc.* 2.62, *QFr.* 1.1.23 = SB 1.

[32] *ORF* (2nd edn.) fr. 80: *rex optimus atque beneficissimus.*

[33] Numa was routinely celebrated for his piety, and Ennius referred to Ancus Marcius as "a good man" (*bonus, Ann.* 149v), but in general royal character was not prominent in evaluations of Rome's "good" kings, which tended to focus instead on their founding of important institutions. Comprehensive collection of references in Classen 1965, esp. 387–94 on Fabius Pictor, Naevius, Ennius, Plautus, and Terence; cf. Rawson 1975: 151, n. 28. For various literary engagements with the regal period during the late Republic and age of Augustus, see discussion in Fox 1996.

[34] For the rise of Greek honorific practice at Rome, Wallace-Hadrill 1990.

[35] A central thesis of Clark 2007, which has put the study of these concepts on a new footing.

It took many years, however, for such an association to become normative. In fact, for the public image of senators in the mid-Republic, virtues were a secondary concern at best. The Scipionic epitaphs do publicize both character and achievement, citing courage (*virtus*) and wisdom (*sapientia*) alongside military victories and public offices, but this public commemoration of virtues seems to be somewhat anomalous.[36] More telling is Q. Caecilius Metellus' funeral oration for his father, who died in 221 BC. In this speech, paraphrased by Pliny the Elder, personal qualities are clearly subordinated to achievements and, above all, status:

Quintus Metellus . . . has left it in writing that his father had achieved the ten greatest and highest objects in the pursuit of which wise men pass their lives: for he had made it his aim to be the best warrior, the best public speaker and the bravest general, for the most important matters to be conducted under his authority, to enjoy the greatest honor, to be supremely wise, to be judged the most eminent senator, to obtain great wealth in an honorable way, to leave behind many children, and to be the most famous man in the state.[37]

Metellus acknowledges wisdom and bravery in war as important aristocratic qualities, but what evidently mattered most was to be the best – or, more accurately, to be recognized as the best – in several key arenas of public performance and competition.[38]

It is really only in the late Republic that personal virtues became prominent in the public sphere. This formative period was characterized by the efforts of some aristocratic families and individual senators to identify themselves publicly with specific ethical qualities. In 108/7 BC, for example, M. Herennius struck a denarius with a bust of Pietas and the legend PIETAS on the obverse; a generation later, in 71 BC, M. Aquilius produced denarii with obverse portrait of Virtus and the legend VIRTUS.[39] In both cases, the collocation of a virtue on the obverse of a coin with the name of a moneyer on the reverse asserted a close link between that virtue and the family represented by the moneyer. More emphatic was the assumption by Q. Caecilius Metellus of the honorific cognomen Pius, through which he arrogated to himself a virtue, *pietas*, that had traditionally belonged to

---

[36] *Virtus*: *CIL* 1².7 = *ILS* 1, l. 2 (L. Cornelius Scipio, cos. 298 BC); *CIL* 1².10 = *ILS* 4, l. 3 (first half of second century BC); *CIL* 1².11 = *ILS* 7, l. 5 (first half of second century BC). Note that several epitaphs also cite *virtutes* in the plural (*CIL* 1².11 = *ILS* 7, l. 2; *CIL* 1².15 = *ILS* 6, tab. II [mid-second century BC]). *Sapientia*: *CIL* 1².7 = *ILS* 1, l. 2; *CIL* 1².11 = *ILS* 7, l. 1. One epitaph also refers to the deceased's *ingenium* (*CIL* 1².10 = *ILS* 4, l. 4), another indication of attention to character.

[37] Plin. *NH* 7.139–40.

[38] For Republican aristocratic values, see the recent overview in Rosenstein 2006.

[39] Herennius: *RRC* 308/1a–b. Aquilius: *RRC* 401.

the *populus Romanus* as a whole. Sulla's assumption of the cognomen Felix, which implied his appropriation of the ideal of *felicitas*, was another step in this direction.[40] But the watershed moment came with Caesar's introduction of the cults of Victoria Caesaris, Fortuna Caesaris, and especially Clementia Caesaris. Henceforth the worship of these traditional ideals would embrace the person of Julius Caesar. The road to the autocratic monopolization of virtues at Rome now lay wide open.[41]

Cicero's writings offer a valuable perspective on the increasing public identification of powerful aristocrats with particular qualities. In the *Pro Lege Manilia* (66 BC), for example, he defines the ideal commander, understood to be Pompey, as the one who possesses expertise in military matters (*scientia rei militaris*), courage (*virtus*), prestige (*auctoritas*), and luck (*felicitas*) (*Man.* 28) – hardly a Platonic canon of virtues, but a telling nod towards innate qualities rather than concrete achievements in the definition of ideal leadership. In the *Pro Marcello*, a proto-panegyric on Caesar delivered in 46 BC, Cicero praises the dictator for his many characteristic virtues, including gentleness (*mansuetudo*, 1), generosity (*liberalitas*, 19), magnanimity (*magnitudo animi*, 19), fairness (*aequitas*, 12, 31), and, above all, clemency (*clementia, misericordia*) and wisdom (*sapientia*).[42] And Cicero understood the implications of his rhetoric. For it was precisely at this time that he was also extolling the Galatian king Deiotarus for a similar set of virtues, explicitly characterized as royal: "brave, just, stern, dignified, magnanimous, bountiful, beneficent, generous: these are the royal praises," declares Cicero, "the other one (sc. frugality) is for private citizens."[43] This is the prescriptive program of one well versed in both Greek political theory and Hellenistic monarchic ideology.[44]

---

[40] Note, however, that *felicitas* was not, like *pietas*, primarily an ethical quality; see below, chapter 3.

[41] Weinstock 1971: 80–132, 233–42, emphasizes the role of Caesar in the process of monopolization. For a different perspective, see Clark 2007: 205–54, suggesting that increasing control over "resources" by the strongmen of the late Republic facilitated their ability to limit and restrict the meanings of these "divine qualities"; there was no real "monopoly" over these concepts in the late-Republican period, in other words, but rather a systematic (and only partially successful) effort to control their polysemy.

[42] Clemency: 1, 9 (*clementer*), 12, 18. Wisdom: 1, 9 (*sapienter*), 18, 19.

[43] *Deiot.* 26: *fortem, iustum, severum, gravem, magni animi, largum, beneficum, liberalem: hae sunt regiae laudes, illa* (sc. *frugalitas*) *privata est.*

[44] Indeed, Cicero's fluency in Greek philosophical ideas about monarchy, and constitutional theory more generally, had already been on display in the *De Re Publica*, published (i.e., circulated beyond a circle of friends) in 51 BC (Zetzel 1995: 1–3). In this Platonic dialogue, Scipio Aemilianus, the main interlocutor, compares monarchy to other forms of legitimate unitary authority (e.g. Jupiter over the other gods, 1.56; the *paterfamilias* over the rest of the household, 1.61), and argues that legitimate monarchy, based on *virtus* and *sapientia* (2.24), is better than other unmixed constitutions (aristocracy and democracy) because the monarch is uniquely capable of providing security, equality,

This long formative period in the political use of ethical language at Rome culminated in the Golden Shield awarded to Augustus, in which the emperor was honored for his "transfer of the commonwealth" to the senate and people of Rome with a shield set up in the Curia Iulia that proclaimed his *virtus, clementia, iustitia,* and *pietas.*[45] All the key elements in the Greek and Hellenistic tradition are here. An honorific award has been made by an important collectivity to an all-powerful ruler in exchange for a benefaction, an award formally motivated by the ruler's defining virtues, which number four, vaguely suggesting a "canonical" Greek pedigree. The Roman assimilation of the ideology of monarchy and virtue was complete.

With the advent of monarchy at Rome under Augustus came the ever more insistent expectation that the "good" emperor display a number of specific qualities. During the first two centuries AD, a handful of texts addressed to or written about individual Roman emperors focused on imperial virtues and vices. Of these, Seneca's *De Clementia,* addressed to the young Nero, is the most traditionally philosophical in approach.[46] *Clementia,* defined by Seneca as "the moderation of the soul when taking vengeance or the gentleness of the stronger towards the weaker in meting out punishments," is appropriate to men in general, because it distinguishes them from wild beasts (1.3.2, 1.25.1), and to the emperor in particular (1.3.3), not only because it is *clementia* that restrains the emperor's absolute and sometimes terrifying power (cf. 1.1.2), but also because it is the main quality that distinguishes him from a tyrant (1.11–13).[47] The opposite of *clementia* is not strictness (*severitas*), according to Seneca, but rather cruelty (*crudelitas*) (2.4.1), a vice explored by Seneca himself in his *Apocolocyntosis,* which can be read as a sharp criticism of Claudius' distortion of justice. In both texts, the question of the emperor's character is paramount.

While Seneca's treatise was concerned with the exposition of a single virtue, Pliny's *Panegyricus* presents an idealized portrait of Trajan through

---

and peace through his own power (*potestas*), justice (*iustitia*) and wisdom (2.43). Though the *De Re Publica* was not an argument for monarchy – the superiority of a mixed constitution, exemplified by Rome's own commonwealth, is repeatedly stressed (e.g. 1.45, 69–71) – it does show the maturation of Roman ideas about monarchy and the successful application by a Roman writer of Greek constitutional theory to a Roman context. For the argument of the *De Re Publica,* see Zetzel 1995: 1–34, esp. 13–29; cf. Lintott 1997 on the tradition of the mixed constitution in Roman political thought.

[45] *RG* 34.2. See discussion in Hölscher 1967: 102–12; Wallace-Hadrill 1981a: 300–7; Galinsky 1996: 84–8; Scheid 2007 *ad loc.*

[46] On the *De Clementia,* see Braund 2009; on the virtue of *clementia,* Barden-Dowling 2006, esp. 169–271 for the Roman imperial period.

[47] Definition of *clementia* (2.3.1): *clementia est temperantia animi in potestate ulciscendi vel lenitas superioris adversus inferiorem in constituendis poenis.*

the celebration of multiple qualities, as we have seen. Most of these virtues are deployed with a view to shaping the emperor's subsequent behavior towards constitutional propriety, beneficent paternalism, and personal courtesy – for only then will the emperor truly merit the philosophically tinged title of *Optimus*, "the best man."[48] Equally sensitive to imperial character, but operating with a different catalog of key qualities, was the imperial biographer Suetonius. In general, Suetonius concentrates on four main areas of imperial activity and their associated virtues and vices: clemency (*clementia*) or cruelty (*saevitia*) in the dispensation of justice; courtesy (*civilitas*) or hauteur (*arrogantia*) in personal interaction with aristocrats; generosity (*liberalitas*) or parsimony (*avaritia*) in public expenditures; and self-control or profligacy in private behavior.[49] Suetonius' ethical concerns, in other words, were not quite the same as those of Pliny or Seneca, but the important point for the moment is that all three authors, despite differences of genre and period, tended to view Roman emperors through the prism of virtue and vice.

In addition to these texts on or addressed to specific emperors, a number of contemporary works, composed in Greek, explored the nature of rulership in general, some rhetorical in nature, others philosophical, but all overlapping with those of Seneca, Pliny, and Suetonius in their ethical conception of monarchy. Especially pertinent among rhetorical texts are Dio Chrysostom's "kingship orations" (*Or.* 1–4), composed in the early second century and probably written, like Pliny's *Panegyricus*, for the edification of Trajan. Over the course of his four essays, which explore monarchy and tyranny from a range of perspectives, Dio returns again and again to the standard royal virtues: justice, courage, moderation, reverence for the gods, humanity, wisdom, and gentleness.[50] It should be noted that these virtues are often presented in groups of four (e.g. 3.7: *phronēsis, sōphrosynē, dikaiosynē, andreia*; 4.24: *andreiotatos, dikaiotatos, philanthrōpotatos*, and *anikētos*), surely with the intention of giving them a canonical feel. Similar in its consistent emphasis on character is the oration *Eis basilea*, preserved among the writings of Aelius Aristides and now usually regarded as one of

---

[48] *Optimus*: Plin. *Pan.* 88.4–10. Trajan's paternalism is expressed above all by the virtue of *indulgentia*; see below, 280–2. Imperial courtesy (*civilitas*), defined by such virtues as *modestia* and *moderatio*, is analyzed in Wallace-Hadrill 1982. On the title *optimus* and its implications, see below, 288–93.

[49] Wallace-Hadrill 1983: 151–74.

[50] Justice: e.g. 1.45, 2.26, 2.54, 3.7, 3.10, 3.32, 4.24. Courage: e.g. 2.26, 2.54, 3.7, 3.32, 3.58, 4.24. Moderation: e.g. 3.7, 3.32, 3.58, 3.85. Reverence for the gods: e.g. 1.15. Humanity: e.g. 1.17, 1.20, 2.26, 4.24. Wisdom: e.g. 3.7, 3.58. Gentleness: e.g. 2.26. In general on the kingship orations, Moles 1990.

his genuine works (*Or.* 35), probably an encomium for Antoninus Pius.[51] The conventional themes of royal courage (29, 38), self-control (27–9), piety (8, 15), humanity (8), and gentleness (10) are all sounded, but the central royal virtue for Aristides, as for Dio, was justice (8, 15, 17). That the ruler's virtues stood as the basic organizing principle of royal panegyric and encomium is clear from these works and especially from Menander Rhetor, writing in the late third century AD, whose brief manual on how to praise a monarch (*basilikos logos*) explicitly advises speakers to arrange their praise of the ruler's accomplishments according to the four virtues of courage, justice, moderation, and wisdom (373).[52]

Philosophers writing on the theme of monarchy were equally concerned with the question of royal character. This is especially pronounced among the Stoics.[53] In his essay "That Kings Too Should Philosophize," for example, Musonius Rufus, the teacher of Dio Chrysostom, argues that kings must become philosophers – inverting Plato's thesis in the *Republic* that philosophers should become kings – because only the king trained in philosophy will distribute justice (*ta dikaia*, 60.21–62.9), display moderation (*sōphrosynē*, 62.10–23) and courage (*andreia*, 62.23–31), and be bold (*tharraleos*, 66.10), fearless (*adeēs*, 66.10), resolute (*hypostatikos*, 66.10), beneficent (*euergetikos*, 66.11), helpful (*chrēstos*, 66.11), and humane (*philanthrōpos*, 66.11).[54] Epictetus is less inclined to cite the conventional royal virtues, but in discussing Herakles as a paradigm for royalty he does observe the hero's provision of justice (*dikaiosynē*) and holiness (*hosiotēs*) (3.26.32), and in distinguishing between Trajan and Nero he associates a set of virtues with the one and a set of vices with the other (4.5.17–18).[55] And Marcus Aurelius devotes most of his personal spiritual guide to examining his own character, both as an individual and as an emperor, with ample attention to the traditional virtues of justice, courage, moderation, and wisdom.[56] Platonist thinking on monarchy is reflected in Plutarch's "To an Uneducated Ruler"

---

[51] So Jones 1972; for translation and commentary, see Swift 1966, following E. Groag in identifying the speech as an anonymous encomium of Philip the Arab (r. 244–9).

[52] Introduction, text, and translation in Russell and Wilson 1981.

[53] For the complex relationship between Stoic philosophy and politics in the Roman empire, see Brunt 1975; Shaw 1985; Roller 2001, esp. ch. 2.

[54] For a comprehensive introduction to Musonius Rufus, with text, translation and discussion, see Lutz 1947, whose pagination and arrangement are followed here (citation by page and line number).

[55] The good man (Trajan) is gentle (*hēmeros*), courteous (*koinōnikos*), patient (*anektikos*), and affectionate (*philallēlon*), while the bad man (Nero) is irascible (*orgilos*), furious (*mēnitēs*), and querulous (*mempsimoiros*).

[56] Justice: e.g. 3.6.1, 5.12.2, 6.47.6, 6.50.1, 7.54, 7.63.1, 8.39, 10.11.2, 11.1.5, 12.1.2–4, 12.15. Courage: e.g. 3.6.1, 3.11.3, 5.12.2, 11.18.21. Moderation: e.g. 3.6.1, 5.12.2, 7.63.1. Wisdom: e.g. 5.9.5, 18.3. Brunt 1974 is still basic for political thought in the *Meditations*.

(*Mor.* 779d–782f).[57] There Plutarch claims that the ruler must model himself on God, for only then will he participate in true equity (*eunomia*),
justice (*dikē*), truth (*alētheia*), and gentleness (*praotēs*) (*Mor.* 780f–781a).
He also stresses the importance of philosophy to rulership (cf. 779e–f),
implying that sovereignty should be given to the best and wisest man, a
principle stated more directly in his *Life of Solon* (14.3–4; cf. *Numa* 20.8).

Quite different in tenor but with similar emphasis on royal character are
the "pseudo-Pythagorean" kingship treatises (*peri basileias*) of Ecphantus,
Sthenidas, and Diotogenes, the proposed dates of which range from the
fourth century BC to the third century AD, with an emerging consensus
favoring the first two centuries AD.[58] Several familiar virtues crop up in
these somewhat idiosyncratic texts. Ecphantus is perhaps the most conventional, concluding his essay with a celebration of wisdom (*phronasis*), justice
(*dikaiosuna*), self-control (*enkratēa*), and courtesy (*koinōnia*) (84.7–8). The
little that survives of Sthenidas' treatise suggests that the focus was on
wisdom (*sophia*), though he asserts in addition that the good king must be
high-minded (*megalophrōn*), gentle (*hameros*), and self-sufficient (*oligodeas*)
(188.1–4). Justice is the key virtue for Diotogenes, who writes that the king
ought to be most just (*dikaiotatos*) and most lawful (*nomimōtatos*), and that
the king himself is "living law" (*nomos empsychos*) (71.18–23) – an emphatic
and striking association of an ethical ideal with the person of the ruler.[59]
Working in a philosophical tradition in which political and ethical thought
were more or less merged, it is not surprising that these representatives from
the different schools shared the assumption that virtue was the essence of
monarchy.[60]

What all of these texts helped to constitute was the robust discursive
formation, built up over several centuries, from Isocrates and Xenophon in
the fourth century BC to the exponents of the major philosophical schools

[57] See discussion in Dvornik 1966: 270–5, 542–9.

[58] See Goodenough 1928 (dating these texts to the Hellenistic period); Delatte 1942 (second century
AD); Centrone 1990: 13–44 (first century BC–first century AD, in the context of Middle Platonism).
For the texts, Thesleff 1965, whose pagination and arrangement are followed here (citation by page
and line number).

[59] Note that Musonius Rufus also employs the term "living law" to describe the king (64.12). Another
pseudo-Pythagorean author, Archytas, draws a distinction between animate law embodied in the
king and inanimate law located in written legal codes (33.8), a distinction made by Plutarch as well
(*Mor.* 780c), while Xenophon writes that Cyrus regarded the good ruler as "seeing law" (*blepon
nomos*) (*Cyr.* 8.1.22).

[60] Attention to the character of the monarch was prominent in other philosophical traditions, too. In
his *Life of Moses*, for example, the Platonist Philo of Alexandria describes the ideal ruler as a "lover
of justice" and a paradigm of *philanthrōpia* (2.9; cf. Archytas 36.1–5 for a "Pythagorean" account of
royal *philanthrōpia*).

in the second and third centuries AD, in which the representation of the Roman emperor's virtues, the subject of this chapter, operated. Most of the specific virtues of the emperor, as we will see, have deep roots in this longstanding tradition. Here what I would like to emphasize is simply the impressive pedigree of the idea that the emperor could in fact be conceptualized and idealized as an exemplar of personal qualities.

And this tradition on the relationship between monarchy and virtue continued to thrive long after the period covered in this study. The late-antique panegyrics form the main bridge between the classical and post-classical traditions.[61] All the main imperial virtues are commended by panegyrists writing in both Latin and Greek. For the Latin panegyrists, the key imperial virtues were *virtus*, usually linked to *victoria* in order to underline its martial nature, and *pietas* and *clementia*, often coupled together, which helped to soften the hard edges of military autocracy – especially desirable in emperors who had come to power through civil war; other virtues frequently cited include justice, generosity, courage, self-control, fairness, and wisdom.[62] It is more difficult to generalize about the much larger corpus of Greek imperial panegyrics. The speeches of Themistius give some indication of their content and outlook.[63] A longstanding insider at the imperial court in Constantinople who spoke in praise of emperors for nearly half a century, from Constantius II to Theodosius, Themistius made a number of familiar claims about monarchy and imperial character: philosophy and kingship go together (6.72a–b); the emperor is the "living law" (1.15b; 5.64b; 16.212d; 19.227d); the good monarch displays courage, self-control, moderation, gentleness, truthfulness (*alētheia*), and justice (1.5c–d, 6, 8a–b; 4.61c–d; 9.122b–d; 15.189b); he is the paradigm of *philanthrōpia*, which reigns over all the other virtues (1.5a–c, 6b, 8a; 6.78c–d). We find broadly similar language in Julian's first panegyric on Constantius II (*Or.* 1). Writing as newly appointed Caesar (AD 355), Julian declares that Constantius' early education provided him with courage, justice, moderation, and wisdom (1.10c); recounts the emperor's exploits as examples of various virtues

---

[61] For Latin panegyric, see MacCormack 1975; Nixon and Rodgers 1994 (introduction, text, translation, and historical commentary); Rees 2002. For Greek panegyric, Hägg and Rousseau 2000. See also the essays in Whitby 1998, which cover both Latin and Greek panegyrists.

[62] *Virtus*: e.g. *Pan.* 2.7.1, 3.3.1, 4.3.3, 6.5.3, 7.5.2, 8.1.4, 9.7.3, 10.2.2, 11.5.3, 12.3.2. *Pietas*: e.g. 2.24.2, 4.6.5, 5.9.6, 6.7.4, 7.1.4, 8.3.3, 9.17.5, 10.1.4, 11.6.1, 12.4.4. *Clementia*: e.g. 2.24.2, 4.8.1, 5.2.2, 6.5.3, 8.19.3, 12.4.4. See discussion and further references to other virtues (*iustitia, liberalitas, fortitudo, prudentia, temperantia, aequitas, sapientia,* etc.) and ideals (esp. *victoria* and *felicitas*) in Seager 1984; cf. Nixon and Rodgers 1994: 23–4.

[63] Selection of texts, translated with introduction and commentary, in Heather and Moncur 2001.

(e.g. courage, 1.11d–12c; wisdom, 1.12c–13a; self-control, 1.13b–d; magnanimity, 1.19b, 38b; humanity, 1.16b, 20d, 26d); and concludes the speech with a systematic recitation of Constantius' defining virtues (1.41b–49a) – identified at the beginning of the speech as more important than his achievements (1.5a–b) – including, in addition to those emphasized earlier in the panegyric, virtue (*aretē*), reverence for the gods (*eusebeia*), ambition (*philotimia*), generosity (*megaloprepeia*), and goodwill (*eunoia*). In format the speech follows Menander's prescriptions very closely, and as an expression of royal ideology it draws on language and themes that reach back to the ideals and values of Hellenistic monarchy.[64]

It would be tedious and unhelpful to cite further examples. What should already be clear enough is the remarkable stability, over centuries of political and ideological change, in the vocabulary employed to define monarchy and to praise individual rulers. Of course the precise meanings of these key terms could and did change over time, and it goes without saying that careful attention to the contexts in which any one essay, speech, treatise, or document was produced is necessary in order to comprehend the full significance of its intended message. But the salient feature of these texts for our purposes is simply the tenacity with which this basic idiom endured, together with the underlying assumption that monarchy was best idealized not through reference to the ruler's achievements, but rather through emphasis on royal character in general, and on individual ethical qualities in particular. This was a deep structure of western political thought, from democratic Athens to the courts of the later Roman empire (and beyond), and it stands as the wider ideological context in which we should locate the official representation of the Roman emperor's virtues.

A TAXONOMY OF IMPERIAL CHARACTER

One question that has loomed over the discussion thus far is why ancient authors were so invested in examining, defining, praising, and prescribing royal virtues in the first place.[65] This enduring concern can be ascribed in part to the nature of classical political thought, in which politics and ethics were mostly overlapping categories – indeed, there was hardly any question relevant to public life that did not involve deeper and more pressing questions about the motivations, dispositions, and character of

---

[64] Julian follows a similar arrangement and promotes a similar set of ideals in the second panegyric on Constantius (*Or.* 2), esp. 2.86a–88b on monarchic virtues (not explicitly attached to Constantius himself); cf. 2.88b–89b on justice and respect for the law.

[65] The following points are argued in greater detail in Noreña 2009.

the individual agents who acted in it. Another distinctive feature of classical political thought was typological analysis of different constitutions (*politeiai*), a mode of inquiry that flourished in the fluid and labile world of Greek city-states in the fifth and fourth centuries BC. But under large and apparently stable monarchies, and under the Roman imperial monarchy in particular, in which the ideal of imperial eternity (*aeternitas*) was regularly promoted, the prospect of imminent constitutional change must have seemed unrealistic.[66] As a result, there was no longer any practical point in debating the relative merits of monarchy, aristocracy, and democracy.[67] The only critical political variable that remained was the personal character of the reigning emperor, which therefore became the focus of contemporary political thought. The awesome power of the Roman emperor did, at least, provide ample scope for the detailed and sometimes dazzling exploration of the myriad virtues and vices attributed to real emperors and imagined monarchs.

There was also an important political dimension to the discourse of imperial virtue. Unconstrained by the laws or any other formal checks on their notionally absolute power, emperors were guided, in principle, by nothing other than their own character.[68] Contemporary authors were very sensitive to this. Near the beginning of the *De Clementia*, for example, Seneca presents a striking vision of imperial absolutism through the eyes of Nero (1.1.1–2); the young emperor then turns immediately to the qualities that will restrain this power, promising not to be motivated by anger (*ira*), youthful passion (*iuvenilis impetus*), rashness (*temeritas*), or stubbornness (*contumacia*), and pledging to display mercy (*clementia*) instead of severity (*severitas*) (1.1.3–4). Nearly all writers of the imperial age shared the view that the emperor's actions, free from institutional constraints, flowed from his character alone, and that the emperor's cultivation of virtues and suppression of vices was therefore the vital political issue in the Roman empire.

What these writers created through their unremitting focus on imperial character was nothing less than the normative framework in which emperors operated. The ethical program outlined in these texts, in other words, not only defined the ideal monarch, but also produced a real-world model

---

[66] On imperial *aeternitas*, see below, 174–5.

[67] Following Cicero's constitutional analysis in the *De Re Publica* – written, of course, before the advent of monarchy at Rome – there were no sustained typological investigations of this sort until the Severan period and the debate between Agrippa and Maecenas in Dio Book 52.

[68] It is worth reiterating that the absolute power of the emperor was largely a construct, and that in practice emperors faced various constraints on their power; see above, 7.

of behavior for emperors to follow. It should be emphasized that emperors during our period belonged to the same social elite that produced these texts, shared their aristocratic outlook, and had been exposed from childhood to all the same historical *exempla* that pervaded upper-class education and culture. An emperor knew exactly what was expected of him. And the imperial regime itself, through its regular advertisement of the reigning emperor's virtues, contributed to and reinforced this normative framework. Roman emperors did not always live up to these ideals, of course, but the insistent celebration of imperial virtues by aristocratic writers, and the equally insistent commemoration of these virtues by the imperial regime, gave a pronounced ethical thrust to public discourse in the Roman empire, and conditioned the manner in which aristocratic Romans, including the emperor, understood the nature and ends of political power.[69]

This public discourse put a high premium not just on imperial character in general, but also on the specific imperial virtues that manifested themselves in specific contexts. But which virtues? After all, any conceivable ethical quality could be ascribed to a ruler, as the preceding discussion has shown. Roman emperors were not unique among ancient monarchs in being praised for a myriad of virtues. Not all virtues, however, were equally important, nor did the ideological importance of the different virtues, relative to one another, remain constant over time. This is a key point. In order to discern the ethical profile of the "good" emperor, I would like to suggest, it is necessary to examine which virtues in particular were most valued at which times, and to consider how the different virtues related to one another as parts of what I hope to show was a coherent semantic and ideological system.

One approach is to survey the literary record. At one end of the literary spectrum of imperial virtue stood justice, the royal virtue *par excellence.* "Mistress and queen of all the virtues," in Cicero's words (*Off.* 3.28), justice was central both to Greek ethical theory and Roman imperial ideology, the two strands coming together in the notion of the emperor as *nomos empsychos*, and remained dominant down through the Middle Ages, the ideal that "triumphs over every other virtue, life, reputation, and science," as one fourteenth-century Italian jurist put it.[70] At the other end of the

---

[69] The effect of conceptual schemas on individual action has been explored by many scholars in a range of disciplines. For the specific effect of public language on political action, see esp. Skinner 1988a (1974) and 1988b (1980), stressing the ways in which the regular attachment of normative terms to certain actions often constrains those employing such terms to match their actions to the values implied by them. Further discussion below, 292–7, 318–20.

[70] On the medieval tradition, see, e.g., Kantorowicz 1957: ch. 4, with quotation at 137, n. 156. It is worth noting here that justice was one of the few virtues promoted by near-eastern monarchs;

spectrum were the countless second- and third-order qualities that make only rare appearances in the record, such as self-sufficiency or sense of humor.[71] Among the scores of virtues in between, certain canons and rankings developed over time, but such hierarchies were rarely uncontested, and they were always susceptible to change.[72] The most famous and influential set of virtues was the Platonic canon of justice, wisdom, moderation, and courage.[73] But Greek authors, including Plato himself, sometimes added a fifth virtue, reverence for the gods (*eusebeia*), or, more commonly, substituted it for one of the other four. And there were differing views on how these four (or five) canonical virtues should be ranked with respect to one another. Naturally, different contexts called for different hierarchies. In the *Republic*, for example, justice seems to be elevated over the other virtues, since it operates in all three parts of the soul, but in the *Laws* wisdom reigns supreme.[74] Stoic writers of the Roman period more or less adopted the Platonic canon, but other writers favored different groups of virtues, often numbering four, such as Cicero's four qualities of the ideal general, or the four Augustan virtues of the Golden Shield. Beyond such canon-oriented groups of virtues, a wide range of different ethical qualities, as we have seen, came to prominence in different historical contexts – *enkrateia* in the Hellenistic period, *pietas* in the Roman period, etc.[75] Despite the prevalence of certain qualities and sets of virtues, then, the language of imperial and royal virtue was quite fluid.

The evidence from the literary sources is invaluable, but the picture of imperial virtue that emerges from these texts is not only unofficial (with the exception of the *Res Gestae*, a documentary text), but also somewhat vague and necessarily impressionistic. Greater precision is possible in the analysis of the virtues officially publicized by the imperial regime, especially

---

see Dvornik 1966: 13–14, 33–41, 65–8; Raaflaub 2000: 52–7, noting the influence of near-eastern ideas on early Greek political thought. Justice was also important to the ideology of Achaemenid kingship. Both at Behistun and especially at the royal tombs at Naqš-i Rustam, for example, Darius represented himself as dispenser of justice; see Briant 2002: 210–16.

[71] Self-sufficiency: e.g. Sthen. 188.4. Sense of humor: e.g. Suet. *Vesp.* 22.

[72] Convenient collection of evidence in North 1966; see also Wallace-Hadrill 1981a: 300–7.

[73] *Rep.* 4.428b ff. This collocation is first attested in Pindar (*Isthm.* 8.24–8); cf. Isoc. *Or.* 9.22–3 (the four defining virtues of Evagoras). For Plato's own varying canons prior to the *Republic*, see North 1966: 170, n. 15.

[74] North 1966: 172–3.

[75] Some of the virtues that crop up in the post-classical world would have struck a discordant note in the Hellenistic or Roman periods. A Byzantine emperor in the thirteenth century, for example, was praised for his "love of the poor" (*philoptochia*), while another was hailed as "living light" (*phōs empsychos*) (Angelov 2007: 93); in the sixth-century west, Theodebert I was commended both for traditional qualities and for his *humilitas* (Aurelian, *Ep. Aust.* 10), a distinctly non-Roman imperial value. Ideas about which qualities in particular were important in a monarch were not static.

in terms of the varying degrees to which these virtues were emphasized with respect to each other and over time. It is the imperial coinage that makes such analysis possible. Official, serial, and quantifiable, imperial coins offer unparalleled insight into the emperor's official virtues, and allow us to reconstruct a basic "taxonomy" of imperial character, as defined by the regime itself.

Quantitative analysis of the virtues advertised on the imperial coinage depends first on the definition of what constitutes a "virtue." Virtues should be distinguished from personifications, figures giving visual shape and human embodiment to abstract ideals and values, most of which received cult at Rome.[76] Most of the personifications on the imperial coinage, such as Libertas, Pax, and Victoria, are not "virtues" at all, as they are sometimes called by numismatists, since they are not ethical qualities possessed by the emperor.[77] Virtues were also personified on imperial coins, and therefore form a distinct subset of personification types as a whole. During our period, eleven such virtue types appeared on the imperial coinage: Aequitas, Clementia, Indulgentia, Iustitia, Liberalitas, Munificentia, Patientia, Pietas, Providentia, Pudicitia, and Virtus. These virtue types constituted between one fifth and one quarter of all personification types, on both denarii and base-metal coins, for the period 69–235.[78] Depicted on the reverse of imperial coins bearing the emperor's portrait on the obverse, and regularly glossed with the label AUGUSTA/AUGUSTI (or with the abbreviation AUG), the virtues represented by these personifications were not just values associated in some vague way with the emperor, but were emphatic claims of the emperor's paradigmatic possession of these specific ethical qualities. Measuring the relative frequency of these virtue types, therefore, reveals the varying degrees to which these qualities were emphasized, and provides us with something like an official taxonomy of imperial character. The results of this quantitative analysis, undertaken for the period 69–235 as a whole, are shown in tables 2.1 and 2.2.

The first point to note is the broad correspondence between the two sets of data. Aequitas, Pietas, Virtus, and Providentia were all prominent on precious-metal denarii and on the various base-metal denominations (though Virtus was notably more frequent on the latter), while Indulgentia, Clementia, Iustitia, Munificentia, and Patientia were all marginal on

---

[76] Clark 2007 refers to this whole set of personifications as "divine qualities" (26–7).

[77] See discussion in Wallace-Hadrill 1981a: 308–10. Many of these non-virtue personifications, which advertised the benefits of imperial rule, are examined in the next chapter.

[78] Among denarii, virtues made up 23 percent of all personification types (N = 77,853); on base-metal coins, 21 percent (N = 20,845).

Table 2.1 *Relative frequency on denarii of individual*
imperial virtues, expressed as a percentage of all
imperial virtues, AD *69–235 (N = 18,187)*

Type	Percentage	Type	Percentage
Aequitas	24%	Indulgentia	4%
Pietas	20%	Clementia	2%
Virtus	13%	Iustitia	2%
Liberalitas	12%	Munificentia	<1%
Providentia	12%	Patientia	<1%
Pudicitia	11%		

Table 2.2 *Relative frequency on base-metal coins of*
individual imperial virtues, expressed as a percentage
of all imperial virtues, AD *69–235 (N = 4141)*

Type	Percentage	Type	Percentage
Pietas	26%	Indulgentia	3%
Virtus	23%	Clementia	3%
Aequitas	19%	Iustitia	3%
Providentia	12%	Munificentia	2%
Liberalitas	6%	Patientia	0
Pudicitia	3%		

both. The only significant discrepancies between metals are reflected in the relative frequencies of the Liberalitas and Pudicitia types. That Liberalitas types were relatively common on denarii and relatively rare on base-metal coins can be accounted for by the different visual and conceptual modes employed to express the ideal of imperial generosity – abstract personification of Liberalitas on the precious-metal coins, circulating amongst wealthier and better-educated users, and concrete representation of the emperor literally distributing coin on the base-metal coins, circulating amongst the masses (see below, 88–90). Pudicitia types were minted almost exclusively on coins with obverse portraits of the imperial women. Among emperors, only Hadrian experimented with the proclamation of *pudicitia*, "chastity."[79] The type was produced during a transitional phase in the

[79] *RIC* 2, Hadrian 135, 176–8, 343.

ideology of the imperial couple as a model of marital bliss and domestic harmony (*concordia*), but *pudicitia* was too strongly associated with the feminine sphere to become a standard imperial virtue.[80] However the discrepancy between metals in the relative frequency of Pudicitia types is to be explained, then, it does not bear directly on the representation of imperial character. The examples of Liberalitas and Pudicitia are, in any case, the exceptions that prove the rule. In general, the profile of imperial virtues was quite consistent across the denominations.

Taking the denarii and base-metal coins together, we see five core virtues expressed by these personifications: *aequitas, pietas, virtus, liberalitas* and *providentia*. Though it would be misleading to think of these qualities as some sort of "official canon" of imperial virtues, they did nevertheless constitute the five most publicized ethical qualities of the emperor, on the most pervasive medium of official communications, over the course of the period 69–235. It must be emphasized that this set of five core imperial virtues does not match up exactly with any pre-existing canon or contemporary set of key virtues. It does not derive from either Augustus' Golden Shield (no *iustitia* and no *clementia*) or Plato's canon (no wisdom, no moderation, no justice – *aequitas*, as we will see, was not a synonym for *iustitia*), and does not correspond precisely to the sets of ethical qualities stressed by contemporary writers such as Pliny, Dio Chrysostom, and Suetonius. There is, of course, significant overlap between this set of official qualities and those of earlier texts and contemporary authors, but these five virtues form a discrete set of virtues in their own right, and should be interpreted as such. As we will see, this particular constellation of virtues is not only coherent, in symbolic and ideological terms, but also illuminating for its emphasis – in contrast with the philosophical canons of the Greek tradition – on the specific contexts, concrete outcomes, and practical applications of these virtues for the community as a whole.

A preliminary glance at how these five core virtues relate to the broader discourse of monarchy and virtue in the Roman imperial period highlights what is not included. Strikingly absent from this group is any virtue unambiguously expressing the concept of justice. Iustitia types themselves were minted in very small numbers. *Clementia*, a virtue with some bearing on the dispensation of justice, was also only marginally represented.[81]

---

[80] Evidence and argument in Noreña 2007b.

[81] *Clementia* was not simply a despotic quality, as is sometimes suggested (by, e.g., Charlesworth 1937: 113; Béranger 1953: 271; Wickert 1954: 2,243); see discussion in Konstan 2005; for the coinage, see also Barden-Dowling 2006: 127, 158–60, 177–81, 190–1, 213–14, 260–1, 269–70 (but without reference to the relative infrequency of the type).

And while *aequitas* was often understood as denoting imperial fairness in the judicial sphere, the history and iconography of Aequitas types on the imperial coinage suggest that the principal message was fairness in the administration of the imperial mint (see below, 66–71). The canonical virtue of justice, as conceived by Greek and Roman theorists and rhetoricians, played a very minor role on the coinage in the official representation of the emperor's virtues. There are several interpretations of this apparent anomaly. Béranger has suggested that Iustitia on the imperial coinage did not refer to the abstract ideal of justice, but was simply one of the many qualities expressing the "personal attitude" of the monarch towards his subjects, but this does not explain why this particular quality, so important to conceptions of monarchy in the ancient Mediterranean world, was so marginal in this official medium of communications.[82] According to Wallace-Hadrill, there already existed so many other vehicles for the public advertisement of imperial justice – published imperial edicts, imperial tribunals in the Forum, the giving of justice during imperial travels, and the imperial *rescripta* inscribed in cities and towns everywhere – that the coinage was not needed to communicate this particular virtue.[83] It could also be the case that justice was not underrepresented on the imperial coinage, but overrepresented in other sources – in texts written by aristocratic authors hoping to encourage emperors to submit to the laws, and in the epigraphic record, which surely reflects the incentive to make a public and permanent record of favorable imperial judgments, often ascribed to the emperor's *iustitia*.

Iustitia, then, did not belong to the primary set of official virtues advertised on the coinage. Though a major virtue, it was subordinated, like the minor qualities listed in tables 2.1–2, to *aequitas, pietas, virtus, liberalitas*, and *providentia*. Evidently, from the official perspective of the Roman imperial state, these were the specific imperial virtues that warranted extensive and regular promotion on the coinage over the long term. It is to these core virtues that we now turn.

FIVE CORE VIRTUES

Identifying which virtues in particular were emphasized on the imperial coinage between 69 and 235 is only the first step in understanding the official representation of imperial character during this period. The second and equally important step is to examine what these virtues actually meant.

[82] Béranger 1953: 270–1.   [83] Wallace-Hadrill 1981b: 37.

And it will be necessary to examine their meaning in some detail, since there has been a tendency in the scholarship on imperial ideology either to present a bare list of imperial virtues, glossed with simple translations of Latin terms and only very cursory analysis of their sense and usage, or to consider the iconography of the coin types in isolation from the conceptual and expressive schemas in which these types were embedded.[84] Such treatments are not very illuminating if we really want to grasp the contemporary significance of these qualities. Only through detailed literary and iconographic analysis together can we begin to comprehend the full semantic range and ideological resonance of imperial *aequitas, pietas, virtus, liberalitas,* and *providentia*.[85]

Aequitas

Aequitas is a straightforward term with a somewhat complicated history as an imperial virtue.[86] In its narrowest application *aequitas* denotes the proportion between two or more elements necessary for symmetry or balance. This usage could be metaphorical, as when Cicero observes that "*aequitas* is most inequitable when the best and worst men have equal honor," or literal, as in the equilibrium of a scale that uses properly calibrated weights.[87] *Aequitas* can also refer to evenness, whether topographical (*aequitas loci*) or mental (*aequitas animi*).[88] From these senses of *aequitas* come the term's principal meanings as justice or as fairness in decision-making, especially in judicial contexts. As a principle of jurisprudence *aequitas* was treated as one component of law (*ius*), frequently distinguished from other components

---

[84] The approach here is inspired in part by the work of the "Cambridge School," which emphasizes, among other things, the importance of attempting to flesh out the full social, linguistic, and especially discursive contexts of the key words and concepts selected for analysis; for a basic orientation, see e.g. Pocock 1987; Tully 1988, esp. 7–25; Ball *et al.* 1989: 1–5.

[85] In what follows, analysis of linguistic usage is mainly synchronic, drawn from texts ranging from the late Republic through the high empire. Significant chronological changes in usage are noted where relevant, but in general, barring evidence to the contrary, it is assumed that the basic meanings of these terms were relatively stable.

[86] Literary evidence for the meaning of *aequitas* is collected in *TLL* 1.1013.73–1017.2. For *aequitas* as an imperial virtue, see references in Wickert 1954: 2,248–53 (note that Wickert treats *aequitas* and *iustitia* interchangeably); cf. Hellegouarc'h 1963: 150–1 for Republican usage. For the meaning of the Aequitas type on the imperial coinage, a much debated question, see Strack 1931–1937: 1.154–64; Mattingly in *BMCRE* II, xlviii–xlix, III, xxxv–xxxvi, IV, lvii; Wallace-Hadrill 1981b, with earlier bibliography at 20–1, n. 4.

[87] Cic. *Rep.* 1.53; cf. Sen. *Nat.* 3.10.3. For *aequitas* as equilibrium in weighing or measuring, see Wallace-Hadrill 1981b: 24–5, citing mainly epigraphic evidence.

[88] *Aequitas loci*: B.Hisp. 29.7. *Aequitas animi*: e.g. Cic. *Font.* 23, *Marcell.* 25, *Tusc.* 1.97, *Or.* 2.102; Caes. *BG* 6.22.4; Nep. *Thras.* 4.2.

of *ius* such as statutes (*leges*) or customs (*mores*).[89] For the jurists *aequitas* was a force that could influence judges or "require" certain judgments.[90] Sometimes it is paired with *iustitia*.[91] More instructive is Cicero's collocation of *aequitas* with moderation (*temperantia*), bravery (*fortitudo*) and wisdom (*prudentia*), a set of four qualities clearly intended to suggest a philosophical canon of virtues, and one in which *aequitas* is employed as the equivalent of the Platonic *dikaiosynē*.[92] *Aequitas* in this sense of justice easily shaded into a personal quality, most often construed as fairness in legal judgment. In a letter addressed to his brother Quintus during Quintus' governorship of Asia, for example, Cicero, articulating a set of principles of provincial governance, in which the administration of justice was a central duty, writes, "For you will constantly do what you have done so that everyone praises your *aequitas*, moderation, strictness and integrity."[93] Indeed, *aequitas* as fairness is often linked with other characteristics of an honorable judge, such as *iustitia*, *fides*, *integritas*, *misericordia*, *mansuetudo* and *humanitas*.[94] Facing a charge of magic, Apuleius surely hoped to encourage just these sorts of qualities in Claudius Maximus, the judge trying his case, when he announced that he was relying in his self-defense on his own innocence and on Maximus' *aequitas*.[95]

It is this broad and central meaning of *aequitas* as justice or fairness and, in particular, the term's semantic overlap between an abstract principle of jurisprudence and a personal quality of individuals, especially those formally empowered to pass legal judgment, that makes *aequitas* so resonant as an imperial virtue. Justice was not only considered an essential quality for monarchs in the ancient world, but would also have been a particularly acute concern for the subjects of the Roman emperor, above all because of the advent and spread of *cognitio*. In this judicial procedure, employed mainly by emperors and provincial governors, the judge conducted all relevant investigations and then pronounced a summary and

---

[89] E.g. Cic. *Top.* 31: *ut si quis ius in legem, morem, aequitatem dividat*; *Part. Or.* 129: *quod* (sc. *ius*) *dividitur in duas primas partes, naturam atque legem, et utrius generis vis in divinum et humanum ius est distributa, quorum aequitatis est unum, alterum religionis*; cf. *Phil.* 9.11; Quint. *Inst.* 7.1.63; many similar references in *TLL* 1.1015.38–1017.2.

[90] *Dig.* 11.1.21 (Ulpian); 12.4.3.7 (Ulpian); 18.4.2.3 (Ulpian); 3.1.7 (Marcellus); 3.3.46.6 (Gaius).

[91] *Aequitas* and *iustitia*: Cic. *Or.* 1.86, *Lael.* 82; cf. Cic. *Off.* 1.50; Nep. *Arist.* 2.2.

[92] Cic. *Cat.* 2.25: *denique aequitas, temperantia, fortitudo, prudentia certant cum iniquitate, luxuria, ignavia, temeritate.*

[93] Cic. *QFr.* 1.1.45 = SB 1.

[94] *Iustitia*: Cic. *Off.* 1.50; Nep. *Arist.* 2.2; *fides*: Cic. *Cluent.* 81, 159, *Off.* 2.27; *integritas*: Cic. *Mur.* 41; *misericordia*: Cic. *Marcell.* 12; Liv. 3.56.10; *mansuetudo*: Cic. *Cluent.* 199; *humanitas*: Cic. *Verr.* 3.86. Note also Cic. *Verr.* 4.195, where *aequitas* is contrasted with *improbitas* and *impudentia*.

[95] Apul. *Apol.* 3.

final verdict. Because the judges in these cases were not bound by any external laws or rules whatsoever, unlike *iudices* in the traditional formulary system, there was nothing in the *cognitio* procedure to prevent arbitrary judgment.[96] Clearly such a procedure put a high premium on the inherent fairness of the judge himself. The emperor's *aequitas* could proclaim precisely that quality. There are accordingly a number of literary references to imperial *aequitas* that invoke *iustitia* or allude to the emperor's justice or fairness, especially in judicial contexts. Velleius Paterculus, for example, credits Tiberius with the restoration of both *aequitas* and *iustitia* (2.126.2). Praising Trajan's jurisdiction as consul, Pliny associates the emperor's "scrupulousness towards *aequitas*" (*religio aequitatis*) with his "reverence for the laws" (*legum reverentia*).[97] Claudius judges even a trivial matter, according to Suetonius, with "unprejudiced *aequitas.*"[98]

Reference to this imperial virtue can also be found in official texts. In the *senatusconsultum de Gnaeo Pisone Patre* of AD 20 (*SCPP*) the senate thanks Tiberius for his *aequitas* and *patientia* in requesting a formal enquiry of the patently guilty Cn. Piso, an expression of gratitude in which the emperor's fairness and regard for proper justice is held up as a model for the senate's own judgment.[99] In fact, we can trace this specific usage of imperial *aequitas* as "judicial fairness" from the reign of Tiberius into the later empire. Ammianus Marcellinus, for example, declares that Julian "never strayed from the straight path of *aequitas*" when pronouncing judgment, and Marcus Aurelius is commended by the biographer of the *Historia Augusta* for judging "with the highest *aequitas*" when hearing capital cases involving upperclass defendants.[100] And in his panegyric to Julian, Mamertinus speaks in lyrical vein about the beauty of the emperor's *aequitas, temperantia, fortitudo,* and *providentia,* echoing Cicero's version of the Platonic canon (with

[96] On the procedural aspects of *cognitio*, the standard treatment is Kaser 1966: 339–409; for the emperor and *cognitio*, Millar 1977: 236–40, 516–37.

[97] Plin. *Pan.* 77.3. Pliny also extols Trajan's *iustitia, gravitas,* and *comitas* in a letter describing his own participation in Trajan's *consilium* (*Ep.* 6.31.2), and Trajan himself refers in a letter to Pliny to the *iustitia nostrorum temporum* (*Ep.* 10.55). Further references to Trajan's *iustitia* in Wickert 1954: 2,250–1.

[98] *Claud.* 15.2: *aequitas integra.*

[99] *SCPP* (*CIL* 2²/5.900), ll. 17–20: *cuius aequitatem et patientiam hoc quoq(ue) nomine | admirari senatum quod cum manufestissuma sint Cn. Pisonis patris scelera | et ipse de se supplicium sumpsisset nihilominus causam eius cognosci volue|rit.* For the significance of *aequitas* in this passage, see discussion in Eck *et al.* 1996: 140–1, 299.

[100] Amm. Marc. 22.10.2; *M. Aur.* 24.2 (*summa aequitate*); cf. H.A. *Max. et Balb.* 17.4, where Pupienus and Balbinus are praised for their restoration of *aequitas* and *clementia,* a pairing of virtues redolent of the judicial sphere.

Illustration 2.1 Reverse of denarius (*RIC* 2, Nerva 13): Aequitas holding a cornucopia and a pair of scales. AEQUITAS AUGUST

providentia for *prudentia*) and revealing the long-term stability of the term *aequitas* as a reference to justice or fairness.[101]

Valerius Maximus, after describing a verdict delivered by Augustus against a widow who had disinherited her children, asks, "If Aequitas herself had heard the case, could she have judged more justly (*iustius*) or in a more dignified manner?"[102] Here we find the personification Aequitas administering justice in an exemplary manner, and in light of the literary references to imperial *aequitas* it is tempting to conclude that the Aequitas coin type was designed to advertise the judicial fairness of the emperor. But the intent behind the coin type depicting the personification Aequitas was evidently rather different. Iconography provides one clue to its meaning. On the imperial coinage the female personification Aequitas is depicted standing or seated, holding in her left hand either a rod, a cornucopia, or a palm, and in her right hand always a pair of scales (illustration 2.1).[103] The pair of scales, the attribute that identifies Aequitas, did not symbolize justice in the visual vocabulary of the Romans, but instead represented the simple act of weighing, symbolic of the economic world of weights and measures in general and of the proper valuation of coins in particular, and consistent

---

[101] *Pan.* 3.5.4.
[102] Val. Max. 7.7.4; cf. Amm. Marc. 22.6.5: *unde velut Aequitate ipsa dictante lex est promulgata.*
[103] Aequitas with scales: e.g. *RIC* 2, Vespasian 5; *RIC* 2, Titus 121; *RIC* 2, Nerva 1; *RIC* 2, Trajan 119; *RIC* 2, Hadrian 228; *RIC* 3, Antoninus Pius 3; *RIC* 3, Marcus Aurelius 178; *RIC* 3, Commodus 13; *RIC* 4.1, Pertinax 14; *RIC* 4.1, Septimius Severus 122; *RIC* 4.1, Geta 189; *RIC* 4.2, Macrinus 52–3; *RIC* 4.2, Elagabalus 163A; *RIC* 4.2, Severus Alexander 51. In general on the iconography of Aequitas, *LIMC* 1.1.241–3, 2.1.176–7 (G. G. Belloni).

with one of the basic meanings of *aequitas* as equilibrium in weighing.[104] The historical context in which the type was introduced under Galba also militates against the "judicial fairness" interpretation. Every personification type minted under Galba had a precedent on the coinages produced by the rebel mints in 68. The one apparent exception to this pattern was Galba's Aequitas type. But this type did in fact respond to one personification promoted by the rebel mints, that of Moneta. The close numismatic association between Moneta and Aequitas is confirmed by the subsequent history of the two types, as their iconography and legends become largely interchangeable.[105] The iconography and history of the Aequitas coin type, therefore, suggest that its primary message was monetary and financial, not judicial. The Aequitas type was never intended to advertise imperial fairness, broadly conceived, or even judicial fairness, but rather the honest administration of the imperial mint.[106]

The fact that the Aequitas coin type did not publicize imperial justice or fairness does not mean that it should be dismissed as irrelevant to the representation of imperial virtues. For honesty and integrity in the administration of the imperial mint could certainly be thought of as important personal qualities of the emperor himself, even if day-to-day decisions at the mint were made by anonymous, low-level officials. After all, what was done under the Roman emperor was often imagined to have been done by the Roman emperor. It was precisely the Aequitas coin type, in fact, that announced the emperor's notional responsibility for the mint and its product. It also made *aequitas* the imperial virtue that guaranteed the intrinsic value of the imperial coinage. In this sense it could be claimed, with some justification, that the monetary economy and financial structure of the empire as a whole depended on imperial *aequitas*.

Long-term patterns in the production of the Aequitas type, intended to advertise the just administration of the imperial mint and the value of its

---

[104] See Wallace-Hadrill 1981b: 25–31 for details. Scales came to represent justice only by the Carolingian period (references in Wallace-Hadrill 1981b: 26, n. 41; for a doubtful example on a coin produced in Antioch under Pescennius Niger, see *LIMC* 8.1.662, no. 10, with discussion by M. C. Caltabiano, 663); on the imperial coinage, the identifying attributes of Iustitia are sceptre and patera (see indices to *BMCRE* or *RIC*).

[105] Wallace-Hadrill 1981b: 31–2; Strack 1931–1937: 1.154–64 provides a more thorough overview of the iconography and history of the Aequitas and Moneta types (but his conclusions are untenable; see next note).

[106] So Mattingly, *BMCRE* III, xxxvi–xxxvii, convincingly refuting Strack's assertion that Aequitas always advertises imperial fairness in general, and only refers specifically to the mint when glossed by the legend MONETA. Moneta was certainly a goddess in her own right, as Mattingly recognized, and not a mere epithet of Aequitas; see discussion in Meadows and Williams 2001, esp. 33 for the evidence that Moneta could be her own goddess – not always treated, that is, as just an epithet of Juno.

product, the coins themselves, reveal a particularly effective convergence of medium and message. In the case of precious-metal aurei and denarii, "value" refers primarily to the amount of gold or silver contained in each coin. From the second half of the second century AD, when the Roman state began to face increasing financial pressures, the debasement of coins issued by the central mint was one of the main techniques employed to maintain fiscal solvency.[107] Because of these periodic reductions in the weight and fineness of the precious-metal coins, especially denarii, the state was sometimes compelled to persuade the public to continue using its newly minted coins. During the more acute financial crisis of the third century, even formal legislation was brought to bear on the problem. A prefect of Egypt, for example, issued an edict requiring banks and others involved in monetary transactions to accept imperial coins, with penalties for non-compliance.[108]

During our period, by contrast, attempts to ensure the use of newly minted imperial coins were persuasive rather than coercive. One way to advertise the value of imperial coins was through the Aequitas type itself. The extent to which emphasis on the Aequitas types matched or did not match the value of imperial coins can be measured by comparing the fluctuating relative frequency of the type on denarii, on the one hand, with stages in the debasement of the silver coinage, as measured by the number of denarii struck per pound of silver, on the other. The results are shown in figures 2.1 and 2.2.[109]

The data reveal – perhaps surprisingly – an inverse relationship between the commonness of the Aequitas type on denarii and the debasement of the silver coinage. In other words, the frequency of the Aequitas type matched the quality of the denarii produced by the imperial mint. This correlation is not perfect, of course, and there are a few exceptions to the pattern, but it is positive and statistically significant.[110] Virtue types were uncommon on the coins of Vespasian, Titus, and Domitian, so the Flavian period is a bit of an outlier for this test. The demonstrable correlation begins under

---

[107] The practice goes back to the reign of Nero. See Walker 1976–78: 3.106–48; Duncan-Jones 1994, esp. chs. 15–16. For the more radical debasements of the third century, Callu 1969; Corbier 2005: 330–52.

[108] *P.Oxy.* 12.1411 (*c.* AD 260); cf. Epict. 3.3.3.

[109] Figure 2.2 is based on the evidence collected in Duncan-Jones 1994: 223–8, with Table 15.6 (227) and Fig. 15.7 (229). Duncan-Jones draws on the work of Walker (1976–1978: 3.106–141), the accuracy of which has been questioned (see Metcalf 1995: 157, with n. 21). Walker's data should, however, suffice for this comparison, which requires only broad orders of magnitude. Note that figures 2.1–2 do not include Macrinus (insufficient data).

[110] For the calculations of the correlation coefficients and permutation values noted in the text that follows, see appendix 9.

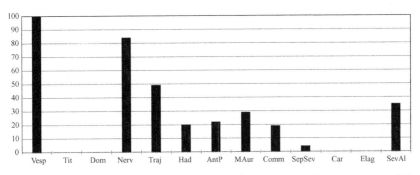

Figure 2.1 Relative frequency of Aequitas types on denarii, expressed as a percentage of all virtue types by reign, AD 69–235 (N = 18,187)

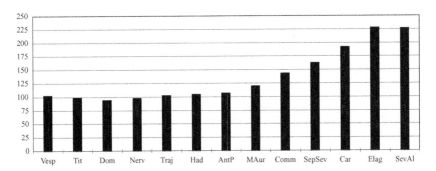

Figure 2.2 Number of denarii struck per pound of silver by reign, AD 69–235

Nerva, Trajan, and Hadrian. The lower-quality denarius produced under Trajan, compared with that of Nerva, is mirrored on the coinage of his reign by decreased emphasis on the Aequitas type; the pattern continues under Hadrian, with a still lower-quality denarius and even less emphasis on Aequitas. Beginning with the reign of Nerva, then, and continuing through the reign of Caracalla, there is a strong, inverse correlation between the frequency of the Aequitas type and the quality of denarii (r = −.73). The statistical significance of this correlation is confirmed by a low permutation value (.04), which indicates that the correlation between the two data sets is not accidental. More significant is the record of the Aequitas type during the period of progressively greater reductions in the weight and fineness of the imperial silver coinage between 161 and 222. Beginning with Marcus Aurelius, the relative frequency of the Aequitas type plummets until it disappears from the coinage entirely. This is exactly when the debasement of the silver coinage during our period was at its most rampant. During this period, the inverse correlation is almost perfect (r = −.96), again reinforced by a low permutation value (.083). This relationship between the commonness of the Aequitas type and the value of the denarius is confirmed by minting practice under Severus Alexander, during whose reign the reappearance of the Aequitas type coincided with the abrupt (and ultimately ephemeral) halt to the long-term debasement of the denarius.

This evidence indicates that fluctuations in the relative frequency of the Aequitas type were not random. Fluctuations in the relative frequency of the Liberalitas type were also meaningful, as we will see (below, 90–2), which suggests that the commonness or rarity of individual coin types in general was either deliberate or at least not random – even if we may not always understand what these fluctuations signify. These data also show that the imperial state did not employ the Aequitas type in an attempt to deceive the public about the value of the coins it produced. Instead, *aequitas* as an imperial virtue was normally emphasized on denarii only when the silver coinage as a whole – i.e, not just those coins bearing the Aequitas type – embodied the monetary value that this virtue guaranteed.[111] This runs counter to common perceptions of Roman imperial government. In his discussion of currency devaluation, for example, Walker notes that the "three Monetae" medallion of Marcus Aurelius and Lucius Verus was introduced at a time of increasing debasement, and Wallace-Hadrill observes that Domitian's introduction of the legend MONETA in 84 preceded the debasement of 85.[112] When it came to *aequitas*, however, the underlying imperial virtue that manifested itself in the quality of the precious-metal coins themselves, the state was careful to ensure that its public claims corresponded to some objective reality.

An imperial coin bearing the personification of Aequitas on one side and the imperial portrait on the other communicated a potent bundle of ideological messages. It represented a conspicuous convergence of medium and message, as the main application of Aequitas was precisely in the monetary sphere, and it neatly expressed the convergence of two separate regimes of value, the one economic and the other symbolic, as the emperor's portrait guaranteed the intrinsic value of the coin – symbolized, in this case,

---

[111] It must be emphasized that there was no correlation between precious-metal content and coins bearing the Aequitas type itself; coins stamped with the Aequitas type, that is, had no greater intrinsic value than those stamped with other types.

[112] Walker 1976–78: 3.125, drawing attention to Gnecchi 1912: 2.33 (medallion); Wallace-Hadrill 1981b: 36–7, n. 100, on *RIC* 2, Domitian 242A.

by Aequitas – which in turn reinforced the authority of the emperor himself. It is no wonder that Aequitas was the most common virtue type on denarii. And it must be emphasized that this *aequitas* was, ultimately, an ethical quality. Indeed, it was mainly the broader conception of "fairness" that invested the Aequitas type with persuasive force. No type more effectively advertised the moral economy of imperial rule.

Pietas

Pietas was one of the principal ideals of the Roman ethical vocabulary. Cicero refers to it as "the foundation of all the virtues," and right from the very beginnings of Latin literature *pietas* is a central theme.[113] *Pietas* as a Roman value has been much discussed and is well understood.[114] Because *pietas* was such an elastic concept, however, and because it has been variously interpreted in its specific usage as a quality of the Roman emperor, it will be useful to consider the term's basic meaning before examining *pietas* as an imperial virtue.[115]

Pietas was, very simply, the virtue of fulfilling one's responsibilities to anyone or anything to whom or to which one was bound in any way. The fulfillment of these responsibilities could be motivated by the requirements of duty or obligation, in which cases *pietas* often overlapped with the notions of *officium*, *fides*, or *religio*, or by the deeper sentiments of love and affection.[116] *Pietas* was a very expansive ideal, and indeed this virtue was invoked in a wide range of contexts involving relations between humans, between humans and gods, and between humans and abstractions. As a quality that governed human relations, it was familial *pietas* that attracted most attention and comment by the Romans themselves. The literary

---

[113] Cic. *Planc.* 29: *pietas fundamentum est omnium virtutum*; *pietas* towards the gods already in Naevius (fr. 12) and Ennius (fr. 340 Diehl); cf. *TLL* 10.1.14.2088.32–40 for references in Plautus to *pietas* towards the gods.

[114] For a convenient overview, see *TLL* 10.1.14.2086–2105.

[115] I have drawn mainly on the following studies of *pietas*: Wagenvoort 1980 (1924); Ulrich 1930; Liegle 1932; Charlesworth 1937: 113–14; Charlesworth 1943; Beaujeu 1955, esp. 283–6; Weinstock 1971: 248–59; Hellegoarc'h 1963: 276–9; Oliver 1978; Saller 1994: 105–14; Galinsky 1996: 86–8; Kragelund 1998; Roller 2001: 26–8. For the Pietas coin type, see Strack 1931–1937: 1.75–6, 2.51–7, 169–71, 3.115–24; Liegle 1932; Mattingly in the introduction to *BMCRE* iii, esp. xcv, cxlii, cl, and clii; Kragelund 1998: 161–5.

[116] For the overlap between *pietas* and *fides*, *officium*, and *religio*, see Hellegouarc'h 1963: 276–9; for *pietas* as an expression of love and affection, an aspect of the virtue often overlooked by those who stress duty and obligation, see discussion in Saller 1994: 105–14; cf. Galinsky 1996: 86. Wagenvoort 1980 (1924): 2–7 emphasizes connections between *pietas* and both *humanitas* and *religio*.

sources abound with references to *pietas* directed towards parents, children, siblings, and spouses.[117] Vergil's Aeneas is of course the archetype of this strand of *pietas*: *insignem pietate virum*.[118] Familial *pietas* could be a "vertical" virtue, directed either "upwards" towards parents or "downwards" towards children – Aeneas' *pietas* embraced both Anchises and Ascanius – and a "horizontal" virtue, directed towards brothers, sisters, husbands, and wives. This versatility of familial *pietas* is mirrored in the functions of *pietas* within social relationships more generally. And so we find *pietas* directed upwards towards patrons, downwards towards clients, and horizontally towards friends.[119] From these principal objects of duty, obligation, and affection, *pietas* branched out in various directions to touch all sorts of human relationships, between Romans and their allies and between teachers and students, for example, and, in a usage which overlaps with *misericordia*, *clementia*, and *venia*, before those deserving pity such as exiles, grieving mothers, and the deceased.[120] Beyond the sphere of interpersonal relations, *pietas* referred primarily to the ideal attitude of duty and devotion that shaped human interaction with the gods. *Pietas* of men towards the gods in particular was crucial for the stability and prosperity of the Roman community, not only as the basis for securing the *pax deorum*, but also as a major justification for Roman imperialism.[121] In addition to this prominent religious aspect, *pietas* also had a critically important civic dimension,

---

[117] Many examples in *TLL* 10.1.14: *pietas* between children and parents (2092.52–2094.22), between siblings (2094.67–2095.16), and between spouses (2094.31–2094.66). Saller 1994: 111 notes that the majority of juristic references to *pietas* concern relations within the nuclear family.

[118] Verg. *Aen.* 1.10. See briefly Galinsky 1996: 86, 89, 204; cf. Saller 1994: 106, n. 16.

[119] Attestations of *pietas* between patrons and clients are mainly epigraphic. Patronal *pietas*: *CIL* 6.2225 (Rome): *patronis suis fecit . . . pro eorum pietati et sibi et suis*; *CIL* 12.5130 (Narbo): *Apate . . . fecit patrono et sibi ob pietatem eius*; *CIL* 3.3658 (Salvium, Dalmatia): *patronus pietatis causa tit(ulum) me(um) . . . posuit. Pietas* of clients: *CIL* 6.9187 (Rome): *patrono bene merenti . . . pietatis causa*; *CIL* 3.6778 (Khadün Khan, Lycaonia): *patrono pietatis causa*; cf. Pliny's incredulity at the honorific inscription set up by the senate to Claudius' freedman Pallas (*Ep.* 7.29.2): *huic senatus ob fidem pietatem erga patronos ornamenta praetoria decrevit . . . Pietas* among friends: Cic. *Sest.* 3, *Mil.* 100, *Fam.* 1.9.1; Ov. *Ars* 2.321; Val. Max. 4.7.4; Stat. *Silv.* 4 praef.; Apul. *Met.* 8.7.3.

[120] *Pietas* between Romans and allies: Liv. 23.9.5; Vell. 2.16.3; Val. Max. 5.2 ext. 4; Luc. 8.127; *pietas* between teachers and students: Quint. *Inst.* 2.9.2; *pietas* towards exiles: Cic. *De Or.* 2.167; Vell. 2.15.4; Ov. *Trist.* 1.7.11; Sen. *Dial.* 12.4.2; *pietas* towards grieving mothers: Verg. *Aen.* 9.493; *pietas* towards the deceased: Cic. *Leg.* 2.54; Ov. *Fast.* 2.535; Sen. *Phoen.* 97; *Dig.* 3.2.23 (Ulpian).

[121] *Pietas* of men towards the gods: abundant references in *TLL* 10.1.14.2088.25–2089.30; for the special Roman claim to this virtue, see esp. Cic. *Har. resp.* 19; Verg. *Aen.* 12.839; Liv. 44.1.11. For the connection between *pietas* and Roman imperialism, see Wagenvoort 1980 (1924): 12; Weinstock 1971: 249–50. Hellegouarc'h 1963: 276, stressing the "contractual" nature of Roman religion, compares *pietas* in the religious sphere to *fides* in the judicial sphere. The "contractual" nature of Roman religion may explain why the actions of gods towards men could also be dictated, in principle, by the requirements of *pietas* (e.g. Verg. *Aen.* 2.536, 5.688; Sil. 6.410).

especially in the Ciceronian age, as it came to denote the loyal fulfillment of responsibilities towards the fatherland (*patria*).[122]

As the virtue that underpinned model relations within the family, between men and gods, and between Romans and their fatherland, then, *pietas* was indeed one of the core values of the Roman moral universe. Because the categories of persons or entities to which one might have responsibilities were so diverse, however, and because they embraced such a wide range of feelings and practices – from the tender love of a mother for her children to the obligatory fulfillment of official duties towards the state – it is sometimes difficult to see what holds *pietas* together as a unified concept. Perhaps the best way to understand *pietas* is to focus not on the bewildering number of external objects towards which it could be oriented, but rather on the internal, subjective quality that motivated devotion or dutiful conduct. *Pietas*, in other words, should be seen as a general attitude or disposition that manifested itself in any number of specific actions, depending on the context. The unifying element of this protean virtue is precisely that attitude or disposition.

The figure of the Roman emperor fit within most of the standard matrices of *pietas*, both as object and as subject of the virtue. The emperor was owed *pietas* from his subjects, not only from the soldiers, who had taken an oath to the emperor, but also from other groups, such as the urban plebs and senators (and indeed from all loyal subjects).[123] The reciprocity inherent in the ideal of *pietas* ensured that the emperor also displayed this virtue towards his subjects. Near the beginning of the *Panegyric*, for example, in a discussion of Trajan's relationship with his subjects, Pliny praises the emperor for his *pietas* after having identified him as a *parens*, a collocation that underlined the emperor's paternal affection for and duty towards his subjects.[124] The emperor, like all good Romans, was also expected to

---

[122] *Pietas* towards one's *patria*: e.g. Cic. *Flacc.* 96, *Phil.* 6.19, 13.46, *Rep.* 6.16, *Brut.* 126; Caes. *BG* 5.27.7; Liv. 5.7.12, 7.10.4, 23.9.10, 27.9.11; Val. Max. 3.8.2; Sen. *Ep.* 86.1; Plin. *Ep.* 2.5.3. Some municipal inscriptions from Italy also record *pietas* towards the *res publica*: *CIL* 5.532 (Tergeste, mid-2nd c.); 10.1783 (Puteoli, mid-2nd c.).

[123] Soldiers: *SCPP* l. 161: *quam fidem pietatemque domui Aug(ustae) praestarent milites* (cf. l. 164); Sen. *Oct.* 844; Tac. *Hist.* 1.83.2, 2.69.1, 3.36.2; for *pietas* towards the emperor as a military virtue, see Ulrich 1930: 41–9. Urban plebs: *SCPP* 155: *plebis pietas . . . erga principem*. Senators: Tac. *Ann.* 3.51.1; Plin. *Pan.* 75.3 (*pietas nostra*), 79.4. Subjects: Ov. *Pont.* 4.9.105; Mart. 8 pr.; Suet. *Vit.* 3: *pietas immobilis erga principem* (on the father of the emperor Vitellius, who had displayed this virtue towards Claudius). Further references to the emperor as object of *pietas* in *TLL* 10.1.14.2,096.50–2,097.23; see discussion in Charlesworth 1943; cf. Alföldy 2001 on honorific monuments for the imperial family as examples of senatorial *pietas* and loyalty, and Weinstock 1971: 256–9 on Caesar's systematic propagation of the *pietas* owed to him by fellow citizens and subjects: "it was not Augustus who created the bond of loyalty between the ruler and his subjects but Caesar" (259).

[124] Plin. *Pan.* 2.3–6; cf. *Pan.* 7.5.1.

display *pietas* towards his parents, both natural and adoptive, and towards other family members, such as brothers.[125] He was also motivated by this virtue in his actions towards the gods, the *res publica*, the *patria* and, during the Tetrarchic period, his imperial colleagues, all of which naturally took on added significance since the emperor's actions in these spheres affected the empire as a whole.[126] In addition, the emperor's familial *pietas* frequently had a dynastic dimension, since the proper fulfillment of obligations towards his predecessor smoothed the transmission of imperial power to a new emperor and promoted the ideal of dynastic continuity.[127]

As in general usage, then, so too for the Roman emperor, *pietas* was a rather elastic concept. That elasticity explains both why at least one provincial copy of Augustus' Golden Shield specified the precise objects of the emperor's *pietas* (*pietas erga deos patriamque*), and why ancient accounts on the meaning of Antoninus' cognomen "Pius" were so diverse.[128] As the author of the *Historia Augusta* writes:

He was given the cognomen "Pius" by the senate, either because he lent a hand to his elderly father-in-law when he attended the senate . . . ; or because he spared those whom Hadrian, in ill health, had ordered to be killed; or because, against the determination of all, he decreed endless immeasurable honors for Hadrian after his death; or because when Hadrian wished to commit suicide he prevented it with great care and attention (*ingenti custodia et diligentia*); or because he was naturally very gentle (*clementissimus*) and did nothing harsh in his own times.[129]

Even for the emperor whose exemplary claim to this virtue was enshrined in his own name, then, it was unclear exactly how the nature of his *pietas* was to be construed.

[125] Natural parents: Tac. *Ann.* 14.3.3; Amm. Marc. 15.8.14. Adoptive parents: Plin. *Ep.* 10.1, *Pan.* 10.3. Brothers: Val. Max. 5.5.3.

[126] Gods: *AE* 1952.165; *Pan.* 11.6.1; imperial *pietas* towards the gods, on behalf of the state, was especially important: see Charlesworth 1943; cf. Dio Chrys. 1.15 on honor for the gods as the mark of the true king: ἔστι δὴ πρῶτον μὲν θεῶν ἐπιμελὴς καὶ τὸ δαιμόνιον προτιμῶν. *Res publica*: Amm. Marc. 15.8.14. *Patria*: *AE* 1952.165. Imperial colleagues: *Pan.* 7.1.4, 11.6.3.

[127] Two clear cases of new emperors promoting *pietas* for dynastic purposes are those of Galba, whose acts of *pietas* towards Nero's family functioned symbolically to incorporate Galba into the *domus Caesaris*, and of Hadrian, whose *pietas* towards Trajan and his family had a similar effect; see Kragelund 1998 (Galba); Beaujeu 1955: 207–8, n. 1 (Hadrian).

[128] The provincial copy of the *clupeus virtutis* is from Arelate (*AE* 1952.165); see briefly Galinsky 1996: 86 ("the *patria* was Augustus' family"). Note that in the *Res Gestae* (34.2) the exact nature of Augustus' *pietas* is not indicated.

[129] H.A. *AntP* 2.3. The *Historia Augusta* life of Hadrian also reports the anecdote about Antoninus and his father-in-law (24.3); Pausanias attributes the cognomen to Antoninus' *pietas* towards the gods (8.43.5). For modern discussions of Antoninus' cognomen, see Ulrich 1930: 65–72; Beaujeu 1955: 282, 286–91, arguing that the title reflects the emperor's work towards reconciliation between the senate and Hadrian, as manifested both through divine honors for Hadrian and through the recall of condemned senators; Birley 2000: 151: loyalty to Hadrian.

The complexity of *pietas* as an imperial virtue means that there cannot be one, simple interpretation for the meaning of Pietas coin types minted between 69 and 235. The legends that accompanied Pietas types offer little guidance. In several issues from the coinage of Commodus, the legend declares PIETATI SENATUS, but this could be understood either as Commodus' *pietas* towards the senate or as the senate's *pietas* towards the emperor.[130] Otherwise the legends are generic: PIETAS, PIETAS AUG, PIETAS AUGUSTI, etc. The numismatic iconography of *pietas* is more helpful. Pietas is depicted as a female personification, often veiled, and her attributes are overwhelmingly sacrificial in nature. The most common type shows Pietas standing next to an altar, often raising one or both hands (illustration 2.2); in addition to the altar, the most common attributes of Pietas are the patera and scepter (illustration 2.3).[131] Other religious images associated with Pietas types include various sacrificial objects, such as boxes of incense and perfumes, sacrificial victims, and fruits.[132] The iconography of the Pietas type is not, however, invariably religious or sacrificial. Pietas is often shown with one or two children (illustration 2.4), for example, and one of the more common types depicts Pietas standing, with no attributes at all (or sometimes holding a perfume box), raising one or both hands (illustration 2.5).[133] Nevertheless, the iconography of these types is mainly sacrificial, expressed above all through the regular appearance of an altar next to Pietas.[134] That would favor a broadly religious interpretation of Pietas types in general, but the immediate circumstances in which individual types were produced could also bear on their intent and meaning. In particular, a number of Pietas types minted early in a reign with generic

---

[130] PIETATI SENATUS: *RIC* 3, Commodus 194 (AD 186–9). The type recalls an earlier issue of Galba with the legend SENATUS PIETATI AUGUSTI SC (*RIC* 1², Galba 489), also ambiguous as to the subject and object of the *pietas*; see Kragelund 1998: 161–3. Commodus is also styled as AUCTOR PIETATIS on the coinage (*RIC* 3, Commodus 146; AD 186–7), but without further specification about the nature of this *pietas*; see Mattingly in *BMCRE* IV, clxii–clxiii, attributing the type to the celebrations marking the suppression of Maternus' plot to murder the emperor (cf. Hdn. 1.10.11).

[131] Pietas with altar: e.g. *RIC* 2, Hadrian 257, 445; *RIC* 3, Antoninus Pius 13, 53, 373–4, 392–3; *RIC* 3, Marcus Aurelius 774–7, 1,755–7; *RIC* 4.1, Septimius Severus 321a; *RIC* 4.1, Caracalla 12; *RIC* 4.2, Elagabalus 126–7; *RIC* 4.2, Severus Alexander 170. Pietas with patera and scepter: e.g. *RIC* 2, Hadrian 218, 260, 366; *RIC* 3, Marcus Aurelius 380, 1,212.

[132] Pietas with incense, perfumes, sacrificial victims, or fruits: e.g. *RIC* 2, Hadrian 439 (perfumes), 601 (incense), 1,082–4 (perfumes); *RIC* 3, Antoninus Pius 135 (victim and incense), 217 (victim and fruits); *RIC* 3, Marcus Aurelius 560 (incense and perfumes); *RIC* 4.1, Septimius Severus 863 (incense); *RIC* 4.1, Caracalla 595 (incense).

[133] Pietas with children: e.g. *RIC* 2, Titus 73; *RIC* 2, Domitian 214; *RIC* 3, Antoninus Pius 253, 1,045, 1,293. Pietas without attributes: e.g. *RIC* 2, Hadrian 96–7; *RIC* 3, Antoninus Pius 134, 684.

[134] For the iconography of Pietas in all media, see the overview in *LIMC* 8.1.998–1,003, 8.2.659–61 (R. Vollkommer).

Illustration 2.2 Reverse of denarius (*RIC* 2, Hadrian 257): Pietas standing next to an altar. PIETAS AUG

Illustration 2.3 Reverse of denarius (*RIC* 2, Hadrian 260): Pietas holding a patera and a scepter. PIETAS AUG

Illustration 2.4 Reverse of sestertius (*RIC* 3, Antoninus Pius 1281): Pietas with a child. PIETAS

Illustration 2.5 Reverse of aureus (*RIC* 2, Hadrian 439b): Pietas holding a perfume box. PIETAS

sacrificial imagery might have been designed to signal an emperor's proper devotion to his deified predecessor, a type of familial *pietas* with clear dynastic significance.[135]

---

[135] See, for example, Trajan's as of 98–9 (*RIC* 2, Trajan 392), which may be seen as commemorating Trajan's *pietas* towards Nerva; see also, in a similar vein, the denarius of Antoninus Pius, minted under Hadrian in 138 (*RIC* 3, Hadrian 445), which may have signalled Antoninus' devotion towards

Analysis of any one Pietas type must take into account the legend, the iconography, and the circumstances of production. In analyzing the cumulative impact of Pietas types for the period 69–235 as a whole, by contrast, it is important not to focus too narrowly on any one detail of any one type, since the original intent and topical significance of most types will have faded away over the course of the coins' "social life" in circulation. For the bulk of Pietas types in circulation at any one time, it was the more general meaning of the virtue represented on the coin that will have come to the fore. And that meaning, as I have suggested, was the underlying attitude or disposition in the emperor that motivated his dutiful conduct towards all persons or things to which, as emperor, he had obligations of any sort. The standard sacrificial iconography of Pietas types may indeed have set the emperor's *pietas* in a broadly religious framework, and the *pietas* of the emperor naturally had specifically imperial applications, especially in the maintenance of both dynastic harmony and the *pax deorum*, but it was, nevertheless, the underlying attitude of dutiful conduct on the part of the emperor that was idealized by Pietas types. Whatever their original purpose, then, the mass of Pietas types produced between 69 and 235 ultimately served as a celebration of, and testament to, the personal character of the emperor. But we should not overlook the reciprocity inherent in this virtue. Unlike most reverse types, Pietas types not only communicated a core virtue of the Roman emperor, but also served as a ubiquitous reminder that the emperor was himself a proper object of *pietas* from his subjects.

Virtus

There is nothing surprising in the prominence of *virtus* in the official representation of the emperor's virtues. *Virtus* was not as distinctively Roman a virtue as was *pietas*, but it was an equally important value for the Romans, and equally central to conceptions of Roman identity.[136] In etymological terms, *virtus* was derived from *vir*, "man," as the Romans themselves noted.[137] As a result, *virtus* originally denoted the quality of

---

his adoptive father. On Trajan, see briefly Strack 1.75–6; Mattingly in *BMCRE* iii, xcv (*pietas* not only for Nerva); Beaujeu 1955: 88. On Antoninus, Strack 3.169ff.; Mattingly in *BMCRE* iii, clii (*pietas* not only for Hadrian). In general on dynastic *pietas*, Strack 2.51–7, 3.115–24.

[136] Useful discussions of *virtus* in Hellegouarc'h 1963: 242–5, 476–83; Earl 1967, esp. 20–6, 31–5, 45–56, 65–78, 115–16, 127–31; Weinstock 1971: 230–3; Eisenhut 1973; Galinsky 1996: 84, 132–5; Roller 2001: 22–6, 99–108; McDonnell 2006; Harris 2006b.

[137] E.g. Cic. *Tusc.* 2.43; Varr. *Ling.* 5.73.

manly behavior, however defined. In practice that often meant courage in warfare. Literary accounts of pre-battle speeches, for example, frequently included appeals by the general to the troops' *virtus*.[138] The function of *virtus*, whether martial or not, was rarely neutral. An early and enduring strain in the ideal of *virtus* stressed not just manly behavior, not just courage in warfare or in other competitive activities, but valor specifically in the service of the state. The early connection between *virtus* and service to the state is reflected both in the rhetoric of aristocratic self-representation, as seen, for example, in the Scipionic epitaphs, which assert an integral bond between *virtus*, achievement, and public office, and in the religious sphere, where temples to Virtus and Honos (the first vowed already in 222 BC) and games for the two deified abstractions reinforced the link between *virtus* and elective office.[139] This conception of *virtus* as an ideal of valor (however defined) in the service of the state can be traced from the middle Republic through the late Republic and Augustan age to the early empire and down into the fourth century. It is surely this close connection between *virtus* and service to the state that explains the continuing centrality of *virtus* in the Roman system of values.[140]

Though *virtus* was always an important value, the indeterminacy of "manliness," which could be (and has been) defined in countless ways, meant that its precise nature and proper application could be debated. It was during the late Republic and Augustan period in particular that the meanings of *virtus* were hotly contested. Especially fierce, it seems, were the debates over what constituted the vital prerequisite for possession of *virtus*: aristocratic birth or public achievement? The Republican aristocracy perpetuated its standing in part through an exclusionary ideology in which rank, status, achievement, and virtue were represented – at funerals, in particular, but also through other media, such as *imagines maiorum* – as

---

[138] E.g. Caes. *BG* 2.21.2: *milites non longiore oratione cohortatus quam uti suae pristinae virtutis memoriam retinerent*; cf. Sall. *Cat.* 58.12, 60.3, *Iug.* 49.2, 97.5. For *virtus* as courage in warfare, see also Caes. *BC* 1.57.3; Cic. *Sest.* 12, *Prov.* 32, *Phil.* 5.52. Cf. *OLD*, s.v. *virtus*, § 1b. See discussion in McDonnell 2006: 59–71; Harris 2006b, esp. 310–13 on *virtus* in Caesar.

[139] Scipionic epitaphs citing *virtus*: *CIL* 1².7, 10, 11, 15 = *ILS* 1, 4, 6, 7, with Earl 1967: 21–4. Temples of Honos and Virtus: Liv. 27.25.7, 29.11.13; Plut. *Marc.* 28.2 (vowed by Marcellus); *CIL* 11.1831 = *ILS* 59 (vowed by Marius). Weinstock 1971: 231, n. 4, gathers evidence for games in honor of Honos and Virtus at Rome, Terracina, and Ostia. *Virtus* and elective office: Cic. *Brut.* 281: *cum honos sit praemium virtutis*; cf. *Rep.* 3.40.

[140] Cf. Sall. *Cat.* 3.2; Hor. *Carm.* 3.2.17–24; Tac. *Ann.* 11.22; Amm. Marc. 29.2.16. For Tacitus, *virtus* was the very foundation of the Roman empire and the defining characteristic of its people; cf. *Hist.* 2.69, 4.73, *Agr.* 33.2. Cf. Liv. 1.9.3; Prop. 3.22.21–2 (linking *virtus* with *pietas* as the main Roman virtues); Vell. Pat. 2.128.3.

heritable and confined to aristocratic families.[141] And *virtus* was just the sort of quality that could be passed down through the generations, as the Scipionic epitaphs so clearly show. Outsider criticism of this attitude is evident already in the mid-second century BC, as Cato, the *novus homo*, trumpeted his own, individual character and achievements, quite independent of the accomplishments (such as they were) of his ancestors.[142] But the real assault came in the first century, when Cicero postulated an antithesis between *nobilitas*, which depended on nothing more than the accident of birth, and *virtus*, which could only be displayed through individual accomplishments and the public merit they earned. It was those doing great deeds in the public sphere, especially the *novi homines* unable to hide behind the fame of their ancestors, who were the true descendants of the great families of the early Republic.[143] Such views found their sharpest expression in Sallust's version of Marius' speech upon winning the consulship of 107, the *locus classicus* for the valuation of personal merit over aristocratic birth and emblematic of the revolutionary attitudes towards *virtus* that came with the rise of the new men in the late Republic. This was the conception of *virtus* that would become normative under Augustus and his successors.[144]

There were other problematic aspects of *virtus*. One concerned the display of *virtus* and the individual *gloria* that came with it. Signal achievements in the public sphere not only benefited the state, but also brought reputation, honor, and glory to the individuals responsible for them. During the middle Republic, when oligarchic solidarity ensured that aristocratic competition was kept within bounds, the attainment of *gloria* was not troublesome. But the increasing intensity of personal competition in the late Republic put an ever higher premium on public standing, which made individual *gloria* susceptible to condemnation by social critics in the

---

[141] For the self-representation of the Republican aristocracy, see, e.g., Flower 1996; Flaig 2003; Hölkeskamp 2004.

[142] Cf. Cato frr. 93, 128, 252 (*ORF* (2nd edn.)); but Cato could also celebrate his father and the *mos maiorum* when the occasion suited him: frr. 18, 144.

[143] For the antithesis between *nobilitas* and *virtus*, Cic. *Sest.* 136: *vosque, adulescentes, et qui nobiles estis, ad maiorum vestrorum imitationem excitabo, et qui ingenio ac virtute nobilitatem potestis consequi, ad eam rationem in qua multi homines novi et honore et gloria floruerunt cohortabor;* cf. *Verr.* 2.5.180 (on Cato's *virtus*); *Pis.* 2 (valuation of *mores* over *maiores*). New men as true descendants of great families: *Verr.* 2.4.81.

[144] Sall. *Iug.* 85. On the contested relationship between birth, achievement, and *virtus*, see discussion in Earl 1967: 44–58; Hellegouarc'h 1963: 243–4, 476–83. Galinsky 1996: 84 characterizes the notion of *virtus* depending on "ongoing effort" (rather than on descent) as an Augustan ideal. The opposition between *virtus* and *nobilitas* was not a pressing issue during the empire, but was not forgotten entirely; see Syme 1958: 566–84, esp. 572–3, 578; cf. Hellegouarc'h 1963: 578, n. 3.

Augustan period who saw out-of-control competition as partly responsible for the downfall of the Republic. There was no consensus, however, on whether or not individual *gloria* was an appropriate reward for *virtus*. While Vergil and Horace both decouple *virtus* from *gloria*, Livy reasserts the traditional association between the display of *virtus* through the performance of great deeds in the service of the state and the *gloria* that accrues from such accomplishments.[145] The latter conception was more influential in the imperial period, at least among historians, as several passages in Tacitus and Ammianus Marcellinus indicate.[146]

Yet another complication was the existence of competing ideals of manliness. Though martial conceptions of *virtus* seem to have predominated in the middle Republic, by the late Republic, with the increasing influence at Rome of the Greek philosophical ideal of *aretē*, the ethical dimensions of *virtus* became more prominent.[147] Cicero, for example, can speak of the four ethical components of *virtus*, while various authors refer to the *virtutes*, in the plural, as the opposite of *vitia*.[148] The ethical dimensions of *virtus* could also be highlighted through the many qualities with which it was linked by late-Republican authors, including *humanitas, integritas, probitas, constantia*, and *sapientia*.[149] And the martial and ethical conceptions of *virtus* could be set in opposition to one another, as is especially clear from the contrast Sallust draws between Caesar and Cato, in which the former's *virtus* was displayed in war, the latter's through personal character.[150] *Virtus*, in brief, could be much more than just courage on the battlefield.

The flexibility and semantic range of *virtus* made it a useful imperial virtue – especially for emperors with little military glory to their credit. But the martial conception of the quality never disappeared entirely. The military *virtus* of the late-antique panegyrics, amongst the most prominent

---

[145] *Virtus* and *gloria* in Livy, e.g. 28.17.2: *et cum ceteri laetitia gloriaque ingenti eam rem volgo ferrent, unus qui gesserat, inexplebilis virtutis veraeque laudis . . . iam Africam magnamque Carthaginem et in suum decus nomenque velut consummatam eius belli gloriam spectabat*; cf. Earl 1967: 74–9 and 144, n. 75 for the various qualities that Horace links to *virtus*.

[146] Cf. Tac. *Ann.* 15.16; Amm. Marc. 29.2.16.

[147] This is the main thesis of McDonnell 2006, esp. 72–141 for the influence of *aretē*. Note also that the martial aspect of *virtus* could have an ethical component: Galinsky 1996: 132–5.

[148] Ethical components of *virtus*: Cic. *Inv.* 2.159: *prudentia, iustitia, fortitudo, temperantia*. *Virtutes* contrasted with vices: e.g., Cic. *Cat.* 2.25: *hinc . . . aequitas, temperantia, fortitudo, prudentia, virtutes omnes certabant cum iniquitate, luxuria, ignavia, temeritate, cum vitiis omnibus*; further references in *OLD*, s.v. *virtus* § 2b. See discussion in Roller 2001: 26; cf. Eisenhut 1973: 42.

[149] *Humanitas*: Cic. *Balb.* 18; Caes. *BG* 1.47.4. *Integritas*: Cic. *Font.* 39, *Verr.* 2.3.7. *Probitas*: Cic. *Lael.* 28. *Constantia*: Caes. *BC* 1.6.1; Cic. *Sull.* 62; *Planc.* 27. *Sapientia*: Cic. *Pis.* 35, *Rep.* 2.24; Sall. *Cat.* 51.42. Further references in Hellegouarc'h 1963: 245, n. 6; cf. *OLD* s.v. *virtus*, §§ 2–3.

[150] Sall. *Cat.* 54.4–6.

ideals cited in those texts, is identical in meaning to the Augustan *virtus* of the Golden Shield.[151] And it could always serve as a stock indicator of military prowess. Suetonius, for example, writes that the Indians and Scythians sought the friendship of Rome simply because of Augustus' reputation for *virtus* (and *moderatio*).[152] Like their late-Republican predecessors, however, imperial writers could also subsume various ethical qualities under the general rubric of imperial *virtus* (or *virtutes*), and could also contrast *virtutes* and *vitia*.[153] In addition, there are various indications that emperors themselves sought to suppress the martial associations of *virtus* and redefine the term in a manner that valorized non-military achievement. The most conspicuous example is the elevation of the hunt as an appropriate sphere for the display of imperial *virtus*. Domitian seems to have been the first emperor to be publicly represented as a hunter, and Pliny could celebrate Trajan's prowess in the hunt, but imperial hunting imagery did not become prominent until the reign of Hadrian, whose exploits in the hunt were commemorated both by the eight tondi that probably once decorated a major Hadrianic monument in the city of Rome (and which are now preserved on the Arch of Constantine), and by the accompanying medallions depicting similar hunting scenes and each bearing a legend, VIRTUTI AUGUSTI, that left no doubt as to what message they conveyed.[154] Similar medallions struck under Antoninus Pius, Marcus Aurelius, Lucius Verus, and Commodus show that this broadening of what constituted imperial *virtus* was successful. Earlier emperors, such as Gaius and Nero, had attempted more radical departures from the traditional conception of *virtus* as valor in warfare, but their efforts were mostly condemned by contemporaries and later observers.[155]

Despite the flexibility and range in meanings of *virtus*, even as an imperial virtue, the coin types representing this ideal were unambiguously martial

[151] That the *virtus* of the Golden Shield (*RG* 34.2) is primarily military in nature can be inferred both from the centrality of conquest in Augustan ideology (cf. Gruen 1996) and from the record of foreign victories presented in the *Res Gestae* itself (26–7, 29–30); for a different reading, McDonnell 2006: 385–7. For military *virtus* in the late-antique panegyrics, see above, n. 62.

[152] Suet. *Aug.* 21.3.

[153] Cf. Suet. *Cal.* 3.1: *omnes Germanico corporis animique virtutes . . . contigisse satis constat: formam et fortitudinem egregiam, ingenium in utroque eloquentiae doctrinaeque genere praecellens, benivolentiam singularem . . . ; Dom.* 3.2: *mixtura quoque aequabili vitiorum atque virtutum.*

[154] See discussion, with references, in Tuck 2005, interpreting an equestrian statue of Domitian from Misenum as a statue of the emperor as hunter. For the evidence on imperial hunting under Trajan and Hadrian, see also Anderson 1985: 101–21. Pliny on Trajan as hunter: *Pan.* 82.6.

[155] Tuck 2005: 240–1. It is worth noting that Julio-Claudian aristocrats, for whom most traditional paths to military glory had been effectively blocked by the imperial regime, had also worked to redefine *virtus* in a manner advantageous to themselves; see Roller 2001: 99–108.

in nature. Like the other imperial virtues, Virtus is depicted as a female personification – somewhat anomalous, given the term's etymology, but in accordance with its grammatical gender – usually standing and wearing military dress, and almost always wielding her defining attributes, the spear and parazonium (illustration 2.6).[156] Other aspects of the numismatic iconography of Virtus emphasize military valor. Among the objects held by Virtus are a statuette of Victory (illustration 2.7), a legionary eagle, and a shield.[157] In addition, the figure of Virtus is sometimes depicted together with a trophy and a captive, and is normally resting one foot on some object redolent of the military sphere: sometimes the prow of a ship, but most frequently a helmet (illustration 2.8).[158] There is nothing in the iconography or the legends (VIRTUS, VIRT[US] AUGUST[A/I] or VIRTUTI AUG[USTI]) to suggest the ethical conception of the virtue.[159] As Mattingly has emphasized, the numismatic iconography of Virtus is largely interchangeable with that of Roma, another multifaceted abstraction in which military might was nevertheless the dominant theme (illustration 2.9).[160] The mass of imperial coins representing imperial *virtus* conveyed a simple and direct message of the emperor's military valor in the service of the Roman state.

Liberalitas

Liberalitas, an abstract noun derived from the adjective *liberalis*, which was itself derived from the adjective *liber*, was nothing more or less than the specific quality – however defined – that befit a free man.[161] As Seneca

---

[156] Virtus with spear and parazonium: e.g. *RIC* 2, Vespasian 355; *RIC* 2, Domitian 246; *RIC* 2, Trajan 202; *RIC* 2, Hadrian 614; *RIC* 3, Antoninus Pius 1268; *RIC* 3, Marcus Aurelius 1249; *RIC* 3, Commodus 292; *RIC* 4.1, Caracalla 198; *RIC* 4.2, Severus Alexander 77.

[157] Virtus holding Victory, legionary eagle, or shield: e.g. *RIC* 3, Antoninus Pius 452 (Victory), 455 (legionary eagle); *RIC* 3, Marcus Aurelius 1,069 (shield); *RIC* 4.1, Septimius 24 (Victory); *RIC* 4.1, Caracalla 50 (Victory), 51 (shield); *RIC* 4.2, Severus Alexander 90 (shield), 220 (Victory).

[158] Virtus with foot on prow of ship, or with trophy and captive: e.g. *RIC* 2, Vespasian 354 (prow); *RIC* 4.1, Caracalla 456 (trophy and captive); *RIC* 4.2, Severus Alexander 77 (prow). Virtus with foot on helmet: e.g. *RIC* 2, Domitian 246; *RIC* 2, Trajan 202; *RIC* 3, Antoninus Pius 60; *RIC* 4.1, Caracalla 112; *RIC* 4.2, Severus Alexander 222.

[159] This is also true of the iconography of *virtus* in general, which consistently emphasizes the military sphere; see the very full discussion, with many images, in *LIMC* 8.1.273–81, 8.2.195–203 (T. Ganschow).

[160] See discussion in *BMCRE* III, cxxxvii–cxxxix.

[161] The literary evidence for *liberalitas* is collected in *TLL* 7.2.1295.29–1299.22. For the derivation from *liber*, see Ernout and Meillett 1959, s.v. "liberalitas." Interpretations of *liberalitas* in Kloft 1970; Manning 1985. For generosity as an imperial virtue, Kloft 1970, Veyne 1976: ch. 4, and Millar 1977: 133–201, remain basic; see also Griffin 2003 on *beneficia* and aristocratic exchange in early imperial Rome, and Zanker 2010 on imperial *liberalitas* in the city of Rome. For the epigraphic evidence on imperial *liberalitas*, Barbieri 1957.

Illustration 2.6 Reverse of sestertius (*RIC* 2, Hadrian 614): Virtus holding a spear and a parazonium. VIRT. AUG

Illustration 2.7 Reverse of denarius (*RIC* 4.1, Septimius Severus 24): Virtus with a statuette of Victory. VIRT. AUG

Illustration 2.8 Reverse of as (*BMCRE* 2, Domitian 394): Virtus holding a spear and a parazonium and resting a foot on a helmet. VIRTUTI AUGUSTI

Illustration 2.9 Reverse of as (*RIC* 2, Trajan 483): Roma holding Victory and a spear

explains, "*liberalitas* is so-called not because it is given to free men, but because it flows from a free soul."[162] Like *pietas*, *liberalitas* denotes an internal, subjective quality, an underlying attitude or disposition that is expressed by certain visible actions. And it was precisely those actions that

---

[162] Sen. *Vit. Beat.* 24.3: *liberalitatem . . . quae non quia liberis debetur, sed quia a libero animo proficiscitur, ita nominata est*; cf. Ter. *Ad.* 57: *pudore et liberalitate liberos retinere satius esse . . . quam metu*, with the gloss by Donatus *ad loc.*: *liberalitate . . . regendi sunt, propter quod liberi dicuntur*.

came to define the quality itself. Central to the concept were acts of giving or personal generosity. Cicero, for example, identifies two basic types of *liberalitas*: one, the giving of a *beneficium*, and the other, the returning of one.[163] Such *beneficia* were frequently material in nature, and they were exchanged in both the private and the public spheres.[164] But the concept of *liberalitas* was not limited to the material realm. In fact, the range of virtues with which it was associated is quite wide, from *beneficentia* and *benignitas*, which Cicero offers as synonyms, to *probitas, indulgentia*, and *iustitia*.[165] In two passages Seneca includes *liberalitas* among an extended series of "humane" virtues. In the first, asserting the fundamental equality of all the virtues, he includes it with *tranquillitas, simplicitas, constantia, aequanimitas*, and *tolerantia*, and in the second, describing the virtues inherent in the soul of a *vir bonum*, he associates it with *frugalitas, continentia, tolerantia*, and *comitas*.[166] In these passages *liberalitas* emerges as a second-order virtue that expresses friendliness, civility, and humanity. Such concepts were rather vague, of course, and they often required actions in order to give them shape and meaning. In practice, the actions that defined *liberalitas* usually centered on the act of giving, especially in the material sphere.

Unlike the other virtues discussed thus far, *liberalitas* was not an unambiguously positive quality. Indeed, some authors can even write of "vicious," "perverse," or "capricious" *liberalitas*.[167] The distinction between "good" and "bad" *liberalitas* was related specifically to the act of giving, and the key variable in determining its valuation was the motivation behind its exercise. By the end of the first century BC, an entire discourse about the nature of *liberalitas* had developed, especially in philosophical texts. At the heart of that discourse was the principle that generosity, including material generosity, should not be tainted by association with the world of exchange. In particular, the one who gives a *beneficium* should not give with any thought of return or personal material benefit. As Cicero wrote, "We are beneficent and generous not in order to exact approval, since we do not

---

[163] Cic. *Off.* 1.48.

[164] Material dimension of *liberalitas*: Cic. *Part.* 77: *animi magnitudinis . . . est liberalitas in usu pecuniae*; cf. Cic. *Tusc.* 5.91; Sall. *Cat.* 35.3, 52.12; [Caes.] *BAlex.* 49.1. For *liberalitas* in public life, see the numerous passages collected in *TLL* 7.2.1296.30–1297.36. Private *liberalitas*: e.g. Sall. *Cat.* 49.3: *privatim egregia liberalitate*.

[165] *Liberalitas* synonymous with *beneficentia* and *benignitas*: Cic. *Off.* 1.20. *Probitas*: Cic. *Fam.* 13.78.1; *indulgentia*: Petron. 47.7; *iustitia*: Cic. *Off.* 1.42 (where *liberalitas* is treated as one aspect of *iustitia*).

[166] Sen. *Ep.* 66.13, 115.3.

[167] *Prava liberalitas*: *Rhet. Her.* 3.3.6, where *liberalitas* is contrasted with *iustitia* and grouped together with several vices: *quam is, qui contra dicet, iustitiam vocabit, nos demonstrabimus ignaviam esse et inertiam ac pravam liberalitatem*. *Sinistra liberalitas*: Cat. 29.15. *Libidinosa liberalitas*: Val. Max. 8.2.2. Further citations for "negative" *liberalitas* in *TLL* 7.2.1296.19–29.

lend out favors at interest, but because we are by nature inclined towards generosity."[168] The casual reference to *natura* in this passage reminds us that at its core *liberalitas* was thought of as the characteristic quality of a free man. A second variable for identifying virtuous *liberalitas* was the degree of generosity manifested in acts of giving. For it was important in the eyes of social commentators that specific instances of generosity be neither too narrow, which suggested parsimony, nor too broad, which suggested extravagance. That is why *liberalitas* could be contrasted with both *avaritia* and *luxuria*, vices that lay on the distal ends of the spectrum of giving.[169] "Good" *liberalitas*, then, was a finely calibrated quality, requiring both an absence of self-interest and a careful calculation of how much generosity was appropriate in a given situation.

Though the concept of *liberalitas* always retained its sense as a personal quality, its association with particular acts of material generosity was so pronounced that the underlying virtue eventually became equated with its outward manifestation. As a result, we find various references to *liberalitates*, in the plural, which denoted individual instances of material generosity, and which could even be numbered in serial fashion.[170] Sitting at the intersection of *liberalitas* as virtue and *liberalitas* as object was the figure of the Roman emperor. The emperor, like all rulers in the Greek and Roman world, was expected to provide material benefits to his subjects through his own personal generosity, and by the early second century, the key term for expressing that generosity and its attendant benefits was *liberalitas*. The most regular manifestations of imperial *liberalitas* were *congiaria*, distributions of money to the urban plebs of Rome, and *donativa*, distributions of money to Roman soldiers.[171] Such cash handouts reinforced the special bond between the emperor and two of the most important

---

[168] Cic. *Lael.* 30–31 (*natura propensi ad liberalitatem sumus*); see briefly Manning 1985: 74. Seneca admits that a *beneficium* can bring favor and material reward, but claims that these benefits are secondary to the simple consciousness of having done a good deed (*Ben.* 2.33.3); cf. Griffin 2003: 94.

[169] *Liberalitas* opposed to *avaritia*: *Rhet. Her.* 4.38.50; Cic. *Flacc.* 89; Plin. *Ep.* 9.32; Apul. *Plat.* 2.4. Opposed to *luxuria*: Cic. *Off.* 1.92; Quint. 4.2.77, 8.6.36; Tac. *Hist.* 1.30.1.

[170] The earliest examples of plural *liberalitates* come from the second century: Suet. *Claud.* 29.1, *Galb.* 15.1: *liberalitates Neronis*; *CIL* 14.4235 (Tibur, 117–135); *CIL* 2.4269 (Tarraco, *c.* 125–150): *ob plurimas liberalitates in rem public(am) suam*; Apul. *Apol.* 23.2: *crebris liberalitatibus modice imminutum* (sc. *patrimonium*); further examples in *TLL* 7.2.1298.19–32. On the enumeration of *liberalitates* on imperial coins, see discussion in Kloft 1970: 159, with the observation that through this numbering the ethical concept of *liberalitas* is "profaned." A moral value, as he notes, cannot be enumerated.

[171] *Liberalitas* and *congiaria*: Barbieri 1957. *Liberalitas* and *donativa*: Tac. *Hist.* 1.18.3; *CIL* 8.2554a (Castra Lambaesitana): *ex largissimis stipendiis et liberalitatibus, quae in eos optiones conferunt*; *ILS* 9,099, 9,100. Further references in *TLL* 7.2.1298.34–50. See discussion in Kloft 1970: 89–95 (*congiaria*), 104–10 (*donativa*). Duncan-Jones 1994: 45, table 3.7 estimates that these cash handouts to the urban plebs and to soldiers represented roughly 5% of the imperial budget.

collectivities within the state. Other standard forms of imperial *liberalitas* included *frumentationes*, distributions of grain in the city of Rome; the imperial *alimenta* programs in Italy; public building programs in the city of Rome; financial aid to senators; public games and spectacles, mainly in the city of Rome; disaster relief; and remission of debts.[172]

Despite this range of more or less regular instances of the emperor's personal generosity, it was the *congiaria* in particular that became institutionalized, in the first half of the second century, as the form of imperial *liberalitas par excellence* – Herodian, for example, can refer without explanation to the "customary distributions to the people" made at the accession of Elagabalus – and it was precisely in the enumeration of *congiaria* that ordinal numbers were attached to imperial *liberalitates*.[173] These numbered *liberalitates* appeared on the imperial coinage, beginning with Hadrian, but even when this numismatic formula became conventional, the simple type of Liberalitas, publicizing the underlying virtue (without the number), continued to be minted.[174] The emperor's personal generosity, in other words, was never abandoned as a concept worth advertising.

As is well known, the notion that a ruler had a moral obligation to provide his subjects with material benefits had a long history in the ancient world, going back at least to Xenophon's *Cyropaedia*.[175] At Rome most of the characteristic expressions of imperial generosity mentioned above were established already under Augustus, who followed Caesar's lead in making his personal generosity a foundation of his rule.[176] Later generations sometimes associated *liberalitas* with Caesar, but it was perceived as a defining characteristic of Augustus, who spent exorbitant sums from what was identified as his personal wealth on handouts of cash and grain, the provision of games and spectacles, numerous public building projects, loans to senators, and subventions of the *aerarium*.[177] Yet Augustus himself, who

---

[172] For these forms of imperial *liberalitas*, see Kloft 1970: 95–104, 110–25, with ample references.

[173] Hdn. 5.5.8: συνηθεῖς τῷ δήμῳ νομαῖ.

[174] Numbered *liberalitates* under Hadrian: *RIC* 2, Hadrian 253, 582, 648–9, 817; subsequent instances under later emperors listed in the appendices to *RIC* and *BMCRE*.

[175] The *Cyropaedia* was allegedly read by Scipio Aemilianus (above, n. 31) and by Caesar (Suet. *Iul.* 87). For the influence of the *Cyropaedia* on Republican political thought, see briefly Kloft 1970: 20–2; Rawson 1991 (1973): 86–7.

[176] Caesar's *liberalitas* is a major theme in Cicero's writings, e.g. *Rab. Post.* 41; *Fam.* 1.9.18 = SB 20; see *TLL* 7.2.1296.62–81 for further references to Caesar's *liberalitas* in Cicero, Catullus, Sallust, and Caesar himself, with discussion in Kloft 1970: 178–9.

[177] According to Suetonius (*Nero* 10.1), for example, Nero declared that we would rule *ex Augusti praescripto*, glossed as a rule imbued with *liberalitas*, *clementia*, and *comitas*. For Augustus' spending, see discussion, with references, in Kloft 1970: ch. 3. Association of *liberalitas* with Caesar: Suet. *Iul.* 38.2.

devotes nearly one quarter of the *Res Gestae* to his expenditures on behalf of the *res publica*, never employs the term *liberalitas*. In fact, *liberalitas* does not emerge as an officially publicized virtue until the second century, when it first appears on the imperial coinage under Hadrian. After Hadrian, Liberalitas types become a fixture on the coinage, appearing under every emperor for the rest of our period and beyond.[178] How can we explain this strange pattern in the official representation of such a key imperial virtue as *liberalitas*?

There was a good political reason why Augustus did not emphasize his *liberalitas* in a text as public as the *Res Gestae* and why the Liberalitas type never appeared on his coinage. Augustus' gifts to senators to help them meet the new census requirement were substantial but, like his personal subventions of the *aerarium*, made clear the degree to which the central institutions of the state had come to depend on the generosity of one man. And the reality of senatorial subordination and dependence was obviously incompatible with the concept of *libera res publica restituta*. In this sense imperial *liberalitas* represented the antithesis of Augustan ideology. It should also be noted that *liberalitas*, unlike the other imperial virtues, was never the object of a state cult at Rome, and therefore did not translate easily into the idiom of imperial expression established under Augustus. This probably explains why *liberalitas* did not play a role in the official publicity of Augustus' Julio-Claudian successors. There is some evidence, though, that generosity and avarice became political slogans in the struggles of 69. In the opposing speeches of Piso and Otho "reported" by Tacitus, *liberalitas* and *avaritia*, along with *luxuria* and *parsimonia*, emerge as key catchwords that distinguish the various contenders for the throne.[179] We may suspect some rhetorical embellishment here, but it is indeed likely that personal generosity was demanded of potential emperors, especially among the troops and the urban plebs of Rome. Yet *liberalitas* was not advertised on the coins of Galba, Otho, or Vitellius, and probably for this reason failed to enter into the circle of officially advertised imperial virtues under the Flavians.[180]

Before the appearance of the Liberalitas type on the coinage of Hadrian, an earlier, formative period in its development as an official imperial virtue

---

[178] See Gnecchi 1905: 354–9 for a list of all emperors down to Constantine on whose coinage the Liberalitas type appears.

[179] Tac. *Hist.* 1.30.1: *Falluntur quibus luxuria* (i.e. of Otho) *specie liberalitatis imponit*; 1.37.4: *falsis nominibus . . . parsimoniam pro avaritia appellat* (sc. Galba); cf. 1.18.3 and 1.38.1 on Galba's stinginess.

[180] Buttrey 1972a emphasizes the derivative nature of Vespasianic coin types, which borrow types and motifs even from "bad" emperors, such as Nero and Vitellius.

can be identified under Trajan. The celebration of the emperor's personal generosity is emphatically announced in Pliny's *Panegyricus*, in which the term *liberalitas* appears a dozen times.[181] Imperial *liberalitas* is also prominent in inscriptions for Trajan.[182] But the full adoption of *liberalitas* into the official language of imperial expression takes place under Hadrian, on whose coinage the virtue first appears. Contemporary sensitivity to *liberalitas* is also reflected in Suetonius, whose schematization of "good" and "bad" emperors often pivots on public and private expenditure, and in honorific inscriptions that commemorate Hadrian's *liberalitas*.[183] An officially recognized and publicly advertised imperial virtue had been born.[184]

As noted above, Liberalitas types on the imperial coinage publicized both the emperor's generosity and its regular manifestation in the city of Rome, the *congiarium*. This dual message was achieved by the numismatic iconography of imperial *liberalitas*. On the reverse of precious-metal coins, the emperor's *liberalitas* is sometimes commemorated through a scene of the emperor personally distributing coins to the urban plebs, but far more often through a personification of Liberalitas, normally standing and holding what is commonly identified as an abacus (illustration 2.10).[185] On the reverse of base-metal coins, by contrast, the distribution scene is much more common than the personification, especially on the sestertius (illustration 2.11).[186] It has been suggested that this correspondence between

---

[181] Plin. *Pan.* 3.4, 25.3, 25.5, 27.3, 28.4, 33.2, 34.3, 38.2, 38.4, 43.4, 51.5, 86.5.

[182] See below, 223 (official inscriptions), and 252 (honorific inscriptions).

[183] For the importance of imperial expenditure in Suetonius, see Kloft 1970: 155–6; Wallace-Hadrill 1983: 166–71. The epigraphic evidence is discussed in chapters 4–5 below.

[184] For a slightly different account of the long-term trajectory in the valuation of *liberalitas*, see Manning 1985, stressing the problematic expression of superiority implied by the display of *liberalitas*; as Manning notes (1985: 79), *liberalitas* is sometimes paired with *clementia* and *misericordia*, virtues that also define relationships between superiors and inferiors. Griffin 2003, by contrast, draws attention to the horizontal relationships of friendship strengthened (not created) by the exchange of *beneficia* in general. The emperor's generosity normally reflected, and reinforced, his superiority (Manning 1985: 81), but could also be construed as evidence of his *civilitas* towards his "nominal peers" (Griffin 2003: 108–11).

[185] Liberalitas as personification on precious-metal coins: e.g. *RIC* 2, Hadrian 253–4; *RIC* 3, Antoninus Pius 138; *RIC* 3, Marcus Aurelius 144; *RIC* 3, Commodus 10; *RIC* 4.1, Septimius Severus 18; *RIC* 4.1, Caracalla 158; *RIC* 4.1, Geta 11; *RIC* 4.2, Macrinus 78; *RIC* 4.2, Elagabalus 97–104; *RIC* 4.2, Severus Alexander 147.

[186] Distribution scene (with legend LIBERAL[ITAS]) on base-metal coins: e.g. *RIC* 2, Hadrian 552; *RIC* 3, Antoninus Pius 537; *RIC* 3, Marcus Aurelius 1,205–11; *RIC* 3, Commodus 300; *RIC* 4.1, Septimius Severus 654; *RIC* 4.1, Caracalla 527; *RIC* 4.2, Elagabalus 289–91; *RIC* 4.2, Severus Alexander 454. Metcalf 1993: 341–2 provides a useful chart of distribution scenes vs. personification types on the different metals of the coinage from Nero to Trebonianus Gallus. According to Metcalf's figures, 67% of all personification types occur on gold and silver, while 71% of all distribution types occur on the bronze.

Illustration 2.10 Reverse of denarius (*RIC* 3, Marcus Aurelius 206): Liberalitas holding an abacus and a cornucopia. LIBERAL. AUG

Illustration 2.11 Reverse of sestertius (*RIC* 2, Hadrian 552): Hadrian seated on raised platform and distributing coins to urban plebs. LIBERALITAS AUG

image and denomination might have been the result of an official attempt to advertise the emperor's generosity in different ways to different social classes.[187] For the educated upper classes, sensitive to the meanings of abstract concepts and in more regular contact with precious-metal coins, so the argument goes, the quality of *liberalitas* was stressed; for those in the lower classes, some of whom had been recipients of imperial *congiaria* and among whom the base-metal coins circulated more regularly, emphasis was placed instead on representations of the cash distributions that most directly expressed the emperor's generosity. While it is true that the larger surface area of the sestertius made it more suitable than aurei and denarii for the representation of the distribution scene, which may explain this discrepancy between metals, the fact that the distribution scene was in fact shown on the smaller coins as well suggests that its prominence on the sestertius was not the result of aesthetic considerations alone.[188] It seems likely, then, that the correspondence between image and metal in the representation of imperial *liberalitas* was not only intentional, but that the aim was indeed to commemorate different dimensions of the emperor's generosity to different social classes.[189]

Further evidence for the strategic production of Liberalitas types comes from the variable relative frequency with which they were minted between their initial appearance under Hadrian and down to the end of our period in 235. A comparison of fluctuations in the relative frequency of Liberalitas types on a reign-by-reign basis, shown in figure 2.3, with the number of congiaria per reign-year, shown in figure 2.4, reveals a correlation that can hardly be accidental.[190] In fact, the correlation between the reigns of Hadrian and Caracalla, covering the span of a century (117–217), is nearly perfect ($r = .95$); that this correlation is not accidental is shown by the low permutation value between these two data sets (.011). In considering the significance of this correlation, two key points must be kept in mind. First, the numbers of imperial congiaria by reign are known to us from the enumeration of *liberalitates* on the coinage, and not from the numbers of known Liberalitas types. It must be emphasized in this connection that not

---

[187] Metcalf 1993. In general on the iconography of *liberalitas*, *LIMC* 6.1.274–8, 6.2.141–3 (R. Vollkommer).

[188] On the different size of the denarius and sestertius as an explanation for the discrepancy, see Hekster 2003: 23. Distribution scene on denarii: e.g. *RIC* 3, Antoninus Pius 74; *RIC* 4.1, Caracalla 159.

[189] For other attempts to document intentional correspondences between image and denomination, see Carney 1967; Hekster 2003; Marsano 2009. See also below, 144–6, on Concordia, Pax, Fortuna, and Salus.

[190] For the statistical basis of this correlation, and the calculations for the correlation coefficient and permutation value noted in the text that follows, see appendix 10.

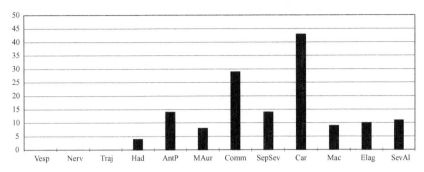

Figure 2.3 Relative frequency of Liberalitas types on denarii, expressed as a percentage of all virtue types by reign, AD 117–235 (N = 18,187)

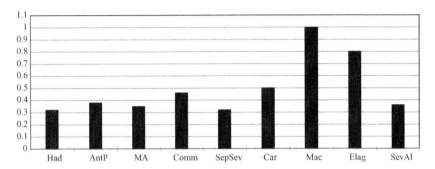

Figure 2.4 Number of congiaria per reign-year, AD 117–235

all Liberalitas types were accompanied by a serial number. The relative frequency of imperial congiaria, in other words, is based on different evidence from that of the relative frequency of Liberalitas types. The demonstrable correlation between the two trends is not circular. The second key point is that the coins bearing the Liberalitas type were not the actual coins distributed at congiaria. Not only were most Liberalitas types minted over the course of two separate occasions for congiaria, but it is also unlikely that Liberalitas types were ever minted in sufficient numbers to cover the necessary payouts for even a single distribution.[191]

The conclusion to be drawn from these two points is that the bulk of Liberalitas types had a commemorative, not an accounting, function. And that makes the correlation between the fluctuating relative frequency of

[191] Metcalf 1993: 343–4.

Liberalitas types and imperial congiaria more significant for our purposes, because it shows that the underlying virtue of the emperor's personal generosity – which was expressed through many other practices in addition to the giving of congiaria – was being advertised and emphasized to the degree that this virtue had actually been demonstrated in the material form of these distributions. Imperial publicity, in other words, could be rational, closely coordinated between different operations of the central state, and based in some sense on objective, quantifiable reality.

Providentia

The last of the five virtues especially emphasized on the imperial coinage during our period was *providentia*.[192] In its most basic sense, *providentia* denoted the capacity to see ahead. Sometimes that meant seeing ahead in space, mainly, it seems, in the context of battle.[193] More often it meant seeing ahead in time – "the *providentia* through which something from the future is seen," as Cicero put it, "before it has happened."[194] In the divine sphere, the power to see ahead, *pronoia* or *providentia*, was one of the forces that governed the affairs of the world; in the Stoic doctrine of predestination in particular it was specifically *pronoia* that determined the future.[195] That such views were current among Stoic thinkers during our period is clear from the writings of Marcus Aurelius, for whom *pronoia*, repeatedly cited, was the divine and benevolent force that generated a rational order and prevented the vagaries of chance from creating chaos.[196] Among humans, the power to see ahead was closely associated with rulership. For Aristotle, in fact, it was precisely the ability to foresee that defined a ruler and distinguished him from a subject: "that which is able, through intelligence, to foresee is by nature a ruler and by nature a master."[197] By the late Republic

---

[192] Martin 1982: 7–65 offers a convenient overview of the intellectual and literary background of *providentia* and its Greek antecedent, *pronoia*. For *providentia* as an imperial virtue, see Charlesworth 1936, 1937: 117–22; Béranger 1953: 210–17, 1973: 331–52; Alföldi 1955; Fears 1977: 271–8; Scott 1982; Martin 1982: 67–428.

[193] E.g. Liv. 30.5.5: *ut quantum nox providentiae adimat tantum diligentia expleant curaque*; cf. Tac. *Hist.* 4.29.

[194] Cic. *Inv.* 2.60: *providentia per quam futurum aliquid videtur ante quam factum est.*

[195] Martin 1982: 19–30; cf. Charlesworth 1936: 108. For Greek *pronoia* as the equivalent of Latin *providentia*, see Cic. *Nat. Deor.* 1.18, 2.58.

[196] M. Aur. *Med.* 2.3.1, 2.11.2, 4.3.5, 6.10.1, 9.1.10, 12.1.2, 12.14.1–3, 12.24.1; see also Fro. *de Nepote Amisso* 2.4 (van den Hout p. 235): *hoc ego ita esse facilius crediderim quam cuncta humana aut nulla aut iniqua providentia regi*; Gel. 7.1.7: *providentia, quae compagem hanc mundi et genus hominum fecit.*

[197] Arist. *Pol.* 1.2, 1252a31–2: τὸ μὲν γὰρ δυνάμενον τῇ διανοίᾳ προορᾶν ἄρχον φύσει καὶ δεσπόζον φύσει . . . Clearly the power to see ahead could not be wielded by everyone; see briefly Martin 1982: 37–8.

this ability referred above all to the foresight necessary to ensure political stability. It was his *providentia*, Cicero claims, in addition to his *virtus* and *consilium*, that saved the state from the great dangers of the Catilinarian conspiracy.[198] Because *providentia* was a quality associated with the gods, and because so few humans were endowed with it, it is easy to see how the line between divine and human *providentia* could become blurred. And so the same Cicero who can adduce his foresight in the mundane context of political discord can also make foresight, connected with leadership, a quality shared by gods and men.[199]

Providentia, then, was a benevolent force that shaped the universe; a quality associated with the gods; and an attribute that helped to define a political leader. As such it could hardly be better suited to the discourse of imperial virtues, and indeed *providentia* was established as a virtue of the emperor early in the Principate.[200] Imperial *providentia* was quite elastic, and in principle any action on the part of the emperor could be attributed to it. Nevertheless, three interrelated applications of the virtue stand out: the securing of an orderly imperial succession; the suppression of conspiracies; and the active concern for the well-being of the *populus Romanus*. *Providentia* as the imperial virtue that guaranteed dynastic continuity was first publicized by the Ara Providentiae Augustae, located in the Campus Martius in Rome and probably erected between 14 and 17, and by the Providentia types in Tiberius' Divus Augustus Pater coin series, which depicted the altar and announced Tiberius' legitimate succession from his adoptive father.[201] Subsequent Ara Providentia types minted in the first century often carried a dynastic message, especially under Vespasian, whose Augustan policy in this regard was manifest.[202] The association between *providentia* and the succession continued in later reigns. Galba's adoption of Piso, for example, was celebrated by the Arvals with an offering to

---

[198] Cic. *Cat.* 3.14.

[199] Cic. *Rep.* 6.26 (Scipio speaking): *deum te igitur scito esse, si quidem est deus, qui viget, qui sentit, qui meminit, qui providet, qui tam regit . . .* , with Béranger 1973: 337. For the role of *providentia* in Cicero's philosophical thought in general, see discussion in Martin 1982: 32–65.

[200] Foresight is invoked near the beginning of the *Res Gestae*, when Augustus reports the senatorial decree that empowered him "to see to it" (*providere*) that the state suffer no harm (1.3), and in the well-known decree of the province of Asia reorganizing the calendar to coincide with Augustus' birthday (*OGIS* 458 = *EJ* 98), in the course of which the dedicators attribute to *pronoia* the birth of Augustus during their lifetimes (ll. 32–4).

[201] Ara Providentiae: *LTUR* 4.155–6 (M. Torelli). For the precise location, see the fragment of the *acta Arvalium* from 38 (*AE* 1983.95: *in campo Agrippae ad aram Providentiae Augustae*); for the date, Eck *et al.* 1996: 200–1. Scott 1982: 436–46 discusses the dynastic message of the monument and the coin series under Tiberius.

[202] So Scott 1982: 446–53; for the dynastic associations of the Ara Providentia type, see also Martin 1982: 107–10, 114–19, 134–7, 145–6; cf. Béranger 1973: 344–6, Ando 2000: 34.

Providentia.[203] The theme is articulated in literary texts, too, from Tacitus, who comments on Augustus' provision of heirs, to Eutropius, who attributes Nerva's adoption of Trajan to the former's divine foresight.[204]

An orderly succession, which ensured political stability, depended on the capacity of the emperor to foresee the state of the empire after his death, and to prepare a successor, or successors, accordingly. That is the essential connection between dynastic continuity and the virtue of *providentia*. The same logic explains the frequent celebration of *providentia* in the suppression of conspiracies against the emperor. Contemporaries celebrated the downfall of Sejanus, for example, with allusions to the imperial *providentia* that had foiled Sejanus' plot.[205] Twice during the reign of Nero the Arvals made offerings to Providentia, evidently in connection with the detection of perceived attempts to overthrow the emperor.[206] And during the reign of Septimius Severus, the execution of Popilius Pedo Apronianus, proconsul of Asia, for employing magic in a bid for the throne, seems to have been acknowledged by a dedication in Ephesus that commemorated the *providentia* of the imperial family.[207]

What the suppression of these putative conspiracies shares with the orderly succession of imperial power, and what makes the virtue of *providentia* apposite to both, is the dynastic continuity that results from the emperor's ability to foresee. This dynastic continuity produced by

---

[203] *CIL* 6.1.2042, 4.2.32354.

[204] Tac. *Ann.* 1.8.6: *provisis etiam heredum in rem publicam opibus*, with Béranger 1973, arguing that this clause means that heirs had been provided by Augustus *for* the state; *contra* Goodyear 1972: *ad loc.*, who takes the preposition *in* to mean that heirs had been provided *against* the (traditional Republican) state. Eutrop. 8.1.2: *rei publicae divina provisione consuluit* (sc. Nerva) *Traianum adoptando*.

[205] On the attempted *coup* of Sejanus, Valerius Maximus writes (9.11.ext. 4), *et in primis auctor ac tutela nostrae incolumitatis ne excellentissima merita sua totius orbis ruina collaberentur divino consilio providit*. A municipal dedication from Interamna in Umbria (*CIL* 11.4170 = *ILS* 157) echoes this language: *providentiae Ti(berii) Caesaris Augusti nati ad aeternitatem | Romani nominis, sublato hoste perniciosissimo p(opuli) R(omani)*; see also the dedication of P. Viriasius Naso, proconsul of Crete, to the *providentia* of Tiberius and the senate, to mark the execution of Sejanus (*ILS* 158). See discussion in Charlesworth 1936: 111–13; Martin 1982: 110–15.

[206] The unsuccessful "conspiracy" of 59 was marked by the Arvals through dedications *pro salute Neronis* and to Providentia (*CIL* 6.1.2042, 4.2.32354), surely as part of the official celebration that followed the execution of Agrippina (cf. Tac. *Ann.* 14.12). In 66, the first two sacrifices of the year include offerings to Providentia "*ob detecta nefariorum consilia*" (*CIL* 6.1.2044, 4.2.32355), clearly to celebrate the suppression of a "conspiracy," either that of Vinicianus (Charlesworth 1936: 114) or of P. Anteius and Ostorius Scapula (Martin 1982: 146–9); Martin notes that the Pisonian conspiracy was detected in April of 65, too early for commemoration in 66 (149, n. 49).

[207] Apronianus: Dio 76(77).8.1. Dedication: *CIL* 3.427 = *ILS* 430 (Ephesus): *quod evidenti in[lustri provi]|dentia domini n[ostri Severus et] | Antoninus Pii Au[gusti et Geta | Caesar] cum [Iulia Aug(usta) ubivis spes | parricidiales insid[iatorum sustulerunt] | Helico libertus eorum [. . .] donum [posuit]*. The restorations are by Mommsen (the Latin text is followed by a Greek version, also fragmentary). For the argument that this dedication refers to the suppression of Apronianus' bid for the throne, Martin 1982: 395–6.

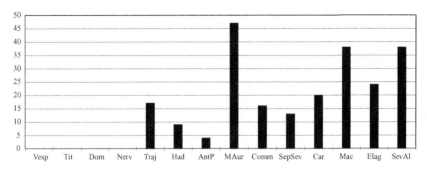

Figure 2.5 Relative frequency of Providentia types on denarii, expressed as a percentage of all virtue types by reign, AD 69–235 (N = 18,187)

imperial *providentia* guaranteed not only political stability, but peace and prosperity as well. As a result, imperial *providentia* could also be generalized as the virtue denoting the emperor's active concern (*cura*) for his subjects.[208] This conceit is visible in a wide range of contexts. In Pliny's correspondence with Trajan, for example, various decisions taken by Trajan are attributed by Pliny to the emperor's foresight and implicitly linked to his interest in the well-being of the inhabitants of Bithynia-Pontus. Other similar applications of imperial *providentia* include the establishment of an *alimenta* program; the reduction of expenses for the sponsorship of gladiatorial combat; the restoration of a road; and payment for a public building.[209] The ultimate effect of this wide-ranging imperial *providentia*, in several formulations, was nothing less than the *aeternitas* of Rome.[210] The emperor's foresight both recognized and produced an ideal world that in principle perpetuated itself indefinitely.

In light of the ideological significance of this virtue, it is unsurprising that Providentia types were so common on the imperial coinage. One way to get a better understanding of the representation of this ideal is to consider the changing relative frequency of the type over time (figure 2.5). Immediately

---

[208] See esp. Béranger 1953: 210–17 for the emperor's *cura* and *providentia*.

[209] Plin. *Ep.* 10.54, 10.61, 10.108. *Alimenta: CIL* 10.6310 = *ILS* 282. Gladiatorial expenses: *CIL* 2S.1168 = *ILS* 5163. Restoration of road: *CIL* 10.5964 = *ILS* 5876. Public building: *CIL* 3.324 = *ILS* 613. See also Alföldi 1955, who connects the coins of Constantine's Providentia series to the reinforcement of the *limes* fortifications on the Danube frontier.

[210] *Providentia* and *aeternitas*: e.g. *CIL* 11.4170 = *ILS* 157 (Interamna, AD 31; see above, n. 205); *CIL* 10.1401 = *ILS* 6,043 (Herculaneum, AD 47): *cum providentia optumi principis tectis quoque | urbis nostrae et totius Italiae aeternitati prospexerit* (relating to Claudius' *ludi saeculares* and censorship); *CIL* 6.1.2044, 4.2.32355 (Arval dedication of 66, with offerings to Providentia and to Aeternitas); cf. Velleius Paterculus on Augustus' adoption of Tiberius and its positive effect on hopes for the *aeternitas* of the Roman empire (2.103). On the connection between *providentia* and *aeternitas*, see the classic discussion in Charlesworth 1936.

apparent is the sharp spike in the production of Providentia types under Marcus Aurelius. It is possible, though perhaps implausible, that Marcus Aurelius, the Stoic emperor, insisted that this core Stoic virtue, *providentia*, was systematically advertised on the imperial coinage. It is also possible, though even less plausible, that this dramatic upsurge in Providentia types under a Stoic emperor is simply fortuitous. The most likely explanation for this marked emphasis on *providentia*, in my view, is that it is simply one part of a broader contemporary discourse on foresight, both as philosophical ideal and imperial virtue, and that this official medium of communications, just like contemporary texts such as Marcus Aurelius' *Meditations*, both reflects and constitutes that discourse.

Another way to grasp the message(s) of the Providentia type is to consider the iconography and legends associated with it. The numismatic representation of Providentia reveals a clear evolution in emphasis on the different aspects of this virtue.[211] From the time of its initial appearance on the imperial coinage under Tiberius down through the reign of Vespasian, the iconography of Providentia is limited to representations of a closed altar precinct, with the legend PROVIDENT, normally taken to depict the Ara Providentiae Augustae (illustration 2.12).[212] The circumstances of its production throughout this period suggest that the message of dynastic continuity, on the Augustan model, was paramount. Then there is a change. Under Titus, a sestertius is produced with the legend PROVIDENT AUGUST SC and an image of Vespasian and Titus, standing face to face, holding a globe between them (illustration 2.13). This type is picked up again under Nerva, with the important difference that Nerva is presented with a globe not by his predecessor, but by a senator, an exchange underlined by the legend PROVIDENTIA SENATUS SC.[213] Two types minted in 98 under Trajan have similar iconography (with Trajan replacing Nerva), one with the legend PROVID, and the other, an exceptional five denarius piece, with the legend PROVIDENTIA SENATUS.[214] On these types *providentia* is still the virtue that guarantees a smooth imperial succession, but the locus of authority has been symbolically transferred from the imperial regime to the senate. Thus these Providentia types produced

---

[211] Martin 1982: 431–3 presents a convenient tabular presentation of all Providentia types between Tiberius and Severus Alexander. General discussion of the iconography of *providentia* in *LIMC* 7.1.562–7, 7.2.432–3 (E. Polito).

[212] Providentia with Ara Providentiae Augustae: *RIC* 1², Tiberius 80–1; *RIC* 1², Galba 499; *RIC* 1², Vitellius 129; *RIC* 2, Vespasian 494; cf. *RIC* 2, Titus 140A, 191. For the core message of dynastic continuity during this period, Scott 1982: 446–53.

[213] *RIC* 2, Nerva 90.   [214] *RIC* 2, Trajan 28; *BMCRE* 3, p. 38.

Illustration 2.12 Reverse of as (*RIC* 2, Vespasian 655): The altar of Providentia Augusta.
PROVIDENT

Illustration 2.13 Reverse of sestertius (*RIC* 2, Titus 97): Vespasian presenting a globe to
Titus. PROVIDENT. AUGUST

Illustration 2.14 Reverse of denarius (*RIC* 2, Hadrian 133): Providentia carrying a scepter and pointing to a globe. PRO. AUG

under Nerva and Trajan expressed the same principles of imperial succession that Pliny articulated near the beginning of the *Panegyricus*.[215]

The subsequent iconography of Providentia reflects an even deeper shift. After the reign of Nerva, the altar type never again appears on the imperial coinage. Sometimes types with the legend PROVIDENTIA (or PROVIDENTIA DEORUM) depict the emperor(s), but far more often the virtue is represented by a female personification, usually standing, carrying a scepter (or wand) and pointing to a globe (illustration 2.14).[216] These attributes suggest a more general application of imperial *providentia*. Beginning in the second century, then, imperial coins no longer proclaimed *providentia* as the specific quality that ensured dynastic continuity, but instead celebrated the wide-ranging imperial foresight that was emblematic of the emperor's *cura* for his subjects. Roughly simultaneous with this shift was the appearance on the imperial coinage, beginning in the reign

---

[215] Plin. *Pan*. 8–10, with Fears 1977: 273–4; Scott 1982: 454–5.
[216] Providentia with emperors: e.g. *RIC* 3, Hadrian 589, 602; *RIC* 3, Marcus Aurelius 1,046. Providentia with scepter/wand and globe: e.g. *RIC* 2, Trajan 240; *RIC* 2, Hadrian 133; *RIC* 3, Antoninus Pius 946; *RIC* 3, Marcus Aurelius 170; *RIC* 3, Commodus 7; *RIC* 4.1, Clodius Albinus 1; *RIC* 4.1, Septimius Severus 92; *RIC* 4.2, Severus Alexander 173.

of Hadrian, of Providentia types with the legend PROVIDENTIA DEO-
RUM. Foresight was, after all, a quality shared by rulers and gods, and
the official representation of both imperial and divine *providentia* on the
imperial coinage not only advertised divine sanction for imperial rule, but
also reminded the inhabitants of the empire that their emperor's virtues
were god-like in nature and effect.[217]

CONCLUSION

The five core virtues of *aequitas, pietas, virtus, liberalitas*, and *providentia*
defined the ethical profile of the good Roman emperor. These virtues did
not form a canon in the Platonic mold, nor was this particular set of qualities ever deliberately packaged together as an official *Regierungsprogramm*
of the imperial regime. Over the course of the period 69–235, though,
these five imperial virtues, systematically emphasized over and above the
other personal qualities of the emperor, came to form a coherent set of
virtues with its own internal logic. Victory and achievement in the military sphere were represented by *virtus*. The religious dimension of Roman
imperial authority was articulated both by *pietas*, the virtue that secured the
maintenance of the *pax deorum* and defined the almost sacred obligations
between emperors and subjects, and by *providentia*, a quality in which the
distinction between imperial virtue and divine attribute was often blurred.
Aequitas and *liberalitas* belonged to the material realm, the one alluding to
the fair administration of the mint and guaranteeing the quality of the coins
it issued, and the other advertising the personal generosity of the emperor
himself.[218] Finally, this set of virtues promoted the ideal of dynastic continuity. *Pietas* characterized the attitude of the reigning emperor towards his
predecessor, and *providentia* referred to the quality that ensured a smooth
succession of imperial power and secured the *aeternitas* of the Roman
empire. All five core virtues, then, had specific applications in the public
sphere, and together they animated the military, religious, material, and

---

[217] Providentia Deorum under Hadrian: e.g. *RIC* 2, 589. See Fears 1977: 271–8 on the ideological
significance of Providentia Deorum types. Because the focus of this chapter is on the emperor's
personal virtues, Providentia Deorum types were not included in the tabulations summarized in
tables 2.1–2.

[218] *Liberalitas* as an expression of imperial generosity was supplemented by the virtues of *indulgentia*
and *munificentia*, both relatively rare on the imperial coinage (cf. tables 2.1–2). *Indulgentia* had
a wide semantic range, signifying not just generosity, but also goodwill and leniency. See *TLL*
7.1.1246.16–1250.38, esp. 1248.24–53 for *indulgentia* as generosity; for *indulgentia* as an imperial
virtue, see below, 280–3. The meaning of *munificentia* was more restricted, referring in general to
generosity in public benefaction (*TLL* 8.1650.68–1651.42), and often more specifically to generosity
in the giving of public games (*TLL* 8.1651.43–68).

dynastic strands of Roman imperial ideology. This is the underlying logic of this particular set of ethical qualities.

This is also a distinctively Roman constellation of monarchic virtues. Comparison with the Platonic canon of justice, wisdom, moderation, and courage is instructive. Justice, as noted above, was fundamental to Greek theories of character and political rule, but is missing from this set of qualities. *Providentia* represents an important form of knowledge, to be sure, but it is a rather shabby substitute for *sophia* or *sapientia* as an expression of royal wisdom. And there is nothing at all in this set of imperial virtues to suggest Platonic moderation (or the Hellenistic royal ideal of self-control). The only real point of contact between the Platonic canon and the core virtues of the Roman emperor, then, is in the ideal of courage.

The differences run even deeper. Plato's qualities are idealized, absolute, and internal – it was in developing his thesis of the tripartite soul in the *Republic*, after all, that Plato fixed his canon in the first place.[219] The emperor's core virtues, by contrast, were usually specific and addressed to concrete outcomes affecting the community as a whole. To put it in different terms, Plato's virtues were mainly "dispositional," indicating subjective attitudes or dispositions to behave in certain ways, while the imperial virtues, though possessing a significant dispositional component, were mainly "enacted," indicating personal qualities regularly made manifest through actions performed in the public eye.[220] This contrast between the dispositional and enacted dimensions of ethical qualities is partly a function of the difference between a philosophical treatise and the official publicity of a monarchic regime, but it also points to a more deep-rooted contrast between Greek and Roman conceptions of ethics and power. For all the influence of Greek ethical ideals on the Roman discourse of monarchy and political power, the valuation of Roman imperial virtues depended ultimately on the tangible, visible, and concrete results that flowed from them.

---

[219] See briefly North 1966: 172.
[220] The terms "dispositional" and "enacted" are borrowed from Roller 2001, esp. 22–7.

CHAPTER 3

The benefits of empire and monarchy

The discourse of monarchy and virtue examined in the last chapter was an aristocratic construct, with most of its animating ideas deriving from Greek philosophy, "the elite in its most elitist of activities." It has been doubted whether any of this really mattered to the fifty million inhabitants of the Roman empire. Indeed, what possible use could "the farmer in Gaul, the grain-shipper in Africa, the shopkeeper in Syria" have for the Socratic virtue of the Roman emperor?[1] We will see that this discourse had an impact beyond the city of Rome and below the educated elite, and that it helped to maintain the local social hierarchies upon which the Roman imperial state depended, but for the moment the point may be conceded. The character of the emperor might have been a pressing concern for the emperor's aristocratic peers, but it is difficult to imagine that his other subjects gave the question much thought. And though the enacted quality of the emperor's virtues helped to bridge the gap between ideal character and concrete outcomes, it was ultimately the practical benefits of monarchy and empire themselves that had the greatest ideological resonance.

Commentators on Roman monarchy, especially those well disposed to individual emperors, naturally recognized the rhetorical value of such benefits. In the last chapter I drew on Pliny's *Panegyricus* to demonstrate the importance of the emperor's virtues to the aristocratic formulation of an ideology of imperial rule, but this address also celebrates the tangible goods that the *optimus princeps* provided for his subjects. Consider Pliny's description of imperial resource allocation under Trajan:

I turn now to the abundance of the grain-supply (*adfluentia annonae*), equal, in my view, to a permanent cash handout. It was this that once brought Pompey no less honor than when he banished bribery from the elections, drove the pirates

---

[1] Questions raised by Wallace-Hadrill 1981a: 299 (with quotations) in criticism of Charlesworth 1937.

from the sea, and illuminated West and East with his triumphs. Nor was Pompey more civic-minded than our Father, who, by his influence, wisdom, and good faith has opened roads that were closed, constructed harbors, created overland routes, brought the sea to the shores and the shores to the sea, and has integrated diverse peoples in trade to such an extent that local products seem to belong to everyone. Is it not clear that every year abounds in the things we need without any harm done to anyone? Harvests are not stolen as if from foreign lands to rot in our granaries while our allies wail in vain. They themselves bring whatever their soil produces, whatever their climate nourishes, whatever the year brings; nor, weighed down by new exactions, do they come up short on their regular taxes. And the imperial treasury makes its purchases openly. The result is this abundance (*copiae*), this grain-supply that benefits both buyer and seller, this plenty (*satietas*) here (sc. in Rome), and the absence of hunger anywhere.[2]

The remarkable individual role that Trajan himself is made to play in this picture is an important point to which we will return. Here I want to draw attention to the notion that imperial rule serves the interests not only of the inhabitants of Rome, but also of the population of the empire as a whole – an idea, it is worth noting, that Pliny expresses in a discussion of the *annona*, the imperial benefit *par excellence* for the city of Rome. As he suggests, the beneficent administration of the empire can be measured both by magnanimous policy, especially in the collection of taxes, and by tangible things, such as the grain and local products found from one end of the empire to the other and the very infrastructure that makes this abundance possible. Even in a consular speech at Rome celebrating the *optimus princeps*, then, the positive impact of imperial rule on the daily lives of the provincials is not neglected.[3]

The full scope of publicized benefits of Roman imperial rule was very wide – much wider, in fact, than the scope of imperial virtues considered in the last chapter – ranging from the abundance of food to the efflorescence of desirable social conditions and even, as we will see, to positive states of mind. There are several ways to conceptualize these putative benefits of empire. One approach is to distinguish between different types of benefit, which may be categorized, very schematically, as material, social, and juridical. The most impressive and enduring material benefits of empire were imperial structures and buildings in the provinces.[4]

---

[2] Plin. *Pan.* 29.

[3] Other imperial benefits mentioned by Pliny include the alleviation of drought conditions in Egypt (30.5, 31.3–6); the spread of fertility (*fecunditas*) everywhere (32.2); the granting of various tax immunities and remissions (38–41); and the settling of rivalries between cities (80.3).

[4] General treatments of imperial building in the provinces in MacMullen 1959 and Mitchell 1987. For more detailed studies of specific areas and periods of more intense imperial building activity, see,

"Imperial building" in the provinces refers to the provision by the central state of materials, labor (esp. from soldiers), architectural or engineering expertise, or financing, whether through direct cash subsidies or temporary tax remissions, for the erection of new buildings and structures or the restoration of old ones. It must be emphasized, however, that most construction and urban restoration in the provinces was funded by local élites from their own private wealth.[5] Nevertheless, building, urbanization, and monumental architecture throughout the empire were often construed as concrete benefits provided by the Roman imperial state. "Now all the Greek cities rise up under your leadership," as Aristides declares, "and the monuments which are dedicated in them and all their embellishments and comforts redound to your honor like beautiful suburbs. The coasts and interiors have been filled with cities, some newly founded, others increased under and by you."[6] But the material benefits of empire were not limited to physical structures. Other benefactions included imperial support for a city's grain supply, cash subsidies, and, above all, temporary remissions of municipal taxes.[7]

Favorable conditions prevailing throughout the empire may be considered under the rubric of social benefits. Good fortune, health, fertility, and happiness were all proclaimed as benefits of empire, but among such propitious conditions it was peace – the "immense majesty of the Roman peace," as Pliny the elder called it – that was most frequently celebrated.[8] As a benefit of empire, peace could be seen as the security that resulted from the military defeat of external enemies – indeed, this is the primary meaning of *pax* – and from the "wall" of Roman soldiers stationed "like a ring around the civilized world."[9] But imperial peace also denoted the elimination of

---

e.g., Jouffroy 1986: 105–6, 137–8, 152, 169–71, 197, 233–4, 279–80, 311–12 (imperial building in Italy and North Africa); MacMullen 2000: 19, 22, 31, 44, 57–8, 62, 95–7, 101–9 (imperial building under Augustus); Boatwright 2000, esp. chs. 6–7 (imperial building under Hadrian). Literary references to imperial building in the provinces are collected in Horster 1997 (with convenient tabular presentation, tab. 1, 114–29); for the epigraphic record, Horster 2001; Alföldy 2002.

[5] Several of Pliny's letters (10.23–4, 90–1) imply that the costs of local building projects could be offset by municipal revenues, but this does not seem to have been the norm, especially if *summa honoraria* are considered "private"; cf. Duncan-Jones 1990: 174–84. For local euergetism and civic benefaction, see below, chapter 5.

[6] Aristid. *Or.* 26.94 (transl. Oliver); cf. 26.101: "You have spanned the rivers with all kinds of bridges and hewn highways through the mountains and filled the barren stretches with posting stations."

[7] Grain supply: Millar 1977: 422; Garnsey 1988: 251–7; Boatwright 2000: 92, 145, 181. Hadrian's support of the grain supply at Athens might have been financed by a permanent endowment: Dio 69.16.2; cf. Garnsey 1988: 252, n. 14; Boatwright 2000: 92. Cash subsidies and remission of taxes: Kloft 1970: 118–20; Millar 1977: 422–5, 428–30; Mitchell 1987: 344–7; Boatwright 2000: 88–9, 93–4.

[8] Plin. *NH* 27.2: *immensa Romanae pacis maiestas.*

[9] Aristid. *Or.* 26.79–94 (quoted); on *pax*, see below, 127–32.

civic discord and internecine conflict that came with incorporation into the Roman empire. It was this internal peace within the Roman empire, in fact, that attracted most comment from Greek authors, who normally contrasted this condition with the endemic strife in the Greek world prior to the Roman conquest.[10] And all of this, as Aristides remarks, without the presence of Roman garrisons in the cities (*Or.* 26.64, 67). The corollaries of peace were prosperity and abundance. Some observers claimed that every conceivable product was exchanged in a free and common market stretching from one end of the empire to the other. Others marveled at the concentration of goods in the city of Rome – the common emporium of the world where everything meets, "trade, shipping, agriculture, metallurgy, all the arts and crafts that are or ever have been, all the things that are engendered or grow from the earth."[11] What I call "social" benefits easily shaded into the material realm.

Juridical benefits concerned matters of formal status, collective and individual, which the Roman imperial state frequently determined or adjudicated. The major juridical benefit of empire was of course Roman citizenship.[12] Greek authors in particular were struck by the unparalleled spread of Roman citizenship. The result of this policy, as Aristides and others claimed, was nothing less than the creation of a single political community, a *communis patria* in which the city of Rome and the entire civilized world (*oikoumenē*) were unified under one benevolent ruler.[13] The Roman state also defined the formal status of communities, and promotion to a more elevated status, from *municipium* to *colonia*, for example, or the award of certain privileges, such as the *ius Latii* or the more highly prized *ius Italicum*, which entailed freedom from *tributum* (land tax and poll

---

[10] Greek authors acknowledge the internal peace of the Roman empire: e.g. Dion. Hal. 1.3.5, 1.5.2; Plut. *Fort. Rom.* 317b–c; App. *praef.* 30–1; Aristid. *Or.* 26.51, 69, 97, 103; Hdn. 3.2.8. Note also the decree of the *koinon* of Asia on the Augustan provision of peace and order: *OGIS* 458 = *EJ* 98, esp. tab. b, ll. 35–6; cf. *EJ* 72 (Augustus); *EJ* 88 (Tiberius). For a Roman perspective, Tac. *Hist.* 4.73 (discord amongst Treveri prior to Roman conquest). See further references and discussion in Gernentz 1918: 129–37; Ando 2000: 54–7.

[11] Free exchange of goods throughout empire: e.g. Plin. *NH* 14.2, 27.2–3; Plin. *Pan.* 29 (quoted above). Abundance of goods in city of Rome: e.g. Aristid. *Or.* 26.11, 13 (quoted); Plut. *Fort. Rom.* 325e; cf. Isoc. *Pan.* 42 on the Piraeus at Athens as the commercial center of the Greek world; Strabo 17.13 on Alexandria as *megiston emporion*. Further references in Gernentz 1918: 137–43.

[12] Sherwin-White 1973 is still the most comprehensive treatment of the juridical details of Roman citizenship. For citizenship as a benefit of empire, see Ando 2000: 10, 57–66; cf. Shaw 2000: 361–72, more skeptical about the practical benefits of citizenship for most provincials. See also Ingelbert 2002b for a discussion of the changing meaning and associations of Roman citizenship and its relation to the nature of Roman identity in the provinces.

[13] On the conceit that the city of Rome embraced the entire civilized world, see discussion in Nicolet 1991: 29–47; Ando 1999.

tax), were eagerly sought.[14] Interventions in the organization of municipalities' territories and in the demarcation of boundaries between cities,
especially when this involved "grants" of land, were also represented as
imperial benefits.[15] Equally valuable were awards of honorific titles for cities,
especially "neocorate" or "metropolis," or titles including imperial names
("Trajanic," "Hadrianic," "Antoninian," etc.) – the currency of municipal
honor in a world of intense competition and bitter rivalry between cities.[16]
And finally, the dispensation of imperial justice to provincials, whether in
the form of primary jurisdiction or appeal, was routinely proclaimed as a
benefit of empire, as was the diffusion of Roman law in general.[17]

Another approach to conceptualizing the benefits of empire is to distinguish between different beneficiaries. Some imperial benefits were enjoyed,
in principle, by the empire as a whole, while others were bestowed upon
individual subjects. Many were targeted at collectivities of various sizes
and compositions, including provinces, cities, the senatorial and equestrian orders, the *plebs urbana* of Rome, priestly colleges, corporations,
synods, and, beginning in the fourth century, the church. Indeed, one
effect of monarchy at Rome was the greater cohesion and public status,
and associated privileges, of the various collectivities that interacted with
the central state.[18] In the representation of these putative imperial benefits,
two countervailing tendencies can be discerned. On the one hand, there
was an impulse to generalize particular benefits and specific privileges as
broader goods of universal, empire-wide significance. This "generalizing"
tendency is clear, for example, in the empire-wide advertisement of military
victories won in particular and sometimes isolated locations, and in the
figuration of the urban plebs of Rome, privileged recipient of all sorts of
gifts and perks (*commoda*), as the equivalent of the Roman citizen body

---

[14] For an overview of the various benefits and privileges granted to cities, see Millar 2002–2006 (1983):
2.336–71; for changes in city statuses and their attendant advantages, see also Boatwright 2000:
ch. 3.

[15] Boatwright 2000: 78–80, 83–8.

[16] Municipal status and honor: Lendon 1997: 126–7, 136–9, 151–3, 171–2. Neocorate: Burrell 2004. For
municipal titulature and inter-city rivalry, Robert 1977 is still basic (further references in Lendon
1997: 136, n. 150); cf. Galsterer-Kröll 1972 for a comprehensive collection of city titles. Inter-city
rivalry was especially intense in the east, but was not unknown in the west; see Syme 1988 (1981):
74–93 on the rivalry between Tarraco and Barcino.

[17] Cf. Aristid. *Or.* 102: "There is no need to write a book of travels to enumerate the laws that each
people uses, as you have assigned common laws to us all" (transl. Oliver, modified); cf. 26.37–9, 65,
103, 107. For the diffusion of Roman law in the provinces, see Galsterer 1986; Crawford 1988; Lintott
1993: 154–60; cf. Ando 2000: 9–10, 339–41, 406–10 for the unifying force and ideological resonance
of Roman law. Galsterer 1996 provides a concise overview of the administration of Roman justice
in the provinces.

[18] A central thesis of Rowe 2002.

as a whole.[19] On the other hand, there was an impulse to underline the particular nature of specific benefits enjoyed by individual members of the imperial community. Nowhere is this "particularizing" tendency more pronounced than in the system of "petition-and-response," whereby even the most humble inhabitants of the Roman empire, including women and slaves, could receive a written judicial decision, formulated and signed as if written by the emperor himself, in response to a legal query, request for judgment, or appeal.[20] These two tendencies were not in tension with one another. Instead, they should be seen as complementary strands of a highly developed ideology of imperial rule that effectively embraced both the individual subject and the empire – or, rather, the civilized world – as a whole.

These material, social, and juridical benefits of empire, then, whether dispensed to individuals, collectivities, or the entire empire, all contributed to the "beneficial ideology" of Roman imperial rule. The benefits of empire, however, were not quite the same thing as the benefits of monarchy – the Roman emperor, after all, was not the Roman state. How to ascribe such wide-ranging imperial benefits to the emperor himself? Indeed, to attribute a virtue, a judicial decision, or even a new building to the emperor was straightforward; to credit him with delivering a regular supply of grain to Rome or with the defense of the entire imperial frontier was rather more complicated. Our own inclination is to ascribe these "benefits" either to the institutional framework of the Roman imperial system, or to its underlying political economy, and to see them either as structural in nature (e.g., frontier defense maintained by an elaborate military-tributary complex) or as a form of redistribution (e.g., public building projects in the provinces financed by the collective surplus of the empire). These benefits, in other words, were systemic and impersonal, so it seems to us, and did not really flow from the character or actions of this or that emperor.[21] And it should be emphasized that contemporary writers could also extol Roman imperial rule with very little attention to the emperor. In Aristides' celebration of

---

[19] For the universalization of Roman military victories (and other events in the imperial household), see Ando 2000: ch. 6, arguing that the systematic advertisement of such events, and the regular expressions of gratitude offered in return, helped to create provincial consensus in Roman imperial rule; see also below, 161–5; for the *plebs urbana*, Rowe 2002: ch. 3; Zanker 2010.

[20] Millar 1977: 240–52, 507–49; Hauken 1998. For the wide social range of petitioners, see also Connolly 2009.

[21] Hopkins 2009 offers a convenient overview of resource allocation in the Roman empire. For general studies of resource allocation in premodern empires, see, e.g., Eisenstadt 1963: 33–49, 121–30; Mann 1986: 24–5, 111, 121–7, 146–55, 417–30, and *passim*; Sinopoli 1994: 170–2. See also Woolf 1990b for the applicability to the Roman empire of Wallerstein's world-systems theory, especially with respect to the flow of resources between center and periphery.

Rome (*Or.* 26), for example, already cited several times, the figure of the emperor only surfaces a few times, when Aristides notes his power and authority (31–2), his administration by correspondence (33), the finality of his judgment (38–9), and his embodiment of justice and law (107). Otherwise the emperor is a non-entity in the speech, his role thoroughly subsumed within the operations of the larger imperial system.

This was certainly not the perception the imperial regime sought to foster. Instead, it promoted the idea that the reigning emperor himself was personally responsible for the myriad benefits of empire, encouraging the notional identification of the emperor with the state. Though it is possible to enumerate the several ways in which the emperor was represented as the author of the benefits of empire – through the configuration of individual grants of Roman citizenship on military diplomas for discharged auxiliaries as personal gifts of the emperor, to take just one example, or through the emperor's nominal authorship of the rescripts written in his name – the association of the emperor with the state also depended on something less deliberate, less rational, and more difficult for the modern observer to grasp.[22] It depended, ultimately, on what Veyne has called "*le style monarchique.*" In the absence of meaningful public opinion, according to Veyne, the emperor, never chosen by his subjects, ruled by "subjective law" (*droit subjectif*) alone, which in turn animated the ideology of imperial euergetism, as even the most routine administrative decisions were attributed to the emperor's personal and beneficent intervention. The regular ascription to the emperor of impersonal, "bureaucratic" actions arose not because the emperor really was the state – the functional separation of the two was "rigorous," as Veyne rightly emphasizes – but because the subjects of a pre-modern empire had difficulty distinguishing between the institutional apparatus of the state and its embodiment in the figure of the emperor, and, even more important, because the ideal of imperial *beneficia* corresponded to popular *mentalité* and to the desire of the emperor's subjects to imagine that they were ruled by a "good" sovereign. Any action of the central state that involved material benefits, therefore, was automatically a benefaction of the emperor himself.[23] That was the essence of "the monarchic style."[24]

[22] Diplomas: Shaw 2000: 365–6; texts in *CIL* 16 (cf. *ILS* 1986–2010 for a representative selection). Rescripts: above, n. 20. For skepticism about imperial authorship, see below, 216, n. 72.

[23] Veyne 1976: 553 (emperor rules by *droit subjectif*); 539–43, 556 (functional separation of emperor and state); 619–25, 635–46 (imperial *beneficia* and popular *mentalité*); 647, 658–9 (state actions as automatic benefactions of emperor).

[24] We might also refer to *le style monarchique* as "the ruler effect," the exact inverse of what Mitchell 1999 has called "the state effect," the idea of an impersonal state that possesses its own agency, an illusion, so Mitchell suggests, produced by a cluster of governmental symbols and official discourses.

In developing his ideas about imperial euergetism, Veyne was focusing mainly on the traditional forms of civic benefaction in the ancient Mediterranean world (public buildings, games, cash handouts, etc.), but the underlying principle of the monarchic style can also be applied to the full range of imperial benefits discussed above. Just as a routine tax remission could be ascribed to the personal intervention of the emperor, in other words, so too could security, peace, prosperity, abundance, fertility, good fortune, or happiness. Such, at least, was the illusion that the imperial regime sought to create, and in light of the social and political conditions discussed by Veyne, it usually found a receptive audience for this message.

In creating, reinforcing, and disseminating the idea that the reigning emperor was the ultimate source of the various benefits of empire, no tool was more effective than the imperial coinage, not only because coins were produced in massive quantities and then circulated from one end of the empire to the other, but also because the physical form of the coins themselves was ideally suited to establishing a conceptual link between the emperor and any concept, however abstract. The inherent duality of an individual coin allowed a complex message to be presented within a single frame of reference, as the obverse and reverse faces of the coin merged to form a unified whole. In the case of imperial benefits, the collocation of the emperor's portrait with the representation of any sort of benefit encouraged the conflation of the benefit with the emperor himself. And any chance that the coin's user would miss this connection was reduced by the regular attachment of the label AUGUSTA/AUGUSTI/AUG to the benefit in question.[25] The simple but potent combination of image and text on the imperial coinage made even tenuous conceptual linkages clear and unambiguous. Imperial coins were the perfect visual and symbolic expressions of *le style monarchique*.

Personifications formed the most common iconographic category on the imperial coinage, on both precious- and base-metal coins (see above, Introduction to Part 1, 34), and it was among the personification types that imperial benefits, like the imperial virtues examined in the last chapter, were primarily represented. For the purposes of this study, I have identified the following personification types, minted at Rome between AD 69 and 235, as representations of imperial benefits: Abundantia, Aeternitas, Annona, Concordia, Fecunditas, Felicitas, Fortuna, Hilaritas, Laetitia, Libertas, Pax, Perpetuitas, Salus, Securitas, Tranquillitas, and Victoria. By measuring the

---

[25] See Hölscher 1980: 279–81, for the synthesis of image and text in Roman visual culture; cf. Eck 1984: 132–3; Woolf 1996: 27–9.

Table 3.1 *Relative frequency on denarii of individual
imperial benefits, expressed as a percentage of all
imperial benefits,* AD *69–235 (N = 52,096)*

Type	Percentage	Type	Percentage
Victoria	16%	Libertas	3%
Felicitas	13%	Abundantia	2%
Pax	12%	Fecunditas	2%
Concordia	12%	Hilaritas	2%
Salus	10%	Securitas	2%
Fortuna	9%	Laetitia	1%
Annona	9%	Tranquillitas	1%
Aeternitas	6%	Perpetuitas	<1%

Table 3.2 *Relative frequency on base-metal coins of
individual imperial benefits, expressed as a percentage
of all imperial benefits,* AD *69–235 (N = 14,166)*

Type	Percentage	Type	Percentage
Victoria	16%	Abundantia	4%
Fortuna	16%	Hilaritas	4%
Salus	14%	Aeternitas	3%
Felicitas	13%	Securitas	3%
Pax	7%	Fecunditas	2%
Concordia	6%	Laetitia	1%
Annona	6%	Tranquillitas	<1%
Libertas	5%	Perpetuitas	0

relative frequency of these sixteen benefit types for the period 69–235, we can assess the varying degrees of official emphasis on the different benefits of empire, and the way in which they related to one another as part of a single ideological structure of advertised benefits. The results are shown in tables 3.1 and 3.2.

Before analyzing the ideals expressed by these types, two preliminary observations are necessary. First, this categorization of reverse types is not quite as clear-cut as the categorization employed in the last chapter. Qualities that constitute personal virtues are unambiguous, so the sort of structural analysis of reverse types undertaken in chapter 2 was straightforward. Determining which personifications should be considered as "imperial benefits," by contrast, is a bit more problematic. On the one hand, some of the types included in these tables, such as Victoria, Salus, or Felicitas, could be interpreted as ideals or qualities relevant to the central state or to the emperor or imperial family alone, and not as real benefits for the emperor's subjects. In what follows, I will argue that this view is mistaken, and that these ideals were indeed represented as benefits of empire. On the other hand, several personifications that could potentially be construed as benefits in a very broad sense, such as Bonus Eventus, Iuventas, Nobilitas, and Spes, were left out of the tabulations, either because they clearly reflected narrowly dynastic concerns, or because there is no evidence that they were ever promoted as imperial benefits.[26] In any case, it must be emphasized that these other personification types were minted in very small numbers, and so would not have upset the hierarchy of benefits reflected in tables 3.1–2 even if they had been included in the calculations.[27] The second observation is that the ideals represented by these types were often represented by other, non-personification types, too. The goddess Ceres, for example, like Annona, could refer to the grain supply, while an image of a cornucopia could allude, like Abundantia, to abundance and material prosperity. All reverse types, of course, should be interpreted in relation to the broader visual and ideological programs of the imperial coinage, but it is especially important in the case of these benefit types to consider how the ideals they expressed were complemented and reinforced, lexically and visually, by related types.

The tabulations summarized in tables 3.1–2 reveal a general correspondence between the two sets of data in the relative frequencies of the individual types. On both precious- and base-metal coins, Victoria and Felicitas were prominent. Pax, Concordia, Fortuna, and Salus were also relatively common, but in the case of these four benefit types, there was some discrepancy between the two metals. This will be examined below. The remaining benefit types were all minted in relatively small numbers on both silver and bronze coins, with several (Laetitia, Perpetuitas, Tranquillitas) barely registering in the sample. As with the virtue types examined in the last chapter, so too with these benefit types, the correspondence in the relative

---

[26] Bonus Eventus, which may be translated as "success," was sometimes conflated with the Genius Populi Romani; see Mattingly in *BMCRE* ii, lxiii. Iuventas types were only minted under Antoninus Pius, always with obverse portrait of Marcus Aurelius (*RIC* 2, Antoninus Pius 423, 1,232–2, 1,238–9, 1,292), which points to the dynastic message of the type. Nobilitas: Gelzer 1969 (1912): 141–61, and below, ch. 5. Spes indicates the "hope" of dynastic succession within the imperial family; see Mattingly in *BMCRE* ii, xxxviii, li, lxvi etc.; Perassi 1991.

[27] For the total numbers of these types, see appendices 3 (silver) and 4 (bronze).

frequencies of the various types across metals and denominations is significant. This strengthens the argument that the typological programs of both the precious-metal and base-metal coinages were being dictated by a single, central source, and militates against the proposition that there existed during our period a separate and autonomous senatorial mint responsible for the bronze coinage.[28]

The figures reveal a broad hierarchy of imperial benefits, then, with *victoria, felicitas, pax, concordia, fortuna,* and *salus* standing out above all the rest. The types representing these ideals were consistently produced in relatively large numbers, and though these six benefits, like the five core virtues examined in the last chapter, were never packaged together as part of an official program, they were repeatedly and regularly emphasized on coins between 69 and 235, indicating that these were the particular benefits of empire and monarchy that the imperial regime intended to promote during this period. At first glance, this set of concepts does not seem to match the specific benefits conventionally associated with the emperor. Some of those benefits, as we will see, were indeed expressed through these particular types, mainly through iconography. But as a group, what these types advertised was something rather more ambitious than a set of discrete benefits. What they really celebrated, as I will argue, were the desirable social conditions that such benefits brought about, and – even more ambitious – the positive emotions and states of mind that arose from such conditions.

As for the types minted in small numbers, these were either minor ideals, such as Perpetuitas, or adjuncts of major ones, such as Securitas and Tranquillitas, which can be seen as corollaries of Pax and Concordia, or Hilaritas and Laetitia, which reinforced the message of Felicitas. The one exception to this pattern is *libertas*, a key value in the Roman social and political lexicon, but only lightly advertised through the Libertas type. This is a significant discrepancy, and we will come back to it in the conclusion to this chapter.

MATERIAL GOODS

No imperial benefits were more immediate in their effects or more probative of the emperor's concern for his subjects than those that could actually be seen and touched. Among such concrete, tangible benefits, the two that

---

[28] See above, Int. Part 1, 35, for the typological programs of the precious- and base-metal coins; for debates about mint organization and agency and intent in type-selection, see below, 191–2.

had the greatest impact on imperial subjects, especially in the city of Rome, were grain and public buildings. Though such material benefits were less prominent on the imperial coinage than we might expect – a point to which we will return – they were nevertheless an indispensable part of the larger message of imperial benefaction.

Several reverse types advertised the ready availability of grain. Especially significant were the Annona, Abundantia, and Ceres types.[29] *Annona* referred originally both to the year's agricultural produce (from the root *annuus*) and to the variable market price of that produce; by the late Republic it also came to denote the *cura publica* that secured the availability of this produce for the inhabitants of Rome.[30] The supply of grain to the city of Rome and its market price became major political issues during the Gracchan period and remained so down to the end of the Republic.[31] Concern over the grain supply is naturally reflected in contemporary sources, and in the writings of Cicero in particular we find a number of references in different contexts to the scarcity of produce, the high cost of grain (*caritas annonae*), and the attendant threat of hunger.[32]

As a term that could refer simultaneously to agricultural produce and to its public provision, *annona* was an ideal expression of the material benefits of imperial rule. Official emphasis on the emperor's personal provision of grain for the city of Rome is visible already in the *Res Gestae*, where Augustus boasts that he did not avoid the *cura annonae* and that with his own money he eradicated a food crisis within a matter of days (5.2). And despite Augustus' creation of an elaborate institutional framework for the regular supply of grain to Rome, headed by an equestrian prefect, the personal role of the Roman emperor in securing the city's grain supply was always an important part of the emperor's own public image.[33] Augustus

---

[29] Another related type, Fecunditas, which first appeared under Antoninus Pius (*RIC* 3, 1,142 [Faustina]), referred mainly to fertility within the imperial house (see Mattingly in *BMCRE* IV, cxliv), but could also denote agricultural fertility (e.g. *B.Hisp.* 8.2: *propter terrae fecunditatem*; cf. Cic. *Div.* 1.94).

[30] Cf. *TLL* 2.110.47–113.70, esp. 110.72–112.12 (market price of annual produce) and 113.18–59 (*cura publica*).

[31] See, e.g., Rickman 1980, esp. 26–66 on the Republican period and the transition to the imperial *cura annonae* under Pompey, Caesar, and Augustus; Garnsey 1988: 198–217.

[32] E.g. Cic. *Dom.* 12: *difficultatem annonae summamque inopiam rei frumentariae, ut homines non iam diuturnam caritatem, sed ut famem plane timerent, nemo negat*; *Har.* 31: *in hac caritate annonae, sterilitate agrorum, inopia frugum*; *Off.* 3.50: *in Rhodiorum inopia et fame summaque annonae caritate.* All three passages make clear the association between the high price of grain, the scarcity of produce in general, and the threat of hunger lurking behind both. See *TLL* 2.112.13–24 for further citations of this sort.

[33] On the imperial grain supply, see, e.g., Rickman 1980: ch. 4; Garnsey 1988: 218–43; Virlouvet 2000; see also Erdkamp 2005 on the Roman imperial grain market in general, esp. ch. 5 on the city of Rome. For the legal superstructure of the *annona* during the imperial period, Sirks 1991.

himself intervened on several occasions to prevent grain crises in Rome, successfully combining dramatic actions in the public eye with his longer-term institutional overhaul of the *annona*.[34] Augustus' successors improved the grain supply to Rome in other ways. Claudius, for example, constructed a new harbor at Ostia (Portus), later improved by Trajan, and both Claudius and Hadrian granted various legal privileges to some of the key personnel involved in the transport of grain from its areas of production to Italy.[35] Commodus even created a new African fleet known as the "Commodiana Herculea," if the *Historia Augusta* can be trusted, designed to fill the void in case the Alexandrian fleet failed to deliver grain from Egypt.[36] From such developments arose the perception that it was the emperor himself who personally guaranteed the supply of grain to Rome. Indeed, when Nero proposed an extended visit to the eastern provinces, the first reaction on the part of the urban populace, according to Tacitus, was fear that the city's grain would run out in the emperor's absence.[37] Pliny knew he was striking a powerful chord when he represented Trajan as literally moving land and sea to guarantee the provision of food for his most favored subjects.[38]

Imperial expenditure on grain for Rome, and the insistence that the emperor himself oversaw the grain supply – Tiberius once declared in the senate that the emperor alone was responsible for the *cura annonae* – were motivated less by benevolent concern for the welfare of the urban populace than by a refined political calculus: in exchange for such imperial benefactions, often carefully choreographed, the urban populace offered honors to the emperor and adopted a particular *modalité d'obéissance* to the regime.[39] It was precisely this notional connection between the emperor, the maintenance of the grain supply, and the acquiescence of the urban populace in the imperial regime that lies behind Fronto's well known observation that "the *populus Romanus* is controlled above all by two things,

---

[34] Aug. *RG* 15, 18; Suet. *Aug.* 41.5; Dio 53.2.1, 54.1.1, 55.10.1, 55.26.2.

[35] For the harbor and port facilities at Ostia (Portus), see Keay *et al.* 2005. Claudian privileges (mainly for *negotiatores* and *mercatores*): Suet. *Claud.* 18–19; Gai. *Inst.* 1.32c; *Dig.* 3.6 (Ulpian); Hadrianic privileges (mainly for *navicularii*): *Dig.* 50.6.6.5–6, 8–9 (Callistratus). See briefly Garnsey 1988: 233–5.

[36] *HA Comm.* 17.7.

[37] Tac. *Ann.* 15.36. For the perception of the emperor's responsibility for the provision of food, see also Suet. *Aug.* 41.5, *Claud.* 18–19.

[38] Plin. *Pan.* 29.2: *litoribus mare litora mari reddidit.*

[39] Tiberius in the senate: Tac. *Ann.* 3.54.6: *hanc curam* (sc. *annonae*) *sustinet princeps*. For imperial benefactions in the city of Rome in exchange for popular honors, see, e.g., Veyne 1976: ch. 4, esp. 621–47 (benefactions), 689–90 (special relationship between emperor and urban plebs), 709–10 ("modality of obedience"); Rowe 2002: ch. 3; Zanker 2010; see also below, chapter 5, on the functioning of this honorific system in the provinces.

the *annona* and the games."[40] And yet the *populus Romanus*, as Fronto knew perfectly well, was a far larger collectivity than the *plebs urbana* that in fact benefited from the *annona* and other imperial benefactions in the city of Rome.[41] The Annona type effectively represented the grain supply to the city of Rome and the emperor's role in securing it, but in order to make the type relevant to those outside of Rome, its underlying message had to be universalized. Two types that were employed to promote this universalization were Abundantia and Ceres.

Abundantia could mean an abundance of anything, and in a number of passages the term denotes an abundance of everything.[42] Though it was sometimes employed in figurative usages (an abundance of fortune, of leisure, of joy, etc.), most often it referred to a profusion of material goods, and especially to a profusion of agricultural produce.[43] And so we find frequent references to an abundance of food, produce, wine, and water, especially when linked to the productiveness of the land.[44] The connection between *abundantia* and agricultural produce is also clear not only from the terms and concepts with which *abundantia* tended to be grouped, such as "the productiveness of the fields," but also, and in particular, from those to which it was opposed, especially hunger.[45]

Ceres was an Italic goddess of agricultural growth, often identified with Demeter, whose cult at Rome was centered on her temple on the Aventine and on the annual Cerialia and *ludi Ceriales* celebrated in her honor.[46]

Annona, abundantia, and Ceres were effectively united on the imperial coinage by means of shared iconography, explanatory legends, and a series of interlocking attributes and adjuncts that drew the ideals represented by

---

[40] Fro. *Princ. Hist.* 20 (A 259): *populum Romanum duabus praecipue rebus, annona et spectaculis teneri.*

[41] Note also the existence of the *plebs frumentaria*, a distinct subset of the urban plebs (or so it seems) eligible for the free grain distributions (*frumentationes*); see discussion in Rickman 1980: 179–85; Rowe 2002: 87–95.

[42] E.g. Cic. *Agr.* 1.18: *propter ubertatem agrorum abundantiamque rerum omnium*; *Lael.* 87; Tac. *Dial.* 6: *in summa rerum omnium abundantia.* For the meaning and usage of *abundantia, TLL* 1.227.12–229.17.

[43] Figurative uses: e.g. *fortunae*: Cic. *De Orat.* 2.242; *otii et amoris*: Cic. *Fam.* 7.1.6 (SB 24); *gratulationis*: Val. Max. 7.1.1. Material goods: *pecuniae*: Val. Max. 1.6 ext. 2; Tac. *Hist.* 2.94, *Ann.* 4.62; *transmarinarum stipendiorum*: Val. Max. 9.1.4; *lapidum*: Colum. *Rust.* 2.2.12; *commeatum* ("provisions"): Tac. *Agr.* 33.

[44] Abundance of food (*cibus*): Vitr. 2 *pr.* 3; Plin. *NH* 21.86; Celsus, *Med.* 1 *pr.*; Sor. *Gyn.* 1.33. Produce: Amm. Marc. 23.6.15 (*frux*); Val. Max. 7.4.3 (*frumentum*). Wine (*vinum*): Val. Max. 2.5.6; Colum. *Rust.* 3.2.23. Water (*aquarum*): Plin. *NH* 7.21 (*ubertas soli*).

[45] *Ubertas frugum/agrorum: TLL* 1.228.47–60. Hunger: Plin. *Pan.* 31: *in suis navibus vel abundantia nostra vel fames esset.* See also Cic. *Agr.* 2.97: *hi ex summa egestate in eandem rerum abundantiam traducti*; the context of the *De Lege Agraria* leaves little doubt about the connection between *egestas, abundantia*, and agricultural produce in this passage.

[46] Spaeth 1996.

Illustration 3.1 Reverse of denarius (*RIC* 2, Vespasian 131): Annona with grain stalks.
ANNONA AUG

the three types into a single conceptual frame.[47] Both *annona* and *abundantia* were represented as female personifications, and they shared the same attributes and adjuncts. The most common were those that advertised the grain itself, especially grain stalks and grain-measures (*modii*) (illustration 3.1); those that referred, directly or indirectly, to agricultural produce, such as baskets of fruit and cornucopias; and those that depicted various nautical symbols, such as ships, anchors, rudders, and prows (illustration 3.2), which alluded to the principal means by which the grain was transported.[48] Indeed, the iconography of Annona and Abundantia

---

[47] For the Annona, Abundantia, and Ceres coin types, see Strack 1931–37: 1.65–7, 164–7, 2.63–4; Mattingly in *BMCRE* III, xlvi–xlvii, lxvi, cxxxv; Rickman 1980: 257–67; Garnsey 1988: 225, n. 17. For the iconography of Abundantia, see *LIMC* 1.1.7–10, 1.2.15–18 (R. F. Barriero), with a distinction drawn, somewhat artificially, between "private" and "public" Abundantia; for Annona, *LIMC* 1.1.795–9, 1.2.644 (H. Pavis D'Escurac); for Ceres, *LIMC* 4.1.893–908, 4.2.599–611 (S. de Angeli).

[48] Annona with grain stalks: e.g. *RIC* 2, Vespasian 131; *RIC* 2, Titus 87; *RIC* 2, Domitian 243; *RIC* 2, Trajan 492–5; *RIC* 3, Marcus Aurelius 372; *RIC* 3, Antoninus Pius 597; *RIC* 3, Commodus 307a–b; *RIC* 4.1, Septimius Severus 57; *RIC* 4.2, Severus Alexander 131–4. *Modius*: e.g. *RIC* 2, Trajan 492–4; *RIC* 2, Hadrian 798; *RIC* 3, Antoninus Pius 597; *RIC* 3, Commodus 307a–b; *RIC* 4.2, Severus Alexander 131–4. Basket of fruit: e.g. *RIC* 2, Vespasian 570; *RIC* 3, Antoninus Pius 910; *RIC* 3, Marcus Aurelius 372. Cornucopia: e.g. *RIC* 2, Titus 86; *RIC* 2, Trajan 1; *RIC* 2, Hadrian 580; *RIC* 3, Antoninus Pius 597; *RIC* 3, Commodus 307a–b; *RIC* 4.1, Septimius Severus 57; *RIC* 4.2, Elagabalus

Illustration 3.2 Reverse of denarius (*RIC* 4.2, Severus Alexander 136): Annona with
nautical symbols (rudder and prow). ANNONA AUG

is so similar that the types are often virtually indistinguishable. It should
also be noted that depictions of Abundantia were very common in domestic contexts (illustration 3.3), indicative of a broad and deep attachment to
this ideal.[49] It is likely that these domestic representations of Abundantia
drew in large part on official iconography. It is also possible, though, that
the relationship between the representation of these concepts was more
dynamic, and that the Annona type, with its shared iconography, drew to
some extent on the "popular" affection for Abundantia. In any case, this
blurring of the distinction between *annona* and *abundantia* was one way
to combine the narrower message of the former with the broader one of
the latter.

Equally effective in this regard was the relationship on the coinage
between Annona and Ceres. Ceres is shown with several of the same
attributes and adjuncts as Annona and Abundantia, including grain stalks,

56; *RIC* 4.2, Severus Alexander 131–4. Ship: e.g. *RIC* 3, Antoninus Pius 520a–b, 525; *RIC* 3, Marcus
Aurelius 142; *RIC* 3, Commodus 325a–b. Anchor: e.g. *RIC* 3, Antoninus Pius 840; *RIC* 4.2, Severus
Alexander 188–9. Rudder: e.g. *RIC* 2, Hadrian 796–7; *RIC* 3, Antoninus Pius 942; *RIC* 4.1, Septimius
Severus 135b; *RIC* 4.2, Severus Alexander 136. Prow: e.g. *RIC* 2, Domitian 262; *RIC* 2, Trajan 492–4;
RIC 3, Antoninus Pius 597; *RIC* 4.1, Septimius Severus 57; *RIC* 4.2, Severus Alexander 135–6.
[49] For Abundantia in the domestic sphere, see *LIMC* 1.1.7–9, with 1.2, nos. 1, 2, 4.

Illustration 3.3 Depiction of Abundantia on a wall painting from Herculaneum (mid-first century AD)

modii, cornucopias, and prows of ships.[50] Such shared imagery naturally encouraged an association between the grain supply to the city of Rome and the goddess who ensured agricultural fertility everywhere. A famous Neronian sestertius minted in *c.* 63–4 depicted the figures of Annona and Ceres facing one another, the one holding a cornucopia and the other

---

[50] Ceres with grain stalks: e.g. *RIC* 2, Vespasian 112; *RIC* 2, Titus 8; *RIC* 2, Domitian 443; *RIC* 2, Trajan 109; *RIC* 2, Hadrian 146; *RIC* 3, Antoninus Pius 358–60; *RIC* 3, Marcus Aurelius 668–9; *RIC* 3, Commodus 276; *RIC* 4.1, Septimius Severus 370–1. *Modius*: e.g. *RIC* 2, Hadrian 146. Cornucopia: e.g. *RIC* 2, Hadrian 146. Prow: e.g. *RIC* 2, Nerva 52 (with torch, her identifying attribute); *RIC* 3, Commodus 230.

Illustration 3.4 Reverse of sestertius (*RIC* I², Nero 137): Annona holding a cornucopia and Ceres holding grain stalks, with a grain measure (*modius*) between them and a ship in the background. ANNONA AUGUSTI CERES

grain stalks, with a *modius* between them and a ship in the background, with the legend ANNONA AUGUSTI CERES (SC) (illustration 3.4). The type was imitated under Domitian, Nerva, and Septimius Severus.[51] Here the connection between Annona and Ceres was explicit. And the fact that Ceres was frequently assimilated to the reigning empress, not only on coins but also on cameos, sarcophagi, and statuary (illustration 3.5), only underlined further the extent to which the imperial regime was the ultimate guarantor of agricultural prosperity.[52] It should also be noted that some of the adjuncts associated with the grain supply were sometimes represented by themselves, especially *modii*, and that occasionally a unique legend pertaining to the grain supply was transmitted on the coinage, as on Nerva's sestertius of 97 depicting a *modius* on the reverse with the legend PLEBEI URBANAE FRUMENTO CONSTITUTO SC, the precise meaning of

[51] Domitian: *RIC* 2, 277a–b; Nerva: *RIC* 2, 52; Septimius Severus: *RIC* 4.1, 756 (with legend ANNONA AUG CERES SC). A similar type was issued under Vitellius, but with the emperor himself standing in for Annona (*RIC* I², 131).

[52] For the empress as Ceres, see *LIMC* 4.1.905–6 and 4.2.609–11; in general on the assimilation of the imperial women to goddesses, see Mikocki 1995.

Illustration 3.5 Marble statue of Julia Domna with the attributes of Ceres (*c.* AD 203)

which is unclear.[53] The cumulative message of all these types, which should be read together, is that the abundance of grain throughout the Roman

[53] Depictions of *modii*: e.g. *RIC* 2, Vespasian 110; *RIC* 2, Domitian 276a–b; *RIC* 2, Hadrian 353; *RIC* 3, Antoninus Pius 40; *RIC* 3, Marcus Aurelius 1,122. Nerva's sestertius: *RIC* 2, Nerva 89, 103, with Rickman 1980: 216.

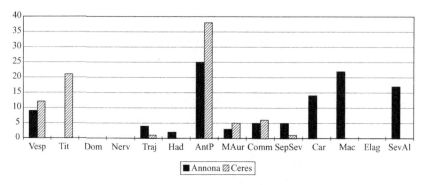

Figure 3.1 Relative frequencies of Annona and Ceres types on denarii, expressed as a percentage of benefit types and deity types, respectively, by reign, AD 69–235 (N = 93,320)
Note: The total number of denarii in figure 3.1 (93,320) equals 52,096 denarii depicting imperial benefits and 41,224 depicting deities; see appendix 3 for tabulations of individual types.

world – especially, but not exclusively, in the city of Rome – was a gift of the imperial regime and an important benefit of empire.

Together, the Annona, Abundantia, and Ceres types were moderately, but not heavily, emphasized on the imperial coinage (cf. tables 3.1–2). Garnsey is probably correct when he observes that individual emissions of these types do not necessarily reflect specific imperial initiatives with respect to the grain supply, but were instead "designed to advertise an emperor's concern in a general way."[54] The fluctuating relative frequencies of these types, however, illuminate some patterns that cannot be discerned when considering individual emissions alone. Figure 3.1 compares the relative frequencies, by reign, of the two most common types representing the grain supply and agricultural prosperity, Annona and Ceres.[55] Immediately apparent is the sharp spike in the production of both types under Antoninus Pius. This can only be understood in connection with a series of measures concerning grain and commerce undertaken by Antoninus, an ambitious and far-reaching program that has not been sufficiently emphasized in general accounts of the period. According to the *Historia Augusta*, Antoninus, in honor of his wife, created a new privileged group of recipients of free grain distributions at Rome (*frumentationes*), the *puellae alimentariae Faustinianae*, and also relieved a shortage of wine, oil, and wheat by

[54] Garnsey 1988: 225, n. 17.
[55] Rickman claims that Ceres was "by no means so prominent as Annona" during the second century (1980: 265). But as these data show, Ceres types were minted more heavily than Annona types throughout most of the period 69–192 (both in relative and absolute terms: see appendix 3); it was only in the Severan period that Annona overtook Ceres.

purchasing these goods with his own funds and distributing them to the people free of charge.[56] Such actions show that Antoninus fulfilled the traditional imperial role of civic benefactor in the city of Rome.

More significant is the evidence for the improvement of port facilities and harbors throughout the empire. An inscription from Puteoli indicates that Antoninus restored the mole of the harbor there.[57] Local coins from Pompeiopolis in Cilicia depicting the city's harbor suggest the completion of an imperial harbor project under Antoninus.[58] And the *Historia Augusta* reports that Antoninus restored "the Farus" – presumably the famous lighthouse at Alexandria (*Pharos*) – as well as the harbors at Caieta and Tarracina.[59] Imperial harbor works under Antoninus, then, seem to have ranged from Italy to the eastern Mediterranean. There is also some evidence for contemporary celebration of the commercial infrastructure of the empire under Antoninus. Two local coins produced in Alexandria, for example, draw attention to the links between Egypt and Rome. The first, minted in 153/54, depicts a personification of the Tiber river, her foot on the prow of a ship, receiving grain stalks from the Nile river, with the legend TIBERIS HOMONOIA, expressing the harmony between the two river deities.[60] The second, minted the following year (154/55), shows the goddess Euthenia (?), representing the imperial grain supply (*annona*), standing with grain stalks and rudder between seated personifications of the Mediterranean and the Nile, the latter also holding a rudder, symbolizing the flow of the Nile river into the Mediterranean sea and the movement of grain from Egypt to Rome.[61] These types evidently advertise the vital commercial connection between east and west and the two critical nodes in this Mediterranean network, the ports of Alexandria and Ostia. Finally, in the administrative sphere, an inscription from Puteoli reveals the existence of an *Augusti dispensator a frumento Puteolis et Ostis*,

---

[56] *HA AntP.* 8.1: *puellas alimentarias in honorem Faustinae Faustinianas constituit*; 8.11: *vini, olei, et tritici penuriam per aerarii sui damna emendo et gratis populo dando sedavit.*

[57] *CIL* 10.1640 = *ILS* 336 (Puteoli, AD 139): *opus pilarum vi | maris conlapsum a divo patre | suo promissum restituit* (sc. Antoninus).

[58] Boyce 1958.

[59] *HA AntP.* 8.2–3: *Fari restitutio, Caietae portus, Terracinensis portus restitutio, lavacrum Ostiense, Antiatium aquae ductus, templa Lanuviana.* Which lighthouse did Antoninus restore? If it were the lighthouse at Ostia, we would expect the biographer to list this in connection with the *lavacrum Ostiense*. Nor is there any evidence for engineering work under Antoninus at Ostia. In light of the Alexandrian coins discussed in the text that follows, it is likely that this passage refers to the famous lighthouse at Alexandria (so Boyce 1958: 76).

[60] *BMCRE Alexandria*, 1.167.

[61] Milne 1923, nos. 2,288–91. There is a good image of the coin at the *RPC* online site (http://rpc. ashmus.ox.ac.uk), temporary number 13,846; there the standing goddess is identified as Isis Euploia (following Milne). Boyce 1958: 71–2 argues persuasively that the goddess represents Euthenia, the Greek personification of the Roman imperial grain supply.

attested only under Antoninus, which may reveal an effort to ensure more effective coordination between the ports at Puteoli and Ostia in the storage and distribution of imperial grain.[62] In light of this extensive and varied evidence, we may speak with some justification of a large-scale imperial policy of developing the Mediterranean's ports, harbors, and commercial infrastructure, begun by Trajan and Hadrian and reaching its culmination in the reign of Antoninus.[63] It was precisely this sort of state intervention that facilitated the Mediterranean-wide availability of agricultural produce during our period, a benefit of empire celebrated by Aristides and others and reflected in the conspicuous prominence of Annona and Ceres types on the imperial coinage of Antoninus.

In addition to grain and agricultural abundance, the other principal material benefit advertised on the imperial coinage was public building. The depiction of buildings, monuments, and other public structures on Roman coins is a topic of perennial interest, attracting sustained attention from numismatists, topographers, and architectural historians.[64] Nearly every discussion of the pertinent methodological issues can be summarized in just two points. First, the appearance of a building or monument on a coin does not by itself prove that the structure was even begun, much less completed.[65] And second, the representation of buildings and monuments on coins does not aim for documentary accuracy, but rather seeks to capture the idea or symbolic message of the building. The variable number of columns shown on the front façade of the same temple is enough to demonstrate that we cannot look to Roman coins for a "photographic" reproduction of the buildings and monuments they depict.[66] It is also worth noting that some structures, such as imperial roads, were represented by means of metonymy, through personifications with identifying legends.

In the extensive scholarship on the depiction of buildings on Roman coins, there has not been much attention to questions of motive, intent, and overall patterning in the numismatic representation of building and

---

[62] *CIL* 11.562 = *ILS* 344 (Puteoli, AD 138–61): *pro salute | imp(eratoris) Caesaris Titi Aelii | Hadriani Antonini Aug(usti) Pii p(atris) p(atriae) et | M(arci) Alli (sic) Aureli Caesaris n(ostri) | Genio coloniae Puteolanorum | Chrysanthus Aug(usti) disp(ensator) a fruminto (sic) | Puteolis et Ostis | l(ocus) d(ecreto) decurionium permissu.* See briefly Rickman 1980: 222–3.

[63] Purcell 1996 discusses Mediterranean ports and Rome's *façade maritime*, with references to earlier and more specialized literature; additional bibliography in Horden and Purcell 2000: 619–20.

[64] General studies of buildings and monuments on Roman coins in Fuchs 1969; Hill 1989; Burnett 1999; see also the 1973 exhibition catalogue, *Bauten Roms auf Münzen und Medaillen* (Munich).

[65] Good discussion of "projected buildings" on Roman coins in Prayon 1982.

[66] See Drew-Bear 1974 on the representation of temples, also pointing to discrepancies in the depiction of the cult statue (usually shown as visible from outside the temple between a gap in the middle columns, though in reality such statues were normally enclosed by the cella wall) and the architrave (often omitted entirely).

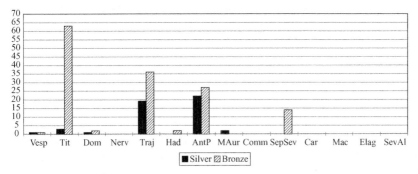

Figure 3.2 Relative frequency of building types on denarii and base-metal coins, expressed as a percentage of object types per reign, AD 69–235 (N = 15,025)

monuments, nor to such imagery as a distinctive feature of Roman civic identity.[67] Another critical issue that has been more or less unrecognized is the rarity of building types on the Roman imperial coinage. Only Burnett has drawn attention to this problem.[68] The data are startling. On Roman imperial denarii minted between 69 and 235, building, monuments, and other structures in Rome make up less than 1 percent of all types. Even on sestertii, with their larger surface areas, and other base-metal denominations, which circulated in large quantities in the city of Rome itself, building types only make up about 1 percent of all types.[69] And even when we isolate object types as a whole, the iconographic category to which building types belong, the relative frequency of such types for the period 69–235 is low. When measured as a percentage of these object types – which were themselves not very common (just 9 percent on denarii, and 7 percent on the base-metal coins) – the building types still comprise only 7 percent of all object types on denarii and 17 percent of all object types on the base-metal coins.[70]

Measuring the fluctuating relative frequency of building types on a reign-by-reign basis provides a useful perspective on the data (figure 3.2).[71] As

[67] Exceptions include Burnett 1999 and Marsano 2009.   [68] Burnett 1999: 156.

[69] Denarii: 881 building types out of a total of 142,798 types (0.6 percent); bronze: 450 building types out of a total of 36,487 types (1.2 percent). For totals and tabulations of individual types, see appendices 3 (silver) and 4 (bronze).

[70] Denarii: 881 building types out of a total of 12,343 object types (7.1 percent); bronze: 450 building types out of a total of 2,682 object types (16.8 percent). For the percentage of object types among all types, see above, Int. Part 1, 34.

[71] Compare Burnett 1999: 161, table 3 (based on data in Hill 1989), listing the total number of different buildings depicted on coins from Rome, from the Republic through the 4th century; note that this is a very different form of tabulation from the measurement of the relative frequency of all building types.

we would expect, such types were always more common on the base-metal coins than on the silver. This is partly a result of the larger surface area of the sestertius, which allowed for more ambitious visual representations of monumental structures (e.g. the Flavian Amphitheater), and partly a result of the greater concentration of such base-metal coins in Rome.[72] The data also show that it was really only under Trajan and Antoninus Pius that types representing buildings and monuments were relatively prominent amongst the object types.[73] The peaks and valleys in the graph, then, do not correspond very well to the changing scale of building activity in the city of Rome. Domitian and Hadrian launched massive public building programs in Rome, but building types are rare on the coinages of both, while Antoninus Pius, on whose coinage such types were not uncommon, built very little.[74] Nor does the selection of specific types for particular emphasis meet our expectations. Among Trajan's building types, for example, the most common, on both silver and base-metal coins, was Trajan's Column (illustration 3.6), which was of course one of the defining monuments of his reign; also relatively common, on the silver, was the Via Traiana (personified, with identifying legend), and on the bronze, an unidentified octastyle temple and an unidentified bridge.[75] Minted in quite small numbers, by contrast, were coins representing several major Trajanic works, including the Forum of Trajan, the Basilica Ulpia, and the harbor at Portus.[76] From these patterns in type selection we can only conclude that Trajan's coinage was not employed as a major vehicle for celebrating his most significant public buildings.[77]

---

[72] Flavian Amphitheater: *RIC* 2, Titus 110. On the circulation patterns of bronze coins, see above, 33–4; cf. Marsano 2009.

[73] The sample of base-metal coins minted under Titus included only eight types depicting objects (five of which were building types), so the figures for Titus must be regarded as inconclusive (and are probably misleading).

[74] For Domitianic construction in Rome, see Darwall-Smith 1996: 101–252; for Hadrian, Boatwright 1987.

[75] Column of Trajan: *RIC* 2, Trajan 235, 238–9, 292–3, 307, 313, 356, 379, 579–80, 600–3, 677–80, 683, with Hill 1989: 57–8. Via Traiana: *RIC* 2, Trajan 266–7. Octastyle temple: *RIC* 2, Trajan 575–6. It is not clear which temple (if any) is being represented by this type. Strack 1931–37: 1.147–9 suggests that this is a temple for the Deified Nerva (but there is no other evidence for such a structure); Hill 1989: 9–10 argues for either a temple of Honos in Regio I, or a generic temple symbolizing Trajan's building activity in Rome. Bridge: *RIC* 2, Trajan 569–70. Again, the identification of this structure is problematic. Strack, followed by Mattingly, argues for a bridge over the Danube (cf. Dio 68.13), alluding to Trajan's conquest of Dacia (1931–7: 1.127–9), while Hill suggests the Pons Sublicius in Rome (1989: 105–6).

[76] Forum of Trajan: *RIC* 2, Trajan 255–7 (aurei), 630, 654, with Hill 1989: 42–43. Basilica Ulpia: *RIC* 2, Trajan 246–8 (aurei), 616–18, with Hill 1989: 43–4. Portus: *RIC* 2, Trajan 471, 631–2.

[77] For Trajan's building types in general, see discussion in Strack 1931–37: 1.145–54, 202–7, 211–13; Mattingly in *BMCRE* III, ci–cii; Marsano 2009.

Illustration 3.6 Reverse of denarius (*RIC* 2, Trajan 292): Trajan's Column. SPQR
OPTIMO PRINCIPI

This conclusion can perhaps be generalized for building types as a whole on the Roman imperial coinage. It seems that such types were intended not so much to advertise periods of intense building activity or to publicize specific monuments – though clearly they could serve these functions, too – but rather to commemorate the symbolic centrality of the empire's capital city and magnify its ideological resonance. Rome, the "city of wonders" where visitors could experience marvels from every corner of the empire, could itself be construed as a benefit of empire, and it was primarily this experience of imperial centrality, I would like to suggest, that building types were designed to evoke.[78] Viewed in this light, the peaks in the relative prominence of building types under Trajan and Antoninus may be seen as the reflection of a broader discourse in the first half of the second century on the centrality of Rome, punctuated in 148 by the celebration of the nine hundredth anniversary of the founding of the city, an official emphasis temporarily disrupted by a pronounced drop in such types under Hadrian, who celebrated the world of the provinces instead, and whose famous province series on the imperial coinage effectively replaced the

---

[78] For imperial Rome as "city of wonders," see Purcell 2000, esp. 405–23.

Rome-centered types of his predecessor and successor.[79] But it must be emphasized that the moderate emphasis on building types under Trajan and Antoninus was anomalous. In general, building types were extremely rare, and were surely overwhelmed by the mass of other types in circulation at any one time.

Neither types representing grain and agricultural abundance, then, nor those representing public buildings, were very prominent on the Roman imperial coinage. There are several reasons why such material benefit types were not more common. First, much of the work of advertising the material benefits of empire was done by the attributes and adjuncts associated with other ideals (see below). Second, types representing both the *annona* and monuments in Rome were perhaps too Rome-centered for an empire-wide medium of communications. The message of the *annona* could be universalized, as we have seen, and building types could stand for civic benefaction in general, but it is nevertheless unlikely that such types resonated very strongly with provincials or soldiers stationed on the frontiers.[80] In addition, material benefits often stood as their own best advertisement. Grain and public buildings, in other words, were themselves tangible evidence of the benefits of empire, and so did not really require further official publicity in order to promulgate the underlying message of imperial benefaction. But another and more compelling explanation lies in the very nature of imperial representation. The provision of material goods was of course a vital component of Roman imperial ideology, but such goods held little emotional appeal or affective force. And when it came to the official communication of imperial benefits, the imperial regime placed a higher degree of emphasis, as I will argue, on the personal, spiritual, and psychological benefits that came with Roman imperial rule.

THE SOCIAL DISTRIBUTION OF IMPERIAL BENEFITS

To an even greater extent than the virtues examined in the last chapter, the numerous benefits of empire and monarchy, and their underlying messages, overlapped and reinforced one another, evident both in the frequent collocation of the relevant terms in literary texts and in the regular sharing of attributes and adjuncts in official iconography. In addition, there were more benefits than virtues represented on the imperial coinage between

---

[79] 900th anniversary: *HA AntP.* 10.8–9. On Hadrian's province series, see Strack 1931–37: 2.139–66; Mattingly in *BMCRE* III, cxlii–cxliv, clxxi–clxxxi; cf. Ando 2000: 318–20.

[80] For the circulation patterns and intended audience(s) of imperial coins, see below, chapter 4.

69 and 235, and the hierarchies reflected in the relative frequencies with which these benefit types were produced were generally less pronounced. And these relative frequencies, as we have seen, were quite similar across the denominations. An exception to this pattern comes with the Pax, Concordia, Fortuna, and Salus types, which stand out from the other benefit types, and from most of the virtue types, in their discrepant frequencies between silver and bronze, with Pax and Concordia more common on the former, and Fortuna and Salus more common on the latter. In order to assess the significance of this patterning in the data, we should begin with an analysis of the ideals themselves.

Pax

Pax had a dual meaning.[81] Within Roman civil society, *pax* referred to the absence of civil war. This "domestic" or "civilian" *pax*, often glossed as *pax civilis* ("civic peace"), was the sort of *pax* that, following the convulsions of civil conflict, "brought back cultivation to the fields, respect for religion, and safety to men," in the words of Velleius Paterculus.[82] As such, *pax civilis* was frequently grouped together with other civic ideals such as *otium* ("leisure, repose"), *iustitia* ("justice"), and *concordia* ("harmony, concord").[83] The close connection between this civilian *pax* and domestic concord is most explicit in the writings of Cicero. As he writes, "When there is a lack of *concordia*, there is no *pax civilis* at all."[84]

Pax in this domestic and civilian sense – essentially the absence of civil war and conflict – comes close to our modern, moral understanding of the word "peace." But it must not be confused with the sort of *pax* that the Romans imposed upon conquered peoples. This other, militaristic *pax*, which originally referred to a "pact" concluding a war (from the verb *pacisci*, "to make an agreement"), but which came to take on the more general meaning of capitulation to Rome, was the product of foreign conquest and depended on the military *virtus* of the Roman soldiers and generals who had brought it about. This "imperialist" *pax* came to the fore with the

---

[81] The literary evidence for *pax* is collected in *TLL* 10.1.6.863–78. For discussion of the term's meaning, see Weinstock 1960; Jal 1961; Gruen 1985; Woolf 1993; Kuttner 1995: 104–06; Noreña 2003, esp. 34–5; Barton 2007.

[82] Vell. Pat. 2.89.3: *finita . . . bella civilia . . . revocata pax . . . rediit cultus agris, sacris honos, securitas hominibus.*

[83] *Pax* and *otium*: Cic. *Agr.* 1.8.23, *Mur.* 1.1.78, *Att.* 9.11A.1 (SB 178A); Tac. *Agr.* 1.24. *Pax* and *iustitia*: Sen. *Clem.* 1.19.8: *sub quo* (sc. the good monarch) *iustitia, pax, pudicitia, securitas, dignitas florent.* For *pax* and *concordia*, see below, nn. 105, 112.

[84] Cic. *Phil.* 7.23.

emergence of monarchy at Rome. In the *Res Gestae*, for example, in the same rubric in which his closures of the Temple of Janus are recorded, Augustus highlights the foundation of military might upon which the *pax Romana* rested, as *pax* is unambiguously presented as the result of military victory: "peace gained through military victories" (*parta victoriis pax*).[85] Similarly, the Ara Pacis Augustae was a monument not to domestic concord, but to imperialism and the military pacification of the *oikoumenē*.[86] In just the same way, Vespasian's Templum Pacis was not intended to celebrate the termination of the civil war of AD 69, as is often claimed, but rather to commemorate the military victory over Judaea, housing the spoils taken from Jerusalem and displayed in the triumph of Vespasian and Titus in 71, and therefore publicizing the pacification of foreign peoples and the power of the Roman war machine under the guidance of the Flavian dynasty.[87] This was evidently the sort of *pax* that Tacitus had in mind when he assigned to the Caledonian chieftain Calgacus the famous phrase, "they make a wasteland and call it peace," a *pax Romana* that was not a desirable condition at all, but an object of fear.[88]

On the imperial coinage, *pax* was represented as a female personification, and her defining attribute was the olive branch, the principle symbol of peace (illustration 3.7).[89] Other attributes associated with Pax included the scepter, emblem of supreme authority; the cornucopia, symbol of abundance; and the caduceus, which she shared with Felicitas (see below, p. 170), evoking the world of commerce and exchange (illustration 3.8).[90]

[85] *RG* 13. The military aspects of *pax* are examined in Gruen 1985, a study of *pax* in Augustus' public image; for a more general treatment of this theme, see also Gruen 1996, esp. 188–94; cf. Woolf 1993 and Barton 2007 on the imperialist ethos encapsulated by the notion of *pax Romana*.

[86] So Gruen 1985: 61–2 and 1996: 193–4; cf. Kuttner 1995: 104–6, who argues that the children depicted on the procession friezes represent barbarian youths – the *pacati* themselves. For iconographic analysis of the visual program of the Ara Pacis, see in general Rehak 2006: 96–137, with ample bibliography.

[87] Noreña 2003. As an anonymous reviewer for the Press points out, imperial monuments often embraced multiple levels of allusion, and it is not impossible that some contemporaries associated the Templum Pacis with the cessation of the civil war of AD 69. But this does not appear to have been the official message of the complex. For the spoils taken from Jerusalem, see Joseph. *BJ* 7.162.

[88] Tac. *Agr.* 30.4: *solitudinem faciunt, pacem appellant*; *Ann.* 12.33: *qui pacem nostram metuebant*; cf. *Agr.* 20.1.

[89] Pax and olive branch: e.g. *RIC* 2, Vespasian 18; *RIC* 2, Titus 113; *RIC* 2, Domitian 452; *RIC* 2, Nerva 66; *RIC* 2, Trajan 16; *RIC* 2, Hadrian 7; *RIC* 3, Antoninus Pius 78; *RIC* 3, Marcus Aurelius 145; *RIC* 3, Commodus 17; *RIC* 4.1, Septimius Severus 37; *RIC* 4.1, Caracalla 184; *RIC* 4.2, Elagabalus 262; *RIC* 4.2, Severus Alexander 164–8. For the *pax* type on the imperial coinage, see briefly Strack 1931–37: 1.52–6; Mattingly in *BMCRE* III, xxxviii, xlvii.

[90] Pax and scepter: e.g. *RIC* 2, Vespasian 18; *RIC* 2, Nerva 66; *RIC* 2, Trajan 16; *RIC* 2, Hadrian 770; *RIC* 3, Antoninus Pius 200a–c; *RIC* 3, Commodus 30; *RIC* 4.1, Septimius Severus 283; *RIC* 4.1, Caracalla 138; *RIC* 4.2, Elagabalus 262; *RIC* 4.2, Severus Alexander 164–8. Pax and cornucopia:

Illustration 3.7 Reverse of denarius
(*RIC* 3, Antoninus Pius 117): Pax holding
an olive branch and a cornucopia

Illustration 3.8 Reverse of as (*RIC* 2, Titus
129): Pax holding a caduceus and a branch.
PAX AUGUST

The imperialist roots of *pax* had no place in this official iconography, which instead publicized the material benefits of the *pax Romana*.[91] Nor do the legends emphasize the military dimension of *pax*, declaring simply PAX AUGUSTA/I, PAX AETERNA ("Eternal Peace"), or, most frequently, just PAX.[92] An excellent visual expression of this non-military *pax* is the type minted under Caracalla with the rather martial legend FUNDA-TOR PACIS ("Founder of Peace"), but depicting the emperor holding a branch and wearing a toga, the latter an unambiguous marker of the civilian sphere.[93] Only on those few types on which Pax is represented with symbols from the military sphere, such as weaponry or a statuette of Victory (illustration 3.9), is the imperialist strand of *pax Romana* visible on the imperial coinage.[94] Otherwise the main message of the Pax type is the prevalence of peaceful conditions rather than the processes that had brought them about – surely more appropriate than images of conquest and subjugation as an advertised benefit of empire.

[91] e.g. *RIC* 2, Vespasian 403; *RIC* 2, Titus 94; *RIC* 2, Trajan 6; *RIC* 2, Hadrian 7; *RIC* 3, Antoninus Pius 78; *RIC* 3, Marcus Aurelius 145; *RIC* 3, Commodus 17; *RIC* 4.1, Septimius Severus 37; *RIC* 4.2, Elagabalus 29. Pax and caduceus: e.g. *RIC* 2, Vespasian 776; *RIC* 2, Titus 113; *RIC* 2, Domitian 452; *RIC* 3, Antoninus Pius 130; *RIC* 3, Commodus 210.

[91] The same was true of the iconography of Pax in the private sphere, as one would expect; for an excellent overview, see *LIMC* 7.1.204–12, 7.2.134–8 (E. Simon).

[92] See indices to *RIC* or *BMCRE*.

[93] *RIC* 4.1, Caracalla 154a.

[94] Pax and military imagery: e.g. *RIC* 2, Trajan 190a (standing on Dacian); *RIC* 2, Hadrian 95 (holding Victoria); *RIC* 4.1, Caracalla 138 (seated between helmet and cuirass).

Illustration 3.9 Reverse of denarius (*RIC* 2, Hadrian 95): Pax holding a statuette of
Victory and a branch

Pax was at the center of a much wider circle of ideals and values. Three
ideals associated with *pax* that were also advertised on the imperial coinage
as benefits of empire were *securitas*, *tranquillitas*, and *concordia*. *Securitas*
normally meant freedom from undesirable conditions, whether from dis-
agreeable feelings, such as anxiety or worry, or from physical danger.[95] It was
not primarily a military concept. In Frontinus' *De aquaeductu urbis Romae*,
for example, the post of *curator aquarum* is called "a duty concerning the
securitas of the city," clearly referring to the material welfare of the city's
inhabitants, and in Pliny's *Panegyricus*, *securitas* is conjoined to *libertas*,
and placed alongside *alimenta* and *congiaria*, in a list of things one would
expect from a "good" emperor.[96] *Securitas*, then, referred mainly to internal
or domestic safety and stability and, like so many other imperial values, was
often attributed to the emperor himself.[97] *Tranquillitas* originally referred

---

[95] *OLD*, s.v., esp. § 1, "freedom from anxiety or care, calmness," and § 3, "freedom from danger, safety,
security." *Securitas* could also refer to the security for the payment of a debt (§ 5), and could even
be used negatively, to denote carelessness (§ 2).

[96] Front. *Aq.* 1: *officium ad securitatem urbis pertinens*; cf. Tac. *Ann.* 15.18: *securitas annonae*. Plin.
Pan. 27.1: *magnum quidem est educandi incitamentum tollere liberos in spem alimentorum, in spem
congiariorum; maius tamen in spem libertatis, in spem securitatis*. For the intimate connection between
securitas, *pax*, and *libertas*, see Wickert 1954: 2,096–8; cf. Wirszubski 1950: 158–9.

[97] See, for example, Suet. *Tit.* 6.2: *quibus rebus sicut in posterum securitati satis cavit*, referring to
Titus' murder of Aulus Caecina and the prevention of civil conflict (since Caecina, according to

Illustration 3.11 Reverse of denarius
(*RIC* 2, Hadrian 222): Tranquillitas
holding a scepter. TRANQUILLITAS
AUG

Illustration 3.10 Reverse of sestertius
(*RIC* 3, Antoninus Pius 641): Securitas
holding a scepter. SECURITAS
PUBLICA

to fair weather and specifically to calmness on the sea, but it came to denote
the calmness of affairs, especially in terms of domestic politics at Rome.[98]
Like *felicitas* it could serve as a catchword for pleasant times – *tranquillitas
temporum, tranquillitas rerum,* or *tranquillitas saeculi* – and as such was
easily associated with other characteristics of civic serenity and quiet such
as *pax* and *otium*, and, as always, with the personal agency of the emperor.[99]
On the coinage, both *securitas* and *tranquillitas* were represented as female
personifications with various attributes, but the most common attribute for
each was the scepter (illustrations 3.10–11), which they shared with Pax.[100]
In general, the numismatic iconography of both Securitas and Tranquillitas

Suetonius, had been preparing to read an inflammatory speech to the troops). Here *securitas* refers
not to protection against a foreign enemy but to the preservation of peaceful conditions in the
civic sphere. For the connection between the emperor and *securitas*, see, e.g., Vell. Pat. 2.103.4:
spem conceptam perpetuae securitatis aeternitatisque Romani imperii; Plin. *Pan.* 50.7: *tanta benignitas
principis, tanta securitas temporum est.*
[98] *OLD*, s.v., esp. § 2, "quiet condition or state of affairs."
[99] Cic. *Att.* 1.20.2 (SB 20): *ad tranquillitatem meorum temporum*; Liv. 4.12.6: *sequitur hanc tranquillitatem rerum annus . . . periculo insignis.* Tac. *Agr.* 1.24: *summam tranquillitatem pacis atque oti.*
Emperor and *tranquillitas*: Plin. *Ep.* 10.3a.2: *tranquillitas saeculi tui* (sc. Trajan).
[100] Securitas with scepter: e.g. *RIC* 2, Vespasian 22a; *RIC* 2, Titus 82; *RIC* 2, Hadrian 271; *RIC* 3,
Antoninus Pius 640–1; *RIC* 3, Marcus Aurelius 325; *RIC* 3, Commodus 23; *RIC* 4.1, Caracalla
43–44a–b; *RIC* 4.1, Elagabalus 121; *RIC* 4.2, Macrinus 90–1; *RIC* 4.2, Severus Alexander 611–14;
for the iconography, *LIMC* 8.1.1,090–3, 8.2.732–3 (U. W. Gottschall). Tranquillitas with scepter:
e.g. *RIC* 2, Hadrian 222–3. See Mattingly in *BMCRE* ii, xlviii, iii, xcvii, n. 2 (Securitas); iii, cxl
(Tranquillitas); for the iconography, *LIMC* 8.1.50–1, 8.2.28–9 (R. Vollkommer).

was emblematic of the civilian, not military, sphere.[101] Both semantic and iconographic overlap, then, bound *pax, securitas,* and *tranquillitas* together as closely related benefits of empire. The latter two types, however, were very rare (cf. tables 3.1–2).

Concordia

Another ideal with which *pax* was closely associated was *concordia*.[102] *Concordia* normally meant the condition of "union" or "entente" between men, especially political partisans, or between spouses.[103] During the Republic, *concordia* in political discourse often referred to the union between potential rivals that produced "harmony" in the state – musical harmony, in fact, was just the metaphor Cicero employed to describe this ideal condition.[104] In the often violent conflicts of the late Republic, *concordia* was naturally a highly charged and topical theme with important religious, political, and social dimensions. Together with *pax,* it could serve as a sort of shorthand for social and political stability, especially in the writings of Cicero.[105] And though the term does not appear in the *Res Gestae,* Augustus' claim to have controlled the state "through the consensus of all men" clearly reflects the importance attached to concord as a basis for political action.[106]

The emergence of monarchy eventually gave rise to a number of new usages for the term *concordia,* all related to the concerns of the imperial

---

[101] It should be noted that a military sense of *securitas* does begin to emerge in the Severan period, reflected in the legend SECURITAS IMPERI (e.g. *RIC* 4.1, Caracalla 168; *RIC* 4.1, Geta 20a–b).

[102] See *TLL* 4.83.22–87.39. On *concordia* in the Roman political lexicon, see Jal 1961; Amit 1962; Hellegouarc'h 1963: 81–5, 125–7; Béranger 1973 (1969): 367–82; Weinstock 1971: 260–6; Levick 1978; Zanzarri 1997 (mainly on the coin type).

[103] *Concordia* between political partisans: Cic. *Att.* 8.15A.1 (SB 165A), Balbus to Cicero: *obsecro te . . . ut Caesarem et Pompeium . . . in pristinam concordiam reducas; Leg. Agr.* 2.103; *Phil.* 3.2; Liv. 3.33.8, 4.7.1, 10.22.4 (*ex concordia consulum*); Vell. Pat. 2.47.2; Luc. 1.98; Sen. *Ep.* 95.72; further references in *TLL* 4.84.49–86.4. *Concordia* between spouses: e.g. Plaut. *Amph.* 475; Cic. *Cluent.* 12; Catull. 66.87; Tac. *Agr.* 6; Plin. *Ep.* 3.16.10.

[104] Cic. *Rep.* 2.69: *quae harmonia a musicis dicitur in cantu, ea est in civitate concordia*; cf. 1.49.

[105] Cic. *Agr.* 1.8.23: *nihil tam populare quam pacem, quam concordiam, quam otium reperiemus; Mur.* 1.1: *pacem, tranquillitatem, otium concordiamque;* 37.78: *pacis, oti, concordiae; Att.* 9.11A.1 (SB 178A): *de otio, de pace, de concordia civium;* 9.11A.3: *me . . . et pacis . . . amicum et ad civium concordiam . . . quam accommodatissimum;* cf. *Deit.* 4.11, *Fat.* 1.2, *Phil.* 4.15.40, 10.4.8, *Att.* 9.9.2 (SB 176), *Fam.* 4.2.3 (SB 151), *Phil.* 2.10.24, 4.16.4. Note also that in early 49 BC, as civil war loomed, Cicero considered writing a treatise on *concordia: Att.* 8.11.7 (SB 161); cf. Weinstock 1971: 264. Other writers, too, picked up the theme: cf. [Sall.] *Ep. ad Caes.* 1.6.5; *Hist.* 1.55.24M, 1.77.5M, 1.77.10M; Liv. 4.10.8, 9.19.17. Further passages in Jal 1961: 217, nn. 11–12, 220, nn. 6–8, 221, nn. 1–9.

[106] Aug. *RG* 34.1: *per consensus universorum potitus rerum omnium;* cf. 25.2: *iuravit in mea verba tota Italia sponte sua.* Note that Caesar, too, largely eschews the term *concordia* in his writings, preferring the term *consensus* (cf. Weinstock 1971: 263, nn. 6–9).

house, a transformation announced right at the beginning of the imperial period by Tiberius' rededication of the Temple of Concordia in
AD 10 or 12 as the Temple of Concordia Augusta.[107] With the decline of
independent senatorial authority and concurrent ascent to power of those
individuals who had privileged access to the emperor, especially emperors'
wives, *concordia* within the imperial family, above all between emperor
and empress, became paramount. Indeed, the symbolism of domestic *concordia* between the imperial couple was potent. For just as this *concordia*
expressed the harmonious conjugal union between emperor and empress,
so too did this conjugal union itself symbolize the *concordia* that prevailed
within the state.[108] Official emphasis on the domestic *concordia* between
emperor and empress first arose under Antoninus Pius and Marcus Aurelius, reflected in the regular production of imperial coins with obverse
portraits of empresses and reverse designs of the personification Concordia
or, in more concrete terms, vignettes depicting imperial spouses in the
traditional marital pose of *dextrarum iunctio*, always accompanied by the
personification of Concordia, and sometimes glossed by the legend CON-
CORDIA (illustration 3.12).[109] But imperial *concordia* was not limited to
marital harmony. Out of the military struggles of 69, for example, came
the new ideal of "the harmony of the soldiers" (*concordia exercituum*), as
both Vitellius and Vespasian sought to proclaim the unanimity of their
armed support.[110] That the theme of *concordia exercituum* continued even
during periods of stability, as under Antoninus Pius, shows that *concordia*
was not always a desperate plea or tendentious claim, as scholars often
imply, but could be a publicized benefit of empire that corresponded to
real conditions.[111] And here we may note the continuity into the imperial period of the late-Republican association between *concordia* and *pax*,
especially in the writings of Tacitus.[112] Finally, the development of two or
more emperors ruling simultaneously placed an especially high premium

---

[107] Temple of Concordia Augusta: Ov. *Fast.* 1.647–8; *Fast. Praen.* 115, *Fast. Verul.* 161 (*Inscr. Ital.* 13.2);
Dio 56.25.1; Suet. *Tib.* 20. See briefly Béranger 1973: 380; Levick 1978: 224. For the temple itself,
LTUR 1.316–20 (Ferroni); Packer 2010.

[108] So Béranger: "la Concorde symbolise-t-elle l'union conjugale ou l'union conjugale symbolise-t-elle
la Concorde? Passer de l'alternative au dilemme serait méconnaître la psychologie romaine. Les
deux opérations mentales allaient à la recontre l'une de l'autre et s'entremêlaient" (1973: 379).

[109] Empresses and *concordia*: *RIC* 3, Antoninus Pius 328–30, 335–7, 1,074–6 (Faustina I); *RIC* 3,
Marcus Aurelius 1,625–7 (Faustina II). Imperial spouses: *RIC* 3, Antoninus Pius 402, 434, 441, 1253
(Faustina II and Marcus Aurelius). On this visual program of imperial *concordia*, and the larger
ideological context of which it was a part, see Noreña 2007b, esp. 308–11.

[110] Zanzarri 1997: 44 (Vitellius), 49 (Vespasian), with references.

[111] Cf. Béranger 1973: 375; Levick 1978: 229.

[112] E.g. *Hist.* 1.56.6, 2.20.4, 3.70.6, 3.80.4; cf. Curt. 10.8.23.

Illustration 3.12 Obverse and reverse of sestertius (*RIC* 3, Antoninus Pius 601): Obverse: portrait of Antoninus Pius. Reverse: Antoninus Pius and Faustina I in the marital pose of *dextrarum iunctio* ("a joining of the right hands"); between them, Marcus Aurelius and Faustina II in the marital pose of *dextrarum iunctio*. CONCORDIAE

on *concordia*, as harmony within the state depended to a large extent on harmony between the two emperors, *concordia Augustorum.*[113]

Like the other benefits of empire, *concordia* was primarily represented on the imperial coinage as a female personification with a range of attributes.[114] Her identifying attributes were the patera and the cornucopia (illustration 3.13), the former alluding to the act of sacrifice and, indirectly, to divine support for imperial harmony, and the latter to the material abundance that arises from stable conditions.[115] This iconography is not particularly illuminating for the underlying messages of imperial *concordia*. More informative are several of the legends accompanying the Concordia type between 69 and 235, especially when combined with more striking designs. In addition to CONCORDIA and CONCORDIA AUG(USTI/A), which are very common, we find CONCORDIA EXERCITUUM and CONCORDIA MILITUM, which advertised the (putative) military harmony and consensus of the legions upon which the stability of the state ultimately depended;

[113] Amit 1962: 153; Béranger 1973: 379–80; Zanzarri 1997: 61–2.
[114] For a comprehensive discussion of the iconography of Concordia in all media, see *LIMC* 5.1.479–98, 5.2.333–40 (T. Hölscher). Zanzarri 1997 provides a convenient overview of the Concordia coin type on the imperial coinage.
[115] Concordia with *patera* and cornucopia: e.g. *RIC* 2, Vespasian 43; *RIC* 2, Titus 112a–c; *RIC* 2, Trajan 2; *RIC* 2, Hadrian 799; *RIC* 3, Antoninus Pius 66; *RIC* 3, Marcus Aurelius 1–6; *RIC* 3, Commodus 278 (Crispina); *RIC* 4.1, Septimius Severus 313–14; *RIC* 4.1, Caracalla 580 (Plautilla); *RIC* 4.2, Elagabalus 210 (Julia Paula); *RIC* 4.2, Severus Alexander 275.

Illustration 3.13 Reverse of denarius (*RIC* 3, Antoninus Pius 335): Concordia holding a
patera and a cornucopia. CONCORDIA AUG

CONCORDIA SENATUI ("Harmony of the Senate"), on a sestertius of
Vespasian depicting a personification of the senate crowning the emperor;
CONCORDIA COMMODI ("Harmony of Commodus"), with an image
of Commodus holding patera and scepter; CONCORDIA AUGUST-
ORUM ("Harmony of the Emperors"), as on denarii minted in 161 showing
Marcus Aurelius and Lucius Verus facing one another and clasping hands
(illustration 3.14); and CONCORDIA FELIX ("Propitious Harmony")
and CONCORDIA AETERNA ("Eternal Harmony"), on types showing
Severan emperors and empresses in the pose of *dextrarum iunctio*, recalling
the Antonine imagery of marital bliss in the imperial household.[116] As these
types suggest, *concordia* as an advertised benefit of empire belonged to the
world of the imperial court, high politics, and the army, and denoted the
harmony prevailing between these powerful individuals and institutions.
And it was precisely that harmony that underpinned the stability of the
empire as a whole.

[116] CONCORDIA EXERCITUUM/MILITUM: e.g. *RIC* 2, Nerva 2–3; *RIC* 2, Hadrian 581a–e; *RIC*
4.1, Septimius Severus 256. CONCORDIA SENATUI: *RIC* 2, Vespasian 418. CONCORDIA
COMMODI: e.g. *RIC* 3, Commodus 198a–b. CONCORDIA FELIX/AETERNA: e.g. *RIC* 4.1,
Septimius Severus 547 (Julia Augusta); *RIC* 4.1 Caracalla 123–4; *RIC* 4.2, Elagabalus 386–7 (Julia
Paula).

Illustration 3.14 Obverse and reverse of aureus (*RIC* 3, Marcus Aurelius 42): Obverse: portrait of Marcus Aurelius. Reverse: Marcus Aurelius and Lucius Verus clasping hands. CONCORDIA AUGUSTORUM

Fortuna

Sometimes conceptualized as a goddess, other times as a protean force or *numen* beyond human control, *fortuna* was usually seen as a superhuman agent that could impinge at any time on the affairs, large or small, of individuals, groups, institutions, places, or peoples.[117] It could also refer simply to a given condition or set of circumstances or, in a passive sense, to effects in general.[118] The countless manifestations of this multifaceted quality, especially when construed as an active agent in the affairs of men, tend to fall into one of two broad conceptions of Fortune, the one emphasizing the unpredictable, fickle, and frequently malevolent workings of "chance," and the other imagining this force as a benevolent goddess, the bringer of "good luck." The "fickle" conception of *fortuna* developed under the influence of Greek *tychē*.[119] This sort of *fortuna* denoted the unexpected and

---

[117] For the literary evidence for *fortuna*, see *TLL* 6.5.1175.48–1195.65. For discussions of the term's meaning and usage, and the public cult of Fortuna, see Erkell 1952: 129–82; Combès 1966: 408–34, esp. 424–34; Weinstock 1971: 112–26; Kajanto 1981; Champeaux 1982–1987. The papers in Matheson 1994 examine Fortuna/Tychē in the visual record. For the coin type, see Mattingly in *BMCRE* ii, xxxvii–xxxviii, iii, lxxiv, n. 1.

[118] *Fortuna* as condition or circumstances: e.g. Cic. *Inv.* 2.30: *et ex fortuna saepe argumentatio nascitur, cum servus an liber, pecuniosus an pauper, nobilis an ignobilis, felix an infelix, privatus an in potestate sit aut fuerit aut futurus sit, consideratur. Fortunae*, plural, often meant simply "effects," though it is sometimes difficult to distinguish between active and passive senses of the term; cf. *TLL* 6.5.1176.71–22, 1179.81–1181.44.

[119] For Hellenistic *tychē*, and its influence on Roman conceptions of *fortuna*, see Erkell 1952: 131–46; Kajanto 1981: 525–32; Champeaux 1982–87: 2.37–59.

incalculable occurrences that somehow altered the flow of events. It was often a harmful and malicious force, especially in the context of warfare, in which unpredictable occurrences frequently wrought havoc with the best laid strategic plans and most brilliant tactical arrangements.[120] Malevolent *fortuna* was also credited with the rise and especially downfall of powerful men, such as Sejanus, and of states, especially with respect to the moral decline and eventual collapse of the Roman Republic.[121]

Fortuna could also be seen, by contrast, as a benign and non-arbitrary force – not as mere chance, that is, for which Latin had other words (*fors*, *casus*), but as a benevolent agent that brought good luck in a consistent or "logical" manner. This conception belongs to the earliest stratum of Roman *fortuna*, uninfluenced by Greek *tychē*.[122] *Fortuna* in this sense overlapped with the idea of a "guardian spirit" (*genius*), and could often be used interchangeably with *felicitas*, "good fortune." It was both communal and individual. Especially significant for Roman writers was the conceit of the *Fortuna populi Romani* (or *rei publicae*), the supernatural force that systematically advanced the interests of the Roman state as a whole.[123] This "benevolent" *fortuna* could also denote the good luck that attended favored individuals, an idea that flourished during the late Republic, as Sulla, Pompey, and Caesar promoted an association between their own exploits, above all in the military sphere, and the special *fortuna* that

---

[120] Cf. Cic. *QFr.* 1.1.5 (SB 1): *quemadmodum gubernatores optimi vim tempestatis, sic illi fortunae impetum superare non possent.* From the context it is clear that Cicero is thinking about governors in their military capacity. The pernicious effects of *fortuna* in warfare were also regularly noted by Caesar, e.g. *BG* 6.30 on the escape of Ambiorix, *BC* 3.68 on the defeat at Dyrrhachium, etc.; for the impact of *fortuna* on warfare in general, cf. *BG* 6.30.2, 6.35.2; *BC* 3.10.6 (*quantum in bello Fortuna posset*), 3.68.1 (*sed Fortuna . . . praecipue in bello, parvis momentis magnas rerum commutationes efficit*), with Champeaux 1982–1987: 2.262–4. The idea goes back (at least) to Thucydides (cf. 1.140.1).

[121] Sejanus: Tac. *Ann.* 4.1. Decline of states: e.g. Sall. *Cat.* 10.1: *sed ubi labore atque iustitia res publica crevit . . . saevire fortuna ac miscere omnia coepit*; Flor. 4.7.10, where the defeat of the Republican cause at Philippi revealed that *virtus* had been defeated once and for all by *fortuna*: *sed quanto efficacior est fortuna quam virtus.*

[122] Cf. Plaut. *Poen.* 973: *aliqua fortuna fuerit adiutrix tibi*; see discussion in Kajanto 1981: 522–3, with further references to Plautus and Terence.

[123] *Fortuna populi Romani*: e.g. Cic. *Verr.* 1.16, *Man.* 45, *Cat.* 1.15, *Mil.* 83, *Phil.* 5.39; Liv. 1.46.5; Sen. *Ep.* 51.11; Flor. 3.18.13. *Fortuna rei publicae*: e.g. Rhet. Her. 4.54–5; Cic. *Man.* 28, *Sull.* 62, *Mil.* 20, *Sest.* 17, *Phil.* 5.29. Despite the native celebration of *fortuna*, some Roman writers insisted that the rise of Rome was not due to *fortuna* alone, but also to characteristic Roman qualities such as *virtus*, *consilium*, and *disciplina*; cf. Cic. *Rep.* 2.30: *intellegesque non fortuito populum Romanum sed consilio et disciplina confirmatum esse, nec tamen adversante fortuna*, with the final clause tacked on as a sort of grudging admission that *fortuna* had not been an obstacle to Roman success. The question of the role of *fortuna/tychē* in driving the rise of Rome was often taken up by Greek authors, most famously by Plutarch in his essay on the theme (*Mor.* 316C–326C).

they enjoyed.[124] From the increasing public association between the late-Republican dynasts and the benevolent quality of *fortuna* it was a short step to the autocratic monopolization of this concept under Augustus. Emblematic of this transformation was the rise of three new ideals and objects of worship, Fortuna Augusti and Fortuna Augusta, the guardian spirit of the emperor and the supernatural force that brought good luck to his subjects, respectively, and Fortuna Redux, the protectress of the emperor whenever he returned to Rome from afar, all of which, sharing, as they did, in the positive connotations of Fortuna, became nearly ubiquitous throughout the western empire.[125] And Fortuna was evidently seen by the emperors themselves as a critical patroness of their power, always present in the imperial bedchamber in the form of a golden statue.[126]

Fortuna, then, was an ambivalent quality, sometimes fickle and sometimes dependable, sometimes malicious and sometimes benevolent. As an advertised benefit of empire, it was naturally the positive conceptions of *fortuna*, and the central role of the emperor himself in securing "good luck" for the empire as a whole, that were emphasized. The numismatic iconography of *fortuna*, always personified, is especially illuminating. Though many different attributes and adjuncts could be associated with Fortuna – e.g. grain stalks, scepter, globe, caduceus, branch, patera, and thunderbolt – befitting the penchant of this goddess to intervene anywhere and at any time, her two defining attributes were the rudder and the cornucopia (illustration 3.15).[127] Both were significant for the specific messages the coin type was intended to project. The rudder was not a vague nautical symbol, but an unambiguous marker of Fortuna's direction and purpose in guiding the lives of men.[128] The cornucopia equated good luck with

---

[124] Here the coinage had an important role to play. Note, for example, the denarius minted in 49 BC by the Pompeian Q. Sicinius, with obverse bust of Fortuna and legend FORT(UNA) (*RRC* 440/1), and the "response" by Caesar, a quinarius of 44, minted by P. Sepullius Macer, with obverse bust of Victoria and reverse design showing Fortuna standing with rudder and cornucopia (*RRC* 480/25). On *fortuna* and the late-Republican dynasts, see Combès 1966: 424–34; Weinstock 1971: 112–17; Champeaux 1982–1987: 2.215–91. These aristocrats were equally aggressive in publicizing their special *felicitas*: see below, n. 206.

[125] See briefly Fears 1981b: 931–2; Kajanto 1981: 517–18; cf. below, chapter 5, for some of the epigraphic evidence.

[126] Cf. *HA AntP.* 12.5.

[127] Fortuna with rudder and cornucopia: e.g. *RIC* 2, Vespasian 487; *RIC* 2, Titus 33; *RIC* 2, Domitian 264; *RIC* 2, Nerva 4; *RIC* 2, Trajan 253; *RIC* 2, Hadrian 242; *RIC* 3, Antoninus Pius 558; *RIC* 3, Marcus Aurelius 183–5; *RIC* 3, Commodus 513; *RIC* 4.1, Septimius Severus 110; *RIC* 4.1, Caracalla 37; *RIC* 4.1, Geta 168a–b; *RIC* 4.2, Elagabalus 80; *RIC* 4.2, Severus Alexander 196. For the other attributes, consult the indices to *BMCRE* or *RIC*; for the iconography of Fortuna in general, *LIMC* 8.1.125–41, 8.2.90–109 (F. Rausa).

[128] Cf. Dio Chrys. 63.7.

Illustration 3.15 Reverse of dupondius (*RIC* 2, Domitian 392): Fortuna holding a rudder and a cornucopia. FORTUNAE AUGUSTI

material prosperity. Amongst Fortuna's most common attributes in literature, by contrast, were the wheel, suggesting mutability, and blindness, symbolizing the arbitrary dispensation of good and bad luck.[129] These were not the qualities advertised on the Fortuna coin type.[130] The legends that accompanied these designs add different nuances.[131] Many simply declared FORTUNA AUG(USTA/I), the good fortune that attended, and flowed from, the emperor. Others put a particular spin on Fortuna, such as FORTUNA SPES ("Hopeful Fortune"), FORTUNA FELIX ("Propitious Fortune"), FORTUNAE MANENTI ("Abiding Fortune"), or FORTUNA

[129] Fortune and the wheel: e.g. Cic. *Pis.* 22: *ne tum quidem Fortunae rotam pertimescebat*; Amm. 26.8.13 (*rota Fortunae*); sometimes Fortune was depicted as a winged figure, too, e.g. Ov. *Trist.* 5.8.7, *Pont.* 4.3.31, implying that she could simply take off and disappear at any moment. Blind Fortune: Cic. *Phil.* 13.10; Ov. *Pont.* 3.1.125–6; Plin. *NH* 2.22; Apul. *Met.* 7.2; Amm. 31.8.8. Wheels and wings are virtually absent from the visual representations of Fortuna in the private sphere (cf. *LIMC* 8.2.90–109). See discussion in Kajanto 1981: 530–2.

[130] The wheel sometimes appears on the coinage, too, but it is a relatively late development (first under Marcus Aurelius: *RIC* 3, 343–4), and it is usually shown under Fortuna's seat, clearly subordinated to the rudder and cornucopia.

[131] For FORTUNA AUG(USTA/I) and FORTUNA REDUX, see indices to *BMCRE* or *RIC*.

Illustration 3.16 Reverse of denarius (*RIC* 4.1, Septimius Severus 78c): Fortuna holding a cornucopia and a rudder on a globe. FORTUNAE REDUCI

POPULI ROMANI ("The Fortune of the Roman People").[132] Most common, however, was FORTUNA REDUX ("Home-Bringing Fortune"), the iconography of which was identical to that of the other manifestations of Fortuna (illustration 3.16). The type originally advertised the Altar of Fortuna Redux voted to Augustus upon his return from the east in 19 BC.[133] Eventually it referred to any safe return of the emperor from abroad. This was not a bland announcement of the emperor's travels, however, but a highly symbolic statement about the return of the monarch to his capital city, reaffirming Rome's status as the center of the empire.

Salus

Personal safety and well-being, physical health, communal security, the means of deliverance from danger – all of these could be denoted by the

---

[132] FORTUNA SPES: e.g. *RIC* 2, Hadrian 246. FORTUNA FELIX: e.g. *RIC* 4.1, Caracalla 154. FORTUNAE MANENTI: e.g. *RIC* 3, Commodus 191a–b. FORTUNA POPULI ROMANI: e.g. *RIC* 2, Nerva 5.

[133] *RIC* 1², Augustus 53a–56b. For the vote of the senate, see Aug. *RG* 11; Dio 54.10.3. Annual games were associated with the altar: *Inscr. Ital.* 13.2, 519–20 (*Fasti Amiternini*). For the altar itself, *LTUR* 2.275 (F. Coarelli).

term *salus*.[134] Salus was also prominent in the religious sphere. The public cult of Salus at Rome seems to date to the late fourth century BC, when a temple to the goddess was built on the Quirinal.[135]

As a value that denoted the welfare of both communities and individuals, celebrated through a public cult that went back to the early Republic, *salus* was an obvious choice for official advertisement as a benefit of empire. What made the message especially potent was its deep association with the figure of the emperor. The monarchic personalization of what had been, under the Republic, communal ideals, is a defining feature of imperial ideology, as we have seen, but the case of *salus* was particularly pronounced because of the overlap, frequently remarked, between the *salus* of the emperor and that of his subjects. The roots of this overlap can be traced back to the Greek title *sōtēr*, "savior," originally a divine epithet but increasingly attached to rulers as well, especially in the Hellenistic period.[136] It is in the writings of Cicero that we find the first explicit connection between *sōtēr* and *salus*: "He who has given *salus* is clearly a *sōtēr*."[137] It was this connection with the idea of the *sōtēr* that invested *salus* with the notion of salvation. Closely related, and equally significant, is Cicero's repeated ascription of the *salus* of individuals, and even of the state as a whole, to prominent aristocrats, including (in addition to himself) Scipio Aemilianus, Marius, Pompey, Caesar, and Octavian.[138] But individual *salus* could also depend on the *salus* of the state: "All men of every order," as Cicero notes, "reckon their own *salus* to lie in that of the *res publica*" (*Rab Post*. 20).

With the emergence of monarchy, when the *res publica* became increasingly associated with the figure of the emperor, the *salus* of the state, of the community of citizens, and of the reigning emperor became, in principle,

---

[134] Cf. *OLD*, s.v., esp §1 (personal safety), §2 (health), §5 (communal security), and §6 (means of deliverance). For *salus* (both as public cult and as political concept), see Weinstock 1971: 163–74; Schwarte 1977; Fears 1981b: 859–61; Le Glay 1982; Marwood 1988; Winkler 1995.

[135] The temple was vowed in 313 BC, during the Samnite Wars, and was dedicated in 302, building having begun four years earlier: Liv. 9.43.25, 10.1.9; cf. Val. Max. 8.14.6; Plin. *NH* 35.19; see discussion in Clark 2007: 50–3. Winkler 1995: 16–19 considers the temple and its topographical context; cf. *LTUR* 4.229–30 (F. Coarelli).

[136] Already in the fifth century BC, Gelon of Syracuse was celebrated by his subjects as *Sōtēr* (Diod. 11.26); for subsequent developments, see Fears 1981b: 860–1; Winkler 1995: 25–6. For *Sōtēr* as an epithet of Hellenistic kings, see also above, 45, n. 25.

[137] *Verr*. 2.2.154: *is est nimirum soter, qui salutem dedit*.

[138] *Verr*. 2.5.129: *me suam salutem appellans*; *Red. pop*. 11: *parens, deus, salus nostrae vitae, fortunae, memoriae nominis* (of P. Cornelius Lentulus Spinther, who had been instrumental in securing his return from exile); *Mar*. 18, 22: *nam quis est omnium tam ignarus rerum . . . tam nihil umquam nec de sua nec de communi salute cogitans, qui non intellegat tua salute contineri suam et ex unius tua vita pendere omnium?*, 29; *Phil*. 3.27: *O C. Caesar . . . adulescentem appello – quam tu salutem rei publicae attulisti, quam improvisam, quam repentinam*; further references in Weinstock 1971: 166–9, 172. For Cicero's influence on Roman conceptions of *salus*, see also Winkler 1995: 30–6.

interdependent.[139] Pliny makes the connection explicit in several contexts. In the *Panegyricus*, for example, he notes that senators have been accustomed to offer vows for the *salus* of the emperors and, through them, for the eternity of the empire, and he concludes the speech with a declaration to Jupiter Capitolinus that senators will not pray for peace, harmony, security, wealth, or public office, but only for the simple and all-encompassing promise of the emperor's welfare, *salus principis*, earlier identified as the object of everyone's prayers, since it was the emperor's well-being that guaranteed one's own *salus* and that of one's children.[140] And in two letters to Trajan from his province of Bithynia-Pontus he reports the fulfillment of vows for the emperor's safety, through which the public welfare is assured.[141]

As these passages indicate, the ideal of *salus principis* had a pronounced religious dimension. Oaths taken to the emperor, both on the anniversary of his accession date (*dies imperii*) and annually on 3 January, were regularly made *pro salute imperatoris*, effectively replacing the annual Republican oath *pro rei publicae salute*.[142] Salus is especially prominent in the prayers of the Arval Brothers, honored on various occasions in addition to the emperor's *dies imperii* and 3 January, including the accession of a new emperor, the emperor's birthday, and the return of the emperor to the city of Rome.[143] The goddess to whom sacrifice was made on such occasions was usually identified as Salus Publica, and was usually mentioned right after, or together with, the Capitoline triad. Sometimes the titulature is more revealing. The record for 3 January, AD 91, for example, identifies Salus as SALUS AUGUSTA P(UBLICA) P(OPULI) R(OMANI) Q(UIRITIUM), a formulation in which the welfare of the *populus Romanus* is not just dependent on Salus Augusta, but is in fact equated with it.[144] The putative

---

[139] So Schwarte 1977; Le Glay 1982.

[140] Plin. *Pan.* 67.3: *nuncupare vota et pro aeternitate et pro salute principum, immo pro salute principum ac propter illos pro aeternitate imperii solebamus*; 94.2: *non te* (sc. Jupiter) *distringimus votis; non enim pacem, non concordiam, non securitatem, non opes oramus, non honores: simplex cunctaque ista complexum omnium votum est, salus principis*; 23.5: *ut in unius salutem collata omnium vota, cum sibi se ac liberis suis intellegerent precari, quae pro te precarentur*; cf. 8.1 (Nerva's adoption of Trajan conduces to *libertas, salus,* and *securitas*).

[141] *Ep.* 10.35 (for oaths sworn on Jan. 3); cf. 10.100; 10.52 (for oaths sworn on Trajan's *dies imperii*).

[142] Oaths on 3 Jan: Plut. *Cic.* 2.1; Plin. *Ep.* 10.35, 100; Gai. *Inst.* 2.33.1; Tert. *Apol.* 35.4. Oaths on the *dies imperii*: Plin. *Ep.* 10.52; Tac. *Hist.* 2.79; *Feriale Duranum* (Fink 1971, no. 117) col. 1, ll. 2–3. For regular oaths to the emperor, see Herrmann 1968; Ando 2000: 359–61; for the language of the emperor's *salus*, see also Schwarte 1977, esp. 226–8; Winkler 1995: 62, n. 281.

[143] See discussion, with many texts quoted in full, in Marwood 1988: 37–52.

[144] So Schwarte 1977: 229–38. For the text, see Scheid 1998, no. 59, l. 17. Note that a formal cult of Salus Augusta is first attested under Tiberius, but probably existed under Augustus, too, and may even go back to a cult of Salus Caesaris; see Weinstock 1971: 167–74; Marwood 1988: 5–9; Winkler 1995: 42, n. 180.

community of interests between the emperor and his subjects could hardly be more pronounced.

On the imperial coinage, legends and iconography worked together to promote this association between the emperor and the communal welfare of the empire's inhabitants.[145] SALUS PUBLICA proclaimed the *salus* of the imperial community, while SALUS GENERIS HUMANI announced, more grandiosely, the welfare of the entire human race. The emperor's own well-being, and his power to bring health to others, were advertised by legends declaring SALUS AUGUSTI (or, when there were two or more emperors ruling jointly, SALUS AUGUSTORUM) and SALUS AUGUSTA, respectively.[146] With coins bearing all of these legends circulating simultaneously, the dual message of communal welfare and imperial well-being was effectively transmitted. And the numismatic iconography of Salus increasingly conflated the various conceptions of the ideal.[147] When the SALUS AUGUSTI legend first appeared, under Galba, Salus was depicted as a female personification, standing and feeding a snake. This iconography is borrowed from Hygieia, Greek goddess of health, and seems to have been intended to publicize the health of the emperor himself.[148] The imagery accompanying the SALUS AUGUSTA type under Galba was different, showing Salus, seated, holding scepter and *patera*, symbols of authority and sacrifice, probably intended to publicize not the emperor's own health, but rather to suggest the idea of his health-giving power.[149] By the reign of Trajan, the iconography of the two types was blended into a single design, showing Salus, seated, holding *patera* (Galba's Salus Augusta) and feeding a snake (Galba's Salus Augusti) wrapped around an altar, sometimes bearing the ambiguous legend SALUS AUG, other times bearing no legend at all. This composite design was picked up under Hadrian, now glossed by the unambiguous legend SALUS AUGUSTI, suggesting the confluence of the emperor's health/welfare and his power to bring these conditions to others.[150] The trend culminated during the reign of Antoninus Pius, as the

---

[145] Convenient overview of the Salus coin type in Marwood 1988: 21–36; cf. Strack 1931–37: 1.171–3, 191–2. For the legends, see appendices to *BMCRE* or *RIC*.

[146] Note that whatever distinctions might have been intended between the adjectival (Augusta) and genetival (Augusti) epithets were regularly effaced by the ambiguous abbreviation SALUS AUG. See discussion in Fears 1981b: 886–9, esp. 887–8, n. 284 (denying any significant distinction), with references to earlier studies.

[147] For what follows, see Schwarte 1977: 238–46; Marwood 1988: 22–5.

[148] *RIC* 1², Galba 500–3. Winkler 1995: 92–100, 142–71 examines the shared iconography of Salus and Hygieia; for a shorter overview, see *LIMC* 7.1.656–61, 7.2.499–501 (V. Saladino).

[149] *RIC* 1², Galba 395–6. The conceit of the emperor as healer and "wonder worker" seems to have taken off during the Flavian period; see discussion in Luke 2010.

[150] *BMCRE* 3, Hadrian 1,348.

Illustration 3.17 Reverse of sestertius (*RIC* 3, Antoninus Pius 637): Salus holding a patera and feeding a snake wrapped around an altar. SALUS PUBLICA

legend SALUS PUBLICA accompanied the now standard iconography of snake and altar, implying the final conflation between the health of the emperor himself (snake = Salus Augusti), the health-giving power of the emperor (*patera* and altar = Salus Augusta), and the communal welfare of the empire's inhabitants (SALUS PUBLICA) (illustration 3.17). From this point forward the iconography changes only in minor details, with the snake and altar firmly established as Salus' defining attributes.[151] *Salus* was a multifaceted imperial benefit, then, a powerful ideal through which the central state could artfully declare the interdependent welfare of the monarch and his subjects.

***

Pax, concordia, fortuna, and *salus* stood as four of the most important benefits of empire and monarchy during the period 69–235, and each has been the subject of many studies. What has not been recognized is that the production of the types representing these ideals on the imperial coinage hints at an arresting convergence of medium and message. The key lies in

---

[151] Salus with snake and altar (after reign of Antoninus Pius): e.g. *RIC* 3, Marcus Aurelius 53–6 (SALUTI AUGUSTOR); *RIC* 3, Commodus 515 (SAL AUG); *RIC* 4.1, Septimius Severus 119 (SALUTI AUG); *RIC* 4.1, Caracalla 196 (no legend); *RIC* 4.2, Macrinus 197 (SALUS PUBLICA); *RIC* 4.2, Elagabalus 141–2 (SALUS AUGUSTI); *RIC* 4.2, Severus Alexander 177–8 (SALUS PUBLICA).

the variable relative frequencies of the types between metals.[152] On silver coins, Pax and Concordia each comprised 12 percent of all benefit types, putting both of them amongst the more common types, while on the bronze coins, they comprised just 7 and 6 percent of all benefit types, respectively, putting them closer to the group of less common types. Fortuna and Salus, by contrast, comprised 9 and 10 percent, respectively, on the silver, putting them somewhere between the common and rare types, but 16 and 14 percent, respectively, on the bronze, placing both in the top tier of benefit types on the base-metal denominations. We can also consider the four types as two pairs. Pax and Concordia, together, make up nearly one quarter of all silver benefit types (24 percent), but only 13 percent of bronze benefit types, while Fortuna and Salus together make up 19 percent of silver benefit types, but comprise almost one third of bronze benefit types (30 percent). These data seem to indicate, then, that Pax and Concordia were major ideals on the silver coins, but marginal ones on the bronze, while Fortuna and Salus were middling ideals on the silver, but major ones on the bronze.

In attempting to understand the significance of these patterns, it is important not to exaggerate the extent of the discrepancy between metals in the relative frequencies of the Pax, Concordia, Fortuna, and Salus types, and also to recognize that the thresholds for "more" or "less" common, "major," "middling," and "marginal" are somewhat loose. The discrepancy is unmistakable, however, especially in light of the remarkably consistent correspondence between metals in the relative frequencies of the other benefit types (and reverse types in general). And it does not appear to be an accident. If, as seems likely, the precious-metal denominations circulated primarily amongst upper-class users, while the base-metal denominations were more common amongst the lower classes, then we may reasonably conclude that the promotion of these four benefits was "targeted" to different social groups. This distinction between precious-metal denominations and upper-class users, on the one hand, and base-metal denominations and lower-class users, on the other, is of course schematic, and in practice there must have been a lot of overlap in between social classes and the use of different coins, but it may help us to understand the logic of this typological patterning across the various denominations.[153]

---

[152] For the figures, see above, tables 3.1–2; for the tabulations, see appendices 7 (silver) and 8 (bronze).

[153] The circulation patterns of the various denominations will be considered in more detail in the next chapter; see also above, 90–2, on patterns in the representation of Liberalitas on precious- and base-metal coins.

Both *pax* and *concordia* were "political" ideals. They pertained mainly to matters of state and to the affairs of aristocrats. In the case of *pax*, this is reflected in the various ideals with which it tended to be grouped, especially *otium*, "leisure" (above, n. 83), a defining aristocratic value. And the Concordia coin type, as we have seen, announced the harmony prevailing at the imperial court, in the world of high politics, and in the army, all matters of perennial concern to the political elites who ran the empire. Both *fortuna* and *salus*, by contrast, were "social" – or, perhaps better, "popular" – ideals. In the visual universe of the private sphere, for example, Fortuna was nearly omnipresent, depicted in many different media and contexts.[154] Indeed, the realm of both Fortuna and Salus was that of private experience: the quality of the annual harvest, the performance of the gladiator one has wagered on, the outcome of a board game, the reciprocation of amorous interest, the state of one's health, the welfare of one's family, etc.[155] Such were the everyday concerns of the non-political classes. In consistently emphasizing Pax and Concordia on the silver coins, and Fortuna and Salus on the various base-metal denominations, in other words, the mint officials at Rome were evidently sensitive to the different interests of its coins' users. We may reasonably conclude, with the caveats noted above, that in this case the official publicity of the central state had been effectively coordinated in order to produce an appropriate distribution of advertised benefits across social classes.

VICTORIA AND THE POLITICS OF EMPIRE

The cluster of benefits associated with *pax*, *concordia*, *fortuna*, and *salus* were proclaimed as benefits of monarchy that flowed from the emperor himself. All of these benefits, however, and in particular those arising from conditions of peace, harmony, stability, and prosperity, depended on the larger structures of state and empire. Especially important were administrative centralization, control over material resources, and the capacity to

---

[154] Even in the sample of images collected in *LIMC* 8.2.90–109, private and domestic media, e.g. gems, cameos, mosaics, wall paintings, lamps, statuettes, and mirrors, seem to predominate over public media (e.g. relief sculpture), a configuration of evidence that distinguishes Fortuna from all the other ideals examined in this and the previous chapter. For the popularity of Fortuna as reflected in the epigraphic record, see below, 306.

[155] For the various areas of life in which Fortune was thought to operate in the "popular" imagination of the Roman empire, see Morgan 2007: 33 (evidence from proverbs), 77 (fables), 111–13 (*gnomai*); for Salus as a deity of personal welfare, see, e.g., Plaut. *Asin.* 712, *Capt.* 529, *Cas.* 801; Ter. *Ad.* 761; Cic. *Font.* 10.21, *Verr.* 2.3.131. Fortuna and Salus are explicitly linked by Plautus in several passages, e.g. *Asin.* 727, *Capt.* 863; see briefly Marwood 1988: 12.

project power through the deployment of armed force. Underpinning these structures, and prior to them, was Roman military conquest. As a result, Victory always stood as the central imperial ideal around which all others circled. The ideological centrality of Victory is particularly clear from the numismatic evidence. Indeed, not only was Victoria the most common benefit type on both silver and base-metal coins (tables 3.1–2), it was also the single most common reverse type on the Roman imperial coinage as a whole for the period 69–235.[156]

It has long been recognized that Victory was "the linchpin" of Roman imperial ideology, and the meanings and representations of *Victoria Romana* have been much discussed.[157] Most of the key issues in the history and interpretation of this core Roman value, therefore, can be reviewed relatively quickly. Two questions that will then require closer examination are, first, how the abstract concept of "victory" could be converted into a structure of power for the reigning emperor, for the institution of monarchy, and for the Roman imperial state – all of which must be distinguished from one another for analytical purposes – and second, how it could be translated symbolically from an expression of Roman conquest over provincial subjects into a benefit enjoyed by all the inhabitants of the empire.

The official cult of Victoria at Rome began in 294 BC.[158] Throughout the middle Republic, when Rome was laying the foundations of its Mediterranean empire, Victoria was a state goddess of the Roman people. This is especially clear from the Republican coinage of the third and second centuries, on which Victoria, a common reverse type, is normally collocated with Roma, Jupiter, or the Dioscuri on the obverse.[159] Beginning in the first century, however, the ideal of Victoria became increasingly personalized as a result of the more intense political competition of the late Republic. The

---

[156] For the tabulations, see appendices 3 (silver) and 4 (bronze).

[157] Modern scholarship on the ideology of Victoria begins from Gagé 1933, a seminal article that synthesized the results of several of his earlier studies on the theme, and Weinstock 1958, a tremendous collection of evidence. Two major and influential works that focus on the monumental and visual evidence for Victoria are Picard 1957 and Hölscher 1967; see also M. Alföldi 1999: 83–116. Fears 1981a provides a useful overview of evidence and ample bibliography through the 1970s. For the ideology of imperial victory in general, see also Charlesworth 1943; Storch 1972 (later empire); McCormick 1986: 11–34; Ando 2000: 175–90, 253–9, 277–303, 320–35; Hölscher 2006; Koortbojian 2006. For the Victoria coin type, Bellinger and Berlincourt 1962: 44–64; Mattingly in *BMCRE* II, xxxv, n. 4; III, xxxix, lxvi.

[158] Liv. 10.33.8–9.

[159] E.g. *RRC* 22 (265–42 BC), 28/1–4 (225–12 BC); especially common was the victoriatus, from 211 BC: *RRC* 44, 53, 57–8, 67, 70–2, 83, 89–98, 101–3, 105–6, 112, 119–22, 124, 132–3, 159, 162, 166, 168; see Crawford 1974: 628–30.

personalization of ideals and values that had traditionally been associated with the *populus Romanus* as a whole has already been noted in various contexts, but no step on the road to monarchy was more significant, in political and ideological terms, than the autocratic monopolization of Victory.

The stages in the process are clear.[160] Open competition over public identification with Victory began with Marius and Sulla, and accelerated with Pompey. Caesar was especially intent on attaching the ideal of Victory to his own person. Following Sulla and Pompey, he paid tribute to Venus Victrix, fighting in her name at Pharsalus and vowing a temple to the goddess before the battle.[161] Among the many honors bestowed upon Caesar by the senate were a statue of him, with his foot atop a globe (*oikoumenē*), emblematic of world conquest, and originally inscribed *hēmitheos*, "semi-divine," set up in the Temple of Jupiter Optimus Maximus, and another statue in the Temple of Quirinus with the inscription *Deo Invicto*, "to the Invincible God."[162] Both conveyed an emphatic message of Caesar's claim to the ideal of Victory. Contemporary coins also sounded the theme, including a gold issue of 47 showing a laurel wreath, symbol of victory; a number of issues between 47 and 45 portraying Victory; and a long series of issues from 44 with obverse portrait of Caesar and various representations of Venus, Caesar's patron goddess, holding a statuette of Victoria.[163] Even more momentous was the inauguration of the *ludi Victoriae Caesaris* in 45 (perhaps replacing the *ludi Veneris Genetricis*, instituted in 46), celebrated between July 20 and 30, which represents the first unambiguous attachment of Victoria to an individual Roman.[164] Together with the coinage, which neatly expressed an almost symbiotic association between Caesar and Victoria, the personalization of Victory at Rome was almost complete.

The dynasts of the late Republic effectively transformed Victoria from a goddess of the *populus Romanus* into a symbol of personal power. But

---

[160] Gagé 1933: 2–6; Weinstock 1958: 2,513–18; Hölscher 1967: 138–164; Fears 1981a: 778–808, drawing attention to Scipio Africanus, Flamininus, and prominent second-century *gentes* as precursors to the late-Republican dynasts in their association with the ideal of Victory (779–87); M. Alföldi 1999: 28–41.

[161] App. *BC* 2.68. Caesar later decided to dedicate the temple to Venus Genetrix.

[162] Statue in Temple of Jupiter (voted after victory at Thapsus, 46): Dio 43.14.6, 43.21.2, with Hölscher 1967: 151; Weinstock 1971: 40–53. Statue in Temple of Quirinus (voted after Munda, 45): Cic. *Att.* 12.45.2 (SB 290), 13.28.3 (SB 299); Dio 43.45.2 ff., with Hölscher 1967: 151–2, n. 949; Weinstock 1971: 186–8.

[163] Laurel wreath (47 BC): *RRC* 456/1a–b. Victory (47–5 BC): *RRC* 454/3, 464/4–5, 472/3, 473/3, 474/6. Caesar and Venus (44 BC): *RRC* 480/3–5b, 7a–18.

[164] *Ludi Victoriae Caesaris*: *Inscr. Ital.* 13.2.47, 78, 178, 188; *CIL* 6.37836; Cic. *Fam.* 11.28.6 (SB 349), *Att.* 13.44.1 (SB 336); Sen. *Q Nat.* 7.17.2; Plin. *NH* 2.93; App. *BC* 3.28; Suet. *Aug.* 10.1; Dio 45.6.4, 49.42.1; Julius Obsequens 68. See discussion in Hölscher 1967: 154–5; Weinstock 1971: 91.

visual representations and public rituals were not the only tools employed in this process. Even more significant in the long run was the increasing monopolization of the political and above all religious authority necessary to claim credit for, and reap the benefits of, military success. In Republican legal and religious terms, military command required both *imperium*, the right to command troops, and *auspicium*, the right to take the auspices. In principle these prerogatives and concepts were intimately bound to one another, but beginning with Sulla we find a functional separation between command, on the one hand, and *imperium*, *auspicium*, and *felicitas*, on the other, as military commanders (*legati*) came to fight under the *imperium* and *auspicium* of someone else. And credit for military success went to the latter, whether or not he had actually commanded troops in battle, because it was specifically the holder of *imperium* and *auspicium* who had established the proper relationship with the gods necessary to ensure victory, and to whom, as a result, the mystique of victory was attached.[165]

The twin processes of the legal/religious monopolization and symbolic/ideological personalization of Victoria culminated in the triumviral period and during the long reign of Augustus.[166] A spectacular string of honors awarded by senatorial decree between 40 and 27 BC facilitated this critical development.[167] That so many of these honors came to Octavian by way of senatorial decree is itself an indication of emergent monarchy at Rome, paralleling, as it does, the honorific system of the Hellenistic kingdoms. Naturally, Octavian also contributed to his public association with Victory. Especially important at the very beginning of his rise to

---

[165] The implications of all this are spelled out in Gagé 1933: 2–4; for a much fuller treatment of the tangle of political and legal issues involved, see Vervaet 2007.

[166] Octavian/Augustus and Victory: Gagé 1930, 1933: 4–11; Picard 1957: 229–311; Weinstock 1958: 2,517–18; Hölscher 1967: 157–64; Barnes 1974; Crawford 1974: 510–11; Fears 1981a: 804–10; Zanker 1988a: 79–85, 210–15, 230–6; Kuttner 1995: index, s.v. "victory"; Gruen 1996, esp. 188–94; Ando 2000: 278–92; Rich 2003; Koortbojian 2006.

[167] These honors included the award of a laurel wreath after the victory at Perusia (Dio 48.16.1, 40 BC); the right to wear the laurel wreath at all times and anywhere in the city of Rome (49.15.1, 36 BC); the annual celebration of Octavian's main military victories, at Mutina, Philippi, Naulochus, Actium, and Alexandria, and of his return to the city in 29 (App. *BC* 5.130; Dio 49.15.1, 51.20.3; *CIL* 10.8375 = *ILS* 108 [Apr. 14, Mutina]; *Inscr. Ital.* 13.2.489 [Aug. 1, Alexandria], 505 [Sep. 2, Actium; Sep. 3, Naulochus], 524 [Oct. 23, Philippi]); the right to celebrate a triple triumph in 29 for the Dalmatian campaigns of 35–3, Actium, and Egypt (Aug. *RG* 4.1); the formal right to employ the *praenomen imperatoris*, which Octavian had in fact been using since the early 30s (Dio 52.41.3, 29 BC); the right to wear a "victory crown" (*stephanos epinikios*) at all public games (51.20.2, 29 BC); the right to don triumphal garb in the city every year on the first of January (53.26.5, 25 BC); and the right to plant laurel trees on either side of the door to his home on the Palatine, awarded, as Dio notes, to honor Octavian – now Augustus – for being "perpetual victor over enemies" (27 BC); cf. Aug. *RG* 34.2; Ov. *Trist.* 3.1.39 ff. For this honor, and the imagery of the laurel in general, see the thorough examination in Alföldi 1973.

prominence was his celebration of the *ludi Victoriae Caesaris* in 44 BC, an ostensible act of *pietas* that in fact served to bind Octavian not only to Caesar's memory, but also to the ideal of Victory.[168] Also significant were monuments and memorials in the city of Rome, of which the Altar of Victory, set up by Octavian in the Curia Julia, stood as a particularly powerful expression of Victory's ideological centrality and its connection both to the state and to its leading family, the Julii.[169] And the coinage, too, regularly communicated the message of Augustus' charismatic hold on the ideal of Victory, with a number of issues depicting Victoria in various guises, and many others representing success in warfare more generally, through images of triumphal quadrigas and bigas, laurel wreaths, standards, trophies, and conquered provinces.[170]

The result of all these honors, celebrations, monuments, memorials, and images was a near-total personalization under Augustus of what Gagé famously called the "theology" of Victory. The roots of this personalization lay in the formal monopolization of the essential prerequisites for winning the major military honors at Rome. Especially important were Augustus' *imperium maius*, first awarded in 23 BC, which not only differentiated Augustus' *imperium* from that of Agrippa but also made it superior to that of any other holder of *imperium* anywhere in the empire – including those commanding troops in the field – and his "*summum auspicium*," a *de facto* prerogative that can be inferred from the visual evidence, which entailed supreme authority for reading the will of the gods.[171] Because Augustus

[168] Cic. *Fam.* 11.28.6 (SB 349); Suet. *Aug.* 10.1; Plin. *NH* 2.93; Dio 45.6.4; for Octavian's celebration of the *ludi Victoriae Caesaris*, see Sumi 2005: 150–3.

[169] Cf. Dio 51.22.1; Suet. *Aug.* 100; Hdn. 5.5.7, 7.11.3; *HA SevAl.* 14.2; Symm. *Rel.* 3.3–5; Ambr. *Ep.* 1.17–18, 1.57.4–6. See discussion in Weinstock 1958: 2,521–3; Hölscher 1967: 6–12, 16–18, 38–41, 163; Ando 2000: 280–3. Among the monuments, the most relevant to the theme of Victory were the arch(es) in the Forum, the Temple of Mars Ultor, and the portrait gallery of *summi viri* in the Forum Augustum; good discussion of these monuments, with extensive earlier bibliography, in Rich 1998.

[170] Octavian/Augustus and Victoria on coins: *RRC* 494/33; *RIC* I² Augustus 1a–b, 31–2, 45–9, 61–2, 88–95, 121–3a, 140–1, 143–5, 184–5, 254–5, 260–1, 266, 268, 270 (with Koortbojian 2006), 276, 319–21. Quadriga/biga: *RIC* I² 96–101, 107a–13b, 131–7, 258–9, 263, 280–4, 301, 303, 311, 313, 399–401. Laurel: *RIC* I² 26a–b, 33a–b, 36a–b, 50–2, 285–6, 302. Standards (with legend SIGNIS RECEPTIS): *RIC* I² 41, 58, 60, 80–7b. Trophies: *RIC* I² 4–6, 265a–b. Conquered provinces: *RIC* I² 275a–b (AEGUPTO CAPTA), 287–9, 314 (with reverse image of Parthian kneeling), 290–2, 306 (ARME[NIA] CAPT[A]; cf. 307: ARMINIA CAPTA).

[171] First *imperium maius*: Dio 53.32.5. Bibliography on Augustus' evolving "constitutional" authority is immense; good recent discussions in Ferrary 2001; Cotton and Yakobson 2002; Gruen 2005. The *SCPP* has shed useful light on *imperium maius* and the varying levels of *imperium* within the imperial regime: see *CIL* 2²/5.900, ll. 34–6 and discussion in Eck *et al.* 1996: 158–61. For Augustus' *auspicium* in particular, see also Richardson 1991: 8; Hurlet 2001; Koortbojian 2006, esp. 201–2, 204–7 (emphasizing the prominence of augural imagery).

wielded both *imperium maius* and, in effect, "*summum auspicium*," all military victories throughout the empire were technically ascribed to him – primarily because the commanders in the field no longer held independent *auspicia militiae* – and as a result he monopolized the major military honors, especially imperatorial acclamations and, as is well known, triumphs, which were not celebrated by anyone outside the imperial family after 19 BC.[172] The final personalization of Victory under Augustus and its institutional/religious basis finds perfect visual expression on the Gemma Augustea, a sardonyx cameo engraved in the last years of Augustus' reign, which shows, in the lower register, a trophy being erected by Roman soldiers amidst defeated barbarians, and in the upper register, a triumphal chariot driven by Victory, from which Tiberius descends, looking at Augustus, who sits enthroned next to Roma, holding a *lituus* and receiving a laurel crown from Oecumene, the *lituus* expressing his supreme augural authority (and therefore his "*summum auspicium*"), and the laurel crown signifying that ultimate credit for Tiberius' military victory belongs to the emperor alone (illustration 3.18).[173]

The ideology of *Victoria Romana*, and its close association with the figure of the Roman emperor, was fully established under Augustus and remained quite stable down through the fourth century, even under Christian emperors. While the growing influence of eastern religions, solar theology, and the rising tide of imperial absolutism are all evident in conceptions of Victory from the mid-third century on, the underlying messages of Roman military success and the emperor's unique and personal relationship with Victoria nevertheless remained constant.

The origins of this long-term centrality of Victory to the ideological structures of Roman imperial legitimacy and monarchic authority can be traced back to the high valuation of military glory in the Hellenistic kingdoms and among Roman Republican aristocrats.[174] In each case, the relationship between military success and political power was paramount.

---

[172] Gagé 1933: 5–8; Barnes 1974; Eck 1984: 138–9, emphasizing that there was never any formal ban on triumphs outside the *domus Augusta*; Campbell 1984: 358–9, following Dio 54.24.7, arguing that triumphs outside the imperial house fell into abeyance not because the emperor held *imperium maius* and supreme *auspicia*, but because the ostentatious refusal of Agrippa to hold triumphs in 19 and 14 made it unrealistic for other senators to request this honor (cf. Eck 1984: 139); see also Beard 2007: 297–9, cautioning against too legalistic an interpretation of the *de facto* imperial monopoly on triumphs.

[173] These points have often been made (cf. Gagé 1930: 28–9); see, most recently, Koortbojian 2006: 207–10.

[174] For military success and Hellenistic kingship, see above, 42, 44–5. Harris 1979: 10–41 is still the standard discussion of the Republican aristocratic valuation of success in warfare; for Republican aristocratic values in general, see Rosenstein 2006, with references to earlier literature.

Illustration 3.18 The Gemma Augustea (early first century AD). Sardonyx cameo

For Hellenistic kings, conquest and the definition of "spear-won territory" were important not only for securing their realms, but also for proving that they were, in fact, kings – "the ability to command an army" being a defining feature of Hellenistic monarchy.[175] And for Republican aristocrats, conspicuous service to the state in the public eye, especially in the military sphere, was vital for political advancement, as the notional association between *virtus*, martial valor, and *honos*, elective office, makes clear.[176] That success in war was also crucial for the Roman emperor's power is undeniable, but how, exactly, military achievements could be converted into political power is rather complicated.

---

[175] Suda, s.v. *basileia*, 2 (see above, 42).
[176] For *honos* and *virtus*, see above, 78. The association was an ideal one, of course, as the electoral success of defeated generals shows: Rosenstein 1990.

One approach is to examine the different mechanisms by which Roman citizens could gain a sense of participation in the fruits of particular victories, normally reserved for the emperor and the victorious army.[177] Various types of ritual, for example, especially triumphs and celebrations of *adventus*, allowed citizens to participate in the celebration of victories won in distant and isolated locations. Monuments and other benefactions from war booty converted information and immediate sensation into memory and a "generalizing ideological concept."[178] What rituals and monuments achieved, in brief, was the generalization and universalization of a successful outcome in this or that battle.[179] Other symbols of military victory, such as imperatorial acclamations, honorific titles referring to defeated enemies (Germanicus, Dacicus, Parthicus, etc.), and triumphal dress, could not by themselves project the message of victories through space and time nor broaden their meaning.[180] Rituals and monuments, by contrast, not only invested victories with transcendent meaning, but also gave rise to a collective "experience" of Roman military success and its attendant benefits, signified by the ideal of Victoria, which was uniquely associated with the figure of the emperor. In this way victory could be converted from an isolated event into a structural basis of political power for the reigning emperor.

Roman imperial coins were also essential for advertising specific victories and, more important, for diffusing the broader message of imperial Victory. Individual coins did not have the same emotional or experiential force as imperial rituals, of course, nor did they have the same visual impact as state monuments. But unlike rituals, which were as fleeting as the victories they commemorated, and unlike monuments, which were confined, for the most part, to the public spaces of the larger cities, especially Rome, coins were in constant and widespread circulation. In no other medium could the message and ideology of Victory be transmitted to so many individuals, which made the imperial coinage a powerful vehicle for diffusing the "experience" of military victory across the empire.

It was also by means of coins that most inhabitants of the empire will have learned the basic iconographic conventions of Roman Victory. Though the numismatic iconography of Victoria was rich and diverse,

---

[177] For what follows, see Hölscher 2006; cf. Hölscher 2003, reaching similar conclusions on the basis of vase paintings and sculptural reliefs.

[178] Hölscher 2006: 43; for monuments in particular, see also Hölscher 1984.

[179] Cf. McCormick 1986: 11–34, with even greater emphasis on the universality of imperial Victory.

[180] For imperial salutations, see the evidence collected under each emperor in the *Dizionario Epigrafico*; for honorific victory titulature, Kneissl 1969. Good discussion of both imperial salutations and imperial cognomina in Campbell 1984: 122–33. On triumphal dress, Alföldi 1970 (1935): 143–61.

Illustration 3.19 Reverse of aureus (*RIC* 3, Antoninus Pius 266a): Victory holding a laurel wreath and a palm

Illustration 3.20 Reverse of aureus (*RIC* 3, Marcus Aurelius 525): Victory inscribing VIC AUG onto shield

Illustration 3.21 Reverse of sestertius (*BMCRE* 5, Septimius Severus, Caracalla, and Geta 266): Victory placing hand on trophy, with captive and female figure. VICT. BRIT

Illustration 3.22 Reverse of dupondius (*RIC* 3, Antoninus Pius 674): Victory in triumphal chariot (quadriga). VICTORIA AUG

the numerous reverse types produced between 69 and 235 were nevertheless composed from a relatively small repertoire of poses and attributes. Victory is always represented as a winged female personification, and her principal attributes are the laurel wreath and the palm (illustration 3.19).[181]

---

[181] Victoria with wreath and palm: e.g. *RIC* 2, Vespasian 61–2; *RIC* 2, Titus 34–5; *RIC* 2, Domitian 42–4; *RIC* 2, Nerva 10; *RIC* 2, Trajan 24–6; *RIC* 2, Hadrian 54; *RIC* 3, Antoninus Pius 110–11a–d;

Illustration 3.23 Reverse of quinarius (*RIC* I², Galba 132): Victory standing on a globe. VICTORIA GALBAE AUG

Illustration 3.24 Reverse of quinarius (*RIC* 2, Vespasian 52): Victory holding a palm and placing a wreath on a military trophy. VICTORIA AUGUSTI

She is also frequently depicted with a shield, which often bears an inscription (illustration 3.20).[182] Other attributes associated with Victoria include symbols of conquest and empire, such as trophy (illustration 3.21), triumphal quadriga or biga (illustration 3.22), and globe (illustration 3.23); various military objects, including spear, parazonium, helmet, standard, vexillum, and legionary eagle (illustration 3.24); and sacrificial imagery, such as altar and *patera*.[183]

The most common reverse types of Victoria, then, correspond to the main stages of Roman warfare, from the religious preliminaries (sacrificial

RIC 3, Marcus Aurelius 117–18; *RIC* 3, Commodus 20a–1; *RIC* 4.1, Septimius Severus 332–4; *RIC* 4.1, Caracalla 197; *RIC* 4.1, Geta 91–2; *RIC* 4.2, Macrinus 208; *RIC* 4.2, Elagabalus 151–7; *RIC* 4.2, Severus Alexander 211–12. Laurel was the symbol of victory (military and athletic), and the palm was a sign of rejoicing; see briefly Mattingly in *BMCRE* II, xxxv, n. 4.

[182] Victoria with shield: *RIC* 2, Vespasian 464 (OB CIV[ES] SER[VATOS]), 478 (SPQR); *RIC* 2, Titus 81 (SPQR); *RIC* 2, Domitian 242c (SPQR), 255 (DE GER[MANIS]); *RIC* 2, Trajan 234 (DACICA); *RIC* 2, Hadrian 107; *RIC* 3, Antoninus Pius 732 (BRITAN[NICA]); *RIC* 3, Marcus Aurelius 88–90 (VIC[TORIA] AUG[USTA/I]), 240 (VIC[TORIA] GER[MANICA]); *RIC* 3, Commodus 67; *RIC* 4.1, Septimius Severus 94, 363 (AUG); *RIC* 4.1, Caracalla 297 (VOT[A] XX), 455; *RIC* 4.1, Geta 166; *RIC* 4.2, Macrinus 164; *RIC* 4.2, Elagabalus 44–5; *RIC* 4.2, Severus Alexander 217–19 (VOT[A] X). For the iconography, Hölscher 1967: 98–135.

[183] Victoria with trophy: e.g. *RIC* 2, Vespasian 114–15; *RIC* 2, Trajan 83–4; *RIC* 2, Hadrian 101; *RIC* 3, Antoninus Pius 109a–d; *RIC* 3, Marcus Aurelius 890–1; *RIC* 3, Commodus 374–5; *RIC* 4.1, Septimius Severus 819; *RIC* 4.1, Caracalla 353; *RIC* 4.1, Geta 186; *RIC* 4.2, Severus Alexander 214. Quadriga/biga: *RIC* 3, Antoninus Pius 101a–e; *RIC* 3, Marcus Aurelius 1,506; *RIC* 4.1, Septimius Severus 817a–b; *RIC* 4.1, Caracalla 170; *RIC* 4.1, Geta 55. Globe: *RIC* 2, Vespasian 51; *RIC* 2, Trajan 456–7; *RIC* 3, Antoninus Pius 110; *RIC* 3, Marcus Aurelius 887; *RIC* 4.1, Septimius Severus 486. Spear/parazonium: *RIC* 2, Trajan 288–9. Helmet: *RIC* 2, Trajan 65; *RIC* 3, Commodus 113;

Illustration 3.25 Reverse of sestertius (*RIC* 2, Domitian 322): Victory crowning the emperor Domitian

imagery), through the battle itself, as represented by weapons (spear, para-zonium), armor (helmet, shield) and legionary equipment (standard, vexil-lum, eagle), to the successful outcome, which issued in celebrations (laurel, palm, triumphal chariots) and, ultimately, empire (globe). The Victoria reverse type also served to underline and magnify the relationship between victory and political power. Not only were Victoria types collocated with a portrait of the reigning emperor on the obverse, but several of the reverse types themselves depict the emperor interacting with the goddess, especially in scenes of Victory crowning the reigning emperor (illustration 3.25), a striking visual expression of imperial proximity to the divine source of military success.[184]

RIC 4.1, Caracalla 448a–b; *RIC* 4.1, Geta 186. Standard: *RIC* 2, Domitian 691; *RIC* 2, Hadrian 102; *RIC* 3, Marcus Aurelius 890–1. Vexillum: *RIC* 4.1, Septimius Severus 803. Eagle: *RIC* 2, Domitian 242b; *RIC* 2, Hadrian 284. Sacrificial imagery: *RIC* 2, Trajan 67–8; *RIC* 3, Antoninus Pius 87; *RIC* 3, Marcus Aurelius 239; *RIC* 3, Commodus 123; *RIC* 4.1, Caracalla 171; for Victory in sacrificial pose, see Mattingly in *BMCRE* III, lxvi.

[184] Emperors between 69 and 235 shown crowned by Victory: Vespasian (*RIC* 2, 105, 112), Domitian (*RIC* 2, 287), Trajan (*RIC* 2, 69), Antoninus Pius (*RIC* 3, 889, 897), Marcus Aurelius (*RIC* 3, 264–6), Commodus (*RIC* 3, 125), Caracalla (*RIC* 4.1, 70a–b), Macrinus (*RIC* 4.2, 36), Elagabalus (*RIC* 4.2, 36), and Severus Alexander (*RIC* 4.2, 317).

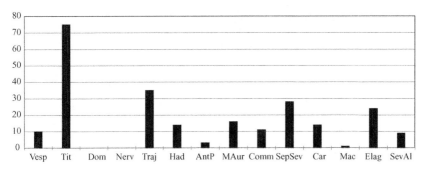

Figure 3.3 Relative frequency of Victoria types on silver coins, expressed as a percentage of all benefit types by reign, AD 69–235 (N = 52,096)

In light of its vital role in imperial ideology, it is no surprise that Victory, depicted in these ways, was the most common reverse type for the period 69–235 as a whole. But not all imperial regimes during this period emphasized Victoria to the same degree. As always, reign-by-reign analysis of the data reveals fluctuations in the relative frequency of the type that can illuminate its changing ideological resonance over time. The results are presented in figure 3.3.

The graph shows a pronounced peak under Titus – potentially misleading, however, since the total number of benefit types minted under Titus was so small – and shorter but still significant peaks under Trajan, Septimius Severus, and Elagabalus.[185] The type was minted in relatively small numbers, or not at all, under Domitian, Nerva, Antoninus Pius, and Macrinus. These fluctuations do not appear to be random. The prominence of Victoria types under Trajan and Septimius Severus, for example, coincides with the large-scale wars of expansion fought during these reigns, and the high relative frequency of the type under Titus may reflect the continued influence of Vespasian's emphasis on military success.[186] The steady decline in the frequency of the type under Hadrian and Antoninus Pius corresponds to the renunciation of further conquest and generally peaceful conditions of these reigns, while the upsurge under Marcus Aurelius surely marks the renewed ideological significance of Victory during a period of

---

[185] There were 51 benefit types under Titus, of which 38 represented Victory; see appendix 7.

[186] For Trajan's military types, see Strack 1931–37: 1.67–8, 105–44, 213–30; for martial ideology under Trajan in general, Beaujeu 1955: 59–67; Picard 1957: 388–418; Seelentag 2004: 259–91. Lusnia 2006 examines military imagery under Septimius Severus. Vespasian and military success: Noreña 2003.

Table 3.3 *Imperatorial acclamations and triumphs, AD 69–235*

Emperor	Imperatorial acclamations	Triumphs
Vespasian	20	1
Titus	17	1
Domitian	22	2
Nerva	2	0
Trajan	13	2
Hadrian	1	0
Antoninus Pius	0	0
Marcus Aurelius	10	2
Commodus	8	2
Septimius Severus	11	0
Caracalla	3	0
Macrinus	0	0
Elagabalus	0	0
Severus Alexander	0	1

Note: The figures listed here include joint triumphs (Vespasian and Titus, during the reign of Vespasian; Marcus Aurelius and Lucius Verus, and Marcus Aurelius and Commodus, both during the reign of Marcus Aurelius), and the totals for Titus and Commodus incorporate these shared triumphs under a senior emperor. Convenient overview of acclamations and triumphs in Kienast 1996.

heavy fighting on the northern frontier.[187] In these cases the correlations between war, peace, and the variable production of the Victoria type are reasonably clear.

Another way to assess the significance of these fluctuations is to compare them to other official metrics of military accomplishment, such as imperatorial acclamations and triumphs (table 3.3). Though there are some discrepancies at the beginning and end of our period between the relative frequency of Victoria types and the numbers of acclamations and triumphs, in general there is a clear relationship between these various indices of military success, especially acclamations. In fact, from the reign of Nerva through that of Macrinus, there is a very strong correlation between fluctuations in the relative frequency of the Victoria type and the number of

---

[187] Another sign of the new mood under Marcus Aurelius is the insistent depiction of violence on the Column of Antoninus Pius; see Pirson 1996.

imperatorial acclamations (r = .844). This is confirmed by a low permutation value (.003), which shows that the correlation is not an accidental one.[188] Naturally, the fit is not perfect for the period 69–235 as a whole. Under Domitian, for example, Victory was overshadowed by other ideals in the advertisement of military success. Domitian was an energetic promoter of his martial accomplishments, boasting no fewer than 22 imperatorial acclamations and celebrating two triumphs – mostly warranted, despite the vicious attacks of his posthumous critics – but the message of victory on the imperial coinage of his reign was transmitted not through the Victoria type, but rather through representations of the emperor's patron goddess Minerva, often depicted in military guise.[189] In light of the correlations noted above, though, this departure from the promotion of Victoria appears to be an anomaly. It should also be noted that the meaning of the concept could be altered to suit circumstances. Under Elagabalus, for example, Victoria seems to have alluded to the circumstances of the emperor's accession, and in particular to the defeat of Macrinus in civil war, a patent distortion of Victory's normal message of conquest over foreign enemies.[190] Overall, though, the picture is one of ideological coherence across different media and institutional agents.

It may seem surprising that Victoria types were not even more common under more emperors. In considering the broader significance of Victory to the structure of Roman imperial ideology, it is important to recognize that this was an ideal that belonged to the institution of Roman monarchy as such, and did not necessarily require constant reiteration by individual emperors. As we have seen, the increasing personalization of Victory characteristic of the late Republic culminated in the autocratic monopolization of this ideal by Augustus. The transfer of this unique and personal relationship with Victory from the person of Augustus to the institution of the monarchy took place in several stages. The first stage came with the reign of Tiberius. Already at the moment of his accession, Tiberius possessed the same *imperium maius* and *"summum" auspicium* that Augustus had wielded, so victories won in the field by his own subordinates,

---

[188] For the calculations, see appendix II. The number of triumphs also seem to correspond, very roughly, to this positive correlation between Victoria types and imperatorial acclamations (between Nerva and Macrinus), but the overall numbers are too small for a statistical comparison.

[189] Syme 1936 is still the best account of Domitian's military activities on the northern frontier. For the typology of the Minerva type under Domitian, which accounted for a remarkable 88% of all reverse types on the silver during his reign, see Mattingly in *BMCRE* II, lxxxv–lxxxvi; for the tabulations, appendix 3.

[190] On the Victoria type under Elagabalus, Mattingly in *BMCRE* v, ccxxxii–ccxxxvii; cf. Potter 2004: 150–3 on Elagabalus' accession. For the use of Victoria imagery in other civil war contexts, M. R. Alföldi 1999: 102–4.

Illustration 3.26 The sheath of the "Sword of Tiberius" (*c.* AD 16). Gilt bronze

including Germanicus, were properly ascribed to him.[191] And Tiberius'
own record of military accomplishment prior to assuming the throne was
unimpeachable. Nevertheless, he seems to have relied to some extent on
the martial charisma of his predecessor, if the visual program of the so-
called "Sword of Tiberius" is any guide (illustration 3.26). On this bronze
sheath, Germanicus, in military dress, presents a statuette of Victory to an
enthroned Tiberius, who rests one arm on a shield inscribed FELICITAS
TIBERI[US]. This central scene is presided over by Mars Ultor and by
Victoria, who stands behind Tiberius and carries a shield with the inscription VIC[TORIA] AUG[USTI]. Here the credit for Germanicus' victory
is shown to belong to Tiberius – just as the credit for Tiberius' victories had
belonged to Augustus, as represented on the Gemma Augustea – but the

[191] In Tacitus' account of Germanicus' campaigns in Germany, the historian is careful to note, where
relevant, that ultimate authority for Germanicus' actions belonged to Tiberius, the *imperator*: e.g.
Ann. 1.38.2, 1.41.1, 1.58.5, 2.18.2, 2.22.1. See discussion in Gagé 1930; Picard 1957: 315–42; Ando
2000: 288–92.

goddess Victory remains the personal agent of Divus Augustus (*Victoria Augusti*), not Tiberius, who never adopted the title "Augustus."[192]

Some blurring in the precise meaning of *Victoria Augusti* occurred under subsequent emperors. The imperial mint under Claudius and Nero, for example, produced coins with the legend VICTORIA AUGUSTI, simultaneously alluding to Augustus and to the name assumed by both Claudius and Nero as members of the Julio-Claudian house.[193] The critical moment in the redefinition of *Victoria Augusti*, however, came with the civil war of 69 and the establishment of Rome's second imperial dynasty under Vespasian. While Galba and Otho minted Victory coins with legends bearing their own names, Vitellius returned to the slogan of *Victoria Augusti*, though he had no connection to the *domus Augusta*.[194] This model was followed by Vespasian, whose ultimate success in the civil war effected the final transfer of *Victoria Augusti* from Augustus and his Julio-Claudian successors to the institution of the principate.[195] Henceforth Victoria belonged to the imperial throne and not to any one emperor or dynasty. During the joint reign of Marcus Aurelius and Lucius Verus (AD 161–9), for example, victories won by Verus' *legati* in the east were credited not only to Verus, but also to Marcus Aurelius, who, like Verus, assumed the titles *Armeniacus*, *Parthicus Maximus*, and *Medicus*. By the late second century, then, Victory was autonomous, indivisible, and a divine attribute of the monarchy itself, whether the imperial throne was occupied by one or more emperors.[196]

As a result of this general association between Victory and the Roman imperial monarchy, it was unnecessary for each successive emperor to advertise his own, personal claims to this goddess. In fact, there were good reasons for detaching the concept of Victory from too close a relationship with any one emperor or specific battle. In ideological terms, the message of imperial Victory was more potent when it was generalized from the concrete and universalized from the particular. In this way it could transcend the

---

[192] On the imagery and meaning of the "Sword of Tiberius," see most recently Koortbojian 2006: 197–200 (with references to earlier studies), whose identification of the figures I follow here.

[193] E.g. *RIC* 1², Claudius 17–18, Nero 115–20.

[194] *RIC* 1², Galba 131–2: VICTORIA GALBAE AUG[USTI]; *RIC* 1 (2nd edn.), Otho 13–17: VICTORIA OTHONIS; *RIC* 1², Vitellius 13, 34–8, 46, etc.: VICTORIA AUGUSTI.

[195] *RIC* 2, Vespasian 52: VICTORIA AUGUSTI. See Gagé 1933: 11–13 ("elle est devenue une divinité autonome, qui veille successivement sur chaque Auguste, et qu'on se passe avec l'empire," 13); cf. Picard 1957: 344–66; Ando 2000: 293–4.

[196] Gagé 1933: 13–16, 33. The indivisibility of Victory is also reflected in the emergence of the legend VICTORIA AUGUSTORUM. Gagé refers to an issue of Verus with this legend (15, n. 1), but this coin does not appear in either *RIC* or *BMCRE*. The earliest example recorded in those catalogues was minted in 204, with obverse portrait of Caracalla (*RIC* 4.1 Caracalla 418b). For Marcus Aurelius' titulature, see Kienast 1996: 139.

contingencies of time and place and stand as one of the permanent and "natural" structures of monarchic authority. *Victoria Romana* could always be employed as a temporal slogan communicated by individual emperors in the advertisement of specific victories – as it was often employed – but its real ideological force lay in its potential universalism.

The coinage was an ideal medium for communicating this broader, universalizing message of imperial victory. The constant repetition in numerous combinations of the same poses, attributes, and adjuncts in the visual representation of Victoria, across reigns and over the long term, helped to blur the distinction between victory in a given battle, the Victory that attended a given emperor, and the Victory that belonged to the imperial monarchy. The frequently ambiguous legends accompanying these types also encouraged a generalized interpretation of imperial Victory. A number of legends, to be sure, referred to specific victories or to individual emperors by name. During the period 69–235, legends on imperial coins celebrated specific victories (whether real or imagined) over Britannia, Germania, and Parthia, while the personal names of Vespasian, Septimius Severus, and Elagabalus were all attached to Victoria.[197] In these cases, the concrete was elevated above the abstract. Far more common, however, were those legends in which Victoria was simply glossed with the abbreviation AUG. Resolved as *Victoria Augusti*, the legend could refer either to Augustus or to the reigning emperor; resolved as *Victoria Augusta*, it denoted the goddess that attended the institution of the monarchy. The ambiguity naturally encouraged some conflation of the three.[198] Even more important than the details of Victoria's iconography and identifying legends were the long lives of imperial coins in circulation. Once minted, coins could stay in circulation for over a century (see below, 194). And because Victory was the most common reverse type, there will have been more Victory types in the coin populations of the empire than any other type. The long-term impact of this regular and indeed monotonous dissemination of Victory

---

[197] Britannia: *RIC* 3, Commodus 440, 452, 459e: VICT(ORIA) BRIT(ANNICA); *RIC* 4.1, Septimius Severus 247: VICT BRIT; *RIC* 4.1, Caracalla 230: VICTORIA BRIT; *RIC* 4.1, Geta 180: VICT BRIT. Germania: *RIC* 3, Marcus Aurelius 1,090–3: VICT(ORIA) GERM(ANICA); *RIC* 4.1, Caracalla 316: VICTORIA GERMANICA. Parthia: *RIC* 3, Marcus Aurelius 160: VIC(TORIA) PAR(THICA); *RIC* 3, Lucius Verus 562: VIC PAR; *RIC* 4.1, Septimius Severus 195b: VICTORIA PARTHICA MAXIMA; *RIC* 4.2, Macrinus 96–8: VICTORIA PARTHICA. Personal names: *RIC* 2, Vespasian 268: VICTORIA IMP(ERATORIS) VESPASIANI; *RIC* 4.1, Septimius Severus 428: VICTOR(IA) SEVER(I) AUG(USTI) (mint of Emesa); *RIC* 4.2, Elagabalus 151–7a: VICTOR[IA] ANTONINI AUG[USTI].

[198] On the distinction between Victoria Augusta and Victoria Augusti, see, e.g., Gagé 1932: 63–5; Mattingly in *BMCRE* III, xxxix; Weinstock 1958: 2,518–21; Hölscher 1967: 161; Fears 1981a: 743, n. 15; Ando 2000: 294.

types will have been to erode the notional connection between Victory and any one battle or emperor, and to generalize the meaning of *Victoria Romana*. In this way the mystique of Victory, which had once belonged to the successful general in the field, now supported the power and authority of the institution of monarchy, a universal ideal that made the "experience" of military success a timeless and defining feature of Roman imperial rule.

In the short term, then, the advertisement of victory helped the reigning emperor to maintain political control. Over the long term, the communication of the universal ideal of *Victoria Romana* increased the authority of the imperial monarchy as a whole. And because there was a natural tendency, fostered by the imperial regime, to equate the emperor with the full apparatus of imperial government (see above, 107–8), the successful dissemination of this ideal also reinforced the legitimacy of the Roman state. In all three cases the ideology of Victory was converted into political power. But such power was not by itself a real benefit for the inhabitants of the empire. The symbolic translation of Victory from an imperial attribute into an imperial benefit was in fact a major challenge. That the challenge was at least partially met can be inferred from the spread of the cult of Victoria throughout the western empire, from the Danubian provinces to North Africa, and from the large number of votive offerings to Victoria Augusta made by provincials in civilian contexts.[199] The decisive shift in the broader meaning of Victory, and the one that made it possible to represent it as an imperial benefit, came with Hadrian's decisions to give up the eastern provinces annexed by Trajan, to stabilize the frontiers of the empire and, implicitly, to renounce further territorial expansion. The effect of these decisions was to define all subsequent opponents of the Roman army as external enemies of the empire – and not, that is, as potential subjects – and to make all the current inhabitants of the empire, whether Roman citizens or not, the beneficiaries of successful military campaigns, now waged, in principle, in the service of communal frontier defense. Hadrian's provincial tour and his celebration of the provinces, most notably through the province series on the coinage, reflect the new conceptualizations of empire and Victory that went with these changes.[200]

---

[199] For the spread of temples to Victoria, see the evidence cited in Weinstock 1958: 2,531–2. For provincial dedications to Victoria Augusta, see below, 305–6.

[200] For Hadrian's renunciation of Trajan's eastern conquests, see Syme 1984 (1981): 1,436–46; on his management of the frontiers in general, see Birley 1997: index, s.v. "frontier policy." For Hadrian's province series, see above, n. 79; for his travels, Halfmann 1986: 188–210. In general on the far-reaching ideological ramifications of Hadrian's frontier policy, see discussion in Ando 2000: 278, 316–20, 330–1.

One specific mechanism that the imperial regime could use to represent Victory as a benefit for its subjects was the institution of the *aurum coronarium*, "gold for crowns," whereby provincial communities sent a "gift" to the imperial court upon learning of some imperial anniversary or beneficial action undertaken by the emperor, especially victory over a foreign enemy.[201] In sending *aurum coronarium* in response to news of a military victory, individual provincial communities formally acknowledged that the defeat of some distant enemy was in fact beneficial for them, too, and as a result they participated, willingly or not, in the ideological construction of Victory as a benefit of empire. The symbolic meaning of the *aurum coronarium*, in other words, had little to do with whether or not those who paid it were conscious of the fact (as they surely were) that they were actually paying a form of tax.

Another mechanism that could be employed to communicate specific ideas about the meaning of Victory was the imperial coinage. Iconography performed some of this work. The sacrificial imagery associated with the Victoria type, for example, advertised divine support for Roman imperialism and connected military victories with the quintessentially Roman virtue of *pietas*, while those attributes symbolizing success and triumph, especially the laurel and palm, imbued military conquest with an aura of jubilant celebration in which everyone could participate. Long-term minting patterns are even more illuminating for the bundle of ideals and values with which Victory was meant to be associated. The second century in particular witnessed a significant convergence of three related concepts. Figure 3.4 compares the fluctuating relative frequencies of Victoria, Felicitas, and Pax types from Nerva through Septimius Severus. As the graph indicates, there was a positive correlation between the fluctuations of Victoria and Pax ($r = .76$), and an even stronger correlation between the fluctuations of Victoria and Felicitas ($r = .8$); again, low permutation values for both correlations ($.048$ and $.038$, respectively) indicate that the relationship between these sets of data is not an incidental one.[202] It bears repeating that long-term patterns of this sort were the result of countless short-term decisions on type selection and mint output, and cannot be seen as a conscious attempt to transmit carefully orchestrated messages over the course of 115 years. These patterns do, however, reflect official perceptions of which values and which sets of values were more or less ideologically resonant at which times. And they also help us to reconstruct the particular combinations

---

[201] Ando 2000: 175–82.

[202] It has long been recognized that Victoria and Pax somehow "went together" on the imperial coinage (see, e.g., Fears 1981a: 812), but it is useful to have some empirical data on which to base such a claim. For the calculations, see appendix 12.

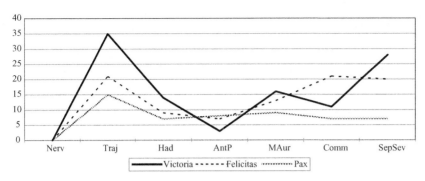

Figure 3.4 Relative frequencies of Victoria, Felicitas, and Pax types on silver coins, expressed as a percentage of all benefit types by reign, AD 96–211 (N = 40,712)

of ideals and values to which provincial populations were most frequently exposed.

The association between Victoria and Pax is straightforward. Pax, as we have seen (above, 127–8), was understood as the result of military pacification, but it was also intimately connected to stability, prosperity, and fertility. To link such desirable conditions with Victory, which the simultaneous minting of Victoria and Pax types could help to bring about, was a particularly effective way to construe Victory as a benefit of empire. The association between Victoria and Felicitas is more complicated. On the one hand, *felicitas* denoted the good fortune that attended the successful and charismatic general. *Felicitas* in this sense is intelligible as a natural counterpart of *Victoria*, but unhelpful in promoting it as somehow beneficial to the empire's inhabitants. On the other hand, *felicitas* could refer to happiness, whether seen as a characteristic of a period or imperial reign or as an individual state of mind. The correlation between the production of Victory and Felicitas types may well point to an official association between military success and the emotional well-being of the imperial community and its individual inhabitants. But did the Roman imperial state really seek to advertise its positive impact on the psychology of its subjects? In order to answer that question, we must take a closer look at *felicitas* and the other "emotional" benefits of empire and monarchy.

FELICITAS AND THE POLITICS OF EMOTION

Felicitas was the product of good fortune (*fortuna*), whether manifested in the actions of men, on the one hand, or in the general bliss and prosperity of the times (*felicitas temporum*), on the other. There has been a tendency in the scholarship on this ideal to treat these two conceptions separately – and to concentrate on the first, especially in the military sphere – but they are closely connected to one another, as we will see, and as a benefit of empire, it was clearly the second that had the greater ideological resonance.[203]

When Cicero included *felicitas* as one of the four defining qualities of ideal generalship, together with expertise in military matters (*scientia rei militaris*), courage (*virtus*), and prestige (*auctoritas*), he was drawing on long-standard terminology for the characterization of Roman military success.[204] By the late Republic these associations were commonplace. Both Cicero and Livy frequently refer to *felicitas* in the context of military achievement.[205] In these passages *felicitas* is the good fortune that attended the successful general, the natural counterpart of martial *virtus* in Roman conceptualizations of victory. Like so many other ideals, *felicitas* became increasingly personalized during the late Republic. In the middle Republic, *felicitas* was the natural corollary of *auspicia*, and was shared by every commander who had correctly taken and followed the auspices. By the late Republic, by contrast, it could also be seen as a special mark of divine favor, going beyond the mere holding of the auspices, and reserved for those charismatic generals, especially Sulla, Pompey, and Caesar, whose military exploits far outstripped those of their aristocratic competitors. Sulla's games in honor of *felicitas* and his assumption of the cognomen Felix are only the most conspicuous examples of the propagandistic advertisement of this ideal's personalization.[206]

---

[203] The literary evidence for *felicitas* is collected in *TLL* 6.426.39–434.59. For general discussions of the term's meaning and usage, see Wagenvoort 1947; Erkell 1952: 41–128; Combès 1966: 208–22, 408–34; Weinstock 1971: 113–15, Gagé 1969; Wistrand 1987. Scholars used to debate whether *felicitas* was a "magical" concept or a "religious" one (cf. Erkell 1952: 43–50), but such distinctions are no longer seen as straightforward, and in any case do not have much significance for our understanding of *felicitas* as a benefit of empire. For the coin type, Strack 1931–37: 1.173–5, 2.181–2; Mattingly in *BMCRE* iii, lxvi, lxxiii, lxxxi, and v, xlii, xcvi; Erkell 1952: 120–7.

[204] Cic. *Man.* 28; cf. Liv. 40.52.5–6 on the inscriptions set up by L. Aemilius Regillus to commemorate his naval victories over Antiochus III in 190 bc: *auspicio, imperio, felicitate, ductuque eius inter Ephesum, Samum Chiumque . . . classis regis Antiochi antehac invicta, fusa, contusa, fugataque est.*

[205] *Felicitas* and *imperium*: e.g. *Leg. agr.* 1.5: *ager Corinthius L. Mummi imperio ac felicitate . . . adiunctus est. Felicitas* and *virtus*: e.g. *Prov. cons.* 35; *Font.* 42: *quorum cognita virtus, industria, felicitas in re militari sit; Dom.* 16; *Phil.* 1.6, 5.40–1, 14.11, 14.28, 14.37; cf. *Rhet. Her.* 4.20.27. *Felicitas* and *victoria*: *Fam.* 1.9.18. Many passages in Livy linking *felicitas* with *imperium, virtus,* and related concepts: 10.24.16, 22.27.3, 22.58.3, 28.32.11, 30.12.12, 30.30.23, 38.48.7, 38.48.15, 39.32.4, 41.16.8. Further passages cited in *TLL* 6.426.71–8, 427.83–428.24.

[206] Games: Vell. Pat. 2.27.6 (for the victory at the Colline Gate in 82). Cognomen: Vell. Pat. 2.27.5; Plin. *NH* 7.44. On Sulla's use of *felicitas*, see Erkell 1952: 71–108; Thein 2009; cf. Gagé 1969: 715–16 on the late Republic in general, and Wistrand 1987: 40–1 on Cicero's celebration of Pompey's special *felicitas* (*Man.* 47–8). Note also that Pompey's triumphal monument inside his theater/portico complex included a dedication to Felicitas (*Inscr. Ital.* 13.2.180, 190; Cic. *Arch.* 10.24), and that

Following the advent of monarchy under Augustus, *felicitas* quickly became a standard imperial attribute. The term did not, however, ossify into a static and empty slogan. Instead, over the course of the first two centuries AD, its primary meaning evolved from good fortune on the battlefield to the happiness of the age, of the community, and of the individual. The *felicitas* of the emperor himself – originally construed as a military ideal – nevertheless remained vital to these broader senses of the term. Consider, for example, the reported words of Valerius Messalla in proposing for Augustus the honorific title of *Pater Patriae*:

May good fortune attend you and your house, Caesar Augustus! For with these words, in our view, we are praying for the perpetual happiness of the state (*perpetua felicitas rei publicae*) and the felicity (*laeta*) of this city. With one voice, the senate, together with the people of Rome, salutes you as Father of the Fatherland.[207]

Though the more general sense of *felicitas* as the defining characteristic of the happy age had already come to the fore by the middle of the first century, the notional connection to the emperor never disappeared. Abundant testimony from authors well disposed to various imperial regimes reveals the emergence of this conception. Seneca, for example, could refer to Nero's accession as "the beginning of the most blessed age," while Tacitus suggests that Trajan himself might increase the *felicitas temporum*: "and though at the dawn of a most blessed age Nerva Caesar brought together two things that were once irreconcilable, the principate and freedom, and though Nerva Trajan daily increases the happiness of the times . . . "[208] Several other passages show that, by the second century, this notion of the emperor's personal role in securing the *felicitas temporum* had become a standard conceit.[209] The diffusion of this idea can also be traced in the official pronouncements of the imperial regime itself. An edict of the emperor Nerva, for example, begins, "The very happiness of the times (*ipsa felicitas temporum*), citizens, proclaims certain things without any doubt . . . "[210]

Caesar had planned to construct a temple to Felicitas in the Forum, eventually built in 44 by M. Aemilius Lepidus (Dio 44.5.2: ναὸν Εὐτυχίας). For the general context, see discussion in Clark 2007: 225–43.

[207] Suet. *Aug.* 58.2 (transl. C. Edwards).

[208] Sen. *Apocol.* 1.1: *initio saeculi felicissimi.* Tac. *Agr.* 3.1: *et quamquam primo statim beatissimi saeculi ortu Nerva Caesar res olim dissociabiles miscuerit, principatum ac libertatem, augeatque cotidie felicitatem temporum Nerva Traianus . . .*

[209] E.g. Curt. 10.9.6: *absit modo invidia, excipiet huius saeculi tempora eiusdem domus utinam perpetua, certe diuturna posteritas. ceterum, ut ad ordinem a quo me contemplatio publicae felicitatis averteram, redeam . . .* ; Sen. *Apoc.* 4.23; Tac. *Dial.* 17 (*sextam iam felicis huius principatus stationem*), *Agr.* 44.5, *Hist.* 1.1. For the role of the emperor in bringing about a "Golden Age," see discussion in Beaujeu 1955: 157–9.

[210] Quoted in Plin. *Ep.* 10.58.7.

The rest of the edict then goes on to announce Nerva's confirmation of his predecessors' *beneficia* – reflecting an important ideological nexus between happiness, on the one hand, and tangible benefits, on the other, to which we will return.

That the imperial coinage was intended to project the dual message of the emperor's *felicitas* and the broader, communal *felicitas* of the age can be inferred from the legends that accompanied the Felicitas types minted between 69 and 235.[211] FELICITAS AUGUSTA/I, which is common throughout the period 69–235, proclaims the state of happiness that the reigning emperor had brought about.[212] Alongside these *Felicitas Augusta* types there were several issues bearing the legends FELICITAS PUBLICA and FELICITAS POPULI ROMANI (the latter only under Hadrian), which identified the beneficiaries of this state of affairs, as well as the more common issues, especially under the later Antonines and the Severans, with legends declaring FELICITAS TEMPORUM and FELICITAS SAECULI, publicizing the communal happiness that defined the current "Golden Age."[213] The Republican and early-imperial association between *felicitas* and military victory is almost entirely effaced by these legends, then, cropping up only once in the Trajanic aureus of 112–14 with reverse legend VIRTUTI ET FELICITATI.[214] The Felicitas types of the imperial coinage clearly denoted happiness and the emperor's role in securing it.

Beyond these official pronouncements on the *felicitas temporum* and *felicitas saeculi*, as seen on the imperial coinage and as expressed by (for example) Nerva's edict, which present *felicitas* as a general state of affairs, a public condition, an external quality, we can also find in the literary sources an understanding of this quality as a state of mind, a personal condition, an internal quality. And it is paradoxically here, I would like to suggest, in the internal and psychological aspect of *felicitas*, that an

---

[211] The type first appeared under Galba: *RIC* I², Galba 273–4, 411–12.

[212] So Mattingly in *BMCRE* III, lxxiii; cf. IV, l, n. 5, and V, xcvi. For the legend, see the relevant indices to either *RIC* or *BMCRE*.

[213] FELICITAS PUBLICA (variously abbreviated): e.g. *RIC* I², Galba 411–12; *RIC* 2, Vespasian 485; *RIC* 2, Titus 89–90; *RIC* 2, Domitian 324; *RIC* 3, Commodus 467; *RIC* 4.1, Septimius Severus 262; *RIC* 4.1, Caracalla 1; *RIC* 4.1, Geta 9a–b; *RIC* 4.2, Severus Alexander 676–81. FELICITAS P(OPULI) R(OMANI): *RIC* 2, Hadrian 238, 756–7, 806–8. FELICITAS TEMPORUM (variously abbreviated, and sometimes expressed as TEMPORUM FELICITAS): e.g. *RIC* 3, Antoninus Pius 857; *RIC* 3, Marcus Aurelius 12–14; *RIC* 3, Commodus 566–7; *RIC* 4.1, Septimius Severus 353–4 (mint of Emesa); *RIC* 4.1, Caracalla 233a; *RIC* 4.1, Geta 1–2; *RIC* 4.2, Macrinus 57–63; *RIC* 4.2, Elagabalus 188; *RIC* 4.2, Severus Alexander 277. FELICITAS SAECULI (variously abbreviated, and sometimes expressed as SAECULI FELICITAS): e.g. *RIC* 3, Antoninus Pius 297; *RIC* 3, Marcus Aurelius 709–11; *RIC* 3, Commodus 113; *RIC* 4.1, Septimius Severus 159; *RIC* 4.1, Caracalla 128; *RIC* 4.1, Geta 126.

[214] *RIC* 2, Trajan 268.

imperial "politics of emotion" is to be found. In his *City of God*, Augustine offers what he represents as an indisputable definition of *felicitas*: "It is well known that happiness is the abundance of everything that is desired."[215] This sense of *felicitas* is certainly related to the meanings discussed above, but without any reference to the emperor or to the community as a whole. The definition, that is to say, is oriented from the perspective of the individual, as the rest of Augustine's discussion makes clear. More revealing is a statement made *en passant* by Pliny in the *Panegyricus*. "For just as happiness is the ability to do whatever you want," he exclaims, "so too is greatness the desire to do whatever you can."[216] In the passage from which this quotation is taken, Pliny is manifestly attempting to direct Trajan's subsequent behavior along moral, and pro-senatorial, lines. But Pliny's casual definition of *felicitas* is illuminating. He equates happiness here with a sort of personal liberty, namely the capacity to do whatever one wants; so, too, Tacitus, who speaks of that "rare happiness of the times," characteristic of the reigns of Nerva and Trajan, "when it is possible to feel what you want and to say what you feel."[217] When the imperial state proclaimed *felicitas*, then, that proclamation of public happiness could perhaps be read, indirectly, as an official declaration of the personal liberty of the emperor's individual subjects.[218] In Roman imperial society, of course, the capacity "to do whatever one wanted," to paraphrase Pliny and Tacitus, was rather narrowly circumscribed, at least in the public sphere. This will not have been lost on the imperial regime. Indeed, the fact that the personal liberty expressed by imperial *felicitas* was only a very pale imitation of the sort of *libertas* that Cicero had championed (see below, 176–7), and one that represented no threat to the supremacy of the emperor, made *felicitas* a very useful condition for the maintenance of the status quo, and may help to explain why this particular value was advertised so regularly.

The imperial politics of emotion runs even deeper than the official celebration of a restricted zone of personal liberty. Hints about what the state may have intended through its advertisement of *felicitas* can be gleaned from the attitudes of contemporary authors, for whom happiness was not an unambiguously positive value. Several authors, in fact, are openly critical of *felicitas*, condemning it as a source of weakness.[219] It is primarily in the writings of Seneca that we find sustained criticism of this emotion.

[215] Aug. *De civ. D.* 5.1: *constat omnium rerum optandarum plenitudinem esse felicitatem.*
[216] Plin. *Pan.* 61.4: *ut enim felicitatis est quantum velis posse, sic magnitudinis velle quantum possis.*
[217] Tac. *Hist.* 1.1: *rara temporum felicitate ubi sentire quae velis et quae sentias dicere licet.*
[218] Cf. Tac. *Agr.* 3.1.
[219] See Morgan 2007: 199–200, drawing on Publilius Syrus' *sententiae* (1st c. BC) and Valerius Maximus.

Characterizing the sort of advice that would be given by one who has turned away from philosophy, Seneca writes:

Virtue, philosophy, justice – it's just a clattering of empty words. The one and only happiness is to live well. Eating, drinking, spending one's inheritance: *that* is living, *that* is remembering that you are a man.[220]

He naturally goes on to disparage this attitude, an elite author combating what he sees as a low, shameful, un-philosophical, and common approach to life. But in his criticism we catch a glimpse, however skewed, of a "popular" understanding of happiness. Seneca's strictures would make no sense if happiness were not regularly construed by his contemporaries as bodily pleasure and the unfettered consumption of food and drink. And he was especially sensitive to the effect that *felicitas* had on the individual. *Felicitas* is a "restless feeling" that incites different men in different ways, he observes, puffing up some, effeminizing others, and enfeebling all.[221] Such conditions were naturally to be avoided. As Seneca counsels, "Shun enticements, shun the enervating happiness that makes the soul grow soft."[222] *Felicitas*, in the Senecan formulation, was not a state of mind conducive to serious thinking. It goes without saying that happiness of this sort, which encouraged depoliticization, would have been welcome to an autocratic regime.

In publicizing *felicitas* on the imperial coinage, the Roman state did not attempt to advertise its effects on those who experienced it, but the numismatic iconography of this ideal did promote a conceptual linkage between happiness and material goods. The two defining attributes of Felicitas, which was always represented as a female personification, were the caduceus and the cornucopia (illustration 3.27).[223] The former represented the world of commerce and the exchange of goods, while the latter symbolized prosperity and agricultural abundance. The standard visual representation of Felicitas, in other words, was unambiguous in its association between the possession of goods and agricultural produce and the personal bliss that these things induced. Nowhere is this association more explicit

---

[220] Sen. *Ep.* 123.10: *virtus et philosophia et iustitia verborum inanium crepitus est. una felicitas est bene vitae facere. esse, bibere, frui patrimonio, hoc est vivere, hoc est se mortalem esse meminisse.*

[221] Sen. *Ep.* 36.1: *res est inquieta felicitas; ipsa se exagitat. movet cerebrum non uno genere; alios in aliud irritat, hos in potentiam, illos in luxuriam. hos inflat, illos mollit et totos resolvit.*

[222] Sen. *Dial.* 1.4.9: *fugite delicias, fugite enervantem felicitatem qua animi permadescunt.*

[223] Felicitas with caduceus and cornucopia: e.g. *RIC* 2, Vespasian 485; *RIC* 2, Domitian 324; *RIC* 2, Trajan 268; *RIC* 2, Hadrian 40a–c; *RIC* 3, Antoninus Pius 535; *RIC* 3, Marcus Aurelius 12–14; *RIC* 3, Commodus 97; *RIC* 4.1, Septimius Severus 261–2; *RIC* 4.1, Caracalla 18; *RIC* 4.1, Geta 2; *RIC* 4.2, Macrinus 57–60; *RIC* 4.2, Elagabalus 148–50; *RIC* 4.2, Severus Alexander 179. See discussion in *LIMC* 8.1.585–91 (T. Ganshow).

Illustration 3.27 Reverse of denarius (*RIC* 2, Hadrian 121): Felicitas holding a caduceus and a cornucopia. FELIC. AUG

than in a sestertius produced under Antoninus Pius, which depicted a personification of Annona, holding a tablet and a rudder, flanked on the left by two ships, one carrying a modius and grain stalks, and on the right by a lighthouse, a scene of robust commerce and agriculture glossed by the legend ANNONA AUG(USTA) FELIX SC.[224] With this image and legend, and with the numismatic iconography of Felicitas in general, we are not too far removed from Augustine's definition of happiness as "the abundance of everything desired," or from Seneca's critique of happiness as nothing more than eating, drinking, and spending money.

Towards the end of the *Panegyricus*, when Pliny acknowledges Trajan's *felicitas*, he feels it necessary to stress that he is not referring to the emperor's material wealth, but rather to his inner spirit.[225] This is a useful reminder that *felicitas*, despite its pronounced material dimension, was ultimately an emotion, an internal and subjective state of happiness, however produced. In advertising happiness as a benefit of empire, the Roman state

---

[224] *RIC* 3, Antoninus Pius 757.

[225] Plin. *Pan.* 74.1: *nihil magis possum proprie dicere, quam quod dictum est a cuncto senatu: "O te felicem!" quod cum diceremus, non opes tuas sed animum mirabamur. ea enim demum vera felicitas, felicitate dignum videri.*

employed two other types on the imperial coinage, *hilaritas* and *laetitia*, that reinforced the message of *felicitas*. Both *hilaritas* and *laetitia* referred mainly to the personal happiness, joy, or merriment of individuals, and the two terms are often used together.[226] *Hilaritas* could serve as a simple contrast to *tristitia*, "sadness," as when Cicero laments to Atticus, "I have lost forever that *hilaritas* with which I used to 'season' this sadness of the times."[227] *Laetitia* also expressed personal joy, and was sometimes paired with another term for gladness, *gaudium*.[228] As with *felicitas*, so too with *hilaritas* and *laetitia*, the connection between these positive emotions and the imperial regime was often drawn. Fronto, for example, writes that it is the happiness of Marcus Aurelius that strengthens his own joy, security, happiness (*hilaritas*), and pride, and Pliny lauds Trajan as the "author" and "cause" of public gladness (*laetitia publica*).[229] Both terms were also connected with public celebrations. In the *acta* of Septimius Severus' *ludi saeculares*, reference is made to the *laetitiae* and *gaudia* (plural) of the human race, an indication that these terms had festive overtones and could be related to public celebrations sponsored by the emperor.[230] And *hilaritas* seems to have been associated with the festival *Hilaria*, which celebrated the resurrection of Attis in the cult of the Magna Mater.[231]

Conceptually, then, *hilaritas* and *laetitia* were closely related to *felicitas*, all three denoting happiness and celebration and, in official discourse, representing pleasant conditions secured by the emperor. But while the numismatic iconography of Hilaritas and Laetitia did overlap somewhat with that of Felicitas, especially through the attribute of the cornucopia that sometimes accompanied Hilaritas – again reminding us of the conceptual

---

[226] *Hilaritas*: *TLL* 6.3.2784.54–2786.8, esp. 2784.67–2785.63 (the "cheerfulness" of men). *Laetitia*: *TLL* 7.2.874.77–879.12, esp. 875.19–43 (personal joy/happiness). *Hilaritas* and *laetitia* together: e.g. Cic. *Tusc.* 4.15: *ut laetitia profusam hilaritatem efficiat*; *Or.* 1.243: *hilaritatis plenum iudicium ac laetitiae fuit*; Sen. *Dial.* 7.4.4: *hilaritas continua et laetitia alta*.

[227] Cic. *Att.* 12.40.3 (SB 281): *hilaritatem illam, qua hanc tristitiam temporum condiebam, in perpetuum amisi*; cf. *Or.* 3.197: *et ad hilaritatem et ad tristitiam saepe deducimur*.

[228] See below, n. 230. According to Cicero, however, *laetitia* was to be distinguished from *gaudium*: *gaudere decet, laetari non decet, quoniam docendi causa a gaudio laetitiam distinguimus* (*Tusc.* 4.66; cf. *Tusc.* 4.13). The implication seems to be that *laetitia* is an "over-exuberant" joy, but this would not have been problematic for the public pronouncements of the imperial regime.

[229] Fro. *ad Marc. Caes.* 2.2.7 (van den Hout): *certe hilaris es, certe bene vales . . . vale meum gaudium, mea securitas, hilaritas, gloria*. Plin. *Pan.* 79.3: *laetitiae publicae auctor eius et causa*; for other expressions of *laetitia publica*, cf. *Act. Arv.* s.a. 89 (Scheid 1998, no. 57), l. 36; Suet. *Cal.* 14.1, 17.2; *Act. Lud. Saec. Sep. Sev.* 2.19.

[230] *Act. Lud. Saec. Sep. Sev.* 1.21: *inter laetitias et gaudia generis humani*; cf. 1.26: *pro temporum laetitia et felicitate . . . p[rincipu]m*.

[231] On the connection between the Hilaritas type and the festival *Hilaria*, see Mattingly in *BMCRE* III, cxxxiii; cf. Strack 1931–37: 2.98–100, who disputes a close connection with the *Hilaria* and argues for a more general meaning for the Hilaritas advertised on the coinage.

Illustration 3.28 Reverse of denarius (*RIC* 3, Commodus 282): Hilaritas holding a palm and a cornucopia. HILARITAS

Illustration 3.29 Reverse of antoninianus (*RIC* 4.3, Gordian III 86): Laetitia holding a laurel wreath and an anchor. LAETITIA AUG. N

link between happiness and material prosperity – the two qualities were more closely associated with Victoria, with which they shared their defining attributes, the palm for Hilaritas (illustration 3.28) and the laurel wreath for Laetitia (illustration 3.29).[232] This iconography brings us back full circle to the structural connection between military victory, guaranteed by the emperor, and its positive effects, including the desirable emotions and states of mind represented by *felicitas*, *hilaritas*, and *laetitia*.

While Hilaritas and Laetitia types were relatively rare on imperial coins, Felicitas was one of the more common benefit types, on both the silver and base-metal denominations. And the three types, as a group, played an important role in the overall typology of the imperial coinage, representing 16 percent of all benefit types on the silver and 18 percent of all benefit types on the bronze (see above, tables 3.1–2). These figures indicate a sustained commitment on the part of the Roman imperial state to the representation of positive emotions as real benefits of empire and monarchy. For through these types, the state not only announced to the coin's users what the current state of affairs was, but also told them how they should feel. Those were

---

[232] Hilaritas with cornucopia: e.g. *RIC* 2, Hadrian 970; *RIC* 3, Antoninus Pius 606; *RIC* 3, Marcus Aurelius 610; *RIC* 3, Commodus 282; *RIC* 4.1, Septimius Severus 556–8. Hilaritas with palm: e.g. *RIC* 2, Hadrian 970; *RIC* 3, Antoninus Pius 606; *RIC* 3, Marcus Aurelius 606; *RIC* 3, Commodus 150; *RIC* 4.1, Septimius Severus 555; *RIC* 4.2, Elagabalus 85. Laetitia with laurel wreath: e.g. *RIC* 3, Antoninus Pius 506; *RIC* 3, Marcus Aurelius 699–702; *RIC* 3, Commodus 632; *RIC* 4.1, Septimius Severus 317; *RIC* 4.1, Geta 10; *RIC* 4.2, Elagabalus 93–6. For the iconography of Hilaritas, see *LIMC* 8.1.631–3, 8.2.390 (T. Ganschow); for Laetitia, *LIMC* 6.1.181–4 (H.-J. Schulzki).

strong claims. Whether the imperial regime actually sought to make the people "happy," as Zanker has suggested, is difficult to judge.[233] It seems unlikely that this was ever a conscious goal, and indeed the continued minting of the Felicitas and Laetitia types amidst the turbulence of the mid-third century is a useful reminder that imperial publicity did not always reflect current conditions.[234]

It is even more doubtful whether the inhabitants of the empire were ever influenced by these types. Of course, the true emotional experience of Rome's imperial subjects is beyond the reach of our evidence. But we can reconstruct the contours of public discourse, and we can study how Romans used language to map various emotional terrains.[235] Among the labels attached to the emotion that we call "happiness" were *hilaritas*, *laetitia*, and especially *felicitas*, which, as we have seen, were invested by the authors of the early empire with a range of meanings. And these meanings, derived from a political and cultural elite, may be taken to represent the dominant cultural construction of the particular psychological state signified by these terms. At the heart of this construction, equally clear in the literary sources and in the official iconography of the imperial coinage, was the cluster of affective experiences associated with festivity, public celebration and merriment, material goods, prosperity, and the abundance of food and drink. The desirability of such experiences surely explains the relative prominence of Felicitas and its satellite ideals, Hilaritas and Laetitia, on the imperial coinage. For the "happiness" of the emperor and that of the empire's inhabitants, intimately connected through this constellation of concepts, helped to maintain the notional community of interests between emperor and subject.

CONCLUSION

Amongst the most common benefit types on denarii minted under Antoninus Pius, comprising about one quarter of all benefit types on the silver coinage from 138 to 161, were those representing *aeternitas*.[236] Some were

---

[233] Zanker 2010. Zanker's suggestion is part of his larger discussion of the motivations behind the imperial provision of games and spectacles for the inhabitants of Rome; as evidence for the notion that emperors sought to make the people "happy" (*glücklich*), he adduces Caracalla's LAETITIA TEMPORUM type of *c.* 202 (*RIC* 4.1, 133).

[234] For the Felicitas and Laetitia types during the "third-century crisis," see the indices to *RIC* 4.2, 4.3, 5.1, and 5.2.

[235] For this approach, see Kaster 2005, esp. 3–12 on the methodological challenges in the study of ancient emotions.

[236] For the tabulations, see appendix 7.

Illustration 3.30 Reverse of sestertius (*RIC* 3, Antoninus Pius 1105): Aeternitas holding a globe with a phoenix on top. AETERNITAS

produced on coins bearing the obverse portrait of the deified Faustina, which sounded the theme of dynastic continuity, while others were collocated with the portrait of Antoninus himself, which hinted at the continuity of the reign and, more broadly, of the institution of the principate.[237] The main attribute associated with the personification of Aeternitas was the globe (illustration 3.30), an emphatic assertion of the eternity of the empire itself. The Aeternitas type, in other words, announced that the golden age of the Roman empire would go on forever, recalling Jupiter's prophecy in the *Aeneid* of an "empire without end," but only under the guidance and protection of the Antonine dynasty.[238]

What gave the message of *aeternitas* real ideological resonance was neither the idea of empire, nor that of monarchy, but rather the spectrum of specific benefits that were associated with both. In the official representation of those benefits, no medium available to the central state was more expressive than the coinage. The physical duality of each coin effectively attached the benefit represented on the reverse to the reigning emperor depicted on the obverse, a potent symbolic expression of "the monarchic style," while the convergence of image and text ensured that the underlying messages were both simple and attractive. In addition, the simultaneous circulation of millions of coins minted over periods of up to a century and more

---

[237] Faustina: e.g. *RIC* 3, 1,099–115. Antoninus: e.g. *RIC* 3, 61a, 114, 125. For the Aeternitas type, see Mattingly in *BMCRE* iv, lxii–lxiii and Strack 1931–37: 3.102–3, both emphasizing the dynastic message; cf. Charlesworth 1936: 122–31, emphasizing the imperial message.

[238] Verg. *Aen.* 1.278–9: *imperium sine fine.*

would have worked to break down neat distinctions between the reigning emperor, the current dynasty, and the Roman imperial system as a whole, which surely helped to generalize and universalize the messages transmitted by individual coins.

Some of the short- and long-term minting patterns discussed in this chapter, in particular those illuminated by the variable relative frequencies with which the different types were minted, show that this medium of communications could be employed more strategically than is normally thought. The promotion of Pax and Concordia on the silver, and of Fortuna and Salus on the base-metal denominations, implies a carefully coordinated targeting of different audiences across social classes, while the fluctuating relative frequencies of the Victoria, Pax, and Felicitas types, especially between the reigns of Nerva and Septimius Severus, show how certain clusters of benefits, mutually reinforcing, could be emphasized simultaneously. The strong correlation between the frequency of the Victoria type and the number of imperatorial acclamations suggests that such fluctuations were meaningful. Iconographic conventions, too, added nuance and complexity. The overlapping iconography of Annona, on the one hand, and of Abundantia and Ceres, on the other, helped to blur the distinction between the narrow message of the former and the universal one of the latter. And the attributes shared between Victoria, Hilaritas, and Laetitia, the latter two connected semantically to Felicitas, established a conceptual link between Roman military conquest and the happiness of the empire's subjects. One attribute in particular that graced many of the types discussed in this chapter is the cornucopia, symbol of material abundance, which appeared with the goddess Ceres and with personifications representing *annona, abundantia, pax, concordia, fortuna, felicitas,* and *hilaritas.* This is an exceptionally diverse set of benefits, ranging from tangible things to desirable conditions to cheerful emotions, all united, visually and ideologically, by the cornucopia, a deeply resonant symbol that subtly forged a broad continuum of ideals advertising the concrete, material goods that came with Roman imperial rule.

But such goods did not come without a price. What was lost in this imperial system that claimed such wide-ranging benefits was the political freedom of those who were supposed to enjoy them; what was lost, in a word, was *libertas.*[239] This trade-off is clearly reflected in the typology of

---

[239] For *libertas* as a political concept at Rome, see Wirszubski 1950; Wickert 1954: 2,080–98; Hellegouarc'h 1963: 542–65; Stylow 1972; Brunt 1988: 281–350 (mainly on the Republican period); Roller 2001: 220–33, 262–4. See also Raaflaub 2004: 250–77 for comparison with Greek ideas of "freedom." For the literary evidence, *TLL* 7.2.1310.57–1319.8.

benefits advertised on the coinage, in which Libertas types were comparatively rare. During our period the Libertas type appeared on the coinage of Vespasian, Nerva, Hadrian, Antoninus Pius, Marcus Aurelius, Commodus, Septimius Severus, Caracalla, Elagabalus, and Severus Alexander, and indeed the coin catalogues give the impression that Libertas types were quite common. In fact, it has been argued that *libertas* was a key imperial ideal, and that its representation on the coinage should be seen as an important form of imperial "propaganda."[240] But here the quantitative evidence stands as an important corrective, as the relatively low frequency with which the type was minted throughout our period suggests that this ideal played only a negligible role in imperial publicity (cf. tables 3.1–2). Nor was this infrequency anomalous. For, as Cicero put it, "*libertas* has a home only in that *civitas* in which the power of the people (*populi potestas*) is supreme."[241] This was patently not the case under the empire, when the emperor could be construed by the jurists as being "above the law."[242] Despite the rhetoric of Tacitus and Pliny, who credit "good" emperors with the reconciliation of *principatus* and *libertas*, monarchy and freedom were inherently incompatible.[243] As a result, Libertas types could hardly have much resonance. The advertised benefits of empire and monarchy, as this chapter has shown, had to be found elsewhere.

---

[240] Stylow 1972. Drawing in particular on the coinage, Stylow also argues that the concepts of *libertas* and *liberalitas* began to merge in the late second century AD, especially under Septimius Severus (58–74), but the relative frequencies of the two types do not fluctuate together in any meaningful way, as far as I can tell.

[241] Cic. *Rep.* 1.47.2.   [242] See above, 6.

[243] Tac. *Agr.* 3.1: *Nerva Caesar res olim dissociabiles miscuerit, principatum ac libertatem.* Plin. *Pan.* 36.4: *eodem foro utuntur principatus et libertas.*

PART II

Circulation

Introduction to Part II: Circulation

The two chapters of Part II turn from the official representation of imperial virtues and benefits to the central communication of these ideals and to their long-term circulation throughout the Roman West. As in Part I, these chapters draw on various sources, but with increasing emphasis on the epigraphic evidence. This introduction discusses the composition of this body of evidence and outlines its main features.

For this study I have assembled a corpus of 575 Latin inscriptions, erected between AD 69 and 235, that include honorific terminology attached to or associated with the Roman emperor.[1] In putting together this corpus I have consulted all the published volumes and supplements of the *Corpus Inscriptionum Latinarum* (*CIL*), and all editions of *L'Année Epigraphique* (*AE*) through *AE* 2004 (published in 2007), and have attempted to record every inscription including honorific terminology for the emperor. I define "honorific terminology" as any term of praise, attached to or associated with the emperor, that does not belong to the emperor's official nomenclature and titulature.[2] Most of these honorific terms are epithets, usually superlatives. Frequently embedded within the emperor's "standard" names and titles, such epithets belong to what some scholars have called the emperor's "unofficial" titulature.[3] In addition to these honorific epithets, we also find a wide range of other evaluative terms associated with the emperor, usually virtues, and almost always cited in the "motivation" clauses of the

---

[1] For a complete list of all 575 inscriptions in the corpus, see appendix 13 (organized by date); cf. appendices 14 (cross-listed by location) and 15 (cross-listed by type).

[2] The indices to *CIL* 16 (military diplomas) and *RIC* are still the best introductions to the evolving typology of the emperor's official titles. For a survey of the epigraphic record in Latin, see Musca 1979; cf. Bureth 1964 and de Jong 2006: 84–97 for the evidence from Egyptian papyri. Kienast 1996 is an indispensable guide to the chronology of imperial titulature. For discussion of the political and ideological significance of the various official titles, see also Hammond 1957; cf. the perceptive comments of H. Nesselhauf in *CIL* 16, p. 153.

[3] Frei-Stolba 1969 collects the evidence (then published) down to Commodus; cf. Berlinger 1935 (somewhat erratic and now out of date); Kuhoff 1990 (focusing on North Africa).

inscriptions in question.[4] Though honorific epithets and evaluative terms tend to appear in different types of inscriptions, both functioned to associate the emperor, directly or indirectly, with the sorts of ideals and values examined in Part I.

It is crucial to note right at the outset that this collection of inscriptions is not a statistical sample, like the sample of imperial coins discussed in the Introduction to Part I. It is, instead, a corpus, and as such is meant to stand as a complete collection of all published inscriptions that meet the criteria noted above. This corpus cannot, however, be taken as representative of all such inscriptions once erected and now lost (or unpublished). Whereas the numismatic sample was designed to be representative of the typological profile of all imperial coins minted at Rome between 69 and 235, these 575 inscriptions provide only a partial picture of a vanished epigraphic landscape. Just how partial that picture is cannot be ascertained. Problems include the difficulty in calculating the total number of inscriptions once erected but now lost; the uneven rate of epigraphic preservation and publication in different areas; and the possibility that discernible patterns in the honorific terminology for the emperor in those inscriptions that do survive have been distorted by these factors.[5] But 575 inscriptions is a sufficient number for various types of quantitative analysis, and in the chapters that follow I hope to show not only that this epigraphic material can be profitably juxtaposed to the sample of numismatic evidence, but also that it can shed new light on the circulation of imperial ideals. Here I want to describe the composition of the corpus in typological, chronological, and geographical terms.

First, the typology. There are several ways in which the inscriptions making up the corpus could be classified into separate categories, but for the purposes of this study, the two key variables for classification are (i) the formal author(s) of the texts, and (ii) the "position" of the emperor in them. Formal authorship ranges on a spectrum between official and unofficial,

---

[4] See briefly Kajanto 1971: 10–12; Salomies 1994: 71, 82–3.

[5] Over 25 years ago, MacMullen estimated that roughly half a million inscriptions from the Roman empire had been published at that time (1982: 238, n. 6a). Using a series of data and calculations from thirteen sites in North Africa, Duncan-Jones estimated that 5 percent of the inscriptions once erected in North Africa have survived (1982: 360–2). The two figures together imply that some 10 million inscriptions had been set up in the Roman empire at one time or another. But MacMullen's figure is probably too low (and not all surviving inscriptions have been published), and Duncan-Jones' estimate too high (as he acknowledges, 362), so the actual number is probably somewhere between 15 million (with a 5 percent survival rate on 750,000 extant inscriptions) and 50 million (with a 1 percent survival rate on 500,000 extant inscriptions), if not higher. The speculative nature of these numbers hardly needs to be stressed. For the variable survival of inscriptions by region, see Duncan-Jones 1982: 360–1; Mann 1985.

with the emperor himself at one end and private dedicators at the other, and various sorts of collectivities and individuals, some associated with the central state, others with municipalities, in between.[6] The "position" of the emperor in these inscriptions denotes his formal place in their grammatical syntax or his degree of centrality to their overall subject matter. In some inscriptions he is the subject of the text, his names and titles in the nominative case. In most he is the object of a dedication (with his names and titles, as we would expect, in the dative).[7] In others the emperor is secondary, incorporated into the inscription only in the context of a dedication to someone or something else. And in some cases the emperor appears in texts that have no honorific or dedicatory function at all, but is nevertheless associated with honorific terminology. With reference both to authorship and to the emperor's position, then, I have identified nine basic types of inscription that include honorific terminology for the emperor; a tenth "type" serves as a catch-all category for all other inscriptions with any sort of honorific terminology for the emperor.[8]

The definitions of these ten types, and the total numbers of inscriptions within the corpus for each type, are presented in table Int. II.1. The ten types making up the corpus of 575 inscriptions may be combined, for analytical purposes, into four separate sub-groups. Type 1 inscriptions, in which the emperor is the formal author of the text, constitutes a sub-group of its own (making up 7 percent of all inscriptions in the corpus). It should be noted that several inscriptions in this category included superlative epithets, in the nominative case, which makes somewhat problematic the conventional identification of these epithets as "unofficial."[9] Types 2–4, which contain all dedications to the emperor made by officials or representatives of the central state, constitute a second sub-group (23 percent of all inscriptions in corpus). Types 5–7 are also made up of dedications to the emperor, but these dedications were all made by any collectivity or individual that was not a representative of the central state (31 percent).

[6] The spectrum of "official" and "unofficial" authorship is discussed below, 214–17, 218–20.

[7] For most of the Republic, the names of honored persons were either in the accusative case, following Greek practice, or in the nominative, perhaps influenced by *elogia*; the earliest attested use of the dative in a Latin honorific inscription is from 91 BC (Delos): *CIL* 1².705 = *ILS* 7172 = *ILLRP* 344. See Kajanto 1971: 7–9.

[8] It goes without saying that some inscriptions straddle the line between two or more types, and that any of these types could be further subdivided. But this scheme should be sufficiently articulated to capture the overall typological shape of the corpus.

[9] The earliest example in the corpus comes from 169, when Marcus Aurelius and Lucius Verus appear as *sacratissimi imperatores* (*CIL* 3.14120, Gortyn, Crete); several years later, between 177–80, Marcus Aurelius and Commodus are styled as *fortissimi* in an inscription from Numidia (*CIL* 8.2488, Mesarfelte [?]).

Table Int. II.1 *Total number of inscriptions employing honorific terminology for the emperor, by type, AD 69–235*

Types	Definition	No. of inscriptions
Type 1	emperor as author (emperor's names/titles in nominative)	38
Type 2	dedication to emperor by senate or SPQR	13
Type 3	dedication to emperor by soldiers or army officials	57
Type 4	dedication to emperor by other imperial officials	64
Type 5	dedication to emperor by city, community, or municipal council	94
Type 6	dedication to emperor by non-state groups or private individuals	38
Type 7	dedication to emperor by unknown dedicator	47
Type 8	dedication to god(s) on behalf of emperor	89
Type 9	dedication to member of imperial family	35
Type 10	miscellaneous inscriptions with honorific terminology for emperor	100
		Total: 575

This stands as a third sub-group. The fourth and final sub-group, with inscriptions belonging to types 8–10, is made up of all inscriptions containing honorific terminology for the emperor in which the emperor was neither the formal author of the text nor the honorand of a dedication (39 percent). This is, of course, a very schematic account of a diverse body of material. One theme that will emerge in the subsequent chapters, in fact, is the remarkably wide range of texts and authors that participated in the circulation of imperial ideals. For some questions, the arguments will draw on this full range of texts. In general, though, chapter 4, which considers the central diffusion of imperial ideals, will draw mainly on types 1–4, while chapter 5, examining the local response to this central communication, will focus on types 5–7. Both chapters will draw, where appropriate, on types 8–10.

We turn now to chronology. Tabulated on a reign-by-reign basis, the number of inscriptions employing honorific terminology for the emperor was very uneven over time. The total numbers are presented in table Int. II.2, which reveals nine emperors for whom substantial material survives: Trajan, Hadrian, Antoninus Pius, Marcus Aurelius, Commodus, Septimius Severus, Caracalla, Elagabalus, and Severus Alexander. But in order to understand the chronological patterning of these inscriptions, we also need to control for the variable lengths of the different imperial reigns.

Table Int. 11.2 *Total number of inscriptions employing*
honorific terminology for the emperor, by reign,
AD 69–235

Emperor	Number	Emperor	Number
Vespasian	3	Commodus	19
Titus	4	Pertinax	1
Domitian	1	Septimius Severus	172
Nerva	0	Caracalla	132
Trajan	28	Geta	10
Hadrian	42	Macrinus	5
Antoninus Pius	33	Elagabalus	29
Marcus Aurelius	21	Severus Alexander	72
Lucius Verus	3		
			Total: 575

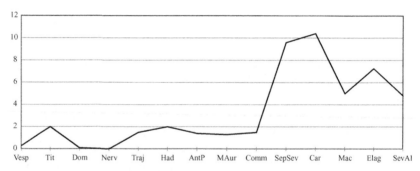

Figure Int. 11.1 Relative frequency of inscriptions employing honorific terminology for the
emperor, per reign-year, AD 69–235 (N = 575)
Note: The figures for Marcus Aurelius (AD 161–180) include those of Lucius Verus (161–9),
and the figures for Caracalla (whose "reign" is here dated from AD 197 to 217) include
those of Geta (211–12). Pertinax was left out of the chart because of the brevity of his reign.

The next step, then, is to tabulate the number of such inscriptions per
reign-year for all emperors from Vespasian to Severus Alexander (figure
Int. 11.1). A very clear pattern emerges. Under the Flavian emperors and
during the reign of Nerva, these inscriptions were comparatively rare –
during these years, in other words, epigraphic references to the emperor, in
honorific and non-honorific inscriptions alike, tended to include his official
names and titles only. Between Trajan and Commodus the use of honorific
terminology was more common. The big upsurge comes with Septimius

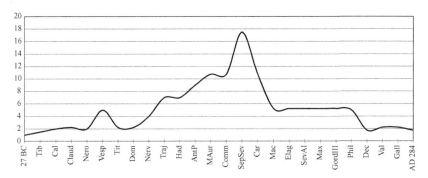

Figure Int. 11.2 Relative frequency of Latin inscriptions, 27 BC–AD 284, expressed as number of inscriptions per reign-year, from Augustus to Numerianus (N = 2892)

Severus and especially Caracalla. After a sharp drop under Geta in inscriptions with honorific terminology for the emperor, the frequency of such inscriptions leveled off between Macrinus and Severus Alexander – but at a significantly higher frequency, it should be noted, than that of the second century.

Another way to assess the chronological fluctuations in these inscriptions is to compare them to the overall frequency curve of all Latin inscriptions, as established by Mrozek (figure Int. 11.2).[10] It has not been sufficiently emphasized that Mrozek's dating criteria were often subjective, and that he employed very rough estimates for dates, employing quarter-century divisions.[11] As a result, it would be misleading to calculate the precise correlation between the number of inscriptions with honorific terminology for the emperor and all Latin inscriptions. Mrozek's curve does at least allow us to place our inscriptions in a very broad chronological context. In general, as the two graphs make clear, the fluctuating relative frequency of inscriptions with honorific terminology for the emperor mirrors the overall frequency curve quite closely. The decision to cite the emperor in an inscription, and to attach honorific terminology to him, in other words, can be seen as one element of the larger epigraphic culture of which these texts were a part. The one exception to this general correlation comes with Caracalla, for whom the inscriptions with honorific terminology are notably more numerous than the frequency curve would predict. This is an important point to which we will return at the end of chapter 5.

[10] Mrozek 1973; cf. 1988. For elaborations of Mrozek's work and attempts to explain the shape of the curve, see MacMullen 1982; Meyer 1990; Woolf 1996; see also below, 279–83.
[11] See discussion in Cherry 1995.

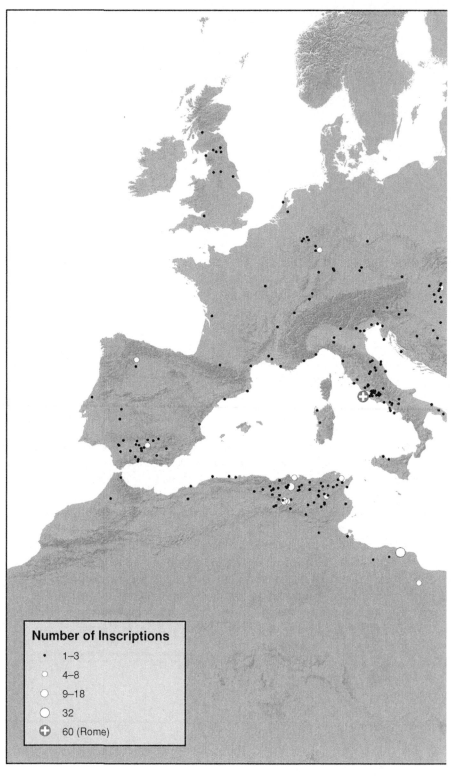

Number of Inscriptions

•	1–3
○	4–8
○	9–18
○	32
⊕	60 (Rome)

Map 1 Inscriptions employing honorific terminology for the emperor AD 69–235

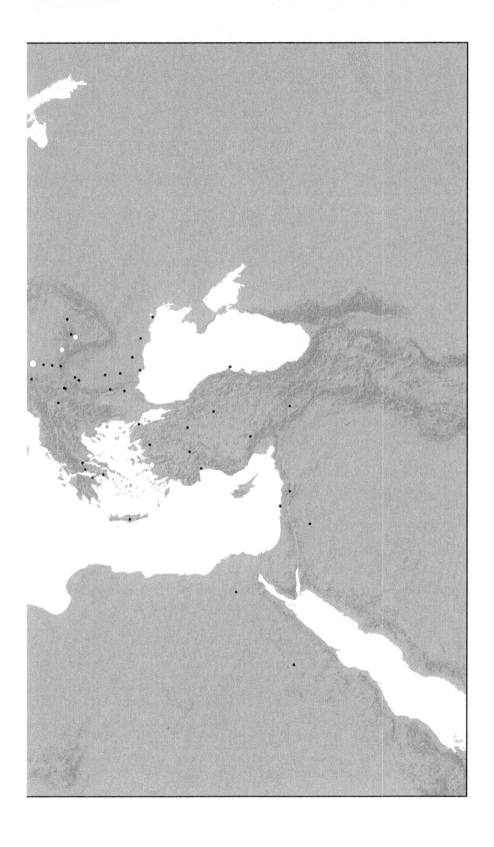

Table Int. 11.3 *Regional distribution of
inscriptions employing honorific terminology
for the emperor, AD 69–235*

Region	Number of inscriptions (% of total)
North Africa	197 (34%)
Italy	150 (26%)
West Continent	99 (17%)
Danube/Balkans	95 (17%)
The East	34 (6%)
	Total: 575

Note: for the definitions of these regions, see above,
table Int. 1.1.

Finally, the geography. Table Int. 11.3 presents the regional distribution of
the 575 inscriptions that make up the corpus. In order to facilitate comparison with the distribution of coin hoards used in the numismatic sample,
this table employs the same regional classification as tables 1.1–2 in the
Introduction to Part 1 (31–2). As the table shows, the spatial distribution of
these inscriptions is very uneven. Roughly one third of these inscriptions
come from North Africa, with another quarter coming from the Italian
peninsula alone. Inscriptions set up in the "West Continent" region, and
those from the "Danube/Balkan" region, each comprise just under one
fifth of the corpus. "The East," as one would expect, is proportionally
less well represented, with only 34 total Latin inscriptions including honorific terminology for the emperor. These numbers are not surprising, of
course, mirroring, as they do, the overall geographical distribution of Latin
inscriptions in the Roman empire.[12]

A map with the locations of all 575 inscriptions provides a more detailed
overview (map 1).[13] The principal concentrations of inscriptions with honorific terminology for the emperor are in central Italy, Africa Proconsularis,
Numidia, and southern Spain, with secondary clusters in north Italy, along

[12] For comparison of the densities of extant inscriptions in different provinces, on the basis of the total
number of inscriptions published in the first edition of *CIL*, see Harris 1989: 266–8, with Woolf
1996: 36 and 1998: 82, fig. 4.1 for a cartographic representation of the data. In interpreting this
data, it is important to bear in mind that a very small number of the inscriptions once erected has
survived and that the ratio of survival varies sharply between regions and even specific sites (above,
n. 5), and also that the first edition of *CIL* is now seriously out of date, especially for the Iberian
peninsula.

[13] See also maps 2 and 3 (below, 230–1), which show the geographical distribution of inscriptions over
two different periods (AD 69–192 and 193–235, respectively).

the middle Rhine (Germania Superior) and middle Danube (Pannonia Inferior), and in Dacia. Lighter concentrations are evident in Tripolitania, central Britannia, through the Rhône corridor, and along the lower Danube (Moesia Inferior). There are also some large areas with notable voids, including central Spain, western Gaul, and southern Britannia. Several arguments in subsequent chapters will draw attention to regional patterns in the choice of honorific terminology for the emperor, but for all global statements about the corpus as a whole, this uneven geographical distribution will have to be kept in mind.

CHAPTER 4

The diffusion of imperial ideals in time and space

REPRESENTATION/COMMUNICATION/CIRCULATION

Through the quantitative analysis of imperial coin types presented in chapters 2 and 3, I have attempted to open up a new perspective on a world of ideas, to examine, in both structural and discursive terms, the constellation of ideals and values associated with the figure of the Roman emperor, from the accession of Vespasian in 69 to the death of Severus Alexander, 166 years later, in 235. Embracing both the emperor's exemplary character, with a strong accent on the virtues of fairness, duty, valor, generosity, and foresight – enacted qualities that operated in the spheres of warfare, benefaction, religion, and dynasty – and the benefits of monarchy and empire, which effectively merged the empire-wide conditions of victory, peace, and harmony, on the one hand, with the more personal experiences of good luck, health, and happiness, on the other, it is an interrelated set of ideals and values that may fairly be described as a system. Though the investigation of this system has traced the genealogies of these concepts and how they came to be attached to the figure of the Roman emperor, how they related to one another, both semantically and iconographically, and what, exactly, they meant, most of the focus has been on how this set of ideas was imagined and, in particular, expressed. It has been an investigation, in other words, of representation. As such, it belongs to the history of ideas, and may stand on its own as a contribution to that history.

But these ideas were neither imagined nor expressed in a vacuum. The coins on which they were represented were mass produced and disseminated from Rome, circulating thereafter for many years and throughout the Roman world, bringing about the long-term diffusion of imperial ideals and values from one end of the empire to the other. It is that process of diffusion and its effects that we now take up, turning from representation to communication and circulation.

The first task is to understand how imperial coins, still critical for the arguments of this and the following chapters, functioned as vehicles of official communications. Scholars have considered this question at length, of course, with much of the discussion centering on problems of agency and intent in type selection, the intelligibility of the types themselves, and, above all, whether or not imperial coins should be seen as instruments of political "propaganda." Those questions are relevant, and will be addressed, briefly, in what follows. Even more important for assessing the communicative functions of imperial coins, however, are the underlying mechanics of coin production and circulation, too often ignored by numismatists and historians in the ongoing debates over the significance of coin types. As we will see, these mechanics are vital to an understanding of the diffusion of imperial ideals by means of coins.

In considering coins as instruments of official communications, we should begin with the problem of agency, and in particular with the administration of the central mint and the decision-making processes that lay behind both mint output (frequently overlooked in this connection) and type selection. Unfortunately, our knowledge of the inner workings of the central mint at Rome is very limited.[1] In terms of personnel, we know of various officials associated with the central mint, but not much about what they actually did. By the early second century AD, the mint was under the overall administrative authority of a *procurator monetae*. What that meant in practice is unclear. The secretary *a rationibus* seems to have been responsible for determining total output. *Triumviri monetales*, "moneyers," are attested through the Severan period, but their precise duties are unknown.[2] Any one of these officials might have chosen the designs for new coins. In addition, some ancient authors, as is well known, write or imply that the emperor himself chose the designs. This is not impossible in individual cases, but rather unlikely on a routine basis.[3] The most plausible guess is that both mint output and routine type selection were determined by the higher-ranking mint officials.[4] For the purposes of this study, though, it

---

[1] See discussion in Carson 1956; Wolters 1999: 85–99.

[2] *Procurator monetae*: *CIL* 6.1607 = *ILS* 1450 (Rome, *c.* 137), 6.1625b = *ILS* 1340 (Rome, 2nd c.). *A rationibus*: Stat. *Silv.* 3.3.104–5: *quae divum in vultus igni formanda liquescat / massa, quid Ausoniae scriptum crepet igne Monetae. Triumviri monetales*: *CIL* 10.3850 = *ILS* 1181 (near Capua, *c.* 233).

[3] E.g. Suet. *Aug.* 94.12, *Nero* 25.2; Eus. *VC* 4.15.1; Soc. *HE* 3.17; Soz. *HE* 5.19.2. We should not forget that what was done for the emperor could often be seen as having been done by the emperor (a point often made).

[4] As Peachin 1986 emphasizes, such officials were usually of equestrian status. In general on type selection in the imperial mint, see Wolters 1999: 255–65. For the administration of the mints under the Republic, see Crawford 1974: 598–620. There can be little doubt that under the Republic, it was the *triumviri monetales* who chose the types on the coins they struck.

does not really matter who chose the types. What does matter is that the designs on imperial coins were selected by officials of the central state; that these coins bore the stamp of imperial authority; and that they carried symbols that were unambiguously official.

Whether or not coin types were intended to transmit specific, topical messages, either to the inhabitants of the empire at large or to particular groups within it, is a different question. It is often impossible to recover the intent behind a particular coin type, and we may suspect that in many cases there was no conscious intent at all. Yet some types were clearly topical and meant to communicate specific messages. Especially topical were those types that announced (or proclaimed) military victories over foreign enemies.[5] Civil wars, too, tended to encourage the production of coin types with topical messages.[6] New or restored buildings in the city of Rome were also commemorated on imperial coins, directly or indirectly, as were new imperial policies and specific civic benefactions.[7] Finally, dynastic politics, especially on the accession coinages of new emperors, were frequently reflected in short-term messaging on imperial coins, usually through reference to the deification of a predecessor.[8] In these cases and others like them, the messages conveyed by coin types were highly topical, and the intent behind them clear. Some officials at the imperial mint, that is to say, sensitive to contemporary developments, were self-consciously producing specific coin types that spoke to an immediate political context.

It is at this level of temporality, topicality, and specificity that the overwhelming bulk of numismatic research on imperial coin types has been focused.[9] Such work is useful and has produced some good results. But too often such research ignores the basic mechanics of coin production

---

[5] In the period 69–235, just to take a small sample, there were coin types referring to victories over Judaea (*RIC* 2, Vespasian 424), Germania (*RIC* 2, Domitian 252), Dacia (*RIC* 2, Trajan 96), Arabia (*RIC* 2, Trajan 94), Parthia (*RIC* 2, Trajan 324; *RIC* 4.1, Septimius Severus 142), Armenia and Mesopotamia (*RIC* 2, Trajan 642), and Sarmatia (*RIC* 3, Marcus Aurelius 340).

[6] Compare the nearly identical legends on coins from the civil wars of 69 (FIDES EXERCITUUM: *RIC* 1², Vitellius 28) and 193–7 (FIDES LEGIONUM: *RIC* 4.1, Clodius Albinus 19).

[7] Under Trajan, for example, coin types celebrated the Forum of Trajan (e.g. *RIC* 2, Trajan 255), the Basilica Ulpia (e.g. *RIC* 2, Trajan 246), the Column of Trajan (e.g. *RIC* 2, Trajan 238), and the Circus Maximus (e.g. *RIC* 2, Trajan 5); for the relative rarity of building types, see above, 123–5. Under Vespasian, Pax types minted in 75 commemorated the dedication of the Templum Pacis in that year (cf. Noreña 2003). Policies and benefactions: e.g. *RIC* 2, Nerva 93 (remission of the *vehiculatio* costs in Italy); *RIC* 2, Nerva 92 (*alimenta* program: TUTELA ITALIAE).

[8] The deification of a predecessor could be communicated either by representations of a funeral pyre (e.g. *RIC* 3, Marcus Aurelius 436, 438: CONSECRATIO, with obverse portrait of Antoninus Pius) or by an eagle (*RIC* 4.1, Septimius Severus 24a: CONSECRATIO, with obverse portrait of Pertinax), which symbolized the deified emperor's flight to the heavens.

[9] Such an approach to imperial coin types was canonized by Mattingly (in Anglo-American scholarship) and by Strack (in the German tradition), whose extensive introductions to coin types in the

and circulation in the Roman empire. It is only through close attention to these factors – total mint output; the mix of new and old coins in that output; the ways in which coins moved from the mint into circulation; where coins actually circulated once leaving the mint; etc. – that we can understand how imperial coins did, and did not, function as a medium of official communications.

In the most elaborate attempt yet to calculate total mint production in the Roman empire, Duncan-Jones estimated that the central mint at Rome could produce as many as 52 million silver coins per year, under the emperor Elagabalus, and that over the course of eleven imperial reigns between AD 64 and 235 it averaged some 22 million silver coins per year (in addition to the gold and bronze coins that it was also minting). Under Septimius Severus alone, according to these estimates, the mint produced 532 million silver coins; under Antoninus Pius, 443 million.[10] Because these figures are based on multi-step extrapolations that ultimately depend on estimates for the average number of coins produced by individual dies – a problematic procedure, because in the pre-modern world the rate of coin production per die was highly variable – they have been met with considerable skepticism.[11] Duncan-Jones' estimates are nevertheless useful for establishing orders of magnitude. In any case, we know from archaeological and literary evidence that Roman imperial coins were more or less ubiquitous, an ordinary and quite unremarkable feature of daily life in the Roman empire.[12] If any medium of communications could saturate the Roman world with specific, topical messages transmitted by the central state, it was the imperial coinage.

The picture becomes more complicated when we consider the emission of coins from the imperial mint and their long "social lives" once in

---

multiple volumes of *BMCRE* and *Untersuchungen zur römischen Reichsprägungen des 2. Jahrhunderts*, respectively, are largely devoted to establishing links between individual types and specific events or other topical matters. Some of the arguments put forward by Mattingly and Strack are very convincing, while others are tendentious; most are (merely) plausible.

[10] Duncan-Jones 1994: 163–8, with tables 11.1–2. The figure of 22 million cited in the text above was derived from the average for the estimates of silver coin production per year listed in table 11.2.

[11] Metcalf 1995. For the debate on calculations of total mint output based on surviving dies, see Buttrey 1993, 1994; De Callataÿ 1995; Lockyear 1999; for problems of numismatic quantification in general, Howgego 1992: 2–4.

[12] The best archaeological evidence for the ubiquity of coins in daily life comes from Pompeii; see Breglia 1950; Duncan-Jones 2003; cf. Kemmers 2006 for coin use in a military context. For some illuminating literary references to coins as a standard feature of civic life, see Strabo 3.3.7, 7.5.5, 11.4.4; Plin. *NH* 5.15, 33.3; Tac. *Germ.* 5.3–5 – all referring to the absence of coinage in peripheral areas of the empire as a sign of backwardness and barbarism. Additional evidence and discussion in Crawford 1970; Howgego 1992: 16–22; Harl 1996: 250–69.

circulation.[13] The principal mechanism for putting newly minted coins into circulation (primary circulation) must have been state expenditure.[14] The imperial budget covered a range of costs, including civilian salaries, cash handouts, and building projects (mainly in the city of Rome), but by far the largest expense was the army, which consumed somewhere between one half and three quarters of the state's budget.[15] We do not know precisely how newly minted coins got from the mint to the various recipients of state payments, but it is likely that procurators, bankers (*argentarii*), and money-changers (*nummularii*) played key, intermediary roles in the process.[16] More important for understanding the potential and limitations of imperial coins as vehicles for official communications is the proportion of state expenditure that was made in newly minted coins, on the one hand, and in older coins collected as tax and then redirected to the recipients of state payments, on the other. Because the regular, large-scale movement of coin (or bullion) between the provinces, the treasury at Rome, and the recipients of state payments, mainly soldiers on the empire's frontiers, will have been prohibitively expensive, it is *a priori* unlikely that most payments were made in new coins. This is corroborated by several quantitative studies of mint output from the first two centuries AD, which indicate that newly minted coins could account for as little as 10 percent of annual state expenditure, and probably for no more than about 25 percent of such expenditure on a regular basis.[17] Most state payments, in other words, were probably made in old coins, which were used and reused for years on end. Indeed, most Roman coins remained in circulation for decades and, in many cases, for over a century.[18]

---

[13] On the circulation of imperial coins, see Callu 1969 (3rd century); Howgego 1994; Duncan-Jones 1994 (*passim*); Harl 1996: 231–49; Hobley 1998: 138–40; Kemmers 2009: 152–5.

[14] Crawford 1970; Hopkins 1980: 112; Duncan-Jones 1994: 106–8; Harl 1996: 209. On the possibility that private individuals during the early empire could have coinage struck by the mint (something we know took place in the fourth century), see Howgego 1990: 19–20.

[15] For some estimates of army costs as a proportion of the central state's budget, see Duncan-Jones 1994: 45 (between 72 and 77 percent); Hopkins 2002 (1995/96): 199–200 (about 50 percent). In addition to their regular salaries (*stipendia*), soldiers were paid discharge bonuses (*praemia*) and given cash handouts (*donativa*).

[16] Harl 1996: 241–7 (note, however, that the evidence for the activities of the money-changers is very sparse; cf. Hobley 1998: 139); for military payments in particular, see also Kemmers 2006, esp. 189–244.

[17] See, e.g., Carradice 1983 on finances under Domitian (new coins as low as 10 percent of total expenditures), with Burnett 1987: 95; Duncan-Jones 1994: 46, 111–12 (25 percent), with the conclusion, "government expenditure must have depended more on tax revenue than on its ability to produce new coin" (112). In general on the prohibitive costs of regular, long-distance movement of coin (and bullion), Millar 2002–6 (1989): 2.89–104; Wolters 2006: 47–9.

[18] In the Reka-Devnia hoard of silver coins, for example, buried in the mid-third century AD, most coins were denarii from the first two centuries AD, going back to the reign of Nero; cf. Depeyrot

Once the coins, whether newly minted at the central mint in Rome or simply redirected from a provincial treasury, arrived in the hands of their recipients, the most common trajectories of their circulation from that point (secondary circulation) can be reconstructed in general outline. Spending by the recipients of state payments, especially soldiers, will have generated the distribution of imperial coins throughout the provinces. Civic spending, mainly on public buildings and municipal festivals, assured continued circulation. And the payment of taxes in coin, facilitated (we think) by the money-changers, together with the growth of interregional trade, enabled by the stability and logistical infrastructure of the empire, both gave rise to the long-distance movement of coin, especially the precious-metal denominations, throughout the Roman world.[19]

These primary and secondary circulation patterns are represented schematically in illustration 4.1. It was as a result of these processes that imperial coins minted at Rome have been found from one end of the empire to the other. But it would be somewhat misleading to say that imperial coins circulated "everywhere." In general, we may infer from the high cost of the army and from the cities' dependence on money that the bulk of coins in circulation at any one time were concentrated in or near military camps and in urban areas. The overall spatial distribution of imperial coins, in other words, must have been very uneven.

These three points – the clustering of coins in camps and cities, the long lives of coins once in circulation, and the predominance of old coin in state expenditure – have significant implications for the role played by imperial coins in official communications, frequently overlooked by those who focus narrowly on the immediate topicality of individual coin types, or who interpret the imperial coinage as an instrument of official "propaganda." While concentrated bursts in the minting of specific types could certainly produce enough coins to communicate a topical message, with real resonance in a short-term context, as a general rule coins cannot

---

2004. In silver hoards buried in the Flavian period, over half the coins were minted under the Republic. Half of the bronze coins in the Garonne hoard, buried *c.* AD 160, were over 40 years old. See Harl 1996: 257–9, with references; cf. Duncan-Jones 1994: 193–212 for some calculations on rates of wastage in Roman imperial coin populations.

[19] The Vindolanda tablets provide good evidence for spending by soldiers (cf. Howgego 1992: 19). Peter 1996 has shown for the area around the camp at Vindonissa that legionary spending largely determined the degree of monetization in the local economy. See also Kemmers 2006 on the coin finds from the legionary base and civilian community at Nijmegen. Civic spending: Harl 1996: 260–9. Interregional trade: Howgego 1994. For the different circulation patterns of precious- and base-metal coins, see Introduction to Part I.

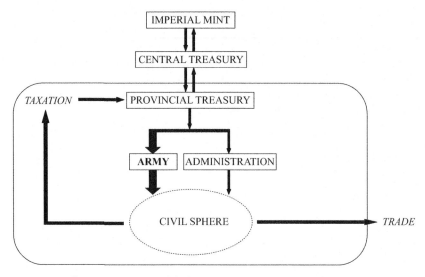

Illustration 4.1 A model of coin circulation in the Roman empire

have functioned in this way on a regular basis.[20] This is not because imperial coin types were unintelligible, as is sometimes argued, or generally ignored, but because the underlying dynamics of coin production and circulation simply did not allow it. Not only were newly minted coins substantially outnumbered by older coins in most state expenditures – more or less ruling out the regular targeting of particular groups, such as soldiers, with specific, topical messages – but more important, once these newly produced coins left the imperial mint, they will have been swallowed up by the ocean of coins circulating at that moment, and the topical messages they conveyed, if any, diluted to the point of disappearance. Though mass-produced and disseminated far and wide, imperial coins were not well suited to the regular communications of specific ideas and messages in the short term.

It would be a mistake, however, to conclude from this that the imperial coinage had no impact as a medium of official communications. This is more or less the position of those scholars who are rightly skeptical about the "propaganda" value of the imperial coinage, but it is no more tenable than the view that imperial coins were efficient instruments of political

---

[20] For a good example of the potential effectiveness of short-term messaging on imperial coins, see Kraay 1978 on the well known IUDAEA CAPTA type of 71 (e.g. *RIC* 2, Vespasian 426–7), heavily minted in May, June, and July of that year to coincide with the Flavian triumph over Judaea, which took place in June.

propaganda, conventionally understood.[21] Imperial coins could indeed be effective vehicles of official communications, but not, in general, by means of individual coin types or in the short term. Instead, it was the cumulative effect of the same (or similar) types, produced in bulk, for years and years on end, that made it possible for imperial coins – or, better, some imperial coins – to disseminate imperial ideals across the Roman empire. For only the most common types will have stood out within the immense population of imperial coins circulating at any one time. And so the focus in chapters 2 and 3 on the most common types was due not only to the arguments offered there about the variable degree of official emphasis on the different ideals and values associated with the emperor, but also to the fact that these were the types that had the most potential to effectively communicate a specific set of imperial ideals. If we wish to understand the imperial coinage as a vehicle of communications, in other words, and not simply as a medium of representation, we must move away from the analysis of individual types in the short term and towards the examination of repeated types over the long term.

Such an approach, it should be noted, runs counter to the tendency of both numismatists and historians to concentrate on those coin types that were new, different, or otherwise striking. By contrast, the most common types are often dismissed as boring or unimportant, especially in the second century, as, in the words of one scholar, "the typology of the peaceful Antonine period . . . sinks to a level of soporific blandness," when "the repetition of types continues, more and more meaninglessly."[22] What I attempted to show in the last two chapters is that the fluctuating relative frequencies of these repeated types, obscured by the standard catalogues, reveals significant patterns over time in official emphasis on certain imperial ideals and values. More important for the argument here is that these endlessly repeated types, whether bland or not, were certainly not "meaningless," at least in terms of official communications. For not only was this typological replication critical, ideologically, for the universalization and naturalization of imperial values, a point to which we will return, but it also contributed to the large-scale dissemination, and long-term communication, of a fairly stable set of ideals associated with the emperor. The more colorful or conspicuous, and therefore rare, types favored by numismatists and collectors could not have had this sort of impact.

---

[21] Skepticism about coins as propaganda: e.g. Jones 1956; Buttrey 1972a; Belloni 1974, 1976; Wallace-Hadrill 1981a, 1981b; Levick 1982, 1999; Lendon 2006: 60–2. On "propaganda," see above, 16–18.

[22] Thus Wallace-Hadrill 1986: 70, 1981a: 311.

In considering the imperial coinage as a medium for the dissemination of ideals and values, it is also important to recognize that imperial coins were firmly embedded within wider networks of communications. Though imperial coins were distinctive in several respects, especially in terms of mass production and portability, the ideas, symbols, and messages they conveyed belonged to larger semiotic systems that almost always transcended individual media. The ideals and values represented on imperial coins, in other words, were not usually themselves distinctive. Even under the Republic, when control over the various public media was spread across multiple institutions and individual actors, coin types frequently reflected contemporary political conditions and closely mirrored the messages transmitted by other media. In the mid-Republic, for example, public monuments in the city of Rome usually celebrated the state as a whole, while in the late Republic they were increasingly pressed into the service of promoting individual families and aristocrats, a broad shift in public expression that is closely paralleled on the coin types of the mid- and late Republic, respectively.[23] And of course we would expect an even closer relationship between coin types and other forms of official representation under the empire, characterized, as it was, by political centralization and increased – but not total – control over messaging in multiple media. Epigraphic texts produced by various representatives of the central state, considered in detail below, will illustrate the point that the messages transmitted by coin types should not be viewed in isolation.

Finally, we come to the effectiveness of the messages communicated by means of imperial coins. A handful of literary references, always cited in this context, mention numismatic imagery in general, and even some specific types in particular.[24] Scholars disagree, however, over whether such references are sufficient to prove that imperial coin types were intelligible or even noticed.[25] Other attempts to document the impact of coin types have focused on the minting of "restoration" types in the second century; on the reflection of imperial motifs on local coinages in the east; and on the presence in domestic contexts of official imagery from the public sphere, as

---

[23] Hölscher 1980: 269–71 (mid-Republic), 1982 and 1984 (late Republic); cf. Meadows and Williams 2001 on the growing interest in the late Republic in "monumentalizing" the past, evident both in public buildings in Rome and on coin types.

[24] Numismatic imagery: e.g. Epict. 3.4.5 (on the coins of Nero and Trajan); Matthew 22:19–21, Mark 12:15–17, Luke 20:22–5 (imperial portrait on coins). Specific types: e.g. Dio 47.25.3 (Brutus' type commemorating the Ides of March); Suet. *Aug.* 94.12 (Augustus' capricorn type); Soc. *HE* 3.17 (Julian's "pagan" bull type).

[25] See, for example, Sutherland 1959; Crawford 1974; Wolters 2003: 189–93.

reconstructed in part from coin types.[26] In these cases and others like them, the influence of coin types on these other forms of expression is plausible, but unproven. The problem lies in the semiotic embeddedness of coin types. Because the ideas, symbols, and messages transmitted by imperial coins were often similar, even identical, to those conveyed by other media, it is usually impossible to pinpoint the specific role, if any, played by coin types in the official communication of imperial ideals and values.[27]

For the argument of this and the subsequent chapters, however, it is really the nature and effectiveness of imperial communications as a whole that is the vital issue. The main reason that coin types are so important for pursuing this question is simply the fact of their survival in large numbers. Because so many coins have survived, in fact, we can use them as a rough index to a whole world of imperial communications, once extensive and vibrant, but now mostly lost. We should not lose sight of the fact that imperial coins, because of their mass production and portability, must have been important bearers of ideas and messages in their own right, especially, as I have stressed, over the long term. Indeed, the long-term diffusion of ideas by means of coins is very important for my overall argument. But equally important for the argument is that these coins can also be used as indices to the many other communications of the Roman imperial state. Imperial coin types, in other words, not only provide us with direct evidence for official communications by means of coins, but also with indirect evidence for official communications by means of all other media, most of which, unlike the coins, have long since disappeared.

One effect of these official communications was the saturation of the public sphere with imperial ideals and values, as well as with other symbolic representations of the Roman emperor. But this saturation, too, must be set in a wider context. For the public sphere was pervaded by imperial symbols produced not only by the central state, but also by a host of other institutions, collectivities, and individuals, some "public" and "official," others "private" and "unofficial."[28] The world of communications in the Roman empire, in fact, must have been quite dynamic and fluid, with many different actors, and many different agendas, operating within it.

---

[26] Restoration types: Komnick 2001; cf. Buttrey 1972a on "imitation" types under Vespasian. Local coinages: e.g. Howgego 2005: 14–15, discussing the prominence on imperial coins and coins from Alexandria of mythological themes in the mid-second century. Official art in the private sphere: Hölscher 1984: 20–32; Zanker 1988b.

[27] This may be related to Ellul's observations about the difficulty of measuring the impact of propaganda (1973: 259–77), since propaganda is always, in his view, "completely integrated and immersed in . . . a general sociological structure" (264).

[28] See below, 214–18, for discussion of these terms.

And it is really this dynamism and fluidity of communications, focused on the Roman emperor, that constitutes the circulation of imperial ideals in its fullest sense. And even though this "circulation" was not quite as natural as the biological metaphor would imply, since it was mediated by various sectional interests, it nevertheless brought about the empire-wide diffusion of these ideals. The most important result of that diffusion, as I will argue in this and the next chapter, was the emergence of an empire-wide symbolic system, centered in general on the idea of the emperor, and in particular on the figure of the emperor as constructed in very specific ways – largely, though not exclusively, through the sorts of virtues and benefits examined in chapters 2 and 3. In order to understand how that symbolic system actually came about, it will be necessary to consider first the different media, in addition to imperial coins, by which imperial ideals were circulated; the different contexts in which this circulation took place; and the different interests that such circulation served.

MEDIUM, CONTEXT, AND AGENCY IN THE PRODUCTION OF IMPERIAL SYMBOLS

The most direct means by which imperial ideals and values were communicated to the inhabitants of the empire – and by which the very idea of the Roman emperor was made most manifest to them – was when the emperor visited in person. This he did with increasing frequency over the course of the first three centuries AD.[29] Because so much of the emperor's time away from Italy was spent on campaign, imperial travels were normally conducted within a more or less military framework. But imperial travels outside of Italy also shaped emperors' relations with their provincial subjects. An imperial visit, celebrated by elaborate ceremonies marking the emperor's arrival (*adventus*), and sometimes requiring months of preparation (not least in order to accommodate the massive entourage that normally traveled with the emperor and his court), not only gave provincials a rare opportunity to see their ruler in person, but also provided the emperor with an ideal context for conferring his patronage directly on favored communities – in principal if not always in practice.[30] The imperial

---

[29] Millar 1977: 28–40; Halfmann 1986, esp. 157–232 for the known itineraries of all emperors from Augustus to Severus Alexander; Wilkes 2005: 241–9 (AD 193–337).

[30] Halfmann 1986: 143–8; Lehnen 1997; cf. MacCormack 1981: 17–89, focusing on the later empire but with much relevant material for the earlier period. For the iconography, Koeppel 1969. Under Hadrian, about whose extended travels we are reasonably well informed, there is no demonstrable correlation between an imperial visit and an imperial benefaction (see briefly Boatwright 2000: 206–7); this is an important point to which we will return (below, 271, 273, 292–3).

adventus thus served in part to consolidate the relationship between center and periphery and, however fleetingly, to invest the local with the presence and aura of the universal. In these respects imperial travels through the provinces were analogous in function to the royal progresses of other pre-modern states.[31] If nothing else an imperial visit at least reminded the emperor's subjects that they were, indeed, ruled by an emperor.

Despite the increasingly itinerant nature of the Roman imperial court, the vast majority of the empire's inhabitants never saw the emperor in person. As a result it was left to imperial images and other symbolic representations of the emperor to maintain his existence in the collective consciousness of his subjects. The ubiquity of visual representations of the Roman emperor was often remarked. In a letter to Marcus Aurelius, for example, Fronto writes, "You know that at all the money-changers' tables and in all the balconies, shops, porches, windows – anywhere and everywhere – your images have been set before the masses."[32] Menander Rhetor advises those praising the emperor to remind him that "the cities are full of his images, some on painted tablets, others on more expensive materials" (377). Even more to the point is the following observation made by Severian, a fourth-century bishop from the province of Galatia:

Consider how many governors there are in all the world. And since the emperor is not with them all, the emperor's image has to be put up in courtrooms, in marketplaces, in places of assembly, in theaters. The emperor's image has to be put up in every place in which the governor governs, in order that his acts have authority.[33]

Abundant evidence from literary sources confirms the high degree of authority inherent in the imperial image. Pliny required those who denied that they were Christians to pray to the gods and to make offerings of wine and incense to Trajan's statue, as proof of their sincerity, while Apuleius, in his speech of self-defense, appeals to a statue of Antoninus Pius in the courtroom to add moral weight to his argument.[34] Presumably such images of the emperor in the tribunals of Roman justice were commonplace. We also know that runaway slaves could take refuge at imperial statues, a practice sanctioned by the Roman jurists.[35] Imperial images, however, were not

---

[31] Cf. Geertz 1983 (1977): 121–46.

[32] Fro. *ad Marc.Caes.* 4.12.6 (van den Hout): *scis ut in omnibus argentariis mensulis pergulis tabernis protectis vestibulis fenestris usquequaque ubique imagines vestrae sint volgo propositae.*

[33] *PG* 56.489.   [34] Plin. *Ep.* 10.96.5; Apul. *Apol.* 85.

[35] *Dig.* 21.1.17.12 (Ulpian): *ego puto non esse eum fugitivum, qui id facit quod publice facere licere arbitratur. ne eum quidem, qui ad statuam Caesaris confugit, fugitivum arbitror: non enim fugiendo*

always treated with respect and veneration. Indeed, riots and even large-scale revolts against imperial authority could begin with attacks against the imperial image. According to Libanius, for example, the Antioch riot of 387 began with attacks against imperial images.[36] And Tacitus, describing the chaotic scene in the Roman Forum that culminated in Galba's murder, notes that "the standard-bearer of the cohort accompanying Galba hurled to the ground Galba's portrait, which had been torn down; by this sign the zeal of all the soldiers for Otho was clear."[37] In general, the literary evidence creates the impression that whenever someone needed an image of the emperor, for whatever purpose, it was readily available.[38]

One way to trace the outlines of this development is to consider the different media in which the emperor was represented visually. In terms of visual impact and "living presence," the most striking form of representation was surely the imperial statue.[39] Statues of the Roman emperor were a defining feature of the public spheres of cities and towns throughout the empire. Precise numbers are beyond the reach of our evidence, but various indications give a sense of scale. Pfanner has calculated that the total number of imperial statues produced during the reign of Augustus alone was between 25,000 and 50,000, which corresponds roughly to an average production of between 500 and 1,000 statues per year.[40] Literary sources help to flesh out the picture. A late Syriac chronicle attributed to Zaccharias Rhetor includes a reference to 4,000 bronze statues of the emperor in fourth-fifth-century Rome.[41] This number is impossible to verify, but it is worth noting that visual depictions of Rome's urban landscape frequently include statues as markers of urban space.[42] More helpful is the archaeological

---

animo hoc facit; cf. Sen. *Clem.* 1.18; Plin. *Ep.* 10.74. For imperial statues as places of asylum, see briefly Pekáry 1985: 130–1.

[36] Lib. 7.23.

[37] Tac. *Hist.* 1.41, with Plut. *Galb.* 26; cf. Plin. *Pan.* 52.4 on the destruction of Domitian's statues: *iuvabat illidere solo superbissimos vultus, instare ferro, saevire securibus* (note that Pliny also speaks here of Domitian's "innumerable statues"). See discussion, with further references, in Pekáry 1985: 134–42.

[38] The ubiquity and various functions of the imperial image in daily life are discussed in Kruse 1934; Niemeyer 1968: 14–27; Hopkins 1978: 219–26; Price 1984: 191–206; Lahusen 1983: 129–43; Pekáry 1985, esp. 107–48; Ando 2000: 232–53; Dahmen 2001: 53–60; cf. Lahusen 1984: 61–91, 111–17 for a good collection of relevant texts.

[39] On Roman imperial statues in general (excluding the many studies of individual emperors), see Kruse 1934; Niemeyer 1968; Zanker 1979, 1983; Lahusen 1983; Pekáry 1985; Smith 1985; Rose 1997a, 1997b; Garriguet 2001; Boschung 2002; Stewart 2003 (*passim*); Højte 2005; Hallett 2005a: 159–83, 224–40, 248–70; Rosso 2006; Fittschen 2010. For the mechanisms of production and distribution, see below, n. 77.

[40] Pfanner 1989: 178–9.

[41] Cited in Hopkins 1978: 220, n. 33; cf. Stewart 2003: 118–56, esp. 123–8.

[42] See discussion in Stewart 2003: 121–3.

evidence, especially from surviving statue bases. Højte has compiled a corpus of 2,300 imperial statue bases, from Augustus to Commodus, from
just under 800 sites in the Roman empire. In twelve cities there were at
least twenty imperial statue bases from this period: Rome (127), Athens
(89), Ephesus (69), Ostia (48), Thamugadi (34), Pergamum (24), Lepcis
Magna (24), Thugga (22), Lyktos (22), Puteoli (20), Lambaesis (20), and
Cuicul (20).[43] These figures naturally depend in part on varying states of
preservation. It cannot be doubted that there were more imperial statues in
the megalopolis of Carthage, for example, where only six statue bases from
this period have survived, than in Lyktos, a smaller but better preserved
city in Crete. The main point, however, is clear. Statues of the emperor
could be found in every city and town of the Roman world, even at the
very edge of the empire.[44]

There is scattered evidence for the placement of imperial portraits in
private and domestic contexts, but it is difficult to know how common this
was.[45] It seems more likely than not that the spread of imperial portraiture
was a predominantly public, and urban, phenomenon. Indeed, from the
combined evidence of literary, epigraphic, and archaeological sources it is
possible to determine where most public imperial statues were erected.[46]
Within urban areas, the majority were erected in the monumental city
center, especially in the forum/agora and the various structures adjacent to
it, such as the basilica or curia.[47] Many were also set up in temples and
associated sacred precincts, as well as in theaters. Outside of urban areas,
it was only in military camps that imperial statues were set up with any
regularity.[48] Imperial statues sometimes adorned extra-urban structures,

---

[43] Højte 2005: 103–8; see also his regional tabulations, Tables SG 1–24 (607–22).

[44] Cf. Arr. *Peripl.* 1.3–4 on a statue of Hadrian in Trapezus, on the Black Sea.

[45] Small busts in *lararia*: Ov. *Pont.* 2.8.1–6, 4.9.105–110; Suet. *Aug.* 7.1, *Vit.* 2.5; *HA SevAl.* 29.2. Statues
in houses in Rome: Tac. *Ann.* 1.73.2 (equestrian residence), 3.70.1 (equestrian), 4.64.3 (senatorial).
Statues on private estates: Plin. *Ep.* 10.8.1; cf. Neudecker 1988: 84–91 for imperial statues in eight
Italian villas. Further references and discussion in Pekáry 1985: 53–4; Dahmen 2001: 58–60; Gradel
2002: 198–212; Højte 2005: 122–3.

[46] On the placement of imperial statues in public spaces, see Niemeyer 1968: 28–36; Lahusen 1983:
7–44 (city of Rome); Pekáry 1985: 42–65 (based on literary sources); Højte 2005: 109–22 (based
on archaeological evidence, esp. statue bases). For regional and local studies, see also Garriguet
2001: 105–22 (cities in Iberian peninsula); Rosso 2006: 121–50 (cities in Gaul); Smith *et al.* 2006:
13–19 (Aphrodisias). The placement of honorific statues for provincial governors followed the same
patterns: Erkelenz 2003: 120–71.

[47] Detailed studies of imperial (and other) statues in fora in Alföldy 1979 (Tarraconensis), 1984 (north-
east Italy); Zimmer 1989 (Cuicul and Timgad); Witschel 1995b: 342–52 (Timgad); Kleinwächter
2001 (North Africa); Garriguet 2001: 105–12 (Iberian peninsula); Rosso 2006: 124–9 (Gaul). For the
symbolism of these public arrays of statues, see below, 273–5.

[48] Sacred precincts: Witschel 1995a: 253–7. Military camps: Kruse 1934: 51–64.

such as bridges and arches, but they must have been extremely rare in the rural areas of the empire.

Statues of Roman emperors were made of marble, bronze, silver, or gold. Most were life-sized, but some were dramatically oversized, colossal sculptures that towered above the viewer.[49] In typological terms, imperial statues may be divided into three broad categories: civilian, military, and "theomorphic."[50] The civilian type was usually marked by the toga (occasionally by Greek civilian dress), which was sometimes pulled over the head (*capite velato*) to denote the act of sacrifice and the emperor's priestly role (illustrations 4.2–3). Breastplate or *paludamentum* defined the military type (illustration 4.4). Theomorphic types were indicated by "ideal" or "divine" nudity or semi-nudity (illustration 4.5), with the emperor sometimes bearing the attributes of Jupiter. Because so few securely identified imperial statues have survived, it is difficult to determine the frequencies of these different statue types, and very different opinions have been expressed.[51] Amongst the 130 securely identified Roman imperial statues assembled by Niemeyer, for what it is worth, the ratio of civilian to military to theomorphic types was roughly 1:1:2.[52] From what we know from other sources on the development of the Roman emperor's public image, this ratio is certainly plausible, but we should be wary of drawing firm conclusions from such a small sample.

Many portraits of Roman emperors were commissioned in connection with what we call "the imperial cult."[53] As a loose bundle of ritual practices, sacred spaces, and monumental buildings, the imperial cult, though characterized by significant regional and local variation, was nevertheless one of the major contexts in which the empire-wide diffusion of the idea

---

[49] On colossal statues of the emperor, Pekáry 1985: 84–7.

[50] On "theomorphic" portraits, i.e. those assuming the form of a god, see discussion in Hallett 2005a: 237–54.

[51] In characterizing the development of imperial imagery after Augustus, for example, Zanker writes, "the qualities of the emperor as field marshal and the preparedness of the army came to play an ever more important role, while the civilian side of the princeps necessarily retreated to a more subsidiary position" (1988a: 377); cf. Alföldi 1970 (1934): 161–86; Gordon 1990: 213. Smith, however, considering Antonine portraits from the eastern empire, writes that these portraits "represented an ideological shift in the imperial image from military *virtus* to an urbane *civilitas*. It is in this period for the first time that genuine visual priority is given to the expression of the *civilis princeps*. The Antonines present the first true image of the civilian Roman emperor" (1998: 62).

[52] Niemeyer 1968. Niemeyer's numbers are as follows: togate: 30 (cat. 1–30); Greek civilian dress: 4 (cat. 31–4); *paludamentum*: 1 (cat. 35); breastplate: 35 (cat. 36–70); hip-mantle (semi-nude): 11 (cat. 71–81); "Jupiter costume": 18 (cat. 82–99); "opus nobile": 5 (cat. 100–4); "generic ideal portrait": 26 (cat. 105–30) (i.e., 34 civilian types, 36 military types, and 60 theomorphic types).

[53] Fishwick 1987–2005: 3.3.273–82.

Illustration 4.2 Marble statue of Titus as a civilian magistrate in a toga (second half of first century AD)

of the emperor, and the imperial family in general, was brought about.[54] Organized both at the provincial level and the municipal level, emperor worship mobilized all of the characteristic features of civic religion in the ancient Mediterranean world, from priests and processions to sacrifices and public banquets. Through such ritual activity, the figure of the emperor was not only associated with divine power and universal order,

---

[54] General studies in Hopkins 1978: 197–242 (with emphasis on the symbolic unification generated by participation in the cult); Price 1984; Fishwick 1987–2005; Beard, North, and Price 1998: 348–63; Clauss 1999; Gradel 2002; Stäcker 2003: 308–67.

Illustration 4.3 Marble statue of Hadrian wearing a toga *capite velato* ("with his head covered") (mid-second century AD)

but was also incorporated into the rhythms of municipal life, as the evidence from several local calendars suggests.[55] Equally significant was the architecture of the imperial cult. Throughout the empire, but especially in the west, the surge in building and monumentalization that began in the late first century BC/early first century AD coincided with, and was often directly initiated by, the spread of emperor worship.[56] Sometimes the new

[55] Rüpke 1995: 538–46; Fishwick 1987–2005: 3.3.229–33. In general on imperial festivals celebrated in the provinces, Herz 1978.
[56] The connection between the emergence of the imperial cult and the first phase of widespread monumentalization is especially clear in the Iberian peninsula (various perspectives in Trillmich and

Illustration 4.4 Marble statue of Trajan in military uniform (cuirass and mantle) (first half of second century AD)

structures consisted of no more than a single altar or small precinct. More often a new temple was constructed to house the local cult for the emperor. And in some of the larger cities, the imperial cult was accommodated in monumental temple and forum complexes, massive structures that dominated the urban landscape.[57] Public building connected with emperor

Zanker 1990; Keay 1998, esp. 74–83), but can also be seen in North Africa (Jouffroy 1986: 183–9), and Gaul (Woolf 1998: 121); cf. Revell 2009: 80–109 for North Africa, Spain, and Britannia. For the eastern empire, see also Price 1984: 133–69; Mitchell 1993: 1.86–90, 100–117; Burrell 2004: 305–30.

[57] The city of Tarraco presents a particularly striking example of large-scale construction driven by the imperial cult. Seat of the provincial cult for Hispania Tarraconensis, the city was adorned by

Illustration 4.5   Bronze statue of Septimius Severus in "divine" nudity (*c.* AD 197)

worship was not always so lavish, of course, but most municipalities of the
Roman empire included at least one architectural expression of the local
cult of the emperor, usually in or near the center of town.

The diffusion of imperial images, and the attendant ideals and values,
did not depend on such grandeur. Nor were imperial coins the only small,

an enormous terraced complex built into a hillside overlooking the city, which included a circus; a
large, porticoed forum for meetings of the provincial council; an adjacent precinct, also surrounded
by porticoes; and, at the rear of the precinct and summit of the complex as a whole, a temple
of Roma and Augustus. On this provincial cult complex, see Fishwick 1987–2005: 3.3.5–40, with
references to earlier studies.

Illustration 4.6 Portraits of Marcus Aurelius and Lucius Verus on a sardonyx cameo
(mid-second century AD)

Illustration 4.7 Portrait of Caracalla on a chalcedony cameo (late second/early third
century AD)

portable objects that conveyed images and symbols of the Roman emperor. Portraits of the emperor were also incised into precious gems, such as agate, onyx, sardonyx, and chalcedony (illustrations 4.6–7), and stamped onto medallions.[58] They were depicted on various items of jewelry as well, especially rings and earrings. In addition, statuettes and small-scale busts of the emperor were carved from a wide range of materials, including

[58] Gems: Megow 1987. Medallions: Gnecchi 1912.

Illustration 4.8 Miniature bust of Domitian in bronze (second half of first century AD)

marble, ivory, plaster, glass, bronze, and precious metals (illustrations 4.8–9). Cameos, jewelry, and statuettes in precious metals were expensive and presumably limited to the upper classes. But depictions of the Roman emperor have been found on much humbler materials as well, including lead seals, clay lamps, bronze scales and mirrors, metal hinges, and even ceramic molds for baking bread and cakes.[59] Such artifacts provide a tantalizing glimpse into a world in which the presence of imperial images could simply be taken for granted.

At the intersection of visual, monumental, and textual media for the spread of imperial symbols were epigraphic texts that included the names and titles of the Roman emperor.[60] In the western empire in particular, the advent of monarchy at Rome brought with it a proliferation of large, public inscriptions throughout the provinces, creating new visual and symbolic

[59] For statuettes, busts, and imperial portraits in all small-scale media, see Dahmen 2001: 15–60, 99–137, 147–73, 204–45.
[60] For imperial representation in epigraphic texts, see Alföldy 1991, 2002, 2003; Kuhoff 1993, esp. 31–6; Horster 2001; Niquet 2003, esp. 156–65; for some recent works on epigraphy and self-representation in general in the Roman world, see also Alföldy and Panciera 2001; Eck and Heil 2005; Corbier 2006.

Illustration 4.9 Miniature bust of Commodus in amethyst (second half of second century AD)

landscapes that were largely defined by what has been called "monumental writing."[61] The total number of inscriptions set up in the Roman empire, the proportion of this total that has survived, and even the total number of published inscriptions are all unknown.[62] All of this will have to be kept in mind when assessing the role played by epigraphic texts in the dissemination of imperial ideals. What is nevertheless clear is that public inscriptions were a defining feature of urban (and military) life in the Roman empire, especially after the advent of monarchy at Rome, and that many related in one way or another to the figure of the Roman emperor.

There were several ways in which inscriptions related to, or publicized, the emperor, depending on the nature of the text inscribed and the type of object onto which it was carved. The official pronouncements of the emperor on all matters of state and society, which themselves could take

[61] Woolf 1996, esp. 24 for the intersection of monuments and writing as constituting what we call epigraphy. Alföldy 1991 discusses the chronological coincidence between the advent of monarchy at Rome and the rapid spread of inscriptions throughout the empire (especially in the west), a correlation that seems to be especially pronounced in the Iberian peninsula (cf. Beltrán Lloris 1995; Alföldy 1998; Stylow 2001). It should be noted that within Italy itself, the upsurge in epigraphic activity begins in the 2nd/1st century BC, i.e., prior to the Augustan settlement; see briefly Gordon in *JRS* 93 (2003): 219–20, drawing on the work of H. Solin.

[62] See above, Introduction to Part II, 181.

various forms (*edicta, epistulae, rescripta,* etc.), were apparently kept in authenticated copies both in Rome and, beginning in the second century, in provincial archives maintained by the governor. These imperial pronouncements could also be inscribed by municipal communities onto durable materials, especially bronze, and then erected in high-profile locations – sometimes at the behest of the central state, sometimes voluntarily.[63] Texts voluntarily chosen for commemoration in this way were naturally seen as useful and advantageous to the community in question, and thus served as an important mechanism for diffusing the idea of a beneficent emperor.[64] The other major form of official pronouncement emanating from the central state was the senatorial decree (*senatusconsultum*).[65] Senatorial decrees were disseminated throughout the provinces in a manner broadly similar to that of imperial edicts and letters, and could also contribute to the circulation of imperial ideals. In several much-discussed senatorial decrees issued under Tiberius, for example, especially the *SCPP*, the virtues of the emperor were stressed.[66] Imperial nomenclature and titulature was also spread far and wide by means of milestones, erected at varying intervals over the course of the thousands of miles of primary and secondary roads that comprised the imperial road network and usually announcing the emperor's role in building or maintaining that stretch of road (illustration 4.10).[67] Dedicatory inscriptions on public monuments "built" or "restored" by the emperor in provincial municipalities, which ensured that the names and titles of various emperors would be highlighted in large and gleaming letters on the biggest and most central buildings in

---

[63] See Millar 1977: 203–72 for the different types of official imperial pronouncement. For copying and authentication of official documents, see Ando 2000: 73–130, with references to more detailed studies; for archives and archival practice, see also Haensch 1992 (provincial); Moatti 1993 and Demougin 1994 (at Rome). Meyer 2004 examines the symbolic significance of bronze as a marker of durability and authority.

[64] In Aphrodisias, for example, an entire wall on one of the entrances to the city's theater was given over to a series of inscribed texts listing multiple imperial benefactions and privileges granted to the city over the course of more than 250 years, clearly intended as a public declaration of the city's honored status and close relationship with the Roman imperial regime; cf. Reynolds 1982: 33–148.

[65] Useful conspectus of *senatusconsulta* in Talbert 1984: 431–59.

[66] See Rowe 2002 for a general treatment of these decrees; for the communication of imperial ideals and values in these texts, see also Millar 2002–6 (1988): 1.350–9; Cooley 1998; Potter 1999. On "publication" and diffusion of senatorial decrees, Talbert 1984: 306–8; Rowe 2002: 64–6.

[67] Imperial milestones are in the process of being collected in the various fascicles of *CIL* 17; cf. Rathmann 2003: App. 6.5.1–52 for the most up-to-date checklist of known imperial milestones from the western empire (down to AD 284). For the spread of imperial names and titles on milestones under Augustus, see Alföldy 1991: 299–302; for milestones as vehicles for the expression of imperial ideals more generally, see also Pekáry 1968: 16–22; König 1973; Kuhoff 1993: 150–70; Ando 2000: 322–3; Witschel 2002; Kolb 2004; see also below, 220–3.

Illustration 4.10 Milestone from Hispania Tarraconensis, set up in AD 98/99, with Trajan's
official names and titles

town, were also common.[68] Finally, provincial communities in the Roman
empire produced a constant barrage of honorific decrees for the emperor,

[68] For imperial building inscriptions, see Horster 2001; Alföldy 2002; cf. Alföldy 1991: 293–9 for the
initial spread of such inscriptions under Augustus. Thomas and Witschel 1992 discuss the rhetoric

many of which were inscribed on various objects, especially statue bases (illustration 4.11).[69] In light of these different epigraphic practices, it is difficult to escape the conclusion that most inhabitants of the Roman empire were regularly confronted by inscribed texts bearing the many names and titles of the emperor, especially that numinous fusion of personal nomenclature and official titulature, AUGUSTUS.[70]

Imperial travels, statues, temples and other cult buildings, small-scale artworks, mundane objects of daily life and public inscriptions, together with imperial coins, all contributed both to the empire-wide diffusion of the simple but potent idea that the Roman world was ruled by an emperor, and to the spread of those ideals and values that, over time, came to be associated with the ruler. To these mechanisms we may add others that are more difficult to trace – literary texts dealing in one way or another with the emperor; documentary paintings commissioned by the imperial regime; rumor, gossip, and word of mouth.[71] Now most of this material is well known to art historians, archaeologists, numismatists, epigraphers, and other specialists. Several important facets and implications of these processes, however, are unclear, debated, or insufficiently emphasized. Especially important for this study are the problems of agency and intent in the production of imperial symbols, and the long-term, cumulative effects of the dissemination and circulation of these symbols through so many different media.

In addressing the question of agency in the production of imperial symbols, we may begin with a basic distinction between those imperial symbols that were produced by the central state, and those produced by all other groups and individuals. Though we may call the former "official" and the latter "unofficial," it will soon become clear that the various actors who produced these symbols ranged across a wide spectrum of statuses and degrees of socio-spatial proximity to the institutions of the central state.

---

of building inscriptions in general, emphasizing that claims of restoration cannot always be taken at face value. See also above, 102–3, on imperial building in the provinces as an advertised benefit of Roman rule.

[69] The conventions of honorific texts inscribed on statue bases are analyzed in Højte 2005: 19–27; for honorific inscriptions for the emperor in general, see below, chapter 5.

[70] Cf. Corbier 2006: 60 for the useful distinction between monumental letters that simply imposed themselves on all passersby, and the smaller letters that required the active decision to stop and read them; most imperial titles in the public sphere must have belonged to the first category.

[71] For literary texts, see Starr 1987: 219–23 and Fedeli 1989b: 354–7 on the growth of the book trade in the western empire in the first two centuries AD. Documentary paintings: Potter 1994: 121–2. Tracing the empire-wide movement and effect of rumor and gossip is nearly impossible, of course, but can sometimes be inferred from unexpected indices, such as the nature of graffiti depicting emperors (MacMullen 1988: 114), the popularity of certain imperial nicknames (cf. Bruun 2003), or gossip about the emperors' sex lives (Vout 2007).

Illustration 4.11 Marble statue base for Marcus Aurelius, with his official names and titles, from Fidenae

The role of the central state in producing imperial images, ideas, and symbols was clear and unambiguous when these were transmitted by the emperor himself, whether in fact, as when the emperor made public appearances in Rome or visited provincial cities and towns with great pomp and ceremony, or in principle, through documents formally authored by the emperor. It is rarely possible to determine on objective grounds whether the emperor was really the author of the words written in his name. It is likely, in fact, that the bulk of texts emanating from the imperial chancery, especially rescripts, were written by secretaries and other court officials.[72] For the purposes of this study, however, this does not matter very much. These documents were produced by the imperial court, and they were therefore, by the definition I propose, official. The same goes for senatorial decrees containing praise for the emperor, as well as for imperial coins and the specific designs they carried.

Equally unambiguous were most images and texts produced within the private sphere. Minor artworks commissioned by individuals, graffiti of all types, rumors, and most literary texts dealing with the Roman emperor were clearly unofficial. These cultural artifacts might have been influenced by official symbols and communications, an important question to which we will return, but they were not themselves produced by the central state, and were therefore unofficial.

More complicated, either because they were sometimes official and sometimes unofficial, or because they straddled the line between the two, were those imperial symbols generated by public inscriptions; produced in the context of the imperial cult; or conveyed through public statuary. In principle, inscriptions were either official or unofficial, depending on whether the central state or other groups and individuals were responsible for the wording used in the text itself and for the decision to display the inscribed text in a public location. A milestone formally placed by the emperor was official, according to the definition proposed above; honorific decrees for the emperor, the result of local initiative, were unofficial; an imperial rescript voluntarily inscribed by local communities was both official and unofficial, since the language was formally the emperor's own, while the decision to display the text publicly belonged to the community in question.[73] The establishment and routine management of the imperial cult was also the product of both official and unofficial directives. In some areas, especially in the eastern empire, the rise of emperor worship was largely spontaneous and the result of local initiative, though the preliminary stages usually involved some sort of negotiations between the local or provincial community and the central authorities; in other areas, the central state itself undertook to establish the ruler cult, usually at the provincial level, in particular at strategic sites in recently conquered areas.[74] Once the institutions of the imperial cult were up and running, however, the routine

---

[72] For procedures and personnel involved in generating official imperial pronouncements, Millar 1977 (esp. 83–110, 203–72, 328–40, 537–49, 556–90) is still fundamental; for secretarial authorship of imperial rescripts, see the arguments of Honoré 1981; Turpin 1991; Connolly 2009: 55–62.

[73] On the precise language of honorific inscriptions – how it was chosen and who chose it – see below, 267–70.

[74] For the origins and development of local and provincial cults for the emperor, see Price 1984: 53–62; Fishwick 1987–2005: 3.1, esp. 5–39, 213–19; Beard, North, and Price 1998: 352–7.

management of the cult was mostly in the hands of the local or provincial community, and its characteristic expressions were mostly unofficial.[75]

The placement of imperial statues on the official/unofficial spectrum is particularly difficult. On the one hand, most statues of the Roman emperor were proposed, paid for, set up, and maintained by local communities on their own initiative – a critical fact that is often overlooked.[76] On the other hand, most portraits of Roman emperors were remarkably uniform from one end of the empire to the other, which can only have resulted from local adherence, whether close or loose, to a central model. No other explanation can account for this iconographic homogeneity. Debate amongst art historians now centers on the precise mechanisms by which these centrally determined models (i.e. "types" or *Urbilder*) were disseminated, for which there is no external evidence before the fourth century AD, and on the appropriate terminology for describing the local version, some preferring terms such as "copying" and "replication," others "emulation" and "adaptation."[77] The key point for our purposes is that any statue of the Roman emperor set up in a provincial community was always simultaneously official and unofficial.

As for the question of intent and motive in the production of these imperial symbols, it will be sufficient for the moment simply to recognize that there were many different interests at work, all made compatible by the fact that the production of these symbols, and the idealization of the emperor that resulted, invariably served to reinforce the power, authority, and status of the different actors who undertook to produce them.[78]

---

[75] Administration: Deininger 1965; Fishwick 1987–2005: *passim*; Clauss 1999; Burrell 2004: 343–71.

[76] Concise discussion in Højte 2005: 167–87.

[77] For many years the main debate was between those who argued for the use of wax or plaster models produced by central workshops and then systematically disseminated to provincial locations for copying (Swift 1923), and those emphasizing instead the role of private workshops and the private art trade (Stuart 1939). The most detailed study is by Pfanner (1989), arguing from multiple, small "bumps" (or "warts," as MacMullen 2000: 130 calls them) on unfinished statues in Rome, evidently for the purpose of guiding the sculptor's hand, that plaster casts (from which those "bumps" derived) were distributed both to central workshops in Rome (controlled by the emperor) and to local workshops in the provinces. Though there is still disagreement about these sorts of mechanisms, there is now a broad consensus on the use of centrally determined models (cf. various perspectives in Smith 1996; Rose 1997a: 57–9; Albertson 2005: 291–9; Fittschen 2010); for emphasis on local adaptation and the workings of the private art trade, Zanker 1983 is basic (cf. Højte 2005: 87, n. 197, for more recent studies of provincial emperor portraits); see also Smith *et al.* 2006: 29–34 for detailed discussion of local procedures and techniques for producing imperial and other statues. Hallett 2005b offers an overview of the ongoing debate over "replication" vs. "emulation."

[78] For some preliminary comments on this key issue, see above, 16–19. More detailed discussion below, 239–43, 270–6, 292–3, 317–20.

This is the wider context in which the diffusion of imperial ideals and values should be seen. Two points deserve emphasis. First, this diffusion was brought about by multiple actors, both institutional and individual, employing different media and operating in different contexts. The symbolic system that arose from the spread of these ideas was not simply dictated from above, but was instead produced collectively. Second, the symbolic system centered on the figure of the emperor was critically shaped by the specific manner in which that figure was constructed, both in terms of these different media and contexts and, as we will see, with respect to the specific ideas that were attached to the emperor. Of the many different ways in which the Roman emperor could be constructed, especially relevant for our purposes were the particular ideals and values, especially virtues and benefits, with which he was associated. And it is by putting together these two basic points – the combined agency of multiple actors, on the one hand, and the variability of specific values, on the other – that we can begin to capture the complexity and dynamism that characterized the circulation of imperial ideals in the Roman empire.

THE CIRCULATION OF IMPERIAL IDEALS: THE "OFFICIAL IMPULSE"

In attempting to chart the empire-wide circulation of imperial ideals and values – asking, in a word, who "said" what about the Roman emperor in the public sphere – it is best to begin with the various official expressions of such ideals, which together constitute the source from which these ideals were ultimately diffused.[79] We have already examined in detail the ideals and values represented on imperial coins, official expressions *par excellence*, and we will return to those findings later. Here we need to cast a wider net, drawing on the epigraphic record in particular, in order to illuminate just how variegated the official expression of imperial ideals could be.

Honorific terminology in public inscriptions is an especially sensitive indicator of the sorts of ideals and values that came to be attached to the figure of the Roman emperor.[80] One of the places in which such terminology appeared is in what we may call, as a matter of convenience, "official" inscriptions, that is texts that were formally authored by institutions, collectivities, officials, and individuals associated in one way or another with

---

[79] As Pocock writes, "It is important that the study of political language takes its departure from the language of ruling groups" (1987: 24). That the conceptualization and diffusion of Roman imperial ideals originated at the center and the top, and not in the periphery nor beneath the level of the ruling elite, cannot be doubted; see discussion below, 239–40, 267–70, 314–16.

[80] See above, Introduction to Part II, for the parameters of this body of evidence.

the central state, in political terms, or which otherwise belonged to the "center," in socio-spatial terms. Before turning to the inscriptions themselves, it will be worthwhile to consider the many different authors of them.

In the city of Rome, in addition to the imperial regime itself, a number of actors, collective and individual, set up inscriptions with honorific terminology for the emperor. Institutions responsible for such texts range in importance and proximity to the imperial regime from the Roman senate – expressing itself either by senatorial decree or, more commonly, on behalf of the *senatus populusque romanus* as a whole – to the 35 tribes and a group of *vicimagistri*. These inscriptions were also set up by groups closely associated with the imperial house, such as the *fratres Arvales*, and those involved in the practices of emperor worship, including the *sodales Titi*, the *cultores larum et imaginorum domus Augustae*, and the *seviri Augustales*. The military presence in the city also generated epigraphic texts with honorific terminology for the emperor, including one produced by an urban cohort, and others by high-ranking officials such as the *praefectus vigilum* and the praetorian prefect. The world of officialdom outside of Rome was also responsible for a number of these inscriptions. Here the Roman army bulked large, with several honorific inscriptions erected not only by whole units, ranging in size from an entire legion to an individual cohort and an individual *ala*, but also from individual officers and soldiers. And finally, amongst the imperial administrators scattered throughout the provinces, we find such inscriptions set up by a variety of officials, including a *conductor*, a *vice praesidis* (of Numidia), and, above all, imperial procurators.

This is a very disparate group, then, extending from emperors to low-level officials, from the senate to marginal collectivities. And the texts themselves come from Rome, Italy, and as far afield as Mauretania Tingitana, Britannia, and Dacia.[81] It goes without saying that there were multiple voices and multiple interests at work here. Indeed, through these inscriptions one can even trace the outlines of a sort of "dialogue" about how the emperor should be represented, as we will see. The rationale for treating these diverse inscriptions together, for analytical purposes, is that they were all produced by representatives or agents of the central state, broadly defined, or by those located at the center (in particular, in the city of Rome itself). As such, these inscriptions belong to what we may call "the first wave" in the diffusion of imperial ideals throughout the Roman West. Because these inscriptions were produced either by imperial officials or by

---

[81] See above, 186–7, for a distribution map.

those close to the regime, in other words, they constitute the first epigraphic expression of those ideals and values initially formulated, as I will suggest below (240), within the orbit of the imperial court. As a result, it is from these inscriptions that we can begin to assess the "official impulse" in the spread of imperial ideals in the public sphere.[82] It is important, though, to remain sensitive to the complexities of authorship and intent that lay behind them.

We may begin with one type of inscription with honorific terminology for the emperor that is especially difficult to situate within the category of "official" inscriptions: the milestone.[83] During the first two centuries AD, milestones were set up, in principle, by the central state, and responsibility for them, and the roads they marked, normally ascribed to the emperor. As a result, most milestones during this period listed the emperor's names and titles in the nominative case.[84] Of these, some included what I have defined as "honorific terminology" for the emperor, usually in the form of superlative epithets. The earliest example in the corpus comes from a milestone in Numidia in which Commodus is styled as "most noble of all men and most blessed emperor."[85] From the same area come two milestones attributed to Caracalla, set up four years apart, in which the emperor is represented, in precisely the same language, as "greatest, most invincible, holiest, bravest, most blessed and, beyond all emperors, most indulgent."[86] Other milestones erected elsewhere under Caracalla identify the emperor as "pacifier of the world" and as "father of the soldiers."[87] From Noricum, three milestones represent Macrinus and Diadumenianus as "most foresightful Augusti."[88] Elagabalus is styled as "most blessed and most invincible and, beyond all emperors, most indulgent" on two nearly

---

[82] The term "official impulse" is borrowed from Wallace-Hadrill 1981b: 24; for the mechanisms by which these ideals were initially formulated ("the first wave"), see discussion below, 240, 314–16. Note that the inscriptions examined in this chapter belong to what I have categorized as "types" 1–4 (cf. Introduction to Part II; appendix 15).

[83] In general on imperial milestones, see above, n. 67.

[84] In index 1A in *CIL* 17.2 (milestones from Gaul and Germany, one of two fascicles of *CIL* 17 published thus far), for example, nearly all milestones up through the reign of Commodus present the names and titles of the reigning emperor in the nominative case. For the imperial *cura viarum*, see Rathmann 2003: 56–90; cf. Pekáry 1968: 71–7.

[85] *CIL* 8.10307 = *ILS* 397 (near Rusicade, 186): *nobilissimus omnium et felicissimus princeps.*

[86] *CIL* 8.22384 (near Milevis, 212), and *CIL* 8.10305 (near Rusicade, 216): *maximus invictissimus sanctissimus fortissimus felicissimus et super omnes principes indulgentissimus.*

[87] *Pacator orbis*: *CIL* 13.9061 (near Noviodonum, Germania Superior, 213), 9068 (Germania Superior, 213), 9072 (near Aquae, 213); cf. *AE* 1996.1141, a milestone from near Augusta Raurica (Germania Superior): [*fortissimus fe*]*licissimusq(ue)* [*magn(us)*] *princeps pacato*]*r orbis* [*vias et pontes vetustate*] *conlab*[*s*]*a*[*s restituit*]. *Pater militum*: *CIL* 2.4676 = *ILS* 454 (near Emerita Augusta, Lusitania, 217).

[88] *AE* 2003.1317 = *CIL* 3.1353 (217–18): [*provi*]*dentissim*[*i Aug(usti)*]; *CIL* 3.5708 (218): *providentissimi Augg(usti)*; *AE* 1980.664 (218): *providentissimi Augusti.*

identical milestones from Numidia.[89] And from a milestone in Moesia Inferior, we find Severus Alexander identified as "holiest Augustus."[90] In all these cases, it must be emphasized, the emperor's names and titles, and the superlative epithets that went with them, were presented in the nominative case.

It is difficult to know what to make of these texts. The anomaly lies in the use of superlative epithets on inscribed monuments for which the central state normally assumed responsibility. Such epithets do not appear in other documentary texts, such as military diplomas, and as a result, most scholars have identified them as parts of the emperor's "unofficial" titulature, found almost exclusively in honorific dedications to the emperor.[91] But the texts in question were set up, at least formally, by the emperor. Now it is difficult to imagine that the emperor himself was responsible for the wording employed in these milestones. Indeed, it seems unlikely that anyone in the emperor's inner circle dictated such terminology. Perhaps it is better to read these milestones as stemming from provincial governors, operating on their own authority, or even as the product of local initiative. One argument in favor of the latter interpretation is the appearance of milestones in which the emperor's names and titles appear not in the nominative case, but rather in the dative, implying that these official monuments should be seen, in some loose sense, as dedications to the emperor.[92] The earliest example comes, once again, under Commodus, on a milestone from Raetia, in which the emperor is hailed as "bravest and most blessed emperor (and) most indulgent master."[93] From Numidia, on a series of four milestones set up by the *colonia* of Sitifis – a rare indication of formal authorship on such milestones – Septimius Severus is honored as "bravest and most blessed (emperor)."[94] On milestones from both Raetia and Noricum, Caracalla is called "bravest and most blessed emperor and most indulgent master."[95] Elagabalus is lauded as "bravest and most

---

[89] *CIL* 8.10304 = *ILS* 471 (near Rusicade, 219): *felicissimus adque invictissimus ac super omnes retro principes indulgentissimus*; *CIL* 8.10308 (near Rusicade, 220): *ibid* (but with *atque* for *adque*); cf. *CIL* 8.22385 (milestone near Milevis, Numidia, 219): *felicissim[us atque] indul[gentissimus]*.

[90] *CIL* 3.12519 (234): *sanctissimus Augustus*.

[91] E.g. Frei-Stolba 1969; see above, Introduction to Part II.

[92] Thus König 1973, followed by Witschel 2002. Such milestones begin to appear in the Severan period, and become the norm in the third and fourth centuries (with quite a bit of regional variation, as we would expect; see references in Witschel 2002: 328, n. 14; cf. Rathmann 2003: App. 6.5).

[93] *CIL* 3.11984 (Raetia, 180–192): *f [ortissi]mo [ac f]elicis[simo pr]inc[ipi] domi[no in]du[lgen]tissi[mo]*.

[94] *CIL* 8.10338 (198), *CIL* 8.10353 (198), *CIL* 8.10362 (198): *fortissimo felicissimo*; cf. *CIL* 8.10337: *fortissimi [felic]issimi (sic)*.

[95] Raetia: *AE* 1978.586 (205–7), 1978.587 (215); *CIL* 3.5997–9 (215). Noricum: *fortissimo ac felicissimo principi domino indulgentissimo* (*CIL* 3.5745, 213).

blessed emperor" on several milestones from Hispania Tarraconensis, and as "invincible, pious, and blessed" on a couple from Numidia.[96] And on milestones in Raetia and Numidia we find Severus Alexander depicted as "invincible" and, in Numidia, as "our greatest and bravest master."[97] On these milestones, at least, the emperor is represented, unambiguously, as the recipient of this praise language, and not as arrogating these epithets to himself, as in the earlier examples.

Several clear patterns emerge from this group of milestones with honorific terminology for the emperor. In chronological terms, they first appear in the last quarter of the second century, under Commodus, and then really proliferate in the Severan period. Geographically, they are found in a number of provinces, but are concentrated in the upper Rhine and upper Danubian provinces (Germania Superior, Raetia, Noricum) and, above all, in Numidia. Because of these geographical concentrations, we could view these inscribed monuments as characteristic of particular regional epigraphies, their honorific terminology shaped largely by local influences.[98] But that cannot be the whole explanation. For another striking feature of these texts, not always noted, is the consistency of honorific terminology on milestones set up at tremendous distances from one another. Caracalla is called "bravest and most blessed" on milestones set up in Numidia and Germania Superior, while Severus Alexander is identified as "invincible" on milestones set up in Raetia and Numidia.[99] And on milestones erected on roads as far apart as Numidia, Pannonia Inferior, Galatia, and Cappadocia, Elagabalus is represented, sometimes in the nominative and sometimes in the dative, as "invincible, pious, and blessed."[100] From these interregional correspondences we may infer some sort of mechanism or framework for the diffusion of a centrally influenced language of honor for the emperor. The possible nature and operations of such a mechanism will be considered below. The important point for the time being is that these milestones were erected in the public sphere, with varying degrees of central authority, and

---

[96] *Fortissimo felicissimoque principi*: CIL 2.4766 (near Asturica, 218), 4767 (219), 4769 (219), 4805 (219). *Invicto pio felici*: CIL 8.10334 (near Biskra, 218–22), AE 1981.909 (218–22).

[97] *Invicto*: AE 1987.790 (Raetia, 226–8); CIL 8.22521 (near Ngaus, Numidia, 222–35). *Domino nostro maximo et fortissimo*: CIL 8.22522–3 (near Ngaus, 222–35).

[98] For the influence of local epigraphic cultures, and local political concerns, in shaping the language of these milestones, see Witschel 2002, focusing on the *territorium* of Aquileia, mainly in the fourth century.

[99] See above, nn. 86, 95, 97.

[100] CIL 8.10267 (Numidia, 218–22): *invictus pius felix*; CIL 8.10334 (Numidia, 218–22): *invicto pio felici*; CIL 3.3713 (Pannonia Inferior, 218–22); AE 1986.684 (Galatia, 218–22); CIL 3.12214 (Cappadocia, 218–22).

so can be seen, on the definition offered above, as official expressions of Roman imperial ideology.[101]

Let us turn now to this set of inscriptions as a whole. It is under Trajan that we first find multiple official inscriptions containing honorific terminology for the emperor. Some of the texts celebrate his military achievements, calling him "enlarger of the world" or "bravest emperor," while others praise his virtues, with epithets such as "most foresightful" or "holiest and greatest."[102] But in most of these inscriptions the language and ideology is that of civic benefaction. On two inscriptions from Rome, for example, he is hailed as "enricher of the citizens" and as "most generous."[103] And in another inscription from Rome, erected by the 35 tribes of citizens, his expansion of the seating at the Circus Maximus is explicitly ascribed to his *liberalitas*:

imp(eratori) Caesari | divi Nervae f(ilio) | Nervae Traiano | Aug(usto) Germanico | Dacico pontifici | maximo tribunic(ia) | pot(estate) vii imp(eratore) iiii co(n)s(ule) v p(atre) p(atriae) | tribus xxxv | quod liberalitate | optimi principis | commoda earum etiam | locorum adiectione | ampliata sint.

To the imperator Caesar Nerva Trajan Augustus Germanicus Dacicus, son of the deified Nerva, pontifex maximus, in the seventh year of the tribunician power, with four imperatorial acclamations, consul five time, father of the fatherland, the 35 tribes (have dedicated this), since, by the *liberalitas* of the best emperor, their perks have been enhanced by the expansion of seats.[104]

In this dedication, the symbolic relationship between the emperor, the supreme benefactor, and the urban plebs of Rome, expressing itself here in corporate terms through the institution of the 35 tribes, is celebrated both by the emperor's benefaction and by the virtue that motivated it, his personal generosity.[105]

Trajan's honorific titles *propagator orbis terrarum* and *locupletator civium*, noted above, actually come from the same inscription, set up in Rome in

---

[101] This does not mean, *contra* Pekáry 1968: 16–22, that these expressions were centrally dictated; see below, 239–40.

[102] *Propagatori orbis terrarum*: *CIL* 6.40500–01 = 6.958 (Rome, 108). *Fortissimo principi*: *CIL* 9.1558 = *ILS* 296 (Beneventum, 115), on Trajan's arch at Beneventum. *Providentissimo principi*: *CIL* 9.5894 = *ILS* 298 (Ancona, 115), on Trajan's arch at Ancona. [*Sacr*]*atissimo m*[*aximoque*]: *CIL* 14.4486a (Ostia, 114–17); for the dedicator, a local patron, cf. *CIL* 3.2909.

[103] *Locupletatori civium*: *CIL* 6.40500–01 = 6.958 (Rome, 108). *Liberalissimo*: *CIL* 6.40493 (Rome, 98–117).

[104] *CIL* 6.955 = *ILS* 286 (Rome, 103). Trajan's work in the Circus Maximus is also celebrated by Pliny (*Pan.* 51.5).

[105] For the ideology of the Roman people's *commoda*, see briefly Purcell 2000: 417–21; see also Rowe 2002: 88–91 for the coalescence of the urban plebs' corporate identity under the early empire.

108.[106] A similar juxtaposition of military achievement and civic benefaction is also found on two honorific inscriptions for Hadrian and one each for Antoninus Pius and Marcus Aurelius, all three emperors lauded by the formulaic coupling, "bravest and most generous." These four inscriptions were erected not in Rome, but in the legionary camp at Lambaesis in Numidia.[107] The tight-knit, military context of these dedications surely accounts both for the replication of the terminology and for the prominence of the martial element in it. In most of the other inscriptions for these three emperors, though, the emphasis continues to fall on virtue and benefaction. Hadrian is honored as "greatest and holiest emperor" and – if the restoration of the text is correct – as "restorer of the commonwealth and of the virtue of the ancestors."[108] And like Trajan before him, he is specifically honored for a public display of *liberalitas*:

s(enatus) p(opulus)q(ue) R(omanus) | imp(eratori) Caesari divi Traiani | f(ilio) divi Nervae nepoti | Traiano Hadriano Aug(usto) pont(ifici) | max(imo) tr[ib](unicia) pot(estate) II co(n)s(ule) II | qui primus omnium principum et | solus remittendo sestertium novies | milies centena milia n(umero) debitum fiscis | non praesentes tantum cives suos sed | et posteros eorum praestitit hac | liberalitate securos.

The senate and people of Rome (dedicated this) to the imperator Caesar Trajan Hadrian Augustus, son of the deified Trajan, grandson of the deified Nerva, pontifex maximus, in the second year of the tribunician power, consul two times, since, in remitting the 900,000,000 sesterces owed to the *fiscus*, he was the first and only emperor to ensure the security not only of his current citizens, but also of their descendants, by means of this *liberalitas*.[109]

Again, what is being commemorated here is not just the imperial benefaction – in this case, the largest tax remission offered by a Roman emperor up to that point – but also the *liberalitas* that had underpinned it.[110] With Antoninus Pius and Marcus Aurelius, we find a wider range of ideals cited in the honorific terminology. Three inscriptions identify Antoninus Pius as "the best (man)," a philosophical ideal which will be examined in

---

[106] Above, nn. 102–3.

[107] *Fortissimo liberalissimoque*: *AE* 2003.2020a = *AE* 1900.33 (117–38); *CIL* 8.2534 (117–38); *AE* 1967.564 (138–61); *CIL* 8.2547 (176). The inscriptions for Hadrian and Marcus Aurelius were found in the praetorium at the camp.

[108] *Maxim[o et sa]nctissimo p[rincipi]*: *CIL* 6.40515 = 6.36915 (Rome, 119–28). *R[estitutori rei publicae atq]ue virtu[tis maiorum]*: *CIL* 6.983 (Rome, 117–38).

[109] *CIL* 6.967 = *ILS* 309 (Rome, 118).

[110] On Hadrian's tax remission, see Dio 69.8.1, 71.32.2; *HA Had.* 7.6–7, with Duncan-Jones 1990: 66–7.

chapter 5, and two others as "most just."[111] And Marcus Aurelius is hailed as "best and most pious" in one inscription, and as "most generous emperor" in another.[112] By the mid-second century, these honorific titles celebrating benefactions and philosophically oriented virtues on official texts begin to appear more consistently throughout the western provinces, in Africa Proconsularis, Numidia, Noricum, and Britannia, for example, but they are mostly attested in Rome and the Italian peninsula.[113]

With Commodus, a transition to a rather different conception of imperial ideals and values begins to come into focus. Some of the traditional concepts retain their currency. He is praised, for example, as "the holiest imperator," and, in an uncharacteristically prosaic nod to the empire's mercantile infrastructure, as "the restorer of commercial transactions."[114] Such titles would have fit well with the ideology of the first half of the second century. In other texts, however, he is styled as "most indulgent master" or, more simply, as "our master."[115] As I will argue in the next chapter, the appearance of this term, "master" (*dominus*), signals a decisive break from earlier conceptions of imperial authority, with important implications for the ways in which that authority was construed in local contexts.

Under Septimius Severus and Caracalla, militarism and imperial absolutism, openly acknowledged, come to the fore. Four themes stand out in these official inscriptions. First, the superlative epithet *fortissimus*, "bravest," proliferates, repeated again and again in a range of contexts. It is no longer paired with *liberalissimus*, however, but rather with *felicissimus*, "most blessed," which in these texts must refer to the emperor's divine support on the battlefield.[116] The ideal of civic benefaction, in other words, has now been wholly elided by that of conquest. Second, the language and ideology of permanent military victory flourishes, the inscriptions making constant

---

[111] *Optimo*: *AE* 1966.428 (Ephesus, Asia, 139: *optumo*), set up by a *legatus* of the proconsul of Asia (who later became a member of the *fratres Arvales*); *CIL* 6.1001 = *ILS* 341 (Rome, 143); *CIL* 3.5654 (Trigisamum, Noricum, 140–4), set up by the *Ala I Augusta Thracum*. *Iustissimo*: *CIL* 6.1001 = *ILS* 341 (Rome, 143); *CIL* 6.40546 = 6.1217 (Rome, 144: *iu[stissimo]*).

[112] *Optimo ac piissimo*: *CIL* 6.1009 = *ILS* 2012 (Rome, 140); on this text, see below, 233–4. *Liberalissim[oque p]rincipi*: *CIL* 8.18067 = *ILS* 2303 (Lambaesis, Numidia, 166).

[113] For the locations of these inscriptions, see appendix 14; see also map 2, 230.

[114] *[Sacra]tissimum imp(eratorem)*: *CIL* 6.31420 (Rome, 186), set up by a group of *vici magistri*. The commercial inscription was erected by a Claudius Xenophon, an imperial procurator, in Porolissum, Dacia, "for the health and victory" of Commodus: *pro salute et victoria . . . restitutori(s) commerc(iorum) secundum sacram subscriptionem domini n(ostri) sanctissimi imp(eratoris)* (*AE* 1988.977, 185–92).

[115] *Dominus indulgentissimus*: n. 93. *D(omino) n(ostro)*: *AE* 1969/70.578 (Baltchik, Moesia Inferior, 180–92).

[116] Inscriptions with the pairing *fortissimo felicissimoque* are too numerous to list here; see appendix 13. For the meaning of *felicitas* in the military sphere, see 166.

reference to the emperors as "invincible" or, in hyperbolic vein, as "most invincible."[117] The ideals of martial bravery, divine support, and invincibility all come together in the honorific title *propagator imperii*, "enlarger of the empire," the third prominent theme in these inscriptions. A version of this title is attested already under Trajan, who was called *propagator orbis terrarum*, but during the reigns of Septimius Severus and Caracalla it becomes common, especially in the North African provinces.[118] Similar in tone and meaning is the title "pacifier of the world," which appears in the texts of four milestones in Germania Superior formally authored by Caracalla in 213.[119] This is also the ideological and discursive context in which we should read the famous dedicatory inscription from the arch of Septimius Severus in the Forum in Rome:

imp(eratori) Caes(ari) Lucio Septimio M(arci) fil(io) Severo Pio Pertinaci Aug(usto) . . . et | imp(eratori) Caes(ari) M(arco) Aurelio L(uci) fil(io) Antonino Aug(usto) . . . | <optimis fortissimisque principibus> | ob rem publicam restitutam imperiumque populi Romani propagatum | insignibus virtutibus eorum domi forisque s(enatus) p(opulus)q(ue) R(omanus).

To imperator Caesar Lucius Septimius Severus Pius Pertinax, son of Marcus . . . and to imperator Caesar Marcus Aurelius Antoninus Augustus, son of Lucius . . . the best and bravest emperors, the senate and people of Rome (have dedicated this monument), on account of the restoration of the commonwealth and the extension of the empire of the Roman people by means of their conspicuous virtues at home and abroad.[120]

In the language of this dedication we may catch a glimpse of competing conceptions of imperial achievement and legitimacy. On the one hand, the senate is plugging the requisite themes of martial valor (*fortissimi principes*) and military conquest (*imperium propagatum*), appropriate for a triumphal arch and consistent with the preferred emphases of the imperial

---

[117] *Invicto*: e.g. *AE* 1967.237 (S. Pedro de la Vina, Hispania Tarraconensis, 197); *CIL* 3.75 (Philae, Egypt, 203); *CIL* 6.1065 (Rome, 213), set up by the *negotiantes Vasculari*; *CIL* 10.6854 = *ILS* 5822 (milestone on the Via Appia, 216: *invictus*); *CIL* 3.207 (milestone in Syria, 212–17). *Invictissimo*: e.g. *AE* 1978.643 (Poetovio, Noricum, 211–12), set up by a procurator; *CIL* 8.22384 (milestone near Milevis, Numidia, 212: *invictissimus*); *CIL* 13.7616 (Holzhausen, Germania Superior, 213); *CIL* 8.10305 (milestone near Rusicade, Numidia, 216: *invictissimus*).

[118] Trajan: n. 102. Mauretania Caesariensis: *AE* 1995.1790 (Tatilti, 198–9: [*pr*]*opagatores* [*imperii*]), in the nominative. Africa: *IRT* 395, 424 (Lepcis Magna, 204), dedicated by a procurator. Numidia: *CIL* 8.2705 (Lambaesis, 197–209: *propagatoribus imperii*), dedicated by the 3rd Augustan Legion; *AE* 1967.567 = *CIL* 8.18256 (Lambaesis, 197), dedicated by a soldier.

[119] *Pacator orbis*: *AE* 1996.1141 (near Augusta Raurica: [*pacato*]*r orbis*); *CIL* 13.9061 (near Noviodunum); *CIL* 13.9068 (location not specified); *CIL* 13.9072 (near Aquae).

[120] *CIL* 6.1033 = *ILS* 425 (Rome, 203). On the arch of Septimius Severus, see most recently Lusnia 2006.

regime itself. On the other hand, it is also representing the emperors as moral exemplars (*optimi principes*) and as propagators of "conspicuous virtues" (*insignes virtutes*), both of which recall the ideals and values of the "good" emperors of the second century.[121] It is a useful reminder that even within the framework of "official" language, there could be multiple voices speaking simultaneously.

The language of invincibility and military conquest evident in so many of the inscriptions set up under Septimius Severus and Caracalla is paralleled by the rise of absolutist conceptions of imperial authority, expressed above all by the term *dominus*, the fourth central theme in the honorific terminology of this period. That militarism and absolutism went together under these two emperors is evident from the frequency with which the term *dominus* is employed in inscriptions erected by military units, officers, and soldiers. It appears in inscriptions erected by entire military units, such as the *cohors* I *Vindelicorum*, stationed in Dacia; by groups of soldiers, whether on active service or after retirement; by officers, such as the *praefectus vigilum* in Rome; and by individual soldiers.[122] In civilian contexts, by contrast, the use of *dominus* is quite rare, and there is no secure case of its usage in a text in which the emperor's names and titles appear in the nominative case.[123] Amongst these official inscriptions, the title *dominus* was evidently limited to the military sphere.

Military power and imperial domination continue to define the honorific terminology of official inscriptions set up under the later Severans.

---

[121] The language of virtue, the reference to the empire of the Roman people, and the dedication by the SPQR are all consistent with the iconography of the arch, which consistently emphasizes the achievements of the Roman imperial state as a whole, subtly downplaying the individual role played by the emperor; see discussion in Mayer 2010: 127–8.

[122] *Cohors I Vindelicorum*: *AE* 1987.848 (Tibiscum, Dacia, 202): *pro salute dd(ominorum) n[n(ostrorum)]*. Active soldiers: e.g. *CIL* 3.75 (Philae, Egypt, 203): *felicissimo saeculo dom(inorum) nn(ostrorum)*; *CIL* 6.1063 (Rome, 212): *pro salute et incolumit[a]te domini nostri*; *RIB* 905 (Old Carlisle, Britannia, 213): *[pro sal(ute) imp(eratoris) do]mini nos[tri]*. Veterans: *AE* 2001.1688 = 1995.1270 = 1993.1302 (Matrica, Pannonia Inferior, 197–209): *numini dd(ominorum) nn(ostrorum) impp(eratorum)*. *Praefectus vigilum*: *CIL* 6.40647 (Rome, 213): *pro salute et reditu et victorias dom(ini) n(ostri)*. Individual soldiers: e.g. *CIL* 13.1766 = *ILS* 4794 (Lugdunum, Lugdunensis, 193–7): *pro salute dom[ini] n(ostri) imp(eratoris)*; *AE* 1994.1408 (Sirmium, Pannonia Inferior, 203): *g(enio) dom(inorum) nn(ostrorum) Augg(ustorum)*, set up by a *beneficiarius*; cf. *AE* 1993.1777 (Sitifis, Mauretania Caesariensis, 201–4); *AE* 1991.1743 (Tamuda, Mauretania Tingitana, 210): *pro salute et incolumitate ddd(ominorum) nnn(ostrorum)*, dedicated to Septimius Severus, Caracalla, and Geta.

[123] One inscription set up in Rome by the *negotiantes Vasculari* refers to the emperor as a *dominus* (*CIL* 6.1065, 213); another was set up by an imperial procurator (*RIB* 2066 = *ILS* 9317), but at Hadrian's Wall, a military zone. An inscription erected at Gorsium in Pannonia Inferior (*AE* 1997.1279 = *CIL* 3.3342) may include the use of *dominus* in the nominative case, but the condition of the text does not permit a secure reading: *[imperat]ores d[d(omini nn(ostri)]*. Finally, one inscription set up by an imperial slave refers to the emperor as *dominus* (*CIL* 3.15184 [4], Poetovio, Noricum, 197–211), but there it could be construed as a legal term.

Under both Elagabalus and Severus Alexander, the coupling *fortissimus felicissimusque* remains common.[124] The language of invincibility also retains its currency during this period.[125] It should also be noted that, during the reign of Severus Alexander, a few echoes of second-century imperial ideology can still be discerned. On a milestone in Moesia Inferior he is styled as "most holy Augustus," for example, and in another inscription, set up in Dacia, he is honored (it seems) as "best and greatest emperor."[126] These terms represent the emperor as a religious and moral exemplar. In general, though, the ethical content of terms such as these was ultimately overwhelmed by martial and autocratic themes, and by the nearly ubiquitous title *dominus*.[127] One formulaic phrase in these official inscriptions that also emerges for the first time is *super omnes retro principes*, "beyond all previous emperors," normally with a superlative epithet attached to it. There were some precursors to this phrase under Septimius Severus, who is identified in two inscriptions from central Italy as "most blessed beyond all."[128] With Elagabalus, though, the group to which he is being favorably compared is specified as "all emperors." It was not enough for Elagabalus to be styled as "most indulgent," in other words, or even as "most indulgent beyond all (men)," but specifically as "most indulgent beyond all previous emperors."[129] This reflects a growing tendency on the part of the imperial regime to "compete" with its predecessors, and is indicative, in general terms, of a pronounced inflation in the honorific language of these official texts.[130]

In considering this set of official inscriptions for the period 69–235 as a whole, two features stand out. The first is a broad shift in emphasis over time. In the first half of the period, roughly through the reign of Marcus

[124] E.g. *CIL* 2.4766–7, 4769, 4805 (milestones near Asturica, Hispania Tarraconensis, 218–19); *AE* 1987.790 (milestone in Raetia, 226–8).

[125] *Invictus*: e.g. *CIL* 8.10267 (milestone near Bisra, Numidia, 218–22); *CIL* 8.8701 = *ILS* 6887 (Castellum Dianense, Mauretania Caesariensis, 234); *AE* 1986.653 (Yuzevler Mahallesi, Bithynia-Pontus, 230–5). *Invictissimus*: *CIL* 8.10304 = *ILS* 471, *CIL* 8.10308 (milestones near Rusicade, Numidia, 219, 220).

[126] *Sanctissimus Augustus*: *CIL* 3.12519 (Moesia Inferior, 234). The Dacian inscription (*CIL* 3.797, Also-Ilosua, 222–35), erected by a *legatus Augusti*, is quite fragmentary: [*optimo maxi*]*moque princi*[*pi*].

[127] See appendix 13.

[128] *CIL* 10.5909 (Anagnia, 207): *fortissimus ac super omnes felicissimus princeps*; *CIL* 14.4388 (Ostia, 211): *fortissimo ac super omnes felicissimo principi*. The correspondence between the terms in these two texts – one listing the emperor's names and titles in the nominative, the other in the dative – can hardly be coincidental.

[129] For the texts, see above, n. 89.

[130] For the phrase *super omnes retro principes*, see discussion in Scheithauer 1988 (not distinguishing, though, between official and unofficial inscriptions); see also below, 280–3, on the use of this formulaic phrase in the contexts of honorific "inflation" and increasing competition between imperial regimes.

Aurelius, the honorific language employed in these texts is primarily that of virtue and civic benefaction. The emperor is consistently represented as a moral exemplar and paradigm of various ethical qualities with distinguished pedigrees in Greek and Roman philosophical and political thought. Several of these qualities denoted the emperor's personal generosity, such as *liberalitas* and *munificentia* (and, perhaps to a lesser extent, *indulgentia*), and many translated into concrete benefactions for the empire's inhabitants, whether explicitly noted in the inscriptions themselves or reflected in titles such as *locupletator civium*, "enricher of the citizens." In the second half of the period, beginning with Commodus and then gathering steam under Septimius Severus and Caracalla, the interrelated themes of martial valor, military conquest, and imperial absolutism become prominent in the texts, effectively displacing the ethical conception of imperial power and authority. That is a significant change, one that can be seen, in fact, as an ideological rupture.[131] The second clear feature of these inscriptions is their changing geographical distribution. In general, most of the inscriptions from the first half of the period (AD 69–192) were set up in Rome, Italy, North Africa, southern Spain, and the Mediterranean coast of Spain and Gaul (map 2), while many from the second half (AD 193–235) were set up along the Rhine-Danube corridor as well (map 3). This implies at least some degree of regional variation in the manner in which the emperor was represented publicly in inscribed monuments, a feature of the epigraphic landscape that will also be clear when we consider the local response to these shifting imperial ideals in the next chapter.

What we are seeing through these inscriptions, then, is both a long-term change in an ideological system and an ideological divergence between the Mediterranean core and the continental periphery in the use of honorific terminology for the emperor. But neither the chronological change nor the geographical divergence should be exaggerated. Inscriptions highlighting martial ideals were set up in the early second century, after all, and texts citing ethical qualities could still be inscribed in the later Severan period; there were inscriptions with honorific terminology for the emperor set up in the provinces in the first half of this period, and in Italy in the second half. Nevertheless, the general pattern in these inscriptions is one of change over time and, less marked, of disparity between center and periphery.

From the epigraphic evidence alone it would be difficult to understand this chronological and geographical patterning, and to assess how the changes over time, on the one hand, and the regional differences, on the

---

[131] Further evidence for this rupture, and its effects, will be discussed in chapter 5.

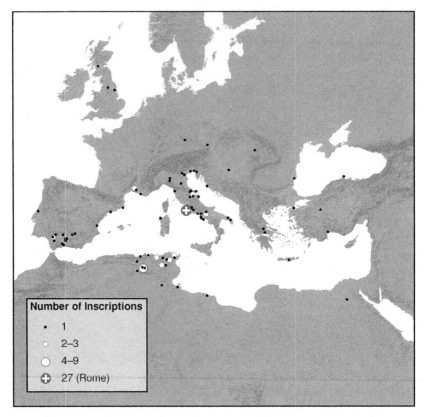

Number of Inscriptions

•   1

○   2–3

◯   4–9

⊕   27 (Rome)

Map 2 Inscriptions employing honorific terminology for the emperor, AD 69–192

other, related to one another. What must be kept in mind in considering these questions is the fact that the bulk of these inscriptions were produced by representatives or agents of the central state, and can therefore be interpreted, as I have argued, as "official" expressions of imperial ideology. This is where the numismatic evidence becomes essential. For imperial coins were also official documents, and by comparing the concepts and values represented on coins with those cited on officially inscribed monuments, we can better comprehend this first wave in the diffusion of imperial ideals.

There are several clues to suggest that the honorific terminology employed in official inscriptions and the ideals and values represented on imperial coins belonged to the same communicative impulse. First, and most clear, is the simultaneous appearance of a new reverse type on the imperial coinage and the first appearance of the corresponding superlative

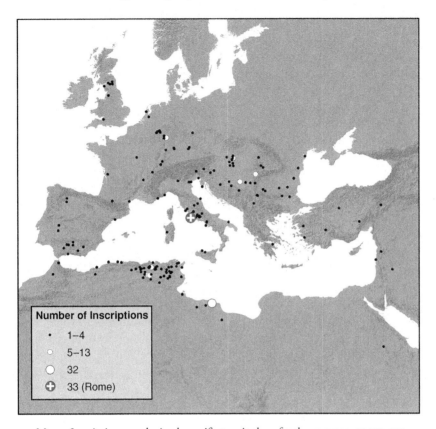

Map 3 Inscriptions employing honorific terminology for the emperor, AD 193–235

epithet in an inscription with honorific terminology for the emperor. A good example comes from the dedicatory inscription from Trajan's arch in Ancona, erected by the senate and people of Rome in 115:

Imp(eratori) Caesari Divi Nervae f(ilio) Nervae | Traiano optimo Aug(usto) Germanic(o) | Dacico pont(ifici) max(imo) . . . | . . . providentissimo principi | senatus p(opuli)q(ue) R(omanus) quod accessum | Italiae hoc etiam addito ex pecunia sua | portu tutiorem navigantibus reddiderit.

To imperator Caesar Nerva Trajan Best Augustus, son of the deified Nerva, Germanicus, Dacicus, pontifex maximus . . . most foresightful emperor, the senate and people of Rome (have dedicated this monument), because by this additional harbor, paid for from his own money, he has rendered the entrance to Italy safer for sailors.[132]

In this inscription, Trajan is lauded as *providentissimus*. This superlative epithet was, as far as we know, unprecedented, and it was precisely under Trajan that the corresponding virtue, Providentia, was first minted on imperial denarii, the denomination with the widest circulation.[133] While it is possible that the senatorial dedicators of this arch sincerely believed that Trajan's construction of a harbor at Ancona displayed real foresight, and that "most foresightful" was therefore the most appropriate honorific epithet for this monument, it seems more likely that they were actively participating, together with the imperial regime, in defining the "good" emperor with reference to specific virtues, and that their choice of the epithet *providentissimus* reflects a contemporary consensus, at the center, that *providentia* was just such a quality.

We find a similar correspondence across official media under Commodus. It was during his reign that the exceedingly rare Nobilitas type was first minted on the imperial coinage, in 186, and also during his reign that we find the first appearance of the superlative epithet *nobilissimus* on an official inscription, a milestone erected in Numidia, also in 186, with the emperor's names and titles in the nominative case.[134] Other examples of the simultaneous appearance of a new coin type and its corresponding epithet on official inscriptions from before and after our period, under Tiberius and then under Constantine, suggest that these correspondences were neither random nor coincidental – nor meaningless.[135]

More often than perfect synchronization in the appearance of new virtues on coins and inscriptions, we find the official inscriptions mirroring the imperial coinage in its fluctuations in emphasis. And it is really here, in fact, that the quantitative analysis of the coinage and the corpus of inscriptions together help us to see patterns and correspondences that would otherwise

[132] *CIL* 9.5894 = *ILS* 298. For infrastructure building as an advertised benefit of empire, see above, 102–3, 121–2.
[133] E.g. *RIC* 2, Trajan 98; note that the type had appeared, in various configurations, on the base-metal denominations; see above, 95–9. For circulation patterns, see above, 30–4.
[134] Nobilitas type: *RIC* 3, Commodus 139. Milestone: *CIL* 8.10307 = *ILS* 397 (near Rusicade, 186): *nobilissimus omnium et felicissimus princeps*. For the appearance of this epithet in unofficial inscriptions, see below, 254–5.
[135] In an inscription from Capena in Etruria (*CIL* 11.3872 = *ILS* 159, 36/37), the senator A. Fabius Fortunatus praises Tiberius as *princeps optimus ac iustissimus*, "best and most just emperor," and it was during Tiberius' reign that the comparatively rare Iustitia type first appeared (*RIC* 1², 42). And the emperor Constantine, on whose coinage the ideal of Gloria made its official debut (*RIC* 7, Rome 279, etc.), is hailed in an inscription from Vaga in Africa Proconsularis as *gloriosissimus*, "most renowned" (*CIL* 8.14436).

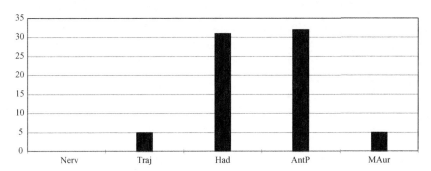

Figure 4.1 Relative frequency of Pietas types on denarii, expressed as a percentage of all virtue types, AD 96–180 (N = 11,658)

be difficult to discern. Consider the following inscription, set up in Rome in 140:

M(arco) Aurelio Caesari imp(eratoris) Caesaris T(iti) Aeli Hadriani Antonini Aug(usti) Pii fil(io) divi Hadriani nep(oti) divi Traiani Parthici pronep(oti) divi Nervae abnep(oti) co(n)s(ule) Petronius Mamertinus et Gavius Maximus pr(aefecti) pr(aetorio) tribuni cohortium praetorium decem et urbanarum trium centuriones cohortium praetoriarum et urbanarum et statorum evocati cohortes praetoriae decem et urbanae x XII XIIII centuriae statorum optimo ac piissimo.

To Marcus Aurelius Caesar, son of the imperator Caesar Titus Aelius Hadrianus Antoninus Augustus Pius, grandson of the deified Hadrian, great-grandson of the deified Trajan Parthicus, great-great-grandson of the deified Nerva, consul: Petronius Mamertinus and Gavius Maximus, praetorian prefects; the tribunes of the ten praetorian and three urban cohorts; the centurions of the praetorian and urban cohorts and administrative attendants; the veterans in active service; the ten praetorian cohorts; the 10th, 12th, and 14th urban cohorts; and the centuries of administrative attendants (have dedicated this monument) to the best and most dutiful (prince).[136]

This dedication to Marcus Aurelius was set up near the beginning of Antoninus Pius' reign. That he was honored specifically as *optimus* and, in particular, as *piissimus*, is significant. Figure 4.1 represents the relative frequency of the Pietas type on imperial denarii minted between 96 and 180. Beginning with the reign of Trajan, as these figures indicate, the Pietas type was being produced in greater and greater relative numbers before reaching its peak under Antoninus Pius. Pietas, in fact, had been the most heavily minted virtue type under Hadrian, and it became even more prominent

[136] *CIL* 6.1009 = *ILS* 2012.

under Pius. *Pietas*, in other words, was an especially resonant virtue at this moment. Indeed, in another inscription set up in 140, in Ostia, Marcus Aurelius is again hailed as *optimus* and *piissimus*.[137] In honoring the heir apparent as *piissimus*, then, the dedicators of these two monuments were not only assimilating Marcus to his adoptive father, by alluding to the latter's cognomen, but were also, like the senatorial dedicators of the arch of Trajan at Ancona, participating in a collective construction of the ideal emperor through the citation of a particular virtue. These dedications are, in any case, the first attestations of the epithet *piissimus*, never particularly common, in inscriptions of this type, and their appearance at a time when the Pietas type was very much in the ascendant on the imperial coinage is unlikely to have been merely coincidental.[138]

Another arresting example of this sort of correspondence between coin type and official inscription comes under Macrinus. Macrinus ruled for just under fifteen months, from April 217 to June 218.[139] During his brief reign, *providentia* was one of the few virtues emphasized on the imperial coinage, with Providentia types accounting for almost 40 percent of all virtue types on denarii during this period.[140] In light of the preceding discussion, it should come as no surprise that of the three surviving milestones set up during Macrinus' brief reign, from Noricum, all three distinguish the emperor and his son, Diadumenianus, as *providentissimi Augusti*, "most foresightful emperors."[141] Especially striking in this case is the long-distance correspondence in ideological expression between officials in the city of Rome, where the coins were minted, and in the province of Noricum, where these milestones were erected, and all within the brief compass of Macrinus' reign. This shows that within the communications networks of the central state, the official diffusion of imperial ideals could be quite systematic and rapid.

In the examples discussed thus far, the coin types have been given implicit priority, as the appearance of new superlative epithets, or the citation of old ones, has been explained with reference either to the appearance of new coin types, or to the fluctuating emphasis on a particular type. There is some logic to this approach, of course, since imperial coins were products of the imperial regime itself, and were therefore closer to the official end of

---

[137] *CIL* 14.4366, found in the *statio vigilum* (dedicators unspecified).

[138] Cf. Harvey 2004 on these two monuments, with emphasis on the dynastic implications of the terminology.

[139] Dates and evidence in Kienast 1996: 169.   [140] See appendix 5.

[141] *AE* 2003.1317 = *CIL* 3.1353 (217–218): [*provi*]*dentissim*[*i Aug*(*usti*)]; *CIL* 3.5708 (218): *providentissimi Augg*(*usti*); *AE* 1980.664 (218): *providentissimi Augusti*.

the official/unofficial spectrum than even the most official inscriptions we have been considering. In some cases, however, the relationship between coin types and official inscriptions may be inverted, with the result that we can perhaps explain the former by the latter. The best example concerns the imperial ideal of *liberalitas*.[142] For in this case, it is in the epigraphic record that the virtue first crops up, in official inscriptions set up under Trajan (see above, 223), and only later, under Hadrian, that it appears as a coin type. It is not impossible that, in producing a Liberalitas type, the imperial mint under Hadrian was responding to the association of the emperor with the virtue of *liberalitas*, as expressed on inscribed monuments set up in Trajanic Rome. But even if in this case the officials of the mint were in fact responding to a new imperial ideal, as I am suggesting, rather than creating it themselves, the underlying dynamic that we have been discussing – the collective definition of the "good" emperor through specific ideals and values – is still at work. That is the key point.

As a final example of ideological convergence across these media, let us examine the articulation of imperial ideals on coins and official inscriptions under Septimius Severus. We have already noted that the dominant honorific themes on the official inscriptions set up during his reign were those of militarism and autocracy, with emphasis on the ideals of martial valor (*fortissimus*), divine support on the battlefield (*felicissimus*), and military invincibility (*invictus/invictissimus*). This cluster of ideals and values has close parallels on the imperial coinage.[143] Among the virtue types on denarii produced under Septimius Severus, for example, nearly one fifth (17 percent) advertised *virtus*. And among the benefit types, 20 percent commemorated the ideal of *felicitas*, and 28 percent *victoria*; roughly one half of all benefit types, that is, were devoted to these two ideologically complementary concepts.[144] The patterns are quite similar on the official inscriptions. In this respect, the configuration of numismatic and epigraphic evidence is analogous to what we have seen in other cases. It should be noted, though, that under Septimius Severus, the overlap between the coin types and the inscriptions is both lexical (*felicitas* and *felicissimus*), as in the examples discussed above, and more broadly conceptual (*virtus* and *fortissimus*; *victoria* and *invictus/invictissimus*). The association, then, is a bit looser. But even without precise lexical correspondence, this honorific

---

[142] *Liberalitas* is discussed in depth above, 82–92; for more detail on the observations here, cf. Noreña 2001: 160–2.

[143] For the figures cited in the text, see the data collected in appendices 5, 7.

[144] For the relationship between *felicitas* and *victoria*, see above, 164–5.

language and set of ideals, expressed both on coins and in inscriptions, is clearly being drawn from the same ideological repertoire.

From these individual texts and sets of inscriptions, then, together with the evidence from the imperial coinage, we can see several lexical and ideological correspondences across different media. It bears repeating that in discerning these correspondences, the quantitative approach has been crucial. Documenting this ideological convergence is not just a matter of juxtaposing any one inscription with any one coin type, in other words, but rather of comparing groups of inscriptions with a mass of coin types, systematically quantified. Analyzing the varying degrees and types of correspondence within the period 69–235 as a whole, and explaining how, exactly, these forms of convergence might have come about, are the problems to which we now turn.

PERIODIZATION AND PROCESS

Considering the period 69–235 as a whole, with reference both to imperial coins and to official inscriptions with honorific terminology for the emperor, there appear to be three distinct phases in terms of lexical and ideological convergence. In the first phase, from Vespasian to Domitian/Nerva (69–98), there were hardly any official inscriptions at all that included honorific terminology for the emperor. In the second phase, from Trajan through Marcus Aurelius (98 180), the ideals and values represented on imperial coins and those cited in official inscriptions mostly converged. Not only were there a number of precise lexical correspondences, but in more general terms, the coin types and the inscriptions both tended to emphasize the emperor's virtues and related ethical ideals, his civic benefactions and, more broadly, the material benefits of monarchy and empire. Then, following a transitional phase, which corresponds roughly with the reign of Commodus (180–192), there arose a third phase, which lasted down to 235. In this phase, the period of the Severan dynasty (193–235), the ideological convergence characteristic of the period *c.* 100–180 begins to unravel. The coins of the Severan period, especially under Septimius Severus, do sound a number of military themes, as we have seen, but in general, the basic idiom of virtues and benefits remains in place. This is not the case with the official inscriptions, which were emphatically martial in nature, thus diverging from the idiom of the imperial coinage and giving rise to something of a rift between coins and inscriptions that had not existed previously. All three phases have important implications for the official diffusion of imperial ideals.

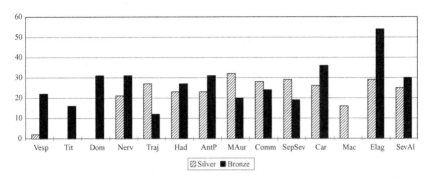

Figure 4.2 Relative frequency of virtue types as a group, expressed as a percentage of all personification types, AD 69–235 (N = 98,698)
Note: Of the 96,698 coins tabulated in figure 4.2, 77,852 are silver, and 20,845 bronze; see appendices 3–4 for details

In the epigraphic sphere, the first phase of our period, 69–98, is characterized by the near-total absence of official inscriptions with honorific terminology for the emperor. Even here, though, we can turn to the numismatic evidence for some insight. Figure 4.2 shows the fluctuating relative frequency of the virtue types, as a group, on both denarii and base-metal denominations. Particularly striking in this graph is the paucity of virtue types on the imperial coinage of the Flavian emperors, especially on the silver coins. In historical terms, this is not too surprising. Despite the importance accorded by Greek and Roman authors to the character of rulers, and despite the absorption of this ideology at Rome in the last two centuries BC, virtues were not central to the public image of Augustus or his Julio-Claudian successors.[145] It is true, of course, that a group of four virtues was highlighted on Augustus' Golden Shield (itself highlighted in the climax of the *Res Gestae*); that in the Tiberian senatorial decrees, especially the *SCPP*, the emperor's virtues were prominent; and that various Julio-Claudian authors, such as Valerius Maximus and Seneca, devoted considerable attention to ethical qualities in general (and, in the case of Seneca, to a single imperial virtue in particular).[146] Nevertheless, imperial

[145] For the role of virtues in Greek and Roman political thought, and the growing importance of ethical conceptions of rulership at Rome in the middle and late Republic, see above, 45–50.
[146] Virtues on the Golden Shield (*virtus, clementia, iustitia, pietas erga deos*): *RG* 34.2 (see above, 50). Virtues in the *SCPP*: *aequitas* (l. 17), *patientia* (ll. 17, 26), *moderatio* (26, 100–1, 133, 146, 167), *indulgentia* (59), *clementia* (90), *iustitia* (90–1, 133), *animi magnitudo* (91), *liberalitas* (95), *modestia* (95), *humanitas* (100), *misericordia* (110), *pietas* (119, 124, 134); for bibliography, see above, n. 66. Valerius Maximus: Bloomer 1992. Seneca's *De Clementia*: Braund 2009.

virtues were not systematically advertised on imperial coins or in official inscriptions during this period. And while the political and ideological ferment unleashed by the events of 69 did bring about some innovations in imperial public representation, the ethical paradigm at the heart of Greek and Roman political thought was not one of them.[147] As a result, virtue types were not common on Flavian coins, nor were they prominent in the official inscriptions of the period. Both imperial coins and official inscriptions were representing the emperor in a positive light, of course, but neither was emphasizing virtues to do it. From this we may infer that the many different actors responsible for producing imperial coins and the various types of inscription pertaining to the emperor were using the same underlying "language."

With the accession of Nerva, virtue types become more prominent on the coinage and, even though there is some fluctuation in emphasis on these types down through the reign of Severus Alexander, they remain significant for the whole period 98–235, especially in the second half of the Severan dynasty (figure 4.2). A related development is the expansion in the number of advertised imperial virtues during this period, especially under Hadrian, on whose coinage four new virtue types were produced for the first time: Indulgentia, Liberalitas, Patientia, and Pudicitia.[148] One broad context in which to place this greater numismatic emphasis on virtues, and the wider range of specific virtues commemorated on the imperial coinage, is the increased attention to the personal qualities of the emperor evident in the literary texts of (roughly) the first quarter of the second century.[149] Pliny's *Panegyricus*, for example, may be read as an extended exposition of more than thirty imperial virtues. A relatively stable set of virtues and vices defines the "good" and "bad" emperor in each of Suetonius' biographies. And much of the political analysis in Tacitus, too, is a meditation on imperial character. The combined evidence of the coinage and the texts suggests that, beginning in the early second century, imperial virtues were resonant and topical in ways that they had not been previously – even if it is difficult to pinpoint why, exactly, this was the case.

---

[147] For various perspectives on imperial ideology in and after the civil war of 69, see e.g. Ramage 1983: 206–9 and Kragelund 1998 (Galba's relationship with his predecessors); Roche 2008 (imperial imagery under Otho); Hurlet 1993 (Vespasian's appropriation of Augustan ideology); Noreña 2003 (ideals of peace and war under Vespasian); Seelentag 2009 (dynastic publicity under Vespasian).

[148] *RIC* 2, Hadrian 212–13, 361, 708 (Indulgentia); 216, 363–4, 712–13, etc. (Liberalitas); 135, 176–8, 343 etc. (Pudicitia); 365 (Patientia).

[149] The following points are made in greater detail, and with supporting bibliography, in Noreña 2007b: 304–6, 312–14; for the timing of these developments, see also Noreña 2001: 155–6; cf. Wallace-Hadrill 1981a: 311–14.

For the argument here, though, more important than the explanation for the rise of virtues on the imperial coinage under Nerva and Trajan, and their diversification under Hadrian, is the fact that it is precisely at the beginning of the second century that such virtues begin to appear with greater frequency in the epigraphic record, too. This chronological correspondence shows that the individuals and groups responsible for the production of coins and inscriptions, as under the Flavians, were employing the same basic idiom in representing the emperor. That is by itself important. But the numismatic and epigraphic evidence takes us far beyond this. For as we have seen, it is not just that these various actors were using the same general idiom, but that, in a number of cases, they were using precisely the same terms, at roughly (and often exactly) the same time, in order to advertise imperial ideals or to honor the emperor. The several examples discussed above have come partly from within the epigraphic record itself, especially in the terminology used on milestones, but mainly from comparisons between coin types and inscriptions. Given the vast extent of the Roman empire, and the pre-modern communications infrastructure within it, these chronological and lexical correspondences – on different media and in widely scattered locations – are very striking. How can they be explained?

In attempting to account for these correspondences, two very different arguments can be imagined. It could be maintained that the specific ideals and values advertised on imperial coins, and the honorific terms cited in official inscriptions, were both dictated by the imperial regime and systematically carried out by representatives of the central state. Or it could be claimed that the correspondences that happen to appear in the epigraphic and numismatic record are simply coincidental. Both of these positions should be ruled out. As remarkable as these chronological and lexical correspondences are, there was always ample diversity of expression on coins and across the epigraphic landscape – too much diversity, in fact, to support the notion of centralized and autocratic control over the initial diffusion of imperial ideals and values.[150] And yet, the number of documented correlations, some very precise, others more conceptual and general, militates equally strongly against the argument that these correlations were only random. Clearly we must look for an explanation between these two extremes.

---

[150] It should be noted that we have considered many different categories of inscription, and that the notion of centralized control over epigraphic terminology is more plausible for some categories, such as milestones, than for others. For sensible discussion of the limits to imperial control over messaging in different media, see Clark 2007: 263–80.

Unfortunately, there is no concrete evidence for how, precisely, the multiple imperial ideals expressed on coins and in inscriptions were disseminated within the communications networks of the central state. What we have to imagine, I think, is an ongoing exchange of ideas, at the top and at the center, in particular between the highest-ranking aristocrats, especially senators, and various members of the imperial family, including the emperor himself. The key social and quasi-institutional establishment that will have enabled such an exchange of ideas was the imperial "court." Participation in the world of the imperial court must have been fluid, but in general, it was composed of the emperor's family, personal servants, and senatorial and equestrian advisors (*amici*), and as such provided a more or less permanent framework for the exchange of ideas between the imperial regime and the imperial aristocracy.[151] Equally important, presumably, was the existence of several channels – some formal, involving explicit directives, and others informal, depending on not much more than word of mouth – by which these ideas were transmitted downwards and outwards through the various layers of officials that together constituted the Roman state.[152] Critical to the success of such transmissions, we might further imagine, were those higher-ranking imperial officials who were in most regular contact both with the center and with the periphery, especially provincial governors and legionary commanders, and perhaps imperial procurators as well.[153] It is likely that it was largely through these officials that the ideas articulated at the center came to be diffused throughout the communications networks of the central state. And what these networks facilitated, in turn, was the diffusion of imperial ideals and values that ultimately derived from what we may call, in an intentionally imprecise way, an "official impulse."[154]

It was precisely this official impulse that began to splinter in the Severan period. While virtues continued to be emphasized on the imperial coinage – becoming more prominent than ever, in fact, under Caracalla, Elagabalus, and Severus Alexander (figure 4.2) – the official inscriptions trumpet military victory and power instead. Now, for the first time, the

---

[151] Social composition of imperial court: Winterling 1999: 83–116, 161–94. Court as *locus* for the production of influential ideas and attitudes: Wallace-Hadrill 1996: 292–4. Emperor's position within court: Paterson 2007. See also Spawforth 2007 for comparative perspectives on court society in ancient monarchies.

[152] For a definition of the "imperial court" and its key role in the articulation of imperial ideals and values, see below, 314–16; for a case-study, cf. Noreña 2007b, esp. 312–14. See also Ando 2000: 73–130 for a different (but complementary) reconstruction of official communications within the Roman empire.

[153] We will return to these officials, especially provincial governors, in chapter 5 below.

[154] For further discussion of the social context in which these ideals were first articulated, see below, 314–16.

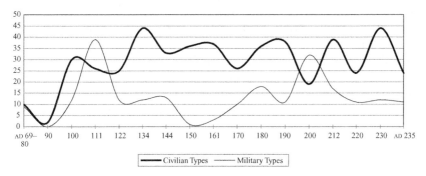

Figure 4.3 "Civilian" and "military" personification types on denarii, expressed as a percentage of all reverse types, AD 69–235 (N = 77,853)

officials responsible for coins and those responsible for the inscriptions were frequently speaking in different voices, no longer sharing the same basic idiom of expression for the public representation of the emperor. There are still some examples of ideological correspondence, to be sure, especially in the language and ideology of military victory, but the overall picture is one of divergence between coins and official inscriptions.

One way to highlight this divergence is to examine the fluctuating relative frequencies of civilian and military personification types on the imperial coinage for the whole period 69–235 (figure 4.3).[155] As this graph indicates, the civilian types predominated throughout most of the second century, and remained frequent into the Severan period, with notable surges in production in the years around 210 and 230. The military types, by contrast, were usually minted in relatively smaller numbers, punctuated by sharp peaks under Trajan and Septimius Severus, and by an upward tick under Marcus Aurelius – periods, that is, when the Roman war machine was in high gear.[156] In general, then, the dominant mode of expression on the reverse types of the imperial coinage was civilian, broadly defined, often articulated by the representation of ethical ideals and the values associated

[155] Figure 4.3 is based on silver coins only, since the sample of silver is both larger and more representative than the bronze sample (cf. Introduction to Part 1). For the full list of personification types, see appendix 3. The types counted here as "civilian" are Abundantia, Aequitas, Annona, Clementia, Fecunditas, Hilaritas, Indulgentia, Iustitia, Laetitia, Liberalitas, Libertas, Moneta, Munificentia, Nobilitas, Pietas, Pudicitia, and Tranquillitas. The "military" types are Victoria and Virtus. Several types blur the line between these two categories, such as Concordia, Fides, and Pax, and several do not fit neatly into either category, such as Aeternitas, Fortuna, and Salus. These types have not been included in Figure 4.3.

[156] On fluctuations in the production of the Victoria type in particular, the single most common reverse type on the imperial coinage, see above, 157–9.

with civic benefaction.[157] And though such themes do appear in the Severan inscriptions, they are clearly overshadowed by the ideals of militarism and absolutism. The underlying language of the official texts is no longer in harmony with that of the coins.

This development, too, requires explanation. If the earlier convergence between coins and inscriptions was indeed facilitated by the successful transmission of ideas through the communications networks of the central state, as I have suggested, then the divergence that opened up in the Severan period may point to the rise of new configurations of communication within those networks. Changes in the organization of the central state introduced by Septimius Severus, or that coalesced during his reign, provide a plausible context for such a development. Purposive changes that may be relevant include the appointment of equestrians to the command of the three new legions raised by Septimius Severus; the replacement of at least seven vacant provincial governorships not with senators, as was traditional, but with equestrians; and the disbanding of the Italian-dominated praetorian guard. Important long-term trends include the empire-wide proliferation in the number of equestrian procuratorships, and the decreasing proportion of Italians in the senate, which dipped below 50 percent for the first time.[158] In the Severan period, in brief, the Roman imperial state was organized in a slightly different way than in the first two centuries, and the communications networks within it may have been partly reconfigured as a result. Nor would it be surprising if the new personnel rising to prominence under Septimius Severus and his successors had their own ideas about what made a "good" emperor. The emergence of two different styles of imperial representation during this period – the one civilian, ethical, and most prominent on coins, and the other militarist, absolutist, and most prominent on official inscriptions – could be seen in this light.

The three phases preliminarily identified above may now be redefined and interpreted as follows. In the first phase, the Flavian period, the language of the coins and inscriptions is unified, but there is very little in the way of imperial virtues. From Trajan (following Nerva) to Marcus Aurelius, the second phase, the coins and inscriptions both continue to employ the same underlying idiom, but it is now characterized by the centrality of the ethical paradigm of imperial authority and the attendant values of

---

[157] It must be emphasized that this statement pertains to the reverse types only. On the obverse of many of these coins, the emperor was shown with various military attributes; for exhaustive treatment of military themes and attributes in the numismatic portraiture of the emperor, see Bastien 1992–4: 1.61–90, 129–37, 201–23, 235–80; 2.435–528.

[158] Good overview of these changes in Daguet-Gagey 1999: 337–80.

virtuous behavior and personal generosity. It is this combination of virtues and civic benefaction, in fact, expressed on both coins and official inscriptions, that defines the imperial ideology of the high Roman empire. The reign of Commodus forms a bridge to the third phase, the Severan period, when the coins and inscriptions diverge, the former continuing to emphasize virtues and civic benefaction, and the latter military conquest and absolute power. There are naturally exceptions to these characteristics in all three phases, but this is the general pattern. And this brings us back to the problem of the relationship between change over time and regional differentiation in the epigraphic record. On balance, it seems that chronological change was primary, and differences between Italy and the provinces secondary. The two were of course interrelated – an inscription from the Danubian frontier hailing Severus Alexander as "invincible" and "bravest and most blessed *dominus*" is at once a product of its place and its time – but it was the changing historical context between 69 and 235, I would like to suggest, in which new ideas about imperial authority and new officials to publicize those ideas came to the fore, that ultimately drove the ideological changes visible in the inscriptions considered above.[159]

CONCLUSION

The Roman imperial state was a big and complex structure. Many different voices within it participated in the expression of imperial ideals and values. And yet, despite this polyphony of expression, it has been analytically useful to examine under one capacious rubric, "official," the various symbols that a wide range of actors, whether operating individually or collectively, produced in the public sphere. For all of the actors who created the coins and inscriptions examined in this chapter were either representatives of the Roman state or belonged, in sociospatial terms, to the center. From this perspective, it makes sense to examine a senator in Italy and a procurator in a distant province, a legionary commander on the frontier and the collectivity of the 35 tribes in the city of Rome, a common soldier and the emperor himself, as constituents of a single, official imperial system. In expressing their various ideas about the "good" emperor, as we have seen, these different actors employed many different media. It is vital not to lose sight of this once vibrant world of communications, even if so much of the evidence for it is no longer extant. The focus here has been on two media for which ample evidence has survived, imperial coins and official

---

[159] Severus Alexander inscription: *AE* 1987.790 (milestone in Raetia, 226–8).

inscriptions. As I hope to have shown, it is really only by considering these two media in quantitative terms, and in relation to one another, that we can effectively trace the diffusion of imperial ideals in time and space.

But with respect to the "circulation" of imperial ideals in the widest sense of the term, this diffusion was only the first stage in a multi-step process. In order to understand that process as a whole, we also need to examine how a very different set of actors, local and unofficial, responded to the dissemination of these ideas. Only then will we be in a position to tackle the really big question: Did the circulation of imperial ideals in the Roman West make any difference at all?

CHAPTER 5

Central communication and local response

LAPIDARY PRAISE FOR THE ROMAN EMPEROR

In the spring of AD 194, while Septimius Severus was in the east, hundreds and hundreds of miles away, hunting down his rival Pescennius Niger, the town council of Norba, in the province of Lusitania, voted to honor Septimius with a statue. The statue itself has long since disappeared, but the statue base upon which the dedication was inscribed has survived. The text reads as follows:

Imp(eratori) Caesari Lucio | Septimio Severo | Pertinaci Aug(usto) pont(ifici) | max(imo) trib(unicia) pot(estate) ii imp(eratori) iii | co(n)s(uli) ii pro co(n)s(uli) p(atri) p(atriae) | optimo fortissimo | providentissimoque | principi ex arg(ento) p(ondo) x | c(urantibus) D(ecimo) Iulio Celso | et L(ucio) Petronio Nigro | iiv(iribus) d(ecreto) d(ecurionum).

To imperator Caesar Lucius Septimius Severus Pertinax Augustus, pontifex maximus, in the second year of the tribunician power, hailed imperator three times, consul twice, proconsul, father of the fatherland, Best, Bravest, and Most Foresightful Emperor, (this was dedicated) by decree of the councilors, from ten pounds of silver. Decimus Julius Celsus and Lucius Petronius Niger, duoviri, oversaw it.[1]

In addition to inscribing the emperor's formal titles on this statue base, the councilors of Norba also decided to laud the emperor with specific honorific terminology, calling him *optimus*, *fortissimus*, and *providentissimus*. That they chose to distinguish the emperor with these particular epithets is noteworthy, for in the very same year the Nepesini, citizens of an Etrurian town about twenty miles northwest of Rome, set up an inscribed monument to Septimius also calling him *optimus* and *fortissimus*.[2] Besides

---

[1] *CIL* 2.693.

[2] *CIL* 11.3201 = *ILS* 416 (Nepet, 194): [*Imp*](*eratori*) *Caesari L*(*ucio*) *Septimio Severo Pertinaci Aug*(*usto*) *pontif*(*ici*) *maxim*(*o*) *trib*(*unicia*) *pot*(*estate*) *II imp*(*eratori*) *IIII co*(*n*)*suli II p*(*atri*) *p*(*atriae*) *Nepesini optimo fortissimoque principi suo devoti.*

this suggestive lexical correspondence, what these inscriptions share is the fact that, through them, the two groups of dedicators – both formally unattached to the central state, and both, apparently, on their own initiative – were actively reproducing specific imperial ideals in the public sphere. These inscriptions, in other words, were "unofficial," unlike the texts examined in the previous chapter, and therefore reflect not an official impulse, but rather (so I will argue) a reaction to it. It is this unofficial and local reaction to the imperial ideals and values diffused from the center that forms the subject of this chapter.[3]

Before attempting to assess the nature of that reaction, it will be useful to consider the characteristics of this epigraphic praise language in general. For one of the distinctive features of the honorific terms employed in these unofficial inscriptions is their tremendous variety. Most of the terms found in these texts were either titles ending with the suffix *–tor*, or superlative epithets; a number of miscellaneous designations may be regarded as a third basic category.

First, the titles ending in *–tor*.[4] One of the principal themes that recurs amongst these titles is that of preservation and restoration. In addition to being called "preserver (*conservator*) of his own," the emperor was hailed as "preserver of the Augustan peace," "preserver of the human race," and as nothing less than "preserver of the world."[5] These honorific titles reflect the ideal of the *cura rei publicae*, "stewardship of the commonwealth," which the emperor automatically assumed upon accession to the imperial purple.[6] Such terms could go beyond the language of preservation, too, as emperors were praised for the actual restoration of a wide range of concepts, institutions, and practices. In this vein, subjects lauded their emperor as the "restorer" (*restitutor*) of "the public peace," "the town," "the colony," and "Italy."[7] In all of these inscriptions the reigning emperor is credited with

---

[3] For the typology of inscriptions, see Introduction to Part II; for the texts examined in this chapter, see appendix 13.

[4] Such titles normally derived from verbal forms; see briefly Salomies 1994: 75–6.

[5] *Conservator suus*: *IRT* 362 (Lepcis Magna, Africa Proconsularis, 132–3); *CIL* 2.5486 (Iluro, Baetica, 180–92). *Conservator pacis Augustae*: *CIL* 2²/14.13 = 2.3732 = *ILS* 259 (Valentia, Hispania Tarraconensis, 69–79); on this inscription, see below, 251–2. *Conservator generis humani*: *CIL* 2²/5.730 = 2.2054 = *ILS* 304 (Aratispi, Baetica, 117), set up by the *res publica Aratispitanorum*. *Conservator orbis*: *IRT* 387 (Lepcis Magna, Africa Proconsularis, 197), set up (*publice*) by the *Lepcitani* (see below, 255–6). Unless otherwise indicated, all titles cited in the footnotes in the nominative case were inscribed in the dative case (i.e., as dedications to the emperor).

[6] On this theme, see discussion in Béranger 1953: 169–217, esp. 186–217 on the imperial *cura*; cf. *SCPP* ll. 162–3 (with Eck *et al.* 1996: 253), where the *salus* of the empire is said to be in the *custodia* of the *domus Augustae*.

[7] *Restitutor pacis publicae*: *CIL* 8.17214 = *ILS* 443 (Thagaste, Numidia, 198), dedicated to Julia Domna: *Iuliae Domnae Augustae . . . matri . . . pacis publ(icae) restitutoris* (i.e., Caracalla). *Restitutor municipii*:

the restoration of something which, by implication, had been lost under earlier reigns. To distinguish the current emperor from his predecessors, in other words, was quite common in these inscriptions, and we will see how dedicators developed specific terminology to make this positive comparison more explicit.

Related to the ideal of preservation and restoration was that of improvement. To convey this idea subjects could praise the emperor as a *locupletator municipii*, "enricher of the town," perhaps (but not necessarily) as a result of specific imperial benefactions.[8] Emperors were also recognized for the actual building of communities, whether in reference to a *municipium* or a *colonia*. The title of *conditor municipii/coloniae* was both straightforward and very likely an accurate description of the emperor's formal role in the foundation of a new community.[9] In some cases the language of building and construction was more grandiose. In one inscription from Thamugadi in Numidia, for example, the dedicators hail Septimius Severus as *vindex et conditor Romanae disciplinae*, "the champion and builder of Roman discipline."[10] Even more laudatory are the inscriptions from Mauretania Caesariensis and Baetica extolling Septimius as "the founder" (*fundator*) of the Roman empire.[11]

In addition to the honorific title *fundator imperii Romani*, a small group of epithets openly identified the emperor as a military conqueror. Most of the inscriptions employing these terms were set up during the reign of Septimius Severus, reflecting that emperor's numerous campaigns and the fact that during his reign the borders of the empire were extended for the first time in nearly ninety years. Septimius was extolled, in particular, as

CIL 2.3239 (Ilugo, Hispania Tarraconensis, 119–38), fragmentary: [*restitu*]*tori m*[*unicipii*]. *Restitutor coloniae*: *CIL* 3.7282 (Athens, Achaea, 132), set up by the Troadenses, with the motivation clause, *ob multa beneficia quae viritim quae publice praestitit*. *Restitutor Italiae*: *CIL* 11.805 = *ILS* 343 (Bononia, Italy, 138–61); cf. *CIL* 11.6939 (Placentia, Italy, 138–61).

8   *Locupletator municipi*: *CIL* 14.2799 = *ILS* 321 (Gabii, Italy, 119–38): *locupletatoribus municipii* (with Sabina).

9   *Conditor municipi*: *CIL* 8.27775a–d (Althiburita, Africa Proconsularis, 117–38), possibly from a triumphal arch; *CIL* 8.83 (Turris Tamalleni, Africa Proconsularis, post 138); *CIL* 8.799 (Avitta Bibba, Africa Proconsularis, 137), fragmentary: [*condito*]*ri munic*[*ipi*]; *CIL* 8.22707 = *ILS* 6779 (Gigthis, Africa Proconsularis, 138–61). *Conditor coloniae*: *CIL* 3.374 (Colonia Iulia Parium, Asia, 117–38): *Iovi Olympio conditori col*(*oniae*). For imperial building in the provinces as an advertised benefit of empire, see above, 102–3.

10 *CIL* 8.17870 = *ILS* 446 (Thamugadi, Numidia, 197), dedicated to Caracalla, *vindicis et conditoris Romanae disciplinae filio*, by decree of the town councilors. In general on the concept of *disciplina*, Phang 2008.

11 *Fundator imperii Romani*: e.g. *CIL* 8.21613 (Portus Magnus, Mauretania Caesariensis, 198), dedicated to Geta: *fundatoris imperi Romani f*[*i*]*l*(*io*), dedicated by the *republica portuensis Magnensis*; *CIL* 2.1969 (Malaca, Baetica, 212–17), dedicated to Caracalla: *fundatoris imperii Romani filio*, dedicated by the *r*(*es*)*p*(*ublica*) *Malacit*(*anorum*).

propagator imperii, "the enlarger of the empire."[12] The many inscribed monuments with this epithet appear to have been concentrated in Numidia,
perhaps reflecting the presence in this province of the only legionary base
in North Africa, at Lambaesis. And because the effect of all these putative
military conquests was the pacification of the world, the *orbis terrarum* – for
this was the principal meaning of *pax Romana* in the Roman imagination –
Septimius was duly honored as *pacator orbis*, "pacifier of the world."[13] That
these particular epithets proliferated under Septimius Severus suggests that
provincials could be well attuned to imperial publicity and the public image
of the reigning emperor.

More common than such titles ending in –*tor*, and with a greater lexical
and conceptual range, were the various superlatives and related epithets
that dedicators attached to the emperor's formal titles.[14] As in the official
inscriptions examined in the previous chapter, so too in these honorific
inscriptions for the emperor there appeared a number of superlative epithets that were concrete expressions of the personified abstractions that
appeared on imperial coins: *indulgentissimus* and Indulgentia, *liberalissimus*
and Liberalitas, *iustissimus* and Iustitia, *clementissimus* and Clementia, *providentissimus* and Providentia, *piissimus* and Pietas.[15] The epigraphic titles
do not always derive from such personifications, of course. In addition to
being hailed as *piissimus*, for example, emperors were also lauded as *sacratissimus* and *sanctissimus*, superlatives without an exact analog on the imperial
coinage.[16] In general, though, there was a broad semantic and ideological

[12] E.g. *AE* 1969/70.697 (Sila, Numidia, 196–7); *CIL* 8.6048 (Arsacal, Numidia, 197); *CIL* 8.19920 (Nechaa, Numidia, 198); *CIL* 8.7970 (Rusicade, Numidia, 203); *CIL* 8.17257 (Wed Scham, Africa Proconsularis, 193–211). There were also numerous dedications to Julia Domna, wife of the *propagator imperii*: e.g. *CIL* 8.5699 (Sigus, Numidia, 197); *CIL* 8. 6702 (Tiddis, Numidia, 197); *AE* 1969.70.699 (Sila, Numidia, 198–9); further examples in appendix 13. On Septimius and the epithet *propagator imperii*, see also Birley 1974; Kuhoff 1990.

[13] *Pacator orbis*: *CIL* 2²/7.60 = 2.2124 (Isturgi, Baetica, 197); *CIL* 2²/5.74 = 2.1669 (Tucci, Baetica, 200), dedicated to Caracalla: *pacatoris orbis filio*; cf. *CIL* 2²/5.77 = 2.1671 (Tucci, 212); *CIL* 2²/5.75 = 2.1670 (Tucci, 200), dedicated to Geta.

[14] Unlike the -*tor* titles, which derived from verbal forms, these superlatives derived mostly from abstract nouns, and were usually, as a result, less specific in their reference; Salomies 1994: 75.

[15] Texts in appendix 13, and a number of specific examples discussed below.

[16] *Sacratissimus*: e.g. *CIL* 5.875 = *ILS* 1374 (Aquileia, Italy, 105); *CIL* 9.23 (Rudiae, Italy, 117–38): [*e*]*xornato eq*(*uo*) *pub*(*lico*) *a sacratissimo principe*, set up by the father of the honorand; *AE* 2000.883 = *CIL* 12.594 = *ILS* 6988 (Ager Arelatensis, Narbonensis, 138–61), set up by the *pagani pagi Lucreti* to a local benefactor who had secured *beneficia* from Antoninus Pius; *CIL* 12.410 (Massilia, Narbonensis, 161–9): *equo p*(*ublico*) *honorato a sacratissimis imp*(*eratoribus*), i.e. Marcus Aurelius and Lucius Verus, set up by the local *decurio*. *Sanctissimus*: e.g. *CIL* 2.5232 = *ILS* 6898 (Collippo, Lusitania, 167); *CIL* 8.5700 (Sigus, Numidia, 195–7); *CIL* 14.2073 (Lavinium, Italy, 213); *CIL* 11.2633 = *ILS* 6597 (Cosa, Italy, 213); *CIL* 8.4598 = *ILS* 463 (Diana, Numidia, 217; on this inscription, see below, 256–7); *CIL* 8.8781 (El-Gara, Mauretania Caesariensis, 222–35). Note also an inscription set up by discharged soldiers to Jupiter Optimus Maximus, the protector of Caracalla and Geta, *pientissimi fratres*: *CIL* 8.2618 (Lambaesis, Numidia, 211–12).

overlap between the two media in the expression of ideals attached to the emperor. In some cases, the usage of a superlative epithet even sheds some light on how the abstractions advertised on imperial coins were understood. *Felicissimus*, for example, a very common title in these inscriptions, as in the official inscriptions, was explicitly attached to the person of the emperor and evidently designated a characteristic of the emperor himself, rather than a general condition. The Felicitas coin type, by contrast, could refer either to the emperor's own good fortune, or to the happiness of the times.[17] In this respect, the superlative epithet was more specific than the coin type. And the fact that *felicissimus* was so often paired with *fortissimus*, as in the official inscriptions, shows that its martial connotations were being emphasized.[18] Militaristic epithets, in fact, such as *invictus* and *invictissimus*, were quite common in these inscriptions.[19] Local dedicators clearly recognized and responded to the emperor's military image.

Though such epithets rarely referred to specific acts or events, their meanings were usually focused within specific ideological spheres. Other epithets honored the emperor for very general qualities or characteristics. In one inscription from Liguria, for example, Caracalla is distinguished as *inclitus*, "renowned." Another group of inscriptions praised the emperor by referring to him as *nobilissimus*, "most noble." And in a display of gratitude and loyalty worthy of his name, a certain M. Cutius Priscus Messius Rusticus Aemilius Papus Arrius Proculus Iulius Celsus from Baetica honored Antoninus Pius as *carissimus*, "most beloved."[20] Some epithets praised the emperor in even more generic terms. In a group of inscriptions from Italy, for example, Caracalla was sometimes referred to simply as *magnus*, "great," an honorific epithet that was perhaps intended to recall the archetypal ruler-conqueror, Alexander the Great. *Magnus* was not a part of Caracalla's official titulature, as the surviving coins and military diplomas from his reign show, but his esteem for and identification with Alexander were evidently well known, at least within Italy.[21] More often

---

[17] See above, 165–74.

[18] For the pairing *fortissimo felicissimoque* in unofficial inscriptions, see below, 261–3.

[19] *Invictus/invictissimus*: e.g. *CIL* 8.9317 (Tipasam, Mauretania Caesariensis, 195); *CIL* 10.5825 = *ILS* 421 (Ferentinum, Italy, 198–201); *CIL* 2.3400 (Acci, Hispania Tarraconensis, 193–211); *CIL* 8.7973 (Rusicade, Numidia, 215); *RIB* 590 (Ribchester, Britannia, 213–17); *CIL* 8.18587 = *ILS* 5793 (Lamasba, Numidia, 218–22); *CIL* 2²/5.442 = 2.1554 (Ucubi, Baetica, 222–35); further examples in appendix 13.

[20] *Inclitus*: *CIL* 5.7780 (Albingaunum, Italy, 214): *fortissimo inclitoque ac super omnes felicissimo principi*, dedicated by the *plebes urbana Albingaunensium*. *Nobilissimus*: e.g. *AE* 1987.470 (Turris Libisonis, Sardinia, 180–92); *CIL* 12.3312 (Nemausus, Narbonensis, 180–92); *AE* 1969/70.698 (Sila, Numidia, 198–9). *Carissimus*: *CIL* 2.1282 (Salpensa, Baetica, 147): *principi optimo et sibi carissimo*.

[21] Caracalla as *magnus*: *AE* 1972.156 (Ciciliano, 212–13); *CIL* 10.5826 (Ferentinum, 213); *CIL* 5.28 (Pola, 213); *CIL* 11.2648 (Colonia Saturnia, 214); cf. *CIL* 10.5802 (Aletrium, 197–217), fragmentary: [*magno e*]*t invicto*.

dedicators chose to praise the emperor in superlative terms by calling him *maximus*, "greatest." The emperor was also hailed as *optimus*, "the best," an honorific title derived ultimately from the Republican notion of the *vir bonus*. During the last years of Trajan's reign (114–17), *optimus* was incorporated into the emperor's official titulature, but was not at any other point during our period one of the emperor's official titles.[22] For subjects to laud the emperor as *optimus*, in other words, was to confer special distinction on him. One striking feature of these honorific inscriptions to the emperor that must be noted is the regularity with which *optimus* and *maximus* are cited together. The collocation of *optimus* and *maximus* in these honorific inscriptions recalled the epithets of Capitoline Jupiter, an epigraphic usage that served at least implicitly to assimilate the emperor to the supreme god of the Greco-Roman pantheon.[23]

Such were the superlative epithets attached to the emperor's names and formal titles in these unofficial inscriptions. There was also, finally, a scattered assortment of miscellaneous titles cited in these texts: Trajan was called *parens publicus*, "public parent," in an inscription from Misenum; the Athenians extolled Hadrian as "Olympius", while the citizens of Colonia Iulia Parium in Asia referred to him as "Jupiter Olympius"; and dedicators from Forum Sempronii praised Antoninus Pius as *adiutor*, "helper."[24] These honorific titles, with the exception of "Olympius," are only attested in a single inscription and were probably quite rare. Another miscellaneous title that appears in the epigraphic record with increasing frequency during our period is *dominus*, "master." Though *dominus* was not really an "honorific" title in the narrow sense of the term, its usage does parallel that of these other honorific terms in that it was never employed in official documents produced by the imperial regime itself, such as coins and military diplomas. For in the public sphere, at least, *dominus* was an absolutist title, implying the domination of a master over his subjects – incompatible, that is, with the aristocratic ideal of the *civilis princeps*. The meaning of this term, and the implications of its spread in the epigraphic record, will be examined in detail below.

---

[22] The earliest Trajanic diplomas with the title *optimus* come from September of 114: *CIL* 14.60–61; see briefly Hammond 1957: 43, n. 149.

[23] For discussion, including examples of the many inscriptions in which *optimus* and *maximus* were cited together, see below, 287.

[24] *Parens publicus*: *AE* 1996.424b = 1993.473 (113), dedicated by the Augustales. *Olympius*: *CIL* 3.7281 (132), dedicated by the *colonia Iulia Augusta Diensium*; *CIL* 3.7282 (132), dedicated by the citizens of the Troad. *Iuppiter Olympius*: *CIL* 3.374 (117–38). *Adiutor*: *CIL* 11.6118 (138–61), dedicators unspecified.

LEXICAL AND IDEOLOGICAL CONVERGENCE

From the preceding discussion it will be clear that the authors of inscriptions with honorific terminology for the Roman emperor had at their disposal an abundance of titles and epithets for praising their ruler. Why and by what processes particular honorific terms were chosen by these authors, at different times and in different places throughout the Roman West, are elusive questions. In what follows, I will argue that these choices in honorific terminology should be interpreted, in general, as a type of local response to the "official impulse" in the dissemination of imperial ideals and values, an impulse that can be partially reconstructed, as I attempted to show in the previous chapter, from surviving coins and official inscriptions. A key interpretive principle should be stated clearly at the outset. I do not claim that in all cases the terms found in these unofficial inscriptions were directly influenced either by imperial coins or by official inscriptions. While such influence is certainly possible, and in some cases likely, it would be nearly impossible to prove. What I am claiming is that the coins and inscriptions provide a reasonably accurate reflection of imperial publicity in a number of different media, now mostly lost, and that it is to this imperial publicity in general that the local authors of these inscriptions were often reacting. In order to sustain this argument, I will first examine a series of individual inscriptions, followed by several groups of inscriptions employing the same or similar terms, and will then turn to a wider analysis of the chronological and spatial patterning in this honorific terminology as a whole.

First, the individual texts. We begin with a short inscription set up in Hispania Tarraconensis during the reign of Vespasian, honoring the heir apparent, Titus:

[Ca]es(ari) T(ito) Imp(eratori) | Vespasiano Aug(usto) | [V]espasiani f(ilio) conser|[v]atori pacis Aug(ustae).

To Caesar Titus Imperator Vespasian Augustus, son of Vespasian, preserver of the Augustan Peace.[25]

As far as we know, this honorific term, *conservator pacis Augustae*, was unprecedented, and it never again appeared in the epigraphic record. Though the dedicator gives no indication of his identity, it is more likely than not that this inscribed monument, probably a statue base, was

---

[25] *CIL* 2²/14.1.13 = 2.3732 = *ILS* 259 (Valentia, 69–79). The editors of the second edition of *CIL* 2 claim that the letter forms of this inscription seem to date to the second or even third century, but the text itself surely rules out a post-Vespasianic date.

commissioned not by a Roman official, but rather by a local actor. The tell-tale sign is the odd arrangement of Titus' titulature.[26] Especially salient for our purposes is the fact that this inscription coheres so closely to the imperial ideals promoted in official media under Vespasian, especially in its celebration of *pax*, a *leitmotif* of early Flavian publicity. The Templum Pacis in Rome was dedicated in 75. An overseas colony was named Colonia Flavia Pacis Deultensium. And Pax types were duly emphasized on the imperial coinage under Vespasian, comprising two thirds of all benefit types on silver coins.[27] These and other public expressions of Pax during Vespasian's reign, emanating from the center, seem to find their echo in this provincial inscription. It should also be noted that another dedication from Spain, set up to Pax Augusta by a *sevir Augustalis* in the Flavian *municipium* of Arva, in Baetica, may also be Vespasianic in date.[28] In these cases, then, we may conclude that these provincial dedicators were effectively responding to a centrally disseminated message.

Less striking, but illuminating nonetheless, is an alimentary inscription set up in Rome to commemorate the civic benefactions of Trajan. In this text, inscribed on a marble tablet, the dedicators, the *pueri et puellae alimentariae*, specifically cite Trajan's *providentia*.[29] In these alimentary inscriptions, as is well known, emperors were honored for a number of different virtues, including *liberalitas*, *indulgentia*, and *munificentia*.[30] Why any one imperial virtue was chosen for commemoration instead of the various alternatives is not often clear. In this particular case, though, we may turn once again to the official publicity of the central state. For it was under Trajan, as we have seen, that the Providentia type first appeared on the precious-metal denominations of the imperial coinage, and also under Trajan that we begin to find official inscriptions touting the emperor's

---

[26] Titus is normally identified as Imperator Titus Caesar Vespasianus Augustus; cf. Buttrey 1980: 18–25 for the chronology of Titus' titulature under Vespasian.

[27] Templum Pacis: *LTUR* 4 (1999), 67–70 (F. Coarelli); date: Dio 65.15.1. Colonia Flavia Pacis Deultensium: *CIL* 6.3828 = *ILS* 6105 (Rome, 82). Pax types: above, 127–32, with appendix 7. For further details, and bibliography, see Noreña 2003.

[28] *CIL* 2.1061 (69–79?): *paci Aug(usatae) sacrum L(ucius) Licinius Crescentis lib(ertus) Hermes IIIIIIIvir Aug(ustalis) d(e) s(ua) p(ecunia) d(edit)*, with Weinstock 1960: 51, n. 92 for the date.

[29] *CIL* 6.40497 = 31298 (Rome, 102–14): [*Imp(eratori)] Caes(ari) [divi Nervae f(ilio)] [Ner]vae Tra[iano Aug(usto) Ger(manico) Dacic(o) po]nt(ifici) max(imo) tri[b(unicia) pot(estate) – – – co(n)s(uli) – – – p(atri) p(atriae) – – – p]ueri et puel[lae – – – ? benefici]o eius civ[ium numero – – – augendo? peten?]te plebe [- – – pr]ovident[ia – – -]*. In general on the terminology and ideology of the alimentary inscriptions, see discussion in Woolf 1990a, esp. 224–5 on the different virtues ascribed to Trajan.

[30] *Liberalitas*: *CIL* 6.1492 = *ILS* 6106 (Rome, 101): *secundum liberalitatem eius*, set up by decree of the senate; cf. *CIL* 11.5956 (Pitinum Mergens, Italy, 138–61); *CIL* 11.5395 = *ILS* 6620 (Asisium, undated). *Indulgentia*: *CIL* 9.1455 = *ILS* 6509 (Ligures Baebiani, 101). *Munificentia*: *CIL* 9.5825 (Auximum, 106).

providentia, as on the Arch of Trajan at Ancona, erected by decree of the senate.[31] Though the inscription in question was set up at the center, in the city of Rome, and cannot, as a result, be considered a "local" response to imperial ideals, it must be emphasized that it was commissioned not by imperial officials, as was the arch at Ancona, but rather by what we may consider an "outsider" group, the *alimentarii*. But they, too, evidently understood the message of the imperial regime, and chose to repeat it in the public sphere.

The next inscription we will consider was carved into a statue base in Cuicul, in the province of Mauretania Caesariensis, during the joint reign of Marcus Aurelius and Lucius Verus (161–9). In this case, both the text and the context of the inscribed monument are clear:

Concordiae | Augustor(um) | imp(eratoris) Caes(aris) M(arci) Aureli Anto|nini Armeniac(i) Medic(i) Par|thic(i) Maximi p(atris) p(atriae) et | imp(eratoris) Caes(aris) L(uci) Aureli Veri Armeniaci | Medici Parthici Maximi p(atris) p(atriae) | L(ucius) Gargilius Q(uinti) fil(ius) Pap(iria) Augustalis aed(ilis) | statuam quam ob honorem | aed(ilitatis) super legitim(am) ex HS ɪɪɪɪ mil(lia) | num(ero) pollicitus est ampli[ata] | pec(unia) anno suo posuit dedicavitq(ue).

To the harmony of the Augusti, imperator Caesar Marcus Aurelius Antoninus Armeniacus Medicus Parthicus Maximus, father of the fatherland, and imperator Caesar Lucius Aurelius Verus Armeniacus Medicus Parthicus Maximus, father of the fatherland, Lucius Gargilius, son of Quintus, of the Papirian tribe, Augustalis and aedile, during his year of office set up and dedicated a statue which, on account of his election to the aedileship, he promised he would set up, at a cost beyond that prescribed by law, the money having been increased, of 4,000 sesterces.[32]

In this inscription we find a characteristic blending of local honors, civic benefaction, and aristocratic self-representation, on the one hand, and the articulation of current Roman imperial ideals, on the other. In order to commemorate his election to the aedileship of Cuicul, this Lucius Gargilius chose to erect a statue, at an even greater expense than that required by law (*super legitimam*), to the Concordia of the emperors Marcus Aurelius and Lucius Verus. The harmony of the imperial house was a natural theme, of course, since this was the first time that two emperors were formally ruling jointly, and we may assume that Gargilius understood the topical significance of this political ideal. But in choosing to celebrate *concordia*, as opposed to any of the other imperial ideals available for commemoration,

---

[31] See above, 231–2. For another senatorial dedication that might have celebrated Trajan's *providentia*, see *AE* 2003.240 (Liternum, Italy, 114–17): [*provide*]*n(tiae)* [*imp(eratoris)* . . . *restitutoris*] *Italiae*.

[32] *CIL* 8.8300 = *ILS* 368 (166–9).

this local aristocrat may well have been influenced by the imperial regime's emphasis on this particular ideal, an emphasis that we can infer from the heavy minting of Concordia types on the imperial coinage during the joint reign of Marcus and Lucius.[33] Another dedication to the *concordia* of the two emperors, set up in Dacia, at the other end of the empire, can also be seen in this light.[34] Once again, we see that provincial dedicators could be closely attuned to what were, at the time, the most resonant imperial ideals.

With the next inscription, set up in Sardinia during the reign of Commodus, we come to a very good example of lexical and ideological correspondence across media and through space. The stone is quite damaged, and the names of both Commodus and his wife, Crispina, were erased in antiquity, but the key honorific term has been preserved:

Imp(eratori) Caes(ari) [[M(arco) Aurelio]] | [[Commodo Antonino Pio Fel(ici)]] | [[Aug(usto) pont(ifici) max(imo) divi Marci]] | Antonini Pi[i Germ(anici) Sarm(atici) filio] | nobilissimo [et feliciss(imo) princ(ipi)] | et [[Bruttiae Crispinae Aug(ustae) – – -]]

To imperator Caesar Marcus Aurelius Commodus Antoninus Pius Felix Augustus, pontifex maximus, son of the deified Marcus Antoninus Pius Germanicus Sarmaticus, most noble and most blessed emperor, and to Bruttia Crispina Augusta . . .[35]

In choosing to honor the emperor specifically as *nobilissimus*, "most noble emperor," the dedicators of this inscribed monument were surely reacting to the official emphasis on *nobilitas* that first emerged during the reign of Commodus. *Nobilitas* was never a major ideal during the imperial period but, as we saw in the previous chapter, it not only appeared for the first time on the imperial coinage under Commodus, in 186, but was also cited as a superlative epithet on a milestone set up in Numidia in the same year.[36] The first Roman emperor to be born to a reigning emperor, Commodus evidently relished his distinguished lineage, even boasting to the troops upon his accession to the throne that he was the first emperor "born in the palace."[37] This is enough to explain the regime's celebration of the atypical

---

[33] During the first three years of the joint reign (161, 162, 163), Concordia types accounted for 91, 100, and 100 percent, respectively, of all benefit types on denarii; and among undated coins for the whole period 161–9, they accounted for 82 percent. See appendix 7; for *concordia* in general, above, 132–5.

[34] *CIL* 3.1412 = *ILS* 7155 (near Sarmizegetusa, 161–9): [*dis*] *faventibus et co[nc]ordia imp(eratorum)*.

[35] *AE* 1987.470 (Turris Libisonis, 180–92).

[36] Above, 232. On the concept of *nobilitas* during the imperial period, see Hill 1969. Note also that, under Septimius Severus, the term *nobilissimus Caesar* became a standard title for designating the heir to the throne; cf. Gelzer 1969 (1912): 157.

[37] Hdn. 1.5.5, with Hekster 2002: 30–2.

imperial ideal of *nobilitas*. More important for our purposes is the fact that these dedicators on the island of Sardinia – a very peripheral location, in both practical and symbolic terms – were actively participating in the commemoration of Commodus' *nobilitas*. Whether they were responding to imperial coins or official inscriptions, or to some other official medium of communications, cannot be determined. In any case, these dedicators, like the *alimentarii* in Rome and Lucius Gargilius in Cuicul, were clearly in touch with the most current trends in imperial publicity.

From Sardinia we turn to Lepcis Magna, in north Africa, and to an inscribed monument erected in 197, just as Septimius Severus was consolidating his hold on the imperial throne. The text, inscribed on a marble statue base and set up in the senate building of the old Forum, reads as follows:

Imp(eratori) Caes(ari) L(ucio) Septi|mio Severo Pio | Pertinaci Aug(usto) | p(atri) p(atriae) trib(unicia) pot(estate) v co(n)s(uli) | ii imp(eratori) viii conser|vatori orbis ob pub|licam et in se pri|vatam pietatem | Lepcitani publice.

To imperator Caesar Lucius Septimius Severus Pius Pertinax Augustus, father of the fatherland, in the fifth year of the tribunician power, consul two times, with eight imperatorial acclamations, the preserver of the world, the citizens of Lepcis (dedicated this) with public funds, on account of his public and private duty towards them.[38]

One noteworthy feature of this dedication is the qualification of Severus' sense of "duty" as both "public and private," a rare collocation in inscriptions of this type, and probably intended to emphasize the unique depth and sincerity of the emperor's benefactions towards his native city. If so, this usage demonstrates some familiarity with the nuances of imperial rhetoric.[39] But it is the attribute to which these adjectives are attached, *pietas*, that really stands out. This is the only inscription in the entire corpus in which the emperor's *pietas*, as an abstract quality, is highlighted for praise. In fact, even the superlative epithet, *piissimus*, was not very common, with two attestations from 140, in official inscriptions erected under Antoninus Pius, and two more from the reign of Severus, both unofficial, dedicated by the *res publica iiii colonia Cirtensis* to members

---

[38] *IRT* 387 (197).
[39] It had become common in rhetorical texts of the imperial period to characterize personal behavior as being consistent in both public and private contexts, as a way of establishing the sincerity of motives for actions in the public sphere; see, e.g., Bartsch 1994: 146–87; Riggsby 1998; Noreña 2007a.

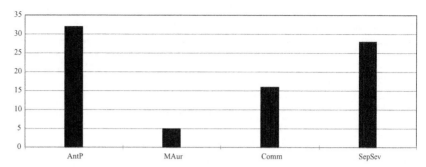

Figure 5.1 Relative frequency of Pietas types on denarii, expressed as a percentage of all virtue types, AD 138–211 (N = 11,349)

of Severus' family and identifying Severus himself as *piissimus*.[40] One way to explain this chronological patterning is to compare the fluctuating relative frequency of the Pietas type on the imperial coinage. As figure 5.1 shows, Pietas types were especially common under both Antoninus Pius and Septimius Severus, indicating, as I argue, a higher degree of official emphasis on this particular virtue during these two reigns.[41] This variable relative frequency of the Pietas type, and especially the changing degree of official emphasis on the virtue that it reflects, may account both for the clustering of inscriptions citing this virtue under Antoninus and Severus, and for the decision of the Lepcitani to single out the latter's *pietas* for commemoration. This inscription may be seen, then, as another example of local response to official communications.

The final individual text that we will consider is, in some ways, the most remarkable of the series. It comes from the epistyle of a triumphal arch constructed (and still extant) in the town of Diana Veteranorum, at the western edge of Numidia. The epistyle has broken into at least sixteen pieces, and several names have been erased, but the text can be reconstructed with little problem:

Imp(eratori) Caes(ari) | M(arco) [[Opellio]] Severo [[Macrino]] Pio Felici Aug(usto) pon[t](ifici) max(imo) trib(unicia) po[tes]t(ate) co(n)s(uli) desig(nato) p(atri) p(atriae) proco(n)s(uli) | providentissimo et sanctissimo principi et [[M(arco) Opellio]] Antonino [[Diadume[niano]]] | nobilissimo Caesari principi iuventutis respu[blica] Dianensium ex dec(reto) dec(urionum).

[40] For the Antonine texts, see above, 233–4. Inscriptions from Cirta: *CIL* 8.19493 = *ILS* 439 (197–209), to P. Septimius Geta, *patri imp(eratoris) Severi Aug(usti) piissimi fili*; *CIL* 8.19494 = *ILS* 440 (193–211), to Paccia Marciana, *coniugi imp(eratoris) Severi Aug(usti) piissimi maximi principis*.
[41] On the type itself, see above, 71–7.

To imperator Caesar Marcus Opellius Severus Macrinus Pius Felix Augustus, pontifex maximus, with tribunician power, consul designate, father of the fatherland, proconsul, most foresightful and most holy emperor, and to Marcus Opellius Antoninus Diadumenianus, most noble Caesar, leader of the youth, the commonwealth of Diana (dedicated this), by decree of the town councilors.[42]

That a triumphal arch could be planned, built, and dedicated within the fourteen months of Macrinus' rule is in itself striking. As this monument shows, the whole machinery of provincial honors for the Roman emperor could be set in motion very rapidly – almost automatically, it seems. What really commands our attention, though, is the fact that the town councilors of Diana decided to honor the new emperor as "most foresightful." There were many different honorific titles and superlative epithets to choose from – including "most holy," which was also employed in this inscription – but the dedicators evidently settled on *providentissimus* as one of the most appropriate options. This cannot be a mere coincidence. As we saw in the previous chapter, Providentia types comprised some 40 percent of all virtue types on the imperial coinage under Macrinus, and three milestones erected in Noricum all identified the emperor and his son, in the nominative case, as *providentissimi*.[43] This suggests that *providentia* had been selected by the short-lived regime as a central ideal, one that was disseminated by means of various media, including (but presumably not limited to) coins and milestones. This monument shows that the message somehow reached the town of Diana Veteranorum. And while Diana was indeed a veteran settlement, there is no indication in this text that the dedicators were acting in any "official" capacity, choosing to represent themselves, in the conventional municipal manner, as having acted *ex decreto decurionum*. It is a prime example, that is, of a local and unofficial response to a central and official message.

From these inscriptions, then, a picture begins to emerge, incomplete but impressive nonetheless, of lexical and ideological correspondence between the central state, on the one hand, and local communities, on the other, in the public representation of the Roman emperor. One way to begin filling out that picture is to turn from individual texts to groups of inscriptions. Though the results are less dramatic in terms of precise lexical correspondences between center and periphery, these groups of inscriptions do provide valuable insight into broader patterns of communication in the Roman empire.

[42] *CIL* 8.4598 = *ILS* 463 (217).   [43] Above, 234.

We begin with a set of inscriptions erected under Hadrian, all in Italy and all lauding the emperor for his *liberalitas*. An honorific inscription from Beneventum, carved into a statue base set up by the Colonia Iulia Concordia Beneventum, celebrates Hadrian as *optimus et liberalissimus*.[44] On two marble tablets, one found in Ostia and the other in Rome, the Colonia Ostia declares that it has been protected and enriched by the emperor's "comprehensive *indulgentia* and *liberalitas*."[45] The deified Hadrian is thanked by the commonwealth of Signia for his "profound" *liberalitas*, while the citizens of Castrimoenium record the role played by the emperor's *liberalitas* in financing a public building project.[46] This group of inscriptions points to the emergence of a new imperial ideal in the collective consciousness of the empire's inhabitants. Public inscriptions lauding the emperor's *liberalitas* first arose under Trajan, as we saw in the previous chapter, but the Trajanic inscriptions, unlike those under discussion here, were all official in nature. The authors of these texts, though (we may assume) occupying positions of authority in municipalities close to the city of Rome, and probably in regular contact with imperial officials, were not, as far as we know, formally associated with the central state. In this respect these inscriptions may be seen as unofficial responses to the central propagation of imperial *liberalitas* under Trajan, evident from the official inscriptions, and under Hadrian, reflected not only on an official inscription from Caesarea, but also in the operations of the imperial mint, which for the first time produced coin types representing this ideal.[47]

As always, it cannot be proven conclusively that the authors of these inscriptions were drawing on any one medium of communications in choosing to honor the emperor for his personal generosity. From at least one inscription, though, we can safely infer that the authors were influenced by imperial coins. The inscription, from Tibur, written in 135 on a marble tablet, commemorates Hadrian's *liberalitates* – in the plural.[48] That is significant. For it was also under Hadrian that *liberalitates*, individual and concrete instantiations of the emperor's generosity, came to be

---

[44] *AE* 1969/70.167 (125–6): *optimo et liberalissimo principi*. The epithet *liberalissimus* was not really "très rare," as the editors of *AE* claim; see above, 223–4, 235.

[45] *CIL* 14.95 (Ostia, 133): *colonia Ostia conservata et aucta omni indulgentia et liberalitate eius*; *CIL* 6.972 (Rome, 133): *ibid.*

[46] *CIL* 10.5963 (Signia, post 138): *profusa liberalita[te]*, dedicated by the *SPQ Signinus*. *CIL* 14.2460 (Castrimoenium, 117–38): *[ex li]ber[alitate]*.

[47] Official inscription under Hadrian: *AE* 1991.694 (Caesarea, Italy, 117–38): *liberalit[ate sua – - -]*, with Hadrian's names and titles in the nominative. On the coin type, see above, 82–92.

[48] *CIL* 14.3577 = 4235 = *ILS* 318: *[libe]ralitates pu[- - -]*. This was probably either an alimentary inscription (*[libe]ralitates pu[eris puellisque]*), or one recording some sort of public benefaction (*[libe]ralitates pu[blicelae – - -]*).

enumerated, on the imperial coinage, and always in connection with the formal occasions of cash handouts to the urban plebs of Rome.[49] This sort of official enumeration of particular examples of the emperor's generosity not only represents the routinization and banalization of an otherwise elaborate moral precept, but also narrows its practical application to a very tiny subset of the empire's population. This peculiar conceptualization of imperial *liberalitas*, as expressed on imperial coins and aimed primarily at the urban populace of Rome, was nevertheless replicated at Tibur, whether or not the dedicators of this inscription realized the implications of their usage. The meanings of imperial ideals, especially in circulation, could be elastic.

Over the course of the reigns of Trajan and Hadrian, then, we can trace a progression across media, from official to unofficial, in the public expression of the imperial ideal of *liberalitas*. A second set of inscriptions set up under Hadrian illustrates a similar evolution in the public expression of a different imperial value, *indulgentia*. Like *liberalitas*, *indulgentia* expressed personal generosity, but it could also denote a number of related ideals, such as goodwill, leniency, and paternal care.[50] During the period 69–235, the first attested example of this term in inscriptions with honorific terminology for the emperor comes under Trajan, in an inscription set up by decree of the senate, commemorating Ferentinum's co-option of a Roman senator who had instituted an alimentary program for the town.[51] In the case of *indulgentia*, the official message seems to have gotten out a bit more rapidly than with *liberalitas*, as we encounter several unofficial inscriptions from the Italian peninsula, erected under Trajan, which commemorate this particular virtue.[52] But the real breakthrough comes with Hadrian. The ideal of *indulgentia* is cited in three official inscriptions during Hadrian's reign, one from Africa Proconsularis, in which Hadrian's names and titles appear in the nominative, and the other two from Mauretania Caesariensis, set up

---

[49] *RIC* 2, Hadrian 253, 582, 648–9, 817. Reference to *liberalitates* in the plural is also attested in Suetonius and Apuleius, both writing in the mid-second century (references in chapter 2, n. 170).

[50] For full discussion of the meaning of *indulgentia*, see below, 280–2.

[51] *CIL* 6.1492 = *ILS* 6106 (101): *ab indulgentissimo imp(eratore) . . . qua aeternitate Italiae suae prospexit secundum liberalitatem eius.* The senator was T. Pomponius Bassus; on this text, see discussion in Woolf 1990a: 218. For an earlier citation of *indulgentia* in an official inscription, see *SCPP* l. 59: *patri optumo et indulgentissimo*, with Eck *et al.* 1996: 182.

[52] E.g. *CIL* 9.215 (Mesagne, 103–11): *[pro salute i]ndulg[entissimi] optimi ma[ximique principis]*; *CIL* 5.875 = *ILS* 1374 (Aquileia, 105): *pleniorem indulgentiam maximi imperatoris*, set up by decree of the town councilors in honor of a local patron. *AÉ* 2000.569 = *CIL* 11.3309 (Forum Clodii, 114–17): *optimo [e]t indulgentissimo principi*, set up by the Claudiani to acknowledge imperial financing of the town's aqueduct.

by an imperial procurator.[53] Even better evidence for the official adoption of this new ideal comes, as we would expect, from the imperial coinage under Hadrian, on which the Indulgentia type first appears.[54] Together, the official inscriptions and imperial coins document the canonization of a new imperial ideal.

It can be no mere coincidence, then, that it is precisely under Hadrian that the language and ideology of imperial *indulgentia* becomes common in unofficial inscriptions. Most of the examples come from Italy – not all set up, however, by inhabitants of the peninsula. We have already considered the two inscriptions set up by the Colonia Ostia, which lauded Hadrian's *indulgentia* in addition to his *liberalitas* (above, 258). Two additional inscriptions found in Rome also celebrate this virtue. The first, carved onto a marble tablet, was set up by the Colonia Iulia Augusta Tertiadecimanorum Uthina, in Africa, and declares that the community was protected by Hadrian's *indulgentia*.[55] The second text, more fragmentary, also celebrates the emperor's *indulgentia*, and was also set up by a *colonia*, perhaps the Colonia Iulia Augusta Pietas Catana, in Sicily.[56] Both texts publicly commemorate imperial benefactions to communities outside the Italian peninsula. Another honorific inscription, from Vicetia, identifies Hadrian as *princeps indulgentissimus*.[57] And finally, the citizens of Ripa Rhodani in Gallia Narbonensis erected a statue to Hadrian, in 119, and honored the emperor on the statue base as *indulgentissimus princeps*.[58] The context in which these last two dedications were made is unknown, but the main point is clear. A number of communities in Italy and various locations in the western Mediterranean were honoring Hadrian in precisely the same terminology, derived from the quality of *indulgentia*, that the imperial regime itself was actively promoting at the time.

From the era of Trajan and Hadrian, and from groups of inscriptions publicizing civilian ideals, mostly set up in Italy, we turn to the reign of Septimius Severus and to a series of inscriptions, mostly erected in North

---

[53] *AE* 1979.658 (Colonia Canopitana, Africa Proconsularis, 117–38): [e]x *indulgentia*. *CIL* 8.8813–14 (Guerria, Mauretania Caesariensis, 117–38): *ex indulgentia . . . fines adsignati*. All three inscriptions pertain to the imperial regulation of municipal boundaries, which could be construed – from the perspective of the beneficiaries – as a benefit of empire. See discussion and further evidence in Boatwright 2000: 78–80, 83–8; see also above, 104–5.

[54] *RIC* 2, Hadrian 212–13, 361, 708.

[55] *CIL* 6.40523 = 3754 = 31302 + 36917 = *ILS* 6784 (Rome, 133); most of the emperor's titles have disappeared, but the text can be dated by the enumeration of the tribunician power (18).

[56] *CIL* 6.40516 (Rome, 119–37); the identification of the colony is the conjecture of the editors of *CIL* 6.

[57] *CIL* 5.3110 (117–138): [*principi i*]*ndulg*[*entissimo*].   [58] *CIL* 12.1797: *indulgentissimo principi*.

Africa, that celebrated military values. The set of texts in question is char-acterized by the formulaic coupling of the superlative epithets *fortissimus* and *felicissimus*. The first point to note about these inscriptions is their con-centration in the north African provinces in general, and in the province of Numidia in particular. No fewer than eleven such inscriptions were set up in Numidia, from the coast to the deep interior of the province, and ranging in date from 198 to 209; three were erected in Phua alone, and another three in Cirta.[59] This density of texts in Numidia hailing the emperor as "bravest" and "most blessed" suggests that these imperial ideals had particular resonance in this area. But a number of inscriptions hailing Septimius Severus as *fortissimus felicissimusque* were set up else-where in North Africa, too. From the province of Africa Proconsularis, for example, we find another six inscriptions employing these two epithets, and from Mauretania Caesariensis one more.[60] These inscriptions were not, however, confined to North Africa. In Narbo, the *decumani Narbo-nenses* honored Septimius as "best, most blessed, and bravest emperor."[61] In Italy, the citizens of Lavinium made two dedications, one in Lavinium and the other in Rome, to Julia Augusta, mother of "the bravest and most blessed emperor."[62] The *ordo et plebs* of Ancona identified Septimius as *fortissimus* and *felicissimus* in an honorific inscription for the emperor's brother, P. Septimius Geta.[63] And on the Arch of the Argentarii in Rome, the *argentarii et negotiantes* honored the emperor, twice, as *fortissimus* and *felicissimus*.[64] Despite the concentration of these inscriptions in the north

---

[59] *CIL* 8.19920 (Nechaa, 198): *propa[g](atori) imp(erii) fortissimo fe[l]icissimoque principi*; *CIL* 8.6340 (Uzelis, 201), dedicated to Julia Augusta, *coniugi . . . fortiss(imi) feliciss(imi) ac sanctissimi principis*; *CIL* 8.7970 (Rusicade, 203); *CIL* 8.19693 (Civitas Celtianensium, 205), dedicated to Julia Augusta by the *republica civitas Celtianensium*; *CIL* 8.7972 (Rusicade, 209). Texts from Phua: *CIL* 8.6305 (200); 6307 (200), dedicated by the *respublica Phuenses*; 6306 (205), dedicated to Julia Augusta. Texts from Cirta: *CIL* 8.6998 (202), dedicated to Julia Augusta by the *respublica Cirtensium*; 6969 (204): *propagatori imperi[i fortis]simi felicissimique principis*, perhaps dedicated to a deity (e.g. Fortuna); 6944 (198–209), a marble base dedicated by a local official to Fortuna Redux Augusta.

[60] Texts from Africa Proconsularis: *AE* 2002.1667a (Mactar, 198–205): *pro salute victori(i)sque et inco-lumitate imperatorum . . . fortissimi felicissimi* (cf. *AE* 2002.1667b, also from Mactar, evidently using the same formula but missing the part of the stone with the two epithets); *CIL* 8.1628 = *ILS* 429 (Sicca Veneria, 208), set up by decree of the town councilors; *AE* 2003.1986 (Giufi, 198–209), set up by a *duumvir*; *CIL* 8.16370 (Aubuzza, 193–211); *CIL* 8.24556 (Carthage, 193–211): *[Iu]lia[e Domnae Augustae] . . . [fortissimi ac fel]icissimi con[iugi]*; *CIL* 8.17258 (Wed Scham, 201–11), set up by a local official. Text from Mauretania Caesariensis: *CIL* 8.20091 (Cuicul, 202).

[61] *CIL* 12.4346 (197): *optim[o] fe[licissimo] fort[issi]mo p[rincipi]*.

[62] *CIL* 14.2072 (Lavinium, 197–209); *CIL* 6.1047 (Rome, 198–210): *Iuliae Aug(ustae) matri . . . fortissimi felicissimi*.

[63] *CIL* 9.5899 = *ILS* 441 (Ancona, 203–11), dedicated by the council and plebs of the city, *ex commodis suis*. In this text the honorifics may in fact apply to Caracalla; see ed. note in *CIL*.

[64] *CIL* 6.1035 (Rome, 204).

African provinces, then, the formulaic use of these two epithets seems to have been a relatively widespread practice.

In attempting to account for this epigraphic practice, it should be noted that these two epithets had already appeared in honorific inscriptions for Commodus, and that both titles, *fortissimus* and *felicissimus*, also appeared individually in honorific inscriptions for Septimius (though the latter rarely appeared without the former).[65] The specific trend that requires attention is the dramatic surge in the coupling of these two terms in unofficial texts during the reign of Septimius Severus. It seems likely, once again, that the authors of these inscriptions were taking their cue from official media of communications. One clue comes from the imperial coinage. Types representing both Virtus and Felicitas, the concepts from which these two epithets were ultimately derived, were minted in relatively large numbers under Septimius, Virtus and Felicitas types both comprising roughly one fifth of all virtue and benefit types, respectively, during his reign.[66] Neither of these two types dominated the typology of Septimius' coinage, however, so it is unlikely that imperial coins were the main vehicles for the communication of these two ideals. In this case, it is rather within the epigraphic record itself that the answer lies. For what we find in the official inscriptions of the period is an unambiguous proliferation in the coupling of these two epithets. The emperor was the formal author of two of the texts. In the first, a milestone from the Via Traiana in Italy, Septimius is identified as "bravest and most blessed," and in the second, a marble tablet found in Anagnia, formally authored by both Septimius and Caracalla, these epithets again appear in connection with the emperor's titulature.[67] Four milestones erected near Sitifis in Numidia also style Septimius as *fortissimus* and *felicissimus* (in the dative).[68] Several additional inscriptions with these terms were set up by other official dedicators, including a *praefectus vigilum* in Rome, the *vigiles Ostienses* in Ostia, and a group of soldiers

---

[65] *Fortissimus* and *felicissimus* in honorific inscriptions for Commodus: e.g. *CIL* 8.802 (Avitta Bibba, Africa Proconsularis, 180–92): [*for*]*tissimo felicissimo p*[*rincipi*]; cf. *CIL* 3.11984 (milestone in Raetia, 180–92): *f* [*ortissi*]*mo* [*ac f*]*elicis*[*simo pr*]*inc*[*ipi*] *domi*[*no in*]*du*[*lgen*]*tissi*[*mo*]. *Fortissimus* by itself for Septimius: e.g. *CIL* 11.3201 = *ILS* 416 (Nepet, 194); *CIL* 8.9317 (Tipasam, Mauretania Caesariensis, 195); *CIL* 2.3343 (Vivatia, Hispania Tarraconensis, 203); further examples in appendix 13. *Felicissimus* by itself: *CIL* 3.6712 (Kiachta, Syria, 193–211); *AE* 1968.429 (Intercisa, Pannonia Inferior, 197–211): [*pro s*]*alute f*[*e*]*licis*[*simi max*]*imi principis.*

[66] These figures are for the silver coinage only, since the bronze data for the Severans is too limited for proper statistical tests; for the overall numbers, see appendices 5 and 7.

[67] *CIL* 9.6011 (milestone, Via Traiana, 210): [*fortissi*]*mus feliciss*(*imus*). *CIL* 10.5909 (Anagnia, 207): *fortissimus ac super omnes felicissimus princeps* (epithets may be attached to Caracalla, not Septimius).

[68] *CIL* 8.10337, 13338, 10353, 10362 (198), formally set up by the *colonia Sitifensis*; see above, 221.

in Numidia.[69] Other examples from the city of Rome may also reflect official authorship.[70]

On the basis of these inscriptions, we may conclude that, under Septimius Severus, the ideals of bravery (*virtus/fortis*) and blessedness (*felicitas/felix*), especially in the military sphere, were systematically publicized by the central state and effectively diffused through different official media of communications. And from the unofficial texts considered above it seems that these particular ideals were widely replicated in local communities throughout the Roman West, especially in the north African provinces. The terminology employed in these unofficial inscriptions, in other words, was not chosen haphazardly.

Correspondences between official and unofficial representations of the emperor in the public sphere were not always lexically precise. In some cases, the correspondence was more broadly ideological in nature. As a brief, final example, again from the reign of Septimius Severus, let us consider a series of unofficial inscriptions celebrating the emperor's piety and sanctity. I have already discussed the honorific inscription from Lepcis Magna commemorating Septimius' "public and private" *pietas*, and attributed the dedicators' selection of this ideal, rare in honorific inscriptions for the emperor, to the regime's emphasis on the concept of *pietas*, as reconstructed from coin types (above, 255–6). That emphasis may also account for the frequency of inscriptions celebrating the emperor's sacred eminence, expressed by the superlative epithets *sanctissimus* and *sacratissimus*. Several dedications to Julia Domna, Septimius' wife, and another to his father, P. Septimius Geta, identify Septimius himself with these epithets.[71] Another dedication, to Jupiter Optimus Maximus, hails that god as the "savior of the most sacred emperors" (i.e., Septimius and Caracalla).[72] An epitaph for a local magistrate in Lepcis Magna states that his election to the quinquennial duovirate came about "by permission of the most sacred emperor."[73] And in the

[69] *Praefectus vigilum*: *CIL* 6.31320 = 3761 (Rome, 198–201): *fort[issimo] felicissimo. Vigiles Ostienses*: *CIL* 14.4388 (Ostia, 211): *fortissimo ac super omnes felicissimo principi*. Soldiers: *CIL* 8.2438 (Thamugadi, 195–8): *fe[l[(icissimo) f]ortissimoque.*

[70] E.g. *CIL* 6.1030 (201); 6.40622 = 31475 (210), very fragmentary.

[71] *CIL* 8.5699 (Sigus, Numidia, 197): *[Iuliae] Augustae… [con]iugi… fortissimi ac sanctissimi princip(is)*, dedicated by the *respublica Siguitanorum*; *AE* 1969/70.699 (Sila, Numidia): *Iuliae Augustae… coniugi… fortissimi [s]anctissimi princip(is)*; *CIL* 8.6340 (Uzelis, Numidia, 201): *fortiss(imi) feliciss(imi) ac sanctissimi principis. CIL* 8.19493 = *ILS* 439 (Cirta, Numidia, 197–209): *P(ublio) Septimio L(uci) f(ilio) Getae patri… avi (sic) imp(eratoris) sanctissimi*, dedicated by the *res publica IIII colonia Cirtensis*. Cf. *AE* 1986.593 (Matrica, Pannonia Inferior, 198), set up to Septimius by a prefect of a cohort, and employing the epithet *sanctissimus*, but attached to Geta, not Septimius.

[72] *CIL* 8.1628 = *ILS* 429 (Sicca Veneria, Africa Proconsularis, 208): *Iovi Opt(imo) Max(imo) conservatori sanctissimorum principum*, set up by decree of the town councilors.

[73] *IRT* 396 (202–11): *[o]b honorem [quinquennalita]tis… permissu sacratiss[imi pr]incipis.*

legionary base at Lambaesis, the soldiers erected a statue to Septimius, "for the health and victory . . . of the bravest and most holy emperor."[74] Though these particular epithets were never especially common, they had in fact appeared in earlier inscriptions with honorific terminology for the emperor, most notably under Antoninus Pius, on whose coinage, like that of Septimius, *pietas* was emphasized.[75] But it is the proliferation of dedications with the honorific terms *sanctissimus* and *sacratissimus* under Septimius that is noteworthy here. What these various dedications seem to point to, again, is a relatively high decree of ideological coherence between the central state and local communities in the public representation of the emperor.

Taking these groups of inscriptions together with the individual texts examined above, what we find is a broad overlap, both lexical and ideological, between the imperial ideals communicated by the central state and those cited in these unofficial inscriptions. We can set these findings in a broader context by considering more general chronological and geographical trends in this epigraphic terminology. These trends may be discussed very briefly, since they are almost identical to the patterns in epigraphic terminology employed in the official inscriptions, examined in the last chapter.[76] The defining feature of this unofficial honorific terminology is the decisive shift that occurs in the last quarter of the second century. For most of the second century, the key terms that appeared in these inscriptions were those that expressed the ideals of ethical value and civic benefaction. Amongst titles, the most frequent were those that alluded to concrete benefactions (*conditor, locupletator, conservator*, etc.), and amongst epithets, the most common were those that derived from personal virtues, especially *optimus, indulgentissimus, liberalissimus*, and *providentissimus*. Beginning with Septimius Severus, by contrast, the language and ideology is far more militaristic and absolutist in nature – *propagator imperii, invictissimus, fortissimus, felicissimus*, and especially *dominus* appearing most frequently in the texts. In the unofficial inscriptions, then, the image of a civilian *princeps* was effectively replaced by that of a military autocrat.[77]

A second feature worth noting is a geographical divergence. In general, much of the earlier, civilian terminology comes from inscriptions set up in

---

[74] *CIL* 8.18249 (Lambaesis, Numidia, 194): [*pro salute et vic*]*toria . . .* [*f*]*ortissimi sa*[*n*]*ctissimi principis*].

[75] E.g. *CIL* 2.5232 = *ILS* 6898 (Collippo, Lusitania, 167): *optimo ac sanctissimo omnium saec*[*u*]*lorum principi*, set up by a local benefactor; *AE* 2000.883 = *CIL* 12.594 = *ILS* 6988 (Ager Arelatensis, Narbonensis, 138–61): *omnium saec*[*ulor*]*um sacratissimo principi*.

[76] Above, 228–9, 236–43. For what follows, see the inscriptions collected in appendix 13, and organized by type in appendix 15.

[77] The implications of this shift, especially the rise of the absolutist title *dominus*, will be examined below, 283–97.

Italy and the Mediterranean core of the empire, while much of the later, militaristic language is found on inscriptions erected in North Africa, which also belongs to the Mediterranean core, and in the Danubian provinces, which were more peripheral in relation to the imperial center. It should be emphasized that these are unofficial inscriptions, so this pattern cannot be explained simply by reference to the disposition of military forces around the empire. Though this geographical divergence is not as pronounced as the chronological shift, these spatial patterns do nevertheless point to a degree of regional variation in the public representation of the emperor.

Because the chronological and geographical trends in this unofficial epigraphic terminology are so similar to those characteristic of the official inscriptions, it would be tempting to conclude that whatever correlation there is between the unofficial and official inscriptions can be explained simply by their shared medium. After all, both sets of texts were subject to the same sorts of constraints and rather unyielding generic conventions. Though there is some merit to such an explanation, it is insufficient by itself because it does not take into account the problem of agency. For even though the two sets of inscriptions look remarkably similar on the surface, the actors who produced them were very different. In brief, some were formally associated with the central state, and others were not – and that is a vital distinction. It is true, of course, that most of the dedicators of these inscriptions, official and unofficial alike, were aristocrats, members of the upper, land-owning class of the empire. In social terms, there was not too much distance between an imperial official of senatorial rank and a local magistrate of equestrian status – at least when both are contrasted with the mass of rural peasantry that made up the majority of the Roman empire. Nevertheless, they were operating in quite different communications networks. The authors of official inscriptions belonged to a web of official communications that was ultimately connected, however tenuously, with the imperial regime itself.[78] The authors of unofficial inscriptions may well have had some contact with that web, but it will have been informal and irregular at best. In choosing the appropriate terms with which to honor the emperor, in other words, they were largely left to their own devices. And yet the terms they chose to employ, and the ideals and values for which those terms stood, were often in strikingly close harmony with the ones chosen by the authors of the official inscriptions.

In attempting to account for this broad and long-term overlap between the official and unofficial inscriptions, we may turn back to the individual

[78] See above, 239–40.

texts and groups of inscriptions discussed above. For if the argument about the terminology used in those inscriptions is correct, then we may reasonably conclude that, in general, the authors of these unofficial texts were taking their cue from some sort of official impulse, an impulse which we are able to reconstruct, in this case, mostly on the basis of the official inscriptions. The underlying dynamic, that is, seems to be the same: the official dissemination of different ideals and values through various media, followed by an unofficial response, in a local context, to those centrally communicated ideals and values. If not probative, the quantitative evidence presented above is at least consistent with this model of communications. Understanding how such long-distance communications were possible in a far-flung, pre-industrial empire, though, and explaining why the authors of these unofficial texts so often chose to follow the official line in representing the emperor, are rather more difficult questions, which we must now take up.

HONORIFIC DEDICATIONS TO THE EMPEROR: LOGISTICS, AUDIENCE, AND MOTIVES

In considering the inscriptions discussed in this and the last chapter, our focus has been on the texts themselves. In order to appreciate the impact of these inscribed texts, though, we also need to consider the processes by which they were actually produced. Most of the texts analyzed above were dedications to the reigning emperor (or to someone else, human or divine, with honorific language for the emperor). They were carved into several different materials, especially marble and bronze, and were associated with a range of structures – public monuments, milestones, plaques, etc. Though we cannot be certain, since the older epigraphic publications such as the first edition of *CIL* rarely specified the nature of the monument on which these inscriptions were written, it seems reasonable to assume that many of these dedications, and perhaps most of them, were inscribed onto statue bases. After all, honorific statuary was a standard feature of every town in the Roman empire, and the archaeological evidence has now made it clear that the public spaces of towns were filled with statues depicting Roman emperors.[79] As a way of understanding how the precise wording employed in honorific dedications to the emperor came to be chosen, then, let us examine the process with reference to statues and statue bases in particular.

---

[79] Evidence and discussion above, 202–4; see also below, 273–5.

As we have seen, most statues for the Roman emperor were proposed, paid for, set up, and maintained by local communities. They were erected all across the empire, and for the duration of an emperor's reign, but with a considerably higher rate of production in the second year of a reign, and higher than average frequencies in the third and fourth years.[80] Though there is some evidence for communities petitioning the emperor for permission to erect an imperial statue, there is no reason to believe that such permission was necessary. Nor is there any indication that the erection of imperial statues was mandatory, even at the accession of a new emperor.[81] Honorific statuary for the Roman emperor was produced spontaneously and by local initiative, a cardinal fact that must be kept in mind in what follows.

More important for our purposes is the question of how the precise wording of the dedications themselves was chosen. It is useful, first, to distinguish between the original decree from which many honorific statues ultimately derived, and the dedication that was carved onto the statue base itself. Rarely in the Latin epigraphic record do we have access to the former (in the much longer inscriptions of the Greek East, by contrast, both the decree and the dedication were often recorded). And amongst Latin dedications to the emperor, most were designed simply to identify the ruler represented by the statue, and therefore contained no additional information beyond a complete listing of the emperor's official nomenclature, in the dative case.[82] Despite occasional errors and infelicities of expression, these simple dedications were usually accurate in recording all of the emperor's current names and titles. That the imperial nomenclature is correctly recorded in these inscriptions is normally taken for granted, but the consistent accuracy of these locally produced texts should give us pause. Imperial titulature was long, complex, and constantly changing (with the serial enumeration of various powers and honors), and the widely dispersed communities of the empire were usually far removed, in time and space, from the emperor. It has been suggested that these communities simply reproduced the titulature that was included in the letter that the emperor had written to them when granting permission for the erection of the statue.[83] This is plausible in some cases, but imperial permission was

---

[80] Højte 2005: 143–56, with fig. 23 (156).

[81] *Contra* Alföldy 1984: 56, and Pekáry 1985: 22, neither of whom cite enough concrete evidence to support their claims.

[82] See discussion in Højte 2005: 65–70; for the divergence between east and west in the epigraphic recording of decrees and dedications, Rose 1997a: 73.

[83] So Rose 1997a: 73, supporting his argument with reference to some oddities in Nero's titulature (reference to both patrilineal and matrilineal descent) that appear in both official documents and honorific inscriptions.

probably not required, and many statues were evidently set up so quickly that there will not have been time to send a letter to the emperor and receive a response.[84] Perhaps imperial letters were just one of the types of official document upon which local communities drew in order to accurately record the emperor's current titulature on a new statue base.

The emperor's official titulature was one thing, the honorific terms we have been discussing quite another. How were these chosen? For even if the copying of the heading from imperial letters can explain the correct reproduction of official titles in honorific dedications to the emperor, it cannot account for the selection of honorific epithets in them. These epithets did sometimes appear in official inscriptions, such as milestones, but it is difficult to believe that any of the superlatives or grandiose titles discussed above were ever employed in letters sent by the emperor or written in his name. In choosing such terms, local dedicators must have drawn on different sources. That they were in fact drawing on some source(s), and not choosing the terms haphazardly, may be inferred from the generally broad, and sometimes precise, overlap between the honorific terms employed in these local dedications and those disseminated through official media by the central state. And unlike the authors of the official texts examined in the previous chapter, the dedicators of these inscriptions had no formal connection with the official communications network of the central state (such as it was).

It is unlikely that there ever existed a single mechanism for the transmission of imperial ideals and values from the central state to local dedicators. Several likely mechanisms can be imagined. Though we have been using imperial coins and official inscriptions primarily as a means of reconstructing an "official impulse" in the dissemination of imperial ideals, the actual coins and inscriptions, it is worth repeating, were themselves important vehicles for the dissemination of these ideas. In choosing appropriate honorific terminology for the emperor, in other words, local dedicators might well have been influenced by what they saw on the mass-produced coins circulating all around them, or by what they read on various official inscriptions, especially imperial edicts, senatorial decrees, and milestones. In addition, some local dedicators might have had access to other categories of official documentation, such as imperial rescripts, which could give some clues about suitable honorific language for the emperor.

In attempting to account for the terminological convergence between local dedications and official media, we should be thinking not only about

---

[84] Højte 2005: 156, n. 361.

documents, but also about individual social actors, and in particular about those actors whose movements bridged the gap between the central state and the myriad municipalities of the empire. This empire-wide traffic moved in two directions. It could be "centripetal," as the cities and towns of the empire generated a constant stream of embassies to the emperor, wherever he happened to be. The ambassadors who undertook such journeys – usually drawn from the same local elite that was mostly responsible for making honorific dedications to the emperor – will have been exposed to current buzzwords and to the most topical imperial ideals, and will have brought this "insider" knowledge back with them to their home towns.[85] If a private dedicator, a local collectivity, or the community as a whole wished to offer a dedication to the emperor, then, these ambassadors, recently returned from a visit to the imperial court, could have advised them on the most appropriate or resonant terminology with which to do so.

The traffic between the central state and local communities was also "centrifugal," of course, as the state regularly sent out a number of imperial administrators into the provinces.[86] And these administrators, whose connection with the imperial regime and whose interactions with one another produced what amounted to an official communications network, naturally came into contact with the cities and towns strewn across the empire. Of the various administrators scattered throughout the provinces, surely the most important for the transmission of imperial ideals from the state to the inhabitants of the empire's municipalities was the provincial governor.[87] Unfortunately, there is almost no empirical evidence for the provincial governor assisting local communities with the precise wording of their honorific dedications. In several cases, it seems that provincial governors provided input on the design of the statue itself.[88] We also know that governors sometimes offered provincial subjects very careful guidelines on the management of religious festivals, cult activities, and, especially, emperor worship.[89] This sort of official intervention in local practice, probably

---

[85] On diplomacy, embassies, and the exchange of ideas in the Roman world, see most recently Eilers 2009; in general on the diplomatic structure of the empire, Millar 1977: 375–85 and 2002–6 (1984): 2.195–228 are still fundamental.

[86] The number of high-ranking officials (of senatorial or equestrian status) sent out each year was remarkably low, no more than about 200; see, e.g., Hopkins 2009: 184. It should be noted, though, that the number of staffers, slaves, and seconded soldiers assisting these officials was probably on the order of 10,000. In general on administrative personnel in the high empire, Eck 2000: 238–65.

[87] On provincial governors in general, see, e.g., Burton 1975; Eck 2000: 272–8; Meyer-Zwiffelhoffer 2002.

[88] For a few documented cases (all in Asia Minor), see Jones 1977/78: 291; Rose 1997a: cat. 109, 123.

[89] Evidence and discussion in Price 1984: 69–71 (Asia Minor); Rives 1995: 76–84 (North Africa); Woolf 1998: 216 (Gaul); cf. Eck 1992 for the religious functions of provincial governors in general.

initiated by the communities in question, is analogous to the plausible scenario of a provincial governor assisting local communities in choosing the most appropriate language for their honorific dedications to the emperor. For most provincials, in fact, the provincial governor was the very face of Roman imperial authority, and will have stood as a reliable source of information for the best way to honor the emperor.

Imperial coins, official inscriptions and documents, ambassadors traveling from their communities to the imperial court, and imperial administrators governing the provinces of the empire – these were surely the key mechanisms and processes by which the most important, and the most topical, imperial ideals and values came to be so widely disseminated throughout the Roman world. Though there is not much concrete evidence for these particular mechanisms and practices, it is difficult to find an alternative explanation for the significant correspondences, presented above, between unofficial dedications to the emperor and the officially publicized imperial ideals reflected in coin types and inscriptions.

If this model of communications is correct, then two simple conclusions follow. On the one hand, the terms employed in these honorific dedications were not mandated by the central state, and did not appear in local contexts as the result of "top-down" directives. There was always some variation in this honorific terminology, after all, and sufficient divergence from official media to rule out the operation of a systematic propaganda machine. On the other hand, these honorific terms were not chosen randomly or in discursive isolation. Instead, they generally reflected the ideals that the imperial regime had publicized. The honorific system as a whole was driven by local initiative and local agency, but its characteristic expressions were largely shaped by the changing concerns of the central state.

This dynamic interaction between imperial ideology and local agency brings us to a more fundamental question that has been postponed until now, which is why these honorific inscriptions were set up in the first place. First we need to consider what their intended "audience" was, for whom they were actually set up. Formally, at least, these statues were public honors offered to the reigning emperor. But it goes without saying that the emperor himself would have seen only the tiniest fraction of these statues and the epigraphic dedications that accompanied them. It is not immediately obvious, then, why they were set up at all. The conventional interpretation is that these honorific statues, and local honors for the emperor more generally, were public expressions of loyalty to the imperial regime.[90] This

---

[90] Representative views in Pekáry 1985: 22–8; Ando 2000: 230–1.

interpretation is not tenable. The Roman imperial state simply did not require such demonstrations of loyalty, and in any case there were hardly enough high-ranking imperial officials in the provinces to form a suitable audience for displays of this sort. Indeed, even the most diligent provincial governor will have remained ignorant of most of them. More plausible is the notion that these local honors for the emperor were given "in gratitude for or in anticipation of imperial benefactions."[91] But the practical mechanics of such a putative exchange are still problematic. If the relationship between imperial benefactions and local dedications to the emperor were really the driving force behind this honorific system, then we would expect the visit of an emperor to have been the critical moment for such an exchange. We now know, however, that there was no correlation whatsoever between an imperial visit and the erection of an honorific statue for the emperor.[92] Nor, for that matter, does there seem to have been a strong correlation between an imperial visit and an imperial benefaction to the community concerned.[93] Imperial benefactions to provincial communities and local honors for the emperor were partly structured by the logic of reciprocity, to be sure, but that reciprocity operated mainly at the level of generalization and abstraction.[94] This is a crucial point to which we will return.

The main obstacle to understanding this honorific system has been to see the primary audience of it as external. I would like to suggest instead that the main audience for these imperial statues and local honors for the emperor was not external but internal – not imperial, that is, but local – and that, over time, these statues, inscriptions, and honors became an important means for provincial communities throughout the Roman West to represent the emperor to themselves in what had become, as a result of official publicity, a familiar symbolic language. This is not to deny that imperial statues could also function as public demonstrations of loyalty to the imperial regime, and that provincial governors and other imperial

---

[91] Rose 1997b: 109; cf. Lendon 1997: 156–7, 163 for ancient views on the exchange of local honors for imperial benefactions, and in deference to imperial honor.

[92] Højte 2000, comparing dated statue bases with the itineraries of Trajan, Hadrian and Antoninus Pius; for a broader analysis, Højte 2005: 159–65, with the conclusion, "there can be no doubt that imperial journeys as a general rule did not cause the cities visited by the emperor or the cities in the general area to erect statues – neither on the occasion of the visit nor in anticipation or in appreciation of it" (165). An imperial visit could be commemorated in other ways, of course. A series of reverse types from the mint at Pergamum, for example, celebrated the visit of Caracalla in 214, which resulted in the city's third neocorate; see Harl 1987: plates 23–4.

[93] Thus Boatwright 2000: 206–7, based on the amply documented record of Hadrian's travels and benefactions.

[94] This observation draws upon the analysis of Ma 1999: 179–242, who argues for a similar dynamic in the interaction between cities and kings in the Hellenistic world, noting that "the commemoration of particular benefactions had a generalizing force" (190).

officials formed a part of their intended audience. But it is to assert the
primacy of the local context. Such an interpretation is consistent with a
series of studies that have emphasized the local impact of imperial symbols
and practices in the Roman empire. In terms of images and visual culture,
for example, it has been argued that imperial portraits, though ultimately
based on models created at the center, were nevertheless adapted, subtly,
to local interests.[95] The characteristic rituals of the imperial cult, too,
have been seen as a sophisticated means of incorporating an alien power
structure, represented by a distant ruler, into local symbolic systems.[96]
And it has been shown that the practical link between religious authority
and civic benefaction, so crucial to the display and reinforcement of social
status in the municipalities of the western empire, was partly inspired by
the figure of the emperor as model priest and benefactor.[97]

The dedication of honorific statues to the emperor can also be seen
as a strategic incorporation of imperial symbols into a local context. In
that respect these statues played a vital semiotic role. These local honors
for the emperor not only functioned as a system of meanings, however,
but also contributed to the reproduction of social hierarchy. For when we
consider the practical, immediate effect on the local community of this
honorific system for the emperor, it becomes clear that these local honors
for the Roman emperor served to legitimate and reinforce the power of local
aristocrats. And it was this legitimating function, I contend, that motivated
this local honorific system in general, and the erection of imperial statues
in particular.[98]

The practice of offering public honors to the Roman emperor reinforced
the power of local aristocrats in at least two ways. First, the idealization of
the emperor through this honorific system entailed a positive valuation
of imperial power in general, which in turn entailed a positive valuation
of local power. For municipal aristocrats were active participants in and
beneficiaries of the Roman imperial system. In the Roman West in particular, the incorporation of communities into the empire tended to strengthen
social hierarchies, to increase the distance between rich and poor, and to

---

[95] Zanker 1983; for the relationship between provincial portraits and official models, see above, 217.
[96] Price 1984.   [97] Gordon 1990.
[98] Lendon 1997 is also sensitive to the local impact of honors ostensibly offered to the emperor (e.g.
174: "The emperor's subjects insisted that their emperor was splendid and glorious as much for
themselves as for him"), but where he emphasizes the roles of deference and especially reciprocity
(again, 174: "And this conspiracy of loyal sentiment was reinforced by anyone who looked forward
to receiving, or had received, an honour from the emperor"), I want to draw attention instead
to how the "conspiracy of loyal sentiment" articulated through a system of public honors for the
emperor served the interests of local aristocrats within their own community, quite independent of
their actual relationship with the emperor or the imperial state.

solidify structures of dependence.[99] The big "winners" in this particular configuration of power therefore had a strong incentive to maintain it. And so throughout the Roman West, local aristocrats, whether acting individually or collectively, willingly offered countless public honors to the emperor, including statues, since the effect of this practice was to universalize and naturalize imperial power in both its empire-wide and local aspects. And this is why the abstract reciprocity of this whole honorific system was so important. For the system was driven not so much by concrete exchanges – this honor for that benefaction – but rather by a more generalized and idealized principle of exchange.[100] Indeed, in reinforcing their own positions through the offering of public honors to the emperor, local aristocrats did not depend upon imperial visits or specific events for commemoration, nor upon concrete imperial benefactions requiring symbolic requital.

The second way in which this honorific system reinforced the power of local aristocrats was in its regular blurring of the lines between divine, imperial, and local authority. This blurring was achieved by means of a very careful arrangement of statues in the most public space of each town, the forum. Detailed studies on the spatial arrangement of statues in the fora of towns in northeastern Spain, north Italy, and North Africa have shown that the statues of gods, emperors, and local aristocrats were regularly erected in close proximity to one another, but in a manner that expressed the hierarchy between them. Indeed, this pattern of exhibition was remarkably consistent in widely separated parts of the empire.[101] This articulation of public space by means of statues, then, probably replicated in town after town throughout the Roman West, stood as a striking visual expression of the political and social order of the Roman world.[102] The forum in Cuicul in North Africa provides a good example of this effect (illustration 5.1).[103]

---

[99] See Woolf 1998 for a model study of how this process worked in one region of the empire; see also the essays collected in Navarro Caballero and Demougin 2001 for various aspects of the process in the Iberian peninsula; cf. Millett 1990 for Britain.

[100] Cf. Ma 1999: chapter 4, stressing the way in which local honors for Hellenistic kings could shape royal action, by creating a set of expectations, and emphasizing the role played by these honors in generating local knowledge and symbolic capital for the community as a whole. The interpretation offered here differs in laying emphasis instead upon the way in which such honors furthered sectional interests within a community, with or without the emperor's participation in the script.

[101] See esp. Alföldy 1979 and 1984 (Venetia and Histria), and Zimmer 1989 (Cuicul and Thamugadi). Further references above, chapter 4, nn. 46–7, to related studies on Gaul, Iberia, and Asia Minor; contrast Stewart 2003: 174–9 on the limited use of public statuary in Britain.

[102] The social hierarchy of the empire was also represented visually in the seating arrangements in the theater, often regulated by law; see discussion in Shaw 2000: 388–90, with references.

[103] Adapted from Zimmer 1989: 35, Abb. 15; for the inscriptions on these statue bases, Zimmer 1989: 54–63. Key to statues in figure 3: emperor/cults related to emperor: 1–3, 7, 9–10, 14, 16; deities: 4–6, 11–13, 15, 26, 28; local aristocrats: 8, 17, 27.

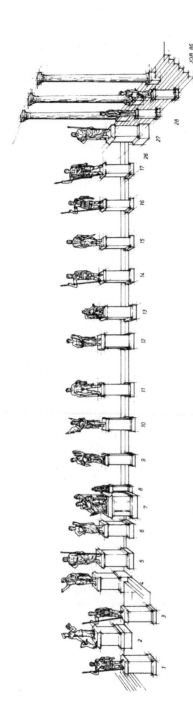

Illustration 5.1 Arrangement of statues on the east side of the Forum, Cuicul, Mauretania Caesariensis

It was in this characteristic intermingling of public statues to emperors, to cults related to the emperor, to other deities, and to local aristocrats that the overlapping and mutually reinforcing power of gods, emperors, and local "big men" must have been impressed upon the collective consciousness of the empire's inhabitants. The fact that it was the local aristocrats themselves who set up all three types of statues leaves little doubt about whose interests such a program served. And so when a rural peasant strolled into the local forum and saw there a statue of his landlord flanked by statues of a god on one side and the emperor on the other, he could hardly miss the point that the wealth and status of his landlord was legitimate, and that his power was supported by imperial and even divine authority. The message, after all, was not very difficult to understand.[104]

The ideological function of these stereotyped arrangements of public statues is now widely acknowledged.[105] Most studies, however, tend to note the important role played by the emperor in this scheme and leave it at that.[106] But it is not enough to speak about "the" Roman emperor, as if he were just some sort of neutral or generic figure. In order for the idea of the Roman emperor to have real symbolic resonance, it had to be invested with specific meaning(s). Some of the necessary work of signification was performed by the imperial statue itself, and in particular by the different ways in which the emperor could be represented visually.[107] But much of the work of signification was performed by the inscribed statue base, which not only identified the emperor as the individual represented by the statue, but also provided a formal justification for the public honor itself through its use of honorific language. That is why the precise language with which the emperor was praised in these dedications is so important for understanding the impact of this honorific system. For the terms employed in these inscriptions not only expressed a set of ideals and values which together formed a coherent semiotic system, but also shaped the manner in which the emperor was imagined in provincial communities, which in turn structured the way in which local aristocrats could represent their own authority.

---

[104] The low rates of provincial literacy argued for by Harris 1989 (5–10 percent in the western provinces: 272), with which I am in substantial agreement, do not affect this argument. All that was necessary to appreciate the message behind this spatial and visual expression of social hierarchy was a bare minimum of cultural literacy.

[105] See, e.g., Stewart 2003, esp. 157–83; cf. Whittaker 1997, who also exploits the evidence for the placement of statues in his discussion of the city as a locus of Roman "cultural imperialism."

[106] E.g. Stylow 2001 (still a very perceptive study of the relationship between imperial honorific and local power); Zuiderhoek 2009: 111, n. 78.

[107] For different portrait types, and attempts to quantify them, see above, 204.

And this brings us back, finally, to the mechanisms and processes by which the various terms employed in these dedications were chosen. In light of the interpretation offered here, this whole communications apparatus takes on greater significance. As I have argued, the terminological and ideological convergence between official media and local dedications resulted both from the central dissemination of imperial ideals, designed to project a positive public image for the reigning emperor, and from local dedicators responding to these same ideals, but on their own initiative and for their own purposes. The imperial regime and the local aristocrats, in other words, were each acting to further their own interests. And even though those interests were distinct, they were fully compatible. For the ultimate result of this ideological convergence was the reinforcement of both Roman imperial power and local aristocratic power. It was a very tidy arrangement.

We will return to this nexus of imperial and local power in the final chapter. For the remainder of this chapter, I propose to examine two major epigraphic trends in honorific terminology for the emperor, both of which will help to illuminate imperial communications and to reveal the deep impact of imperial ideals on local configurations of power. The first concerns the association between Caracalla and the ideal of *indulgentia*, and the second the changing relative frequencies of two diametrically opposed terms attached to the emperor, *optimus* and *dominus*.

CARACALLA'S *INDULGENTIA*

At some point in the second half of Caracalla's reign, in the city of Vienna in Gallia Narbonensis, a religious official, most likely a priest of the imperial cult, offered a dedication to the emperor Caracalla. The text, inscribed on a tablet, reads as follows:

Imp(eratori) Cae[sari] | M(arco) Aurel(io) [Severo] | Antoni[no Pio Feli]|ci Aug(usto) Pa[rthico maximo] | Britann[ico maximo] | German[ico maximo] | fortissi[mo invictis]|simo fe[licissimo] | indulge[ntissimoque] | prin[cipi] | C(aius) Ulatt[ius – - -] | sacerd[os Rom(ae) et Aug(usti)] | devotus [numini] | maiestat[ique eius] | civis Se[gusavius].

"To imperator Caesar Marcus Aurelius Severus Antoninus Pius Felix Augustus . . . strongest, most invincible, most blessed, and most generous Emperor, Gaius Ulattius [- – -], Priest of Roma and Augustus, devoted to his divinity and majesty, a citizen of Segusio (dedicated this)."[108]

---

[108] *CIL* 12.1851 (Vienna, 214–17).

In most respects this inscription is unremarkable. Indeed, as will now be clear, honorific dedications to the emperor offered by local aristocrats, employing a mix of the emperor's formal titles and a series of superlative epithets, were an everyday feature of urban landscapes in the Roman empire. It is only in the wider context of all honorific inscriptions erected under Caracalla that this text becomes significant. For in choosing to honor the emperor as *indulgentissimus*, the author of this text, Gaius Ulattius, was contributing to a dramatic proliferation in the number of dedications employing this particular epithet and its derivatives. As we will see, the configuration of evidence fits the now familiar pattern, as the upsurge in the use of this term mirrors the increased emphasis on the ideal of *indulgentia* reflected in the official media of the imperial regime. In this case, however, the semantic and ideological content of this term, and the historical context in which it became so prominent, were of much greater importance. Public inscriptions hailing Caracalla as *indulgentissimus*, I will argue, represent the culmination of the local honorific system for the emperor that had been developing over the course of the first two centuries AD.

We begin with the inscriptions themselves. Several surviving honorific dedications to Caracalla, celebrating the emperor's *indulgentia*, were set up in Rome by various unofficial collectivities.[109] Also in the city of Rome we find a more official dedication to Caracalla, a marble tablet offered by the senator M. Asinius Sabinianus to the emperor "on account of his conspicuous *indulgentia*."[110] In Cosa in Italy, the *respublica Cosanorum* set up a statue to Caracalla and, on the statue base, hailed the emperor for his "untiring and pre-eminent *indulgentia*."[111] From the north African provinces several more honorific inscriptions celebrated Caracalla's *indulgentia*, from Cirta, Lepcis Magna, and Volubilis.[112] And from Gallia Narbonensis came the honorific text cited above. In addition to these dedications to the emperor himself, we find an additional honorific inscription in Germania Superior, offered by a cohort, to Julia Domna, "mother of the most generous emperor."[113] Also worth noting in this context are two somewhat anomalous dedications to Indulgentia as a personified abstraction. The first comes from an

---

[109] *CIL* 6.1066 (Rome, 213): *domino nostro invictissimo [et] omnium principum v[irtute] benivolentia indulgentia exuperantissimo,* set up by the *Laurentes Lavinates* (cf. *CIL* 14.2073); *CIL* 6.1065 (Rome, 213): *domino indulgentissimo,* set up by the *negotiantes Vasculari.*

[110] *CIL* 6.1067 (Rome, 214): *ob insignem indulgentiam beneficiaque eius erga se.*

[111] *CIL* 11.2633 = *ILS* 6597 (Cosa, Italy, 213): *infatigabili indulgentia eius exuperantissimo.*

[112] Cirta: *CIL* 8.7000 (211–13): *[in honorem] . . . fortis[simi fe]licissimique et super o[mnes prin]cipes indulgentissimi,* set up by a local official. Lepcis Magna: *IRT* 429 (216): *[pro cont]inua indulgentia eius,* on a marble base dedicated by the *Lepcitani Septimiani.* Volubilis: *CIL* 8.21828 (216): *ob si[ngular]em eiu[s erga mun]icipes [indu]lgenti[am].*

[113] *CIL* 13.6351 (Murrhardt, 211–17): *matri [i]nd[u]lgentis[si]mi princi[pis].*

arch erected in Cirta, built by a local notable to celebrate his election to the quinquennial duovirate, and including a bronze statue dedicated to "the Indulgentia of our lord" (i.e., the emperor).[114] The second, set up by a local official in Tinfadi, belonged to a composite dedication made to Jupiter Optimus Maximus, Juno, and Minerva, together with Indulgentia – a rather odd addition to the standard Capitoline Triad.[115] And finally, no fewer than six milestones, five from Raetia and one from Noricum, identify Caracalla, in the dative case, as *indulgentissimus*.[116] It should be noted that the honorific language of these milestones, probably to be interpreted as local and semi-official dedications to the emperor, is broadly interchangeable but not precisely identical (slightly different ordering of terms, differing abbreviations, etc.), which implies a common source but not a single blueprint.[117]

These markedly diverse inscriptions, set up by a range of dedicators throughout the Roman West, and for the duration of Caracalla's reign, demonstrate that the idea of the emperor's *indulgentia* was very much "in the air" during these years. One indication that this idea was promoted by the central state comes from the epigraphic record itself, as we find two milestones from Numidia, one set up near Milev in 212, and the other near Rusicade in 216, with Caracalla's names and titles in the nominative case, and identifying the emperor with a string of identical epithets culminating with the phrase "and beyond all emperors most generous (*indulgentissimus*)."[118] But it is really the imperial coinage that provides the best evidence for this official emphasis on *indulgentia*. Figure 5.2 shows the fluctuating relative frequency of Indulgentia types on silver coins minted over the course of a century, from their initial appearance under Hadrian through the reign of Macrinus. The salient feature of the graph, of course, is the sharp peak in the frequency of Indulgentia types minted under Caracalla. *Indulgentia*, as these data suggest, was central to the public image that the imperial regime sought to project.

---

[114] *CIL* 8.7094–98 = *ILS* 2933 (Cirta, Numidia, dated by the editors to 197–217, but very likely erected during Caracalla's sole reign, 212–17): *Indulgentiae domini nostri*.

[115] *CIL* 8.2194 (Tinfadi, Numidia, 214), set up by a local official.

[116] Raetian milestones: *AE* 1978.586 (205–7): *fort]issimo ac felic[issi]mo principi do[mino i]ndulgentissim[o]*; *AE* 1978.587 (215): *[f]ort(issimo) A[u]g(usto) f[e]l[i]c(issimo) principi [d]omino indulgent(i)ss(imo)*; *CIL* 3.5997 (215): *fort(issimo) Aug(usto) fel(icissimo) princ(ipi) dom(ino) ind[ul]g(entissimo)*; *CIL* 3.5998 (215): *felic(issimo) prin(cipi) [dom]in(o) indul[gent]issimis (sic)*; *CIL* 3.5999 (215): *fort(issimo) Aug(usto) felic(issimo) pr[incipi do]mino indulg[e]n[tiss(imo)]*. Norican milestone: *CIL* 3.5745 (213): *fortissimo ac felicissimo principi domino indulgentissimo*.

[117] On the authorship of the texts inscribed on milestones, see above, 220–3.

[118] *CIL* 8.22384 (near Milev, 212): *maximus invictissimus sanctissimus fortissimus felicissimus et super omnes principes indulgentissimus*; *CIL* 8.10305 (near Rusicade, 216): *ibid.*

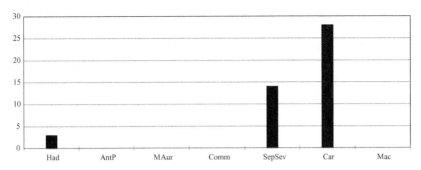

Figure 5.2 Relative frequency of Indulgentia types on denarii, expressed as a percentage of all virtue types, AD 117–218 (N = 14,185)

The proliferation of honorific inscriptions celebrating Caracalla's *indulgentia*, together with the regime's emphasis on this ideal, parallels the other cases of epigraphic and numismatic correspondence discussed above. In this case, though, two contemporary trends in the epigraphic culture of the Roman empire in general invest the spread of *indulgentia* terminology with particular significance. The first is the upsurge in all inscriptions with honorific terminology for the emperor that took place under Caracalla, itself related to the overall peak in epigraphic production that occurred around the turn of the third century.[119] One way to understand these inscriptions hailing Caracalla's *indulgentia*, then, is to set them in the larger context of this empire-wide rise in the frequency of Latin inscriptions. Several seminal works on the "epigraphic habit" in the Roman empire have addressed this issue, stressing the historical conditions that may account for the rise and fall in epigraphic production.[120] MacMullen, for example, invoked a distinctive "sense of audience" that was characteristic of the high Roman empire. In Woolf's view, monumental writing served to define one's identity at a time when the expansion of Roman society was opening up numerous avenues of social mobility. And Meyer has argued that the Roman-style epitaph – always the most common type of inscription – was a conscious claim to Roman status on the part of the commemorator, and that the rise in the number of such epitaphs in the second century AD reflects the diffusion of Roman citizenship and the high value placed on it.

Situating the spread of Latin inscriptions in the contexts of audience, identity and, in particular, citizenship, seems promising. But it is really the

[119] See above, Int. Part II, 184–5.   [120] MacMullen 1982; Meyer 1990; Woolf 1996.

second epigraphic trend that helps us to connect these overlapping contexts with the inscriptions hailing Caracalla's *indulgentia*. That trend was the significant increase under Caracalla in the use of the phrase *super omnes (retro) principes*, employed to distinguish the reigning emperor from his predecessors. This formula appeared far more often in unofficial inscriptions to Caracalla than to any other emperor, even allowing for the greater number of such inscriptions produced during his reign.[121] While this phrase is certainly emblematic of a general inflation in the language of praise offered to emperors, and does not signal a widely held belief in Caracalla's superiority with respect to his predecessors, the conspicuous frequency in its usage is unlikely to be wholly arbitrary or without topical significance. Like the increase in epigraphic production in general, and like the rise in inscriptions citing Caracalla's *indulgentia*, the spread of this formulaic phrase can be documented throughout the Roman West. In order to explain it, then, we should look to other contemporary developments of similar, or even empire-wide, scope. The only other development of such empire-wide significance during Caracalla's reign, of course, was the universal grant of citizenship of 212, the so-called *constitutio Antoniniana*.[122] And it was the official publicization of that grant, I would like to suggest, that provides the key to understanding the widespread commemoration of Caracalla's *indulgentia*.

That there was any official publicization at all of the *constitutio Antoniniana* might seem doubtful, since the grant of universal citizenship was never explicitly advertised on imperial coins. But if we read the symbolic language of the coinage correctly, we see that this grant was in fact commemorated, if only indirectly. For it is likely that it was precisely the Indulgentia coin type that was meant to publicize this grant, and that the sustained emphasis on this type reflects a systematic effort by the regime to communicate the emperor's spectacular generosity in granting citizenship to all free inhabitants of the empire – an effort, that is, to attach a specific meaning to the edict that announced this extraordinary decision, and then to disseminate that meaning as broadly as possible.

So what, exactly, did *indulgentia* mean? The term had a fairly wide semantic range, and may be translated as "generosity," "lenience," or

---

[121] Scheithauer 1988. Scheithauer's figures for the number of attestations of this phrase per emperor (for the emperors during our period) are: Marcus Aurelius (1); Commodus (1); Septimius Severus (2); Caracalla (26); Elagabalus (4); Severus Alexander (1?). Note, though, that among what I have called "official" inscriptions, this phrase only begins to appear under Elagabalus; see above, 228.

[122] On the grant of 212 see Sherwin-White 1973: 275–87, 380–435; for full bibliography, see also Oliver 1989, no. 260, and, most recently, Garnsey 2004.

"indulgence."[123] It was often employed in literary and epigraphic texts in conjunction with two other virtues, *liberalitas* and *clementia*, "mercy," "mildness," or "humanity." The term also had a strong, paternalistic aspect, frequently used to express the normative disposition of a parent towards a child.[124] In the *pro Caelio*, for example, Cicero bids the jurors to "support them (i.e. Caelius and his father) either through the recollection of your parents or through your affection for your children, so that in your sorrow for another you yield either to your *pietas* or to your *indulgentia*."[125] This juxtaposition is telling. Just as *pietas* denoted the proper attitude towards one's parents, so too did *indulgentia* designate the proper attitude towards one's children. *Indulgentia*, in other words, could be an appropriate expression of the emperor's own "paternal" responsibilities towards his subjects.

In connection with the Roman emperor, a paradigmatic paternal figure, *indulgentia* was construed as a virtue to which imperial *beneficia* could be ascribed, from *alimenta* programs and patronage of the arts to the remission of debts owed to the treasury and the abolition of judicial sentences. Numerous texts make it clear that the concrete favors bestowed by the emperor were thought to flow directly from his *indulgentia* and other personal qualities. An explicit formulation comes from the Trajanic jurist Iavolenus Priscus, who writes, "we ought to interpret a favor of the emperor as amply as possible, since it comes from his divine *indulgentia*."[126] Imperial virtue and imperial favor were intimately bound.

Among the many *beneficia* at the emperor's disposal, grants to individuals that enhanced their personal status, including the conferral of various honors, offices, promotions, and legal privileges, were regularly traced back to the emperor's *indulgentia*. Within this sphere of personal patronage, imperial grants of Roman citizenship naturally bulked large. And here, in particular, we find the routine employment of *indulgentia* terminology to characterize the basis of imperial favor. I cite just two examples. In a letter to Trajan, Pliny, after describing a recent illness, writes, "I brought in a therapist, whose care and consideration I can repay only with the favor of your *indulgentia*. I ask, therefore, that you grant him Roman citizenship."[127] Here the notional connection between imperial *indulgentia* and Roman

---

[123] Full conspectus of usages in *TLL* 7.1.1246.16–1250.38; for discussion of *indulgentia* as an imperial virtue, see also Gaudemet 1962; Cotton 1984; Griffin 2003: 110–11.

[124] Stressed by Cotton 1984.

[125] Cic. *Cael.* 79: *vel recordatione parentum vestrorum vel liberorum iucunditate sustentate, ut in alterius dolore vel pietati vel indulgentiae vestrae serviatis.*

[126] *Dig.* 1.4.3 (Iavolenus Priscus): *beneficium imperatoris, quod a divina scilicet eius indulgentia proficiscitur, quam plenissime interpretari debemus.*

[127] Plin. *Ep.* 10.5.1–2.

citizenship is manifest. More revealing for our purposes is an imperial letter of AD 168 preserved on the *Tabula Banasitana*, in which the emperors Marcus Aurelius and Lucius Verus preface a grant of Roman citizenship to a tribal leader in Mauretania with the observation that "Roman citizenship, unless occasioned by great services, is not normally granted to those peoples by imperial *indulgentia*."[128] So even in the official language of the Roman state, a grant of citizenship could be represented as a concrete expression of the emperor's *indulgentia*.

Now *indulgentia* was not used exclusively with reference to imperial *beneficia*, nor were grants of citizenship attributed exclusively to the emperor's *indulgentia*. But the frequent association of this term with paternalism and generosity in general, and with imperial grants of citizenship in particular, suggests that *indulgentia* would have been the most appropriate imperial virtue through which to commemorate and publicize the grant of universal citizenship. That would explain the prominence of the Indulgentia type on Caracalla's coinage and, if correct, would suggest that the regime sought to characterize the citizenship grant in ethical rather than legal or administrative terms.[129]

This interpretation also helps to explain both the spread of honorific inscriptions to the emperor lauding him for this particular virtue, and the increased frequency of the formulaic phrase *super omnes retro principes*. In publicly honoring their emperor as *indulgentissimus*, Caracalla's subjects were evidently sensitive to the regime's emphasis on the emperor's *indulgentia*, which manifested itself most emphatically in the citizenship grant. And in declaring that his virtue in general, and generosity in particular, was "beyond that of all other emperors," they appear to have been responding to this unprecedented and empire-wide benefaction. If nothing else, these inscriptions at least serve as another particularly strong indication that the imperial regime could be very successful in disseminating specific messages. For it is simply inconceivable that the simultaneous increase in the use of the epithet *indulgentissimus* to honor Caracalla, on multiple local inscriptions from widely scattered parts of the empire, was spontaneous. Nor can the sudden and equally widespread increase in the use of the formulaic phrase *super omnes retro principes* have been spontaneous. It, too, must have

---

[128] *Tabula Banasitana*, ll. 4–5 (*CRAI* 1971, p. 470 = *AE* 1971, 534 = *ILM* 2.94): *civitas Romana non nisi maximis meritis provocata in[dul]gentia principali gentibus istis dari solita sit.*

[129] The official meaning that the regime wished to attach to the edict is sometimes deduced from the much discussed Giessen papyrus 40 (Oliver 1989, no. 260), in which the themes of piety and *megaleiotēs* ("majesty") are prominent, but it is unclear whether this papyrus is a reference to the edict, or preserves a copy of the edict itself; see discussion in Stroux 1933; Sherwin-White 1973: 281–3, 86–7; Potter 2004: 138–9.

been a response, local and unofficial, to a centrally disseminated message. And the most compelling grounds on which the regime could have based its message that Caracalla was a paradigm of *indulgentia*, and that he had surpassed all his predecessors, was the grant of universal citizenship.

It is important to remember that in honoring Caracalla for his *indulgentia*, local dedicators were not necessarily responding – and in fact probably were not responding – to the impact of the citizenship grant on their particular communities. This honorific system, as I have argued, was mostly generalized and abstract, more ideological than concrete. In this respect, the proliferation of dedications honoring Caracalla as *indulgentissimus* may be seen as the culmination of this honorific system, since the citizenship grant was the empire-wide benefaction *par excellence*. In another way, however, the citizenship grant and its commemoration contributed to the eventual demise of this system, since the universality of Roman citizenship eroded one of the principal markers of social differentiation in the municipalities of the Roman West. Being a Roman citizen no longer conferred any distinction, with the result that many local aristocrats effectively lost a weapon in their symbolic arsenals.[130] But this was by no means the most important challenge to local aristocratic standing. For in the Severan period there arose a much more serious threat in the form of a new and more menacing conception of monarchic authority, one that offered no symbolic support to the empire's municipal elite.

THE EMPEROR AS SYMBOL: FROM MODEL TO MASTER

In examining the epigraphic record for public representations of the Roman emperor, we have analyzed individual texts, groups of related inscriptions, and several longer-term patterns in the use of honorific terminology. Much of the discussion has focused on those texts or groups of texts that were particularly common or conspicuous for short periods, often no longer than a single imperial reign. In fact, most of the fluctuations in the frequency of the various honorific terms we have considered were dramatic and significant, but ephemeral nonetheless. We have also examined some slower-moving changes, especially the shift from an honorific terminology derived from the language of ethical value and civic benefaction to one based on militarism and autocracy. This shift was no mere fluctuation, but rather a major transformation which took place, roughly, between the Antonine and Severan periods, and one that is evident in both official

---

[130] So Meyer 1990.

and unofficial inscriptions. It is possible to go deeper, however, and to consider even longer-term fluctuations in honorific terminology over the whole period 69–235. In so doing, the purpose is no longer to analyze short-term changes that can be described and explained in topical terms, but rather to illuminate the underlying rhythms and "deep structure" of this honorific system as a whole. To turn to this level of historical change is to turn to a rather different temporality, then, very slow moving and largely imperceptible to contemporaries. But the structural revolution that occurred at this deep level, as we will see, underpinned many of the changes discussed in this and the previous chapter, and helps to explain both the essence and the slow transformation of this entire honorific system.

In turning to fluctuations in honorific terminology over the course of these 169 years, we will no longer consider the full range of terms that appeared in these inscriptions, but will instead focus on the two most common terms, *optimus* and *dominus*.[131] For much of the second century, the single most common epithet for the emperor in these honorific inscriptions was indeed *optimus*, "the best." From the accession of the emperor Vespasian in 69 to the beginning of the reign of Septimius Severus in 193, the term *optimus* by itself accounted for one quarter of all honorific terminology employed in these inscriptions, and for much of the second century the figure is closer to 40 percent. In the last quarter of the second century, however, the frequency of this epithet drops precipitously, and during the first half of the third century, it is comparatively rare in honorific inscriptions for the emperor. The slow fading away of the epithet *optimus* created, in effect, a terminological void in these inscriptions, which continued to be set up well beyond the period covered in this book (but in much smaller numbers). That void was filled not by one of the other traditional epithets for the emperor, but rather by a very different sort of title, *dominus*. *Dominus* may be translated as "lord" or "master," and was among other things the term used for a master in relation to his slaves. The use of this term for the emperor had appeared intermittently in inscriptions going all the way back to Domitian, but it did not become common until the reign of Septimius Severus.[132] The relative frequency of the term *dominus* rose steadily during the Severan period, and by the middle of the third century had very nearly crowded out all other honorific terminology in inscriptions for the emperor, accounting for no less than three quarters of all such terminology in this honorific epigraphy.

---

[131] For the data on which the following discussion is based, see appendix 13.

[132] Domitian as *dominus*: CIL 10.444 = *ILS* 3546 (Vallis Silari Superior, Lucania, 81–96): *pro salute optum[i] / principis et domini*; cf. CIL 3.6998 (Nacolia, Asia) for Hadrian as *dominus*.

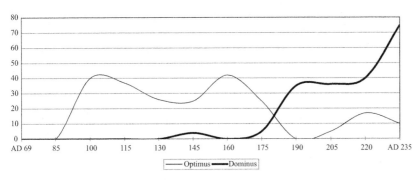

Figure 5.3 Relative frequency of the terms *optimus* and *dominus* in honorific inscriptions for the emperor, expressed as a percentage of all honorific terms (N = 575)
Note: N = number of inscriptions.

The changing frequencies of the honorific terms *optimus* and *dominus* are presented graphically in figure 5.3. As the graph shows, there was a decline over the long term in the frequency of the term *optimus*, and a corresponding increase in the frequency of the term *dominus*. Now it has long been recognized that the term *dominus* for the emperor became common in the epigraphy of the Severan period.[133] The timing of this development, however, has not been properly understood. While it is true that the title *dominus* proliferated during the reign of Septimius Severus, figure 5.3 indicates that the tendency to hail the emperor as *dominus* really began under Commodus. That was the axial moment in this long-term change.

More important is the context in which the term *dominus* for the emperor became prominent. And what has not been recognized in this respect is that the title *dominus* did not just crop up in the epigraphic sphere in general, but precisely in the very honorific inscriptions that we have been considering. Like the other honorific epithets discussed thus far, the term *dominus* was not an official imperial title during this period and did not appear in official imperial documents. In fact, *dominus* was not incorporated into the emperor's official titulature until the end of the third century.[134] It cannot be stressed too strongly that this term never appeared in official inscriptions in which the emperor's names and titles appeared in the nominative case. It was, therefore, a properly honorific term, if a somewhat anomalous one. Moreover, and even more important, it has not been recognized that the autocratic *dominus* effectively replaced the traditional *optimus* as

---

[133] See already K. Neumann in *RE* v (1905): 1308. [134] Hammond 1957: 45, n. 164, with references.

the most common honorific epithet for the emperor in these inscriptions. This is significant. In the middle of the second century, throughout the Roman West, the public sphere was flooded with honorific inscriptions identifying the emperor as *optimus*.[135] In the middle of the third century, throughout the Roman West, the public sphere was flooded with honorific inscriptions identifying the emperor as *dominus*.[136] For the purposes of this argument no one inscription is terribly important. It is instead the cumulative impact of all these Italian and provincial inscriptions on the collective consciousness of the empire's inhabitants that matters. And when we consider the cumulative impact of all these inscriptions, it becomes clear that there was, over the long term, a slow change in the way the local dedicators of these honorific inscriptions represented and conceptualized the emperor, a profound shift in which they went from representing the emperor as being the best to representing him as being, simply, a master.

While the timing and context of this fundamental change in honorific language for the emperor can be pinpointed with some precision, its causes are more difficult to identify. That this change was entirely the result of local initiative is implausible. The roughly simultaneous replacement of *optimus* by *dominus* in honorific inscriptions for the emperor can be documented in scores of widely separated regions, from Italy to various points throughout the periphery. It is difficult, therefore, to escape the conclusion that these changes were the product of a common source. Some evidence from the eastern empire helps us to set this change in a wider context. In Greek inscriptions of the first three centuries AD, the standard translation of *dominus* as a title for the emperor is *kurios*.[137] The indices to *IGRR* 3–4 give a very rough-and-ready sense of long-term trends in the use

---

[135] Emperor as *optimus* in second century: e.g. *CIL* 11.1147 (Veleia, Aemilia, 102–13); *CIL* 2.2010 (Nescania, Baetica, 109–10); *CIL* 10.676 = *ILS* 312 (Surrentum, Latium, 121–2); *AE* 1969/70.167 (Beneventum, Apulia, 125–6); *CIL* 2.1371 (Callenses, Baetica, 128); *CIL* 14.4366 (Ostia, Latium, 140); *CIL* 3.5654 (Trigisamum, Noricum, 140–4); *CIL* 2.1282 (Salpensa, Baetica, 147); *AE* 1976.351 (Castulo, Hispania Tarraconensis, 155); *CIL* 8.27776 (Althiburos, Africa Proconsularis, 138–61); *CIL* 8.12513 = *ILS* 345 (Carthage, Africa Proconsularis, 145–61); *CIL* 2.5232 = *ILS* 6898 (Collippo, Lusitania, 167).

[136] Emperor as *dominus* in third century: e.g. *IRT* 414 (Lepcis Magna, Africa Proconsularis, 201); *AE* 1993.1777 (Sitifis, Mauretania Tingitana, 201–4); *CIL* 8.17835 (Thamugadi, Numidia, 209–11); *RIB* 905 (Old Carlisle, Britannia, 213); *CIL* 5.824 (Aquileia, Venetia, 211–17); *AE* 1992.892 (Muru de Banguis, Sardinia, 211–17); *CIL* 5.7866 (Cemenelum, Alpes Maritimae, 211–17); *AE* 1993.668 (Forum Clodii, Etruria, 222–3); *CIL* 3.8173 (Ulpiana, Moesia Superior, 226); *CIL* 13.2922 (Autessiodurum, Gallia Lugdunensis, 228); *CIL* 8.26262 (Uchi Maius, Africa Proconsularis, 222–35); *AE* 1983.608 (Tutugi, Hispania Tarraconensis, 222–35).

[137] Dickey 2001: 9. As Dickey notes, *despotēs* begins to replace *kurios* at the beginning of the fourth century.

of *kurios* as an imperial title in one large region of the eastern empire.[138] *Kurios* as an honorific title for the emperor appears as early as the reign of Tiberius, becomes slightly more common during the joint rule of Marcus Aurelius and Commodus (176–80) and the sole rule of the latter, and seems to become standard under Septimius Severus and especially Caracalla.[139] The eastern pattern in the use of *kurios*, in other words, appears to mirror the western pattern in the use of *dominus*. The late-second-century rise of the title *dominus/kurios* for the Roman emperor in public inscriptions may well have been an empire-wide phenomenon.[140]

In light of the evidence presented above for indirect influence from the center in the choice of honorific terminology, we can safely infer such influence in the cases of both *optimus* and *dominus*. Unfortunately, tracing the mechanisms of that influence is, once again, beyond the reach of our evidence. As possible inspirations for hailing the emperor as *optimus* one could point to the term's brief incorporation into Trajan's official titulature between 114 and 117; to the spread throughout the Roman West of temples to Jupiter Optimus Maximus, which gave provincials an obvious model for imperial authority – and indeed they often honored the emperor as *optimus* and *maximus*; or to the general ideal of the *optimus princeps* that emerged under the adoptive emperors of the second century.[141]

The rise of the title *dominus* under Commodus is more puzzling, though it hardly escaped contemporaries that his accession marked a departure from the meritocratic ideal of the *optimus princeps*.[142] The record of Commodus' reign also suggests that this was an imperial regime in which an official conception of the Roman emperor opposed to the senatorial ideal of the *civilis princeps* began to prevail.[143] The use of the title *dominus* in

---

[138] *IGRR* 3 covers Bithynia and Pontus, Cappadocia, Armenia, Galatia, Lycia, Pamphylia, Cilicia, Cyprus, Syria, Palestine, and Arabia; *IGRR* 4 covers Mysia, Phrygia, Lydia, and the larger islands of the eastern Aegean.

[139] Roman emperors as *kurios* in Greek inscriptions from the east: Tiberius: *IGRR* 3.1086; Marcus Aurelius and Commodus: e.g. *IGRR* 3.1109, 1116, 1195, 1220, 1245, 4.676, 1519; Commodus: e.g. *IGRR* 3.351, 1128, 1133, 1250; Septimius Severus: e.g. *IGRR* 3.838, 1151, 1161, 1248; Caracalla: e.g. *IGRR* 3.60, 806, 1132, 1239–40, 1314, 4.1251, 1354, 1519.

[140] The Egyptian evidence (papyri and inscriptions) does not really fit the pattern. *Kurios* is attested already under Augustus (as is *despotēs*), and becomes common beginning with Nero. See Bureth 1964: 25, 33–4; Dickey 2001: 3. In general on imperial titles in the Egyptian papyri, de Jong 2006.

[141] *Optimus* in Trajan's titulature: below, n. 151. Temples to Jupiter Optimus Maximus: Barton 1981; MacMullen 2000: 39, 60, 66, 75, 77, 104, 112. Emperor as *optimus* and *maximus*: e.g. *CIL* 2.2010 (Nescania, Baetica, 109–10); *CIL* 9.215 (Mesagne, Apulia, 103–11); *CIL* 2.2054 = *ILS* 304 (Aratispi, Baetica, 117); *AE* 1966.182 (Municipium Flavium Muiguense, Baetica, 132); *CIL* 8.12513 = *ILS* 345 (Carthage, Africa Proconsularis, 145–61); further examples in appendix 13. On the political rhetoric and reality of imperial succession in the second century, see discussion in Hekster 2002: 16–30.

[142] Cf. Hdn. 1.5, with Whittaker's note in the Loeb edition on 1.5.5.

[143] In general on Commodus' public image, Hekster 2002.

honorific inscriptions for Commodus may echo that shift. There is also an intriguing piece of evidence from Dio. Complaining about Commodus' treatment of senators in the amphitheater, Dio writes, "For in addition to other things, we used to shout out whatever we were commanded, especially the following words continuously: 'you are master (*kurios*) and you are first and you are of all men most fortunate'."[144] So Commodus evidently wanted to be called "master," and this information may have seeped out, informally, from Rome.[145] But it is unlikely that there was ever an official directive under Commodus compelling provincials to honor the Roman emperor as *dominus*. The evidence presented above has shown that specific terms could be rapidly and widely diffused without any sort of imperial mandate. In this case the argument from silence is a strong one. It should also be noted that the slow change from identifying the emperor primarily as *optimus* to identifying him primarily as *dominus* took place over many years, and would hardly have been perceptible to contemporaries.

Many of the texts identifying the emperor as either *optimus* or *dominus* were inscribed onto statue bases, and therefore played a major role in shaping local representations of the Roman emperor. And therein lies the real importance of this transformation. For as a result of this terminological change in the late second century, local communities were now representing the emperor to themselves in a fundamentally different manner than before. Above all, this change brought with it a conceptual passage from the emperor's moral exemplarity, implied in the title *optimus*, to his mere domination, expressed forcefully by the title *dominus*. And this transformation from imperial exemplarity to imperial domination had serious implications both for the legitimation of local aristocratic power and, as I will suggest, for the public behavior of the aristocrats themselves. In order to comprehend this transition from imperial exemplarity to imperial domination, we will have to examine what the terms *optimus* and *dominus* meant and how they were used, and how the antithetical meanings of these two terms functioned, discursively and practically, in local contexts.

The term *optimus*, "best," is the superlative form of the adjective *bonus*, "good."[146] When applied to a person, the term *optimus* normally implied moral excellence. As such it is redolent of the Ciceronian notion of the

---

[144] Dio 72[73].20.2.

[145] Commodus was not, however, the first emperor to insist on the title; see below, n. 166.

[146] See *TLL* 2.2079.21–2098.41 (s.v. *bonus*) for a useful collection of evidence, esp. 2081.74–2084.50 for *bonus/optimus* as a moral quality. For *optimus* as an imperial title under Trajan, see Hammond 1957: 42–5; Frei-Stolba 1969: 21–31 (as part of the emperor's "unofficial" titulature); cf. *TLL* 2.2085.56–2086.14 for *bonus/optimus* as an honorific term.

vir bonus, "the good man," an ideal with strong philosophical and ethical undertones.[147] Indeed, it very nearly encapsulates all the imperial virtues discussed in chapter 2. The person described as *optimus* was also by definition an exemplar. And educated Romans were extremely sensitive to the power of example.[148] The moral exemplarity inherent in the term *optimus* is especially pronounced when attached to the Roman emperor, who was indeed expected to play a paradigmatic role for society as a whole.[149] The theme that the emperor as *optimus* was an ethical model for others abounds in imperial literature. An explicit formulation can be found in a statement by Velleius Paterculus in which the historian, lauding the emperor Tiberius, writes, "For the emperor who is best (*princeps optimus*) instructs his citizens to do right by doing it, and even though the emperor is greatest in power, he is even greater through his example."[150] In his *Panegyricus*, Pliny weaves the ideal of the *optimus princeps* throughout the speech. Not only does he repeatedly refer to Trajan as *optimus princeps* (e.g. *Pan.* 36.1, 56.1, 91.1, 95.4), he also offers a short lecture on the meaning of the term *optimus* and explains why it applies especially to Trajan (*Pan.* 88; cf. 2.7).[151] And Pliny, like Velleius, can be explicit about the emperor's paradigmatic role: "for we do not need power [sc. over us] so much as an example. Indeed, fear is an unreliable teacher of what is right. Men learn better from examples."[152] In fact, the idea of imperial exemplarity was present right from the very advent of monarchy at Rome, and can be found stated clearly in the *Res Gestae*. In this text Augustus claims that, "By new laws passed under my authority I brought back many exemplary practices of our ancestors that were disappearing in our time, and I myself have transmitted many

---

[147] Vogt 1933; Hellegouarc'h 1963: 495–500.

[148] Cf. Quint. 12.2.30 (a *locus classicus*): *an fortitudinem, iustitiam, fidem, continentiam, frugalitatem, contemptum doloris ac mortis melius alii docebunt quam Fabricii, Curii, Reguli, Decii, Mucii aliique innumerabiles? Quantum enim Graeci praeceptis valent, tantum Romani, quod est maius, exemplis.* In general on exemplarity in Roman culture, see Roller 2004, with references.

[149] Emperor as model: Ov. *Met.* 15.833–4, *Fast.* 6.647–8; Vell. Pat. 2.126.5; Sen. *Clem.* 2.2.1; Plin. *Pan.* 45–6; Tac. *Ann.* 3.55; Dio 52.34.1–3; Hdn. 1.2.4; *HA Pert.* 8.10, *SevAl.* 41.2, *Valer.* 5.4–7. The idea that the ruler was a model for the ruled had a distinguished pedigree (cf. Plato *Laws* 711b).

[150] Vell. Pat. 2.126.5: *nam facere recte civis suos princeps optimus faciendo docet, cumque sit imperio maximus, exemplo maior est.*

[151] Pliny also refers to Trajan as *optimus* in his correspondence (*Ep.* 2.13.8, 3.13.1, 3.18.3, 4.22.1, 5.13.7, 10.1.2, 10.4.1, 10.14). *Optimus* was eventually incorporated into Trajan's official titulature during the last three years of his reign: *CIL* 16.60–1 (military diplomas from 114); see Hammond 1957: 43, n. 149. With the exception of the years 114–17, the term *optimus* was not part of the emperor's official titulature at any point during the period 69–235.

[152] Plin. *Pan.* 45.6: *nec tam imperio nobis opus est quam exemplo. quippe infidelis recti magister est metus. melius homines exemplis docentur . . .* ; this entire section of the speech (45–6) develops the theme of imperial exemplarity.

exemplary practices to posterity for imitation."[153] The theme also emerges in official documents of the early principate. It is especially prominent in the *SCPP*. In one telling passage, the senate declares, "Likewise the senate, mindful of its own clemency, justice, and great-heartedness, virtues which it had inherited from its ancestors, and then learned even more from the deified Augustus and Tiberius Caesar Augustus, its *principes . . .* "[154] From the very beginning of imperial rule, then, the emperor's moral exemplarity was a proclaimed and officially recognized basis of imperial authority.[155]

It might be objected that this notion of the emperor as a model for society is just an elaborate literary conceit concocted by self-serving authors and absorbed by the imperial regime, an absurd fiction with no effect on actual practice. But the impact of this idea can actually be traced in the Italian and provincial epigraphic record, especially in local honorific inscriptions set up not for the emperor, but for local aristocrats. The salient point here is that the honorific terminology of these inscriptions drew heavily on the language of imperial virtues. So, for example, among the most common qualities cited in these inscriptions for local aristocrats were *liberalitas*, "generosity," *munificentia*, "munificence," and *pietas*, "duty," all virtues associated with the Roman emperor and, as we have seen, systematically advertised on imperial coins and other media.[156] Through this surely intentional overlap in value terms, these municipal notables were, in a sense, representing themselves as local versions of the emperor, sharing in many of the emperor's particular virtues, and indeed claiming them as their own. Together with the blurring of statue types in a shared civic space, this was the most direct way in which local aristocrats modeled their own authority on that of the emperor.[157]

In general, however, these inscriptions did not go so far as to employ the superlative epithets accorded the emperor. Local aristocrats, in other words,

---

[153] *RG* 8.5: *legibus novis me auctore latis multa exempla maiorum exolescentia iam ex nostro saeculo reduxi et ipse multarum rerum exempla imitanda posteris tradidi.*

[154] *SCPP* ll. 90–2: *item senatum, memorem clementiae suae iustitiaeq(ue) animi magnitudinisque, virtutes quas a maioribus suis accepisset, tum praecipue ab divo Aug. et Ti. Caesare Aug. principibus suis didicisset . . .*; cf. the *SC* on funeral honors for Germanicus, also explicit on the didactic function of the imperial family: *TabSiar.* IIb.11–17.

[155] For the impact of monarchy on Latin historiography, in which exemplarity always bulked large, see Kraus 2005.

[156] *Liberalitas*: e.g. *CIL* 5.1012 = *ILS* 6686, *CIL* 5.5128 = *ILS* 6726, *CIL* 9.1686 (Italy); *CIL* 8.980, 8.5365, 8.10523 (North Africa); *CIL* 12.1585, 12.3165, 12.4406 (Gaul). *Munificentia*: e.g. *CIL* 10.5928 = *ILS* 6264, *CIL* 10.5392, 14.2120 = *ILS* 6199, *CIL* 11.4579 = *ILS* 6633 (Italy); *CIL* 8.5368 (North Africa). *Pietas*: e.g. *CIL*.14.2408 = *ILS* 5196, *CIL* 10.1818 (Italy).

[157] This discourse of aristocratic virtue and honor was also thriving in the eastern empire; see most recently Zuiderhoek 2009: 122–33.

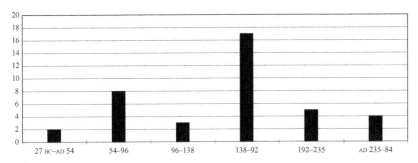

Figure 5.4 Number of datable Italian honorific inscriptions for local aristocrats employing the term *optimus*, 27 BC–AD 284 (N = 39)

were not generally lauded as *felicissimus, fortissimus,* or *indulgentissimus*. In this particular respect, there was a clear dividing line between emperors and aristocrats. But there was one critical exception to this pattern. Like the Roman emperor, these local notables were frequently hailed as *optimus*. The practice of identifying local aristocrats as *optimus* in honorific inscriptions erected on their behalf is attested throughout the Roman West in the high empire.[158] An honorific inscription for a local notable, set up in the middle of the second century in Aratispi, in the province of Baetica, is a typical example:

M(arco) Fulvio Senecioni / Aratispitano optum[o et praes]/tantissumo civi ob m[erita eius] / amici posuerunt . . .

To Marcus Fulvius Senecio, the best and most eminent citizen of Aratispi, on account of his merits, his friends have set up (this statue) . . .[159]

In this inscription, Senecio's friends were proclaiming publicly that the honorand, just like the emperor, was *optimus*. In fact, the convergence of the ideals of the *optimus princeps* and *optimus civis* implicit in this inscription seems to have been common in the honorific epigraphy of the mid-second century, as indicated by figure 5.4.[160] This graph indicates that

[158] Local aristocrats as *optimus*: e.g. *CIL* 5.903, *CIL* 14.373 = *ILS* 6141, *CIL* 10.1783 = *ILS* 5919, *CIL* 11.7265 = *ILS* 6596, *CIL* 11.5712, 11.6061 = *ILS* 6648, *CIL* 11.421 = *ILS* 6662, *CIL* 9.4970 = *ILS* 6559, *CIL* 9.5843 (Italy); *CIL* 12.1853 (Gaul); *CIL* 2.3231, 2²/14.1.796 = 2.4062, 2.4114, 2.4122 (Spain).

[159] *CIL* 2²/5.733 = *CIL* 2.2056.

[160] Data taken from Forbis 1996: 255–6, appendix 7. Note that these are absolute numbers, not percentages, and that the chart does not account for changing frequencies in the total number of

the largest number of datable inscriptions employing the term *optimus* for local aristocrats occurs during the period 138 to 192, when it was very common for emperors, too (at least through 180), and that this number drops precipitously in the third century, again mirroring the sharp drop in the use of the epithet *optimus* to honor emperors. In addition, in the second century the term *optimus* was increasingly reserved for those local notables who were prominent benefactors of the community. In the first century, by contrast, *optimus* was used as a more general term of praise. As Forbis has written, "to many Italians (sc. in the second century) *optimus* became more than a sign of simple respect, but a term especially appropriate for dignifying the efforts of their own local benefactors."[161] The shape of the evidence, then, creates the strong impression that, in the mid-second century, these local aristocrats – at least in Italy, and probably throughout the Roman West – were consciously and explicitly modeling themselves on the Roman emperor, especially in his role as model civic benefactor.[162]

Local aristocrats were formally rewarded with these honorific inscriptions in exchange for services performed on behalf of the municipality, above all for civic benefactions such as paying for a new building or sponsoring an afternoon of gladiatorial combat. These aristocrats, in other words, were prominent benefactors of their local communities. And here, too, these local magnates were copying the emperor, for the emperor was the grand patron at the center of a vast, empire-wide network of patronage, displaying his paradigmatic generosity through the dispensation of gifts and benefactions far and wide. It was this patronal role of the emperor that in part generated the reciprocal exchange of imperial benefactions for local honors, though this exchange mainly operated, as I have suggested, at the level of abstraction. But in the case of these local notables, the reciprocity of honors for benefactions was not abstract at all. They really were spending their own money on their towns, and were being directly rewarded for it through this honorific system of statues and inscriptions.[163] And here we are witnessing a potent convergence of ideology and practice

---

Latin inscriptions. If anything, though, the "Mrozek curve" (see Int. Part II) would only make more pronounced the decline in the use of *optimus* after 193.

[161] Forbis 1996: 24.

[162] See also Nicols 1980: 371 on the second-century convergence of the ideals of the *optimus princeps* and *optimus civis* as model civic benefactors. This finding may be contrasted with Zuiderhoek's assertion that the emperor was not an essential model for the euergetism of local aristocrats in Asia Minor (2009: 110–11).

[163] See briefly Lendon 1997: 84–9, with ample references; see also Rogers 1991. In considering the motivations behind this elaborate system of honors for benefactions, so apparently useful for the legitimation of local aristocratic power (cf. Zuiderhoek 2009: 113–53), we should not lose sight of its irrational elements. See Veyne 1976: 406, emphasizing nothing more than the prestige that

in the second century. The Roman emperor was the most powerful figure in the empire, he was a moral exemplar through his empire-wide generosity and patronage, and he was honored by local communities, as a result of this particular nexus, as *optimus*. Local aristocrats, in turn, were also honored as *optimus*, an honorific title rewarded for their voluntary benefactions to their towns, and one that not only confirmed their power, wealth, and elite status in the local community, but also legitimated it. The economy of this ideal system is elegant in its simplicity, but it depended, critically, on the availability of the emperor as a suitable model for local aristocrats.[164]

It was this ideal system of imperial honorific, local honorific, and local benefaction that crumbled in the early third century with the virtual disappearance of the term *optimus* in honorific inscriptions for the emperor and its effective replacement by the term *dominus*. The term *dominus*, when used as a title in the public sphere, meant "lord" or "master" and, as noted above, was the term used to describe a master in relation to his slaves.[165] The autocratic associations of the term *dominus* made it inappropriate for the "good" Roman emperor, and in fact acceptance or refusal of the title became a conventional marker of imperial character. Modest emperors like Augustus, Tiberius and Claudius all ostentatiously rejected the title *dominus*, while "bad" emperors like Caligula, Domitian, and Commodus insisted on it.[166] Suetonius, for example, in a trenchant and often quoted critique of Domitian's public image, writes, "With the same arrogance, when he issued a rescript in the name of his procurators, he began thus: 'Our Master and God order this to be done.' Hence the custom came about that he was called nothing else even in writing or in conversation."[167] And much of Pliny's panegyric of the emperor Trajan was designed to articulate

---

resulted from civic benefaction (a principal theme of his *magnum opus*); cf. MacMullen 1990 (1980): 13–24, noting the challenge this level of causation presents to historians: "how difficult . . . to give persuasive force to explanations of conduct that rest on nothing but people's alleged feelings" (1990: 23)!

[164] Gordon 1990 examines a similar nexus of imperial exemplarity and local benefaction, with a focus on the emperor's dual paradigmatic role as sacrificer and benefactor. For the mutual benefit that accrued to both emperors and local aristocrats in this idealized relationship, see, e.g., Carrié 1992, emphasizing the language of personal generosity, and Zuiderhoek 2008, exploring the symbolic roles of emperors and local patrons as "father figures."

[165] On the meanings of the term *dominus*, see Dickey 2002: 77–99. For *dominus* as an imperial title, see also Alföldi 1970 (1934/35): 62, 209–13; Béranger 1953: 62–8; Wickert 1954: 2,127–35; Hammond 1957: 45, n. 164.

[166] Emperors refuse title *dominus*: Suet. *Aug.* 53.1, *Tib.* 27; Tac. *Ann.* 2.87 (Tiberius), 12.11 (Claudius). Emperors insist on title *dominus*: Aur. Vict. *Caes.* 13.3 (Caligula); Suet. *Dom.* 13.2; Dio 72(73).20.2 (Commodus).

[167] Suet. *Dom.* 13.2: *pari arrogantia, cum procuratorum suorum nomine formalem dictaret epistulam, sic coepit: dominus et deus noster hoc fieri iubet. unde institutum posthac, ut ne scripto quidem ac sermone cuiusquam appellaretur aliter.*

a clear contrast between the *optimus princeps* Trajan and the hated *dominus* Domitian. As Pliny announces near the beginning of his speech, for example, "Nowhere shall we flatter him as a god, nowhere as a divinity: for we are discussing not a tyrant (*tyrannus*) but a citizen, not a master (*dominus*) but a father."[168] Pliny's casual assimilation of the *dominus* to the *tyrannus* shows how easily the term *dominus* could assume odious connotations, and makes its increasing prominence in honorific inscriptions to the emperor so striking.[169]

The late-second and third-century proliferation of the term *dominus* in honorific inscriptions for the emperor had at least two important consequences. First, this autocratic title had no ethical content, unlike the term *optimus* and many of the other honorific epithets that *dominus* crowded out of these inscriptions. As a result, when local communities represented the emperor to themselves as a *dominus*, they were actively stripping imperial authority of its moral basis. Second, and even more important for our purposes, the title *dominus* had no exemplary or paradigmatic potential whatsoever. In the relationship between emperors and subjects, there could only be one *dominus*. Though the local aristocrats we have been considering could be quite brazen in their public self-representation, they were never, as far as I know, identified in these honorific inscriptions as *dominus*. That title was reserved for the emperor alone. The effective replacement in the late second century of the term *optimus* by the term *dominus* in honorific inscriptions for the emperor, therefore, should have transformed the ideal system of imperial honorific, local honorific, and local patronage that I argued for above. For if the emperor were no longer *optimus*, then local aristocrats would have had little to gain by continuing to call themselves *optimus*. How much resonance could this generic term have retained when no longer associated with the ruler of the empire? And if the ideal emperor implied by the title *optimus* were no longer available for imitation, since the emperor had become an inimitable *dominus*, then local aristocrats would have had less incentive to continue modeling their own

---

[168] Plin. *Pan.* 2.3: *nusquam ut deo, nusquam ut numini blandiamur. non enim de tyranno sed de cive, non de domino sed de parente loquimur*; cf. *Pan.* 7.6: *non enim servulis tuis dominum, ut possis esse contentus quasi necessario herede, sed principem civibus daturus et imperatorem*; *Pan.* 45.3: *scis ut sint diversa natura dominatio et principatus*; *Pan.* 55.7: *sedemque obtinet principis ne sit domino locus.* The theme appears in other authors, too, e.g. Martial (10.72.8: *non est hic dominus sed imperator*).

[169] It should be noted that the vocative *domine* was a standard form of polite address in late-Republican and early-imperial usage, whether between lovers (e.g. Prop. 1.1.21), as a term of affection among family members (e.g. Suet. *Aug.* 53.1), or as an address to social equals and superiors (e.g. Ap. *Met.* 2.14); see Dickey 2002: 81–94, with references. What was often found offensive was the referential use of *dominus* as a title in public contexts – precisely the situation with these honorific inscriptions. For the public/private dichotomy in the use of this term, see discussion in Noreña 2007a: 247–50.

behavior on that of the emperor, and as a result would have curtailed their activities as benefactors of their communities. How much resonance could civic benefaction have retained when the ruler of the Roman world was no longer imagined primarily as a model civic benefactor? The consequence of such a change would have been that the power, wealth, and status of these local notables would no longer be legitimated primarily through civic benefaction and local patronage. And that would have been a change with empire-wide ramifications, since the empire depended on the vitality of its cities and the municipal aristocracies who controlled them.[170]

What is being offered here, then, is a model of public behavior in the Roman West. Now we have to ask if the outcomes predicted by this model really took place. The decline in the use of the honorific epithet *optimus* for local aristocrats, corresponding to the decline in its use for the emperor, has already been discussed. Equally important is the record of civic benefaction in the Roman West over the course of the first two and a half centuries of the empire.[171] Because if the argument offered here about the significance of the shift from emperor as *optimus* to emperor as *dominus* is correct, especially in its impact on local benefaction, then we should be able to observe the effects of this shift in the archaeological record. And the effects of this shift are indeed discernible in the archaeological record of what has traditionally been called "the third-century crisis" in the Roman empire, the fifty-year period between the murder of the emperor Severus Alexander in 235 and the accession of Diocletian in 284.[172] This period was characterized, according to the conventional narrative, by continuous warfare (external and internal), acute political instability, debasement of the coinage, rampant inflation, economic decline, a pervasive sense of "crisis" among contemporaries, and several features that bear directly on the thesis of this chapter, in particular markedly fewer honorific statues for emperors or local patrons, fewer honorific inscriptions, and the near-total absence of evidence, whether archaeological or epigraphic, for new urban development, especially in Italy and the western empire.[173]

It is true that recent work on conditions in the third-century west has modified the traditional picture in a number of ways. Contemporary despair was voiced above all by Christians, it is now recognized, and their cries might have been triggered by imperial persecutions rather than by

---

[170] See above, 11–14, and below, 318–24.

[171] To document that record properly is, of course, far beyond the scope of this chapter.

[172] Useful overviews of the period 235–84 in Potter 2004: 167–280; Drinkwater 2005; Hekster 2008.

[173] On the sharp decrease in traditional honorific inscriptions and statues in the third century, Borg and Witschel 2001; cf. Liebeschuetz 2001: 11–19 for the decrease in epigraphic production in general.

any general feeling of crisis.[174] In terms of the demonstrable signs of urban change in the third century, there is now ample evidence to show that such change varied widely by region.[175] Some areas in the Roman West, such as Gaul, were hit particularly hard by the overlapping problems of the third century, while others, such as North Africa, passed through these years relatively unscathed. And there are now competing interpretations about what these signs of change actually indicate. Several scholars, for example, while acknowledging that the tempo of urban munificence slowed considerably in the third century, have demonstrated that civic benefactions by local patrons did not completely disappear, but were less frequently commemorated by means of honorific inscriptions.[176] Drawing on this finding, Borg and Witschel have argued for a broad shift in elite self-representation in the third-century west, one that valued the re-use of old inscriptions and inscriptions in new media (e.g. mosaics on church floors), and one that favored forms of public display that were not as enduring as honorific statues and inscriptions.[177] The change, it is argued by these and other scholars, was not the product of any "crisis," but instead reflects a deeper change in *mentalité*.

This new work on the third century has provided a fuller and more detailed picture of the complex changes, and continuities, that characterized the years between Severus Alexander and Diocletian. But the revisionist pendulum is in danger of swinging too far, to the point that it can be claimed that during this period the empire was "a remarkably stable system," and that changes in the third-century west "concerned external forms rather than fundamental structures."[178] No amount of scholarly ingenuity, however, can explain away the facts on the ground. There was surely some regional variation in the timing and intensity of the changes associated with the third-century crisis.[179] Moreover, the old notion of a widespread and violent destruction of towns all along the frontiers of the empire in the third century, and the simultaneous near-total abandonment of cities within its Mediterranean core, is not supported by the archaeological and material evidence. And not only did the empire survive, but many of the

---

[174] Thus Strobel 1993, mainly arguing against Alföldy 1974.

[175] Witschel 1999, with very extensive references (for an updated summary of the work, see Witschel 2004); for regional studies, see also Duncan-Jones 2004; Krause and Witschel 2006; Johne *et al.* 2006. The general trend of these works is to minimize or even deny the existence of a "crisis" in the third century. For earlier works arguing against the notion of third- and fourth-century decline in civic benefaction, see Lendon 1997: 85–6, n. 271.

[176] See, e.g., Krause 1987; Lepelley 1997.   [177] Borg and Witschel 2001; cf. Alföldy 1998, esp. 298.

[178] Quotations from Strobel 1993: 347 (*ein bemerkenswert stabiles System*) and Witschel 2004: 257.

[179] For periodization within the years 235–84, see De Blois 2006, with references.

developments we associate with Diocletian and his successors had roots going back to the early empire. But the unassailable fact, and the one most relevant to the argument of this chapter, is that there is almost no evidence for new construction and new development of cities in the third-century west. In this respect the third century differed profoundly from the first two. Indeed, the disappearance of the traditional practices of civic benefaction, monumental construction, and urban development may be seen, in the words of one scholar, as nothing less than "the end of the early empire."[180]

It is in this larger context that we should place the broad shift in identifying the emperor as *optimus* to identifying him as *dominus* in honorific inscriptions. I am not, of course, claiming that this shift caused the third-century "crisis" (however that crisis is defined). But I am suggesting that this terminological revolution undermined the traditional legitimation of local aristocratic power through imitation of the emperor as model benefactor, which in turn discouraged the traditional practice of civic benefaction, effectively sapping western cities of the vitality that had made them so critical to the stability of the empire in the first two centuries. It is ultimately, then, a question of individual motive. Naturally, there existed a whole host of interrelated problems that deterred local aristocrats from voluntarily expending their own material resources on the monumental development of their cities. But if we interpret traditional civic benefaction as having been motivated primarily by the legitimation and reinforcement of aristocratic status that such public displays of generosity brought about, and if that legitimation depended at least in part on the collective representation of the emperor as a model benefactor and paradigm of personal virtue – the *optimus princeps* – then the disappearance of that model, and with it the disappearance of an important source of aristocratic legitimation, should be seen as an important cause of the disappearance of traditional urban munificence in the Roman West. The symbolism of social power mattered.

---

[180] Liebeschuetz 2007: 18, identifying 240–50 as the critical decade of change.

PART III

Power

CHAPTER 6

Ideological unification and social power in the Roman West

IDEOLOGICAL UNIFICATION

The systematic diffusion of Roman imperial ideals and values throughout the Roman West, in several different media of official communications, and the nearly simultaneous replication of these ideals and values in public inscriptions set up in widely dispersed communities – in Italy, in the Mediterranean core of the western empire, and (to a lesser extent) throughout the region's continental peripheries – may appear to provide evidence for the workings of an elaborate propaganda machine, on the one hand, and for widespread acquiescence in the imperial order and loyalty to the person of the emperor, on the other. They do not. While there may have been a propagandistic element to the central diffusion of imperial ideals, the communications infrastructure of the Roman empire was simply incapable of supporting a concerted campaign of political "propaganda" – as that term is normally understood.[1] And while the repeated, public expressions of these ideals may indicate a degree of popular consensus in the Roman imperial order, such displays may equally reflect a strategic calculus on the part of those who authored them that they effectively served their particular interests.[2] What this communication and replication actually indicates, as I argue, is the intensity of ideological unification within the Roman empire, reflecting, in turn, the achievement of a finely calibrated equilibrium between two distinct, but ultimately compatible, sets of interests: those of the central state, and the imperial aristocrats who controlled it, and of the empire's municipalities, and the local aristocrats who controlled them.

"Ideology" and "ideological unification" are notoriously slippery concepts.[3] "Roman imperial ideology," as it has been employed in this

---

[1] See chapter 1, 15–18 (propaganda), and chapter 4, 195–6, 239–40 (communications infrastructure).
[2] For the logic of such displays, see chapter 5, 270–6; further discussion below, 318–20.
[3] What follows is a modest attempt to define my usage of these terms in the context of this book's main argument.

study, refers to the more or less coherent set of ideals and values, associated both with the empire and with the emperor – the conflation inherent in the term "imperial" is significant – that served, ultimately, to legitimate the larger configuration of power that we call "the Roman empire." This working definition is not meant to imply that only ruling groups within the Roman empire possessed ideologies, nor does it require an *a priori* judgment about either the truth or the normative value of the claims made by the ideals we have been considering.[4] In both epistemological and normative terms, that is, this definition of ideology is intended to be neutral, designed simply to facilitate the analysis of how, specifically, a set of ideas could reinforce and even strengthen a particular configuration of power – the main problem addressed in this chapter.

In the study of empires, ideology has normally been seen to serve three principal functions: the justification and, in particular, the motivation for imperial conquest and expansion; the fostering of cohesion within key sectors of imperial societies, especially aristocracies; and the legitimation of the dramatically unequal distributions of wealth, status, and power characteristic of empires.[5] Ideology appears to have served all three functions in the Roman empire. It has long been recognized, for example, that the values of militarism, conquest, and triumph were cherished by the Roman elite, and that the aristocratic association and identification with these imperialist ideals helps to explain the aggressive expansion of the Roman state from the mid-Republic through the Augustan age.[6] While the ideals of militarism and expansionism influenced the elites of other states in the ancient Mediterranean world, too, the collective embrace of this ethos seems to have been particularly pronounced in the Roman case – perfectly captured in Anchises' declaration to Aeneas that Rome's unique calling was "to rule peoples," "impose peace," "spare the meek" and "crush the proud."[7]

Our focus, however, has been on the role played by ideology in fostering aristocratic cohesion and in legitimating an unequal distribution of

---

[4] By the same token, the definition does not prevent us from making such judgments.

[5] Bibliography on these topics is vast. Convenient overviews and discussions, with references, in Sinopoli 1994: 167–8; Alcock and Morrison 2001; Mann 2006: 344–50; Goldstone and Haldon 2009: 10–15.

[6] Militarism and aristocratic ideology in Republican Rome: Harris 1979: 10–41; Rosenstein 2006. For the connection between imperialist ideals and imperial expansion in the Augustan period, Brunt 1990 (1963): 96–109; 1990 (1978): 288–323, 506–11; 1990: 433–80 is fundamental; cf. Gruen 1996. For some hints of doubt or anxiety about imperialism in (and around) the ceremony of the triumph itself, see also Beard 2007: 135–42, 177–8.

[7] Militarism and expansionism not unique to Rome: Eckstein 2006. Verg. *Aen.* 6.851–3: *tu regere imperio populos, Romane, memento | hae tibi erunt artes, pacique imponere morem | parcere subiectis et debellare superbos.*

power. In terms of promoting cohesion within specific segments of society, we may say that specific ideals and values help to define the conceptual and normative framework, or structure, within which social practice takes place – even as that practice may ultimately transform the structure itself.[8] And it is when different groups and collectivities within a given polity can be shown to subscribe to the same ideals and values that we can speak of the "ideological unification" of those groups. It should be emphasized that such groups and the individuals within them can actively promote these ideals and values, declare their allegiance to them – and even be influenced by them – without actively believing in them. Ideological unification, in other words, does not necessarily imply widespread belief in the normative claims implied by a set of ideals and values, though such belief may of course arise, with varying degrees of social depth and emotional intensity.

The connection between ideological unification and the reinforcement of a particular social and political order is more complex. One way to approach this problem is to consider what this type of ideological unification entailed not just for the layered aristocracies of the Roman world, but for the Roman empire as a whole. If nothing else, the public representation and idealization of the emperor in broadly similar terms, both at the center and throughout the periphery, must have provided a measure of "symbolic glue" for the empire, a necessary condition for the long-term maintenance of such an immense and conspicuously diverse political system.[9] The importance of such "symbolic glue" is now widely recognized, both for the Roman empire in particular and for pre-modern empires in general.[10] But how far down the social spectrum did this ideological unification really go? The focus thus far has been on the top of the empire's social and political hierarchy, and on its collective representations of the ideal Roman emperor, but it will be worthwhile to pause for a moment to consider the depth to which these imperial ideals and values might have penetrated provincial societies.

One potential constraint on such penetration was illiteracy. The imperial ideals and values that appeared on coins and in inscriptions were mainly

---

[8] Sewell 2005 (1992): 124–51 provides an exceptionally lucid analysis, with abundant references, of this dialectic.

[9] For the size and internal diversity of the empire, see above, 2–5.

[10] For the Roman empire's partial dependence on some form of "symbolic glue" in order to maintain its integrity over the long term, see, e.g., Hopkins 1978: 197–242 (imperial cult); Gordon 1990 (sacrifice, euergetism, and religious authority). The theme is prominent in Alcock *et al.* 2001 (cf. Alcock and Morrison 2001: 281), with chapters exploring different aspects of symbolic and ideological unification in the contexts of the Achaemenid empire, the Roman empire, the Inca empire, the Spanish colonial empire in the Americas, and the imperial systems of ancient Nubia and South Asia.

expressed in words, after all, and if literacy rates in the Roman world were anywhere near as low as Harris has suggested – no higher than 5–10 percent in the western provinces during our period – then very few provincials can have actively assimilated these ideals for themselves.[11] We may quibble with Harris' methods and conclusions, but there is a real problem here, especially given the fact that most of the honorific terminology for the emperor that appeared in inscriptions was embedded within sometimes lengthy texts that would have required the active decision on the part of passersby to stop and read. It is difficult to imagine anyone doing this on a regular basis, much less the rural peasantry that made up the bulk of the empire's population.

In reminding ourselves of the empire's rural peasants, and distinguishing them from the inhabitants of urban centers, we should also recall the over-whelmingly public nature of those symbols that expressed different aspects of imperial ideology – another potential constraint on social penetration. Indeed, one of the most striking features of the evidence for the diffusion of imperial ideals and values is the near-total concentration of these symbols in the public sphere.[12] Surviving depictions of the emperor on small-scale media, such as precious gems, medallions, miscellaneous items of jewelry, clay lamps, and bronze mirrors, and the discovery of imperial portraits and images in several domestic contexts, are useful reminders that impe-rial imagery was not wholly absent from private and domestic contexts.[13] Nevertheless, the balance of evidence is heavily tilted towards the public end of the public/private spectrum.[14] That this imbalance is not simply a matter of the differential survival of different types of evidence is suggested by the fact that, despite the widespread dissemination of imperial worship throughout the empire, not a single votive inscription unambiguously ded-icated to a living emperor has ever been found.[15] The public rituals of the imperial cult may have imbued the emperor with an aura of divinity, but for private assistance the emperor's subjects turned to other gods.

---

[11] Harris 1989: 175–284 on the Roman empire, esp. 272 for the percentage cited in the text above.

[12] See above, 200–18.

[13] Depictions of the emperor on small-scale media: 208–10. Imperial portraits in domestic contexts: 203, n. 45. That imperial imagery might have been perfectly common in domestic contexts is suggested by Price 1984: 117–21 and by Gradel 2002: 198–212.

[14] Even Zanker, who has argued for the spontaneous reproduction in the private sphere of styles and motifs from the official art of the Augustan period (see below, n. 30), has drawn attention to "the subordinate role that the political themes associated with the myth of the emperor played in the imagery of private homes and graves" in and around Pompeii (1998: 24).

[15] A point repeatedly made by A. D. Nock and confirmed by Fishwick 1990 (with 121, nn. 1–2 for citations of Nock's discussions of the issue); cf. Veyne 1976: 561–3.

Despite such constraints, there are a few reasons to believe that imperial ideals and values could achieve some currency beneath the level of the social and political elite. First, and most important, these ideals were not only expressed through words, but were also represented by images. An imperial coin type, for example, was a composite of image and text, as was an imperial statue, comprising, as it usually did, a visual representation of the emperor together with an inscribed statue base. Indeed, as we have seen, some of the most important work of signification in these material expressions of imperial ideology was performed by the visual images, which could be understood on their own terms and without reference to the accompanying texts. At least partial understanding of the messages conveyed by coins, statues, and related media, in other words, could be achieved with a bare minimum of "visual literacy." And this must have been relatively high in the Roman empire, which we may reasonably infer from the omnipresence of public images in everyday life (at least in urban settings).[16]

Another feature of this mode of communications that will have encouraged broad understanding and assimilation was the sheer, almost ceaseless repetition, through different media and in different contexts, of the same few ideals and values, again and again and again. In fact, it was the very dullness and monotony of this repetition that will have maximized the potential impact of these ideals, effectively translating these social constructs into ideas that could be seen as self-evident and natural. In this respect, it was not the most dramatic and spectacular expressions of imperial ideology that were most effective in promoting and naturalizing its normative claims, but rather the most mundane and even banal ones.[17] That these ideas were regularly conveyed by everyday material objects, especially coins, must have facilitated this process. This was an ideology made manifest.

The multi-stage process by which imperial ideals and values were diffused also bears on the question of social penetration. Here we can take our cue from some work on modern communications systems. In their study of mass communications in the modern world, for example, Katz and Lazarsfeld showed that advertising campaigns were not necessarily more

---

[16] The prominence of public images in ancient Mediterranean cultures is examined in a set of illuminating case studies in Hölscher forthcoming; for the symbolic dimension of ancient writing, and its frequent collocation with imagery, see also Woolf 2000: 895–7.

[17] Naturalization, of course, is a defining feature of most successful ideologies – ideology as "common sense" (cf. Eagleton 1991: 58–61, tracing the idea back to Marx and Engels) – and has been the object of much work in social theory, of which the most influential has surely been Bourdieu's notion of *doxa*, "the universe of the undiscussed," i.e., the general condition in which the social world appears as self-evident, to be contrasted with the sphere of opinion, the "universe of discourse," which is recognized as subjective and therefore open to debate (1977: 159–97).

effective when repeated endlessly, but instead achieved the best results when the messages seemed to come not from a distant and unknown source, but rather from persons of local influence and authority, whose opinions were most valued by members of local communities.[18] This observation highlights the critical importance of the local aristocratic replication of imperial ideals, since most provincial subjects, we might imagine, would be more influenced by local authorities than by distant and unseen ones. Studies of the temporal and spatial diffusion of various phenomena, including ideas, support this interpretation. These studies suggest that the spread of ideas tends to begin slowly, to accelerate to a point of "saturation," and then to level off, while in spatial terms, the degree of assimilation to these ideas tends to be a function of distance from the source(s) of information.[19] In general, this is a plausible model of communications that fits both the temporal diffusion of imperial ideals by means of coins and other official media – not very well suited to short-term, topical messaging, as we have seen, but ideally suited to the slow and steady dispersal of ideals – and the spatial diffusion of those ideals, with marked concentrations of coins and inscriptions in and around urban agglomerations and military installations.[20]

One clue that imperial ideology might have penetrated provincial societies relatively deeply is furnished by the many humble, votive dedications to various "divine qualities" associated with the emperor, offered by members of the non-ruling classes, including women and freedpersons.[21] It appears that the most common object of such dedications was Victoria Augusta – not just the abstract quality of Victory, that is, but the more ideologically charged concept of Augustan Victory.[22] Typical is this small altar from the territory of the Vocontii in the province of Gallia Narbonensis:

Victoriae | Aug(ustae) | Cornelia | Decumina | v(otum) s(oluit) l(ibens) m(erito).

Cornelia Decumina fulfilled her vow to Victoria Augusta, willingly and deservedly.[23]

Similar votive offerings to Victoria Augusta abound in the western provinces, from Lusitania and Gaul to Noricum and Pannonia Superior,

---

[18] Katz and Lazarsfeld 1955.   [19] Morrill 1970; Brown 1986.
[20] The model is also a reasonable fit with what we know about the diffusion of other phenomena in the Roman world, such as law (cf. Crawford 1988) and technology (Greene 1992; Wilson 2002, esp. 9–15 on the diffusion of the water mill).
[21] The term "divine qualities" is borrowed from Clark 2007 (discussed at 26–7). For what follows, see the useful collection of evidence in Fears 1981a: 743–4, 1981b: 931–6; for Fortuna, see also Kajanto 1981: 517–18.
[22] See above, 159–63.   [23] *CIL* 12.1707.

as well as the Italian peninsula, dedicated not by imperial officials or local magistrates, but by private persons, and not infrequently in extra-urban contexts.[24] It seems rather unlikely that the widespread proliferation of such votives to Victoria Augusta is unrelated to the long-term emphasis on this very ideal by the imperial regime. These dedications were not, however, an isolated phenomenon. Almost as common were votive offerings to Fortuna Augusta. This plain altar from Risingham in the province of Britannia may be taken as representative of such dedications:

Fortunae | Aug(ustae) | Ael(ia) | Proculina | v(otum) s(oluit).

Aelia Proculina fulfilled her vow to Fortuna Augusta.[25]

Again, similar vows to Fortuna Augusta have been found at widely scattered spots throughout the western provinces.[26] Other objects of such votive offerings include Concordia Augusta, Salus Augusta, Virtus Augusta, Pietas Augusta, Pax Augusta, and Aequitas Augusta – all of them closely associated with the emperor, and all, as we have seen, widely advertised on official media of communications, including imperial coins.[27] It bears repeating that in making such vows, the dedicators of these objects were celebrating not just Harmony, Health, and Peace etc., but *Augustan* Harmony, *Augustan* Health, and *Augustan* Peace. The notional connection between these ideals and the figure of the emperor was not only recognized, that is, but actively and spontaneously replicated. These simple votives, distributed across the Roman West, provide a tantalizing glimpse of a wider world of religious practice beneath the level of the social and political elite, and show that some of the most characteristic expressions of Roman imperial ideology could be found here, too.

Another perspective on this wider world is provided by unofficial works of art, in various small-scale media, that represented different imperial ideals, almost always personified as female figures. A particularly striking

---

[24] E.g. *CIL* 12.1537 (territory of the Vocontii, Gallia Narbonensis); *CIL* 2.457 (territory of the Igaeditani, Lusitania), 927 (Caesarobriga, Lusitania); *CIL* 3.5612 (valley between Iuvavum and Ovilava, Noricum), 10766 (Emona, Pannonia Superior), 11745 (valley between Leibnitz and Bruck, Noricum), 11760 (Iuvavum, Noricum). Italian examples: e.g. *CIL* 5.4915 (Trumplini), 4986 (Riva), 7695 (Augusta Bagiennorum), 7831 (Forum Germanorum), 7643 (Ager Saluzzensis).

[25] *RIB* 1211.

[26] E.g. *CIL* 3.1014 (Apulum, Dacia), 13186 (Delminium, Dacia); *CIL* 13.1539 (Cadurci, Aquitania); *CIL* 8.16522 (Theveste, Africa Proconsularis), 18216 (Civitas Lambaesis, Numidia), 18892 (Thibilis, Numidia).

[27] Concordia Augusta: 254, n. 34. Salus Augusta: e.g. *AE* 1962.74, on a small bronze bull (Mantanegra, Lusitania). Virtus Augusta: e.g. *RIB* 845 (Netherhall, Britannia). Pietas Augusta: e.g. *CIL* 2.332, 396, 1474 (Spanish provinces). Pax Augusta: 251–2. Aequitas Augusta: e.g. *CIL* 8.26487, coupled with Mercury (Thugga, Numidia).

Illustration 6.1 Depiction of Victory on a carnelian intaglio (second-fourth century AD)

feature of such representations is their high degree of iconographic fidelity to the official versions. Consider, for example, visual representations of Victoria in such unofficial artworks. Such representations have been found in a very wide range of media, including intaglios (illustration 6.1), clay lamps (illustration 6.2), statuettes made of marble, limestone, and bronze (illustration 6.3), works of bronze applique, marble urns, wall paintings, and cameos, to name only a few.[28] Such artifacts create the impression that Victoria was rather commonplace in private contexts – and almost always represented in more or less the same manner as on state reliefs, imperial coins, and other official media. So, too, Fortuna, also represented visually in many different media (illustrations 6.4–5), and again, almost always in harmony with official iconographic conventions.[29] Though we cannot be sure about the different meanings with which such images were invested, we can at least say with some confidence that visual representations of ideals and values that had come to be closely associated with the Roman emperor were nearly ubiquitous in the private and domestic sphere.[30]

---

[28] Intaglios: *LIMC* 8.2, s.v. "Victoria," nos. 19, 21, 73, 94, 126, 144, 167, 181, 190; clay lamps: nos. 33, 68, 69 (handle), 92, 169b; statuettes: nos. 58, 71, 116; bronze applique: nos. 27, 158; marble urns: no. 62; cameos: nos. 88, 102, 367; wall painting: no. 278. This is only a small selection of the different media illustrated in the plates of *LIMC*.

[29] *LIMC* 8.2.90–109; for the prominence of Fortuna in the private sphere, see 146, nn. 154–5.

[30] For attempts to document this proposition with reference to a single emperor, see Hölscher 1984: 20–32 and Zanker 1988a: 265–95, both focusing on the Augustan period.

Illustration 6.2 Depiction of Victory on a clay lamp (first century AD)

Illustration 6.3 Bronze statuette of Victory carrying a shield with legend CAIS. SACERD (second-third century AD)

Illustration 6.4 Depiction of Fortuna on a wall painting from Pompeii (second half of first century AD)

This evidence from votive inscriptions and small-scale artworks sheds some useful light on the social depth to which imperial ideology might have penetrated, but the major problem with these categories of evidence is that they can rarely be dated with any precision – educated guesses within a given

Illustration 6.5 Depiction of Fortuna on a mosaic from Britannia (Lincolnshire)

century or two are the norm.[31] As a result, it is impossible to document influence from any one source on the expression or representation of this or that concept. Of course it can always be argued, in a general way, that there existed a substantial overlap in representation between the official and the unofficial, the central and the peripheral, but no way to show that the former was influencing the latter in any chronologically meaningful manner. And for the main thesis of this book, which depends in large measure on quantification and correspondence, such chronological precision is essential. Only by means of precisely dated imperial coins and precisely dated inscriptions with imperial titulature, in fact, has it been possible to build up my larger argument about ideas, communications, and power in the Roman empire.

Despite this critical problem of interpretation, this evidence is illuminating for the question of ideological diffusion. Indeed, these more humble inscriptions and small-scale, private objects, together with the official media of communications and public expressions of imperial ideals and values examined in previous chapters, suggest the possibility of a broad and potentially deep ideological penetration of the provinces, centered mainly on the figure of the Roman emperor and the ideals associated with imperial rulership. This cumulative evidence also reveals a sufficient quantity of the mass-produced imperial symbols necessary for those who encountered

---

[31] In the case of inscriptions, the main criterion for dating (in the absence of explicit chronological markers) is usually orthography, but this is a rather blunt tool, and in any case the editors of the first edition of *CIL* often chose to omit proposed dates altogether. Individual works of art can be dated by a wider range of criteria, especially style and material, and sometimes burial context, but these criteria rarely permit chronological resolution finer than a quarter century. Even in a reference work as comprehensive as *LIMC*, furthermore, many items are left undated.

them to be able to imagine their place within an enormous, but apparently unified, political and cultural system. And this imagination was necessary, in a sense, because the Roman empire, like all large-scale polities, was far too big to be anything but imagined as a unified whole. Many historians of the empire now recognize this, and as a result it has become conventional to refer to the Roman empire, following Anderson's much-cited phrase, as an "imagined community."[32]

Similarities between the Roman empire and the modern nations examined by Anderson are indeed suggestive, but the analogy is probably more misleading than helpful. For what seems to have gone unremarked by Roman historians who cite Anderson is the very serious mismatch between "empire" and "community."[33] Acknowledging that a nation may be riven by inequalities and exploitation, Anderson nevertheless insists that "the nation is always conceived as a deep, horizontal comradeship," and should therefore be treated analytically as a "community."[34] What was being imagined in the Roman empire, however, was very far from being a community, much less a "horizontal comradeship." The empire was an order, and a particularly steep and stratified one at that – and that is exactly how it was imagined. The hierarchical arrays of statues at Cuicul and elsewhere, and the strict, class-based seating arrangements at the big venues of public entertainment, show this quite conclusively.[35]

This does not mean that culture and the collective imagination were any less significant for the socio-political structure of the Roman empire than they were for that of late-eighteenth century nation-states. But they functioned in a very different manner, as Gellner's work on complex agrarian societies and modern industrial nations shows. For Gellner, the fundamental difference between the two lies in the social distribution of high culture. Whereas modern nationalism, according to Gellner, is defined by the spread of high culture throughout the whole of society, enabled by the mass education provided by the state and the mass literacy required by the needs of capitalist economies, in "agro-literate polities" such as the Roman empire, high culture is confined to the ruling class(es). In the modern industrial nation, state and culture are inextricably linked, and individual members are therefore anonymous and functionally "interchangeable." In agrarian societies, by contrast, individuals belong either to a narrow,

---

[32] Anderson 1991 (1st edn. 1983). Roman empire as "imagined community": e.g. Habinek 1998: 44–5; Beard, North, and Price 1998: 214; Ando 2000: 8; Potter 2004: xii.
[33] See also Laclau 2003, noting some conceptual fuzziness in Anderson's usage of the term "community."
[34] Anderson 1991: 7.
[35] Arrays of statues: 203, 273–5. Seating arrangements: 273, n. 102.

horizontal ruling class, ideologically unified by its monopoly on high culture, or to the "laterally insulated" majority of direct agricultural producers, detached from high culture and often culturally disconnected even from adjacent groups of agricultural producers.[36] Though there was often social stratification within the ruling class itself, the defining cleavage in agrarian societies was between a narrow ruling class and a wide mass of peasants, and this cleavage was particularly marked, so the argument goes, by differential access to high culture.

Gellner's sketches of agrarian and industrial societies should be understood as ideal types, of course, and not as historical descriptions. His account of the typical agro-literate polity, for example, is not perfectly consistent with the Roman empire, where a shared imperial culture appears to have penetrated a bit further down the social pyramid than his model would predict. But Gellner's core insight into the function of high culture in complex agrarian societies is a useful corrective to the conceptualization of the Roman empire as a "community," reminding us that culture usually serves as an instrument of social control in those configurations of power in which access to high culture was so dramatically unequal. And so it was in the Roman empire, where the collective production of a symbolic system centered on the figure of the emperor manifestly served the interests of those who produced it, the central state and local aristocrats. For the upper-tier aristocrats who controlled the central state, this symbolic system universalized and naturalized the supreme authority of the state's principal symbol, the emperor. For the lower-tier aristocrats who controlled the empire's municipalities, this system not only helped to naturalize a social and political order from which they themselves had secured a privileged position, but also provided a useful vehicle for class cohesion and social differentiation – it was the aristocrats, after all, and not the masses, who were the ones expending their own resources on the production of such symbols, especially imperial statues and the monumental complexes constructed in connection with the imperial cult.

Roman imperial ideals and values were spread far and wide, then, and ideological penetration of the provinces might have reached beneath the level of the social and political elite, but for the central argument of

---

[36] The changing social distribution of high culture from the agrarian to the industrial world is the central theme of Gellner 1983. For the notion of individual "interchangeability" in modern nations, essential both for the industrial division of labor and for social cohesion, see also Gellner 1987; cf. Anderson 1991: 55–6. Culture and society in the agrarian world are discussed in Gellner 1983: 8–18, with fig. 1; 1987: 13–16; for discussion of cultural patterning, social organization, and social hierarchy in complex agrarian societies, see also Crone 1989, esp. 81–122.

this book, it does not really matter whether or not the masses of the empire "bought in" to the normative claims of the central state. This is not because the beliefs of those excluded from the networks of power are intrinsically unimportant or unworthy of study, but because the masses, caught up in power structures controlled by others, and therefore incapable of collective action, could not bring about social or political change on their own.[37] What was essential was that those who were in control of these structures were ideologically unified. And the collective representation and idealization of the figure of the Roman emperor, both at Rome and throughout the provinces, in official and unofficial media alike – in the same terms, at the same times, but in very different places – indicates that the dispersed aristocracies of the Roman world, both central and local, had indeed achieved a high degree of ideological unification. Whether such unification was a necessary condition for the long-term maintenance and reproduction of this particular configuration of power is the question to which we now turn.

IDEALS, IDEOLOGIES, INSTITUTIONS, AND PRACTICES

In assessing the impact of this ideological unification, it is necessary to take seriously the specific ideas upon which it was based. This is not quite as obvious as it sounds. Indeed, even in the works of Anderson and Gellner – focused on the role of culture and ideas in the formation of large-scale political systems – there is not much space given to analysis of the ideas themselves.[38] By now it should be clear that for the central thesis of this book, the underlying ideas that made up what we call "Roman imperial ideology" were in fact critical. For the figure of the emperor was not some dull or static symbol of absolute power, but a complex and multivalent symbol that could be invested with many different meanings, some of

---

[37] As Mann puts it, the failure of the masses to revolt is not due to "value consensus," but because they are, in practice, "organizationally outflanked" (1986: 7); cf. Crone 1989: 41–2 on logistical constraints to the collective action of the masses as a key feature of pre-industrial societies. The culture of loyalism that bulks so large in Ando's theory of imperial ideology and "provincial loyalty" (2000), even if true, has no bearing on the thesis argued here.

[38] This interpretive dichotomy is especially patent in Gellner's chapter on nationalist ideas (1983: 123–36), where he writes that nationalist "thinkers did not really make much difference," and that "their precise doctrines are hardly worth analyzing" (124). It is also partially true of Anderson 1991, a work sometimes criticized for not paying enough attention to what was actually written in the novels that bulk so large in his theory (cf. Culler 2003). In general on the downgrading of ideas in the recent scholarship on state formation and nationalism, see Steinmetz 1999b; for an exception to the trend, see Gorski 2006 (a critique of Mann 1986–93, drawing on his own earlier work on the constitutive role of Calvinist doctrine in European state-formation in the early modern period).

which, as I have argued, had a transformative impact on configurations of power within the empire.

The quantitative approach employed in this study has provided a new perspective on the ideas and meanings attached to the figure of the emperor, allowing us to compare the commonness or rarity of imperial ideals and values in numerical terms, and to determine, empirically, how these frequencies changed over time. From the imperial coinage in particular it has been possible to measure these frequencies quite precisely. Several findings stand out. Personification, which gave concrete expression to a wide range of abstract ideas, was the major mode of representation.[39] Among the various personifications depicted on the imperial coinage, the most common categories were virtues, the personal qualities of the emperor himself, and benefits, the advertised advantages of empire and monarchy. For the period 69–235, five virtues predominated: *aequitas, pietas, liberalitas, virtus,* and *providentia*.[40] Among benefit types, the most common during our period were *victoria, felicitas, fortuna, pax, concordia,* and *salus*.[41] At no time were these five virtues or six benefits formally packaged together as an official set of ideals, nor do they correspond precisely to any other collection of virtues or benefits, but they were the most emphasized concepts on the most pervasive medium of communications available to the central state, and should therefore be seen as the core ideals and values of the Roman emperor from Vespasian to Severus Alexander.

Identifying the most common ideals and values is an important step in its own right, but it is only a first step. It is also vital, as I hope to have shown, to understand what these concepts actually stood for, and to investigate how they worked together as constituent parts of a larger semiotic and ideological system. Much of the discussion in chapters 2 and 3 focused on these issues. The two main conclusions about the virtues were, first, that together they effectively embraced the military, religious, material, and dynastic strands of Roman imperial ideology – this was the underlying logic of this set of virtues – and second, that unlike the Platonic virtues, which were mainly "dispositional" in nature, denoting internal qualities, these virtues were mainly "enacted," deriving their particular resonance from their outward manifestation in the public sphere.[42] With respect to the benefits, emphasis was placed on the way in which a wide range of concrete benefactions, favorable conditions, and even

---

[39] Cf. Introduction to Part 1, with table Int. 1.3.
[40] Chapter 2, with tables 2.1–2 for the percentages, and appendices 5 and 7 for the raw data and tabulations.
[41] Chapter 3, with tables 3.1–2, and appendices 6 and 8.　　[42] Chapter 2, 99–100.

desirable states of mind was ascribed to the person of the emperor – the essence of *le style monarchique* – and on the key role of numismatic collocations and iconographic conventions in creating notional associations between seemingly different ideas, especially military conquest, material abundance, and personal happiness. Such associations were particularly significant, in ideological terms, in helping to magnify and universalize the message of those particular benefits that were enjoyed, in reality, by narrow subsets of the empire's population.[43] In considering these two sets of core ideals together, what really stands out is their joint emphasis on, and characteristic blending of, the spheres of personal ethics and material benefaction. This conceptual convergence of ethics and benefaction was the defining feature of Roman imperial ideology during the high empire.

The ideals and values associated with the Roman emperor were quite dynamic, then, their potency further distinguished by the imposing weight of an intellectual tradition of political thought that went back to the most authoritative thinkers of the classical Greek period. In fact, it is in the very breadth and diversity of that intellectual tradition, and in the profusion of different virtues and benefits claimed on behalf of rulers in the ancient Mediterranean world, that we can perceive the historical distinctiveness and specificity of the particular constellation of ideals and values ascribed to the emperor. A full understanding of exactly how the specific virtues and benefits analyzed in chapters 2 and 3 happened to coalesce in the high empire as the definitive set of ideals associated with the emperor is probably beyond the reach of our evidence, but a big part of the explanation must lie in the social and institutional context in which these virtues and benefits, and the underlying nexus of ethical value and material benefaction they expressed, was first articulated. The key site within this context, as I suggested above, was the imperial court.[44]

It is instructive to compare the Roman imperial court with some of the other social and institutional contexts in antiquity within which monarchic ideals developed. In the Greek city-states of the classical period, as we have seen, the formulation of monarchic ideals was mostly theoretical in nature, evolving in tandem with the rise of speculative thinking and the diversification of literary genres, especially encomiastic biography, but was eventually shaped at least in part by the appearance of "big men" on the periphery of the classical Greek heartland. The situation in Republican Rome was analogous, as a number of aristocratic writers, especially Cicero, elaborated a theoretical vocabulary for ideal rulership that was

---

[43] Chapter 3, 175–6.   [44] Chapter 4, 240.

heavily influenced by classical Greek political thought, but that also came to be structured, at least in the case of Cicero, by the extraordinary careers of the political "dynasts" of the late Republic.[45] So the "city-state mode" in the development of monarchic ideals did not, in either classical Greece or Republican Rome, share much in common with the conceptualization and valuation of such ideals in the Roman imperial court, mainly because in the Roman imperial case, this process, which we may call "the Roman imperial mode," was driven by a regime in which political power was actually concentrated in, and represented by, the figure of a ruling monarch.

At first glance, the royal courts of the Hellenistic kingdoms might seem to have functioned in a manner like the Roman imperial court in the generation and communication of particular monarchic ideals, but the social and political context in which the Hellenistic courts operated was structurally quite different. For in the Hellenistic world, ideologies of rulership seem to have arisen through a sort of dialectic between kings and their inner circles, on the one hand, and the local communities of their kingdoms, on the other. The dialogic nature of this process is evident in the different sorts of values stressed by the two sets of actors. Whereas the royal courts in general promoted the ideals of militarism, conquest, and divine authority, the local communities – especially those of the Greek world – tended to stress the kings' virtues and civic benefactions. The symbolic interactions between kings and cities were regular, intense, and dynamic, to be sure, and Hellenistic royal ideology was clearly informed by both monarchs and communities, but the royal court nevertheless remained an institution apart, socially and administratively autonomous from the subject population over which it ruled.[46] It was this dialectical process that characterized the "Hellenistic mode" in the development of monarchic ideals and that distinguishes it from the "Roman imperial mode." For a defining feature of the Roman imperial court during our period is that it was deeply embedded within an aristocratic society in which the articulation and valuation of monarchic ideals was the result not of a dialectical process between discrete sets of actors (kings and cities), but rather of a collective one involving emperors themselves and their families, advisors, and aristocratic *amici*.[47] This does not mean that local communities in the Roman empire did not participate

---

[45] See discussion above, 38–41 (classical Greek city states), 46–9 (Republican Rome).

[46] See above, 43–5; cf. Herman 1997 for Hellenistic court society.

[47] The social embeddedness of the Roman imperial court is rightly stressed by Wallace-Hadrill 1996. Indeed, nowhere is Kautsky's claim (1982: 235–7) that a monarchy is part of an aristocracy more true than in the case of the Roman empire; but see also Paterson 2007 on the changing position of the emperor within the world of the imperial court in the first two centuries AD.

in the process of expressing and publicizing imperial ideals, which they clearly did, but that in so doing, they were never engaged in a true dialogue with the imperial regime. In other words, these local communities actively celebrated a number of imperial ideals, spontaneously and for their own purposes, but the ideals themselves always came from the top and the center.

In associating the imperial court with the "top" and the "center," and identifying it as the key site in which different sets of imperial ideals first coalesced as "official" ideals, I do not mean to suggest that such ideals emanated from the imperial regime itself, narrowly defined. Indeed, in terms of personnel the imperial court must have been very fluid. Structurally, however, it was quite stable, functioning as a more or less permanent bridge between the imperial regime and the Roman aristocracy, and indeed facilitating the social merger of the two groups. In this respect, it is misleading to speak of "imperial" and "senatorial" ideals for the Roman emperor, since both tended to be produced by the same sets of actors. In the later Roman empire, by contrast, the court became ever more detached from the senatorial aristocracy.[48] As a result, the public image of late Roman emperors diverged markedly from what had prevailed in the first two centuries AD. No longer a civilian *princeps* administering his realm in a beneficent manner, the emperor had become a distant, god-like, aggressively militaristic, and mostly terrifying autocrat.[49] So an important element in the historical distinctiveness of the high Roman empire was the extent to which the imperial court was embedded within aristocratic society, a quasi-institutional configuration of social interaction in which the high valuation of personal ethics and material benefaction, and the particular ideas that expressed this nexus – the virtues and benefits examined in chapters 2 and 3 – first coalesced and became "official."[50]

Imperial ideals not only drew on the authority of a Greek intellectual tradition, then, but also came to be identified as definitive within a highly influential social and institutional context. But ideas cannot do anything

---

[48] Smith 2007.

[49] For the public image of the emperor in the later empire, see e.g. Alföldi 1970 (1934–5), on Roman monarchic representation in general, but drawing in particular on late-antique sources; Kelly 1998: 139–50; Kolb 2001. In general on late-Roman emperors, see also Demandt 1989: 212–31; Matthews 1989: 231–52.

[50] The relationship between the imperial court, aristocratic society, and an ideology of personal ethics and material benefaction was not, of course, automatic. Though the royal courts of early modern Europe were similarly embedded within their respective aristocratic societies, for example, the emphasis within them was not on virtue and moral value, but rather on etiquette and social courtesy. See the classic treatment in Elias 1983 (1969).

by themselves; they have no independent agency.[51] In order to assess their impact, it has been necessary to examine by whom, by what means, and how effectively they were communicated. And it was precisely in analyzing the communications infrastructure within which imperial ideals and values circulated that we have been able to begin sorting out the different uses to which these ideas were being put not only during the period 69–235 as a whole, but also during different phases within it. Examination of the various media of representation and the specific mechanisms by which these ideals were communicated revealed a multiplicity of actors involved in the collective process of idealizing the emperor.[52] The simultaneous participation of so many different actors – individual and collective, official and unofficial, central and local, all acting in accordance with their own perceived interests – rules out any analysis of the process as a whole in terms of propaganda or autocratic monopolization of media and communications. Analyzing the circulation of imperial ideals in diachronic terms, with reference both to the official dissemination of these ideals and to the local, unofficial response to them, indicated several important chronological shifts within the period 69–235. The most important of these shifts, by far, and the only one that constitutes a true ideological rupture, was the emergence, in the last third of our period, of a more militaristic and despotic imperial image, expressed above all by the term *dominus*, that effectively replaced the "ethical-benefactor" paradigm that had characterized most of the second century AD.[53]

Consideration of the multiplicity of actors involved in the public expression of imperial ideals and values, together with careful attention to chronological patterns in these forms of expression, highlights a major ideological convergence between the reigns of Trajan and Marcus Aurelius (AD 98–180). For it was during this period that the main vehicles of imperial communications, especially coins and official inscriptions – the latter, as we have seen, set up by a wide range of authors – and the main forms of local response to this central dissemination of ideals, especially honorific dedications to the emperor, were all in harmony in idealizing the emperor as a model of human virtues and as an exemplary benefactor for the empire as a whole. This convergence was documented both by a series of chronologically and lexically precise correspondences, and by a broader semantic and ideological overlap, between official and unofficial media. It is unlikely

---

[51] An obvious point, perhaps, but worth stating explicitly so that my overall argument is not misunderstood.
[52] Chapter 4, 200–18.   [53] Chapter 4, 228–9, 236–43; chapter 5, 264–6, 283–97.

to be merely coincidental, then, that it was also during this period that we discovered several other, statistically significant correspondences between different forms of imperial expression and institutional action: the frequency of Aequitas types and the quality of the silver coinage produced by the imperial mint; the frequency of Liberalitas types and the number of congiaria per reign-year; the frequency of Victoria types and the number of imperatorial acclamations per reign-year; and the frequencies of Victoria types and of types representing *pax* and *felicitas*.[54] These data indicate that it was during the period 98–180 – the "high empire," roughly three quarters of a century – that ideological unification in the Roman empire reached its peak of intensity.

And this brings us to the main reason that the specific ideals underpinning this unification were so important. This was not just an ideology unified around the Roman emperor. It was an ideology unified around a particular conception of the Roman emperor – and that conception changed substantially over the period 69–235, as the quantitative evidence has shown.

For most of the second century AD, ideological unification was based less upon the emperor himself than upon a robust ideal of ethical value and civic benefaction for which the emperor served as an especially resonant symbol. The promotion of this ideal advanced the interests of all the key actors in this configuration of power. For the central state, it helped to justify and legitimate imperial rule, which was embodied in the figure of the emperor. It should be stressed, once again, that such legitimation was useful not only for the imperial regime itself, but also for the upper-tier aristocrats who sat atop the empire's social and political hierarchy, especially senators and those equestrians who served in the imperial administration. This does not mean that these actors cleverly dreamed up these ideals and communicated them in propagandistic fashion as part of a self-conscious "strategy of legitimation."[55] But the discourse of imperial virtue and benefaction was clearly a legitimating discourse, insofar as it idealized the figure of the Roman emperor and, by extension, the Roman imperial state as a whole, and we may reasonably infer from the sheer variety of virtues and benefits ascribed to the emperor and from their underlying logic that those who

---

[54] Chapter 2, 67–70, 90–2; chapter 3, 158–9, 164–5; appendices 9–12.

[55] On this particular point I am in substantial agreement with Lendon 2006, but his conclusion that the imperial regime "needed no such strategies" (63), which implies either that it could rely on force alone (clearly untenable) or that the "practical inducements, whether tangible or psychological, to obedience" (53) – i.e., patronage – were not themselves part of a legitimating discourse, is difficult to accept.

publicized them in official media of communications understood that they were conducive to the widespread acceptance of Roman imperial authority as legitimate.

This legitimation was also helpful for the lower-tier aristocrats, the local ruling classes of the empire, since they, too, were clear beneficiaries of this political system, and so stood to gain from broad acquiescence in the system as a whole. For these local aristocrats, though, the promotion of this particular ideal of ethical value and civic benefaction was even more useful as a way of fashioning a potent model upon which they could base their own, local authority. Indeed, as we have seen, they frequently identified themselves in honorific inscriptions in the same terms with which they also praised the emperor, highlighting their own *liberalitas*, *munificentia*, and *pietas*, for example, and even referring to themselves, when the occasion suited, as *optimus*.[56] In this way, these local aristocrats could claim some share in the authority and legitimacy of the emperor himself. But in order for this strategy to work for the advancement of their own perceived interests, they also had to pattern their public behavior on the normative claims implicit in this particular model of political authority. Whether or not they actively believed in those claims may be debated, but the very fact that they seem to have defined their self-interest in terms of holding political office, expending their personal resources, and enhancing their social status in the public arena – none of which can simply be taken for granted as self-evident or obvious social goals – suggests that they had indeed adopted a characteristically "Roman" outlook about the proper ends of public life.[57]

In any case, what this strategically motivated public behavior meant, in practice, was the regular display of personal generosity and active participation in the competitive world of civic euergetism that we associate with the municipal life of the high empire.[58] And this strategy worked brilliantly. These local aristocrats expended their own resources in part on the monumentalization of their cities, and were honored by their communities, in return, with a range of commemorative symbols, especially statues, which is precisely the way in which these aristocrats had themselves publicly honored the emperor. That imperial benefaction and local honorific was

---

[56] Chapter 5, 290–3.

[57] Eagleton suggests, rightly, that we should attempt to distinguish between "normative" and "pragmatic" acceptance of ruling ideologies (1991: 56), but the distinction loses some of its urgency if it can be shown, simply, that a set of public practices was closely tied to a set of publicly expressed ideals, as I attempted to demonstrate above (chapter 5), inspired in part by Skinner's work on the relationship between language and action (see above, 56–7).

[58] For references, see above, 11, n. 41.

mostly idealized and abstract, while their own benefactions were quite real, does not seem to have upset this interlinked set of exchanges and practices. Such was the veil of ideological unification in the high Roman empire.[59]

Ideological unification in the Severan period, by contrast, was both less intense than it had been in the period 98–180, though still significant, and was based upon a different conception of the emperor, one that stressed his military and autocratic power. This shift can be explained in part by the changing institutional context in which imperial ideals were formulated, not only in terms of an imperial court that was perhaps not as deeply embedded in aristocratic society as it had been during the high empire, but also in terms of the more general changes in the organization and personnel of the central state that took place during this period.[60] Ideological unification around this absolutist conception of the emperor nevertheless remained useful to the central state since it continued to promote the universal authority of the Roman emperor, even if in a different guise. For the local aristocracies of the empire, by contrast, this transformation in the emperor's public image had a deep and ultimately adverse impact. In brief, what local aristocrats really lost in the Severan period, with the rise of the absolutist conception of the emperor, was a suitable model for their own authority. In symbolic terms, this meant that they could no longer honor themselves in the same way that they honored the emperor. There could be only one *dominus*. And in practical terms, because they could no longer pattern their own public behavior on the model of the emperor as paradigm of ethical value and material generosity, they found less reason to expend their own resources on civic benefaction in their own communities. Ideologies, institutions, and social practices, then, were all changing together in this critical period. This further underlines, once more, the distinctiveness and empire-wide effects of the ideological, institutional, and practical conjuncture characteristic of the high Roman empire.

SOCIAL POWER

It will be useful at this point to spell out, briefly, what I am not arguing in this book. The first important point relates to periodization. The association between ideological unification and a particular configuration of social power for which I have argued pertains mainly to the first three quarters of the second century AD. The nexus between the idealization of

---

[59] The metaphor is borrowed from Gordon 1990, to which the analysis in this chapter is indebted.
[60] Chapter 4, 242.

the emperor as ethical paradigm and model benefactor, ideological convergence between center and periphery, imperial power, and local power was looser during the period 69–98, before virtues became prominent in imperial ideology, and unraveled almost completely during the period 180–235, when the construction of the emperor as *dominus* came to the fore. Yet the Roman empire managed to function during both periods – not to mention under Augustus, the Julio-Claudians, and into the fifth century AD. A related point concerns geography. The focus has been almost entirely on the Roman West.[61] Yet the Roman empire managed to function in the East, too. The conclusion to be drawn is simple. Ideological unification between the layered aristocracies of the western empire, based on the specific idea of a virtuous and beneficent emperor, was not by itself a necessary condition for the functioning of the Roman imperial state as a whole, and it is no part of my argument to claim that such ideological unification was in fact necessary (much less sufficient).

But it should go without saying that this is not a question of the presence or absence of either ideological unification or social power, since both are always matters of degree. So what the book does argue is that during the period 98–180 (or thereabouts), the degree of ideological unification among several key sectors of the Roman world reached its peak, which in turn, so the argument goes, helped to bring about a convergence of social power in the Roman world that was broader and deeper than during any comparable period before or after. What is also distinctive about these decades is that the particular version of unification that was peaking at this time was especially conducive to the overall functioning of the Roman imperial state, since it virtually obligated local aristocrats in the western empire to align their public behavior with a set of ideals and values that worked to solidify Roman imperial rule in general. For during this period, these local aristocrats were not only honoring the emperor, imitating his beneficence in their own communities, and being honored in similar terms – all of which reinforced their own local status and authority – but they were also actively playing all the other roles that allowed the imperial state to operate, above all by maintaining local order and by ensuring that the taxes were being collected in full and delivered to the appropriate imperial officials, which were necessary in turn to support the imperial court, the city of Rome, and, above all, the Roman army.[62] That the Roman imperial state

---

[61] The methodological rationale for this focus is explained in chapter 1, 25.

[62] On these basic foundations of the Roman imperial state, see above, 11–14; for more detail and references, Noreña 2010.

as a whole ran more efficiently during what we call "the high empire" than it ever did before or after can hardly be doubted, and a critical part of that success, I argue, was not just the ideological unification that was characteristic of this period, but the specific form that it took.

This larger argument about the relationship between ideological unification and social power naturally depends in part on a particular understanding of "power."[63] By "social power" I refer to control over territories, resources, and persons, and to the manner in which such control is organized, both logistically and symbolically. It is mainly collective and institutional instead of individual, and it is situated not within societies, but rather within sets of overlapping and interconnected networks.[64] And the intensity of this form of power is, once again, a matter of degree, which can be measured in terms of centralization, hierarchy, and socio-spatial extent and depth. In the case of the Roman empire, it is especially appropriate to interpret the operations of power with reference to networks of actors and institutions as opposed to society, since what we call "Roman society" was neither unitary nor bounded, and so not a framework within which the sort of large-scale power investigated here can be neatly located.[65] Moreover, because states and cultures in the pre-modern world were rarely if ever isomorphic, the only way to understand the interrelationship between the two is to examine the apparatuses and processes that brought them into regular and dynamic contact with one another.[66] The multiple networks that facilitated communications between the key actors of the Roman world – the institutions of the central state, its most influential collectivities (senate and army), and the upper- and lower-tier aristocracies of the empire – will have served precisely this function.

These networks could be quite complex. A legionary officer conducting a military campaign in Dacia; a procurator collecting rents from an

---

[63] The following brief comments, inspired by Mann 1986 and 1993, should not be taken as comprehensive, nor are they meant to imply that other forms of power did not operate within the Roman empire. For critical reactions to Mann's work, see Wickham 1988; Hall and Schroeder 2006, with Mann's response (Mann 2006).

[64] For a recent study of networks in the ancient Mediterranean, explicitly drawing on Social Network Theory, but focusing in practice on commercial and religious networks, see Malkin *et al.* 2009.

[65] Cf. Wickham 1988: 65–6.

[66] Gellner 1983 emphasizes the lack of overlap between states and cultures in the pre-modern world (see above, 310–11). But it should be noted that there was probably a higher degree of isomorphism between state and culture in the Roman empire than in any other configuration of state power and culture in the ancient Mediterranean; see the brief but stimulating discussion in Woolf 1998: 246–9, contrasting the spread of Roman culture, "firmly limited by the boundaries of the empire" (246), with that of Hellenism, Judaism, and Christianity, "the seductiveness of [which] did not derive from any material rewards open to those who adopted Greek, Jewish or Christian identities, but rather from the content and organization of those cultural systems" (248).

imperial estate in North Africa; a senator dictating the text of senatorial decree in Rome; a local magnate in Tarraco dedicating a new public building; an imperial secretary in Mogontiacum handling the emperor's correspondence; a provincial governor in Britannia settling a local dispute; a decurion in Lugdunum voting to honor a local benefactor with a statue – social actors such as these, and thousands more like them, were operating within institutions and interlinked networks that not only enabled them to exercise their own wills in countless small ways on a day-to-day basis, but also made it possible for these interconnected groups of individuals, over time, to dominate an empire of 60 million persons. And it was the Roman emperor above all, both as actor and as symbol, that functioned as the critical "node" for all of these overlapping networks, harmonizing a number of discrete interests and helping to bring about, as a result, the general convergence and intensification of social power outlined in chapter 1.

One way to contextualize this claim is to consider the very long-term history of Roman imperial state-formation, from the mid-Republic through the late empire. Throughout these centuries, the Roman state relied mainly on force and various coercive mechanisms in order to control the human and material resources within the territory it ruled.[67] The capacity to project military force and to impose such coercive mechanisms on conquered areas were clearly necessary for the long-term maintenance of imperial rule. But they were not sufficient. Indeed, no imperial system can survive over the long term through reliance on coercion alone.[68] As a result, it seems clear that the decisive moment in this history of state-formation was the advent of monarchy at Rome, which coincided, roughly, with the end of large-scale imperial expansion and with the rapid spread of Roman/Italic cultural forms throughout the western empire, a process that was mainly advanced by the local aristocracies of this region, who found themselves increasingly bound to the larger social and political order that we call "the Roman empire." What the decades around the turn of the first century witnessed, in brief, was a momentous convergence of social power, a convergence in which the social and political functions and, in particular, symbolic significance of monarchy were far from incidental. For what the rise of monarchy in the late first century BC brought about was the existence of a resonant symbol of empire-wide scope, which by itself provided the empire

---

[67] See, briefly, Hopkins 2009: 178–81, 192–5, with references.
[68] Recent comparative analyses of ancient empires are unanimous on this point; see, e.g., Sinopoli 2001; Goldstone and Haldon 2009: 9, 11–15, 25–7.

with a measure of the "symbolic glue" that it had lacked under the Republic. This in turn enabled at least a measure of ideological unification between the multiple actors who controlled the main power networks of the Roman world. Eventually, by the second century AD, the Roman imperial monarchy also served as the catalyst for a conjuncture of ideologies, institutions, and practices that underpinned an unprecedented, empire-wide intensification of social power.

In conclusion, then, we may say that at least a degree of ideological unification amongst the layered aristocracies of the Roman world was necessary, along with the instruments of coercion, for the long-term maintenance and reproduction of this larger configuration of power. And if the arguments offered in this book are correct, then we may also say that there was a structural relationship between the degree and, more critically, the particular *form* of ideological unification, on the one hand, and the extent and depth of Roman imperial power, on the other – an uncomfortable reminder that systematic exploitation on the grand scale is consistent with the logic and normative claims of ideals and values to which many of us still subscribe.

List of appendices

Sources for the tabulation of silver coin types

This appendix provides the sources for the tabulations of silver reverse types represented in appendices 3, 5, and 7. It contains the following information: the conventional name of the hoard; the number of silver coins found in the hoard minted for all Roman emperors between Vespasian and Severus Alexander (with the exception of Didius Julianus and Pertinax); its approximate burial date, based on internal evidence; and the bibliographic reference. The 105 hoards have been divided into five regional zones, following Duncan-Jones 1994: appendix 10 (though I have added the data from the one North African hoard, Volubilis, to the figures for Italy, Zone C). For discussion of the geographical spread of my sample, see above, Introduction to Part I, 30–2. Within each zone the hoards are listed by order of burial date. Note that the column showing the number of coins for each hoard includes hybrids, forgeries, unidentified coins, and coins minted outside Rome. Because I have not included such coins in my study, the total number of silver coins from the hoards, 148,421, is greater than the number of coins tabulated in appendix 3 (142,798).[1]

Abbreviations (see also *L'Année Philologique* for standard abbreviations):

AMN	*Acta Musei Napocensis*
BBCS	*Bulletin of the Board of Celtic Studies*
Besly and Bland 1983	Besly, E. and R. Bland (1983) *The Cunetio Treasure: Roman Coinage of the Third Century A.D.* London.
Carson 1979	Carson, R. A. G. and A. M. Burnett (1979) *Recent Coin Hoards from Roman Britain*. London.
CH	*Coin Hoards* (Royal Numismatic Society, London)

---

[1] Hybrids, forgeries, unidentified coins, and coins from mints other than Rome represent 3.8 percent of all silver coins minted between 69–235 (except those of Didius Julianus and Pertinax) found in these 105 hoards. See above, 28.

CHRB	*Coin Hoards of Roman Britain*
DM	*Deutsche Münzblätter*
FMRD	*Die Fundmünzen der römischen Zeit in Deutschland*
FMRÖ	*Die Fundmünzen der römischen Zeit in Österreich*
FMRSL	*Die Fundmünzen der römischen Zeit in Slowenien*
Göbl 1954	Göbl, R. (1954). *Der römische Münzschatzfund von Apetlon.* Wiss. Abhandlungen aus dem Burgenland 5.
JIAN	*Journal international d'archéologie numismatique*
Krzyzanowska 1976	Krzyzanowska, A. (1976). *Skarb denarow rzymskich z Drzewicza.* Wroclaw.
Lightfoot 1991	Lightfoot, C. S. (ed.) (1991). *Recent Turkish Coin Hoard and Numismatic Studies.* Oxford.
MA	*Memoria Antiquitatis*
Mihailescu-Bîrliba 1977	Mihailescu-Bîrliba, V. (1977). *Tezaurul de Magura.* Bucharest.
Mitkowa-Szubert 1989	Mitkowa-Szubert, K. (1989). *The Nietulisko Male Hoards of Roman Denarii.* Warsaw.
Mouchmov 1934	Mouchmov, N. A. (1934). *Le trésor numismatique de Reka Devnia (Marcianopolis).* Sofia.
NK	*Numizmatikai Közlöny*
NSb	*Numismatický Sborník*
Ondrouch 1934	Ondrouch, V. (1934). *Der römische Denarfund von Vyskovce aus der Frühkaiserzeit.* Bratislava.
PSAS	*Proceedings of the Society of Antiquaries of Scotland*
Robertson 2000	Robertson, A. S. (2000). *An Inventory of Romano-British Coin Hoards.* London.
Schaad 1992	Schaad, D. *et al.* (1992). *Le trésor d'Eauze.* Toulouse.
SCN	*Studii Si Cercetâri de Numismaticâ*
TCWAAS	*Transactions of the Cumberland and Westmorland Antiquarian and Archaeological Society*
TM	*Trésors Monétaires*

van Es 1960	van Es, W. A. (1960). *De romeinse muntvondsten vit de drie noordelijke provincies.* Groningen.
VHAD	*Vjesnik Hrvatskoga Arkheolockoga Drustva*
Weber 1932	Weber, S. H. (1932). *An Egyptian Coin Hoard of the Second Century A.D.* New York.
WN	*Wiadomósci Numizmaticzne*

Hoard	No. of coins	Burial date (*AD*)	Reference
Zone A: Britain			
Beck Row Mildenhall	105	80	*CHRB* 4 (1984), 15–24
Howe	31	87	*CHRB* 10 (1997), 62–3
Lavenham	160	103/111	*NC²* 15 (1875), 140–3
Verulamium	26	112/117	*NC⁶* 20 (1960), 271–3
Ormskirk	77	119/122	*NC⁶* 8 (1948), 232
Hastings	42	125	*CHRB* 9 (1992), 34–8
Waddington	11	135	*CHRB* 9 (1992), 39–40
Mallerstang	102	136/138	*TCWAAS* 7 (1927), 205–17
Swaby	123	137/138	*NC⁵* 14 (1934), 216–19
Londonthorpe	398	153/154	Carson 1979: 9–25
Lawrence Weston	579	157	*CHRB* 8 (1988), 23–31
Allerton Bywater	271	162	*NC⁵* 5 (1925), 400–1
Barway	395	180	*CHRB* 10 (1997), 128–30
Ollerton (Edwinstowe)	404	180	*CHRB* 9 (1992), 46–9
Briglands	173	186/187	*PSAS* 90 (1956–7), 241–46
Bletchley	872	187	*CHRB* 9 (1992), 50–64
Postwick	171	192	*CHRB* 10 (1997), 131–4
Handley	414	194/195	*NC⁶* 10 (1950), 311–15
Abergele	317	201/206	*BBCS* 8 (1935–7), 188–201
Bristol	1,388	208	*NC⁵* 18 (1938), 85–98
Muswell Hill	633	209/210	*NC⁵* 9 (1929), 315–18
Much Hadham	89	210/211	*CHRB* 9 (1992), 73–80
Darfield II	469	215	*NC⁶* 8 (1948), 78–80
St. Mary Cray	319	226	*NC⁶* 15 (1955), 62–6
Llanarmon	400	226/227	Robertson 2000, no. 426
Falkirk	1,828	230	*NC⁵* 14 (1934), 1–30
East England	3,147	231/235	*NC³* 18 (1898), 126–84
Elveden	928	246/247	*NC⁶* 14 (1954), 204–8
Brickendonbury	369	251	*NC³* 16 (1896), 191–208
Dorchester	161	257	*NC⁵* 19 (1939), 21–61
Edlington Wood	422	258	*NC⁶* 5 (1945), 155–8
Stevenage	372	263	*CHRB* 8 (1988), 73–83
Caister-by-Yarmouth	482	263	*NC⁶* 7 (1947), 175–9
Cunetio	598	266/267	Besley and Bland 1983

(*cont.*)

Hoard	No. of coins	Burial date (*AD*)	Reference
Zone B: West Continent			
Middels Osterloog	77	140/143	*ZfN* 29 (1912), 207–41
Amiens XIII	42	148/149	*TM* 5 (1983), 125–30
Jever	328	162/163	*FMRD* 8.1, no. 3,019
Stockstadt III	1,337	167/168	*FMRD* 1.6, no. 6,020
Neunkirchen	26	167/168	*NZ* 101 (1990), 17–28
Bargercompascuum	309	187/188	van Es 1960: 106–12
Obererbach	844	218/222	*FMRD* 4.5, no. 5,028
Baden Baden	342	225	*FMRD* 2.2, no. 2,196
Kirchmatting	1,049	231	*FMRD* 1.2, no. 2,116
Wiggensbach	382	233	*FMRD* 2.7, no. 7,199
Niederaschau	738	235	*FMRD* 1.1, no. 1,229
Cologne	4,303	236	*FMRD* 6.1.1, no. 1–3
Köngen	312	247	*FMRD* 2.4.n.1, no. 4,135/1
Viuz-Faverges	1,607	251/253	*TM* 3 (1981), 33–76
Wiesbach	337	253	*FMRD* 3, no. 1,082
Nanterre	181	255	*RN*5 9 (1946), 47–8
Eauze	3,802	261	D. Schaad 1992
Zone C: Italy and North Africa			
Volubilis	92	119/122	*AA* 12 (1978), 180–4
Castagnaro	730	126	*RIN* 27 (1914), 349–64
Rome, Via Tritone	714	244	*AIIN* 5 (1925), 57–72
Zone D: Danube			
Tiszanagyrev	48	134/138	*NK* 23–4 (1924–5), 38–40
Erla	451	136	*NZ* 82 (1967), 26–48
Dîmbau	129	140/143	*SCN* 1 (1957), 113–31
Vyskovce	1,036	152/153	Ondrouch 1934
Salasuri	3,097	157/158	*AMN* 2 (1965), 269–94
Visá	82	157/158	*NK* 7–8 (1908–9), 120
Mocsolad	1,120	164/165	*NK* 4 (1905), 75–9
Kurd Gyulaji	1,099	164/165	*NK* 34–5 (1935–6), 77–8
Osijek	1,136	165	*DM* 12 (1937), 289–93, 311–17
Lengowo	209	165/166	*ZfN* 26 (1908), 304–16
Sotin	1,617	165/166	*VHAD* 2 (1910–11), 241–77
Carnuntum II	15	166	*FMRÖ* 3.1, 200–1
Apetlon II	77	166/167	Göbl 1954
Carnuntum III	102	168/169	*FMRÖ* 3.1, 201–3
Szombathely	966	176/177	*NK* 64–5 (1965–6), 69–70
Piatra Neamt I	443	177/178	see note below.[2]
Piatra Neamt II	241	177/178	*ibid.*

[2] Two lots treated as one: *Carpica* 1 (1968), 209–31 and 2 (1969), 157–78; cf. *Muzeul National* 3 (1976), 143–51.

(cont.)

Hoard	No. of coins	Burial date (*AD*)	Reference
Simoniesti	100	177/178	*SCN* 4 (1968), 385–91
Gîrla Mare	297	179/180	*Historica* 3 (1974), 67–91
Butoiesti	157	180	*SCN* 9 (1989), 37–42
Prelazko	569	186	*FMRSL* 2, no. 353
Przewodowa	146	186/187	*WN* 9 (1965), 203–8
Saskut	779	187	*Bucurestii* 2 (1935), 218–32
Puriceni	1,119	194	*MA* 4–5 (1972–3), 125–30
Nietulisko Male I	1,357	195	K. Mitkowa-Szubert 1989
Nietulisko Male II	3,135	195	K. Mitkowa-Szubert 1989
Magura	2,758	196	Mihailescu-Bîrliba 1977
Drzewicz	1,153	193/196	A. Krzyzanowska 1976
Vidin	329	201/206	*NSb* 4 (1957), 49–72
Mastacan	333	206/211	*SCN* 7 (1980), 83–93
Ercsi	363	228	*NK* 62–3 (1963–4), 9–17
Börgönd	546	230	*NK* 34–5 (1935–36), 24–35
Postojna	249	237	*FMRSL* 1, no. 91/2
Taga	940	239	*SCN* 4 (1968), 139–73
Plevna	540	251	*NC⁵* 3 (1923), 210–38
Rustschuk	1,127	251	*NZ* 51 (1918), 43–51
Reka Devnia	77,911	251	Mouchmov 1934[3]
Zone E: The East			
Acarnania	32	97	*CH* 4 (1978), 33
Sakha	255	114/117	Weber 1932
Murabb'at	37	119/122	*RN6* 1 (1958), 11–26
Eleutheropolis	128	128/132	*JIAN* 10 (1907), 230–48
Barbura	71	166?	*NK* 14 (1915), 70
Larnaka	448	183/184	*NC⁷* 19 (1979), 25–34
Syria	153	214	*AIIN* 5 (1925), 57–72
Kecel	2,544	215	*Cumania* 9 (1986), 27–71
Tell Kalak	1,942	222	*ANSMN* 20 (1975), 39–108

[3] The Reka Devnia (ancient Marcianopolis) hoard alone constitutes over one half of all the silver coins in the sample; on this hoard in general, see Depeyrot 2004. The overwhelming size of this one hoard might be suspected of having an inordinate effect on the overall hoard profile, but a few test cases show that the composition of Reka Devnia, although far larger than other hoards, is remarkably similar to that of smaller hoards. The variable annual percentages of Trajanic denarii and denarii of Severus Alexander in the Reka Devnia hoard, for example, closely mirror those of the via Braccianese hoard in Rome (6,409 denarii, unpublished), and the Elveden hoard in Britain, respectively (Duncan-Jones 1994: 114, fig. 8.2; 116, fig. 8.3). Caracalla's antoninianus, introduced in 215, represents 11.5 percent of Caracalla's silver at Reka Devnia, and 12.2 percent of his silver at Colchester (Duncan-Jones 1994: 138). At least three other hoards, then, are demonstrably similar in composition to Reka Devnia, and the combined evidence of these test cases suggests indeed that Reka Devnia "should provide something like a directory of central silver coin-output" (Duncan-Jones 1994: 133).

(*cont.*)

Hoard	No. of coins	Burial date (*AD*)	Reference
Sulakyurt	426	235/236	Lightfoot 1991: 213–47
Yatagan	184	243	Lightfoot 1991: 249–73
E. Turkey	1,090	251	*NC*[7] 6 (1966), 165–70
Turkey	423	251/253	*CH* 2 (1976), 236; 3 (1977), 156
Haydere	1,084	264	Lightfoot 1991: 91–180

Regional Totals:

England	16,276		
West Continent	16,016		
Italy/North Africa	1,536		
Danube	105,776[4]		
The East	8817		
TOTAL:	148,421		

---

[4] Without the Reka Devnia hoard the total for the Danube region is 27,865.

Sources for the tabulation of bronze coin types

This appendix provides the sources for the tabulations of bronze reverse types represented in appendices 4, 6, and 8. It contains the following information: the area in which the coins were found (including the two major individual hoards of bronze coins); the number of bronze coins found in the area minted for all Roman emperors between Vespasian and Severus Alexander (with the exception of Didius Julianus and Pertinax); and the source of the data. For discussion of the geographical spread of the sample, see Introduction to Part 1, 32–4. On the discrepancy between the total number of coins tabulated (37,140) and the number of coins in appendix 4 (36,487), see explanatory note to appendix 1.

Abbreviations:

Hobley 1998	Hobley, A. S. (1998). *An Examination of Roman Bronze Coin Distribution in the Western Empire A.D. 81–192.* BAR International Series 688. Oxford.
Étienne 1984	Étienne, R. *et al.* (1984). *Le trésor de Garonne.* Paris.
FMRD	*Die Fundmünzen der römischen Zeit in Deutschland*
FMRL	*Die Fundmünzen der römischen Zeit in Luxemburg*
FMRN	*Die Fundmünzen der römischen Zeit in Niederlanden*
FMRSL	*Die Fundmünzen der römischen Zeit in Slowenien*
Turcan 1963	Turcan, R. (1963). *Le trésor de Guelma.* Paris.

Area	No. of Coins	Source
Britain	2,439	Hobley 1998[1]
Gaul	4,822	Hobley 1998[1]

[1] The numismatic data for Britain, Gaul, and Italy have been taken from Hobley 1998, Tables 5.3 (27–9), 6.5 (35–6), 7.3 (44–7), 8.3 (58–62), 9.4 (73–80), 10.6 (89–95), and 11.2 (99–103). Hobley discusses his methods of data collection at 1–2. For my use of Hobley's data, see above, Introduction to Part 1, 32–3.

(cont.)

Area	No. of Coins	Source
Germany	13,191	*FMRD*[2]
Netherlands	190	*FMRN*[3]
Luxembourg	1,022	*FMRL*[4]
Italy	8,268	Hobley 1998[1]
Slovenia	1,366	*FMRSL*[5]
(individual hoards)		
Garonne	3,131	Étienne 1984
Guelma	2,711	Turcan 1963
TOTAL:	37,140	

[2] I have consulted the following volumes of *FMRD*: 1.1 (1960), 1.2 (1970), 1.3–4 (1978), 1.5 (1963), 1.6 (1975), 1.7 (1962), 2.1 (1963), 2.2 (1964), 2.1–2n1 (1980), 2.3 (1964), 2.3n1 (1993), 2.4 (1964), 2.4n1 (1994), 3 (1962), 4.1 (1960), 4.2 (1965), 4.3/1 (1970), 4.5 (1985), 5.1.1 (1994), 5.1.2 (1994), 5.2.1 (1989), 5.2.2 (1989), 6.1.1 (1984), 6.4 (1971), 6.5 (1972), 6.6 (1975), 7.1–3 (1988), 7.4–9 (1988), 8 (1994), 9 (1994), 11 (1994), 12 (1994) and 14 (1994).

[3] I have consulted the following volumes of *FMRN*: 1 (1992), and 2 (1996).

[4] I have consulted the following volumes of *FMRL*: 1 (1972), 3 (1983), and 4 (1990).

[5] I have consulted the following volumes of *FMRSL*: 1 (1988), 2 (1988), and 3 (1995).

APPENDIX 3

Silver reverse types, by reign

This appendix provides the tabulations for silver reverse types, by reign, from Vespasian to Severus Alexander. Reverse types have been tabulated according to the identifications presented in *RIC*. All tabulations are listed under the reigning emperor (or senior emperor, in the case of joint ruler-ship), regardless of the portrait depicted on the obverse. Please note that the last numerical column provides the figures for the period 69–235 as a whole.

Totals:	Vesp 6,665	Tit 1,550	Dom 2,146	Nerv 1,044	Traj 13,073	Had 15,261	AntP 25,533	MAur 18,493	Comm 5,736	SepSev 24,015	Car 5224	Mac 730	Elag 10,117	SevAl 13,211	69–235 142,798
Personifications															
Abundantia	–	–	–	–	475	307	–	–	–	–	–	–	313	112	**1,207**
Aequitas	51	–	–	158	1,039	485	788	974	176	149	–	41	–	569	**4,430**
Aeternitas	–	–	–	–	115	166	2,600	97	–	–	–	–	–	–	**2,978**
Annona	223	–	–	–	–	111	2,659	220	108	437	63	63	–	711	**4,595**
Bonus Eventus	–	18	–	–	–	–	–	87	86	14	–	–	–	–	**205**
Clementia	–	–	–	–	–	155	275	87	86	14	–	–	–	–	**430**
Concordia	90	–	–	248	225	2,094	1,020	1,071	276	500	1	–	423	116	**6,064**
Fecunditas	–	–	–	–	–	–	–	724	–	14	–	–	124	249	**1,111**
Felicitas	–	–	–	–	1,137	628	753	883	415	1,569	1	89	740	530	**6,745**
Fides	25	–	–	–	17	305	91	13	198	86	173	103	620	292	**1,923**
Fortuna	70	2	1	248	796	646	1,193	559	237	911	1	–	217	16	**4,897**
Hilaritas	–	–	–	–	–	82	–	413	145	355	–	–	–	–	**995**
Honos	–	–	–	–	–	–	686	–	–	–	–	–	–	–	**686**
Indulgentia	–	–	–	–	–	65	–	–	–	502	92	–	–	–	**659**
Iustitia	–	–	–	29	–	293	–	8	–	–	–	–	–	–	**330**
Iuventas	–	–	–	–	–	–	120	–	–	–	–	–	–	–	**120**
Laetitia	–	–	–	–	–	–	49	80	36	104	–	–	177	–	**446**
Liberalitas	–	–	–	–	–	91	501	257	269	492	142	7	187	184	**2,130**
Libertas	–	–	–	150	–	410	39	–	244	78	98	–	519	192	**1,730**
Moneta	–	–	–	–	–	364	20	–	–	75	304	–	–	–	**763**
Munificentia	–	–	–	–	–	–	–	–	–	81	–	–	–	–	**81**
Nobilitas	–	–	–	–	–	–	–	–	89	345	–	–	–	–	**434**
Patientia	–	–	–	–	–	4	–	–	–	–	–	–	–	–	**4**
Pax	1,643	–	–	–	837	478	822	638	147	554	104	–	115	1093	**6,431**
Perpetuitas	–	–	–	–	–	–	–	–	–	–	–	–	–	101	**101**
Pietas	–	–	1	–	98	763	1,161	163	149	979	86	–	276	16	**3,606**
Providentia	–	–	–	–	349	209	143	1,583	150	438	86	30	443	613	**4,044**

(*cont.*)

335

(cont.)

	Vesp 6,665	Tit 1,550	Dom 2,146	Nerv 1,044	Traj 13,073	Had 15,261	AntP 25,533	MAur 18,493	Comm 5,736	SepSev 24,015	Car 5,224	Mac 730	Elag 10,117	SevAl 13,211	69–235 142,798
Totals:															
Pudicitia	–	–	–	–	–	363	219	146	–	256	10	–	940	–	**1,934**
Salus	186	11	3	62	26	1,042	799	1,164	124	453	110	53	352	685	**5,070**
Securitas	28	–	–	–	3	12	18	38	38	760	–	80	–	–	**977**
Spes	38	–	–	–	264	244	465	33	–	205	–	33	–	357	**1,639**
Tranquillitas	–	–	–	–	–	65	265	–	–	–	–	–	–	–	**330**
Victoria	240	38	–	–	1,920	959	276	1,093	228	2,264	64	3	963	371	**8,419**
Virtus	–	–	–	–	619	–	505	215	183	587	–	–	–	230	**2,339**
Deities															
Aesculapius	–	–	–	–	–	–	–	–	–	–	166	–	–	–	**166**
Apollo	–	–	–	–	–	–	102	–	139	49	311	–	–	–	**601**
Bacchus	–	–	–	–	–	–	–	–	–	5	–	–	–	–	**5**
Capricorn	21	32	–	–	–	–	–	–	–	–	–	–	–	–	**53**
Castor	–	–	–	–	–	–	–	–	–	33	–	–	–	–	**33**
Ceres	135	50	–	–	27	11	2,751	230	92	51	73	–	–	–	**3,347**
Cybele	–	–	–	–	–	–	–	60	2	320	–	–	–	–	**455**
Diana	–	–	–	1	–	119	119	302	–	156	329	–	–	–	**1,026**
Dionysus	–	–	–	–	–	–	–	–	–	154	–	–	–	–	**154**
Genius	–	–	–	–	652	260	725	–	–	646	147	–	–	–	**2,430**
Hercules	–	–	–	–	236	65	422	–	45	160	291	–	–	–	**797**
Juno	–	–	–	–	–	214	1	1,073	189	413	403	–	132	779	**3,222**
Jupiter	300	–	2	–	–	–	–	120	291	619	–	57	85	1,466	**3,344**
Luna	–	–	–	–	–	–	–	–	–	–	25	–	–	–	**25**
Mars	272	–	–	–	917	161	69	1,240	175	1,520	480	–	302	1,856	**6,992**
Mercury	–	–	–	–	–	–	–	78	–	–	–	–	–	–	**78**
Minerva	–	47	1,877	–	–	172	667	223	179	768	–	–	–	–	**3,933**
Nemesis	5	–	–	–	–	–	–	–	–	–	–	–	–	–	**5**
Neptune	29	–	–	–	–	74	–	–	–	236	–	–	–	–	**339**
Oceanus	–	–	–	–	–	24	–	–	–	–	–	–	–	–	**24**

Ops	–	–	–	–	–	–	–	3	–	–	–	–	–	**3**
Pluto	–	–	–	–	–	–	–	–	–	–	22	–	–	**22**
Roma	–	–	–	–	629	1,540	102	378	207	479	3	200	–	**3,538**
Romulus	–	–	–	–	–	64	–	–	–	–	–	–	–	**64**
Serapis	–	–	–	–	–	–	–	–	23	–	514	–	–	**537**
Sol	–	–	–	–	18	–	–	–	–	555	224	481	543	**1,821**
Tellus	–	–	–	–	–	182	–	–	–	–	–	–	–	**182**
Triton	–	–	–	–	–	–	–	–	–	2	–	–	–	**2**
Venus	22	91	–	–	–	230	633	735	217	734	505	790	217	**4,174**
Vesta	359	13	–	–	365	79	1,683	261	–	328	288	–	476	**3,852**
*Objects*¹														
Altar	–	114	25	–	–	–	–	473	85	–	–	–	–	**697**
Arch	–	–	–	–	–	–	–	–	–	1	–	–	–	**1**
Arms	–	–	–	–	–	–	–	–	8	–	–	–	–	**8**
Bull	3	–	–	–	–	–	–	–	–	–	–	–	–	**3**
Caduceus	305	–	–	–	–	–	28	–	–	–	–	–	–	**333**
Captive(s)	218	58	–	–	1,027	–	–	569	–	694	–	–	–	**2,566**
Clasped hands	66	12	–	10	–	–	450	1	–	–	–	–	–	**539**
Club of Herc.	–	–	–	–	–	–	–	–	–	–	20	–	–	**20**
Column	23	38	–	8	–	–	–	–	–	–	–	–	–	**69**
Column AntP	–	–	–	–	–	–	–	64	–	–	–	–	–	**64**
Column Traj.	–	–	–	–	196	–	–	–	–	–	–	–	–	**196**
Cornucopiae	3	–	–	–	–	–	–	–	–	–	–	–	–	**3**
Dolphin	–	223	43	–	–	–	–	–	–	–	–	–	–	**266**

(cont.)

¹ This is *not* a list of attributes and adjuncts, but rather of those reverse types in which *various* objects were depicted, usually without an identifying legend. The cornucopiae, for example, was one of the most common attributes on the imperial coinage (see 176), but was only rarely shown by itself (three examples in the entire sample, all minted under Vespasian).

(cont.)

	Vesp 6,665	Tit 1,550	Dom 2,146	Nerv 1,044	Traj 13,073	Had 15,261	AntP 25,533	MAur 18,493	Comm 5,736	SepSev 24,015	Car 5224	Mac 730	Elag 10,117	SevAl 13,211	69–235 142,798
Totals:															
Eagle	268	—	—	—	129	16	18	567	379	106	—	—	—	—	1,483
Elephant	—	98	—	—	—	—	—	—	—	—	7	—	—	—	105
Galley	—	—	—	—	—	49	—	—	—	33	—	—	—	—	82
Globe	—	—	1	—	—	—	—	—	—	—	—	—	—	—	1
Goat/Goatherd	17	25	—	—	—	—	—	—	—	—	—	—	—	—	42
Grain stalks	124	—	—	—	—	13	91	—	12	—	—	—	—	—	240
Heifer	38	—	—	—	—	—	—	—	—	—	—	—	—	—	38
Herald	—	—	19	—	—	—	—	—	—	—	—	—	—	—	19
Laurel	15	—	—	—	—	—	—	—	—	—	—	—	—	—	15
Lion	—	—	—	—	—	—	—	—	—	—	23	—	—	—	23
Oxen	98	—	—	—	—	—	—	—	—	—	—	—	—	—	98
Peacock	—	—	—	—	—	—	281	315	—	—	—	—	—	—	596
Pegasus	188	—	—	—	—	—	—	—	—	—	—	—	—	—	188
Prow	20	—	—	—	—	—	—	—	—	—	—	—	—	—	20
Pulvinar	—	—	—	—	—	—	—	—	—	2	—	—	—	—	2
Pyre	—	—	—	—	—	—	—	—	—	9	—	—	—	—	9
Quadriga	9	59	—	—	—	—	—	—	—	—	—	—	—	—	68
Relig. tools	450	—	—	138	—	86	107	—	—	200	—	—	—	—	981
Rogus	—	—	—	—	—	—	—	661	—	—	—	—	—	—	661
Seasons	—	—	—	—	—	—	—	—	—	1	—	—	—	—	1
She-wolf	125	—	—	—	—	—	20	—	—	—	—	—	—	—	145
Shield	—	195	—	—	—	—	—	—	—	—	—	—	—	—	195
Sow	106	—	—	—	—	—	—	—	—	—	—	—	—	—	106
Standards	—	—	—	—	4	—	—	—	—	—	—	—	—	—	4
Star/crescent	—	—	—	—	—	204	—	19	—	—	—	—	—	—	223
Temple	—	1	2	—	—	—	414	—	—	4	—	—	—	—	421
Throne	—	227	41	—	—	—	97	105	—	—	—	—	—	—	470
Thunderbolt	—	113	45	—	—	—	322	—	—	—	—	—	—	—	480
Tripod	—	—	52	—	—	—	—	—	—	—	—	—	—	—	52

338

													Total
Trophy	–	–	–	308	–	62	37	–	–	–	–	–	**407**
Via Traiana	–	–	–	138	–	–	–	–	–	–	–	–	**138**
Woman	–	–	–	–	–	–	–	6	–	–	–	–	**6**
Wreath	31	–	–	–	15	103	–	–	–	–	–	1	**150**
Emp./Imp. Family[2]	821	–	452	719	880	395	338	3,402	164	171	1,718	1,436	**10,496**
Geography													
Aegyptos	–	–	–	164	–	–	–	–	–	–	–	–	**164**
Africa	–	–	–	123	–	–	–	121	–	–	–	–	**244**
Alexandria	–	–	–	48	–	–	–	–	–	–	–	–	**48**
Asia	–	–	–	43	–	–	–	–	–	–	–	–	**43**
Danube	–	–	55	–	–	–	–	–	–	–	–	–	**55**
Germania	–	2	–	50	–	–	–	–	–	–	–	–	**52**
Hispania	–	–	–	80	–	–	–	–	–	–	–	–	**80**
Italia	–	–	–	57	66	–	–	–	–	–	–	–	**123**
Nile	–	–	–	73	–	–	–	–	–	–	–	–	**73**

[2] Because the number of different types in this category is so large, the tabulations list only the totals, rather than the numbers for individual types.

Bronze reverse types, by reign

This appendix provides the tabulations for bronze reverse types, by reign, from Vespasian to Severus Alexander. Reverse types have been tabulated according to the identifications presented in *RIC*. All tabulations are listed under the reigning emperor (or senior emperor, in the case of joint ruler-ship), regardless of the portrait depicted on the obverse. For the small numbers of bronze coins under the Severan emperors, see above, Introduction to Part I, 34, n. 25. Please note that the last numerical column provides the figures for the period 69–235 as a whole.

	Vesp 867	Tit 449	Dom 3,317	Nerv 855	Traj 4,915	Had 6,896	AntP 7,652	MAur 6,918	Comm 2,218	SepSev 230	Car 91	Mac 10	Elag 67	SevAl 2,002	69–235 36,487
Totals:															
Personifications															
Abundantia	–	–	–	–	511	–	35	–	–	–	–	–	–	–	**546**
Aequitas	90	32	–	85	38	212	120	152	17	2	–	–	–	31	**779**
Aeternitas	–	17	3	1	–	60	213	81	–	5	–	–	–	83	**374**
Annona	2	15	39	1	–	174	461	53	47	5	–	–	–	83	**880**
Bonus Eventus	–	–	–	–	–	–	37	–	–	–	–	–	–	–	**37**
Clementia	–	–	–	–	2	73	21	24	–	–	–	–	–	–	**120**
Concordia	10	9	–	144	79	266	168	66	61	–	–	–	5	3	**811**
Fecunditas	–	–	–	–	–	–	2	309	5	–	–	–	–	25	**341**
Felicitas	92	9	2	–	282	590	284	227	110	15	1	1	4	200	**1,817**
Fides	34	1	102	–	–	137	167	41	3	3	–	1	1	21	**511**
Fortuna	58	–	551	270	354	545	193	129	147	11	8	–	1	–	**2,267**
Hilaritas	–	–	–	–	–	237	71	216	80	11	1	–	–	–	**616**
Honos	–	–	–	–	–	–	75	–	–	–	–	–	–	–	**75**
Indulgentia	–	–	–	–	–	23	95	–	–	6	–	–	–	–	**124**
Iustitia	–	–	–	1	–	99	18	–	–	–	–	–	–	22	**140**
Iuventas	–	–	–	–	–	–	65	–	–	–	–	–	–	–	**65**
Laetitia	–	–	–	–	–	–	28	84	73	–	–	–	–	–	**185**
Liberalitas	–	–	–	–	–	28	56	88	47	2	–	–	–	25	**246**
Libertas	9	–	–	223	–	95	250	83	50	6	–	–	8	–	**718**
Moneta	–	–	497	–	–	177	70	–	14	6	–	–	–	17	**781**
Munificentia	–	–	–	–	–	–	70	–	2	1	–	–	–	–	**73**
Nobilitas	–	–	–	–	–	–	–	–	21	–	–	–	–	–	**21**
Patientia	–	–	–	–	–	–	–	–	–	–	–	–	–	–	**0**
Pax	46	58	3	15	382	70	217	26	21	3	–	–	2	110	**953**
Perpetuitas	–	–	–	–	–	–	–	–	–	–	–	–	–	–	**0**

(*cont.*)

341

(cont.)

	Vesp 867	Tit 449	Dom 3,317	Nerv 855	Traj 4,915	Had 6,896	AntP 7,652	MAur 6,918	Comm 2,218	SepSev 230	Car 91	Mac 10	Elag 67	SevAl 2,002	69–235 36,487
Totals:															
Pietas	—	—	—	—	100	235	485	202	29	2	4	—	10	—	1,067
Providentia	40	—	—	—	127	34	163	71	53	—	12	—	—	233	733
Pudicitia	—	—	—	—	—	18	64	29	21	—	—	—	7	—	139
Salus	2	2	90	—	95	714	423	569	148	1	—	2	1	3	2,050
Securitas	24	10	—	—	9	43	167	32	29	4	15	1	—	26	360
Spes	118	78	—	—	104	257	111	39	—	—	—	—	—	—	837
Tranquillitas	—	—	—	—	—	5	—	—	—	—	—	—	—	—	5
Victoria	112	27	123	—	903	36	94	704	80	25	3	1	2	133	2,243
Virtus	—	—	633	—	—	187	64	25	27	7	—	—	—	9	952
Deities															
Aesculapius	—	—	—	—	—	—	—	—	—	—	6	—	—	—	12
Apollo	9	16	1	—	—	—	80	—	46	2	—	—	—	—	128
Ceres	—	—	—	—	23	124	400	72	4	7	—	—	—	—	656
Cybele	—	—	—	—	—	—	15	87	5	7	—	—	—	—	114
Diana	—	—	—	—	—	193	77	193	6	3	5	—	—	—	477
Genius	—	13	—	—	—	25	115	4	27	2	—	—	—	—	186
Hercules	—	—	—	—	11	—	11	1	100	5	—	—	—	—	128
Honos	3	—	—	—	—	—	—	—	—	—	—	—	—	—	3
Janus	—	—	—	—	—	24	11	—	12	—	—	—	—	—	47
Juno	—	—	—	—	—	24	262	544	107	6	6	—	—	23	972
Jupiter	—	—	297	—	—	91	47	187	86	2	5	2	—	78	795
Mars	18	2	41	—	37	—	125	317	20	15	3	—	2	251	831
Mercury	—	—	—	—	1	—	—	44	—	—	—	—	—	—	45
Minerva	—	67	383	—	—	102	291	126	97	8	—	—	—	—	1,074
Nemesis	—	—	—	—	—	50	—	—	—	—	—	—	—	—	50

												Total
Neptune	–	–	–	113	–	–	–	–	–	–	–	**113**
Ops	–	–	–	–	29	–	–	–	–	–	–	**29**
Roma	51	4	221	161	124	242	128	12	1	5	21	**970**
Romulus	–	–	–	2	20	–	–	–	–	–	33	**55**
Serapis	–	–	–	–	–	–	2	–	–	–	–	**2**
Sol	–	–	–	1	–	–	–	–	1	2	242	**246**
Tellus	–	–	–	10	–	–	–	–	–	–	–	**10**
Venus	–	–	–	32	247	310	52	8	3	5	93	**750**
Vesta	–	9	–	86	271	81	–	10	2	–	75	**535**
*Objects*¹												
ANN NAT URB	–	–	–	1	–	–	–	–	–	–	–	**1**
Aqua Traiani	–	–	32	–	–	–	–	–	–	–	–	**32**
Arch	–	4	14	–	–	–	–	–	–	–	–	**18**
Basilica	–	–	4	–	–	–	–	–	–	–	–	**4**
Ulpia	–	–	–	–	–	–	–	–	–	–	–	–
Boar	–	–	45	–	–	–	–	–	–	–	–	**45**
Bridge	–	1	56	–	–	–	–	–	–	–	–	**57**
Caduceus	–	16	–	1	18	–	–	1	–	–	–	**36**
Carpentum	–	1	–	–	3	–	–	–	–	–	–	**4**
Circus Max.	–	–	14	–	–	–	–	–	–	–	–	**14**
Clasped hands	–	2	–	3	7	14	–	–	–	–	–	**26**
Club	–	–	32	2	8	–	–	–	–	–	–	**42**
COH	–	–	–	3	–	–	–	–	–	–	–	**3**
PRAETOR	–	–	–	–	–	–	–	–	–	–	–	–
Colosseum	5	–	–	–	–	–	–	–	–	–	–	**5**
Column	–	–	43	–	–	–	–	–	–	–	–	**43**
Col. Traj.	–	–	68	–	–	–	–	–	–	–	–	**68**
CONGIARIUM	2	–	–	–	–	–	–	–	–	–	–	**2**

¹ This is *not* a list of attributes and adjuncts, but rather of those reverse types in which various objects were depicted, usually without an identifying legend. The cornucopiae, for example, was one of the most common attributes on the imperial coinage (see 176), but was only rarely shown by itself (three examples in the entire sample, all minted under Vespasian). Types listed in all capitals (ANN NAT URB, etc.) were those depicting prominent legends but little or no imagery.

(cont.)

Totals:	Vesp 867	Tit 449	Dom 3,317	Nerv 855	Traj 4,915	Had 6,896	AntP 7,652	MAur 6,918	Comm 2,218	SepSev 230	Car 91	Mac 10	Elag 67	SevAl 2,002	69–235 36,487
CONSECRATIO	–	–	–	–	–	–	77	196	157	–	3	–	–	–	**433**
Cornucopiae	–	–	3	–	–	4	2	–	–	–	–	–	–	–	**9**
Cuirass	–	–	–	–	17	–	–	–	–	–	–	–	–	–	**17**
Debts burning	–	–	–	–	–	20	–	–	–	–	–	–	–	–	**20**
Eagle	67	–	–	–	41	39	2	–	–	3	–	–	–	–	**152**
Elephant	–	–	–	–	–	–	–	–	–	–	1	–	–	–	**1**
EQ ORDO PRIN	–	–	–	–	–	–	–	5	–	–	–	–	–	–	
FISCI IUDAICI	–	–	–	10	–	–	–	–	–	–	–	–	–	–	**10**
Forum Traiani	–	–	–	–	2	–	–	–	–	–	–	–	–	–	**2**
Gaming table	–	–	–	–	11	–	–	–	–	–	–	–	–	–	**11**
Globe	–	–	–	5	–	–	–	–	–	–	–	–	–	–	**5**
Goat	–	–	–	–	–	1	–	–	–	–	–	–	–	–	**1**
Grain stalks	–	–	14	5	–	–	1	5	–	–	–	–	–	–	**25**
Griffin	–	–	–	–	–	5	–	–	–	–	–	–	–	–	**5**
Helmet	–	–	1	–	–	–	–	1	–	–	–	–	–	–	**2**
Lion	–	–	–	–	–	–	–	–	–	–	1	–	–	–	**1**
Lyre	–	–	1	–	–	16	–	–	–	–	–	–	–	–	**17**
Mules	–	–	–	15	–	–	–	–	–	–	–	–	–	–	**15**
Olive branch	–	–	13	–	–	–	–	–	–	–	–	–	–	–	**13**
Owl	–	–	32	–	2	–	6	–	–	–	–	–	–	–	**40**
Palm tree	1	–	–	–	–	–	–	–	–	–	–	–	–	–	**1**
Pegasus	–	–	–	–	–	47	–	–	–	–	–	–	–	–	**47**
Portum Trai.	–	–	–	–	5	–	–	–	–	–	–	–	–	–	**5**
PRIMI DECENN	–	–	–	–	–	–	3	105	9	–	–	–	–	–	**117**
PROFECTIO	–	–	–	–	3	–	–	–	–	–	–	–	–	–	**3**
Pulvinar	–	–	–	–	–	–	5	–	–	–	–	–	–	–	**5**

	1	2	3	4	5	6	7	8	9	10	11	12	13	14	**Total**
Raven	—	—	13	—	—	—	—	—	—	—	—	—	—	—	**13**
Relig. tools	—	—	—	—	—	—	—	21	6	—	—	—	—	—	**27**
REX PARTH	—	—	—	—	71	—	—	—	—	—	—	—	—	—	**71**
Rhinoceros	—	—	40	—	—	—	—	—	—	—	—	—	—	—	**40**
Rostrum	—	—	—	—	6	—	—	—	—	—	—	—	—	—	**6**
SC in wreath	3	—	68	—	47	39	2	—	—	—	—	—	—	—	**159**
She-wolf	—	—	—	—	—	73	—	16	12	—	—	—	—	—	**101**
Shields	—	—	3	—	—	18	24	—	—	—	—	—	—	—	**45**
Ship	—	—	—	—	52	—	—	—	—	—	—	—	—	—	**52**
Sow	—	—	—	—	—	—	19	—	—	—	—	—	—	—	**19**
OB CIV SERV	6	—	—	—	—	—	—	—	—	—	—	—	—	—	**6**
Standards	2	—	—	—	11	—	—	2	—	—	—	—	—	—	**15**
Star/crescent	—	—	—	—	2	—	—	39	—	—	—	—	—	—	**41**
Table	—	—	—	—	—	4	—	—	—	—	—	—	—	—	**4**
Temple	1	—	—	—	67	6	—	99	—	—	—	—	—	—	**173**
Throne	1	—	—	—	—	—	—	—	—	—	—	—	—	—	**1**
Thunderbolt	—	—	—	—	—	2	3	29	—	—	—	—	—	—	**34**
Titulature	—	—	8	—	115	—	1	50	—	—	—	—	—	—	**174**
Tripod	—	—	3	—	—	—	—	—	—	—	—	—	—	—	**3**
Trophy(ies)	—	—	—	—	106	—	—	18	—	—	—	—	—	—	**124**
Vexillum	2	—	26	—	—	—	—	—	—	—	—	—	—	—	**28**
Via Traiana	—	—	—	—	29	—	—	—	—	—	—	—	—	—	**29**
VOTA	—	—	—	—	—	—	21	8	—	—	—	—	—	—	**29**
Woman	—	—	—	—	40	16	—	1	—	3	—	2	—	—	**62**
Emp/Imp. Family[2]	33	29	294	12	581	632	465	729	242	20	9	2	12	95	**3,155**
Geography[3]	33	7	15	—	244	607	245	293	22	15	—	—	—	—	**1,481**
Restoration[4]	—	39	13	47	—	—	—	—	—	—	—	—	—	—	**99**

[2] Because the number of different types in this category is so large, the tabulations list only the totals, rather than the numbers for individual types.

[3] Because the number of different types in this category is so large, the tabulations list only the totals, rather than the numbers for individual types.

[4] On the restoration types, see Komnick 2001.

345

Totals and percentages of silver virtue types, by reign

This appendix includes two tables. The first provides the totals of all silver virtue types, by reign and for the period 69–235 as a whole, and the second provides the percentages of these types, by reign and for the period 69–235. Note that the total for Providentia types (2,244) is different from the total listed in appendix 3 (4,044), since the Providentia Deorum types were not tabulated here as they do not represent imperial "virtues." Note also that in the second table, the totals do not always add up exactly to 100 percent, since the percentages have been rounded off to the nearest whole number; the last row is presented for the sake of clarity.

	Vesp	Tit	Dom	Nerv	Traj	Had	AntP	MAur	Comm	SepSev	Car	Mac	Elag	SevAl	69–235
Totals:	51	0	1	187	2,105	2,428	3,552	1,924	927	3,262	244	48	1,846	1,612	18,187

TOTALS

	Vesp	Tit	Dom	Nerv	Traj	Had	AntP	MAur	Comm	SepSev	Car	Mac	Elag	SevAl	69–235
Aequitas	51	–	–	158	1,039	485	788	974	176	149	–	41	–	569	4,430
Clementia	–	–	–	–	–	155	275	–	–	–	–	–	–	–	430
Indulgentia	–	–	–	–	–	65	–	–	–	502	92	–	–	–	659
Iustitia	–	–	–	29	–	293	–	8	–	–	–	–	–	–	330
Liberalitas	–	–	–	–	–	91	501	257	269	492	142	7	187	184	2,130
Munificentia	–	–	–	–	–	–	–	–	–	81	–	–	–	–	81
Patientia	–	–	–	–	–	4	–	–	–	–	–	–	–	–	4
Pietas	–	–	1	–	98	763	1,161	163	149	979	–	–	276	16	3,606
Providentia	–	–	–	–	349	209	103	161	150	216	–	–	443	613	2,244
Pudicitia	–	–	–	–	–	363	219	146	–	256	10	–	940	–	1,934
Virtus	–	–	–	–	619	–	505	215	183	587	–	–	–	230	2,339

PERCENTAGES

	Vesp	Tit	Dom	Nerv	Traj	Had	AntP	MAur	Comm	SepSev	Car	Mac	Elag	SevAl	69–235
Aequitas	100	–	0	84	49	20	22	29	19	4	0	53	0	35	24
Clementia	0	–	0	0	0	6	8	0	0	0	0	0	0	0	2
Indulgentia	0	–	0	0	0	3	0	0	0	14	28	0	0	0	4
Iustitia	0	–	0	16	0	12	0	0	0	0	0	0	0	0	2
Liberalitas	0	–	0	0	0	4	14	8	29	14	43	9	10	11	12
Munificentia	0	–	0	0	0	0	0	0	0	2	0	0	0	0	<1
Patientia	0	–	0	0	0	0	0	0	0	0	0	0	0	0	<1
Pietas	0	–	100	0	5	31	32	5	16	28	0	0	15	1	20
Providentia	0	–	0	0	17	9	4	47	16	13	26	38	24	38	12
Pudicitia	0	–	0	0	0	15	6	4	0	7	3	0	51	0	11
Virtus	0	–	0	0	29	0	14	6	20	17	0	0	0	14	13
Totals	100	–	100	100	100	100	100	100	100	100	100	100	100	100	100

347

Totals and percentages of bronze virtue types, by reign

This appendix includes two tables. The first provides the totals of all bronze virtue types, by reign and for the period 69–235 as a whole, and the second provides the percentages of these types, by reign and for the period 69–235. Note that the total for Providentia types (501) is different from the total listed in appendix 4 (733), since the Providentia Deorum types were not tabulated here as they do not represent imperial "virtues." Note also that in the second table, the totals do not always add up exactly to 100 percent, since the percentages have been rounded off to the nearest whole number; the last row is presented for the sake of clarity.

Totals:	Vesp 130	Tit 32	Dom 633	Nerv 86	Traj 267	Had 909	AntP 1,048	MAur 520	Comm 143	SepSev 20	Car 16	Mac 0	Elag 17	SevAl 320	69–235 4,141

TOTALS

	Vesp	Tit	Dom	Nerv	Traj	Had	AntP	MAur	Comm	SepSev	Car	Mac	Elag	SevAl	69–235
Aequitas	90	32	–	85	38	212	120	152	17	2	–	–	–	31	779
Clementia	–	–	–	–	2	73	21	24	–	–	–	–	–	–	120
Indulgentia	–	–	–	–	–	23	95	–	–	6	–	–	–	–	124
Iustitia	–	–	–	1	–	99	18	–	47	2	–	–	–	22	189
Liberalitas	–	–	–	–	–	28	56	88	2	1	–	–	–	25	200
Munificentia	–	–	–	–	–	–	70	–	–	–	–	–	–	–	70
Patientia	–	–	–	–	–	–	–	–	–	–	–	–	–	–	0
Pietas	–	–	–	–	100	235	485	202	29	2	4	–	10	–	1,067
Providentia	40	–	–	–	127	34	55	–	–	–	12	–	–	233	501
Pudicitia	–	–	–	–	–	18	64	29	21	–	–	–	7	–	139
Virtus	–	–	633	–	–	187	64	25	27	7	–	–	–	9	952

PERCENTAGES

	Vesp	Tit	Dom	Nerv	Traj	Had	AntP	MAur	Comm	SepSev	Car	Mac	Elag	SevAl	69–235
Aequitas	69	100	0	99	14	23	12	29	12	10	0	–	0	10	19
Clementia	0	0	0	0	1	8	2	5	0	0	0	–	0	0	3
Indulgentia	0	0	0	0	0	3	9	0	0	30	0	–	0	0	3
Iustitia	0	0	0	1	0	11	2	0	33	10	0	–	0	7	5
Liberalitas	0	0	0	0	0	3	5	17	1	5	0	–	0	8	5
Munificentia	0	0	0	0	0	0	7	0	0	0	0	–	0	0	2
Patientia	0	0	0	0	0	0	0	0	0	0	0	–	0	0	0
Pietas	0	0	0	0	38	26	46	39	20	10	25	–	59	0	26
Providentia	31	0	0	0	48	4	5	0	0	0	75	–	0	73	12
Pudicitia	0	0	0	0	0	2	6	6	15	0	0	–	41	0	3
Virtus	0	0	100	0	0	21	6	5	19	35	0	–	0	3	23
Totals	100	100	100	100	100	100	100	100	100	100	100	–	100	100	100

Totals and percentages of silver benefit types, by reign

This appendix includes two tables. The first provides the totals of all silver benefit types, by reign and for the period 69–235 as a whole, and the second provides the percentages of these types, by reign and for the period 69–235. Note that in the second table, the totals do not always add up exactly to 100 percent, since the percentages have been rounded off to the nearest whole number; the last row is presented for the sake of clarity.

TOTALS

Totals:	Vesp 2,480	Tit 51	Dom 4	Nerv 708	Traj 5,534	Had 7,000	AntP 10,493	MAur 6,980	Comm 1,998	SepSev 7,999	Car 442	Mac 288	Elag 3,943	SevAl 4,176	69–235 52,096
Abundantia	–	–	–	–	475	307	–	–	–	–	–	–	313	112	**1,207**
Aeternitas	–	–	–	–	115	166	2,600	97	–	–	–	–	–	–	**2,978**
Annona	223	–	–	–	–	111	2,659	220	108	437	63	63	–	711	**4,595**
Concordia	90	–	–	248	225	2,094	1,020	1,071	276	500	1	–	423	116	**6,064**
Fecunditas	–	–	–	–	–	–	–	724	–	14	–	–	124	249	**1,111**
Felicitas	–	–	–	–	1,137	628	753	883	415	1,569	1	89	740	530	**6,745**
Fortuna	70	2	1	248	796	646	1,193	559	237	911	1	–	217	16	**4,897**
Hilaritas	–	–	–	–	–	82	–	413	145	355	–	–	–	–	**995**
Laetitia	–	–	–	–	–	–	49	80	36	104	–	–	177	–	**446**
Libertas	–	–	–	150	–	410	39	–	244	78	98	–	519	192	**1,730**
Pax	1,643	–	–	–	837	478	822	638	147	554	104	–	115	1,093	**6,431**
Perpetuitas	–	–	–	–	–	–	–	–	–	–	–	–	–	101	**101**
Salus	186	11	3	62	26	1,042	799	1,164	124	453	110	53	352	685	**5,070**
Securitas	28	–	–	–	3	12	18	38	38	760	–	80	–	–	**977**
Tranquillitas	–	–	–	–	–	65	265	–	–	–	–	–	–	–	**330**
Victoria	240	38	–	–	1,920	959	276	1,093	228	2,264	64	3	963	371	**8,419**

PERCENTAGES

	Vesp	Tit	Dom	Nerv	Traj	Had	AntP	MAur	Comm	SepSev	Car	Mac	Elag	SevAl	69–235
Totals:	2,480	51	4	708	5,534	7,000	10,493	6,980	1,998	7,999	442	288	3,943	4,176	52,096
Abundantia	0	0	0	0	9	4	0	0	0	0	0	0	8	3	**2**
Aeternitas	0	0	0	0	2	2	25	1	0	0	0	0	0	0	**6**
Annona	9	0	0	0	0	2	25	3	5	6	14	22	0	17	**9**
Concordia	4	0	0	35	4	30	10	15	14	6	0	0	11	3	**12**
Fecunditas	0	0	0	0	0	0	0	11	0	0	0	0	3	6	**2**
Felicitas	0	0	0	0	21	9	7	13	21	20	0	31	19	13	**13**
Fortuna	3	4	25	35	14	9	11	8	12	11	0	0	6	0	**9**
Hilaritas	0	0	0	0	0	1	0	6	7	4	0	0	0	0	**2**
Laetitia	0	0	0	0	0	0	1	1	2	1	0	0	5	0	**1**
Libertas	0	0	0	21	0	6	0	0	12	1	22	0	13	5	**3**
Pax	66	0	0	0	15	7	8	9	7	7	24	0	3	26	**12**
Perpetuitas	0	0	0	0	0	0	0	0	0	0	0	0	0	2	**<1**
Salus	8	22	75	9	1	15	8	17	6	6	25	18	9	16	**10**
Securitas	1	0	0	0	0	0	0	1	2	10	0	28	0	0	**2**
Tranquillitas	0	0	0	0	0	0	3	0	0	0	0	0	0	0	**1**
Victoria	10	75	0	0	35	14	3	16	11	28	15	1	24	9	**16**
Totals	100	100	100	100	100	100	100	100	100	100	100	100	100	100	**100**

352

Totals and percentages of bronze benefit types, by reign

This appendix includes two tables. The first provides the totals of all bronze benefit types, by reign and for the period 69–235 as a whole, and the second provides the percentages of these types, by reign and for the period 69–235. Note that in the second table, the totals do not always add up exactly to 100 percent, since the percentages have been rounded off to the nearest whole number; the last row is presented simply for the sake of clarity.

Totals:	Vesp 355	Tit 147	Dom 811	Nerv 653	Traj 2,615	Had 2,835	AntP 2,606	MAur 2,579	Comm 851	SepSev 75	Car 28	Mac 5	Elag 15	SevAl 591	69–235 14,166
Abundantia	–	–	–	–	511	–	35	–	–	–	–	–	–	–	**546**
Aeternitas	–	17	3	–	–	60	213	81	–	–	–	–	–	–	**374**
Annona	2	15	39	1	–	174	461	53	47	5	–	–	–	83	**880**
Concordia	10	9	–	144	79	266	168	66	61	–	–	–	5	3	**811**
Fecunditas	–	–	–	–	–	–	2	309	5	–	–	–	–	25	**341**
Felicitas	92	9	2	–	282	590	284	227	110	15	1	1	4	200	**1,817**
Fortuna	58	–	551	270	354	545	193	129	147	11	8	–	1	–	**2,267**
Hilaritas	–	–	–	–	–	237	71	216	80	11	1	–	–	–	**616**
Laetitia	–	–	–	–	–	–	28	84	73	–	–	–	–	–	**185**
Libertas	9	–	–	223	–	95	250	83	50	–	–	–	–	8	**718**
Pax	46	58	3	15	382	70	217	26	21	3	–	–	2	110	**953**
Perpetuitas	–	–	–	–	–	–	–	–	–	–	–	–	–	–	**0**
Salus	2	2	90	–	95	714	423	569	148	1	–	2	1	3	**2,050**
Securitas	24	10	–	–	9	43	167	32	29	4	15	1	–	26	**360**
Tranquillitas	–	–	–	–	–	5	–	–	–	–	–	–	–	–	**5**
Victoria	112	27	123	–	903	36	94	704	80	25	3	1	2	133	**2,243**

PERCENTAGES

	Vesp	Tit	Dom	Nerv	Traj	Had	AntP	MAur	Comm	SepSev	Car	Mac	Elag	SevAl	69–235
Totals:	355	147	811	653	2,615	2,835	2,606	2,579	851	75	28	5	15	591	14,166
Abundantia	0	0	0	0	20	0	1	0	0	0	0	0	0	0	4
Aeternitas	0	12	<1	0	0	2	8	3	0	0	0	0	0	0	3
Annona	1	10	5	<1	0	6	18	2	6	7	0	0	0	14	6
Concordia	3	6	0	22	3	9	7	3	7	0	0	0	33	1	6
Fecunditas	0	0	0	0	0	0	<1	12	1	0	0	0	0	0	2
Felicitas	26	6	<1	0	0	21	11	9	13	20	4	20	27	4	13
Fortuna	16	0	68	41	14	19	7	5	17	15	29	0	7	34	16
Hilaritas	0	0	0	0	0	8	3	8	9	15	4	0	0	0	4
Laetitia	0	0	0	0	0	0	1	3	9	0	0	0	0	0	1
Libertas	3	0	0	34	0	3	10	3	6	0	0	0	0	1	5
Pax	13	40	<1	2	15	2	8	1	3	4	0	0	13	19	7
Perpetuitas	0	0	0	0	0	0	0	0	0	0	0	0	0	0	0
Salus	1	1	11	0	4	25	16	22	17	1	0	40	7	1	14
Securitas	7	7	0	0	<1	2	6	1	3	5	54	20	0	4	3
Tranquillitas	0	0	0	0	0	<1	0	0	0	0	0	0	0	0	<1
Victoria	32	18	15	0	35	1	4	27	9	33	11	20	13	23	16
Totals	100	100	100	100	100	100	100	100	100	100	100	100	100	100	100

Calculations for the correlation coefficients and permutation values derived from figures 2.1–2

This appendix provides the data and calculations for the correlation coefficients and permutation values derived from figures 2.1–2, and discussed in chapter 2, 68–70, where it was argued that there was a statistically significant, inverse correlation between the relative frequency of the Aequitas type on the silver coinage, expressed as a percentage of all silver virtue types, and the quality of the silver coinage produced by the imperial mint, as reflected in the number of denarii produced per pound of silver.

For the period 98–217, the correlation coefficient (r) was −.73; for the period 161–217, it was −.96. The data upon which these calculations were made are as follows:[1]

Reign	Aequitas relative frequency	Denarii per pound of silver
Nerva	84	98
Trajan	49	103
Hadrian	20	105
Antoninus Pius	22	107
Marcus Aurelius	29	120
Commodus	19	143.4
Septimius Severus	4	163
Caracalla	0	192

For the period 96–217, the average figure for the relative frequency of Aequitas types on the silver coinage was 28.375, and the average figure for denarii per pound of silver was 128.925. The following equation produces

---

[1] For the totals and percentages of Aequitas types on the silver coinage, see appendix 5. The data for the quality of the silver coinage was taken from Duncan-Jones 1994: 223–8, with table 15.6 (227) and figure 15.7 (229).

the correlation coefficient (A_i = Aequitas relative frequency, D_i = Denarii per pound of silver):

$$\frac{\sum(A_i - 28.375)(D_i - 128.925)}{\sqrt{\sum(A_i - 28.375)^2 \sum(D_i - 128.925)^2}} = -.7258$$

For the period 161–217, the average figure for the relative frequency of Aequitas types on the silver coinage was 13, and the average figure for denarii per pound of silver was 169.28. The following equation produces the correlation coefficient (A_i = Aequitas relative frequency, D_i = Denarii per pound of silver):

$$\frac{\sum(A_i - 13)(D_i - 169.28)}{\sqrt{\sum(A_i - 13)^2 \sum(D_i - 169.28)^2}} = -.9614$$

In order to test the significance of these correlation coefficients – to test that the association between the data was not simply the result of chance – I employed non-parametric permutation tests of the null hypothesis that there was no association between the relative frequency of Aequitas types and the number of denarii produced per pound of silver, both for the period 96–217 and for the period 161–217. The relative frequencies of the Aequitas types were shuffled into a random order, then paired with the number of denarii produced per pound of silver (in their original order, as in the chart above). For each of 1,000,000 such random permutations, the correlation coefficient between the relative frequency of the Aequitas type and the number of denarii per pound of silver was calculated. The permutation values (p-values) for the null hypothesis were estimated to be the fraction of those random permutations for which the correlation coefficient was at least −.7258 or −.9614, in absolute value, for the periods 96–217 and 161–217, respectively, i.e., the values of the correlation coefficients for the actual ordering of the data (as in the chart above). Based on these 1,000,000 permutations, the p-value for the period 96–217 was calculated to be 0.04, and for the period 161–217, 0.083.

Calculations for the correlation coefficient and permutation value derived from figures 2.3–4

This appendix provides the data and calculations for the correlation coefficient and permutation value derived from figures 2.3–4, and discussed in chapter 2, 90–2, where it was argued that between 117 and 217, there was a statistically significant correlation between the relative frequency of the Liberalitas type on silver coins, expressed as a percentage of all silver virtue types, and the frequency of imperial *congiaria*, as calculated by the number of known congiaria per reign-year.

The correlation coefficient (r) was .95. The data upon which this calcuation was made are as follows:[1]

Reign	Liberalitas relative frequency	Congiaria per reign-year
Hadrian	4	.32
Antoninus Pius	14	.38
Marcus Aurelius	8	.35
Commodus	29	.46
Septimius Severus	14	.32
Caracalla	43	.5

For the period 117–217, the average figure for the relative frequency of Liberalitas types on the silver coinage was 18.667, and the average figure for congiaria per reign-year was .388. The following equation produces the

---

[1] For the totals and percentages of Liberalitas types on the silver coinage, see appendix 5. The data for the number of congiaria per reign-year are taken from Barbieri 1957: 843–64.

correlation coefficient (L_i = Liberalitas relative frequency, C_i = congiaria per reign-year):

$$\frac{\sum (L_i - 18.667)(C_i - .388)}{\sqrt{\sum (L_i - 18.667)^2 \sum (C_i - .388)^2}} = .9462$$

In order to test the significance of this correlation coefficient, I employed a non-parametric permutation test, using 1,000,000 permutations of the data (see above, appendix 9, for a description of the test). Based on these 1,000,000 permutations, the p-value was calculated to be 0.011.

Calculations for the correlation coefficient and permutation value derived from figure 3.3 and table 3.3

This appendix provides the data and calculations for the correlation coefficient and permutation value derived from figure 3.3 and table 3.3, and discussed in chapter 3, 158–9, where it was argued that between 96 and 218, there was a statistically significant, positive correlation between the relative frequency of the Victoria type on the silver coinage, expressed as a percentage of all silver benefit types, and the number of imperatorial acclamations per reign.

Table 3.3 *Imperatorial acclamations and triumphs,* AD *69–235*

Emperor	Imperatorial acclamations	Triumphs
Vespasian	20	1
Titus	17	1
Domitian	22	2
Nerva	2	0
Trajan	13	2
Hadrian	1	0
Antoninus Pius	0	0
Marcus Aurelius	10	2
Commodus	8	2
Septimius Severus	11	0
Caracalla	3	0
Macrinus	0	0
Elagabalus	0	0
Severus Alexander	0	1

Note: The figures listed here include joint triumphs (Vespasian and Titus, during the reign of Vespasian; Marcus Aurelius and Lucius Verus, and Marcus Aurelius and Commodus, both during the reign of Marcus Aurelius), and that the totals for Titus and Commodus incorporate these shared triumphs under a senior emperor. Convenient overview of acclamations and triumphs in Kienast 1996.

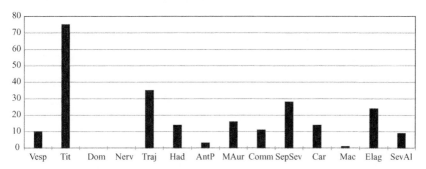

Figure 3.3 Relative frequency of Victoria types on silver coins, expressed as a percentage of all benefit types by reign, AD 69–235 (N = 52,096)

The correlation coefficient (r) was .844. The data upon which these calcuations were made are as follows:

Reign	Victoria relative frequency	Imperatorial acclamations
Nerva	0	2
Trajan	35	13
Hadrian	14	1
Antoninus Pius	3	0
Marcus Aurelius	16	10
Commodus	11	8
Septimius Severus	28	11
Caracalla	15	3
Macrinus	1	0

For the period 96–218, the average figure for the relative frequency of Victoria types was 13.667, and the average number of imperatorial acclamations per reign was 5.333. The following equation produces the correlation coefficient (V_i = Victoria relative frequency, and A_i = number of imperial acclamations):

$$\frac{\sum (V_i - 13.667)(A_i - 5.333)}{\sqrt{\sum (V_i - 13.667)^2 \sum (A_i - 5.333)^2}} = .844$$

In order to test the significance of this correlation coefficient, I employed a non-parametric permutation test, using 1,000,000 permutations of the data (see above, appendix 9, for a description of the test). Based on these 1,000,000 permutations, the p-value was calculated to be .003.

Calculations for the correlation coefficients and permutation values derived from figure 3.4

This appendix provides the data and calculations for the correlation coefficients and permutation values derived from figure 3.4, and discussed in chapter 3, 164–5, where it was argued that, between 96 and 211, there was a statistically significant, positive correlation on the silver coinage between the relative frequencies of the Victoria and Pax types, each expressed as a percentage of all silver benefit types, and between the relative frequencies of the Victoria and Felicitas types, each expressed as a percentage of all silver benefit types.

During this period, the correlation coefficient (r) between Victoria and Pax types was .76, and between Victoria and Felicitas types .8. The data upon which these calcuations were made are as follows:[1]

Reign	Victoria rel. freq.	Pax rel. freq.	Felicitas rel. freq.
Nerva	0	0	0
Trajan	35	15	21
Hadrian	14	7	9
Antoninius Pius	3	8	7
Marcus Aurelius	16	9	13
Commodus	11	7	21
Septimius Severus	28	7	20

For the period 96–211, the average figure for the relative frequency of Victoria types on the silver coinage was 15.286, and for Pax types 7.571. The following equation produces the correlation coefficient

---

[1] For the totals and percentages of Victoria, Pax, and Felicitas types on the silver coinage, see appendix 7.

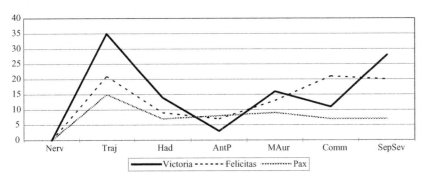

Figure 3.4 Relative frequencies of Victoria, Felicitas, and Pax types on silver coins, expressed as a percentage of all benefit types by reign, AD 96–211 (N = 40,712)

(V_i = relative frequency of Victoria types, P_i = relative frequency of Pax types):

$$\frac{\sum (V_i - 15.286)(P_i - 7.571)}{\sqrt{\sum (V_i - 15.286)^2 \sum (P_i - 7.571)^2}} = .7635$$

For the period 96–211, the average figure for the relative frequency of Victoria types on the silver coinage was 15.286, and for Felicitas types 13. The following equation produces the correlation coefficient (V_i = relative frequency of Victoria types, F_i = relative frequency of Felicitas types):

$$\frac{\sum (V_i - 15.286)(F_i - 13)}{\sqrt{\sum (V_i - 15.286)^2 \sum (F_i - 13)^2}} = .7946$$

In order to test the significance of these correlation coefficients, I employed non-parametric permutation tests, using 1,000,000 permutations of each of the two sets of data (see above, appendix 9, for a description of the test). Based on these 1,000,000 permutations, the p-value for the first correlation (between Victoria and Pax) was calculated to be 0.048, and for the second correlation (between Victoria and Felicitas), 0.038.

Master list of inscriptions in epigraphic corpus

This appendix presents the corpus of inscriptions with honorific terminology for the emperor discussed in the Introduction to Part II and employed as the empirical basis for chapters 4 and 5. The list of inscriptions is organized chronologically, and provides the following information for each text: a number, in order to facilitate cross-checking with appendix 14 (inscriptions organized by location) and appendix 15 (inscriptions organized by type); the type of inscription (see Int. Part II, 181–3); the date; the honorific terms, titles and/or praise language employed in the inscription; the location of the text; the dedicator(s) or author(s) (note: DD = *decreto decurionum*); the honorand(s), where applicable; and the reference number in the standard epigraphic corpora and publications. Wherever the information in one of these categories was not applicable or unknown, the space has been left blank.

No.	Type	Date	Honorific term(s), Title(s), Praise language	Location	Dedicator(s)/ Author(s)	Honorand(s)	Reference
			VESPASIAN				
1	2	71	quod vias urbis neglegentia superior(ibus) tempor(ibus) corruptas inpensa sua restituit	Roma	SC	Vespasian	CIL 6.931 = ILS 245
2	10	75	beneficio imp(eratoris) Caesaris Aug(usti) Vespasiani	Igabrum (Baetica)	municipes Igabrenses		CIL 2²/5,208 = 2.1610 = ILS 1981
3	10	77	benef[icio]	Cisimbrium (Baetica)	local official (?)		CIL 2²/5,292 = 2.2096 = AE 1986,334b
			TITUS				
4	3	72	p(rincipi) o(ptimo)	Patavium (Reg x)	G(aius) Papirius Aequos leg(atus)	Titus	AE 1986.250
5	7	69–79	conser[v]atori pacis Aug(ustae)	Valentia (HispTarr)		Titus	CIL 2²/14,13 = 2.3732 = ILS 259
6	4	81	conservatori caerimoniarum publicarum et restitutori aedium sacrarum	Roma	Sodales Titi	Titus	CIL 6.934 = ILS 252
7	2	81	quod praeceptis patri[is] consiliisq(ue) et auspiciis gentem Iudaeorum domuit et urbem Hierusolymam omnibus ante se ducibus regibus gentibus aut frustra petitam aut omnino intemptatam delevit	Roma	SPQR	Titus	CIL 6.944 = ILS 264

(cont.)

365

No.	Type	Date	Honorific term(s), Title(s), Praise language	Location	Dedicator(s)/ Author(s)	Honorand(s)	Reference
DOMITIAN							
8	10	81–96	beneficio	Cordoba (Baetica)			*CIL* 2²/5,291 = *AE* 1981.496
TRAJAN							
9	10	101	ab indulgentissimo imp(eratore)… qua aeternitate Italiae suae prospexit secundum liberalitatem eius	Roma	SC		*CIL* 6.1492
10	10	101	[ex praecepto optimi] maximiq(ue) principis; ex indulgentia	Ligures Baebiani (Reg II)	Ligures Baebiani	Trajan	*CIL* 9.1455 = *ILS* 6509
11	4	103	quod liberalitate optimi principis commoda earum etiam locorum adiectione ampliata sint	Roma	Tribus xxxv	Trajan	*CIL* 6.955 = *ILS* 286
12	10	105	sacratissimus princeps; pleniorem indulgentiam maximi imperatoris	Aquileia (Reg X)	Decr(eto) Dec(urionum)	municipal patron	*CIL* 5.875 = *ILS* 1374
13	7	107	[opti]mo ac m[aximo]	Rusicade (Numidia)		Trajan	*CIL* 8.7967
14	4	108	propagatori orbis terrarum locupletatori civium	Roma	cultores Larum et imaginum domus Aug	Trajan	*CIL* 6.40500–01 = 958
15	5	109–10	optumo maxsumoque principi	Nescania (Baetica)	Nescanienses publice	Trajan	*CIL* 2²/5,846 = 2.2010
16	5	103–11	[pro salute i]ndulg[entissimi optimi ma[ximique principis]	Mesagne (Reg II)		Trajan	*CIL* 9.215

17	5	106–11	[per mu]nificentiam suam	Auximum (Reg v)	Auximates publice	Trajan	*CIL* 9.5825
18	2	112	optime de republica merito domi forisque	Roma	SPQR	Trajan	*CIL* 6.959 = *ILS* 292
19	10	102–13	ex indulgentia optimi maximique principis	Veleia (Reg viii)			*CIL* 11.1147
20	2	113	ad declarandam quantae altitudinis mons et locus tantis operibus sit egestus	Roma	SPQR	Trajan	*CIL* 6.960 = *ILS* 294
21	10	113	optimo maximoq(ue) principi; parenti publico	Misenum (Reg i)	Augustales		*AE* 1996.424b = 1993-473
22	5	102–14	[… benefici]o eius; [pr]ovident[ia…]	Roma	pueri et puellae alimentariae	Trajan	*CIL* 6.40497 = 31298
23	4	102–14	[p]ro salute et victoria … conditoris col(oniae)	Thamugadi (Numidia)	conductor	Trajan	*CIL* 8.17841 = *ILS* 6842
24	2	115	fortissimo principi	Beneventum (Reg ii)	SPQR	Trajan	*CIL* 9.1558 = *ILS* 296
25	2	115	providentissimo principi	Ancona (Reg v)	SPQR	Trajan	*CIL* 9.5894 = *ILS* 298
26	5	117	optumo maximoque principi conservatori generis humani	Aratispi (Baetica)	res publica Aratispitanorum	Trajan	*CIL* 2².5.730 = 2.2054 = *ILS* 304
27	4	98–117	liberalissimo	Roma		Trajan	*CIL* 6.40493
28	10	98–117	[iussu] sacratissimi princi[pis]	Iader (Dalmatia)	Trajan (?)		*CIL* 3.2909
29	10	98–117	beneficio optimi principis	Delphi (Achaea)			*CIL* 3.567
30	7	103–17	in honorem imp Nervae Traiani … ex beneficiis eius	Iliturgicola (Baetica)		Trajan	*CIL* 2².5.252 = 2.1640
31	2	114–17	[provide?]n(tiae) [imp(eratoris)…] [restitutoris] Italiae	Liternum (Reg i)	SC	Trajan	*AE* 2003.340
32	4	114–17	[sacr]atissimo m[aximoque]	Ostia (Reg i)	seviri Augustales Claudian[i]		*CIL* 14.4486a
33	5	114–17	optimo [e]t indulgentissimo principi	Forum Clodii (Reg vii)		Trajan	*AE* 2000.569 = *CIL* 11.3309

(cont.)

(cont.)

No.	Type	Date	Honorific term(s), Title(s), Praise language	Location	Dedicator(s)/Author(s)	Honorand(s)	Reference
34	10	114–17	hos honores beneficio optumi princip(is) maturius quam . . .	Nemausus (Narbonensis)		imp. official	CIL 12.3164 = ILS 1048
35	10	114–17	beneficio o[ptumi princi]pis	Nemausus (Narbonensis)	decreto decurionum	imp. official	CIL 12.3165a
36	2	118	qui primus omnium principum et solus remittendo sestertium novies milies centena milia n debitum fiscus non praesentes tantum cives suos sed et posteros eorum praestitit hac liberalitate securos	Roma	SPQR	Divus Traianus	CIL 6.967 = ILS 309
HADRIAN							
37	5	119	indulgentissimo principi	Ripa Rhodani (Narbonensis)	Rhodanici	Hadrian	CIL 12.1797
38	5	121–2	optimo maximoq(ue) princ(ipi)	Surrentum (Reg I)	Decurions/Municipes of Surrentum	Hadrian	CIL 10.676 = ILS 312
39	5	125–6	optimo et liberalissimo principi	Beneventum (Reg II)	Colonia Iulia Concordia Beneventum	Hadrian	AE 1969/70.167
40	4	126	inso[l]itae munificentiae eius erga fratres Arvales . . .]	Roma	fratres Arvales	Hadrian	CIL 6.40517, = 917
41	1	127	munificentia sua templum deae cuprae restituit	Cupra Maritima (Reg v)	Hadrian		CIL 9.5294 = ILS 313

				Roma	SPQR	Hadrian	*CIL* 6.40515 = 36915
42	2	119–28	maxim[o et sa]nctissimo p[rincipi]	Roma	SPQR	Hadrian	*CIL* 6.40515 = 36915
43	6	128	optimo principi	Callenses (Baetica)	imp. official	Hadrian	*CIL* 2.1371
44	5	129	optimo maximoque principi	Teanum Sidicinum (Reg 1)	Teanenses	Hadrian	*CIL* 10.4782
45	5	132	optumo maximumque principi	MunFlavMuniguense (Baetica)	res [publica . . .]	Hadrian	*AE* 1966.182
46	5	132	Olympio	Athens (Achaea)	colonia Iulia Augusta Diensium	Hadrian	*CIL* 3.7281
47	5	132	Olympio; restitutori coloniae suae	Athens (Achaea)	Troadenses	Hadrian	*CIL* 3.7282
48	5	132	[fragmentary]	Athens (Achaea)	colonia Caesarea Antiochia	Hadrian	*CIL* 3.7283
49	5	132–3	per omnia conser[v]atori suo	Lepcis Magna (Africa)	Lepcitani publice	Hadrian	*IRT* 362
50	5	133	omni indulgentia et liberalitate eius	Ostia (Reg 1)	Colonia Ostia	Hadrian	*CIL* 14.95
51	5	133	colonia Ostia conservata et aucta omni indulgentia et liberalitate eius	Roma		Hadrian	*CIL* 6.972
52	5	134–5	indulgentia eius au[cta et ornata]	Roma	colonia Iulia Augusta	Hadrian	*CIL* 6.40523 = 3754 = *ILS* 6784
53	2	135	[quod summo pugnandi a]rdore mi[ss]o [exercitu suo superatis imperat]oribus max[imis Syriam Palaestinam ab hoste] liberaverit	Roma	SPQR	Hadrian	*CIL* 6.40524 = 974
54	7	135	[libe]ralitates pu[. . .]	Tibur (Reg 1)		Hadrian	*CIL* 14.3577 = 4235 = *ILS* 318

(cont.)

No.	Type	Date	Honorific term(s), Title(s), Praise language	Location	Dedicator(s)/ Author(s)	Honorand(s)	Reference
55	5	119–37	ind[ulgentia eius aucta et ornata] max[imo et... principi]	Roma	colonia – – –	Hadrian	*CIL* 6.40516
56	7	137	condito]ri munic[ipi]	Avitta Bibba (Africa)		Hadrian	*CIL* 8.799
57	10	117–38	[ex li]ber[alitate]	Castrimoenium (Reg I)	municipes Castrimoenienses		*CIL* 14.2460
58	10	117–38	optimus imperator	Formia (Reg I)	freedman	municipal patron	*CIL* 10.6090 = *ILS* 6295
59	10	117–38	[e]xornato eq pub a sacratissimo principe	Rudiae (Reg II)	father of honorand	municipal patron	*CIL* 9.23
60	10	117–38	adlecto a sacratissimo imp(eratore) Hadriano Aug(usto)	Auximum (Reg V)	Auximi	municipal patron	*CIL* 9.5833 = *ILS* 1059
61	1	117–38	liberalit[ate sua...]	Caesarea (Reg VIII)	Hadrian	Hadrian	*AE* 1991.694
62	7	117–38	[principi i]ndulg[entissimo]	Vicetia (Reg X)			*CIL* 5.3110
63	5	117–38	conditori municipi	Althiburita (Africa)	DD	Hadrian	*CIL* 8.27775a–d
64	1	117–38	[e]x indulgentia	Colonia Canopitana (Africa)	Hadrian		*AE* 1979.658
65	3	117–38	for[tissim]o libera[lissimo]que	Lambaesis (Numidia)	Legio III	Hadrian	*AE* 2003.2020a = *AE* 1900.33
66	3	117–38	fortissimo liberalissimoq[ue]	Lambaesis (Numidia)	soldiers	Hadrian	*CIL* 8.2534
67	10	117–38	[e]x indulgenti[a] ... fines adsignati	Guerria (MaurCaes)	procurator		*CIL* 8.8813
68	10	117–38	ex indulgentia... fines adsignati	Guerria (MaurCaes)	procurator		*CIL* 8.8814

69	10	117–38	ob legationem qua gratuita aput maximum princ(ipum) Hadrianum Aug(ustum)	Tarraco (HispTarr)	heirs		*CIL* 2.4201 = *ILS* 6927
70	10	117–38	cum optimus maximusque princeps Traianus Hadrianus Aug(ustus) scripsit . . .	Lamia (Macedonia)	procos		*CIL* 3.586
71	5	117–38	Iovi Olympio conditori col(oniae)	Colonia Iulia Parium (Asia)		Hadrian	*CIL* 3.374
72	10	117–38	domini n(ostri)	Nacolia (Asia)			*CIL* 3.6998
73	4	117–38	r[estitutori rei publicae atq]ue virtu[tis maiorum]	Roma		Hadrian	*CIL* 6.983
74	5	119–38	locupletatoribus municipii	Gabii (Reg 1)	[publice]	Hadrian and Sabina	*CIL* 14.2799 = *ILS* 321
75	5	119–138	[restitu]tori m[unicipii]	Ilugo (HispTarr)	Ilugonenses	Hadrian	*CIL* 2.3239
76	5	post 138	profusa liberalita[te]	Signia (Reg 1)	SPQ Signinus	Divus Hadrianus	*CIL* 10.5963
77	5	post 138	[divo] Hadrian[o] condito[ri m]unicip[i(i)]	Turris Tamalleni (Africa)	DD	Divus Hadrianus	*CIL* 8.83
78	5	post 138	conditori suo	Mursa (PannInferior)	Mursenses	Divus Hadrianus	*CIL* 3.3279
ANTONINUS PIUS							
79	10	139	ex lib[eralitate] ei[us]	Pitinum Mergens (Reg vi)			*CIL* 11.5956
80	3	139	optumo et indulgentissimo principi	Ephesus (Asia)	legatus of procos Asia	Antoninus Pius	*AE* 1966.428
81	7	140	indulgentissim[o princip]	Pisae (Reg vii)		Antoninus Pius	*CIL* 11.1424
82	10	142	ad optimum maximumque bis imp(eratorem)	Synope (Asia)	decreto decurionum	local benefactor	*AE* 1969/70.592

(*cont.*)

371

(cont.)

No.	Type	Date	Honorific term(s), Title(s), Praise language	Location	Dedicator(s)/ Author(s)	Honorand(s)	Reference
83	2	143	optimo maximoq(ue) principi et cum summa benignitate iustissimo ob insignem erga caerimonias publicas curam ac religionem	Roma	SPQR	Antoninus Pius	CIL 6.1001 = ILS 341
84	10	140–4	ob honor[em] domus divi[nae]	Brough-on-Humber (Brit)	local aedile	Antoninus Pius	RIB 707
85	3	140–4	optimo principi	Trigisamum (Noricum)	Ala 1 Augusta Thracum	Antoninus Pius	CIL 3.5654
86	4	144	iu[stissimo]	Roma		Antoninus Pius	CIL 6.40546 = 1217
87	6	147	principi optimo et sibi carissimo	Salpensa (Baetica)	imp. official	Antoninus Pius	CIL 2.1282
88	10	155	statuam imp(eratoris) . . . optimi maximique	Castulo (HispTarr)		Antoninus Pius	AE 1976.351
89	10	138–61	[ex indu]lgenti[a]	Roma			CIL 6.40530
90	10	138–61	consecuti ab indulgentia optimi maximique imp(erator) . . . beneficio interpretationis	Camerinum (Reg VI)	vicani Censorglacenses	municipal patron	CIL 11.5632 = ILS 2735
91	7	138–61	adiut[or . . .	Forum Sempronii (Reg VI)		Divus Had, Antoninus Pius	CIL 11.6118
92	10	138–61	ab optimo maximoque principe; optimus imp(erator)	Tuficum (Reg VI)	decr[e]t(o) decur(ionum)	Antoninus Pius	CIL 11.5694 = ILS 2666a

372

93	7	138–61	rest[itutori It]aliae	Bononia (Reg VIII)		Antoninus Pius	CIL 11.805 = ILS 343
94	7	138–61	[restit]utor[i Italiae?]	Placentia (Reg VIII)		Antoninus Pius	CIL 11.6939
95	10	138–61	optimus princeps; iustitia divini principis	Tergeste (Reg X)	decuriones et plebes Tergestinorum	Antoninus Pius	CIL 5.532 = ILS 6680
96	6	138–61	optimo principi ob singularem eius in se indulgentiam	Althiburita (Africa)	local official	Antoninus Pius	CIL 8.27776
97	5	138–61	[c]onditori munic[ipii]	Gigthis (Africa)	Gigthenses publice	Antoninus Pius	CIL 8.22707 = ILS 6779
98	4	138–61	fortissimo liberalissimoq(ue)	Lambaesis (Numidia)	soldier	Antoninus Pius	AE 1967.564
99	6	138–61	indul]gentia eijus	Hispalis (Baetica)	centonarii	Antoninus Pius	CIL 2.1167 = ILS 7223
100	6	138–61	[ex indulg]entia	Hispalis (Baetica)	centonarii	Antoninus Pius	AE 1987.496
101	10	138–61	omnium saec[ulor]um sacratissimo principi; ut omnium saeculorum sacratissimi principis... beneficia durarent permanerentque...	Ager Arelatensis (Narbonensis)	Pagani pagi Lucreti	local benefactor	AE 2000.883 = CIL 12.594 = ILS 6988
102	10	138–61	Virtus Aug(usta)	Duntocher (Britannia)	soldiers		RIB 2200
103	4	139–61	ex indulgentia eius	milestone ad Milev (Numidia)			CIL 8.10327 = ILS 5874
104	4	139–61	ex indulgentia eius	milestone ad Milev (Numidia)			CIL 8.10328
105	4	139–61	ex indulgentia eius	milestone ad Milev (Numidia)			CIL 8.22391
106	5	141–61	ob insignem eorum concordiam	Ostia (Reg I)	decurionum decreto	AntP & Faustina	CIL 14.5326

(cont.)

(cont.)

No.	Type	Date	Honorific term(s), Title(s), Praise language	Location	Dedicator(s)/Author(s)	Honorand(s)	Reference
107	10	142–61	allecto ab optimo imp(eratoris)	Tuficum (Reg VI)	d(ecreto) d(ecurionum)	municipal patron	CIL 11.5697 = ILS 5891
108	10	145–61	[ex] permissu [et voluntate?] optimi maximique principis; colonia co[ndita] … beneficiis eius au[cta]	Carthago (Africa)			CIL 8.12513 = ILS 345
109	3	160–4	Divo Antonin[o] ex cuiu[s] indulgent[ia]	Verecunda (Numidia)	soldier	Divus Antoninus	CIL 8.4205 = ILS 5752
110	6	167	optimo ac sanctissimo omnium saec[u]lorum principi	Collippo (Lusitania)	local patron	Divus Antoninus	CIL 2.5232 = ILS 6898
111	4	post 161	conservatori [ge]neris humani	milestone ad Milev (Numidia)		Divus Antoninus	CIL 8.19919

MARCUS AURELIUS

No.	Type	Date	Honorific term(s), Title(s), Praise language	Location	Dedicator(s)/Author(s)	Honorand(s)	Reference
112	3	140	optimo ac piissimo	Roma	officers of urban cohort	Marcus Aurelius	CIL 6.1009 = ILS 2012
113	7	140	optimo ac piissimo	Ostia (Reg I)		Marcus Aurelius	CIL 14.4366
114	3	161	pro salute im[p(eratorum)] … d(ominis) n(ostris)	Fayoum (Egypt)	army officials	MAur & LVer	AE 1987-974
115	6	162	optimo et indulgentissimo principi	Ficulea (Reg I)	pueri et puellae alimentari Ficolensium	Marcus Aurelius	CIL 14.4003 = ILS 6225
116	3	166	liberalissim[oque p]rincipi	Lambaesis (Numidia)	soldiers	Marcus Aurelius	CIL 8.18067 = ILS 2303

117	5	166	[-]ficientissim[o]	coloni (or colonia)	Mena'a (Numidia)	Marcus Aurelius senator/official	*CIL* 8.17958
118	10	167	trib. lat. ... donatum ab o[pt]imis maximisque imperator[ibus]		Ephesus (Asia)		*AE* 1979.601 = 1972.576
119	5	168	pagus Thugg(aritanus) caelesti beneficio eorum auctus	pagus Thuggaritanus	Thugga (Africa)	Marcus Aurelius municipal patron	*CIL* 8.26528b = *ILS* 9399
120	10	161–9	a sanctissimis imp(eratoribus) mandata; providentia maximorum imperat(orum) missus	Ordo Concordiensium	Concordia (Reg x)		*CIL* 5.1874 = *ILS* 1118
121	10	161–9	adlecto in decurias ab optimis maximisque imp Antonino et Vero	scapharii Hispalenses	Hispalis (Baetica)	local benefactor	*CIL* 2.1180 = *ILS* 1403
122	10	161–9	equo p(ublico) honorato a sacratissimis imp(eratoribus)	local council	Massilia (Narbonensis)	local benefactor	*CIL* 12.410
123	3	161–9	[pro salute imperato]rum... Antonini et Veri Iovi dilect(orum)	pref of cohort	Ilkley (Britannia)	MAur & LVer	*RIB* 636
124	1	169	sacratissimi imperatores; indulgentia sua	MAur and LVer	Gortyn (Crete)		*CIL* 3.14120
125	10	174	a sacratiss(imo) [imp(eratore)] ordinibu[s adscriptum sum]	soldiers	ain-Rua Gergur (MaurCaes)		*CIL* 8.21567
126	2	176	quod omnes omnium ante se maximorum imperatorem glorias supergressus bellicosissimis gentibus deletis aut subactis	SPQR	Roma	Marcus Aurelius	*CIL* 6.1014 = *ILS* 374
127	3	176	fortissimo [libe]ralissimoq(ue) [prin]cipi	soldiers	Lambaesis (Numidia)	Marcus Aurelius	*CIL* 8.2547

(*cont.*)

375

No.	Type	Date	Honorific term(s), Title(s), Praise language	Location	Dedicator(s)/ Author(s)	Honorand(s)	Reference
128	10	175–7	[pro salu]te et re[ditu et vi]ctoria; [ut eius ben]eficio [c(ivitatem R(omanam c(onsecutus]	Roma			*CIL* 6.40560 = 1015 = 31226
129	10	161–80	[ob m]erita quod su[ffragio eius ab sacra]tissimo ac [indulgent(issimo) imp(eratore)	Perge (Lycia/ Pamphylia)		proconsul	*AE* 2000.1453
130	10	169–80	adlectus in decurias ab optimis maximisq(ue) impp(eratores)	Mactar (Africa)	local citizen		*AE* 1983.976
131	1	177–80	fortissimi	Mesarfelta (?) (Numidia)	MAur and Comm		*CIL* 8.2488
132	10	177–80	magni imperatores; fructus tantae vestrae providentiae; sanctissimi imperatores; maximis imp(eratoribus) gratias; maximi principes	Italica (Baetica)	SC		*CIL* 2.6278 = *ILS* 5163
LUCIUS VERUS							
133	6	166	[pro]pagatori [imperii]	Roma	navicularii	Lucius Verus	*CIL* 6.1022
134	6	166	quod providentia et liberalitate indulgentiss[imi principis]	Ostia (Reg 1)	colleg fabr tign ostis	Lucius Verus	*CIL* 14.105
135	6	166	[pro]pagatori [imperii]	Ostia (Reg 1)	[codica]ri navicula[ri]	Lucius Verus	*CIL* 14.106
COMMODUS							
136	4	186	[sacra]tissimum imp(eratorum)	Roma	vici magistri	Commodus	*CIL* 6.31420
137	1	186	nobilissimus omnium et felicissimus princeps	milestone Rusicadem (Numidia)	Comm		*CIL* 8.10307 = *ILS* 397

No.	n	date	inscription	location	role	emperor	reference
138	3		fortissimo principi	Brixia (Reg x)	coss. 201	Commodus	*CIL* 5.4318
139	3	189	indulgentissimo principrincipi (sic!)	Bir Haddada (MaurCaes)	procurator	Commodus	*CIL* 8.8702
140	7	190	nobilissimo [et felicissimo principi]	Turris Libisonis (Sardinia)		Commodus	*AE* 1987.470
141	7	180–92	[for]tissimo felicissimo p[rincipi]	Avitta Bibba (Africa)		Commodus	*CIL* 8.802
142	10	180–92	opus dol(iare) ex pred(is) Staton(iensibus) Comm(odi) Aug(usti) domini n(ostri)	Carthago (Africa)		Commodus (?)	*CIL* 8.22632, 6
143	5	180–92	conservatori suo	Iluro (Baetica)	Ilurenses	Commodus	*CIL* 2.5486
144	10	180–92	sub specie nobilissimi pri[ncipis]	Nemausus (Narbonensis)	decreto decurionum	Commodus (?)	*CIL* 12.3312
145	8	180–92	pro salute et victoria domini n(ostri)	Castra Regina (Raetia)	soldier	Genius centuriai	*AE* 1986.532
146	4	180–92	f[ortissi]mo [ac f]elicis[simo pr]inc[ipi] domi[no in]du[lgen]tissi[mo]	milestone (Raetia)		Commodus	*CIL* 3.11984
147	4	180–92	d(omini) n(ostri)	Baltchik (Moesia Inferior)	Ennius Repertus	Commodus	*AE* 1969/70.578
148	4	185–92	pro salute et victoria . . . restitutori(s) commerc(iorum) secundum sacram subscriptionem domini n(ostri) sanctissimi imp(eratoris)	Porolissum (Dacia)	Cl. Xenophon, procurator	Commodus	*AE* 1988.977
149	4	192	[p]aca[t]or[i] orbis felici invicto romano herculi; omnium virtutum exsuperant(issimo)	Treba Augusta (Reg 1)	ordo decurionum commodianor(um)	Commodus	*CIL* 14.3449 = *ILS* 400

No.	Type	Date	Honorific term(s), Title(s), Praise language	Location	Dedicator(s)/Author(s)	Honorand(s)	Reference
150	10	180–93	[ius]sum divinae providentiae [tuae invo]care; sacratissime imperator; secundum sacram subscriptionem domini n(ostri) sanctissimi imp(eratoris)	Saltus Burunitanus (Numidia)			*CIL* 8.10570 = *ILS* 6870
151	6	197	divo Comm[odo]...fr[atri]... propagato[ris imperi]	Cirta (Numidia)	local benefactors	Divus Commodus	*CIL* 8.6994
152	7	197	divo Commodo...fratri... propagator(is) imp(eri)	Cirta (Numidia)		Divus Commodus	*CIL* 8.19679
153	6	202–3	Divo Commodo...fratri... propagatoris imperi(i)	Cuicul (MaurCaes)	local citizen	Divus Commodus	*AE* 1989.900
154	5	209	divo Commodo...fr[atri]... propagator(is) imp(erii) fortissimi [feli]ciss[imi] [patruo]...fortissim(i) [fe]licissimique prin[cipis] et super omnes p[rin]cipes nobi(li)ssim(i)	Nattabutes (Numidia)	Nattabutes	Divus Commodus	*CIL* 8.4826
			PERTINAX				
155	5	193	fortissimo duci et omnium virtu[t]uum (sic) principi	Capena (Reg VII)	Capenates	Pertinax	*CIL* 11.3873 = *ILS* 409

SEPTIMIUS SEVERUS

156	5	194	optimo fortissimoque principi	Nepet (Reg VII)	Nepesini	Septimius Severus	CIL 11.3201 = ILS 416
157	7	194	[pro salute et vic]toria… [f]ortissimi sa[nctissimique principis]	Lambaesis (Numidia)		Septimius Severus	CIL 8.18249
158	5	194	optimo fortissimoque providentissimoque principi d(omino) n(ostro)	Norba (Lusitania)	duumviri of Norba	Septimius Severus	CIL 2.693
159	5	195	dom[ino] n(ostro)	Saltus Aurasius (Numidia)	decurio	Septimius Severus	CIL 8.17950
160	7	195	dom[ino n(ostro)]	Cartenna (MaurCaes)		Septimius Severus	CIL 8.21506
161	6	195	fortissimo … invicto imperatori	Tipasam (MaurCaes)	magistri	Septimius Severus	CIL 8.9317
162	6	196	Aug(usto) Invicto	Ravenna (Reg VIII)	Rufinus Lib(ertus)	Septimius Severus	CIL 11.8
163	8	196	pro salute ddd[[d]](ominorum) nnn[[n]](ostrorum)	Singidunum (Moesia Sup)	Cilices	Jupiter Opt Max	AE 1990.854
164	3	193–7	pro salute dom[ini] n(ostri) imp(eratoris)	Lugdunum (Lugdunensis)	soldier	Septimius Severus	CIL 13.1766 = ILS 4794
165	8	193–7	pro salute do[mi]ni n(ostri)	Berytus (Syria)	Mummeus Ingenuus	Septimius Severus	CIL 3.158
166	8	194–7	pro salute et victoria domini n(ostri)	Aqua Flavianae (Numidia)	soldier	Aesculapius, Hygia	CIL 8.17726
167	7	196–7	propagatori imperi(i); prop[agatori]s imp(erii) … [filio]	Sila (Numidia)		Septimius Severus	AE 1969/70.697
168	6	197	indulgentissimo et clementissimo principi	Thermae Himeraea (Sicily)	local elites	Septimius Severus	CIL 10.7343
169	5	197	conservatori orbis ob publicam et in se privatam pietatem	Lepcis Magna (Africa)	Lepcitani publice	Septimius Severus	IRT 387

(cont.)

(cont.)

No.	Type	Date	Honorific term(s), Title(s), Praise language	Location	Dedicator(s)/ Author(s)	Honorand(s)	Reference
170	5	197	propagatori [i]mperi	Arsacal (Numidia)	res publica Arsacalitanorum	Septimius Severus	CIL 8.6048
171	10	197	iudicio dom[ini] n(ostri) sanctissimi et fortissi[mi]; legati... ad eundem dominum	Cirta (Numidia)	local citizen	local aristocrat	CIL 8.7062 = ILS 1143
172	9	197	[Iuliae] Augustae... [con]iugi... propagatoris imperi... fortissimi ac sanctissimi princip(is)	Sigus (Numidia)	res publica Siguitanorum	Iulia Augusta	CIL 8.5699
173	9	197	Iuliae Augustae... coniugi... propag(atoris) imp(erii)	Tiddis (Numidia)	res publica Tidditanorum	Iulia Augusta	CIL 8.6702
174	5	197	pacatori orbis	Isturgi (Baetica)	res publica Isturgitanorum	Septimius Severus	CIL 2²/7,60 = 2.2124
175	3	197	invicti Aug(usti)	S. Pedro de la Vina (Tarraconensis)	military unit	Septimius Severus	AE 1967.237
176	6	197	optim[o] fe[licissimo] fort[issi]mo p[rincipi]	Narbo (Narbonensis)	decumani Narbonenses	Septimius Severus	CIL 12.4346
177	3	195–8	fe[l[icissimo) f]ortissimoque	Thamugadi (Numidia)	soldiers	Septimius Severus	CIL 8.2438
178	6	198	indulgentissimo	Pola (Reg x)	local benefactor	Septimius Severus	CIL 5.27
179	5	198	indulgen[tis]simo et clementissimo principi [dom]ino nostro	Panhormus (Sicily)	res publica Panhormitanus	Septimius Severus	CIL 10.7274

180	6	indul[genti]ssimo et clementissi[mo] [pr]incipi domino n(ostro)	198	Panhormus (Sicily)	local elites	Septimius Severus	*CIL* 10.7276
181	5	optimo maximoque principi	198	Thibaris (Africa)	pagus Thibaritanus	Septimius Severus	*AE* 1991.1680 = 8.26179
182	7	propa[g](atori) imp(erii) fortissimo fe[l]licissimoque principi	198	Nechaa (Numidia)		Septimius Severus	*CIL* 8.19920
183	9	Iuliae Domnae Augustae... matri... pacis publ(icae) restitutoris	198	Thagaste (Numidia)	DD	Iulia Augusta	*CIL* 8.17214 = *ILS* 443
184	4	fortissimi [felic]issimi (sic)	198	milestone ad Sitifim (Numid)	colonia Sitif.		*CIL* 8.10337
185	4	fortissimo felicissimo	198	milestone ad Sitifim (Numid)	colonia Sitif.		*CIL* 8.10338
186	4	fortissimo felicissimo	198	milestone ad Sitifim (Numid)	colonia Sitif.		*CIL* 8.10353
187	4	fortissimo felicissimo; fortissimi felicissimi	198	milestone ad Sitifim (Numid)	colonia Sitif.		*CIL* 8.10362
188	10	sanctissim(i)	198	Matrica (PannInferior)	soldier		*AE* 1986.593
189	5	pro salute et victoria domin(orum) nn(ostrorum)	198–9	Gnathia (Reg II)	publice	SepSev, Car	*AE* 1993.503
190	9	Iuliae Augustae... coniugi... [pr]o[p]agatoris imperi(i)... fortissimi [s]anctissimi princip(is); matri... indulgentissimiq(ue) pr(i)ncipis	198–9	Sila (Numidia)	res publica Silensium	Iulia Augusta	*AE* 1969/70.699
191	1	[pr]opagatores [imperii]	198–9	Tatilti (MaurCaes)		SepSev and Car	*AE* 1995.1790
192	5	domino indulgentissimo	199	Panhormus (Sicily)	res publica Panhormitanus	Septimius Severus	*CIL* 10.7275

(cont.)

No.	Type	Date	Honorific term(s), Title(s), Praise language	Location	Dedicator(s)/ Author(s)	Honorand(s)	Reference
193	6	199	sedem quoque domino nostro Severo Augusto... posuit idemque dedicavit	Bulla Regia (Africa)	local official	Septimius Severus	AE 2004.1874
194	8	199	pro salute et reditu domm(inorum) nn(ostrorum) Impp(eratorum)	Sirmium (PannInferior)	imp. official (beneficiarius)	Jupiter Opt Max	AE 1994.1406
195	5	200	fortissimo]que prin]cipi; [patri felicis(issimi)... [fe]llicissimi [fortissimique et] super omne[s retro principes in]victissimi [principis]	Phua (Numidia)		Septimius Severus	CIL 8.6305
196	5	200	fortissimo felicissimoque principi p(atri) p(atria) et super omnes principes indulgentissimo	Phua (Numidia)	res publica Phuenses	Septimius Severus	CIL 8.6307
197	9	200	[Iuliae Augustae]... coniugi invic[ti] imp(eratoris)	Lepcis Magna (Africa)	local citizens	Iulia Augusta	IRT 402
198	3	198–201	fort[issimo] felicissimo... ob maximam erga se domu[s divinae]	Roma	praefectus vigilum	Septimius Severus	CIL 6.31320 = 3761
199	6	198–201	caelestem indulgent[iam] invicto imper(atore)	Ferentinum (Reg 1)	Ferentinates Novani	Septimius Severus	CIL 10.5825 = ILS 421
200	4	201	fortissimo [felicissimo]; fortissimi felicissimi filio	Roma		SepSev and Car	CIL 6.1030

201	9	201	Iuliae Augustae…coniugi invicti imp(eratoris)	Lepcis Magna (Africa)	procurator	Iulia Augusta	IRT 403
202	9	201	P(ublio) Septimio Getae patri domini n(ostri) imp(eratoris)	Lepcis Magna (Africa)	Curia Nervia ex voto		IRT 414
203	8	201	ubi domini nnn(ostri) castra fieri iusserunt	Bu Njem (Africa)	centurion	Genius Gholaiae	AE 1976.700
204	9	201	Iuliae August[ae]… coniugi…propa(gatoris) imp(erii)…fortiss(imi) felicis(imi) ac sanctissimi principis	Uzelis (Numidia)		Iulia Augusta	CIL 8.6340
205	6	201	pro sal(ute) dom(inorum) nn(ostrorum)	? (Dacia)	Cultores Iovis?	SepSev, Car, Geta	CIL 3.1602
206	5	202	ob eximiam ac divinam in se indulgentiam	Lepcis Magna (Africa)	Lepcitani Septimiani publice	Septimius Severus	IRT 393
207	5	202	ob eximiam ac divinam in se indulgentiam	Lepcis Magna (Africa)	Lepcitani Septimiani publice	Septimius Severus	IRT 423
208	9	202	avo d(omini) n(ostri)	Lepcis Magna (Africa)	Lepcitani publice		IRT 412
209	9	202	[Iu]liae Augustae… coniugi…[pr]opagatoris imperii fortissimi felicissimique prin[cipis]; matri…[fort]issimi felicissimique principis…[for]tissimi et super omnes principes indulgentissimi	Cirta (Numidia)	res publica Cirtensium	Iulia Augusta	CIL 8.6998
210	7	202	[pro salute]…for[tissimi f]elicissimiq(ue) principis super o(mnes) prin(cipes) – – –	Cuicul (MaurCaes)		Septimius Severus	CIL 8.20091

(cont.)

No.	Type	Date	Honorific term(s), Title(s), Praise language	Location	Dedicator(s)/ Author(s)	Honorand(s)	Reference
211	1	202	[imperat]ores d[d(omini nn(ostri)	Gorsium (PannInferior)	SepSev and Caracalla		AE 1997.1279 = CIL 3.334²
212	3	202	pro salute dd(ominorum) n[n(ostrorum)]	Tibiscum (Dacia)	Cohors I Vindelicorum	SepSev and Car	AE 1987.848
213	1	203	fortunatissimus nobilissimusque	Roma	SepSev		CIL 6.1032
214	2	203	optimis fortissimisque principibus ob rem publicam restitutam imperiumque populi Romani propagatum insignibus virtutibus eorum domi forisque	Roma	SPQR	SepSev and Car	CIL 6.1033 = ILS 425
215	7	203	[pro salute] . . . propagat(oris) imperi [fortissimi fe]llicissimiq(ue) principis; felicis(simi); [fortissimi fel]icissimiq(ue) principis et . . . indulgentissimi ac fortissimi Caes(aris)	Rusicade (Numidia)		Septimius Severus	CIL 8.7970
216	5	203	[fortissimo] invi[ctissimoque princi]pi; [fortissimi invi[ctissimique principis]	Thamugadi (Numidia)	res publica coloniae Thamugad.	Septimius Severus	CIL 8.17872
217	5	203	optimo [fortissimoque prin]cipi	Vivatia (HispTarr)	res publica Vivatiensium	Septimius Severus	CIL 2.3343
218	3	203	G(enio) dom(inorum) nn(ostrorum) Augg(ustorum)	Sirmium (PannInferior)	imp. official (beneficiarius)	SepSev, Car, Geta	AE 1994.1408

219	3	203	felicissimo saeculo dd(ominorum) nn(ostrorum) invictor(um); piissimorum	Philae (Egypt)	imp. soldiers	SepSev and Car	*CIL* 3.75
220	3	201–4	pro salute Augg[[g(ustorum)]] dominor(um) nn[[(ostrorum)]]	Sitifis (MaurCaes)	beneficiarius	SepSev, Car, Geta	*AE* 1993.1777
221	3	202–4	[a]mpla beneficia de indulgentia [Au]gustorum suffragio patris eius consecutus	Roma	imp. official		*CIL* 6.1074 = *ILS* 456
222	4	204	fortissimo felicissimoque; fortissimo felicissimo principi	Roma	argentari et negotiantes	SepSev and Car	*CIL* 6.1035
223	8	204	propagatori imperi[i fortis]simi felicissimique principis. . . [invi]ctissimi fortissimi felicissimi et super omnes principes indulgentissimi dominorum nostrorum	Cirta (Numidia)		Fortuna (?)	*CIL* 8.6969
224	3	204	p[ro]pagatori imperi ob cael[est]em in se indulgentiam eius	Lepcis Magna (Africa)	procurator	Septimius Severus	*IRT* 395
225	3	204	propagatori imp(eri) ob caelestem in se indulgentiam eius	Lepcis Magna (Africa)	procurator	Septimius Severus	*IRT* 424
226	3	204	pro salute dd(ominorum) nn(ostrorum)	Welzheim (GermSup)	soldier	SepSev and Car	*CIL* 13.6659 = *ILS* 428

(*cont.*)

(*cont.*)

No.	Type	Date	Honorific term(s), Title(s), Praise language	Location	Dedicator(s)/Author(s)	Honorand(s)	Reference
227	6	204	pro s[alute] dd(omini) nn(ostri) Augg(ustorum); [nobi]lissimi Caes(are)	Castra Regina (Raetia)	negotiatores?	SepSev and Car	*CIL* 3.5943
228	8	198–205	pro salute victori(i)sque et incolumitate imperatorum.... fortissimi felicissimi	Mactar (Africa)		Apollo	*AE* 2002.1667a
229	8	198–205	pro salute victori(i)[sque] et i[ncolumi]t[a]te imp[era]torum.... [fortissimi felicissimi]	Mactar (Africa)		Aesculapius	*AE* 2002.1667b
230	9	202–5	C. Bruttio Praesenti... Commodi nobilissimi et felicissimi p. socero	Urso (Baetica)	res publica Ursonensium		*CIL* 2²/5,1027 = 2.1405
231	10	205	[[Gaio Fulvio Plautiano... necessario]] dominorum nostrorum i[mp]eratorum	Lepcis Magna (Africa)	local citizens		*AE* 1973.572
232	10	205	dominorum nostrorum invictissimorum Augustor(um)	Ostia (Reg 1)	[-]	[-]	*CIL* 14.4570
233	9	205	Iuliae Aug(ustae)... coniugi... propag(atoris) imp(erii) fortissimi felicissimiq(ue)	Civitas Celtianensium (Numidia)	res publica civitas Celtianensium	Iulia Augusta	*CIL* 8.19693

			Text	Place	Dedicator	Honorand	Reference
234	9	205	p[rin(cipis)]; [matri] . . . fortissimi felicissimiq(ue) pr(incipis) . . . nobilissimi et [sup]er omnes prin(cipes) indulgen[tissim]o / Iuliae Augustae . . . coniugi . . . propagatoris imperi fortissimi felicissimiq(ue) principis / matri . . . felicis(simi) . . . fortissimi felicissimiq(ue) principis p p et super omnes / retro principes invictissimi	Phua (Numidia)	res publica Phuenses	Iulia Augusta	CIL 8.6306
235	10	205	dominis nn(ostris)	Rigomagum (GermInferior)	soldiers		CIL 13.7797
236	8	206	Geniis dd(ominorum) nn(ostrorum) Augg(ustorum)	Sirmium (PannInferior)	imp. official (beneficiarius)	Jupiter Opt Max	AE 1994.1411
237	10	206	evidenti in[l]ustrique provi]dentia domini n[ostri	Ephesus (Asia)	imp. freedman		CIL 3.427
238	3	207	restitutori castrorum ostiensium	Ostia (Reg 1)	vigiles Ostienses	Septimius Severus	CIL 14.4381 = ILS 2155
239	1	207	fortissimus ac super omnes felicissimus princeps	Anagnia (Reg 1)	SepSev and Car		CIL 10.5909
240	10	208	Iovi Opt(imo) Max(imo) conservatori sanctissimorum principum / ddd(ominum) nnn(ostrorum); fortissimi felicissimi; ob conservatam eorum salutem detectis insidiis hostium publicorum	Sicca Veneria (Africa)	DD		CIL 8.1628 = ILS 429

(cont.)

No.	Type	Date	Honorific term(s), Title(s), Praise language	Location	Dedicator(s)/Author(s)	Honorand(s)	Reference
241	4	197–209	[pro sal(ute) et v]ic(toria) impp(eratorum) domi[norum nn(ostrorum)]	Roma		SepSev and Car	*CIL* 6.40603 = 1039
242	9	197–209	fortissimi et felicissimi	Lavinium (Reg 1)	Laurentes Lavinates	Iulia Aug	*CIL* 14.2072
243	8	197–209	pro salute et felicissimo reditu . . . fortissimi felicissimique . . . fortissimi et super omnes principes indulgentissim(i)	Cirta (Numidia)	local official	Fortuna Red Aug	*CIL* 8.6944
244	9	197–209	P Septimio L f Getae patri . . . piissimi fili(o) maximi principis avi (sic) imp(eratoris) sanctissimi . . . fortissimi et indulgentissimi principis	Cirta (Numidia)	res publica IIII colonia Cirtensis		*CIL* 8.19493 = *ILS* 439
245	3	197–209	piis(simis) Augg(ustibus) ac fortissimis principibus propagatoribus imperii	Lambaesis (Numidia)	Leg III Aug	SepSev and Car	*CIL* 8.2705
246	3	197–209	pro salute . . . felicis(simi) maximi fortissimique principi iuventutis	Lambaesis (Numidia)	Leg III Aug	SepSev and Car	*CIL* 8.2706
247	7	197–209	[pro salute] d[d](ominorum) nn(ostrorum)	Lambaesis (Numidia)		SepSev, Car, Iulia	*CIL* 8.2707
248	8	197–209	Marti Aug(usto) conservatori dominorum nn[n](ostrorum)	Thamugadi (Numidia)		Mars Augustus	*CIL* 8.17835

388

249	8	197–209	Concordiae Augg(ustorum) dominorum nn[n](ostrorum)	Thamugadi (Numidia)	local official	Concordia Augusta	CIL 8.17829 = ILS 434
250	10	197–209	secundum mandata impp(eratorum) dominor(um) nn(ostrorum) Augg(ustorum)	Ara Romae et Augusti (Lugdunensis)		soldier/ benefactor	CIL 13,1680 = ILS 1390
251	10	197–209	dominor(um) nn(ostrorum)	Ara Romae et Augusti (Lugdunensis)		Plautianus	CIL 13,1681 = ILS 1328a
252	7	197–209	pr[o salute et reditu] impp(eratorum) inv[ictorum]	Mediolanum (Aquitania)		SepSev and Car	AE 1977.535
253	5	197–209	in h(onorem) . . . invicti	Mogontiacum (GermSup)	civitas Treverorum	SepSev and Car	CIL 13,6800 = ILS 419
254	1	197–209	maximo perp(etuo) Aug(usto)	Egmond (GermInferior)		SepSev and Caracalla	CIL 13,8829
255	8	197–209	pro sal(ute) dd(omini) nn(ostri); nobil(issimo) Caes(are)	Campona (PannInferior)	C. Iulius Euticus	Jupiter Opt Max	CIL 3,3391
256	3	197–209	Numini dd(ominorum) nn(ostrorum) impp(eratorum)	Matrica (PannInferior)	vet(erani) et [cives Romani]	SepSev, Car, Geta	AE 2001.1688 = 1995,1270 = 1993.1302
257	8	197–209	pro salu[te domin]orum nn(ostrorum)	Szekesfehervar (PannInf)	soldiers	Deus Sol Elagabalus	AE 1973.437bis
258	8	197–209	pro salute dd(ominorum) nn(ostrorum) impp(eratorum) Augg(ustorum)	Gracanica (Moesia Superior)	priests of IOM Dolichenus	IOM Dolichenus	AE 1966.340
259	8	197–209	pro salute dominorum [im]p(eratorum) n(ostrorum)	Tyra (Moesia Inferior)		Tempus Bonus	CIL 3.13747

(cont.)

(cont.)

No.	Type	Date	Honorific term(s), Title(s), Praise language	Location	Dedicator(s)/ Author(s)	Honorand(s)	Reference
260	8	197–209	p[ro] salute dominorum nn(ostrorum)	Tyra (Moesia Inferior)		Tempus Bonus	CIL 3.12510
261	8	197–209	pro salu(te) dd(ominorum) nn(ostrorum)	Aulutrene (Asia)	soldiers	IOM and Juno Reg	AE 1995.1512
262	1	197–209	[fort]issimor(um) Augu(storum)	milestone (Asia)	(SepSev and Car)		CIL 3.7168
263	8	197–209	pro salu(te) dd(ominorum) nn(ostrorum) Impp(eratorum) Augg(ustorum)	Apollonia (Galatia)	soldiers	IOM and Juno Reg	AE 1987.941
264	10	198–209	in h(onorem) dd(ominorum) impp(eratorum)... Auggg(ustorum) nnn(ostrorum) max(imorum)	milestone/boundary stone (Asia)	quaestor		AE 1997.1448
265	5	198–209	pro salute... fortissimi felicis[simi]; fortissimi felicissimi fili; for[ti]ssimi felicissimi [[fili]]	Giufi (Africa)	civitas Giufitana	SepSev, Car, Geta	AE 2003.1986
266	5	198–209	pro salute dd(ominorum) nn(ostrorum) im]p[p(eratorum)	Virunum (Noricum)	IIvir	SepSev and Car	AE 2001.1587
267	8	198–209	pro salute felicissimorum impp(eratorum)	Montana (Moesia Inferior)	centurion	Apollo	AE 1987.887

						SepSev/Car	CIL 8.7972
268	7	209	[f]ortissimo f[elicissimoque principi]; [f]elicis(simi); [f]or[t]issim[i et] felicissim[i et supra omnes re]tro pri[ncip]e[s i]nd[ulgentissimi] ac forti[s]sim[i et]; [fortissimo f]eli[c]issim[o]que [p]rincipi [et supra omnes retro princ]ipes	Rusicade (Numidia)			
269	8	209	pro salute ddd(ominorum) nn[[n]](ostrorum) Augg[[g]](ustorum)	Sirmium (PannInferior)	imp. official (beneficiarius)	Jupiter Opt Max	AE 1994.1414
270	9	198–210	Iuliae Aug(ustae) matri . . . fortissimi felicissimi	Roma	Laurentes Lavinates	Iulia Aug	CIL 6.1047
271	4	198–210	for[tissimo]; indul]gentiss[imo]	Roma		Septimius Severus	CIL 6.40608 = 31323
272	4	210	fort[issimo felicissimoque]	Roma		Septimius Severus	CIL 6.40622 = 31475
273	1	210	[fortissi]mus feliciss(imus)	Via Traiana (Reg II)		Septimius Severus	CIL 9.6011
274	5	210	caelesti eius indulgentia in aeternam securitatem adque gloriam	Camerinum (Reg VI)	Cameres	Septimius Severus	CIL 11.5631 = ILS 432
275	10	210	[Indulgentiae . . .] fortissimi nobilissimiq(ue)	Cirta (Numidia)	local official		CIL 8.6996
276	3	210	pro salute et incolumitate ddd(ominorum) nnn(ostrorum)	Tamuda (MaurTing)	soldier		AE 1991.1743

(cont.)

(cont.)

No.	Type	Date	Honorific term(s), Title(s), Praise language	Location	Dedicator(s)/ Author(s)	Honorand(s)	Reference
277	9	193–211	[matri] domini nostr[i]	Roma	imp. freedpersons	SepSev and Iulia	CIL 6.40646 = AE 1983,28
278	10	193–211	inulcti (sic) Severi fortis[simi felicissimi]	Pola {Reg x}			CIL 5,61
279	9	193–211		Aubuzza (Africa)			CIL 8.16370
280	9	193–211	[Iu]lia[e Domnae Augustae]... [fortissimi ac fel]icissimi con[iugi]	Carthago (Africa)		Iulia Augusta	CIL 8.24556
281	7	193–211	[pro salute et victorii]s... [i]nvic[ti	Mactar (Africa)			CIL 8.23411
282	10	193–211	[fo]rtissimi	Mbudja (Africa)			CIL 8.23655
283	6	193–211	propagatori imperi	Wed Scham (Africa)	local official	Septimius Severus	CIL 8.17257
284	4	193–211	[fortis]simo f[e]licissimo	milestone (Africa)		Septimius Severus	CIL 8.25416
285	9	193–211	Pacciae Marcianae quondam coniugi... piissimi maximi principis	Cirta (Numidia)	res publica IIII colonia Cirtensis	Paccia Marciana	CIL 8.19494 = ILS 440
286	7	193–211	[i]nvict[o]	Acci (HispTarr)		Septimius Severus	CIL 2.3400
287	8	193–211	pro salute et victoria...domini indulgentissimi	Poetovio (PannSup)	imp. freedman	Jupiter Opt Max	CIL 3.402c
288	8	193–211	pro [s]alu[te] d(ominorum) n(ostrorum)	Veczel (Dacia)	soldiers	Jupiter Opt Max	AE 1977,705 = CIL 3.1343
289	8	193–211	pro [sal(ute)] d(ominorum) n(ostrorum) imp(eratorum)	Cabyle (Thrace)	soldiers	(multiple deities)	AE 1999,1374a

290	5	193–211	princip(em) felicissimum; principem [iu]stissimum	Kiachta (Syria)	quattuor civitates Commag	Septimius Severus	CIL 3.6712
291	7	195–211	optimo fortissimo	Marsi Marruvium (Reg IV)		Septimius Severus	CIL 9.3665
292	10	197–211	[fel(icibus?)] invict(is) A[ugg]	Caiatia (Reg I)		municipal patron	CIL 10.4584
293	5	197–211	ex indulgentia dominorum	Lanuvium (Reg I)	SPQ Lanivinus	SepSev and Car	CIL 14.2101 = ILS 5686
294	9	197–211	Iuliae Augustae... coniugi invicti imp(eratoris)	Lepcis Magna (Africa)	Curia Augusta	Iulia Augusta	IRT 405
295	9	197–211	Iulia[e] Augustae... coniugi invicti imp(eratoris)	Lepcis Magna (Africa)	Curia Iulia	Iulia Augusta	IRT 406
296	9	197–211	Pac[cia]e M[a]rcianae quondam [u]xoris domini n[o]str[i] imp(eratoris)	Lepcis Magna (Africa)	Curiae tres Plotina et Nervia et Matidia	Paccia Marciana	IRT 411
297	9	197–211	Fulviae Piae matris domini nostri imp(eratoris)	Lepcis Magna (Africa)	Lepcitani Septimiani publice	Fulvia Pia	IRT 415
298	9	197–211	Fulviae Piae matri domini nostri imp(eratoris)	Lepcis Magna (Africa)	Curiae tres Severae Pia et Ulpia et Augusta	Fulvia Pia	IRT 416
299	3	197–211	piis(simis) A[ugg(ustibus) et fortissi[mis(i) principibus]	Lambaesis (Numidia)		SepSev and Car	CIL 8.18071
300	8	197–211	pro salute dd(omini) [nn(ostrorum)]	Ain-Rua Gergur (MaurCaes)		Deus Frugiferus Aug	CIL 8.20318
301	10	197–211	[aet]ernit[ati imperii d]omino[rum nostrorum]	Caesarea (MaurCaes)			CIL 8.20981
302	8	197–211	[pro salute do]minorum [nostrorum]	Volubilis (MaurTing)	DD	IOM and Juno Reg	AE 1987.1105
303	8	197–211	pro salute dominorum nn(ostrorum)	Celeia (Noricum)	soldier	Fortuna Stabilis	CIL 3.5156a

(cont.)

(cont.)

No.	Type	Date	Honorific term(s), Title(s), Praise language	Location	Dedicator(s)/Author(s)	Honorand(s)	Reference
304	4	197–211	pro salute dominorum nostrorum	Poetovio (PannSup)	imp. slave	SepSev and Car	CIL 3.15184 (4)
305	8	197–211	[pro s]alute f[e]licis[simi max]imi princip<i>s sacratissimi imper(atores)	Intercisa (PannInferior)	soldiers	Diana Tifatina	AE 1968.429
306	10	197–211	[pro salut]em do[minoru]m nn[[n]](ostrorum)	Apulum (Dacia)	heirs	soldier	CIL 3.1193
307	8	197–211	pr(o) sal(ute) domino(rum) (sic) nn(ostrorum) Augg(ustorum)	Apulum (Dacia)	eques singularis	IOM Dolichenus	AE 1994.1490 = 1978.662
308	8	197–211	pro salute dominorum nostrorum	Apulum (Dacia)	imp. freedman	Minerva Victrix	CIL 3.14215 (16)
309	8	197–211	[pr]o sal(ute) ddd(ominorum) [nnn(ostrorum) A]ugg(ustorum)	Mediam (Dacia)	legatus	Hercules	CIL 3.1564
310	8	197–211	pro sal(ute) d(ominorum) n(ostrorum) [Au]g(ustorum)	Tibiscum (Dacia)	veteran	Deus Malachbelus	AE 1983.797
311	8	197–211	pro salute domino[r](um) nn(ostrorum)	Tibiscum (Dacia)	veteran	Deus Malachbelus	AE 1967.393
312	8	197–211		Viminiacum (Moesia Sup)			CIL 3.14217 (3)
313	7	197–211	pro salute et incolumitate dominorum nn(ostrorum) Impp Augg	Qasr el Uweinid (Syria)		SepSev and Car	AE 1978.827
314	8	201–11	[pr]o salute et victoria [dom]inor(um) nostor(um) imp(eratorum)	Ain Wif (Africa)	soldier	IOM Dolichenus	IRT 868

(cont.)

315	6	201–II	[pro salute in]vi[ctorum] Augustoru[m]... fortissimi felicissimi; feliciss(imi)	Wed Scham (Africa)	local official		*CIL* 8.17258
316	10	202–II	pr pr ac necessario dd(ominorum) nn(ostrorum)	Patavium (Reg x)		Plautianus	*AE* 1979.294
317	10	202–II	[o]b honorem [quinquen-nalita]tis...permissu sacratiss[imi pr]incipis	Lepcis Magna (Africa)	local magistrate		*IRT* 396
318	10	202–II	iussu Fulvi Plautiani... [ne]cessari dominorum nostrorum	Lepcis Magna (Africa)			*IRT* 530
319	10	205–II	[[G(aio) Fulvio Plautiano... necessario]] dominorum nostrorum	Lepcis Magna (Africa)	local citizens		*AE* 1967.537
320	10	209–II	felicissimo saeculo do[minorum nostrorum]	Roma	official from schola urbana		*CIL* 6.40623
321	7	209–II	ex indulgentia d(ominorum) n(ostrorum)	Praeneste (Reg I)		SepSev, Car, Geta	*CIL* 14.3036
322	10	209–II	pro felicitate et incolumitatem saeculi dominorum nn(ostrorum)	Lambaesis (Numidia)	Cornicines Leg III Aug		*CIL* 8.2557 = *ILS* 2354
323	7	209–II	pro salute dd[d](ominorum) nn[n](ostrorum); pii(ssimi) fortissimiq(ue)	Thamugadi (Numidia)	local official		*CIL* 8.17837
324	10	209–II	ex indulg[entia] dominorum	Thibilis (Numidia)			*CIL* 8.18903
325	3	211	fortissimo ac super omnes felicissimo principi	Ostia (Reg I)	vigiles Ostienses	Septimius Severus	*CIL* 14.4388
326	8	211	[p]ro salute d(omini) n(ostri) [i]m[p](eratoris)	Campona (PannInferior)	Oeticus VB Corvinus	Hercules Augusti	*CIL* 3.3390

(cont.)

No.	Type	Date	Honorific term(s), Title(s), Praise language	Location	Dedicator(s)/Author(s)	Honorand(s)	Reference
327	9	post 211	fortissimi felicissimi princ(ipis)	Ancona (Reg v)	ordo et plebs ex commodis suis	Julia Domn.'s brother	CIL 9,5899 = ILS 441
CARACALLA							
328	5	195–7	filio . . . propaga[t]oris imperi . . . fortissimi [e]t [sa]nctissimi principis f(ortissimi) f(elicissimi)	Sigus (Numidia)	res publica Siguitanorum	Caracalla	CIL 8,5700
329	7	197		Uriunum Hortanse (Reg vi)		Caracalla	AE 1995.448
330	5	197	M Aurelio Antonino [C]aes[ar]i [fil]io . . . fortissimi felicis[simi]que p[r]inci[pis]	Cirta (Numidia)	res publica Cirtensium	Caracalla	CIL 8.19495
331	3	197	propagatoris imperi(i) filio	Lambaesis (Numidia)	soldier/patron of community	Caracalla	AE 1967.567; = 8.18256
332	5	197	vindicis et conditoris Romanae disciplinae filio	Thamugadi (Numidia)	DD	Caracalla	CIL 8.17870 = ILS 446
333	6	198	domino indulgentissimo	Roma	paedagogi puerorum a capite Africae	Caracalla	CIL 6.1052
334	5	198–9	fortissimo felicissimoque principi filio . . . propagatori[s] imperi(i) p(atris) p(atriae) fortissimi felicissimiqu[e] principis indulgentissimi nobilissimiq(ue)	Sila (Numidia)	res publica Silensium	Caracalla	AE 1969/7c.698
335	6	199	fortis[simi f]elic[issimique principis filio	Thamugadi (Numidia)	local official	Caracalla	CIL 8.17871

(cont.)

336	4	200	fortissimi felicissim(i) p(atris) p(atriae) filio	Roma	tibicines Romani	Caracalla	CIL 6.1054
337	6	200	felicissimi p(atris) p(atriae) filio	Lepcis Magna (Africa)	local citizens	Caracalla	IRT 419
338	5	200	imp Caesari M Aurelio Antonino Aug.... pacatoris orbis filio	Tucci (Baetica)	res publica Tuccitanorum	Caracalla	CIL 2²/5,74 = 2.1669
339	5	201	felicissimi p(atris) p(atriae) filio	Lepcis Magna (Africa)	Curia Pia Severiana ex voto	Caracalla	IRT 420
340	5	201	felicissimi p(atris) p(atriae) filio	Lepcis Magna (Africa)	Curia Ulpia	Caracalla	IRT 421
341	3	201	felicissimi p(atris) p(atriae) filio	Lepcis Magna (Africa)	procurator	Caracalla	IRT 422
342	5	202	fortissimi f[elicissi]mi principis... filio	Uchi Maius (Africa)	res publica Uchitanorum Maiorum	Caracalla	AE 2000.1733
343	4	205–7	forti]ssimo ac felic[issi]mo principi do[mino i]ndulgentissim[o]	milestone (Raetia)		Caracalla	AE 1978,586
344	4	198–209	forti[ssimi felicissimique... fil(io)]	Roma		Caracalla	CIL 6.40667 = 1041
345	4	198–209	fortiss[imi felicissimique... fil(io)]	Roma		Caracalla	CIL 6.40668 = 31346
346	4	198–210	fortiss[imi felicissimique... fil(io)]	Roma		Caracalla	CIL 6.40652 = 31452
347	4	198–210	f]ortissi[mi felicissimique... fil(io)...]	Roma		Caracalla	CIL 6.40653 = 31476
348	4	202–10	felici[ssimi principis filio]	Roma		Caracalla	CIL 6.40636a = 31385a
349	7	210	fortissim(i) felicissimi... filio	Falerii (Reg VII)		Caracalla	CIL 11.3087
350	5	210	fortissimi felicissimi... filio	Alsium (Reg VII)	decur(iones) colon(iae) Alsiensis	Caracalla	CIL 11.3716
351	7	193–211	[for]tissimi [f]elicissimi[q]ue	Chaouat (Africa)		Caracalla	CIL 8.25370
352	5	193–211	fortissimi felicissimi filio	Giufi (Africa)	civitas Giufitana	Caracalla	CIL 8.23993

(cont.)

No.	Type	Date	Honorific term(s), Title(s), Praise language	Location	Dedicator(s)/Author(s)	Honorand(s)	Reference
353	4	197–211	felicissimi [f]o[r]ti[ssimi p(atris) p(atriae) filio]	Roma		Caracalla	CIL 6.1061
354	7	197–211	[fortissimi feli]cissimi[i principis... filio]	Capena (Reg VII)		Caracalla and Geta	CIL 11.3876
355	7	197–211	felicissimi p(atris) p(atriae) filio	Lepcis Magna (Africa)		Caracalla	IRT 426
356	5	197–211	felicissimi p(atris) p(atriae) fil(io)	Lepcis Magna (Africa)	Lepcitani Septimiani publice	Caracalla	IRT 435
357	4	211	[o]ptimo; [t]onistratori Aug(usto); orbis terrarum [propagatori; domino] maximo; providens imperi sui mai[estatem finesque eius] ampliavit; largam gloriam pac[e data auxit]; [f]elicia tempora	Roma	corpus piscatorum et urinatorum		AE 1996.90 = CIL 6.40638 = 1080
358	10	211–12	[pro s]alu[te] ... f(elicis) Aug(usti) invicti	Aures (Numidia)	veteran		AE 1976.722
359	3	211–12	IOM con[s(ervatori)] Augg(ustorum) nn(ostrorum) pien(tissimorum) fratrum	Lambaesis (Numidia)	discharged soldiers	Caracalla and Geta	CIL 8.2618
360	10	211–12	quaestor candidatus a domin[o] nostr[o] invictissim[o]	Thibilis (Numidia)			CIL 8.5528
361	3	211–12	[pro salute... i]nvic[ti]ssimorum imp[p(eratorum)]	Poetovio (PannSup)	procurator	Caracalla and Geta	AE 1978.643

362	8	211–12	pro sal(ute) domin[[n(orum)]] n[[n(ostrorum)]]	Porolissum (Dacia)	prov. gov.	Nymphis Augustor	*AE* 1977.666
363	8	211–12	pro salute<m> d[[d(ominorum)]] n[[n(ostrorum)]] Aug[[g(ustorum)]]	Tibiscum (Dacia)	veteran/decurion of Sarm	Deus Sol Ierhabolus	*AE* 1977.697
364	8	211–12	pro salute dd(ominorum) nn(ostrorum)	Varmezo (Dacia)	soldiers (?)	IOM Dolichenus	*CIL* 3.7645
365	3	212	pro salute et incolumit[a]te domini nostri	Roma	soldiers		*CIL* 6.1063
366	5	212	pacatori orbis	Tucci (Baetica)	res publica Tuccitanorum	Caracalla	*CIL* 2².5.77 = 2.1671
367	1	212	maximus invictissimus sanctissimus fortissimus felicissimus et super omnes principes indulgentissimus	milestone ad Milev (Numid)	Caracalla		*CIL* 8.22384
368	6	211–13	[in honorem] … fortis[simi fe]licissimique et super o[mnes prin]cipes indulgentissimi	Cirta (Numidia)	local official	Caracalla	*CIL* 8.7000
369	5	212–13	magno et [invicto ac] super omnes principes [fortissimo] et felicissimo	Ciciliano (Reg IV)	[ex d(ecurionum)] d(ecreto)	Caracalla	*AE* 1972.156
370	4	213	invicto; domino indulgentissimo; conservatori suo	Roma	negotiantes Vasculari	Caracalla	*CIL* 6.1065
371	5	213	domino nostro invictissimo [et] omnium principum v[irtute] benivolentia indulgentia exuperantissimo; optimo sanctissimoque	Roma	Laurentes Lavinates	Caracalla	*CIL* 6.1066

(cont.)

(cont.)

No.	Type	Date	Honorific term(s), Title(s), Praise language	Location	Dedicator(s)/Author(s)	Honorand(s)	Reference
372	10	213	magnus et invictus ac super omnes principes fortissimus felicissimusque; divina providentia eius	Roma			CIL 6.31338a
373	10	213	fe[l]icissimus]	Roma			CIL 6.31339
374	3	213	pro salute et reditu et victorias dom(ini) n(ostri)	Roma	praefectus vigilum		CIL 6.40647
375	5	213	magno [e]t invicto ac fortissimo principi	Ferentinum (Reg 1)	SPQFerentinas	Julia and Car	CIL 10.5826
376	5	213	domino nostro invictissimo [et] omnium principum v[irtute] benivolentia indulgentia exuperantissimo; optimo sanctissimoque	Lavinium (Reg 1)	Laurentes Lavinates	Caracalla	CIL 14.2073
377	5	213	infatigabili indulgentia eius	Cosa (Reg VII)	res publica Cosanorum decr(eto) dec(urionum)	Caracalla	CIL 11.2633 = ILS 6597
378	5	213	magno imperatori	Pola (Reg x)		Caracalla	CIL 5.28
379	5	213	d(omino) n(ostro)	Horrea (MaurCaes)	saltus Horreorum et Kalefacelenses	Caracalla	CIL 8.8426 = ILS 6890
380	1	213	[fortissimus fe]licissimusq(ue) [magn(us) princeps pacato]r orbis [vias et pontes vetustate] conlab[s]a[s restituit]	ms. Augusta Raur. (GermSup)		Caracalla	AE 1996.1141
381	1	213	fortissimus felicissimus magnus imp(erator) pacator orbis	ms. Noviodonum (GermSup)		Caracalla	CIL 13.9061

382	1	213	fort(issimus) felici[ss(imus) . . .]; pac(ator) orb(is)	milestone (GermSup)		Caracalla	*CIL* 13.9068
383	3	213	invictissimo Aug(usto)	Holzhausen (GermSup)	cohort	Caracalla	*CIL* 13.7616
384	10	213	[invictis]si(mo) inno[centissimoque]	Saalburg (GermSup)		Caracalla	*CIL* 13.7465a
385	1	213	fortissim(us) felicissimusque magn(us) princeps pacator orb(is)	milestone AdAqHelv (GermSup)		Caracalla	*CIL* 13.9072
386	8	213	pro salute M(arci) [A]ur[eli . . .] bono generis humani imperante	High Rochester (Britannia)	leg aug prpr	Matunus	*RIB* 1265 = *ILS* 4727
387	3	213	[pro sal(ute) imp(eratoris) do]mini nos[tri]	Old Carlisle (Britannia)	soldiers		*RIB* 905
388	10	213	d(omino) n(ostro)	Mogontiacum (GermSup)	soldiers		*CIL* 13.6762
389	3	213	[fortissi]mo ac [fe]lici[issimo principi	Abusina (Raetia)	Leg. III Italica	Caracalla	*CIL* 3.11950
390	4	213	invicto; fortissimo ac felicissimo principi domino indulgentissimo	milestone (Noricum)		Caracalla	*CIL* 3.5745
391	6	213	pro salute d(omini) n(ostri) imp(eratoris)	Szekesfehervar (PannInf)	IIvir and decurion of colony	Caracalla	*AE* 1973.437
392	3	214	magno et invicto; ob insignem indulgentiam beneficiaque eius erga se	Roma	M. Asinius Sabinianus vc	Caracalla	*CIL* 6.1067
393	10	214	dominus noster invictissimus	Mogontiacum (GermSup)			*AE* 1975.620

(*cont.*)

No.	Type	Date	Honorific term(s), Title(s), Praise language	Location	Dedicator(s)/ Author(s)	Honorand(s)	Reference
394	5	214	magno et invicto et super omnes princ(ipes) fort(issimo) felic(issimo)	Colonia Saturnia (Reg VII)	d(ecreto) d(ecurionum)	Caracalla	CIL 11.2648
395	6	214	fortissimo inclitoque ac super omnes felicissimo principi	Albingaunum (Reg IX)	plebes urbana Albingaunensium	Caracalla	CIL 5.7780
396	5	214	optimo maximoque principi	Ucubi (Africa)	decuriones	Caracalla	CIL 8.15669 = ILS 6807
397	8	214	Iovi Optimo Ma[ximo]; Iunoni; Minervae; Indulgentiae	Tinfadi (Numidia)	res publica Tinfadi	Caracalla	CIL 8.2194
398	6	214	pro salute d(omini) n(ostri)	Aquincum (PannInferior)	local benefactor (IIvir)	Caracalla	CIL 3.10439
399	3	214	[felicissimo f]ortissi[m]oq[ue] princ(ipi)	Porolissum (Dacia)	cohors V Lingonum Antoniniana	Caracalla	AE 1979.492 = AE 1958.231
400	8	212–15	[ma]x[i]mi [sa]nctis[si]miq(ue) [i]mp(eratoris) n(ostri)	Tibiscum (Dacia)	legatus	Apollo Conservator	AE 1987.849
401	5	215	optimo maximoque principi	Colonia Iulia Assuras (Africa)	Colonia Iulia Assuras	Caracalla	CIL 8.1798 = ILS 437
402	6	215	domino nostro invictissimo Augusto	Rusicade (Numidia)	local citizen	Caracalla	CIL 8.7973
403	5	215	op[timo] princ(ipi)	Siagitana (Africa)	civitas Siagitanorum	Caracalla	CIL 8.966
404	4	215	i[nv]ict[o]; [f]ort(issimo) A[u]g(usto) f[e]l[i]c(issimo) principi [d]omino indulgent(i)ss(imo)	milestone (Raetia)		Caracalla	AE 1978.587
405	4	215	invicto; [fortiss(imo) ac] felic(issimo) princ[ipi]	milestone (Raetia)		Caracalla	CIL 3.5980

406 4	215	invict(o); fort(issimo) Aug(usto) fel(icissimo) princ(ipi) dom(ino) ind[ul]g(entissimo)	milestone (Raetia)		Caracalla	CIL 3.5997
407. 4	215	invic[to]; felic(issimo) prin(cipi) [dom]in(i) indul[gent]issimis (sic?)	milestone (Raetia)		Caracalla	CIL 3.5998
408 4	215	invicto; fort(issimo) Aug(usto) felic(issimo) pr[incipi do]mino indulg[e]n[tiss(imo)]	milestone (Raetia)		Caracalla	CIL 3.5999
409 8	215	pro sal(ute) d(omini) n(ostri)	Celeia (Noricum)	soldier	IOM Conservator	CIL 3.5185
410 8	215	pro salute domini n(ostri); pii felicis	Apulum (Dacia)	legionary tribune		CIL 3.1063 = ILS 2178
411 8	215	pro salu(te) d(omini) n(ostri)	Abritus (Moesia Inferior)	beneficiarius consularis legionis XI Claud	Dea Epona Regina	AE 1993.1370
412 1	216	invictus	milestone Via Appia		Caracalla	CIL 10.6854 = ILS 5822
413 5	216	[pro cont]inua indulgentia eius maximus invictissimus	Lepcis Magna (Africa)	Lepcitani Septimiani	Caracalla	IRT 429
414 1	216	sanctissimus fortissimus felicissimus et super omnes principes indulgentissimus	milestone Rusicadem (Numidia)		Caracalla	CIL 8.10305
415 10	216	ob si[ngular]em eiu[s erga mun]icipes [indul]genti[am]	Volubilis (MaurTing)			CIL 8.21828
416 3	216	pro salu[te et incolumitate domini nostri . . . pii felicis] invicti	Aquincum (PannInferior)	legionary cohorts (?)	Caracalla	AE 1990.805
417 7	197–217	[magno e]t invicto	Aletrium (Reg 1)		Caracalla	CIL 10.5802
418 6	197–217	numini victoriae . . . invicti principis	Ager Saluzzenis (Reg IX)	Eulalius libertus	Caracalla	CIL 5.7643

(cont.)

No.	Type	Date	Honorific term(s), Title(s), Praise language	Location	Dedicator(s)/Author(s)	Honorand(s)	Reference
419	10	197–217	Indulgentiae domini nostri; Virtutis domini n(ostri)	Cirta (Numidia)	local official		CIL 8.7094–8 = ILS 2933
420	4	211–17	salvis dominis nn(ostris)	Roma	Felix Rufinus et Lupercilla	Caracalla	CIL 6.1070
421	4	211–17	fortis[simo principi]	Roma		Caracalla	CIL 6.40650 = 1072
422	10	211–17	eq(uus) rom(anus) ab domino imperatore	Cemelenum (Reg x)	Q. Eniboudius Montanus	local god	CIL 5.7865
423	10	211–17	eq(uus) rom(anus) ab domino imperatore	Cemelenum (Reg x)	Q. Eniboudius Montanus	local god	CIL 5.7866
424	10	211–17	[d]omini n(ostri)	Muru de Bangius (Sardinia)	(restoration)		AE 1992.892
425	5	211–17	optimo maximoque principi	Ain-Zouza (Africa)	DD	Caracalla	CIL 8.23708
426	9	211–17	Iuliae Aug(ustae)...matri sanctissimi [principis]	Althiburita (Africa)		Iulia Augusta	CIL 8.27778
427	8	211–17	pro salute et aeternitate imperi domini nostri	Carthago (Africa)			AE 1998.1538
428	5	211–17	[sa]lutis con[servationi]s et felicita[tis domini] nostri	Gigthis (Africa)	Gigthenses publice	Caracalla	CIL 8.22715
429	6	211–17	optimo m[aximo]que principi	Nibber (Africa)	seniores	Caracalla	CIL 8.15721
430	5	211–17	optimo maxi[mo invicto? p]rincipi	Pupput (Africa)	Pupputenses	Caracalla	CIL 8.24092
431	7	211–17	[A]ug(usto) op[timo]	Thibaris (Africa)	local citizen	Caracalla (?)	CIL 8.15436
432	9	211–17	pro salute... [et Iul]iae Domnae A[ug(ustae) matris...d]omini nostri	Thugga (Africa)		Iulia Augusta	AE 1997.1654

433	8	211–17	pro salute domin(i) [nostri]	Calceus Herculis (Numidia)	soldier	Hercules	*CIL* 8.2496
434	8	211–17	ordinatus ex eq(uite) Rom(ano) ab domino imp(eratore)	Cemenelum (AlpsMaritimae)	Q. Eniboudius Montanus (centurion)		*CIL* 5.7865 = *ILS* 4664
435	8	211–17	ordinatus ex eq(uite) Rom(ano) ab domino imp(eratore)	Cemenelum (AlpsMaritimae)	Q. Eniboudius Montanus (centurion)		*CIL* 5.7866
436	3	211–17	[invic]tiss[imo]	Holzhausen (GermSup)	cohort	Caracalla	*CIL* 13.7617
437	9	211–17	matri [i]nd[u]lgentis[si]mi princi[pis]	Murrhardt (GermSup)	cohort	Iulia Augusta	*CIL* 13.6531
438	8	211–17	pro salute invicti Antonini Aug(usti)	Nettersheim (GermInferior)	M. Aurelius Agrippinus BF COS	Deabus Aufanis	*CIL* 13.11984 = *ILS* 9330
439	5	212–17	pacatoris orbis et fundatoris imperii romani filio	Malaca (Baetica)	r(es) p(ublica) Malacit(anorum)	Caracalla	*CIL* 2.1969
440	10	212–17	pro salute d(omini) n(ostri) maximi ac fort(issimi) imp(eratoris)	Birdoswald (Britannia)			*RIB* 1911
441	3	212–17	pro sal[ute et incolumitate] dom(ini) nostr(i) Invict(i)	Hadrian's Wall (Britannia)	imp. procurator		*RIB* 2066 = *ILS* 9317
442	8	212–17	[pro salute] domini [nostri imp(eratoris)	Chrtrhouse on Mendip (Brit)			*RIB* 185
443	8	212–17	pro sal[l]ute dom(ini) n(ostri); p(ii) f(elicis)	Brod (PannInferior)	dispensator	Iovi Depulsori	*CIL* 3.3269
444	3	212–17	[optimo maxim]o[que] principi	Veczel (Dacia)	Ala I Hisp	Caracalla	*CIL* 3.1378
445	8	212–17	pro s(alute) imp(eratoris) d(omini) n(ostri)	Ratiaria (Moesia Superior)		IOM D(olichenus?)	*CIL* 3.14502 (1)
446	8	212–17	domini imp(eratoris)	Ephesus (Asia)	procurator	Bona Fortuna	*AE* 1972.595

(cont.)

(cont.)

No.	Type	Date	Honorific term(s), Title(s), Praise language	Location	Dedicator(s)/Author(s)	Honorand(s)	Reference
447	6	212–17	invicto Augusto pio felici	Ancyra (Galatia)	Ael Lycinus V E	Caracalla	CIL 3.244
448	1	212–17	[pi]us felix invictus	Podandus (Cilicia)	Caracalla	Caracalla	AE 1969/70.608 = CIL 3.12118
449	8	212–17	pro salut[e et] victoriis d(omini) n(ostri)	Heliopolis (Syria)	local councilors		CIL 3.138
450	4	212–17	invicte imp Antonine pie felix Aug multis annis imperes	milestone (Syria)		Caracalla	CIL 3.207
451	10	213–17	[adlecto] inter patric(ios) a [sanctissimo?] domino nostro	Aquileia (Reg x)		local benefactor	AE 2000.606 = CIL 5.874
452	1	213–17	[invi]ctus Aug(ustus); [libe]ralita[te]	Aquae (GermSup)		Caracalla	CIL 13.6301
453	7	213–17	pro salute et victoria invicti imp(eratoris)	Ribchester (Britannia)		Caracalla	RIB 590
454	6	214–17	fortissi[mo invictis]simo; [felicissimo] indulg[entissimoque] pri[ncipi]	Vienna (Narbonensis)	flamen of imp. cult (civis Seguisavus)	Caracalla	CIL 12.1851
455	7	216–17	invicto et m[ax(imo)]	Tarraco (HispTarr)		Caracalla	AE 1989.483
456	4	217	in]victo; [. . .fel]iciss[imo	Roma		Caracalla	CIL 6.1069
457	6	217	pro salute et incolumitate domini nostri	Lambaesis (Numidia)	cultores dei Ierhobolis iuniores	Caracalla	AE 1967.572
458	1	217	pater militum	milestone via Emerita (Lusitania)		Caracalla	CIL 2.4676 = ILS 454
459	5	222–35	[Div]o An[tonin]o Mag[no] patri do[min]i nostri	Tutugi (HispTarr)	res publica Tutugiensis	Divus Caracalla	AE 1983.608

GETA

460	5	198	pacatoris orbis et fundatoris imperi romani f[i]l(io) [[filio]]	Portus Magnus (MaurCaes)	res publica Portuensis Magnensis	Geta	*CIL* 8.21613
461	6	200	felicissimi p(atris) p(atriae) [[filio]]	Lepcis Magna (Africa)	local citizens	Geta	*IRT* 433
462	5	200	[P. Septimio Getae Nob. Caesari] ... pacatoris orbis filio et M. Aurelio Antonini imp. fratri	Tucci (Baetica)	res publica Tuccitanorum	Geta	*CIL* 2²/5,75 = 2.1670
463	3	200–1	felicissimi p(atris) p(atriae) [[filio]]	Lepcis Magna (Africa)	procurator	Geta	*IRT* 434
464	7	209	[nobilis]simo Caes(ari) ... [ob] eximiam ac divinam in s[e indulgentiam]	Lepcis Magna (Africa)		Geta	*IRT* 441
465	3	209	felicissimi p(atris) p(atriae) [[filio]]	Lepcis Magna (Africa)	procurator	Geta	*IRT* 444
466	5	211	Imp(eratori) Caes(ari) Getae ... pacatoris orbis f(ilio) et M. Aurelio Antonini imper(atoris) frat(ri)	Tucci (Baetica)	res publica Tuccitanorum	Geta	*CIL* 2²/5,76
467	7	193–211	for[ti]ssimi felicissimi pr[inc(ipis) fil(io)	Sicca (Africa)	local official (?)	Geta	*CIL* 8.15857
468	5	197–211	felicissimi p(atris) p(atriae) [[filio]]	Lepcis Magna (Africa)	Curia Matidia	Geta	*IRT* 436
469	3	197–211	fortissimi felicissimi p(atris) p(atriae) filio	Lepcis Magna (Africa)	centurion of urban cohort	Geta	*IRT* 439

MACRINUS

470	5	217	providentissimo et sanctissimo principi	Diana (Numidia)	res publica Dianensium	Macrinus	*CIL* 8.4598 = *ILS* 463

(cont.)

407

No.	Type	Date	Honorific term(s), Title(s), Praise language	Location	Dedicator(s)/ Author(s)	Honorand(s)	Reference
471	7	217–18	[pio felici] invicto	Arqub Abu Busela (Palestine)		Macrinus	*AE* 1969/70.630
472	1	217–18	[provi]dentissim[i Aug(usti)]	milestone (Noricum)		Macrinus and Diadume- nianus	*AE* 2003.1317 = *CIL* 3.13534
473	1	218	nobiliss(imus) Caes(ar); providentissimi Augg(usti)	milestone (Noricum)		Macrinus and Diadume- nianus	*CIL* 3.5708
474	1	218	nobilissimus Caes(ar); providentissimi Augusti	milestone (Noricum)		Macrinus and Diadume- nianus	*AE* 1980.664

ELAGABALUS

No.	Type	Date	Honorific term(s), Title(s), Praise language	Location	Dedicator(s)/ Author(s)	Honorand(s)	Reference
475	8	218	pro salute d(omini) n(ostri); pii felicis	Aquincum (PannInferior)	soldier	Jupiter Opt Max	*CIL* 3.3445
476	4	218	fortissim[o] felicissim[oque] principi	milestone Asturicam (HispTarr)			*CIL* 2.4766
477	4	219	fortissimo felicissimoque principi	milestone Asturicam (HispTarr)			*CIL* 2.4767
478	4	219	fortissimo felicissimoque principi	milestone Asturicam (HispTarr)			*CIL* 2.4769
479	4	219	fortissimo felicissimoque principi	milestone Asturicam (HispTarr)			*CIL* 2.4805
480	1	219	felicissim[us atque] indul[gentissimus]	milestone ad Milev (Numid)		Elagabalus	*CIL* 8.22385

481	1	219	felicissimus adque invictissimus ac super omnes retro principes indulgentissimus d(omino) n(ostro)	milestone Rusicadem (Num)		Elagabalus	CIL 8.10304 = ILS 471
482	8	219	d(omino) n(ostro)	Salorducom (GermSup)	local citizen?	Genius Publicus	CIL 13.5171
483	10	219	ex inl(ustre) imp(eratore) d(omino) n(ostro)	Mogontiacum (GermSup)	Vicani capite limitis		CIL 13.6764 = ILS 7086
484	10	220	dominus noster	Mogontiacum (GermSup)			AE 1966.262
485	1	220	felicissimus atq(ue) invictissimus ac super omnes retro principes indulgentissimus	milestone Rusicadem (Num)		Elagabalus	CIL 8.10308
486	8	220	pro s(alute) d(omini) n(ostri)	Naissus (Moesia Superior)	soldier	Jupiter Opt Max	CIL 3.14561
487	8	221	pro s(alute) dd(omini) nn(ostri)	Naissus (Moesia Superior)	priest	Dea Fortuna	CIL 3.14562
488	1	221	d(omini) n(ostri) filius	milestone (Cappadocia)		Elagabalus	AE 1993.1565 = 1989.731
489	4	218–22	[sup]er omnes [retro principes feli]ci(ssimo)	Roma		Elagabalus	CIL 6.1077
490	5	218–22	[indulgenti]ssim(o) [principi]	Aquileia (Reg x)	[res pub]lic[a Aquileiensis]	Elagabalus	AE 1984.432
491	10	218–22	[domi]ni n(ostri)	Bu Njem (Africa)		Elagabalus	AE 1976.701
492	5	218–22	invicto pio felice Aug(usto) amplissimo [sacerdote dei invicti Solis Elagabali]	Lamasba (Numidia)	decreto ordinis et colonorum		CIL 8.18587 = ILS 5793
493	7	218–22	Iuliae Maesae . . . aviae domini nostri	Lambaesis (Numidia)		Elagabalus, Maesa	CIL 8.2715

(cont.)

No.	Type	Date	Honorific term(s), Title(s), Praise language	Location	Dedicator(s)/Author(s)	Honorand(s)	Reference
494	4	218–22	invicto pio felici	milestone ad Biskram (Numidia)			CIL 8.10334
495	1	218–22	invictus pius felix	milestone ad Biskram (Numidia)		Elagabalus	CIL 8.10267
496	4	218–22	invicto pio felici	milestone (Numidia)		Elagabalus	AE 1981.909
497	8	218–22	pro salute dom(ini) n(ostri)	Traiectum (GermInferior)	soldiers	multiple divinities	CIL 13.8811
498	1	218–22	[p]ius [f]elix Augustus [i]nvictus	milestone (Galatia)		Elagabalus	AE 1986.684
499	4	218–22	domino indulgentissimo	milestone (Cappadocia)	imp. legatus	Elagabalus	CIL 3.6900
500	1	218–22	pi[us] fel[i]x invictus	milestone (Cappadocia)		Elagabalus	CIL 3.12214
501	10	221–2	Virtus Augg(ustorum)	Chesters (Britannia)	soldiers		RIB 1466
502	3	222	nobilissimo Caes(ari) d(omini) n(ostri)... [[fil(io)]]	Bu Njem (Africa)	vice praesidis Numidiae	Elag. and SevAl	AE 1995.1640 = 1990.1028
503	1	222	pio felici invicto	milestone (PannInferior)		Elagabalus	CIL 3.3713
SEVERUS ALEXANDER							
504	4	218–22	[indulgentissimo] ac super omnes principes fortissimo	Roma		Severus Alexander	CIL 6.40679a = 1079
505	10	222	d(omino) n(ostro)	Fauces Bingenses (GermSup)			CIL 13.7607
506	10	222	d(ominis) n(ostris)	Netherby (Britannia)	soldiers		RIB 979
507	3	222	d(omini) n(ostri)	Netherby (Britannia)	soldiers	Severus Alexander	RIB 978 = ILS 2619

508	9		av[iae domi]ni n(ostri)	Forum Clodii (Reg VII)	IIviri of Aquincum	Iulia Maesa	AE 1993.668
509	8	222–3	pro sal(ute) d(omini) n(ostri)	Aquincum (PannInferior)	imp. official (beneficiarius)	IOM Teutanus	AE 1993.1313 = CIL 3.10481
510	8	223	[Genj]o Imp(eratoris) [[[d(omini) n(ostri)]]	Sirmium (PannInferior)		Jupiter Opt Max	AE 1994.1416
511	7	223	[pio] felici invicto	Ancyra (Galatia)		Severus Alexander	CIL 3.316
512	8	225	pro salute et incolumitate domini n(ostri) imp(eratoris)	Bu Njem (Africa)	soldiers	Deus Mars Canapph.	AE 1979.645
513	8	226	d(omino) n(ostro)	Bonna (GermInferior)	soldier	Hercules Magusanus	AE 1971.282
514	8	226	[p]ro salute d(omini) n(ostri) [[imp(eratoris) – – -]]	Bolcske (PannInferior)	IIviri of Aquincum	IOM Teutanus	AE 2003.1413 = 1991.1324
515	8	226	pro s(alute) d(omini) n(ostri) imp(eratoris)	Ulpiana (Moesia Superior)	soldier	IOM UPP	CIL 3.8173
516	10	227	Indu[l]gentiae imp(eratoris)	Sabratha (Africa)			IRT 41
517	10	227	infatigabili indulgentia domini nostri	Perdices (Numidia)	castellani Perdicenses		AE 1966.593
518	8	227	pro salute d(omini) n(ostri)	Novae (Moesia Inferior)	primus pilus	IOM Depulsor	AE 1972.526
519	8	227	pro sal(ute) d(omini) n(ostri) imp(eratoris) . . . optimi principis	Svistov (Moesia Inferior)			AE 1999.1330a
520	4	226–8	invicto; d[om(ino) nost]ro; [forti]ssimo ac felic[issi]mo principi dom[ino] [i]ndulgentissimo	milestone (Raetia)		Severus Alexander	AE 1987.790
521	7	228	pro salute dominorum	Autessiodurum (Lugdunensis)		Severus Alexander?	CIL 13.2922

(cont.)

(cont.)

No.	Type	Date	Honorific term(s), Title(s), Praise language	Location	Dedicator(s)/ Author(s)	Honorand(s)	Reference
522	8	228	pro salute d(omini) n(ostri)	Sirmium (PannInferior)	imp. official (beneficiarius)	Jupiter Opt Max	*AE* 1994.1418
523	8	229	pro salute d(omini) n(ostri)	Sirmium (PannInferior)	imp. official (beneficiarius)	Jupiter Opt Max	*AE* 1994.1419
524	8	229	d(ominus) n(oster)	Bingium (GermSup)	local benefactor	Jupiter Opt Max	*CIL* 13.7502
525	10	229	d(omino) n(ostro)	Mogontiacum (GermSup)	soldiers		*CIL* 13.6752
526	7	230	[domino n]ostro	Sabratha (Africa)		Severus Alexander	*IRT* 42
527	10	230	[pro s]alute imp(eratoris)... domini n(ostri)	Uchi Maius (Africa)	eques; sacerdos bidentalis		*AE* 1999.1852
528	10	230	[ex indulgenti]a domini no[st]r[i]	Uchi Maius (Africa)			*AE* 2001.2086 = *CIL* 8.26262
529	8	230	Genio d(omini) n(ostri)	Sirmium (PannInferior)	imp. official (beneficiarius)	Jupiter Opt Max	*AE* 1994.1420
530	8	231	pro salutem d(omini) n(ostri) Imp(eratoris)	Sirmium (PannInferior)	imp. official (beneficiarius)	Jupiter Opt Max	*AE* 1994.1422
531	8	231	[inv]icti	Bonna (GermInferior)	legion		*CIL* 13.8017
532	8	233	ob salutem e reditum d(omini) n(ostri); p(ii) f(elicis)	Aquincum (PannInferior)	soldier	Hercules Augusti	*CIL* 3.3427
533	1	234	invictus	Castellum Dianense (MaurCaes)	SevAl		*CIL* 8.8701 = *ILS* 6887

534	1	234	sanctissimus Augustus	milestone (Moesia Inferior)	SevAl		*CIL* 3.12519
535	10	218–35	d(omino) n(ostro)	Saalburg (GermSup)	soldier	genius loci?	*CIL* 13,7450
536	3	218–35	[pr]o salu[te] imp(eratoris) domini n(ostri)	Fauces Bingenses (GermSup)			*CIL* 13,7608
537	10	222–35	op[timo]	Capua (Reg 1)	Lugdunenses	patronus	*CIL* 10.3856 = *ILS* 1173
538	1	222–35	[invic]tus pius felix et super [omnes principes . . .]	Misenum (Reg 1)		Elag. or SevAl	*AE* 2002.358 = *CIL* 10.3342
539	10	222–35	ex indulgentia sacra dom(ini) n(ostri) invicti	Iulium Carnicum (Reg x)			*CIL* 5,1837 = *ILS* 5589
540	10	222–35	sacro praecepto d(omini) n(ostri) Antonini Pii felicis(simi) Aug(usti)	Calama (Africa)			*CIL* 8.17521
541	8	222–35	IOM Conservatori . . . invicti pii felicis Aug(usti)	Lambaesis (Numidia)	local official	Jupiter Opt Max	*CIL* 8.2620
542	8	222–35	pro salute d(omini) n(ostri)	Lambaesis (Numidia)	soldier	Dis Mauris	*CIL* 8.2638 = *ILS* 9293
543	10	222–35	[pro aeternitate imp]erii domini nostri	Lambaesis (Numidia)			*AE* 1967.573 = 8.18254 + 18257
544	8	222–35	p(ro) s(alute) d(omini) n(ostri)	Plaine de Guert (Numidia)	collegium Maiorum et Melliorum	Jupiter Opt Max	*AE* 1971,513
545	8	222–35	Marti Aug(usto) protectori d(omini) n(ostri)	Sigus (Numidia)	local official	Mars Augusti	*CIL* 8.19124
546	4	222–35	do[mi]no n(ostro) maximo et fortissimo	milestone ad Ngaus (Numidia)			*CIL* 8.22522
547	4	222–35	domino n(ostro) maximo et fortissimo	milestone ad Ngaus (Numidia)			*CIL* 8.22523
548	4	222–35	invicto	milestone ad Ngaus (Numidia)			*CIL* 8.22521
549	4	222–35	d(omino) n(ostro)	Bordj Medjama (MaurCaes)	officials		*CIL* 8.8812 = *ILS* 5965
550	10	222–35	[incompar]abili indul[gentia]	Castellum Dianense (MaurCaes)			*CIL* 8.20486

(cont.)

413

(cont.)

No.	Type	Date	Honorific term(s), Title(s), Praise language	Location	Dedicator(s)/Author(s)	Honorand(s)	Reference
551	7	222–35	pro sal(ute) d[omini n(ostri)] sanc(tissimi) [fort(issimi)]que; super omn[es] . . .]cent[. . .] princ[ipis]	El-Gara (Msad) (MaurCaes)		Severus Alexander	CIL 8.8781
552	8	222–35	pro salute d(omini) n(ostri); invicti pii fel(icis)	El-Gara (Msad) (MaurCaes)	soldiers		CIL 8.8795 = ILS 4340
553	5	222–35	invict(o); optim[o - - -] principi	Ucubi (Baetica)	res publica Ucubitanorum	Severus Alexander	CIL 2²/5,442 = 2.1554
554	5	222–35	for[tissi]mo maximoq(ue) principi	Ulia Fidentia (Baetica)	res publica Uliensium	Severus Alexander	CIL 2²/5,493 = 2.1533 = AE 1986.375
555	9	222–35	Iuliae Avitae Mameae Aug(ustae) matri domini n(ostri) imp(eratoris)	Ulia Fidentia (Baetica)		Iulia Mamaea	CIL 2²/5,494 = AE 1986.376
556	8	222–35	[p]ro salute . . . invicti	Iversheim (GermInferior)	soldiers		CIL 13.7944 = ILS 4745
557	7	222–35	pro salute d(omini) n(ostri)	Iversheim (GermInferior)			CIL 13.11761
558	9	222–35	[matri . . . Alex]andr[i felicis for]tissimi Aug(usti)	High Rochester (Britannia)		Iulia Mamaea	RIB 1282
559	8	222–35	[pro s]alute . . . [Iul]iae M[ameae matr(is) d(omini)] n(ostri) et c[astr(orum)]	Old Carlisle (Britannia)		Deae Matres	RIB 901
560	9	222–35	[p]ro [sa]l(ute) im[p(eratoris) . . . Iul(iae) Mamaeae ma]t[r]is d(omini) n(ostri)	Ribchester (Britannia)	soldiers		RIB 587

561	8	222–35	pro salute d(omini) n(ostri)	Brigetio (PannSuperior)	soldier	Jupiter Opt Max	*CIL* 3.10984
562	3	222–35	[p]ro s[alute] d(omini) n(ostri); d(omini) sanctissimi Aug(usti)	Cirpi (PannSuperior)	praetorian prefect	Severus Alexander	*AE* 1982.799
563	8	222–35	pro sal(ute) d(omini) n(ostri) p(ii) f(elicis) Aug(usti)	Intercisa (PannInferior)	praepositus stationis Spondill--	Deus Aeternus	*AE* 1990.823
564	8	222–35	pro sal(ute) d(omini) n(ostri) p(ii) f(elicis) Aug(usti)	Intercisa (PannInferior)	praepositus stationis Spondill--	Deus Aeternus	*AE* 1966.302
565	9	222–35	d(omini) n(ostri) invicti	Ulcisia Castra (PannInferior)	cohort	Iulia Mamaea	*CIL* 3.3639
566	5	222–35	pio fel(ice) inv[i]c[t]o; [i]ndulgent[i]ss[imo] principi	Domav (Dalmatia)	local council of Domav	Severus Alexander	*CIL* 3.8359
567	9	222–35	[p]ii [felicis in]v[ic(ti)	Domav (Dalmatia)	local council of Domav	Iulia Mamea	*CIL* 3.8360
568	3	222–35	[optimo maxi]moque princi[pi	Also-Ilosua (Dacia)	Legatus Augusti	Severus Alexander	*CIL* 3.797
569	8	222–35	pro sal(ute) d(omini) n(ostri)	Sacidava (Moesia Superior)	IIvir designatus	IOM Dolichenus	*AE* 1998.1143
570	8	222–35	pro salute d(omini) n(ostri)	Medit. ad Haem. (MoesInf)	Vil VC	Diana Sospita	*CIL* 3.14207 (41)
571	8	222–35	pro salutem imp(eratoris) d(omini) n(ostri)	Noviodonum (Moesia Inf)	local officials (?)	IOM Dolichenus	*CIL* 3.14445
572	1	222–35	aquaeductum divi Hadriani parentis sui liberalitate Dyrrachinis factum. . . .	milestone (Macedonia)		SevAl	*CIL* 3.709
573	10	222–35	proc(uratori) d(omini) n(ostri)	Corinth (Achaea)	procurator	procurator	*CIL* 3.536
574	3	230–5	pio felici invicto Aug(usto)	Yuzevler Mahallesi (BithPont)	imp. official	SevAl and IulMam	*AE* 1986.653
575	3	234–5	salvo [et i]n[victo] domino nostro	Volubilis (MaurTing)	procurator	procurator	*AE* 1966.606

Inscriptions in epigraphic corpus, by location

This appendix is organized geographically, and presents the inscriptions in the epigraphic corpus by location: Rome; Italy; provinces; and several larger areas (mainly in the eastern empire). The number refers to the number of the inscription in the master list of inscriptions (appendix 13). For discussion of the geographical spread of these inscriptions, see Introduction to Part II, 188–9; for the main distribution map (AD 69–235), see 186–7.

Rome:

1, 6, 7, 9, 11, 14, 18, 20, 22, 27, 36, 40, 42, 51–3, 55, 73, 83, 86, 89, 112, 126, 128, 133, 136, 198, 200, 213, 214, 221, 222, 241, 270–2, 277, 320, 333, 336, 344–8, 353, 357, 365, 370–4, 392, 420, 421, 456, 489, 504.

Italy:

4, 10, 12, 16, 17, 19, 21, 24, 25, 31–3, 38, 39, 41, 44, 50, 54, 57–62, 74, 76, 79, 81, 90–5, 106, 107, 113, 115, 120, 134, 135, 138, 140, 149, 155, 156, 162, 168, 178–80, 189, 192, 199, 232, 238, 239, 242, 273, 274, 278, 291–3, 316, 321, 325, 327, 329, 349, 350, 354, 369, 375–8, 394, 395, 412, 417, 418, 422–4, 451, 490, 508, 537–9.

Africa Proconsularis:

49, 56, 63, 64, 77, 96, 97, 108, 119, 130, 141, 142, 169, 181, 193, 197, 201–3, 206–8, 224, 225, 228, 229, 231, 240, 265, 279–84, 294–8, 314, 315, 317–19, 337, 339–42, 351, 352, 355, 356, 396, 401, 403, 413, 425–32, 461, 463–5, 467–9, 491, 502, 512, 516, 526–8, 540.

Numidia:

13, 23, 65, 66, 98, 103–5, 109, 111, 116, 117, 127, 131, 137, 150–2, 154, 157, 159, 166, 167, 170–3, 177, 182–7, 190, 195, 196, 204, 209, 215, 216, 223, 233, 234,

243–9, 268, 275, 285, 299, 322–4, 328, 330–2, 334–5, 358–60, 367, 368, 397, 402, 414, 419, 433, 457, 470, 480, 481, 485, 492–6, 517, 541–8.

Mauretania Caesariensis:
67, 68, 125, 139, 153, 160, 161, 191, 210, 220, 300, 301, 379, 460, 533, 549–52.

Mauretania Tingitana:
276, 302, 415, 575.

Baetica:
2, 3, 8, 15, 26, 30, 43, 45, 87, 99, 100, 121, 132, 143, 174, 230, 338, 366, 439, 462, 466, 553–5.

Hispania Tarraconensis:
5, 69, 75, 88, 175, 217, 286, 455, 459, 476–9.

Lusitania:
110, 158, 458.

Alpine Provinces:
434, 435.

Gallia Narbonensis:
34, 35, 37, 101, 122, 144, 176, 454.

Gallia Lugdunensis:
164, 250, 251, 521.

Aquitania:
252.

Germania Superior:
226, 253, 380–5, 388, 393, 436, 437, 452, 482–4, 505, 524, 525, 535, 536.

Germania Inferior:
235, 254, 438, 497, 513, 531, 556, 557.

Britannia:
84, 102, 123, 386, 387, 440–2, 453, 501, 506, 507, 558–60.

Raetia:
145, 146, 227, 343, 389, 404–8, 520.

Noricum:
85, 266, 303, 390, 409, 472–4.

Pannonia Superior:
287, 304, 361, 561, 562.

Pannonia Inferior:
78, 188, 194, 211, 218, 236, 255–7, 269, 305, 326, 391, 398, 416, 443, 475, 503, 509, 510, 514, 522, 523, 529, 530, 532, 563–5.

Dalmatia:
28, 566, 567.

Dacia:
148, 205, 212, 288, 306–11, 362–4, 399, 400, 410, 444, 568.

Moesia Superior:
163, 258, 312, 445, 486, 487, 515, 569.

Moesia Inferior:
147, 259, 260, 267, 411, 518, 519, 534, 570, 571.

Thrace/Macedonia:
70, 289, 572.

Achaea/Crete:
29, 46–8, 124, 573.

Asia Minor/Anatolia:
71, 72, 80, 82, 118, 129, 237, 261–4, 446–8, 488, 498–500, 511, 574.

Syria/Levant/Egypt:
114, 165, 219, 290, 313, 449, 450, 471.

Inscriptions in epigraphic corpus, by type

This appendix presents the inscriptions in the epigraphic corpus, by type. The number refers to the number of the inscription in the master list of inscriptions (appendix 13). For discussion of the different types into which the epigraphic corpus has been divided, see Introduction to Part II, 181–3.

Type 1 (emperor as author = emperor's names/titles in nominative):
41, 61, 64, 124, 131, 137, 191, 211, 213, 239, 254, 262, 273, 367, 380–2, 385, 412, 414, 448, 452, 458, 472–4, 480, 481, 485, 488, 495, 498, 500, 503, 533, 534, 538.

Type 2 (dedication to emperor by senate/SPQR):
1, 7, 18, 20, 24, 25, 31, 36, 42, 53, 83, 126, 214, 572.

Type 3 (dedication to emperor by soldiers/army officials):
4, 65, 66, 80, 85, 109, 112, 114, 116, 123, 127, 138, 139, 164, 175, 177, 198, 212, 218–21, 224–6, 238, 245, 246, 256, 276, 299, 325, 331, 341, 359, 361, 365, 374, 383, 387, 389, 392, 399, 416, 436, 441, 444, 463, 465, 469, 502, 507, 536, 562, 568, 574, 575.

Type 4 (dedication to emperor by non-military imperial officials):
6, 11, 14, 23, 27, 32, 40, 73, 86, 98, 103–5, 111, 136, 146–9, 184–7, 200, 222, 241, 271, 272, 284, 304, 336, 343–8, 353, 357, 370, 390, 404–8, 420, 421, 450, 456, 476–9, 489, 494, 496, 499, 504, 520, 546–9.

Type 5 (dedication to emperor by city, community, or municipal council):
15, 16, 17, 22, 26, 33, 37, 38, 39, 44–52, 55, 63, 71, 74–8, 97, 106, 117, 119, 143, 154–6, 158, 159, 169, 170, 174, 179, 181, 189, 192, 195, 196, 206, 207, 216, 217, 253, 265, 266, 274, 290, 293, 328, 330, 332, 334, 338–40, 342, 350, 352, 356, 366, 369, 371, 375–9, 394, 396, 401, 403, 413, 425, 428, 430, 439, 459, 460, 462, 466, 468, 470, 490, 492, 553, 554, 566.

Type 6 (dedication to emperor by non-state groups or private individuals):
43, 87, 96, 99, 100, 110, 115, 133–5, 151, 153, 161, 162, 168, 176, 178, 180, 193, 199, 205, 227, 283, 315, 333, 335, 337, 368, 391, 395, 398, 402, 418, 429, 447, 454, 457, 461.

Type 7 (dedication to emperor by unknown dedicator[s]):
5, 13, 30, 54, 56, 62, 81, 91, 93, 94, 113, 140, 141, 152, 157, 160, 167, 182, 210, 215, 247, 252, 268, 281, 286, 291, 313, 321, 323, 329, 349, 351, 354, 355, 417, 431, 453, 455, 464, 467, 471, 493, 511, 521, 526, 551, 557.

Type 8 (dedication to god[s] on behalf of emperor):
145, 163, 165, 166, 194, 203, 223, 228, 229, 236, 243, 248, 249, 255, 257–61, 263, 267, 269, 287–89, 300, 302, 303, 305, 307–12, 314, 326, 362–4, 386, 397, 400, 409–11, 427, 433–5, 438, 442, 443, 445, 446, 449, 475, 482, 486, 487, 497, 509, 510, 512–15, 518, 519, 522–4, 529–32, 541, 542, 544, 545, 552, 556, 559, 561, 563, 564, 569–71.

Type 9 (dedication to member of imperial family):
172, 173, 183, 190, 197, 201, 202, 204, 208, 209, 230, 233, 234, 242, 244, 270, 277, 279, 280, 285, 294–8, 327, 426, 432, 437, 508, 555, 558, 560, 565, 567.

Type 10 (miscellaneous):
2, 3, 8–10, 12, 19, 21, 28, 29, 34, 35, 57–60, 67–70, 72, 79, 82, 84, 88–90, 92, 95, 101, 102, 107, 108, 118, 120–2, 125, 128–30, 132, 142, 144, 150, 171, 188, 231, 232, 235, 237, 240, 250, 251, 264, 275, 278, 282, 292, 301, 306, 316–20, 322, 324, 358, 360, 372, 373, 384, 388, 393, 415, 419, 422–4, 440, 451, 483, 484, 491, 501, 505, 506, 516, 517, 525, 527, 528, 535, 537, 539, 540, 543, 550, 573.

Works cited

Adams, J. N. (2003). *Bilingualism and the Latin Language*. Cambridge.

(2007). *The Regional Diversification of Latin, 200 BC–AD 600*. Cambridge.

Alberston, A. (2005). "The creation and dissemination of Roman imperial portrait types: the case of Marcus Aurelius Type IV," *JdI* 119: 259–306.

Alcock, S. and Morrison, K. (2001). "Imperial ideologies," in Alcock *et al.* (eds.), pp. 279–82.

Alcock, S. *et al.* (eds.) (2001). *Empires: Perspectives from Archaeology and History*. Cambridge.

Alföldi, A. (1970). *Die monarchische Repräsentation im römischen Kaiserreiche*. Darmstadt (orig. 1934, 1935).

(1973). *Die zwei Lorbeerbäume des Augustus*. Bonn.

Alföldi, M. R. (1955). "Providentia Augusti to the question of *limes* fortifications in the 4th century," *AAASH* 3: 245–59.

(1999). *Bild und Bildersprache der römischen Kaiser: Beispiele und Analysen*. Mainz.

Alföldy, G. (1974). "The crisis of the third century as seen by contemporaries," *GRBS* 15: 89–111.

(1979). "Bildprogramme in den römischen Städten des Conventus Tarraconensis: das Zeugnis der Statuenpostamente," in *Homenaje a García Bellido IV*, ed. A. Blanco, pp. 177–275. Zaragoza.

(1984). *Römische Statuen in Venetia et Histria: epigraphische Quellen*. Heidelberg.

(1991). "Augustus und die Inschriften: Tradition und Innovation," *Gymnasium* 98: 289–324.

(1998). "La cultura epigráfica de la Hispania romana: inscripciones, autorepresentación y orden social," in *Hispania: El legado de Roma*, pp. 289–301. Zaragoza.

(2001). "*Pietas immobilis erga principem* und ihr Lohn: öffentliche Ehrenmonumente von Senatoren in Rom während der frühen und hohen Kaiserzeit," in Alföldy and Panciera (eds.), pp. 11–46.

(2002). "Roms Kaiser als Bauherren," review of Horster 2001, *JRA* 15: 489–98.

(2003). "Die Repräsentation der kaiserlichen Macht in den Inschriften Roms und des Imperium Romanum," in De Blois *et al.* (eds.), pp. 3–19.

Alföldy, G. and S. Panciera (eds.) (2001). *Inschriftliche Denkmäler als Medien der Selbstdarstellung in der römischen Welt*. Stuttgart.

Amit, M. (1962). "Concordia, idéal politique et instrument de propagande," *Iura* 13: 133–69.

Anderson, B. (1991). *Imagined Communities: Reflections on the Origin and Spread of Nationalism*. 2nd edn. New York.

Anderson, J. K. (1985). *Hunting in the Ancient World*. Berkeley.

Ando, C. (1999). "Was Rome a *polis?*" *CA* 18: 5–34.

  (2000). *Imperial Ideology and Provincial Loyalty in the Roman Empire*. Berkeley.

Angelov, D. (2007). *Imperial Ideology and Political Thought in Byzantium (1204–1330)*. Cambridge.

Austin, M. M. (1986). "Hellenistic kings, war, and the economy," *CQ* 36: 450–66.

Ball, T. *et al.* (eds.) (1989). *Political Innovation and Conceptual Change*. Cambridge.

Balot, R. (2006). *Greek Political Thought*. Oxford and Malden, MA.

  (2009). *A Companion to Greek and Roman Political Thought*. Oxford and Malden, MA.

Bang, P. (2008). *The Roman Bazaar: A Comparative Study of Trade and Markets in a Tributary Empire*. Cambridge.

Barbieri, G. (1957). "Liberalitas," *DE* 4: 836–86.

Barden-Dowling, M. (2006). *Clemency and Cruelty in the Roman World*. Ann Arbor.

Barnes, T. (1974). "The victories of Augustus," *JRS* 64: 21–6.

Barton, C. (2007). "The price of peace in ancient Rome," in *War and Peace in the Ancient World*, ed. K. Raaflaub, pp. 245–78. Oxford and Malden, MA.

Barton, I. (1981). "Capitoline temples in Italy and the provinces (especially Africa)," *ANRW* 2.12.1: 249–342.

Bartsch, S. (1994). *Actors in the Audience: Theatricality and Doublespeak from Nero to Hadrian*. Cambridge, MA.

Bastien, P. (1992–4). *Le buste monétaire des empereurs romains*, 3 vols. Wetteren.

Beard, M. (2007). *The Roman Triumph*. Cambridge, MA.

Beard, M., J. North, and S. R. F. Price (1998). *Religions of Rome*, 2 vols. Cambridge.

Beaujeu, J. (1955). *La religion romaine à l'apogée de l'empire I: la politique religieuse des Antonins (96–192)*. Paris.

Beik, W. (2005). "The absolutism of Louis XIV as social collaboration," *Past & Present* 188: 195–224.

Bellinger, A. and M. A. Bellincourt (1962). *Victory as a Coin Type*. New York.

Belloni, G. G. (1974). "Significati storico-politico delle figurazione e delle scritte delle monete da Augusto a Traiano," *ANRW* 2.1: 997–1,144.

  (1976). "Monete romane e propaganda: impostazione di una problematica complessa," in Sordi (ed.), pp. 131–59.

Beltrán Lloris, F. (1995). "La escritura en la frontera: inscripciones y cultura epigráfica en el valle medio del Ebro," in *Roma y el nacimiento de la cultura epigráfica en Occidente*, ed. F. Beltrán Lloris, pp. 169–95. Zaragoza.

Bendix, R. (1978). *Kings or People*. Berkeley.

Benoist, S. (2005). *Rome, le prince et la cité: pouvoir impérial et cérémonies publiques, 1. siècle av.-début du 4. siècle apr. J.-C*. Paris.

Béranger, J. (1953). *Recherches sur l'aspect idéologique du principat.* Basel.

(1973). *Principatus: études de notions et d'histoire politiques dans l'antiquité gréco-romaine.* Geneva.

Berlinger, L. (1935). *Beiträge zur inoffiziellen Kaisertitulatur.* Diss. Berlin.

Bertrand, J.-M. (1990). "Formes de discours politiques: décrets des cités grecques et correspondance des rois hellénistiques," in *Du pouvoir dans l'antiquité: mots et réalités,* ed. C. Nicolet, pp. 101–15. Paris and Geneva.

Bilde, P. *et al.* (eds.) (1996). *Aspects of Hellenistic Kinship.* Aarhus.

Birley, A. R. (1974). "Septimius Severus, *propagator imperii,*" in *Actes du IXe congrès international d'études sur les frontières romaines,* pp. 297–9. Bucharest.

(1997). *Hadrian: The Restless Emperor.* New York.

Bloomer, W. M. (1992). *Valerius Maximus and the Rhetoric of the New Nobility.* Chapel Hill.

Boatwright, M. (1987). *Hadrian and the City of Rome.* Princeton.

(2000). *Hadrian and the Cities of the Roman Empire.* Princeton.

Bolin, S. (1958). *State and Currency in the Roman Empire to 300 A.D.* Stockholm.

Borg, B. and C. Witschel (2001). "Veränderung im Repräsentationsverhalten der römischen Eliten während des 3. Jhs. n.Chr.," in Alföldy and Panciera (eds.), pp. 47–120.

Boschung, D. (2002). *Gens Augusta: Untersuchungen zu Aufstellung, Wirkung und Bedeutung der Statuengruppen des julisch-claudischen Kaiserhauses.* Mainz.

Bourdieu, P. (1977). *Outline of a Theory of Practice,* transl. R. Nice. Cambridge.

Bowman, A. and A. Wilson (eds.) (2009). *Quantifying the Roman Economy: Methods and Problems.* Oxford.

Boyce, A. (1958). "The harbor of Pompeiopolis," *AJA* 62: 67–78.

Braund, S. (2009). *Seneca: De Clementia.* Oxford.

Breglia, L. (1950). "Circolazione monetale ed aspetti di vità economica a Pompei," in *Pompeiana: raccolta di studi per il secondo centenario degli scavi di Pompei,* ed. A. Maiuri, pp. 41–59. Naples.

Briant, P. (2002). *From Cyrus to Alexander: A History of the Persian Empire,* transl. P. Daniels. Winona Lake, IN.

Brilliant, R. (2007). "Forwards and backwards in the historiography of Roman art," *JRA* 20: 7–24.

Bringmann, K. (1993). "The king as benefactor: some remarks on ideal kingship in the age of Hellenism," in *Images and Ideologies: Self-Definition in the Hellenistic World,* ed. A. Bulloch *et al.,* pp. 7–24. Berkeley.

Brown, M. (1986). "Diffusion," in *International Encyclopedia of Communications,* 4 vols., ed. E. Barnouw *et al.,* pp. 2.31–6. Oxford.

Brunt, P. A. (1974). "Marcus Aurelius in his *Meditations,*" *JRS* 64: 1–20.

(1975). "Stoicism and the principate," *PBSR* 43: 7–35.

(1977). "*Lex de imperio Vespasiani,*" *JRS* 67: 95–116.

(1988). *The Fall of the Roman Republic and Related Essays.* Oxford.

(1990). *Roman Imperial Themes.* Oxford.

Bruun, C. (2003). "Roman emperors in popular jargon: searching for contemporary nicknames (I)," in De Blois *et al.* (eds.), pp. 69–98.

Bureth, P. (1964). *Les titulatures impériales dans les papyrus, les ostraca et les inscriptions d'Égypte (30 a.C.-284 p.C.)*. Brussels.

Burnett, A. (1977). "The authority to coin in the late Republic and early empire," *NC* 17: 37–63.

(1987). *Coinage in the Roman World*. London.

(1999). "Buildings and monuments on Roman coins," in Paul and Ierardi (eds.), pp. 137–64.

Burrell, B. (2004). *Neokoroi: Greek Cities and Roman Emperors*. Leiden.

Burton, G. (1975). "Proconsuls, assizes, and the administration of justice," *JRS* 65: 92–106.

(2001). "The imperial state and its impact on the role and status of local magistrates and councillors in the provinces of the empire," in De Blois (ed.), pp. 202–14.

Buttrey, T. V. (1972a). "Vespasian as moneyer," *NC*⁷ 12: 89–109.

(1972b). "A hoard of sestertii from Bordeaux and the problem of bronze circulation in the third century A.D.," *ANSMN* 18: 33–55.

(1980). *Documentary Evidence for the Chronology of the Flavian Titulature*. Meisenheim am Glan.

(1993). "Calculating ancient coin production: facts and fantasies," *NC* 153: 335–51.

(1994). "Calculating ancient coin production II: why it cannot be done," *NC* 154: 342–52.

(1999). "The content and meaning of coin hoards," *JRA* 12: 526–32.

Callu, J. P. (1969). *La politique monétaire des empereurs romains de 238 à 311*. Paris.

(1983). "Structure des dépôts d'or au IVe siècle (312–392)," in *Crise et redressement dans les provinces européenes de l'empire (milieu du IIIe-milieu du Ive siècle ap. J.-C.)*, ed. E. Frézouls, pp. 157–74. Strasbourg.

Campbell, J. B. (1984). *The Emperor and the Roman Army, 31 B.C.–A.D. 235*. Oxford.

Carcassone, C. and T. Hackens (eds.) (1981). *Statistics and Numismatics. Statistique et Numismatique*. Paris.

Carney, T. F. (1967). "The political legends on Hadrian's coinage: policies and problems," *The Voice of the Turtle (North American Journal of Numismatics)* 6: 291–303.

Carradice, I. (1983). *Coinage and Finances in the Reign of Domitian AD 81–96*. Oxford.

(1998). "Towards a new introduction to the Flavian coinage," in *Modus Operandi: Essays in Honour of Geoffrey Rickman*, ed. M. Austin *et al.*, pp. 93–117. London.

Carrié, J.-M. (1992). "La 'munificence' du prince: le vocabulaire tardif des actes impériaux et ses antécédents," in *Institutions, société et vie politique au IVe siècle ap. J.-C.*, ed. M. Christol *et al.*, pp. 411–30. Rome.

Carson, R. A. G. (1956). "System and product in the Roman mint," in Carson and Sutherland (eds.), pp. 227–39.

Carson, R. A. G. and C. H. V. Sutherland (eds.) (1956). *Essays in Roman Coinage Presented to Harold Mattingly.* Oxford.

Carson, R. A. G. and C. M. Kraay (eds.) (1978). *Scripta Nummaria Romana: Essays Presented to Humphrey Sutherland.* London.

Casson, L. (1971). *Ships and Seamanship in the Ancient World.* Baltimore.

Centrone, B. (1990). *Pseudopythagorica ethica. I trattati morali di Archita, Metopo, Teage, Eurifamo.* Naples.

Champeaux, J. (1982–7). *Fortuna: recherches sur le culte de la Fortune à Rome et dans le monde romain des origines à la mort de César,* 2 vols. Rome.

Charlesworth, M. P. (1936). "*Providentia* and *aeternitas,*" *HTR* 29: 107–32.

(1937). "The virtues of a Roman emperor: propaganda and the creation of belief," *PBA* 23: 105–33.

(1943). "Pietas and Victoria: The emperor and the citizen," *JRS* 33: 1–10.

Cherry, D. (1995). "Re-figuring the Roman epigraphic habit," *AHB* 9: 143–56.

Clark, A. (2007). *Divine Qualities: Cult and Community in Republican Rome.* Oxford.

Classen, C. J. (1965). "Die Königszeit im Spiegel der Literatur der römischen Republik," *Historia* 14: 385–403.

Clauss, M. (1999). *Kaiser und Gott: Herrscherkult im römischen Reich.* Munich.

Combès, R. (1966). *Imperator: recherches sur l'emploi et la signification du titre d'imperator dans la Rome républicaine.* Paris.

Connolly, S. (2009). *Lives Behind the Laws: The World of the Codex Hermogenianus.* Bloomington, IN.

Cooley, A. (1998). "The moralizing message of the *senatus consultum de Cn. Pisone patre,*" *G&R* 45: 199–212.

Corbier, M. (1991). "City, territory and taxation," in *City and Country in the Ancient World,* ed. J. Rich and A. Wallace-Hadrill, pp. 211–39. New York.

(2005). "Coinage and taxation: the state's point of view, A.D. 193–337," in *CAH²* 12, pp. 303–92. Cambridge.

(2006). *Donner à voir, donner à lire: mémoire et communication dans la Rome ancienne.* Paris.

Cotton, H. (1984). "The concept of *indulgentia* under Trajan," *Chiron* 14: 245–66.

Cotton, H. and A. Yakobson (2002). "Arcanum imperii," in *Philosophy and Power in the Graeco-Roman World: Essays in honour of Miriam Griffin,* ed. G. Clark and T. Rajak, pp. 193–209. Oxford.

Crawford, M. (1970). "Money and exchange in the Roman world," *JRS* 60: 40–8.

(1974). *The Roman Republican Coinage,* 2 vols. Cambridge.

(1983a). "Roman imperial coin types and the formation of public opinion," in *Studies in Numismatic Method Presented to P. Grierson,* ed. C. N. L. Brooks et al., pp. 47–64. Cambridge.

(1983b). "Numismatics," in *Sources for Ancient History,* ed. M. Crawford, pp. 185–233. Cambridge.

(1988). "The laws of the Romans: knowledge and diffusion," in *Estudios sobre la Tabula Siarensis,* ed. J. González and J. Arce, pp. 127–39. Madrid.

Crone, P. (1989). *Pre-Industrial Societies: Anatomy of the Pre-Modern World*. Oxford and Malden, MA.

Crook, J. (1996). "Augustus: power, authority, achievement," in *CAH²* 10, pp. 113–46. Cambridge.

Culler, J. (2003). "Anderson and the novel," in Culler and Cheah (eds.), pp. 29–52.

Culler, J. and P. Cheah (eds.) (2003). *Grounds of Comparison: Around the Work of Benedict Anderson*. New York.

Daguet-Gagey, A. (1999). *Septime Sévère: Rome, l'Afrique et l'Orient*. Paris.

Dahmen, K. (2001). *Untersuchungen zu Form und Funktion kleinformatiger Porträts der römischen Kaiserzeit*. Münster.

Darwall-Smith, R. H. (1996). *Emperors and Architecture: A Study of Flavian Rome*. Brussels.

De Blois, L. (ed.) (2001). *Administration, Prosopography and Appointment Policies in the Roman Empire*. Amsterdam.

(2006). "The onset of crisis in the first half of the third century A.D." in Johne *et al.* (eds.), pp. 25–36.

De Blois, L. *et al.* (eds.) (2003). *The Representation and Perception of Roman Imperial Power*. Leiden.

De Callataÿ, F. (1995). "Calculating ancient coin production: seeking a balance," *NC* 155: 289–311.

(ed.) (forthcoming). *Long-Term Quantification in Ancient Mediterranean History*.

De Jong, J. (2006). *Emperors in Egypt: The Representation and Perception of Roman Imperial Power in Greek Papyrus Texts from Egypt, AD 193–284*. Diss. Nijmegen.

Deininger, J. (1965). *Die Provinziallandtage der römischen Kaiserzeit von Augustus bis zum Ende des dritten Jahrhunderts n. Chr.* Munich.

Delatte, L. (1942). *Les traités de la royauté d'Ecphante, Diotogène et Sthenidas*. Paris.

Demandt, A. (1989). *Die Spätantike: römische Geschichte von Diocletian bis Justinian, 284–565 n. Chr.* Munich.

Demougin, S. (ed.) (1994). *La mémoire perdue: à la recherche des archives oubliées, publiques et privées, de la Rome antique*. Paris.

Depeyrot, G. (2004). *La propagande monétaire (64–235) et le trésor de Marcianopolis (251)*. Wetteren.

Dickey, E. (2001). "Kyrie, Despota, Domine: Greek politeness in the Roman empire," *JHS* 121: 1–11.

(2002). *Latin Forms of Address: From Plautus to Apuleius*. Oxford.

Dietler, M. (2007). "The Iron Age in the western Mediterranean," in Scheidel *et al.* (eds.), pp. 242–76.

Dillon, S. and K. Welch (eds.) (2006). *Representations of War in Ancient Rome*. Cambridge.

Drew-Bear, T. (1974). "Representations of temples on the Greek imperial coinage," *ANSMN* 19: 27–63.

Drinkwater, J. (2005). "Maximinus to Diocletian and the 'crisis'," in *CAH²* 12, pp. 28–66. Cambridge.

Duncan-Jones, R. P. (1982). *The Economy of the Roman Empire: Quantitative Studies*². Cambridge.

(1989). "Mobility and immobility of coin in the Roman empire," *AIIN* 36: 121–37.

(1990). *Structure and Scale in the Roman Economy*. Cambridge.

(1994). *Money and Government in the Roman Empire*. Cambridge.

(1996). "Empire-wide patterns in coin-hoards," in King and Wigg (eds.), pp. 139–52.

(1999). "The monetization of the Roman empire: regional variations in the supply of coin types," in Paul and Ierardi (eds.), pp. 61–82.

(2003). "Roman coin circulation and the cities of Vesuvius," in *Credito e moneta nel mondo romano*, ed. E. Lo Cascio, pp. 161–80. Bari.

(2004). "Economic change and the transition to late antiquity," in Swain and Edwards (eds.), pp. 20–52.

(2005). "Implications of Roman coinage: debates and differences," *Klio* 87: 459–87.

Durry, M. (1938). *Panegyrique de Trajan*. Paris.

Dvornik, F. (1966). *Early Christian and Byzantine Political Philosophy: Origin and Background*, 2 vols. Washington, DC.

Eagleton, T. (1991). *Ideology: An Introduction*. New York.

Earl, D. C. (1967). *The Moral and Political Tradition of Rome*. Ithaca, NY.

Eck, W. (1984). "Senatorial self-representation: developments in the Augustan period," in *Caesar Augustus: Seven Aspects*, ed. F. Millar and E. Segal, pp. 129–67. Oxford.

(1992). "Die religiösen und kultischen Aufgaben der römischer Statthalter in der hoher Kaiserzeit," in *Religio Deorum*, ed. M. Mayer and J. Gomez Pallarès, pp. 151–60. Barcelona.

(2000). "Government and civil administration," in *CAH*² 11, pp. 195–292. Cambridge.

(2005). "Der Senator und die Öffentlichkeit–oder: Wie beeindruckt man das Publikum?" in Eck and Heil (eds.), pp. 1–18.

(2010). "The emperor and senatorial aristocracy in competition for public space," in Ewald and Noreña (eds.), pp. 89–110.

Eck, W. *et al.* (eds.) (1996). *Das senatus consultum de Cn. Pisone patre*. Munich.

Eck, W. and M. Heil (eds.) (2005). *Senatores populi Romani: Realität und mediale Präsentation einer Führungsschicht*. Stuttgart.

Eckstein, A. (2006). *Mediterranean Anarchy, Interstate War, and the Rise of Rome*. Berkeley.

(2009). "Hellenistic monarchy in theory and practice," in Balot (ed.), pp. 247–65.

Eder, W. (2005). "Augustus and the power of tradition," in Galinsky (ed.), pp. 13–32.

Eich, A. (2003). "Die Idealtypen 'Propaganda' und 'Repräsentation' als heuristische Mittel bei der Bestimmung gesellschaftlicher Konvergenzen und Divergenzen von Moderne und römischer Kaiserzeit," in Weber and Zimmermann (eds.), pp. 41–84.

Eich, P. (2005). *Zur Metamorphos des politischen Systems in der römischen Kaiserzeit: die Entstehung einer "personalen Bürokratie" im langen dritten Jahrhundert.* Berlin.

Eilers, C. (ed.) (2009). *Diplomats and Diplomacy in the Roman World.* Leiden.

Eisenhut, W. (1973). *Virtus Romana.* Munich.

Eisenstadt, S. (1963). *The Political Systems of Empires.* New Brunswick.

Elias, N. (1983). *The Court Society,* transl. E. Jephcott (orig. 1969). Oxford.

Ellul, J. (1973). *Propaganda: The Formation of Men's Attitudes.* New York.

Elsner, J. (2007). *Roman Eyes: Visuality and Subjectivity in Art and Text.* Princeton.

Enenkel, K. and I. Pfeijffer (eds.) (2005). *The Manipulative Mode: Political Propaganda in Antiquity: A Collection of Case Studies.* Leiden.

Erdkamp, P. (2005). *The Grain Market in the Roman Empire: A Social, Political and Economic Study.* Cambridge.

Erkelenz, D. (2003). *Optimo praesidi: Untersuchungen zu den Ehrenmonumenten für Amtsträger der römischen Provinzen in Republik und Kaiserzeit.* Bonn.

Erkell, H. (1952). *Augustus, Felicitas, Fortuna.* Diss. Göteborg.

Ernout, A. and A. Meillet (1959). *Dictionnaire étymologique de la langue latine: histoire des mots.* Paris.

Erskine, A. (ed.) (2003). *A Companion to the Hellenistic World.* Oxford and Malden, MA.

Evans, J. D. (1992). *The Art of Persuasion: Political Propaganda from Aeneas to Brutus.* Ann Arbor.

Ewald, B. and C. Noreña (eds.) (2010). *The Emperor and Rome: Space, Representation, and Ritual.* Cambridge.

Fears, J. R. (1977). *Princeps a Diis Electus: The Divine Election of Emperors as a Political Concept at Rome.* Rome.

(1981a). "The theology of Victory in Rome: approaches and problems," *ANRW* 2.17.2: 736–826.

(1981b). "The cult of virtues and Roman imperial ideology," *ANRW* 2.17.2: 827–948.

Fedeli, P. (1989a). "Il 'Panegyrico' di Plinio nella critica moderna," *ANRW* 33.1: 387–514.

(1989b). "I sistemi di produzione e diffusione," in *Lo spazio letterario di Roma antica, vol. 2: la circolazione del testo,* ed. G. Cavallo *et al.,* pp. 343–78. Rome.

Feeney, D. (2006). *Caesar's Calendar: Ancient Time and the Beginnings of History.* Berkeley.

Ferrary, J.-L. (2001). "A propos des pouvoirs d'Auguste," *CCGG* 12: 101–51.

Fishwick, D. (1987–2005). *The Imperial Cult in the Latin West: Studies in the Ruler Cult of the Western Provinces of the Roman Empire,* 3 vols. Leiden.

(1990). "Votive offerings to the emperor?" *ZPE* 80: 121–30.

Fittschen, K. (2010). "The portraits of Roman emperors and their families: controversial positions and unsolved problems," in Ewald and Noreña (eds.), pp. 221–46.

Flaig, E. (1992). *Den Kaiser herausfordern: Die Usurpation im römischen Reich.* Frankfurt.

(2003). *Ritualisierte Politik: Zeichen, Gesten und Herrschaft im alten Rom.* Göttingen.

(2010). "How the emperor Nero lost acceptance in Rome," in Ewald and Noreña (eds.), pp. 275–88.

Flower, H. (1996). *Ancestor Masks and Aristocratic Power in Roman Culture.* Oxford.

Fogel, R. W. (1975). "The limits of quantitative methods in history," *AHR* 80: 329–50.

Forbis, E. (1996). *Municipal Virtues in the Roman Empire: The Evidence of Italian Honorary Inscriptions.* Stuttgart.

Fox, M. (1996). *Roman Historical Myths: The Regal Period in Augustan Literature.* Oxford.

Frei-Stolba, R. (1969). "Inoffizielle Kaisertitulaturen im 1. und 2. Jahrhundert n. Chr.," *MH* 26: 18–39.

Fuchs, A. (1969). *Architekturdarstellungen auf römischen Münzen der Republik und der frühen Kaiserzeit.* Berlin.

Gagé, J. (1930). "La Victoria Augusti et les auspices de Tibère," *RA^s* 32: 1–35.

(1932). "Un thème de l'art impérial romain: La Victoire d'Auguste," *MÉFR* 49: 61–92.

(1933). "La théologie de la Victoire impériale," *RH* 171: 1–43.

(1969). "Felicitas," *RAC* 7: 711–23.

Galinsky, K. (1996). *Augustan Culture: An Interpretive Introduction.* Princeton.

(ed.) (2005). *The Cambridge Companion to the Age of Augustus.* Cambridge.

Galsterer, H. (1986). "Roman law in the provinces: some problems of transmission," in *L'impero romano e le strutture economiche e sociali delle province,* ed. M. Crawford, pp. 13–27. Como.

(1996). "The administration of justice," *CAH²* 10, pp. 397–413. Cambridge.

Galsterer-Kröll, B. (1972). "Untersuchungen zu den Beinamen der Städte des *Imperium Romanum,*" *ES* 9: 44–145.

Garnsey, P. (1988). *Famine and Food Supply in the Graeco-Roman World: Responses to Risk and Crisis.* Cambridge.

(2004). "Roman citizenship and Roman law in the late empire," in Swain and Edwards (eds.), pp. 133–55.

Garnsey, P. and R. Saller (1987). *The Roman Empire: Economy, Society and Culture.* Berkeley.

Garriguet, J. A. (2001). *La imagen del poder imperial en Hispania: tipos estatuarios.* Murcia.

Gaudemet, J. (1962). *Indulgentia principis.* Milan.

Geertz, C. (1973). *The Interpretation of Cultures.* New York.

(1983). *Local Knowledge: Further Essays in Interpretive Anthropology.* New York.

Gellner, E. (1983). *Nations and Nationalism.* Ithaca, NY.

(1987). "Nationalism and the two forms of cohesion in complex societies," in *Culture, Identity, and Politics,* pp. 6–28. Cambridge.

Gelzer, M. (1969). *The Roman Nobility,* transl. R. Seager (orig. 1912). Oxford.

Gernentz, W. (1918). *Laudes Romae.* Rostock.

Gnecchi, F. (1905). "Le personificazioni allegoriche sulle monete imperiali," *RIN* 18: 349–88.

(1912). *I medaglioni romani descritti ed illustrati da Francesco Gnecchi*, 3 vols. Milan.

Goldstone, J. and J. Haldon (2009). "Ancient states, empires, and exploitation: problems and perspectives," in Morris and Scheidel (eds.), pp. 3–29.

Goodenough, E. (1928). "The political philosophy of Hellenistic kingship," *YCS* I: 55–102.

Goodyear, F. (ed.) (1972). *The Annals of Tacitus: Volume I (Annals 1.1–54)*. Cambridge.

Gordon, R. (1990). "The veil of power: emperors, sacrificers, and benefactors," in *Pagan Priests: Religion and Power in the Ancient World*, ed. M. Beard and J. North, pp. 199–231. Ithaca, NY.

Gorski, P. (2006). "Mann's theory of ideological power: sources, applications and elaborations," in Hall and Schroeder (eds.), pp. 101–34.

Gradel, I. (2002). *Emperor Worship and Roman Religion*. Oxford.

Greene, K. (1992). "How was technology transferred in the western provinces?" in *Current Research on the Romanization of the Western Provinces*, ed. M. Wood and F. Queiroga, pp. 101–5. Oxford.

Grierson, P. (1975). *Numismatics*. Oxford.

Griffin, M. (1982). "The Lyons tablets and Tacitean hindsight," *CQ* 32: 404–18.

(2003). "*De Beneficiis* and Roman society," *JRS* 93: 92–113.

Gruen, E. (1984). *The Hellenistic World and the Coming of Rome*, 2 vols. Berkeley.

(1985). "Augustus and the ideology of war and peace," in *The Age of Augustus*, ed. R. Winkes, pp. 51–72. Louvain.

(1990). *Studies in Greek Culture and Roman Policy*. Berkeley.

(1992). *Culture and National Identity in Republican Rome*. Ithaca, NY.

(1996). "The expansion of the empire under Augustus," in *CAH²* 10, pp. 147–97. Cambridge.

(2005). "Augustus and the making of the principate," in Galinsky (ed.), pp. 33–51.

Habinek, T. (1998). *The Politics of Latin Literature: Writing, Identity, and Empire in Ancient Rome*. Princeton.

Habinek, T. and A. Schiesaro (eds.) (1997). *The Roman Cultural Revolution*. Cambridge.

Hadot, P. (1972). "Fürstenspiegel," *RAC* 7: 555–632.

Haensch, R. (1992). "Das Statthalterarchiv," *ZRG* 109: 209–317.

Hägg, T. and P. Rousseau (eds.) (2000). *Greek Biography and Panegyric in Late Antiquity*. Berkeley.

Hahm, D. (2000). "Kings and constitutions: Hellenistic theories," in Rowe and Schofield (eds.), pp. 458–76.

Halfmann, H. (1986). *Itinera Principum: Geschichte und Typologie der Kaiserreisen im römischen Reich*. Stuttgart.

Hall, J. and R. Schroeder (eds.) (2006). *An Anatomy of Power: The Social Theory of Michael Mann*. Cambridge.

Hallett, C. (2005a). *The Roman Nude: Heroic Portrait Statuary 200 BC–AD 300.* Oxford.

(2005b). "Emulation *versus* replication: redefining Roman copying," *JRA* 18: 419–35.

Hamberg, P. G. (1945). *Studies in Roman Imperial Art with Special Reference to the State Reliefs of the Second Century.* Uppsala.

Hammond, M. (1956). "The transmission of the powers of the Roman emperor from the death of Nero in A.D. 68 to that of Severus Alexander in A.D. 235," *MAAR* 24: 61–133.

(1957). "Imperial elements in the formula of the Roman emperors during the first two and a half centuries of the empire," *MAAR* 25: 19–64.

(1959). *The Antonine Monarchy.* Rome.

Hannestad, N. (1986). *Roman Art and Imperial Policy.* Aarhus.

Harl, K. (1987). *Civic Coins and Civic Politics in the Roman East, A.D. 180–275.* Berkeley.

(1996). *Coinage in the Roman Economy, 300 B.C. to A.D. 700.* Baltimore.

Harris, W. V. (1979). *War and Imperialism in Republican Rome 327–70 BC.* Oxford.

(1989). *Ancient Literacy.* Cambridge, MA.

(2006a). "A revisionist view of Roman money," *JRS* 96: 1–24.

(2006b). "Readings in the narrative literature of Roman courage," in Dillon and Welch (eds.), pp. 300–20.

Harvey, B. (2004). "Two bases of Marcus Aurelius Caesar and the Roman imperial succession," *Historia* 53: 46–60.

Hauken, T. (1998). *Petition and Response: An Epigraphic Study of Petitions to Roman Emperors, 181–249.* Bergen.

Heather, P. and D. Moncur (eds.) (2001). *Politics, Philosophy, and Empire in the Fourth Century: Select Orations of Themistius.* Liverpool.

Hekster, O. (2001). "All in the family: the appointments of emperors designate in the second century AD," in De Blois (ed.), pp. 35–49.

(2002). *Commodus: An Emperor at the Crossroads.* Amsterdam.

(2003). "Coins and messages: audience targeting on coins of different denominations?" in De Blois *et al.* (eds.), pp. 20–35.

(2008). *Rome and its Empire, AD 193–284.* Edinburgh.

Hellegouarc'h, J. (1963). *Le vocabulaire latin des relations et des partis politiques sous la République.* Paris.

Herman, G. (1997). "The court society of the Hellenistic age," in *Hellenistic Constructs: Essays in Culture, History and Historiography*, ed. P. Cartledge *et al.*, pp. 199–224. Berkeley.

Herrmann, P. (1968). *Der römische Kaisereid.* Göttingen.

Herz, P. (1978). "Kaiserfeste der Prinzipatszeit," *ANRW* II.16.2: 1,135–200.

Hill, H. (1969). "*Nobilitas* in the imperial period," *Historia* 18: 230–50.

Hill, P. (1989). *The Monuments of Ancient Rome as Coin Types.* London.

Hobley, A. S. (1998). *An Examination of Roman Bronze Coin Distribution in the Western Empire A.D. 81–192.* BAR International Series 688. Oxford.

Hofter, M. (ed.) (1988). *Kaiser Augustus und die verlorene Republik.* Mainz.

Højte, J. M. (2000). "Imperial visits as occasion for the erection of imperial statues," *ZPE* 133: 221–35.

(2005). *Roman Imperial Statue Bases: From Augustus to Commodus*. Aarhus.

Hölkeskamp, K. (2004). *Senatus populusque romanus: die politische Kultur der Republik: Dimensionen und Deutungen*. Wiesbaden.

Hölscher, T. (1967). *Victoria Romana*. Mainz.

(1980). "Die Geschichtsauffassung in der römischen Repräsentationskunst," *JdI* 95: 265–321.

(1982). "Die Bedeutung der Münzen für das Verständnis der politischen Repräsentationskunst der späten römischen Republik," in *Actes du 9ème congrès international de numismatique*, ed. T. Hackens and R. Weiller, pp. 269–82. Louvain-la-Neuve.

(1984). *Staatsdenkmal und Publikum: vom Untergang der Republik bis zur Festigung des Kaisertums in Rom*. Konstanz.

(1990). "Römische Nobiles und hellenistische Herrscher," in *Akten des XIII Internationalen Kongresses für klassische Archäologie Berlin 1988*, pp. 74–9. Mainz.

(2003). "Images of war in Greece and Rome: between military practice, public memory, and cultural symbolism," *JRS* 93: 1–17.

(2006). "The transformation of Victory into power: from event to structure," in Dillon and Welch (eds.), pp. 27–48.

(forthcoming). *Visual Power in Ancient Greece and Rome*. Berkeley.

Honoré, T. (1981). *Emperors and Lawyers*. London.

Hopkins, K. (1978). *Conquerors and Slaves*. Cambridge.

(1980). "Taxes and trade in the Roman empire (200 B.C.–A.D. 400)," *JRS* 70: 101–25.

(1983). *Death and Renewal*. Cambridge.

(2002). "Rome, taxes, rents and trade," in *The Ancient Economy*, ed. W. Scheidel and S. von Reden, 190–230 (orig. 1995/96). New York.

(2009). "The political economy of the Roman empire," in Morris and Scheidel (eds.), pp. 178–204.

Horden, P. and N. Purcell (2000). *The Corrupting Sea: A Study of Mediterranean History*. Oxford and Malden, MA.

Horster, M. (1997). *Literarische Zeugnisse kaiserlicher Bautätigkeit: eine Studie zu Baumassnahmen in Städten des römischen Reiches während des Prinzipats*. Stuttgart.

(2001). *Bauinschriften römischer Kaiser: Untersuchungen zu Inschriftenpraxis und Bautätigkeit in Städte*. Stuttgart.

Howgego, C. (1990). "Why did ancient states strike coins?" *NC* 150: 1–26.

(1992). "The supply and use of money in the Roman world 200 B.C. to A.D. 300," *JRS* 82: 1–31.

(1994). "Coin circulation and the integration of the Roman economy," *JRA* 7: 5–21.

(2005). "Coinage and identity in the Roman provinces," in *Coinage and Identity in the Roman Provinces*, ed. C. Howgego *et al.*, pp. 1–18. Oxford.

(2009). "Some numismatic approaches to quantifying the Roman economy," in Bowman and Wilson (eds.), pp. 287–95.

Hurlet, F. (1993). "La *Lex de imperio Vespasiani* et la légitimité augustéene," *Latomus* 52: 261–80.

(2001). "Les auspices d'Octavien/Auguste," *CCGG* 12: 155–80.

Huttner, U. (2004). *Recusatio imperii: ein politisches Ritual zwischen Ethik und Taktik.* Hildesheim.

Ingelbert, H. (ed.) (2002a). *Idéologies et valeurs civiques dans le monde romaine: hommage à Claude Lepelley.* Paris.

(2002b). "Citoyenneté romaine, romanités et identités romaines," in Ingelbert (ed.), pp. 241–60.

Jacques, F. (1984). *Le privilège de liberté: politique imperiale et autonomie municipale dans les cités de l'Occident romain (161–244).* Rome.

Jal, P. (1961). "*Pax civilis-Concordia,*" *REL* 39: 210–31.

Johne, K.-P. *et al.* (eds.) (2006). *Deleto paene imperio Romano: Transformationsprozesse des römischen Reiches im 3. Jahrhundert und ihre Rezeption in der Neuzeit.* Stuttgart.

Jones, A. H. M. (1956). "Numismatics and history," in Carson and Sutherland (eds.), pp. 13–33.

Jones, C. P. (1972). "Aelius Aristides, *Eis Basileia,*" *JRS* 62: 134–52.

(1977/78). "Some new inscriptions from Bubon," *IstMitt* 27/28: 288–96.

Jones, T. (1963). "A numismatic riddle: the so-called Greek Imperials," *PAPS* 107: 308–47.

Jouffroy, H. (1986). *La construction publique en Italie et dans l'Afrique romaine.* Strasbourg.

Kaczynski, B. and M. Nüsse (2009). "Reverse type selection in sanctuaries? A study of antoniniani found in various contexts," in von Kaenel and Kemmers (eds.), pp. 93–107.

Kajanto, I. (1971). "Un'analisi filologico-letteraria delle inscrizioni onorarie," *Epigraphica* 33: 3–19.

(1981). "Fortuna," *ANRW* 2.17.1: 502–58.

Kantorowicz, E. H. (1957). *The King's Two Bodies: A Study in Mediaeval Political Theology.* Princeton.

Kaser, M. (1966). *Das römische Zivilprozessrecht.* Munich.

Kaster, R. (2005). *Emotion, Restraint, and Community in Ancient Rome.* Oxford.

Katz, E. and P. Lazarsfeld (1955). *Personal Influence: The Part Played by People in Mass Communication.* Glencoe, IL.

Kautsky, J. (1982). *The Politics of Aristocratic Empires.* Chapel Hill.

Keay, S. (1998). "The development of towns in early Roman Baetica," in *The Archaeology of Early Roman Baetica, JRA* suppl. 29 ed. S. Keay, pp. 55–86. Portsmouth, RI.

Keay, S. *et al.* (2005). *Portus: An Archaeological Survey of the Port of Imperial Rome.* Rome.

Kehoe, D. (2007). "The early Roman empire: production," in Scheidel *et al.* (eds.), pp. 543–69.

Kelly, C. (1998). "Emperors, government and bureaucracy," *CAH 13*, pp. 138–83. Cambridge.

Kemmers, F. (2006). *Coins for a Legion: An Analysis of the Coin Finds from the Augustan Legionary Fortress and Flavian canabae legionis at Nijmegen.* Mainz.

(2009). "Sender or receiver? Contexts of coin supply and coin use," in von Kaenel and Kemmers (eds.), pp. 137–56.

Kennedy, D. (1984). Review of *Poetry and Politics in the Age of Augustus*, ed. T. Woodman and D. West (Cambridge, 1982), *LCM* 9: 157–60.

Kienast, D. (1996). *Römische Kaisertabelle: Grundzüge einer römischen Kaiser-chronologie²*. Darmstadt.

King, A. (1999). "Diet in the Roman world: a regional inter-site comparison of the mammal bones," *JRA* 12: 168–202.

King, C. (1999). "Roman portraiture: images of power?" in Paul and Ierardi (eds.), pp. 123–36.

King, C. and D. Wigg (eds.) (1996). *Coin Finds and Coin Use in the Roman World.* Berlin.

Kleinwachter, C. (2001). *Platzanlagen nordafrikanischer Städte: Untersuchungen zum sogennanten Polyzentrimus in der Urbanistik der römischen Kaiserzeit.* Mainz.

Kloft, H. (1970). *Liberalitas principis: Herkunft und Bedeutung: Studien zur Prinzi-patsideologie.* Cologne.

Kneissl, P. (1969). *Die Siegestitulatur der römischen Kaiser.* Göttingen.

Koeppel, G. (1969). "*Profectio* und *adventus*," *BJb* 169: 130–94.

Kolb, A. (2004). "Römische Meilensteine: Stand der Forschung und Prob-leme," in *Siedlung und Verkehr im römischen Reich: Römerstrassen zwischen Herrschaftssicherung und Landschaftsprägung*, ed. R. Frei-Stolba, pp. 135–55. Bern.

Kolb, F. (2001). *Herrscherideologie in der Spätantike.* Berlin.

Komnick, H. (2001). *Die Restitutionsmünzen der frühen Kaiserzeit: Aspekte der Kaiserlegitimation.* Berlin.

König, I. (1973). "Zur Dedikation römischer Meilensteine," *Chiron* 3: 419–27.

Konstan, D. (2005). "Clemency as a virtue," *CP* 100: 337–46.

Koortbojian, M. (2006). "The bringer of Victory: imagery and institutions at the advent of empire," in Dillon and Welch (eds.), pp. 184–217.

Kraay, C. (1956). "The behaviour of early imperial countermarks," in Carson and Sutherland (eds.), pp. 113–36.

(1978). "The bronze coinage of Vespasian: classification and attribution," in Carson and Kraay (eds.), pp. 47–57.

Kragelund, P. (1998). "Galba's *pietas*, Nero's victims and the Mausoleum of Augus-tus," *Historia* 47: 152–83.

Kraus, C. S. (2005). "From *exempla* to *exemplar*? Writing history around the emperor in imperial Rome," in *Flavius Josephus and Flavian Rome*, ed. J. Edmonson *et al.*, pp. 181–200. Oxford.

Krause, J.-U. (1987). "Das spätantike Städtepatronat," *Chiron* 17: 1–80.

Krause, J.-U. and Witschel, C. (eds.) (2006). *Die Stadt in der Spätantike – Nieder-gang oder Wandel?* Stuttgart.

Kruse, H. (1934). *Studien zur offiziellen Geltung des Kaiserbildes im römischen Reich.* Paderborn.

Kuhoff, W. (1990). "Il riflesso dell'autorappresentazione degli imperatori romani nelle province dell'Africa (I-III sec. d.C.)," *AfrRom* 7.2: 943–60.

    (1993). *Felicior Augusto Melior Traiano: Aspekte der Selbstdarstellung der römischen Kaiser während der Prinzipatszeit.* Frankfurt.

Kuttner, A. (1995). *Dynasty and Empire in the Age of Augustus: The Case of the Boscoreale Cups.* Berkeley.

Laclau, E. (2003). "On imagined communities," in Culler and Cheah (eds.), pp. 21–8.

Lahusen, G. (1983). *Untersuchungen zur Ehrenstatue in Rom: literarische und epigraphische Zeugnisse.* Rome.

    (1984). *Schriftquellen zum römischen Bildnis I: Textstellen: von den Anfangen bis zum 3. Jahrhundert n. Chr.* Bremen.

Le Glay, M. (1982). "Remarques sur la notion de *salus* dans la religion romaine," in *La soteriologia dei culti orientali nell'impero romano*, ed. U. Bianchi and M. J. Vermaseren, pp. 427–44. Leiden.

Lehnen, J. (1997). *Adventus Principis.* Frankfurt.

Lendon, J. E. (1997). *Empire of Honour: The Art of Government in the Roman World.* Oxford.

    (2006). "The legitimacy of the Roman emperor: against Weberian legitimacy and imperial 'strategies of legitimation'," in *Herrschaftsstrukturen und Herrschaftspraxis*, ed. A. Kolb, pp. 53–63. Berlin.

Lepelley, C. (1997). "Évergétisme et épigraphie dans l'antiquité tardive: les provinces de langue Latine," in *Actes du Xe congrès international d'épigraphie grecque et latine 1992*, ed. M. Christol and O. Masson, pp. 335–52. Paris.

Levick, B. (1978). "Concordia at Rome," in Carson and Kraay (eds.), pp. 217–33.

    (1982). "Propaganda and the imperial coinage," *Antichthon* 16: 104–16.

    (1999). "Messages on the Roman coinage: types and inscriptions," in Paul and Ierardi (eds.), pp. 41–60.

Liebeschuetz, J. H. W. G. (2001). *The Decline and Fall of the Roman City.* Oxford.

    (2007). "Was there a crisis of the third century?" in *Crises and the Roman Empire*, ed. O. Hekster *et al.*, pp. 11–20. Leiden.

Liegle, J. (1932). "Pietas," *ZN* 42: 59–100.

Lintott, A. (1993). *Imperium Romanum: Politics and Administration.* New York.

    (1997). "The theory of the mixed constitution at Rome," in *Philosophia Togata II: Plato and Aristotle in Rome*, ed. J. Barnes and M. Griffin, pp. 70–85. Oxford.

Lo Cascio, E. (2000). *Il princeps e il suo impero: studi di storia amministriva e finanziaria romana.* Bari.

    (2007). "The early Roman empire: the state and the economy," in Scheidel *et al.* (eds.), pp. 619–47.

Lockyear, K. (1999). "Hoard structure and coin production in antiquity – an empirical investigation," *NC* 159: 215–43.

Lomas, K. (2003). "Public building, urban renewal and euergetism in early imperial Italy," in *Bread and Circuses: Euergetism and Municipal Patronage in Roman Italy*, ed. K. Lomas and T. Cornell, pp. 28–45. New York.

Lostal Pros, J. (1992). *Los miliarios de la provincia tarraconense*. Zaragoza.

Luke, T. (2010). "A healing touch for empire: Vespasian's wonders in Domitianic Rome," *G&R* 57: 77–106.

Lusnia, S. (2006). "Battle imagery and politics on the Severan arch in the Roman Forum," in Dillon and Welch (eds.), pp. 272–99.

Lutz, C. (1947). "Musonius Rufus: the Roman Socrates," *YCS* 10: 38–49.

Ma, J. (1999). *Antiochus III and the Cities of Western Asia Minor*. Oxford.

(2003). "Kings," in *A Companion to the Hellenistic World*, ed. A. Erskine, pp. 177–95. Oxford and Malden, MA.

MacCormack, S. (1975). "Latin prose panegyrics," in *Empire and Aftermath*, ed. T. Dorey, pp. 143–205. London.

(1981). *Art and Ceremony in Late Antiquity*. Berkeley.

MacMullen, R. (1959). "Roman imperial building in the provinces," *HSCP* 64: 207–35.

(1982). "The epigraphic habit in the Roman empire," *AJP* 103: 23–46.

(1988). *Corruption and the Decline of Rome*. New Haven.

(1990). *Changes in the Roman Empire: Essays in the Ordinary*. Princeton.

(2000). *Romanization in the Time of Augustus*. New Haven.

Malkin, I., C. Constantakopoulou, and K. Panagopoulou (eds.) (2009). *Greek and Roman Networks in the Mediterranean*. New York.

Manders, E. (2008). *Coining Images of Power: Patterns in the Representation of Roman Emperors on Imperial Coinage, A.D. 193–284*. Diss. Nijmegen.

Mann, J. C. (1985). "Epigraphic consciousness," *JRS* 75: 204–6.

Mann, M. (1986). *The Sources of Social Power I: A History of Power from the Beginning to A.D. 1760*. Cambridge.

(1993). *The Sources of Social Power II: The Rise of Classes and Nation States, 1760–1914*. Cambridge.

(2006). "The sources of social power revisited: a response to criticism," in Hall and Schroeder (eds.), pp. 343–96.

Manning, C. (1985). "Liberalitas – the decline and rehabilitation of a virtue," *G&R* 32: 73–83.

Marsano, A. (2009). "Trajanic building projects on base-metal denominations and audience targeting," *PBSR* 77: 125–58.

Martin, T. (1982). *Providentia deorum: recherches sur certains aspects religieux du pouvoir impérial romain*. Rome.

Marwood, M. (1988). *The Roman Cult of Salus*. Oxford.

Matheson, S. (ed.) (1994). *An Obsession with Fortune: Tyche in Greek and Roman Art*. New Haven.

Matthews, J. F. (1989). *The Roman Empire of Ammianus*. London.

Mayer, E. (2010). "Propaganda, staged applause, or local politics? Public monuments from Augustus to Septimius Severus," in Ewald and Noreña (eds.), pp. 111–34.

McCormick, M. (1986). *Eternal Victory: Triumphal Rulership in Late Antiquity, Byzantium, and the early Medieval West.* Cambridge.

McDonnell, M. (2006). *Roman Manliness: Virtus and the Roman Republic.* Cambridge.

Meadows, A. and J. Williams (2001). "Moneta and the monuments: coinage and politics in Republican Rome," *JRS* 91: 27–49.

Megow, W.-R. (1987). *Kameen von Augustus bis Alexander Severus.* Berlin.

Melchor Gil, E. (2001). "Consideraciones sobre la munificencia cívica en la Bética romana," in Navarro Caballero and Demougin (eds.), pp. 157–71.

Metcalf, W. (1989). "Rome and Lugdunum again," *AJN* 1: 51–70.

(1993). "Whose *liberalitas*? Propaganda and audience in the early Roman empire," *RIN* 95: 337–46.

(1995). Review of Duncan-Jones 1994, *RSN* 74:145–59.

Meyer, E. A. (1990). "Explaining the epigraphic habit in the Roman empire: the evidence of epitaphs," *JRS* 80: 74–96.

(2004). *Legitimacy and Law in the Roman World: Tabulae in Roman Belief and Practice.* Cambridge.

Meyer-Zwiffelhoffer, E. (2002). *Politikos archein: zum Regierungsstil der senatorischen Statthalter in den kaiserzeitlichen griechischen Provinzen.* Stuttgart.

Mikocki, T. (1995). *Sub specie deae: les impératrices et princesses romaines assimilées à des déesses: étude iconologique.* Rome.

Millar, F. (1977). *The Emperor in the Roman World.* Ithaca, NY.

(2002–6). *Rome, The Greek World, and the East,* 3 vols. Chapel Hill.

Millett, M. (1990). *The Romanization of Britain: An Essay in Archaeological Interpretation.* Cambridge.

Milne, J. (1923). *Catalog of Alexandrian Coins.* Oxford.

Mitchell, S. (1987). "Imperial building in the eastern Roman provinces," *HSCP* 91: 333–65.

(1993). *Anatolia: Land, Men, and Gods in Asia Minor,* 2 vols. Oxford.

Mitchell, T. (1999). "Society, economy and the state effect," in Steinmetz (ed.), pp. 76–97.

Moatti, C. (1993). *Archives et partage de la terre dans le monde romain (IIe siècle avant-Ier siècle après J.-C.).* Rome.

(1997). *La raison de Rome: naissance de l'esprit critique à la fin de la République (IIe-Ier siècle avant J.-C.).* Paris.

Moles, J. (1990). "The kingship orations of Dio Chrysostom," *PLLS* 6: 297–375.

Momigliano, A. (1993). *The Development of Greek Biography.* Cambridge, MA.

Morgan, T. (2007). *Popular Morality in the Early Roman Empire.* Cambridge.

Morley, N. (2007). "The early Roman empire: distribution," in Scheidel *et al.* (eds.), pp. 592–618.

Morrill, R. (1970). "The shape of diffusion in space and time," *Economic Geography* 46: 259–68.

Morris, I. and W. Scheidel (eds.) (2009). *The Dynamics of Ancient Empires.* Oxford.

Motyl, A. J. (2001). *Imperial Ends: The Decay, Collapse, and Revival of Empires.* New York.

Mrozek, S. (1973). "A propos de la répartition chronologique des inscriptions latines dans le haut-empire," *Epigraphica* 35: 13–18.

(1988). "A propos de la répartition chronologique des inscriptions latines dans le haut-empire," *Epigraphica* 50: 61–4.

Murray, O. (1965). "Philodemus on the good king according to Homer," *JRS* 55: 161–82.

(1967). "Aristeas and Ptolemaic kingship," *JTS* 18: 337–71.

(1970). "Hecataeus of Abdera and Pharaonic kingship," *JEA* 56: 141–71.

Musca, D. (1979). *Le denominazioni del principe nei documenti epigrafici romani.* Bari.

Navarro Caballero, M. and S. Demougin (eds.) (2001). *Élites hispaniques.* Bourdeaux.

Neesen, L. (1980). *Untersuchungen zu den direkten Staatsabgaben der römischen Kaiserzeit.* Bonn.

Neudecker, R. (1988). *Die Skulpturenausstattung römischer Villen in Italien.* Mainz.

Neumann, G. and J. Untermann (eds.) (1980). *Die Sprachen im römischen Reich der Kaiserzeit.* Cologne and Bonn.

Nicolet, C. (1991). *Space, Geography and Politics in the Early Roman Empire.* Ann Arbor.

Nicols, J. (1980). "Pliny and the patronage of communities," *Hermes* 108: 865–85.

Niemeyer, H. (1968). *Studien zur statuarischen Darstellung der römischen Kaiser.* Berlin.

Niquet, H. (2003). "Inschriften als Medium von 'Propaganda' und Selbstdarstellung im 1. Jh. n. Chr." in Weber and Zimmermann (eds.), pp. 145–73.

Nixon, C. E. V. and B. S. Rodgers (eds.) (1994). *In Praise of Later Roman Emperors: The Panegyrici Latini.* Berkeley.

Noreña, C. F. (2001). "The communication of the emperor's virtues," *JRS* 91: 146–68.

(2003). "Medium and message in Vespasian's Templum Pacis," *MAAR* 48: 25–43.

(2007a). "The social economy of Pliny's correspondence with Trajan," *AJP* 128: 239–77.

(2007b). "Hadrian's chastity," *Phoenix* 61: 296–317.

(2009). "The ethics of autocracy in the Roman world," in Balot (ed.), pp. 266–79.

(2010). "The early imperial monarchy," in *The Oxford Handbook of Roman Studies,* ed. A. Barchiesi and W. Scheidel, pp. 533–46. Oxford.

North, H. (1966). "Canons and hierarchies of the cardinal virtues in Greek and Latin literature," in *The Classical Tradition: Literary and Historical Studies in Honor of Harry Caplan,* ed. L. Wallach, pp. 168–83. Ithaca, NY.

Oliver, J. H. (1978). "The piety of Commodus and Caracalla and the *Eis Basilea,*" *GRBS* 19: 375–88.

(1989). *Greek Constitutions of Early Roman Emperors from Inscriptions and Papyri.* Philadelphia.

Packer, J. (2010). "Pompey's theater and Tiberius' temple of Concord: a late-Republican primer for an early-imperial patron," in Ewald and Noreña (eds.), pp. 135–67.

Paterson, J. (2007). "Friends in high places: the creation of the court of the Roman emperor," in Spawforth (ed.), 127–56.

Paul, G. M. and M. Ierardi (eds.) (1999). *Roman Coins and Public Life under the Empire*. Ann Arbor.

Peachin, M. (1986). "The Procurator monetae," *NC* 146: 94–106.

Pekáry, T. (1968). *Untersuchungen zu den römischen Reichsstraßen*. Bonn.

(1985). *Das römische Kaiserbildnis in Staat, Kult und Gesellschaft*. Berlin.

Perassi, C. (1991). *Spes: iconografia, simbologia, ideologia nella moneta romana, I-III sec*. Milan.

Peter, M. (1996). "Some aspects of coin circulation on the Rhine in the 2nd century A.D.," in King and Wigg (eds.), pp. 309–20.

Pfanner, M. (1989). "Über das Herstellen von Porträts: ein Beitrag zu Rationalisierungsmaßnahmen und Produktionsmechanismen von Massenware im späten Hellenismus und in der römischen Kaiserzeit," *JdI* 104: 157–257.

Phang, S. (2008). *Roman Military Service: Ideologies of Discipline in the Late Republic and Early Principate*. Cambridge.

Picard, G.-C. (1957). *Les trophées romains: contribution à l'histoire de la religion et de l'art triomphal de Rome*. Paris.

Pirson, F. (1996). "Style and message on the column of Marcus Aurelius," *PBSR* 64: 139–79.

Pocock, J. G. A. (1987). "The concept of a language and the *métier d'historien*: some considerations on practice," in *The Languages of Political Theory in Early-Modern Europe*, ed. A. Pagden, pp. 19–38. Cambridge.

Potter, D. S. (1994). *Prophets and Emperors: Human and Divine Authority from Augustus to Theodosius*. Cambridge, MA.

(1999). "Political theory in the *Senatus Consultum Pisonianum*," *AJP* 120: 65–88.

(2004). *The Roman Empire at Bay A.D. 180–395*. New York.

Prag, J. and J. Quinn (eds.) (forthcoming). *The Hellenistic West*. Oxford.

Prayon, F. (1982). "Projektierte Bauten auf römischen Münzen," in *Praestant Interna: Festschrift für Ulrich Hausmann*, ed. B. Freytag, pp. 319–30. Tübingen.

Préaux, C. (1978). *Le monde hellénistique*, 2 vols. Paris.

Price, S. R. F. (1984). *Rituals and Power: The Roman Imperial Cult in Asia Minor*. Cambridge.

Purcell, N. (1996). "The ports of Rome: evolution of a *façade maritime*," in '*Roman Ostia' Revisited: Archaeological and Historical Papers in Memory of Russell Meiggs*, eds. A. Claridge and A. Gallina Zevi, pp. 267–79. London.

(2000). "Rome and Italy," *CAH²* 11, pp. 405–43. Cambridge.

Raaflaub, K. (2000). "Poets, lawgivers, and the beginnings of political reflection in archaic Greece," in Rowe and Schofield (eds.), pp. 23–59.

(2004). *The Discovery of Freedom in Ancient Greece*. Chicago.

Radice, B. (1968). "Pliny and the *Panegyricus*," *G&R* 15: 166–72.

Ramage, E. (1983). "Denigration of predecessor under Claudius, Galba, and Vespasian," *Historia* 32: 200–14.

(1997). "Augustus' propaganda in Gaul," *Klio* 79: 117–60.

(1998). "Augustus' propaganda in Spain," *Klio* 80: 434–90.

(2000). "Augustus' propaganda in Africa," *Klio* 82: 171–207.

Rathmann, M. (2003). *Untersuchungen zu den Reichsstraßen in den westlichen Provinzen des Imperium Romanum*. Mainz.

Rawson, E. (1975). "Caesar's heritage: Hellenistic kings and their Roman equals," *JRS* 65: 148–59.

(1989). "Roman tradition and the Greek world," in *CAH*² 8, pp. 422–76. Cambridge.

(1991). *Roman Culture and Society: Collected Papers*. Oxford.

Reece, R. (1973). "Roman coinage in the western empire," *Britannia* 4: 227–51.

(1981). "The 'normal' hoard," in Carcassone and Hackens (eds.), pp. 335–41.

Rees, R. (2002). *Layers of Loyalty in Latin Panegyric, AD 289–307*. Oxford.

Rehak, P. (2006). *Imperium and Cosmos: Augustus and the Northern Campus Martius*. Madison, WI.

Revell, L. (2009). *Roman Imperialism and Local Identities*. Cambridge.

Reynolds, J. (1982). *Aphrodisias and Rome*. London.

(1988). "Cities," in *The Administration of the Roman Empire, 241 BC–AD 193*, ed. D. Braund, pp. 15–51. Exeter.

Rich, J. (1998). "Augustus' Parthian honours, the temple of Mars Ultor and the arch in the Forum Romanum," *PBSR* 66: 71–128.

(2003). "Augustus, war and peace," in De Blois *et al.* (eds.), pp. 329–57.

Richardson, J. (1991). "*Imperium Romanum*: empire and the language of power," *JRS* 81: 1–9.

Rickman, G. (1980). *The Corn Supply of Ancient Rome*. Oxford.

Riggsby, A. (1998). "Self and community in the younger Pliny," *Arethusa* 31: 75–98.

Rives, J. B. (1995). *Religion and Authority in Roman Carthage from Augustus to Constantine*. Oxford.

(2007). *Religion in the Roman Empire*. Oxford and Malden, MA.

Robert, L. (1977). "La titulature de Nicée et de Nicomédie: la gloire et la haine," *HSCP* 81: 1–39.

Roche, P. (2008). "The public image of the emperor Otho," *Historia* 30: 108–23.

(ed.) (2011). *Pliny's Praise: the Panegyricus in the Roman World*. Cambridge.

Rogers, G. (1991). "Demosthenes of Oenoanda and models of euergetism," *JRS* 81: 91–100.

Roller, M. (2001). *Constructing Autocracy: Aristocrats and Emperors in Julio-Claudian Rome*. Princeton.

(2004). "Exemplarity in Roman culture: the cases of Horatius Cocles and Cloelia," *CP* 99: 1–56.

Rose, C. B. (1997a). *Dynastic Commemoration and Imperial Portraiture in the Julio-Claudian Period*. Cambridge.

(1997b). "The imperial image in the eastern Mediterranean," in *The Early Roman Empire in the East*, ed. S. Alcock, pp. 108–20. Oxford.

Rosenstein, N. (1990). *Imperatores Victi: Military Defeat and Aristocratic Competition in the Middle and Late Republic*. Berkeley.

(2006). "Aristocratic values," in *A Companion to the Roman Republic*, ed. N. Rosenstein and R. Morstein-Marx, pp. 365–82. Oxford and Malden, MA.

Rosso, E. (2006). *L'image de l'empereur en Gaule romaine: portraits et inscriptions*. Paris.

Rowe, C. and M. Schofield (eds.) (2000). *The Cambridge History of Greek and Roman Political Thought*. Cambridge.

Rowe, G. (2002). *Princes and Political Cultures: The New Tiberian Senatorial Decrees*. Ann Arbor.

(2007). "The emergence of monarchy: 44 BCE-96 CE," in *A Companion to the Roman Empire*, ed. D. Potter, pp. 198–212. Oxford and Malden, MA.

Rüpke, J. (1995). *Kalender und Öffentlichkeit: die Geschichte der Repräsentation und religiösen Qualifikation von Zeit in Rom*. Berlin.

(1997). *Religion of the Romans*, transl. R. Gordon. Cambridge.

Russell, D. A. and N. G. Wilson (eds.) (1981). *Menander Rhetor*. Oxford.

Saller, R. (1994). *Patriarchy, Property, and Death in the Roman Family*. Cambridge.

Salomies, O. (1994). "Observations on the development of the style of Latin honorific inscriptions during the empire," *Arctos* 28: 63–106.

Scheid, J. (1998). *Commentarii Fratrum Arvalium qui Supersunt: les copies épigraphiques des protocoles annuels de la confrérie arvale, 21 av.-304 ap. J.-C.* Rome.

(2007). *Res Gestae Divi Augusti*. Paris.

Scheidel, W. (2006). "Republics between hegemony and empire: how ancient city-states built empires and the USA doesn't (anymore)," *Princeton/Stanford Working Papers in Classics*.

(2007). "Demography," in Scheidel *et al.* (eds.), pp. 38–86.

(forthcoming). "Roman dynastic discontinuity."

Scheidel, W. *et al.* (eds.) (2007). *The Cambridge Economic History of the Greco-Roman World*. Cambridge.

Scheithauer, A. (1988). "*Super omnes retro principes* . . . Zur inoffiziellen Titulatur römischer Kaiser," *ZPE* 72: 155–77.

Schubart, W. (1937). "Das hellenistische Königsideal nach Inschriften und Papyri," *APG* 12: 1–26.

Schwarte, H. (1977). "Salus Augusta Publica: Domitian und Trajan als Heilbringer des Staates," in *Bonner Festgabe J. Straub*, ed. A. Lippold, pp. 225–46. Bonn.

Scott, R. (1982). "Providentia Aug.," *Historia* 31: 436–59.

Scott, S. and J. Webster (eds.) (2003). *Roman Imperialism and Provincial Art*. Cambridge.

Seager, R. (1984). "Some imperial virtues in the Latin prose panegyrics: the demands of propaganda and the dynamics of literary composition," *PLLS* 4 (1983): 129–65.

Seelentag, G. (2004). *Taten und Tugenden Traians: Herrschaftsdarstellung im Principat*. Stuttgart.

(2009). "*Spes Augusta*: Titus und Domitian in der Herrschaftsdarstellung Vespasians," *Latomus* 69: 83–100.

Sewell, jr., W. H. (2005). *Logics of History: Social Theory and Social Transformation.* Chicago.

Shapiro, H. A. (1993). *Personifications in Greek Art: The Representation of Abstract Concepts 600–400 B.C.* Zürich.

Shaw, B. (1985). "The divine economy: Stoicism as ideology," *Latomus* 44: 16–54.

(2000). "Rebels and outsiders," *CAH²* 11, pp. 361–403. Cambridge.

(2001). "Challenging Braudel: a new vision of the Mediterranean," review of Horden and Purcell 2000, *JRA* 14: 419–53.

Sherwin-White, A. N. (1973). *The Roman Citizenship².* Oxford.

Sinopoli, C. (1994). "The archaeology of empires," *ARA* 23: 159–80.

(2001). "Imperial integration and imperial subjects," in Alcock *et al.* (eds.), pp. 195–200.

Sirks, B. (1991). *Food for Rome: The Legal Structure of the Transportation and Processing of Supplies for the Imperial Distributions in Rome and Constantinople.* Amsterdam.

Skinner, Q. (1988a). "Some problems in the analysis of political thought and action," in Tully (ed.), pp. 97–118 (orig. 1974).

(1988b). "Language and social change," in Tully (ed.), pp. 119–32 (orig. 1980).

Smith, R. (2007). "The imperial court of the late Roman empire, *c.* AD 300–*c.* AD 450," in Spawforth (ed.), pp. 157–232.

Smith, R. R. R. (1985). "Roman portraits: honours, empresses, and late emperors," *JRS* 75: 208–21.

(1988). *Hellenistic Royal Portraits.* Oxford.

(1996). "Typology and diversity in the portraits of Augustus," *JRA* 9: 30–47.

(1998). "Cultural choice and political identity in honorific portrait statues in the Greek East in the second century A.D.," *JRS* 88: 56–93.

Smith, R. R. R. *et al.* (2006). *Roman Portrait Statuary from Aphrodisias.* Mainz.

Sordi, M. (ed.) (1974). *Propaganda e persuasione occulta nell'antichità.* Milan.

(ed.) (1976). *I canali della propaganda nel mondo antico.* Milan.

Spaeth, B. (1996). *The Roman Goddess Ceres.* Austin.

Spawforth, A. (ed.) (2007). *The Court and Court Society in Ancient Monarchies.* Cambridge.

Stäcker, J. (2003). *Princeps und Miles.* Hildesheim.

Starr, R. (1987). "The circulation of literary texts in the Roman world," *CQ* 37: 213–33.

Steinmetz, G. (ed.) (1999a). *State/Culture: State-Formation after the Cultural Turn.* Ithaca, NY.

(1999b). "Introduction: culture and the state," in Steinmetz (ed.), pp. 1–49.

Stewart, P. (2003). *Statues in Roman Society: Representation and Response.* Oxford.

Stone, L. (1987). "History and the social sciences in the twentieth century," ch. 1 in *The Past and the Present Revisited*, pp. 3–44. New York.

Storch, R. (1972). "The absolutist theology of Victory," *C&M* 29: 197–206.

Strack, P. (1931–7). *Untersuchungen zur römischen Reichsprägungen des 2. Jahrhunderts*, 3 vols. Stuttgart.

Strobel, K. (1993). *Das Imperium Romanum im '3. Jahrhundert': Modell einer historischen Krise?* Stuttgart.

Stroux, J. (1933). "Die Constitutio Antoniniana," *Philologus* n.s. 42: 272–95.

Stuart, M. (1939). "How were imperial portraits distributed throughout the Roman empire?" *AJA* 43: 601–17.

Stylow, A. (1972). *Libertas und Liberalitas: Untersuchungen zur innenpolitischen Propaganda der Römer.* Diss. Munich.

(2001). "Las estatuas honoríficas como medio de autorrepresentación de las elites locales de Hispania," in Navarro Caballero and Demougin (eds.), pp. 141–53.

Sumi, G. (2005). *Ceremony and Power: Performing Politics in Rome between Republic and Empire.* Ann Arbor.

Sutherland, C. H. V. (1959). "The intelligibility of Roman imperial coin types," *JRS* 49: 46–55.

Swain, S. and M. Edwards (eds.) (2004). *Approaching Late Antiquity: The Transformation from Early to Late Empire.* Oxford.

Swift, E. (1923). "Imagines in imperial portraiture," *AJA* 27: 286–301.

Swift, L. (1966). "The anonymous encomium of Philip the Arab," *GRBS* 7: 267–89.

Syme, R. (1936). "Flavian wars and frontiers," in *CAH* 11, pp. 131–87. Cambridge.

(1939). *The Roman Revolution.* Oxford.

(1958). *Tacitus*, 2 vols. Oxford.

(1984). *Roman Papers* vol. 3. Oxford.

Talbert, R. (1984). *The Senate of Imperial Rome.* Princeton.

Temin, P. (2001). "A market economy in the early Roman empire," *JRS* 91: 169–81.

Thein, A. (2009). "Felicitas and the Memoirs of Sulla and Augustus," in *The Lost Memoirs of Augustus*, ed. C. Smith and A. Powell, pp. 87–110. Swansea.

Thesleff, H. (1965). *The Pythagorean Texts of the Hellenistic Period.* Turku.

Thomas, E. and C. Witschel (1992). "Constructing reconstruction: claim and reality of rebuilding inscriptions from the Latin West," *PBSR* 60: 135–77.

Toynbee, J. C. M. (1956). "Picture-language in Roman art and coinage," in Carson and Sutherland (eds.), pp. 205–26.

Trigger, B. (2003). *Understanding Early Civilizations: A Comparative Study.* Cambridge.

Trillmich, W. and P. Zanker (eds.) (1990). *Stadtbild und Ideologie: die Monumentalisierung hispanischer Städte zwischen Republik und Kaiserzeit.* Munich.

Tuck, S. (2005). "The origins of Roman imperial hunting imagery: Domitian and the redefinition of *virtus* under the principate," *G&R* 52: 221–45.

Tully, J. (ed.) (1988). *Meaning and Context: Quentin Skinner and his Critics.* Princeton.

Turcan, R. (1996). *The Cults of the Roman Empire.* Oxford and Malden, MA.

Turpin, W. (1991). "Imperial subscriptions and the administration of justice," *JRS* 81: 101–18.

Ulrich, Th. (1930). *Pietas (pius) als politischer Begriff.* Breslau.

Vervaet, F. (2007). "The principle of the *summum imperium auspiciumque* under the Roman Republic," *SDHI* 73: 1–148.

Veyne, P. (1976). *Le pain et le cirque: sociologie historique d'un pluralisme politique.* Paris.

(1990). "Propaganda expression roi, image idole oracle," *L'Homme* 114: 7–26.

(2002a). "L'empereur, ses concitoyens et ses sujets," in Ingelbert (ed.), pp. 49–74.

(2002b). "Lisibilité des images, propagande et apparat monarchique dans l'empire romain," *RH* 621: 3–30.

(2005). *L'Empire gréco-romain.* Paris.

Virlouvet, C. (2000). "L'approvvigionamento di Roma imperiale: una sfida quotidiana," in *Roma imperiale: una metropoli antica,* ed. E. Lo Cascio, pp. 103–35. Rome.

Vogt, J. (1933). "Vorläufer des Optimus Princeps," *Hermes* 68: 84–92.

Volk, T. R. (1987). "Mint output and coin hoards," in *Rythmes de la production monétaire, de l'antiquité à nos jours,* ed. G. Depeyrot *et al.,* pp. 141–221. Louvain-la-Neuve.

von Kaenel, H.-M. and F. Kemmers (eds.) (2009). *Coins in Context I: New Perspectives for the Interpretation of Coin Finds.* Mainz.

Vout, C. (2007). *Power and Eroticism in Imperial Rome.* Cambridge.

Wagenvoort, H. (1947). *Roman Dynamism: Studies in Ancient Roman Thought, Language and Custom.* Oxford.

(1980). *Pietas: Selected Studies in Roman Religion.* Leiden.

Walbank, F. (1984). "Monarchies and monarchic ideas," in *CAH²* 7.1, pp. 62–100. Cambridge.

Walker, D. R. (1976–8). *The Metrology of the Roman Silver Coinage,* 3 vols. Oxford.

(1988). "Roman coins from the sacred spring at Bath," in *The Temple of Sulis Minerva at Bath, vol. 2: The Finds from the Sacred Spring,* ed. B. Cunliffe, pp. 281–358. Oxford.

Wallace-Hadrill, A. (1981a). "The emperor and his virtues," *Historia* 30: 298–323.

(1981b). "Galba's Aequitas," *NC* 141: 20–39.

(1982). *Civilis princeps:* between citizen and king," *JRS* 72: 32–48.

(1983). *Suetonius: The Scholar and his Caesars.* New Haven.

(1986). "Image and authority in the coinage of Augustus," *JRS* 76: 66–87.

(1989). "Rome's cultural revolution," review of Zanker 1988, *JRS* 79: 157–64.

(1990). "Roman arches and Greek honours: the language of power at Rome," *PCPS* 216 (n.s. 36): 143–81.

(1996). "The imperial court," in *CAH²* 10, pp. 283–308. Cambridge.

(1997). "*Mutatio morum:* the idea of a cultural revolution," in Habinek and Schiesaro (eds.), pp. 3–22.

(2000). "The Roman revolution and material culture," in *La révolution romaine après Ronald Syme: bilans et perspectives,* ed. A. Giovannini, pp. 283–321. Geneva.

(2005). "*Mutatas Formas:* the Augustan transformation of Roman knowledge," in Galinsky (ed.), pp. 55–84.

(2008). *Rome's Cultural Revolution.* Cambridge.

Ward-Perkins, J. B. (1970). "From Republic to Empire: reflections on the early imperial provincial architecture of the Roman west," *JRS* 60: 1–19.

Weber, G. and M. Zimmermann (eds.) (2003). *Propaganda-Selbstdarstellung-Repräsentation im römischen Kaiserreich des I. Jhs. n. Chr.* Stuttgart.

Weber, M. (1968). *Economy and Society*, 2 vols., ed. G. Roth and C. Wittich. Berkeley (orig. 1921).

Weinstock, S. (1958). "Victoria," *RE* 8.A2: 2,501–42.

(1960). "Pax and the 'Ara Pacis'," *JRS* 50: 44–58.

(1971). *Divus Julius*. Oxford.

Welles, C. (1934). *Royal Correspondence in the Hellenistic Period*. New Haven.

Wesch-Klein, G. (1990). *Liberalitas in rem publicam: Private Aufwendungen zugunsten von Gemeinden im römischen Afrika bis 284 n. Chr.* Bonn.

Whitby, M. (ed.) (1998). *The Propaganda of Power: The Role of Panegyric in Late Antiquity*. Leiden.

Whittaker, C. R. (1997). "Imperialism and culture: the Roman initiative," in *Dialogues in Roman Imperialism: Power, Discourse, and Discrepant Experience in the Roman Empire, JRA* suppl. 23, ed. D. J. Mattingly, pp. 143–63. Portsmouth, RI.

Wickert, L. (1954). "Princeps (civitatis)," *RE* 22.2: 1,998–2,296.

Wickham, C. (1988). "Historical materialism, historical sociology," review of Mann 1986, *New Left Review* 177: 63–78.

Wilkes, J. J. (2005). "Provinces and frontiers," in *CAH²* 12, pp. 212–68. Cambridge.

Wilson, A. (2002). "Machines, power and the ancient economy," *JRS* 92: 1–32.

Winkler, L. (1995). *Salus: vom Staatskult zur politischen Idee: eine archäologische Untersuchung*. Heidelberg.

Winterling, A. (1999). *Aula Caesaris: Studien zur Institutionalisierung des römischen Kaiserhofes in der Zeit von Augustus bis Commodus (31 v. Chr. – 192 n. Chr.)*. Munich.

Wirszubski, C. (1950). *Libertas as a Political Idea at Rome during the Late Republic and Early Principate*. Cambridge.

Wistrand, E. (1987). *Felicitas imperatoria*. Göteburg.

Witschel, C. (1995a). "Römische Tempelkultbilder und römische Kaiserstatuen als Tempelkultbilder," in *Standorte: Kontext und Funktion antiker Skulptur*, ed. K. Stemmer, pp. 250–7. Berlin.

(1995b). "Statuen auf römischen Platzanlagen unter besonderer Berücksichtigung von Timgad (Algerien)," in *Standorte: Kontext und Funktion antiker Skulptur*, ed. K. Stemmer, pp. 332–58. Berlin.

(1999). *Krise, Rezession, Stagnation? der Westen des römischen Reiches im 3. Jahrhundert n. Chr.* Frankfurt.

(2002). "Meilensteine als historische Quelle? Das Beispiel Aquileia," *Chiron* 32: 325–93.

(2004). "Re-evaluating the Roman west in the 3rd c. AD," *JRA* 17: 251–81.

Wolters, R. (1999). *Nummi Signati: Untersuchungen zur römischen Münzprägung und Geldwirtschaft*. Munich.

(2003). "Die Geschwindigkeit der Zeit und die Gefahr der Bilder: Münzbilder und Münzpropaganda in der römischen Kaiserzeit," in Weber and Zimmermann (eds.), pp. 175–204.

(2006). "Geldverkehr, Geldtransporte und Geldbuchungen in römischer Republik und Kaiserzeit: das Zeugnis der schriftlichen Quellen," *RBN* 152: 23–49.

Woolf, G. (1990a). "Food, poverty and patronage: the significance of the epigraphy of the Roman alimentary schemes in early imperial Italy," *PBSR* 58: 197–228.

(1990b). "World systems analysis and the Roman empire," *JRA* 3: 44–58.

(1993). "Roman peace," in *War and Society in the Roman World*, ed. J. Rich and G. Shipley, pp. 171–94. New York.

(1995). "The formation of Roman provincial cultures," in *Integration in the Early Roman West: The Role of Culture and Ideology*, ed. J. Metzler *et al.*, pp. 9–18. Luxembourg.

(1996). "Monumental writing and the expansion of Roman society in the early empire," *JRS* 86: 22–39.

(1998). *Becoming Roman: The Origins of Provincial Civilization in Gaul.* Cambridge.

(2000). "Literacy," in *CAH*² 11, pp. 875–97. Cambridge.

(2001). "The Roman cultural revolution in Gaul," in *Italy and the West: Comparative Issues in Romanization*, ed. S. Keay and N. Terrenato, pp. 173–86. Oxford.

(2005). "Provincial perspectives," in Galinsky (ed.), pp. 106–29.

Zanker, P. (1979). "Prinzipat und Herrscherbild," *Gymnasium* 86: 353–68.

(1983). *Provinzielle Kaiserporträts: zur Rezeption der Selbstdarstellung des Princeps.* Munich.

(1988a). *The Power of Images in the Age of Augustus*, transl. A. Shapiro. Ann Arbor.

(1988b). "*Bilderzwang*: Augustan political symbolism in the private sphere," in *Image and Mystery in the Roman World (papers given in memory of Jocelyn Toynbee)*, ed. J. Huskinson, *et al.*, pp. 1–22. Gloucester.

(1998). *Pompeii: Public and Private Life*, transl. L. Schneider. Cambridge, MA.

(2010). "By the emperor, for the people: 'popular' architecture in Rome," in Ewald and Noreña (eds.), pp. 45–87.

Zanzarri, P. (1997). *La concordia romana: politica e ideologia nella monetazione dalla tarda repubblica ai Severi.* Rome.

Zetzel, J. (ed.) (1995). *Cicero De Re Publica: Selections.* Cambridge.

Zimmer, G. (1989). *Locus datus decreto decurionum: zur Statuenaufstellung zweier Forumsanlagen im römischen Afrika.* Munich.

Zuiderhoek, A. (2008). "Feeding the citizens: municipal grain funds and civic benefactors in the Roman east," in *Groningen-Royal Holloway Studies on the Greek City after the Classical Age I: Feeding the Ancient Greek City*, ed. R. Alston and O. van Nijf, pp. 159–80. Leuven.

(2009). *The Politics of Munificence in the Roman Empire: Citizens, Elites and Benefactors in Asia Minor.* Cambridge.

General index

Note: individuals are listed by their common names in English, not by their *nomina* (e.g. "Trajan," not "Ulpius Traianus, M.").

447

Printed in Great Britain
by Amazon

48756004R00268